ROBERT A. POWELL

HERMETIC ASTROLOGY

TOWARDS A NEW WISDOM OF THE STARS

Volume II

Astrological Biography

Lives of great men remind us
We can make our lives sublime,
And, departing, leave behind us
Footprints on the sands of time.

Footprints, that perhaps another,
Sailing o'er life's solemn main,
A forlorn and shipwrecked brother,
Seeing, shall take heart again.

(From Longfellow's poem *A Psalm of Life*)

SOPHIA FOUNDATION PRESS

SAN RAFAEL, CA

Second edition, 2006
Sophia Foundation Press
An imprint of Sophia Perennis
Copyright © 1989 by Robert Powell

All rights reserved.

No part of this book may be reproduced or transmitted,
in any form or by any means, without permission

For information, address:
Sophia Foundation Press, PO Box 151011
San Rafael, CA 94915

Library of Congress Cataloging-in-Publication Data

Powell, Robert A.
Hermetic astrology: towards a new wisdom of the stars /
Robert A. Powell.—2nd ed.

v. cm.
Includes bibliographical references.
Contents: v. 1. Astrology and reincarnation—v. 2. Astrological biography.
ISBN 1 59731 155 3 (v. 1 : pbk. : alk. paper)
ISBN 1 59731 157 X (v. 1 : cloth : alk. paper)
ISBN 1 59731 156 1 (v. 2 : pbk. : alk. paper)
ISBN 1 59731 158 8 (v. 2 : cloth. : alk. paper)
1. Astrology. 2. Hermeneutics. 3. Reincarnation. I. Title.
BF1711.P745 2006
133.5—dc22   2006033841

Author's acknowledgements

With grateful acknowledgements to Dr. Michael Frensch for his initiative and support with regard to this book and to Martin Schmidt of Hermetika for publishing it; to Ernstfried Prade for designing the cover; to Willi Sucher (1902-1985) for the encouragement he gave to my research work; to friends who contributed their help in one way or another; and to my wife who made it all possible.

Preface to Second Edition

In the first chapters of this book we simultaneously follow two threads. While considering the lives of Richard Wagner, Friedrich Nietzsche, and King Ludwig II of Bavaria in their nineteenth-century incarnations and in earlier incarnations, we examine the planetary configurations accompanying not only their conception, birth, and death, but also various significant events in their lives. In this way we experience how these two perspectives — the biographical and the astrological — weave together and are intimately interconnected. As illuminating as this is, the author also indicates however that astrological calculation alone can never suffice for the truly deep biographical research into karma and reincarnation demonstrated in this work.

The author shows that although it is clear that an individual's destiny is connected with the positions of the celestial bodies — that certain regular occurrences are evident — nonetheless no *strict* regularities exist. He maintains moreover that a certain level of clairvoyance is requisite for any serious astrological study of destiny; even more — that *real* astrology requires initiation. Such astrological research, when successfully carried out as it is here, relating salient celestial configurations to the life-drama of well-known historical personalities, reads like fine literature.

On a practical level this work illustrates several important new tools for the astrologer: how to calculate *hermetic charts*, how to cast horoscopes not only of birth and death but also of *conception* (including the astrological significance of the *embryonic period* between conception and birth), and then also how to apply these various horoscopes in describing the *spiral of life* that unfolds in seven-year periods during the course of a person's earthly existence. All this reveals profound and fascinating regularities — among them the discovery that stellar configurations during the embryonic period are reflected again and again in the subsequent periods of life.

Quite new for most readers will be the author's treatment of Uranus, Neptune, and Pluto, indicating that the names given these planets are deeply meaningful in the light of spiritual science. To make his case he extends Rudolf Steiner's description of cosmic evolution by drawing upon Greek mythology, particularly Orphic cosmology. This book by Robert Powell is of the greatest possible interest.

Professor Konrad Rudnički
Astronomical Observatory
Jagiellonian University
Cracow, Poland

Hermetic Astrology
Volume II
Astrological Biography

TO THE READER	xi
PREFACE	xii
FOREWORD	xiii
INTRODUCTION	xv
CHAPTER 1: Karmic Relationships	1
CHAPTER 2: Further Aspects of Karmic Relationships	34
CHAPTER 3: An Example of Astrological Biography	63
CHAPTER 4: The Spiral of Life (up to 21)	101
CHAPTER 5: The Spiral of Life (21 onwards)	136
CHAPTER 6: The Hermetic-Astrological Science of Destiny	178
CHAPTER 7: The Hermetic House System	246
CHAPTER 8: Uranus, Neptune and Pluto	287
CHAPTER 9: The Second Coming and the New Age	327
CHAPTER 10: The Hermetic Calendar	354
APPENDIX I: The 7-year Periods (Septennaries)	398
APPENDIX II: Computations	403
APPENDIX III: The Jewish Calendar	413
AFTERWORD	417

Footnotes are located at the end of each chapter to which they belong

Figures

The following figures are listed in this book.

1.	The fundamental principle of astrological biography	75
2.	The spiral of life	104
3.	Different levels of astrological significance	118
4.	The formation of the solar system	145
5.	The further formation of the solar system	145
6.	The two axes of the zodiacal man	174
7.	The destiny image of the stroke	186
8.	The karmic background of the moment of death (John Addey)	203
9.	Normal length embryonic period	230
10.	The completion of the circle	232
11.	Return to the image	234
12.	Different length embryonic periods	235
13.	Archetypal relationship of the head to the zodiacal sphere	239
14.	The house system of Porphyry	246
15.	Seven steps in each ring of the spiral of life	249
16.	Planetary correspondences between the steps	251
17.	Hermetic house system (third demotic horoscope)	256
18.	Hermetic house system (example: John Addey)	257
19.	(a) The sevenfold and twelvefold divisions	273
19.	(b)The sevenfold and twelvefold divisions	274
20.	The heliocentric system	292
21.	The cosmic self and the earthly self	355
22.	The cycle of sunlight in the course of the year	374

Tables
The following tables are listed in this book.

1.	St. Teresa/Wagner chart comparison for zodiacal alignments	21
2.	St. Teresa/Wagner chart comparison for aspect metamorphoses	22
3.	St. John/Ludwig II chart comparison for zodiacal alignments	60
4.	St. Teresa/Wagner (conception) chart comparison	74
5.	Cosmological systems relating to different levels of consciousness	109
6.	The first three 7-year periods of life	115
7.	The spiral of life	136
8.	Maestlin/Addey zodiacal alignments at John Addey's birth	199
9.	Maestlin/Addey zodiacal alignments at John Addey's conception	200
10.	The zodiacal periods in John Addey's life	211
11.	The human being's development through the 7-year periods	214
12.	Juxtaposition of the lunar and solar rythms in John Addey's life	216
13.	Lengths of the zodiacal periods in life	217
14.	The names of the houses (from four demotic horoscopes)	247
15.	Traditional one-word designations for the twelve houses	259
16.	The twelve houses in relation to Wagner's biography	267
17.	Solar zodiacal periods in Wagner's life	279
18.	Lunar zodiacal periods in Wagner's life (Aug. 1874 to Sep. 1882)	280
19.	The manvantaras of Orphic cosmology and the stages of evolution	295
20.	Mu'awiya/Woodrow Wilson chart comparison	299
21.	Louis the Pious/Wallenstein chart comparison	303
22.	Hermetic calendar: 19-year intercalation cycle, 1981-2000	389

Charts

The following charts are listed in this book.

Symbols and abbreviations: ∅ = conception; * = birth; † = death;
e.c. = embryonic correspondence.

1. *Richard Wagner — 5
2. *Friedrich Nietzsche — 6
3. *St. Teresa of Avila — 12
4. †St. Teresa of Avila — 13
5. *St. John of the Cross — 45
6. †St. John of the Cross — 46
7. *Ludwig II of Bavaria — 58
8. ∅Richard Wagner — 73
9. e.c. Wagner's meeting with Ludwig II of Bavaria — 80
10. *Stroke patient — 183
11. ∅Stroke patient — 184
12. e.c. Stroke at 46 years 5 months — 185
13. *Michael Maestlin — 195
14. †Michael Maestlin — 196
15. ∅John Addey — 197
16. *John Addey — 198
17. †John Addey — 202
18. e.c. paralysis at 23 years 6 months — 207
19. *Wallenstein — 301
20. †Louis the Pious — 302
21. *Emmanuel Swedenborg — 311
22. *Johannes Kepler — 314
23. *Nero — 317

Note concerning the astrological charts listed in this book:

Each chart indicates the positions in the sidereal zodiac of the Sun, Moon, Moon's nodes and planets (plus Ascendant and Midheaven in cases where the time is known). See Appendix II for the computations of the planetary positions — geocentric and heliocentric — at the conception/birth/death of the person under consideration. The charts comprise an outer circle and an inner circle. In the outer circle the hermetic chart, based on the Egyptian-Tychonic system, is given; and in the inner circle the traditional geocentric horoscope is shown. Thus the hermetic chart (outer circle) is superimposed on the geocentric chart (inner circle). All planetary positions are listed in the sidereal zodiac to the nearest degree. Uranus, Neptune and Pluto are included in the hermetic chart (outer circle), but have not to been entered onto the inner circle of the geocentric planetary configurations (since their geocentric sidereal positions hardly differ from their sidereal longitudes in the hermetic chart)

To the reader

This work is addressed to those who are seeking a *true astrology* such as was cultivated in the mystery temples of antiquity. It has little in common with the popular astrology of today, which for the most part represents a profanation of the sacred science of the stars. *Hermetic astrology* is intended to serve as a stepping-stone to the mystery wisdom of the stars, in the spirit of the *Mercury Star Journal,* which the author edited from 1975 to 1981. Mercury = Hermes, and in a deeper sense *Hermetic Astrology* can be viewed as a continuation of the impulse that was represented in the *Mercury Star Journal.*

The *Mercury Star Journal* came into being in order to continue the *Star Journal* (1965-1974) of Willi Sucher, whose life's work was devoted towards the development of a new star wisdom (astrosophy). Owing to the esoteric nature of Willi Sucher's work, however, it has not become widely known. Similarly, owing to the intimate nature of the content of *Hermetic Astrology,* especially on account of the indications concerning the previous incarnations of various historical personalities, this work belongs ideally to a circle of friends who are prepared to go beyond an intellectual appraisal, to allow the content to become a concern of the heart. It is in this spirit — for those who bear the impulse towards a new star wisdom in their hearts — that this work is being published.

Thereby it is hoped that the research presented in the following pages may serve as a stimulus to encourage others to take up hermetic astrology. In order to avoid any misunderstanding, however, a word of warning must be added here — at the outset — concerning the interpretation of the results of this research. The astrological «laws» of reincarnation discovered by the author and published in this work do NOT enable previous incarnations to be calculated. For, the mystery of reincarnation is inaccessible to intellectual speculation. No amount of speculative reasoning combined with computational skill can ever penetrate this mystery. It is along other paths — whereby, instead of the brain, the heart becomes an organ of knowledge — that knowledge of reincarnation becomes attainable. In this deeper sense is this work truly a concern of the heart. And those who read it from this point of view will recognize that the contents of the following pages are only scattered fragments serving as indicators on the way towards a new wisdom of the stars. Truth to tell, this new wisdom of the stars can hardly be communicated in book form; for it is a matter of inner knowledge and experience attained during the course of spiritual growth. But for those who feel called to embark upon this path of inner development leading to a new wisdom of the stars, *Hermetic Astrology* may help to provide a basic orientation with regard to the essential nature of the human being's relationship to the world of stars.

Preface

Volume II of *Hermetic Astrology* supplements and develops further the research findings described in Volume I. The two main findings in Volume I, arising from astrological reincarnation research, are:

(1) the sidereal zodiac is the authentic astrological zodiac; and

(2) the hermetic chart (based on the Egyptian-Tychonic system) is of major significance in the field of astrological reincarnation research.

The hermetic chart forms a foundation for hermetic astrology, which comprises a new science of destiny (karma). Whereas Volume I («Astrology and Reincarnation») is concerned with the nature of birth and death (the mystery of reincarnation), Volume II focuses upon the course of life between birth and death (how karma comes to expression in biography).

Volume II can be read independently of Volume I, provided that the two findings referred to above are acknowledged, at least as a «working hypothesis». To begin with in Volume II («Astrological Biography»), the question of karmic relationships, i.e. relationships between human beings from one incarnation to the next, is examined with reference to some historical examples. Then the science of astrological biography is discussed, and some viewpoints concerning the astrological houses and the outermost planets (Uranus, Neptune and Pluto) are outlined. Lastly, the spiritual aspect of hermetic astrology — considered as a spiritual path — is looked at in relation to spiritual impulses active in the twentieth century.

Foreword

«Who am I? Where do I come from? What is my task in life?» These are fundamental questions — existential questions — which many people in our time are asking.

Astrology has long sought to answer these questions, and — as many have found — it goes a long way towards providing insight into the basic questions of human existence. Yet astrology — as it has developed up until now — has its limitations. This is because the key to astrology — that which explains the foundations of this ancient science — has not been taken into account up until now. The key to astrology is *reincarnation*, and it is this key which is taken into consideration and applied in hermetic astrology.

Reincarnation is not only the key to astrology — it also helps to answer the existential questions posed above.

«Who am I?» The answer to this question provided by traditional astrology is expressed in terms of the horoscope of birth. Hermetic astrology goes a stage further by viewing the birth horoscope in terms of the horoscope of death from the previous incarnation. (The relationship between the horoscope of birth and that of death in the previous incarnation comes to expression in terms of the «laws» of reincarnation.) It is in gaining insight into previous incarnations that the deeper answer to the question «Who am I?» lies, and it is into this mysterious realm — that of reincarnation — that hermetic astrology endeavours to penetrate. Hermetic astrology thus represents an extension of traditional astrology — extending it to take account of previous incarnations.

«Where do I come from?» To look back into previous incarnations is an initial step towards answering this question. A further step is to look into the realm in which the human being dwells between incarnations — the realm of the planetary spheres, reaching up to the zodiacal sphere of fixed stars. Hermetic astrology seeks not only to take account of previous incarnations, but also of the human being's cosmic life — his cosmic existence in the realm of the planets and the zodiac between incarnations on the Earth.

«What is my task in life?» Knowledge acquired through looking back into previous incarnations should not be an end in itself. It becomes of value when it is directed towards the future. In this respect hermetic astrology is essentially future-orientated, in that it seeks to view the sequence of the human being's earthly incarnations in the context of his mission in relation to the Earth and mankind. The nature of the human being's task in his present life can be understood from his previous incarnation(s), whereby in hermetic astrology an overview is sought — an overview of the human being's mission which unfolds step by step from incarnation to incarnation.

In embarking upon a study of hermetic astrology, the reader will find that he encounters a new world — a world with its own unique cosmological system. This was already known in the cosmology of the ancient Egyptians, but has long

In embarking upon a study of hermetic astrology, the reader will find that he encounters a new world — a world with its own unique cosmological system. This was already known in the cosmology of the ancient Egyptians, but has long since been forgotten. However, there is a major difference from the days of ancient Egypt: since the Crucifixion and Resurrection the moral center of this cosmological world is Jesus Christ. He it is, who is to be found at the center of hermetic-astrological cosmology, and it is through Him — ultimately — that knowledge of previous incarnations is gained. For He is the *Lord of karma*, who has an overview of each human being's sequence of earthly incarnations, who knows each human being's mission, and who helps each human being to fulfil his karma (destiny). Hermetic astrology is essentially *Christian astrology*, for it looks to Him — the Lord of karma — as the ultimate source of all knowledge concerning reincarnation and human destiny.

The first volume of *Hermetic Astrology* provides an introduction to hermetic-astrological cosmology and reincarnation research. Thus, Volume I — *Astrology and Reincarnation* — opens up the domain of reincarnation and karma in the light of astrology. In addition, this volume contains what is possibly the world's first scientific proof of reincarnation, presented in terms of the first and second «laws» of reincarnation.

Volume II — *Astrological Biography* — is concerned with karmic relationships, i.e. with human relationships which are carried over from one incarnation to the next, and how destiny unfolds in the «spiral of life», where each ring of the spiral amounts to seven years of life. In Volume II, therefore, the foundations are laid for the hermetic-astrological science of destiny, which is something completely new in the history of astrology.

Hermetic astrology is a new science of the stars concerned with and based upon reincarnation, and embodying a new science of destiny. These two volumes are intended to serve as an introduction to this new science of the stars, for all those who are interested in the deeper, existential questions of life.

Introduction

For many people interested in astrology who have read *Hermetic Astrology Vol.I: Astrology and Reincarnation*, since its publication in 1987, a central question has been: How reliable are the reincarnation examples given there? This question is of fundamental importance, since the whole basis of the research findings presented in *Hermetic Astrology* I, which form the foundation of a new astrology, depends upon the reliability of these reincarnation examples. The principal research findings established in *Hermetic Astrology* I may be summarized as follows: (1) the sidereal zodiac is the authentic astrological zodiac, since the reincarnation of the soul is guided by the movements of the Sun, Moon and planets through the signs of the sidereal zodiac; (2) it is not only the geocentric but also the heliocentric movements of the planets through the signs of the sidereal zodiac which are of importance for the birth configuration chosen by the reincarnating soul.

Substantial evidence for these research findings (1) and (2) could not have been arrived at without the study of numerous reincarnation examples, which the author carried out over a long period of time. It was for this purpose – and not for the sake of publicly revealing deep mysteries – that the step was taken of publishing the reincarnation examples given in Volume I. Moreover, as discussed at length in Volume I, the most important principle of reincarnation research is moral development. For, it is through taking up a path of moral-spiritual development that each individual is able to arrive for himself or herself at the truth of reincarnation statements – this being an essential step on the way towards carrying out reincarnation research.

Focusing now upon the question of the truth of the reincarnation statements presented in this work on hermetic astrology, a distinction must be drawn between Volume I: *Astrology and Reincarnation* and Volume II: *Astrological Biography*. Volume I includes a total of eighteen reincarnation examples (twelve in Table 18 and an additional six in Table 24). Of these examples, fourteen are referred to directly by Rudolf Steiner in his lectures entitled *Karmic Relationships*, and another concerning himself is referred to indirectly. With respect to this latter example, in a confidential letter written by Rudolf Steiner on May 14, 1904, which was published in 1984 (see Rudolf Steiner, *Complete Works*, Vol. 264, p.55), he wrote: "In my earlier life several centuries ago a personality played the role of withdrawing me from a certain family situation and made it possible for me to take the necessary steps leading to my calling (in that life) as a Catholic priest." This confirms the research finding indicated in *Hermetic Astrology* I that there was no incarnation between the death of this Catholic priest on March 7, 1274 and Rudolf Steiner's birth on February 25, 1861 – see Table 18, reincarnation example (9)

In the case of reincarnation examples (10), (11) and (12) in Table 18 of *Hermetic Astrology* I, although also referred to indirectly by Rudolf Steiner in *Karmic Relationships,* they are essentially the result of independent research. Thus these three reincarnation examples from Volume I must be distinguished from the remaining fifteen examples presented there. Whereas Rudolf Steiner is the direct source for these fifteen examples, he may not be held responsible for the other three. Thus, in considering the truth of the eighteen reincarnation examples listed in *Hermetic Astrology* I, Rudolf Steiner is the "guarantor", so to say, of fifteen of these examples, the truth of which will not be disputed by anyone who is thoroughly acquainted with his life's work. But who can guarantee the truth of the other three reincarnation examples?

Here it is necessary to look more closely at the source of these three reincarnation examples. In fact, it is a matter of three different sources, all anonymous: two who communicated with the author (examples 10 and 11), and one who communicated with Willi Sucher (example 12). In each of these three cases the author applied not only hermetic-astrological methods for testing their validity (including the "laws" of reincarnation discussed in *Hermetic Astrology* I), but also the method of "biographical comparison". It is a basic truth of the working of karma (destiny) that each incarnation is a metamorphosis of the preceding incarnation(s), and that a biographical comparison of successive incarnations of an individuality generally reveals certain underlying relationships between the biographies of the different incarnations. This is brought out in a remarkable way in the biographical studies of the reincarnation examples (from Rudolf Steiner's *Karmic Relationships*) presented in the five-volume series *Destiny in Repeated Earthly Lives (Schicksal in wiederholten Erdenleben),* ed. Wolfgang Schuchhardt, Philosophisch-Anthroposophischer Verlag, Dornach, 1982–1987). In the last analysis, however, neither the method of biographical comparison nor the astrological comparison of birth and death horoscopes between different incarnations can give absolute certainty with regard to the validity of a reincarnation statement. Ultimately it is spiritual cognition – of a very highly developed kind – that can verify with absolute certainty the truth of a reincarnation statement.

Rudolf Steiner's entire life's work demonstrates that he had developed this high level of spiritual cognition, and therefore the fifteen reincarnation examples in *Hermetic Astrology* I stemming directly from him are trustworthy on an altogether different level from the other three presented there. With regard to these three reincarnation examples, it is in each case a matter of inspiration stimulated by means of an intensive occupation with Rudolf Steiner's indications on the individualities concerned in these three examples. This means that there is no one "guarantor" of the truth of these three reincarnation examples, but the author nevertheless included them in *Hermetic Astrology* I together with the other fifteen examples, being convinced – through his own research – that they are fundamentally true.

Of these three examples, one (example 12, concerning Friedrich Nietzsche) is also included in the following pages comprising Volume II. Partly on account of this reincarnation example communicated by Willi Sucher, the author was enabled to conduct his own reincarnation research, some of the results of which are presented here in Volume II. Apart from this example concerning Friedrich Nietzsche, and apart from two further brief references (in Chapter 8 to President Woodrow Wilson and in Chapter 9 to Novalis – these being reincarnation examples stemming from Rudolf Steiner), all the reincarnation examples presented in Volume II derive from the author's own reincarnation research. Thus the author is the "guarantor" of the truth of the reincarnation examples presented in the following pages. Whilst not claiming to be infallible, the author is nevertheless certain enough of the results of his own reincarnation research to be in a position to commit these findings to print. Again, as with the reincarnation examples presented in Volume I, it is not for the sake of publicly revealing deep mysteries that these findings are published here, but in order to clarify certain far-reaching issues.

In taking this step the author does not seek to claim that his capacity for reincarnation research can in any way be compared with the highly developed faculty of Rudolf Steiner. Nevertheless the author is fully conscious of the validity of his own findings through spiritual research, and for him it is a matter of certainty that he stands upon the secure foundation of truth. This level of certainty, however, is the result of years of careful and painstaking research. For the author – and in this respect he has been helped through studying and teaching mathematics for a number of years – the findings of his own reincarnation research are as trustworthy and certain as those of any tried and tested mathematical formula. Just as the truth of Pythagoras' theorem is self-evident to every mathematician, so the statements concerning reincarnation examples to be found in the following pages are self-evident to the author, who has rigorously avoided all elements of speculation and fantasy in the research he has conducted. In this respect the author is the "guarantor" of the reincarnation research presented in Volume II, just as Rudolf Steiner is the "guarantor" of all but three of the reincarnation examples given in Volume I.

However, it is not the intention of the author to be taken as an "authority". He asks that his research findings be taken simply as indications, and that they be treated critically, but with openmindedness to the possibility of their being true. Thus, the findings presented in the following pages should not be accepted unconditionally, but should be tested by the reader, each through his own sense for truth. It is essentially the quest for truth which motivates the author, and in his pursuit of a new astrology it is – he believes – above all *insight* that may serve as the foundation for a new science of the stars, and not superstition or belief in authority. It is in this spirit that *Hermetic Astrology* has been written. And it is the author's hope that these two volumes on hermetic astrology may serve as research material that may be taken up to help insight to become the common foundation linking all those concerned with the development of a new wisdom of the stars.

In this respect I feel united in a spirit of brotherhood with the many people working with the cosmological ideas of Rudolf Steiner and the related research of Willi Sucher, including the American researcher Paul Platt, who has recently published (1986/87) a three-volume work entitled *The Qualities of Time* (Golden Stone Press, Box 233A RD2, Ghent, NY 12075, USA). Some of the questions touched upon in *Hermetic Astrology* are to be found also in Paul Platt's work. In fact, Paul Platt shares with myself a debt of gratitude to Willi Sucher (1902–1985), whose work has been an important stimulus to both of us.

For myself, I look to Willi Sucher as a prime source – if not the major source – of inspiration for my astrological work. And as indicated in the following pages, it is Willi Sucher who may be regarded as the original pioneer of the science of astrological biography outlined in *Hermetic Astrology* II. It is as a tribute to him – as the founder of a new science of the stars in the twentieth century – that I would like this work on astrological biography to be viewed.

Chapter 1

Karmic Relationships

The karmic relationship between
Richard Wagner and Friedrich Nietzsche

One of the most famous relationships of the last century was that between the composer Richard Wagner and the philosopher Friedrich Nietzsche. It started in 1869 with Nietzsche as a fervent admirer — he signed himself in his earliest letter to Wagner as «your most faithful and devoted follower and admirer»[1] — but developed seven years later into an intellectual divorce, which resulted in a severe alienation between the two men.

The beginning of Nietzsche's «conversion» to Wagner took place on October 28, 1868, shortly after Nietzsche's twenty-fourth birthday. (He was born on October 15, 1844.) On this occasion the 24-year old student heard a performance of the preludes to Wagner's operas *Tristan* and *Die Meistersinger*.

I find it impossible to keep a critically cool head where this music is concerned... I am quivering in every fibre, every nerve, and I have never experienced such a lasting feeling of ecstasy as I did when listening to the last-named overture (the MEISTERSINGER prelude).[2]

The first meeting between Nietzsche and Wagner took place eleven days later — on November 8, 1868 — at a small gathering of Wagner's admirers in Leipzig. Nietzsche later described this first encounter with Wagner.

Before and after dinner Wagner played (the piano) and included all the important sections of the MEISTERSINGER, imitating all the vocal parts and growing very exuberant. For he is a wonderfully lively and animated man who speaks very fast, is very witty and makes a gathering of this private sort very cheerful. In between times, I had a longish talk with him about Schopenhauer; and you can imagine what joy it was for me to hear him speak of him with a quite indescribable warmth, saying how much he owed to him and how he was the only philosopher who understood the nature of music... Afterwards he read a portion of the autobiography he is now writing, an extremely amusing scene from his Leipzig student days, which I still! cannot think about without laughing... At the end of the evening, as we two were about to leave, he pressed my hand very warmly and cordially invited me to visit him to play music and talk philosophy.[3]

At the time of this meeting Richard Wagner was 55 years old. He was already famous and was approaching the zenith of his career as a composer. On the surface, his invitation to the 24-year old student appears to have been nothing more than a matter of conventional politeness. On a deeper level, however, it was a matter of a *karmic relationship* between the two men. It was a relationship «written in the stars», having its origin in a previous incarnation on Earth. As such, the meeting between Nietzsche and Wagner was not simply a matter of chance, but was the result of the higher guidance of destiny. It was the outcome of a relationship which already existed between these two individuals in a previous earthly incarnation.

The study of karmic relationships is intrinsic to hermetic astrology and — as we shall see in the case of Richard Wagner and Friedrich Nietzsche — it can open up totally new perspectives concerning the nature of human relationships. Hermetic astrology, as outlined in Volume I, is concerned with — and based upon — astrological reincarnation research.

Essential to an understanding of reincarnation is the concept of *karma*. As discussed in Volume I, Chapter 6, there are two perspectives of karma: either it is future karma, or it is past karma. Future karma — comprising the future destiny of the human being — is essentially positive in nature, and concerns the mission of the individuality in relation to mankind and the Earth. On the other hand, past karma — arising from the human being's past destiny — generally has positive and negative aspects. On the whole it can be said that past karma is positive in so far as it accords with the individuality's mission, and it is negative in so far as it constitutes a departure from — or hindrance to — the unfolding of his mission. Past karma — comprising the consequences deriving from the human being's previous incarnations upon the Earth — generally has positive and negative sides mixed together, and when the human being reincarnates he has to cope with the negative aspects — to make good the wrongs of the past — as well as receiving the blessing of the positive aspects.

The meeting between Friedrich Nietzsche and Richard Wagner was essentially the outcome of positive past karma. As we shall see, it resulted from a positive cooperation in the preceding incarnation. They had known each other, and it had been a positive relationship, in their previous lives on Earth. It was this positive karma that blessed their relationship from the beginning, which developed rapidly through Nietzsche's frequent visits to Wagner at Triebschen (near Lucerne, Switzerland), commencing in 1869. Before long Nietzsche was addressing Wagner as *Meister* («Master»). His letters to his friends were filled with praise for Wagner's genius and were permeated with a sense of joy at his own good fortune in knowing Wagner.

> *I have found a man who reveals to me as no other the image of what Schopenhauer calls «the genius» and who is quite possessed by that wonderfully intense philosophy (Schopenhauer's). He is none other than Richard Wagner, about whom you should believe none of the judgements to be found in the press, the writings of musical scholars, etc. NO ONE knows him and is capable of judging him because all the world stands on a different footing from him and is not at home in his atmosphere. There dwell in him such uncompromising idealism, such deep and affecting humanity, such exalted seriousness of purpose, that when I am near him I*

I. Karmic Relationships

feel as if I am near the divine.[4]

Recent joyful proximity to Richard Wagner, in the warmest and most cheerful way — Wagner: the greatest genius and greatest human being of our time, incomparably great! Every two or three weeks I spend a few days on his property at the Lake of Lucerne and consider this as the greatest attainment of my life, next to that which I owe to Schopenhauer.[5]

Nietzsche first went to Triebschen on May 15, 1869, but as on that day Wagner was deep in composing the *Ring of the Nibelungen*, Nietzsche left and returned two days later, on Whit Monday. This first visit was highly successful, and in his letter of appreciation Nietzsche wrote thanking Wagner for the «best and highest moments» of his life.[6] In the space of the next three years — until April 1872, when Wagner left Switzerland to settle in Bayreuth, Germany — Nietzsche was a guest at Triebschen twenty-three times.

Triebschen was (and is) a large house overlooking Lake Lucerne, about half-an-hour's walk from Lucerne. Wagner had moved there from Munich in April 1866. He was joined later by Cosima, the daughter of Franz Liszt and wife of one of Liszt's most gifted pupils, Hans von Bülow. (Cosima obtained a divorce from Hans von Bülow and married Wagner in August 1870. Nietzsche was asked to be a witness, but at the time of the wedding he was serving with the Prussian forces in France.)

In 1869 the chair of classical philology at Basel University fell vacant and was offered to the young Friedrich Nietzsche, Nietzsche then became a university professor at the age of 24, and he arrived in Basel to take up this post on April 19, 1869. The proximity of Basel to Lucerne — they are about fifty miles apart — enabled Nietzsche's frequent visits to Triebschen to take place without too much difficulty. (The first visit, referred to above, took place within a month of Nietzsche's arrival in Basel.) These were idyllic times, summed up by Nietzsche in the following words:

I offer all my other human relationships cheap; but at no price would I relinquish from my life the Triebschen days, those days of mutual confidence, of cheerfulness, of sublime incidents — of PROFOUND moments. I do not know what others may have experienced with Wagner: over OUR sky no cloud ever passed.[7]

This early phase of the relationship between Nietzsche and Wagner — the Triebschen days — was imbued with the «heavenly blessing» of their positive karma, carried over from the previous incarnation. Nietzsche recognised Wagner to be a genius and wanted to do everything in his power to help Wagner. Wagner, in his turn, felt genuinely touched by the young professor's devotion. As a sign of how close Nietzsche had grown to him, he entrusted Nietzsche with the task of arranging the printing of his autobiography and of checking the proofs. During this time Nietzsche became more or less a member of the Wagner household, with a room for his own use in House Triebschen. Alongside this relationship to Wagner, a friendship developed between himself and Cosima, and Cosima's children treated him almost like an elder brother.

The early phase of the relationship between Wagner and Nietzsche — one of friendship and mutual respect, whereby Nietzsche sought to place himself at Wagner's service — reflects the relationship between these two individuals as it had developed in the preceding incarnation in the sixteenth century. It was a karmic relationship of a positive nature which united the two and which blossomed forth again through their renewed contact in the nineteenth century. The karmic relationship between Nietzsche and Wagner helps to explain the powerful alliance that arose between these two human beings, despite their polar opposite natures, which can be characterized briefly as follows:

Wagner: composer, sociable, sensual, drinking in everything into his ongoing life-drama, laughing and crying according to the dictates of his heart.

Nietzsche: philosopher, solitary, ascetic*, removed from life through his immersion in books, not displaying his feelings outwardly.

*(In his student days Nietzsche had practised self-chastisement and self-punishment, and when he took up vegetarianism, Wagner regarded this, also, as a form of self-punishment.)

The horoscopes of Wagner and Nietzsche

The polarity in personality between Wagner and Nietzsche comes to expression in their birth horoscopes, where the Ascendants are diametrically opposite. The Ascendant at Wagner's birth was 6° Taurus (see Chart 1) and at Nietzsche's birth was opposite at 6° Scorpio (see Chart 2). The Ascendant, as well as indicating the personality, has much to do with the human being's outlook, his way of relating to the world. The Taurean Ascendant of Richard Wagner — strengthened by the presence of the Sun and Venus, which were rising at his birth — fits well the sensual human being «drinking in everything into his ongoing life-drama». Here it is the *will* — the life-will — which is of paramount importance. On the other hand, the Scorpionic Ascendant of Friedrich Nietzsche applies well to the ascetic philosopher, who — like an eagle — hovers above the world of events. (In antiquity the Scorpion was seen as an Eagle, as is evident from Christian iconography, where an Eagle is often depicted above John the Evangelist.) In this latter case it is *intelligence* that comes to the fore.

The soaring intelligence of the Eagle stands diametrically opposite the rampant life-will of the Bull. Thus Nietzsche's personality was constituted quite differently from the personality of Wagner. Whereas Wagner lived life to the full (the nature of the Bull), Nietzsche was more an observer of life, whose spirit repeatedly soared to heights from which he could look down and contemplate the world (the nature of the Eagle). Wagner became for Nietzsche an object of knowledge, and the purpose of Nietzsche's first book — *The Birth of Tragedy out of the Spirit of Music* (1871) — was to shed light upon Wagner in relationship to Greek tragedy. In his second book — *Untimely Meditations*

I. Karmic Relationships

Chart 1
*Richard Wagner
Richard Wagner *4.00 a.m. on May 22, 1813 at Leipzig

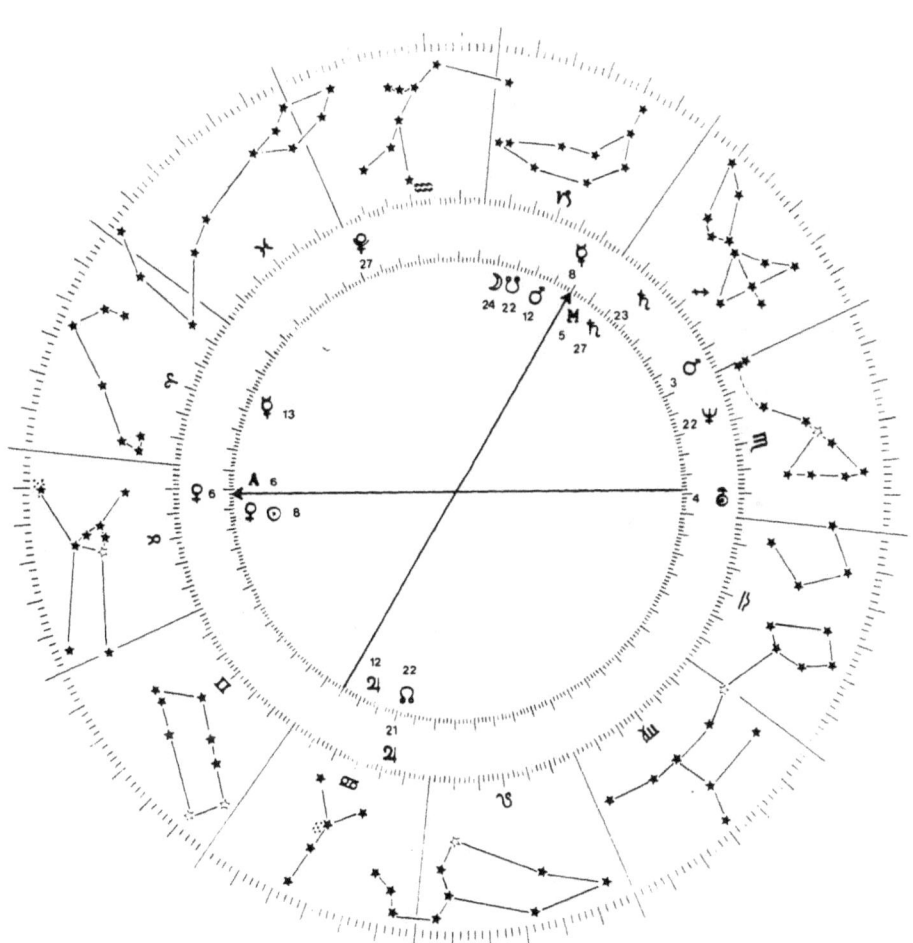

Chart 2
*Friedrich Nietzsche
Friedrich Nietzsche *10.00 a.m. on October 15, 1844 at Rocken

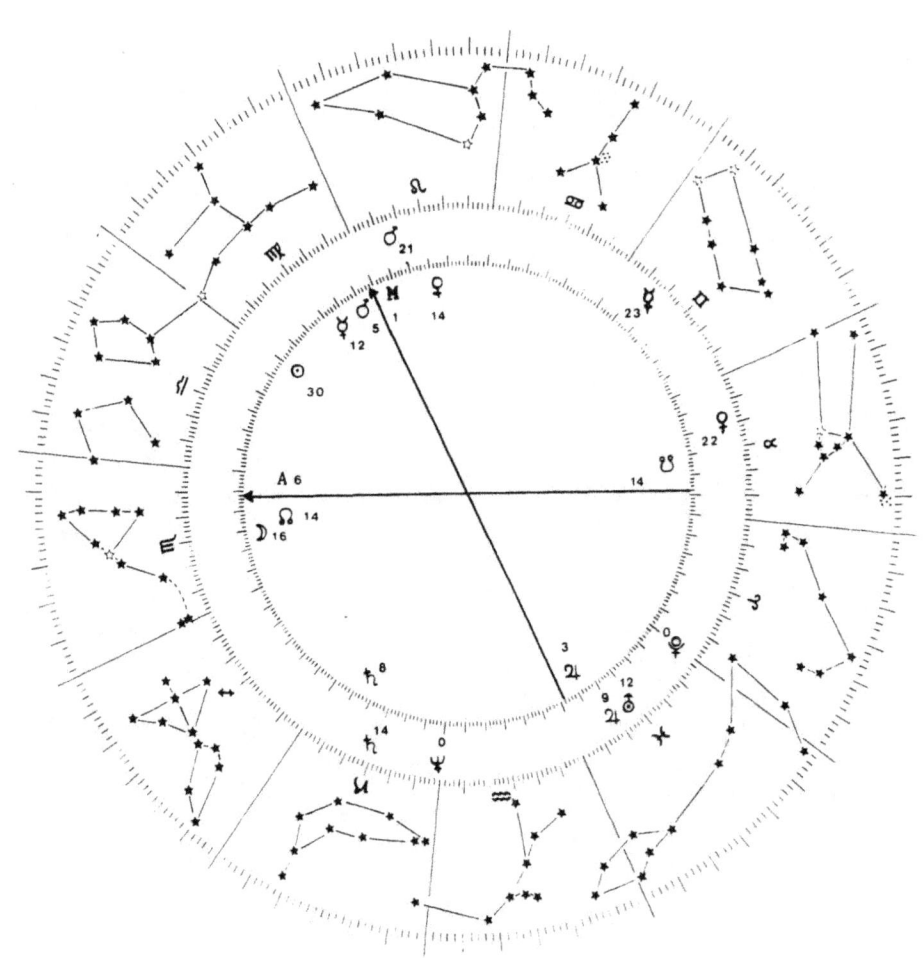

(1876) — the fourth *Meditation* is entitled: *Richard Wagner in Bayreuth*. Here, in his observation of Wagner, the seeds for some of Nietzsche's later ideas — especially that of the *will to power* — were born:

> *When the RULING IDEA of his (Wagner's) life — the idea that an incomparable amount of influence... could be exercised through the theatre — seized hold of him, it threw his whole being into the most violent ferment... this idea appeared at first... as an expression of his obscure personal will, which longed insatiably for POWER AND FAME. Influence, incomparable influence — how? over whom? — that was from now on the question and quest that ceaselessly occupied his head and heart. He wanted to conquer and rule as no artist had done before, and if possible to attain with a single blow that tyrannical omnipotence for which his instincts obscurely craved.*[8]

Through his observation of Richard Wagner at first hand, evidently Nietzsche gained the first intimations of ideas that were later to become central to his philosophy. The work *Richard Wagner in Bayreuth* — published in 1876 to coincide with the first Bayreuth festival — is sympathetic towards Wagner. This is indicated by the composer's reaction. Upon receiving a copy, Wagner wrote to Nietzsche: «Friend! Your book is prodigious! However did you learn to know me so well?»[9]

But by 1876 the intellectual divorce between Nietzsche and Wagner was already under way, and the first Bayreuth festival — at which the complete *Ring of the Nibelungen* (comprising four operas) was performed for the first time — was the occasion at which Nietzsche's estrangement from Wagner first began noticeably to assert itself. It was around the time of this festival that Nietzsche commenced work on his next book — *Human, All Too Human*, published in 1878 — which is definitely anti-Wagnerian, as was recognized by Wagner himself.

The alienation between Nietzsche and Wagner

The psychological motivation for Nietzsche's estrangement from Wagner is readily understandable. For seven years, from 1869 to 1876 (especially during the early part of this period), the brilliant young professor had lived in a condition of intellectual admiration for Richard Wagner — with Wagner as an object of knowledge — at the expense of and neglection of his own inner impulses. By the time of the first Bayreuth festival in 1876 he was approaching the age of 32, and already during his thirtieth year[10] the need had arisen within him — which asserted itself with ever-increasing intensity — to distance himself from Wagner in order to find himself. As one who had experienced Wagner at close proximity over a period of several years, he had become all too aware of Wagner's human failings. It was no longer the image of Wagner's genius — the manifestation of Wagner's higher self — which dominated his perception of the composer, but rather the «human, all too human» side (the lower self).

Nietzsche, who was a profound thinker and intellectual genius, whilst acknowledging Wagner's creative ability as a composer, began increasingly to distance himself from Wagner's intellectual pontifications.

> *Wagner's pose as a philosopher and seer had no justification; his brain was intensely alive, but his reasoning powers were of the slightest; he pontificated on matters he was utterly ignorant of; and he had the habit of decking out his writings with half-understood terminology from Feuerbach and Schopenhauer, giving them a spurious air of profundity. That Nietzsche (originally) admired some of them must be accounted a demonstration of love's proverbial blindness.*[11]

Nietzsche's early admiration of (some of) Wagner's writings developed later into outright hostility. This first came out into the open — although still in a relatively mild form — with the publication of Nietzsche's work *Human, All Too Human* in 1878. In 1888, however, *The Wagner Case* was published, which constituted an outright attack on Wagner. In this work, as well as casting aspersions on Wagner's character, Nietzsche protested at the composer's writings. His attack culminated in his designation of Wagner as *neurotic* and *decadent*.

The extent of Nietzsche's alienation from Wagner is emphasized by the fact that *The Wagner Case* appeared five years after Wagner's death. (Wagner died on February 13, 1883). Realising that he might be charged with apostacy against his deceased Master, Nietzsche published privately in 1889 *Nietzsche contra Wagner*, consisting of passages drawn from two works — *Human, All Too Human* and *Towards a Genealogy of Morals*, passages written between 1876 and 1878 — to show that his critical views of Wagner had already been established at least five years *before* Wagner's death.

The previous incarnation of Friedrich Nietzsche

At the beginning of the year in which *Nietzsche contra Wagner* was privately issued, Nietzsche, who at that time was living in Turin, collapsed and suffered a complete mental breakdown, which took place on January 3, 1889. From Turin he sent out short, cryptic notes to various friends and public personages, signing himself: «*Dionysus*» or «*the Crucified*». To Cosima Wagner he sent the note: «*Ariadne, I love you. Dionysus.*» Later, whilst at the psychiatric clinic in Jena, he is reported to have said: «*My wife Cosima Wagner brought me here.*» Nietzsche never recovered. He had entered into a twilight mental existence, which lasted almost twelve years, until his death on August 25, 1900.

During this period towards the end of Nietzsche's tragic life he was visited one day by the young Rudolf Steiner, who wrote of

> *the wonderful sensation that — while we were busy downstairs arranging his manuscript treasures for the world — he sat enthroned on the veranda above us in solemn awfulness, unconcerned with us, like a god of Epicurus. Whoever saw Nietzsche at this time — as he reclined in his white, pleated robe, with the glance of a Brahman in his wide- and deep-*

set eyes beneath bushy eyebrows, with the nobility of his enigmatic, questioning face and the leonine, majestic carriage of his thinker's head — had the feeling that this man could not die, but that his eye would rest for all eternity upon mankind and the whole world of appearance in this unfathomable exaltation.[12]

Some twenty-four years after Nietzsche's death, Rudolf Steiner described the karmic background to Friedrich Nietzsche and indicated how — considered from the standpoint of Nietzsche's destiny — Nietzsche's mental breakdown could be understood. He described how Nietzsche in his last incarnation had been a Franciscan monk, who had engaged in extreme self-chastisement.[13] Through severe self-flagellation the monk had created an unusually strong bond of awareness with his physical body, which was often racked with self-inflicted pain. This led in the next incarnation (as Friedrich Nietzsche) eventually to a condition of withdrawal from the physical body, which came to full expression from the time of Nietzsche's breakdown until his death. (Gabriele Reuter's words, after visiting Nietzsche during this time, were: «Who can tell how much of that great, unhappy soul still lived on in the secluded body?»[14])

The law of karma — «As ye sow, so shall ye reap» — is inexorable. In his previous incarnation Nietzsche — or rather, the Franciscan monk who he had been — had severely punished his physical body. In accordance with the law of karma (destiny) the consequences of this abuse revisited him in the next incarnation as Friedrich Nietzsche. Nietzsche was plagued with illness, much of which was of a psychosomatic nature: headaches, eye trouble, vomiting, stomach problems. «In April 1879... for several weeks he was in a state of permanent collapse, racked by attack after attack of the most agonizing headaches, his eyes almost useless from pain and his stomach in continual revolt.»[15] The consequences of the self-inflicted abuse of his physical body in the one incarnation returned in the next incarnation as a constitutional weakness combined with a psychological predisposition to suffer pain. Remarkably enough, in spite of suffering almost continual pain, Nietzsche managed to produce his philosophical works. «Continual and painful suffering has not up to this moment subdued my spirit... Read my latest manuscript through, dear friend, and ask yourself if any trace of suffering or depression can be discovered in it.»[16]

Eventually, however, Nietzsche's soul was driven out of his tortured body. The breakdown on January 3, 1889 — whereby the ensuing mental twilight existence lasted until his death — constituted a release, a separation from his physical body. This condition can be understood against the karmic background of Nietzsche's former incarnation as an ascetic Franciscan monk, who had inflicted pain — amounting to torture — upon his physical body.

Although Rudolf Steiner indicated the former incarnation of Friedrich Nietzsche, thereby explaining the karmic background to Nietzsche's mental breakdown, he did not divulge the name of the Franciscan monk. Through astrological karma research — applying the first «law» of reincarnation — the identity of the monk in question was established in *Hermetic Astrology I* as St. Peter of Alcantara (see Volume I, Appendix III: *The first «law» of reincarnation;* see also Appendix IV, which contains a brief biography of St. Peter of Alcantara). It is the life of St. Peter of Alcantara to which we shall now turn in order to understand the karmic relationship between Friedrich Nietzsche and Richard Wagner.

«Fray Pedro is on the way! He is coming to Avila! Fray Pedro de Alcantara! Fray Pedro, the saint! God has sent him to us!» This jubilant cry from faithful believers rang out one day in the year 1558/9 (or possibly 1560), as Peter of Alcantara came to visit the flourishing cathedral city of Avila, some seventy miles north-west of Madrid, Spain. It was well-known that the monk practised the most severe self-mortification, that his life was spent in active apostolic service or in praying on his knees, that for some forty years he had allowed himself only one hour's sleep each night — and this in sitting, with «his head resting on a block of wood».[17] His fame — as an ascetic Franciscan reformer, on account of his miracles, raptures and unheard-of austerities — had spread throughout the land. He was known as a man blessed by God, attributed with the gift of «wondrous repentance and sublime contemplation».

The relationship between St. Peter of Alcantara and St. Teresa of Avila

Upon hearing the news of Peter of Alcantara's arrival in Avila, an illustrious widow of this city, Dona Guiomar de Ulloa, hurried to the Carmelite convent of the Incarnation not far from her house. There she managed to persuade the prioress of the Incarnation to allow the Carmelite nun Teresa of Avila to come and stay with her at her house for eight days. She wanted to arrange a meeting between her friend — Teresa — and Fr. Peter, so that Teresa's case could be investigated by one who was renowned for the divine favours he had received. Dona Guiomar was convinced that Teresa was also the recipient of divine favours — that her visions and locutions stemmed from God — despite the opinion of Father Gaspar Daza that her supernatural experiences were diabolical, not divine.

Soon it became apparent that Fr. Peter was overjoyed at his meeting with the Carmelite nun, Teresa of Avila. «He says, her presence strengthened him greatly, that his greatest consolation in life consists in meeting those upon whom God has bestowed his favours in great abundance.»[18]

Fr. Peter openly declared his regret that Teresa had to suffer the severest of all trials, i.e. to be attacked by prominent personages, to have to suffer their denigrating criticism, their negation of her supernatural experiences. He added: «No one in Avila is in a position to understand her.»[19] He himself was able to understand her — not by virtue of his knowledge of theology, but on account of his own inner experiences. He understood because he himself had been blessed by the presence of God and knew the ecstasies, visions and divine locutions that result from such meetings with the Divine.

At last — through Fr. Peter of Alcantara — came the confirmation for Teresa of that which the Jesuit Father Diego de Cetina, and also St. Francis Borgia, had assured her: that she was «very evidently being led by the Spirit of God».[20] During a period of some five years Teresa had taken as her confessor the Jesuit father Balthasar Alvarez, who had begun to lead her «to greater perfection».[21] During this time she was sorely tried by «a number of people in whom (she) had great confidence» but who ascribed her experiences to the devil, so that she became «quite upset and worn out, with not the least idea what to do».[22] Father Alvarez and his fellow Jesuits, however, had maintained all along that her supernatural experiences were of divine origin.

So much was Fr. Peter of Alcantara convinced of the genuineness of Teresa's experiences that he told Father Alvarez and some of his Jesuit colleagues that «apart from the Holy Scripture and all that which the Church teaches us to believe, nothing is truer than this: that the things which this woman sees are of divine origin.»[23]

In Peter of Alcantara Teresa had found a true friend and supporter. Their friendship lasted until Peter's death, at which Teresa reports that she saw his soul — in light-illumined form — sore towards heaven. Even after his death their relationship continued, and the departed saint appeared to her several times «in a state of great glory... full of bliss».[24]

Apart from Peter of Alcantara's reassurance concerning the validity of Teresa's supernatural experiences, she also listened to his accounts of «his own affairs and undertakings» as a reformer of the Franciscan Order.[25] It was as a result of this that she became encouraged in her own plan to reform the Carmelite Order, which she had first conceived of in about 1558. Her idea was to found a small convent where several nuns could follow a more penitential life than was possible at the convent of the Incarnation. She wanted to return to the Primitive Rule of Our Lady of Carmel, to restore an austerity typified by the word *discalced* («barefooted»). It was thus that her plan for the Discalced Reform came into being, which gained the support of Peter of Alcantara, himself a Discalced Franciscan.

In view of the fierce opposition which Teresa of Avila met in trying to carry through her plan, and the incredible difficulties she had to overcome before the Carmelite Reform triumphed, the advice and support of Peter of Alcantara proved invaluable in helping to set the reform in motion. Something of this relationship between St. Teresa of Avila and St. Peter of Alcantara recurred — in metamorphosed form — in the next incarnation, where St. Peter reincarnated as Friedrich Nietzsche and St. Teresa as Richard Wagner. (The hermetic-astrological confirmation that St. Peter of Alcantara reincarnated as Friedrich Nietzsche is presented in *Hermetic Astrology* I, Appendix III, Table 20, and that St. Teresa reincarnated as Richard Wagner is presented below.)

Chart 3
*St. Teresa of Avila
St. Teresa of Avila *5.30 a.m. on March 28, 1515 at Avila

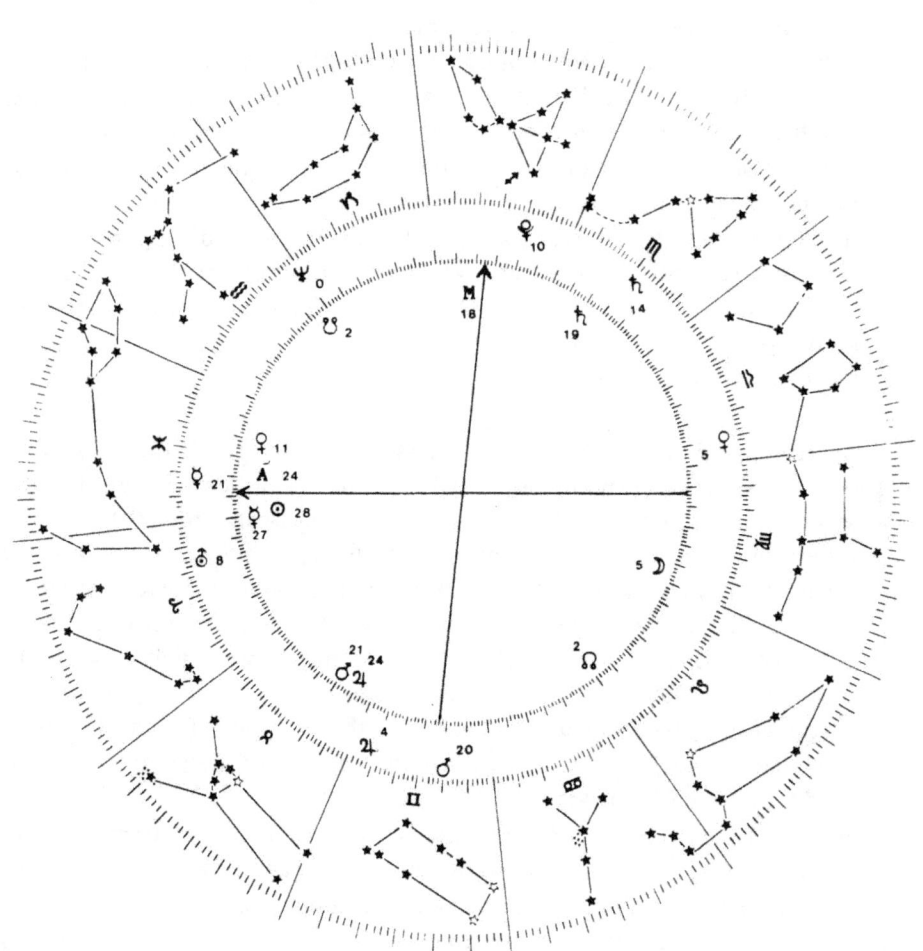

I. Karmic Relationships

Chart 4
†St. Teresa of Avila

St. Teresa of Avila †6.15 a.m. on October 4, 1582 at Alba de Tormes

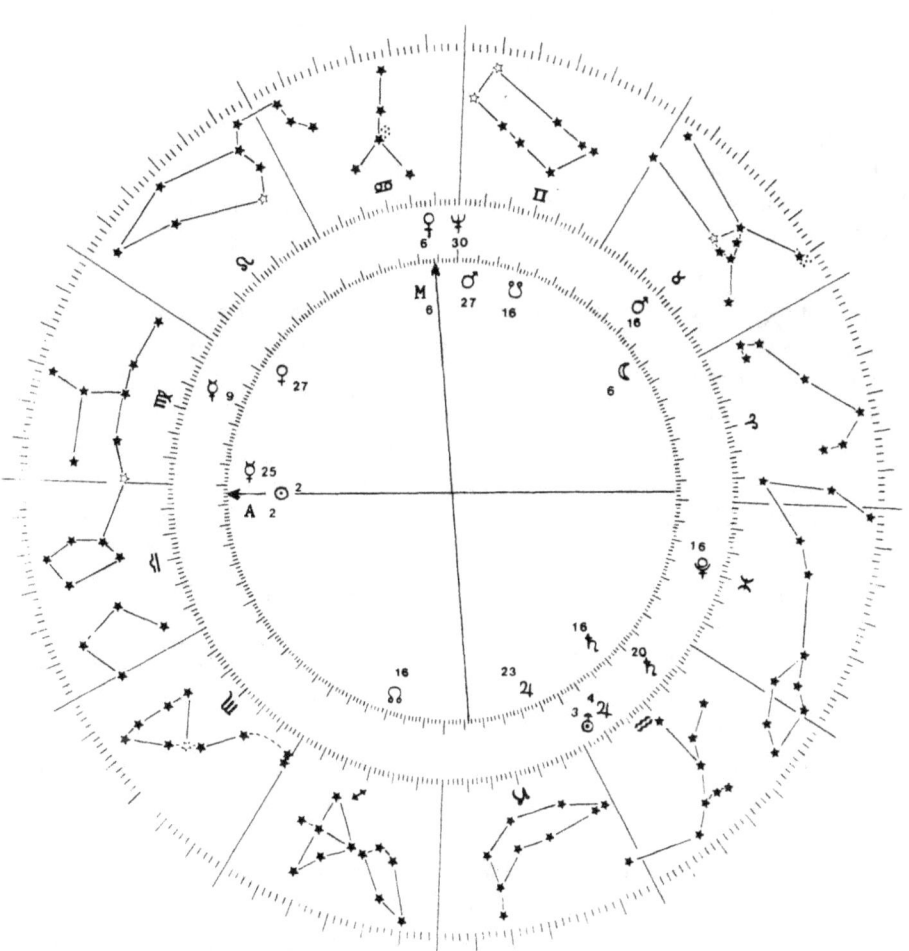

The reincarnation of St. Teresa of Avila as Richard Wagner

Just as St. Teresa had been concerned with a reform, the driving motivation of Richard Wagner's life was a reform — or even a revolution — leading to what he called the «art-work of the future» in which the «total art-work» would be restored. One of the visions which inspired him — that of a new «sacred theatre» — led him to the founding of the opera house at Bayreuth, dedicated to the fulfilment of his idea for the art-work of the future. There is, in fact, a remarkable parallel in the colossal difficulties confronted by Richard Wagner in the struggle to establish his theatre at Bayreuth for the performing of his operas, and the immense problems confronted by St. Teresa of Avila in the struggle to found convents for the Carmelite reform. The contexts of their respective struggles are, of course, very different. But in both cases it is a matter of a single personality fighting against tremendous odds in a heroic struggle to realise far-reaching aims.

However, before looking in further detail at the karmic relationship involved here, it is important — in the context of hermetic astrology — to seek confirmation of the reincarnation statement referred to above: St. Teresa of Avila — Richard Wagner.

According to the method of approach developed in hermetic astrology, the first step is to compare the birth horoscope of Richard Wagner (Chart 1) with the birth/death configurations of St. Teresa of Avila (Charts 3 and 4). Hermetic-astrological karma research has revealed the existence of the first «law» of reincarnation, discussed in Volume I, Appendix III. The first «law» of reincarnation states that the angular relationship (aspect) between the Sun and Saturn at an individual's birth is the same as — or is the complement of (with respect to 180 degrees) — that at death in the previous incarnation. (This is not a strict law, since there are examples in which it does not apply, and therefore the word «law» is written in inverted commas.)

Looking at the birth horoscope of Richard Wagner (Chart 1), the angle between the Sun and Saturn amounts to 132 degrees. From Chart 4, the planetary configuration at the death of St. Teresa of Avila, it can be seen that the Saturn-Sun angle is 134 degrees. The first «law» of reincarnation thus supports the reincarnation statement: St. Teresa of Avila — Richard Wagner.

Hermetic-astrological karma research

The «laws» of reincarnation in hermetic astrology are based upon the following principle, which was first formulated by Rudolf Steiner in the year 1912:

> When a person passes through the gate of death he dies under a certain configuration of stars. This configuration is significant for his further life of soul because it remains there as an imprint. In his soul there remains the endeavour to enter into this same configuration at a new birth, to do justice once again to the forces received at the moment of death. It is an

interesting point that if one works out the configuration at death and compares it with the configuration of the later birth, one finds that it coincides to a high degree with the configuration at the former death.[26]

Hermetic-astrological karma research has been able to confirm this general principle formulated by Rudolf Steiner, by finding concrete manifestations of it — the so-called «laws» of reincarnation. There are three astrological domains in which the search for the «laws» of reincarnation may be conducted, when configurations at birth are compared with those at the former death. These three astrological domains are:

(i) the houses — the positions of the planets in the houses (the spatial positioning of the planets geographically with respect to the Earth, i.e. whether the planets are above or below the Earth, to the east or to the west, etc., at the moment of birth/death; this is brought to expression by the positions of the planets in the houses, where the houses constitute geographical sectors defined in relation to the time and place of birth/death);

(ii) the aspects (the mutual relationships of the planets to one another, expressed in terms of angular relationships between the planets; here there are two levels to be taken into consideration: geocentric and heliocentric, i.e. both the geocentric and heliocentric planetary aspects need to be taken into account);

(iii) the zodiac — the locations of the planets in the signs of the zodiac (here again there are two levels, i.e. both the geocentric and heliocentric planetary positions in the sidereal zodiac need to be taken into consideration).

With regard to (i) — the houses, more specifically, the locations of the planets in the houses — the comparison of the birth configuration with the death configuration in the previous incarnation entails looking for similarities in the locations of the planets (including the Sun and Moon) in the houses. For example, it could be that there is a tendency if someone dies with a given planet on the Ascendant (marking the first house) to reincarnate at a moment when the same planet is again on the Ascendant, or when it is opposite (on the Descendant). However, there are certain difficulties involved in astrological karma research with respect to the positions of the planets in the houses, which means that research in this astrological domain has been very limited until now. One difficulty is that there is no consistent agreement as to how the houses are defined. The location of the planets (including the Sun and Moon) at the time and place of birth in twelve geographical sectors defined by the houses is by no means unique. Different house systems lead to the location of the planets in different houses. (The hermetic house system is discussed in Chapter 7.) This fact constitutes one reason as to why astrological karma research in the domain of the houses has been limited hitherto. Another more serious reason hindering astrological karma research with respect to the positions of the planets in the houses is that it is rare to have accurate times of birth and/or death in two successive incarnations. It is only if both the time of death in one incarnation and the time of birth in the next incarnation are known that a comparison of planetary positions in the houses between the two charts is possible. As this condition is seldom fulfilled, there are very few reincarnation examples in which it is possible to compare the charts with respect to planetary positions in the houses. Consequently — at least, up until now — it has not been possible to discover any «laws» of reincarnation that hold in the astrological domain of the houses.

Of course, if the time of birth/death in a given incarnation of a particular reincarnation example is known, then the houses — or rather, the Ascendant and Midheaven, which are the main determinants of the houses — can be included in the comparison of birth/death charts from one incarnation to the next. (The Ascendant is the degree of the zodiac rising on the eastern horizon at the moment of birth, and the Midheaven is the degree of the zodiac culminating overhead at the moment of birth.)

The Ascendant axis (the zodiacal axis from the Ascendant to the opposite point, the Descendant) and the Midheaven axis (the zodiacal axis from the Midheaven to the opposite point, the Nadir) specify the primary division into four house quadrants, where each of the four quadrants are subdivided into three sectors to obtain twelve houses. The Ascendant axis and the Midheaven axis thus provide a «partial representation» of the houses. Like the Moon node axis, the Ascendant and Midheaven axes can also be included in the search for zodiacal alignments when comparing birth/death configurations from one incarnation to the next — see (iii) below for a discussion of zodiacal alignments and their significance.

With respect to (ii) — the aspects — the comparison of the birth horoscope with the configuration at the death in the previous incarnation entails looking for *aspect metamorphoses* from one chart to the other. Nine different aspect metamorphoses are defined in *Hermetic Astrology* I, Appendix V, Table 28. (See also Table 27 for an example of aspect metamorphosis — the reincarnation example Cardinal Mazarin/Georg Hertling — where the heliocentric conjunction between Venus and Neptune at Mazarin's death became metamorphosed to become a heliocentric opposition between Venus and Neptune at Hertling's birth.) These nine are the main aspect metamorphoses. Further aspect metamorphoses have been excluded from the author's astrological karma research in hermetic astrology so far, owing to the complexity introduced by the consideration of aspects other than three main aspects of conjunction, opposition and square. (There is a further reason — discussed below — for considering only these three aspects when looking for aspect metamorphoses.)

These three main aspects alone yield nine aspect metamorphoses, and each additional aspect would raise the number of aspect metamorphoses considerably. For example, four aspects would yield sixteen aspect metamorphoses; five aspects would yield twenty-five aspect metamorphoses, etc.

The comparison of charts from death in one incarnation to birth in the next incarnation, looking for aspect metamorphoses, is complicated further by the two levels: geocentric and heliocentric (hermetic). On the one hand, aspect metamorphoses have to be looked for from the geocentric death configuration to the geocentric birth horoscope in the next incarnation, and on the other hand they have also to be looked for from the heliocentric (hermetic) death configuration to the heliocentric (hermetic) birth horoscope. In *Hermetic Astrology* I, Appendix V, it is shown that the hermetic chart — which astronomically is essentially equivalent to the heliocentric chart — is an astrologically valid chart, and that the search for aspect metamorphoses should be looked for in terms of the hermetic charts rather than in terms of the corresponding heliocentric charts. (Much of *Hermetic Astrology* I is concerned with the significance of the hermetic chart, which is based on the Egyptian-Tychonic system, in contrast to the heliocentric chart based on the Copernican system.)

Therefore two levels of search for aspect metamorphoses are given by the planetary aspects in (a) the hermetic chart and (b) the geocentric chart. (The charts presented in this book are drawn in terms of two concentric circles, the hermetic chart being given in the outer circle and the geocentric chart in the inner circle.) Thus, in comparing the planetary configuration at birth with the planetary configuration at death in the previous incarnation, aspect metamorphoses may be found either in the respective hermetic charts or in the respective geocentric charts.

The first «law» of reincarnation is a special case — belonging to the astrological domain of aspects — in which the angular relationship between the Sun and Saturn at birth in one incarnation is compared with that at death in the previous incarnation. It is a special case, because often the angle between the Sun and Saturn does not correspond to any known astrological aspect at all. If the angle between the Sun and Saturn at death in one incarnation is denoted by α, then in terms of the first «law» of reincarnation the metamorphosis of α (from death in one incarnation to birth in the next incarnation) can be expressed

either as $\alpha \rightarrow \alpha$ (in which case the angle remains the same)

or as $\alpha \rightarrow 180 - \alpha$ (in which case the angle becomes the complement of 180 degrees).

In the reincarnation example Teresa of Avila/Richard Wagner, the metamorphosis is $\alpha \rightarrow \alpha$, where α at St. Teresa's death was 134 degrees and α at Richard Wagner's birth was 132 degrees. In this case the angle α does correspond approximately to a traditional astrological aspect, namely the aspect of a sesquiquadrate (135 degrees), which lies midway between the aspects of square and opposition. But this is pure coincidence, as there are numerous examples of the first «law» of reincarnation in which the angle α does not correspond to any known traditional astrological aspect (see, for example, the angles listed in the reincarnation examples presented in *Hermetic Astrology* I, Appendix III, Table 18).

In the reincarnation example Teresa of Avila/Richard Wagner — and in all the reincarnation examples in *Hermetic Astrology* I, Appendix III, Table 18 — the angle α is the angle between the Sun and Saturn in the *geocentric* chart, i.e. it is the angle between the Sun and g-Saturn. As the difference between Saturn's heliocentric position (h-Saturn) and geocentric position (g-Saturn) can amount to at most 6 degrees, the angle between the Sun and Saturn in the hermetic chart cannot differ from its equivalent in the geocentric chart by more than 6 degrees. Therefore it does not make a great deal of difference, when applying the first «law» of reincarnation, whether the comparison of angles between the Sun and Saturn — from death in one incarnation to birth in the next incarnation — is made in terms of the hermetic charts or in terms of the geocentric charts. (The angle between the Sun and Saturn in the hermetic chart at St. Teresa's death was $138\frac{1}{2}$ degrees, and in the hermetic chart at Richard Wagner's birth it was 136 degrees — also closely fulfilling the first «law» of reincarnation.) Sometimes it is the angle between the Sun and Saturn in the geocentric charts (death → birth) and sometimes it is the angle between Sun and Saturn in the hermetic charts (death → birth) which better fits the first «law» of reincarnation.

Above it was said that the first «law» of reincarnation can be regarded as a special case. However, this does not mean that it is a special case of aspect metamorphosis, since — as referred to already — the angular relationship between the Sun and Saturn, in applying the first «law» of reincarnation, often does not correspond to any known traditional astrological aspect. Rather, the aspect metamorphoses referred to above must be regarded as special cases of that which is indicated by the first «law» of reincarnation. This is one reason for considering only the aspects of conjunction, opposition and square, when looking for aspect metamorphoses. For these three aspects also obey the principle of the first «law» of reincarnation. This «law» — as formulated above — states: either $\alpha \rightarrow \alpha$, or $\alpha \rightarrow 180 - \alpha$. The aspects of conjunction (0 degrees), opposition (180 degrees) and square (90 degrees) fit this, since

$180 - 0 = 180$, i.e. the complement of a conjunction is an opposition;

$180 - 180 = 0$, i.e. the complement of an opposition is a conjunction;

$180 - 90 = 90$, i.e. the complement of a square is a square.

That is, when applying the relationship $\alpha \rightarrow \alpha$ or $\alpha \rightarrow 180 - \alpha$ to the three aspects conjunction, opposition and square, the result is again always conjunction, opposition or square.

With regard to (iii) — the zodiac, i.e. the locations of the planets in the zodiacal signs — the comparison of the birth horoscope in one incarnation with the configuration at death in the previous incarnation entails looking for *zodiacal alignments* from one chart to the other. This is the third possible concrete manifestation of the general karmic-astrological principle formulated by Rudolf Steiner in 1912 (quoted above). It was through looking for zodiacal alignments from death in one incarnation to birth in the next incarnation that the author discovered the objectively verifiable result that it is the sidereal zodiac which is the authentic astrological zodiac, and not the tropical zodiac currently enjoying widespread use in astrology. The authenticity of the sidereal zodiac becomes apparent when comparing death/birth charts for zodiacal alignments in reincarnation examples where the successive incarnations are widely separated in time. During the intervening period of time a significant difference arises — owing to precession — between the zodiacal locations of the planets in the sidereal zodiac (S) and the tropical zodiac (T). If the successive incarnations are sufficiently far apart, the difference between S and T arising on account of precession becomes noticeable.

If the number of years between successive incarnations is Y years, then the difference between S and T amounts to Y/72 degrees, since the (average) rate of precession is one degree in 72 years. Thus, if 720 years elapses between death in one incarnation and birth in the next incarnation, the difference between S and T amounts to $720/72 = 10$ degrees. This means in this case that an exact zodiacal alignment in terms of S is 10 degrees away from being an exact zodiacal alignment when looked at in terms of T, and *vice versa*. (Note: a zodiacal alignment from death in one incarnation to birth in the next incarnation signifies that a planet's position in the zodiac at death in one incarnation is either the same, or is opposite in the zodiac, when compared with its or another planet's position at birth in the next incarnation. It need not be the same planet which aligns at a given zodiacal degree, and the Moon's nodes — and likewise the Ascendant and Midheaven axes, as referred to in (i) above — can also be taken into consideration when looking for zodiacal alignments.)

Applying the principle outlined here (of looking for zodiacal alignments from death in one incarnation to birth in the next incarnation), but applied only to reincarnation examples with at least 8 degrees of precession — corresponding to a period of $8 \times 72 = 576$ years between the successive incarnations — the results presented in *Hermetic Astrology* I, Appendix IV, show conclusively that the sidereal zodiac is the authentic astrological zodiac. (In Appendix IV it emerges that certain specific kinds of zodiacal alignment occur predominantly in the sidereal zodiac rather than in the tropical zodiac. Of course, some zodiacal alignments occur in the tropical zodiac also, but these can be regarded as purely a matter of coincidence, since the majority of the alignments take place in the framework of the sidereal zodiac.) As part of this verification of the sidereal zodiac as the authentic astrological zodiac in Appendix IV of *Hermetic Astrology* I, the second «law» of reincarnation is referred to. This is the «law» of alignment of h-Mercury and/or h-Venus from death in one incarnation to birth in the next incarnation. (See Table 25 in Appendix IV, where h-Mercury/h-Venus zodiacal alignments occur in the sidereal zodiac in five of the six reincarnation examples listed.)

Just as with the first «law» of reincarnation (which comes under the astrological domain of *aspects*), so the «law» of alignment of h-Mercury/h-Venus (which comes under the astrological domain of *zodiacal positions of the planets*) is a pseudo-law, i.e. it does not always apply, which is why it — also — is written in inverted commas.

As in the search for aspect metamorphoses, the search for zodiacal alignments — when comparing charts from death in one incarnation to birth in the next incarnation — must take account of both the hermetic and the geocentric charts. Just as with the search for aspect metamorphoses, so the search for zodiacal alignments in the sidereal zodiac is in terms of (a) the respective hermetic charts (death → birth) and (b) the respective geocentric charts (death → birth). The zodiacal alignment of h-Mercury/h-Venus from death in one incarnation to birth in the next incarnation is an example of a regularly recurring zodiacal alignment in the respective hermetic charts (death → birth), whereby h-Mercury and/or h-Venus at death in one incarnation aligns in the sidereal zodiac with h-Mercury and/or h-Venus at birth in the next incarnation.

The non-occurrence of this h-Mercury/h-Venus zodiacal alignment does not mean that a reincarnation example is invalid, just as the non-fulfilment of the first «law» of reincarnation does not mean that a reincarnation example is invalid. On the other hand, the fulfilment of either the first «law» of reincarnation and/or the «law» of h-Mercury/h-Venus zodiacal alignment lends weight to support the validity of a given reincarnation statement. These «laws» of reincarnation are, in the last analysis, merely corroborators of something that can only be known by way of spiritual faculties of cognition.

Chart comparison between the two incarnations

The identification of Richard Wagner's previous incarnation as St. Teresa of Avila was arrived at by way of spiritual cognition. (See *Hermetic Astrology* I, Chapter 7, under the heading «Four principles of karma research» for a description of the conditions pertaining to the spiritual cognition necessary for reincarnation research.) Nevertheless, it is of significance that St. Teresa of Avila's reincarnation as Richard Wagner, which was arrived at by way of spiritual cognition, is corroborated not only by the first «law» of reincarnation — as already discussed above — but also by the «law» of zodiacal alignment of h-Mercury/h-Venus. This second reincarnation «law» is fulfilled by virtue of h-Mercury (h-ME) at Wagner's birth (*) having aligned on the opposite ($\mathcal{S}$) side of the zodiac to h-Venus (h-VE) at the death (†) of St. Teresa of Avila. In terms of the sidereal zodiac (S), this zodiacal alignment can be expressed as

$$S: \dagger h\text{-VE} \; \mathcal{S} \; *h\text{-ME} \quad (6CN/7\tfrac{1}{2}CP, \text{ orb: } 1°27')$$

Since both the time of birth of Richard Wagner and the time of death of St. Teresa of Avila are known, the above equation of zodiacal alignment is

I. Karmic Relationships

accurate, the orb of difference from exact alignment being approximately $1\frac{1}{2}$ degrees.

The two reincarnation «laws» applied to (and corroborating) the reincarnation statement: Teresa of Avila = Richard Wagner, refer strictly to the relationship between the death configuration in one incarnation and the birth configuration in the next incarnation. In general, however, the search for zodiacal alignments and aspect metamorphoses in astrological karma research can be extended from the death configuration of the previous incarnation to include the birth configuration as well, if it is known, i.e. if the date of birth in the previous incarnation is known. The birth configuration in the new incarnation is then compared with the birth and death configurations of the preceding incarnation, in the search for zodiacal alignments and aspect metamorphoses. As an example, let us consider Richard Wagner's birth horoscope in relation to the birth and death configurations of St. Teresa of Avila. (See Table 1 for a summary of the zodiacal alignments, and Table 2 for a summary of the aspect metamorphoses, arising from a comparison of Wagner's horoscope with the birth/death configurations of St. Teresa.)

Table 1
St. Teresa of Avila/Richard Wagner
chart comparison for zodiacal alignments

See Appendix II for the computation of the planetary positions — geocentric and heliocentric — listed in the following table.

Abbreviations:

h = heliocentric sidereal longitude (hermetic chart)
g = geocentric sidereal longitude (geocentric chart)
* = birth
† = death

St. Teresa of Avila		Richard Wagner	
†h-Venus	(6° Cancer)	*h-Mercury	($7\frac{1}{2}°$ Capricorn)
†Moon	(6° Taurus)	*Ascendant	($5\frac{1}{2}°$ Taurus)
		*h-Venus	($6\frac{1}{2}°$ Taurus)
		*g-Venus	($7\frac{1}{2}°$ Taurus)
		*Sun	($8\frac{1}{2}°$ Taurus)
†g-Jupiter	($23\frac{1}{2}°$ Capricorn)	*Moon	(24° Capricorn)
		*Moon's node	(22° Cancer)
		*h-Jupiter	($21\frac{1}{2}°$ Cancer)
*h-Jupiter	($3\frac{1}{2}°$ Gemini)	*h-Mars	($3\frac{1}{2}°$ Sagittarius)
†g-Mars	(27° Gemini)	*g-Saturn	(27° Sagittarius)
*h-Mars	($20\frac{1}{2}°$ Gemini)	*h-Saturn	($22\frac{1}{2}°$ Sagittarius)
*g-Mars	(21° Taurus)	*g-Neptune	($22\frac{1}{2}°$ Scorpio)
*g-Jupiter	($24\frac{1}{2}°$ Taurus)		
†g-Venus	($27\frac{1}{2}°$ Leo)	*g-Pluto	($28\frac{1}{2}°$ Aquarius)

Table 2
St. Teresa of Avila/Richard Wagner
chart comparison for aspect metamorphoses

See Appendix II for Computations.
Abbreviations:
☌ denotes conjunction, ☍ opposition and □ square. The orb of difference from exact conjunction (0 degrees 0 minutes), exact opposition (180 degrees 0 minutes) and exact square (90 degrees 0 minutes) is also listed (in brackets), where the maximum orb of difference allowed for the aspects of conjunction and opposition is 8 degrees and for the aspect of square is 4 degrees. (Note: only the aspects of conjunction and opposition of a planet to the Ascendant, Midheaven and Moon's north node are taken into consideration, and not the aspect of square.)
h denotes that the aspect is in the hermetic chart
g denotes that the aspect is in the geocentric chart
* = birth
† = death

St. Teresa of Avila				Richard Wagner			
*g:	A ☌ SU	(4°25')		*g:	A ☌ SU	(2°57')	
†g:	A ☌ SU	(0°00')**					
*h:	VE ☌ SU	(7°02')		*h:	VE ☌ SU	(2°08')	
				*g:	VE ☌ SU	(0°53')	
†g:	ME □ MA	(1°39')		*g:	ME □ MA	(1°42')	
*h:	ME □ MA	(0°52')					
*h:	VE ☍ UR	(2°40')		*h:	VE ☍ UR	(2°26')	
				*g:	VE ☍ UR	(4°00')	
*g:	MA ☌ JU	(3°34')		*g:	MA ☍ JU	(0°12')	
*h:	MO □ JU	(1°18')		*h:	MO ☍ JU	(2°39')	
†h:	MO □ JU	(1°53')					

(** Here the time of death is given as «around sunrise», at which time the Sun is exactly conjunct the Ascendant, in which case the orb of difference would be 0 degrees 0 minutes. However, it is unlikely that the Sun was exactly conjunct the Ascendant, and therefore in actual fact the orb of difference would not have been exactly 0 degrees 0 minutes.)

Symbols: A = Ascendant; SU = Sun; MO = Moon; ME = Mercury; VE = Venus; MA = Mars; JU = Jupiter; UR = Uranus.

From the zodiacal alignments and aspect metamorphoses listed in Tables 1 and 2, it is evident that a close relationship exists between the birth/death charts of St. Teresa of Avila and the birth chart of Richard Wagner — in addition to the fulfilment of the two «laws» of reincarnation referred to already. (The fulfilment of the «law» of alignment of h-Mercury/h-Venus is indicated by the first entry in Table 1, whereas the fulfilment of the first «law» of reincarnation — as it does not correspond to any aspect metamorphosis involving conjunction, opposition and square — is not listed at all.) Most striking is that the conjunction of Venus and the Sun on the Ascendant at Richard Wagner's birth aligned with the zodiacal location of the Moon at St. Teresa's death, and that the conjunction of Mars and Jupiter in the geocentric chart at St. Teresa's birth metamorphosed to become an exact opposition between the two planets in the geocentric chart at Richard Wagner's birth.

In *Hermetic Astrology* I, Appendix VI, where Richard Wagner's birth chart is given as an example (see Chart 38), it is pointed out that in the hermetic chart there is an opposition (☍) between the Moon and Jupiter along the axis of the Moon's nodes, and that this configuration has much to do with the deep inspiration in Wagner's music. The importance of the relationship between the Moon and Jupiter in the hermetic chart is emphasized by the fact that in the hermetic chart at the birth *and* at the death of St. Teresa the Moon is square (□) to Jupiter. This Moon-Jupiter aspect metamorphosis in the hermetic charts from birth to death in one incarnation and then to birth in the next incarnation can be represented as: □ → □ → ☍.

The mission of the individuality

As indicated several times in *Hermetic Astrology* I, the significance of the hermetic chart is that it relates to the level of the individuality — in contrast to the geocentric chart, which refers more to the levels of the personality and the soul. From the hermetic chart it is possible to gain insight into the human being's mission, which is connected with his individuality. In particular, the planetary configuration in the hermetic chart portrays the structure of the human being's psycho-spiritual organism — bound up with the system of lotus flowers — the key to which is given by the *hermetic man*. In the figure of the hermetic man (see *Hermetic Astrology* I, Chapter 5, Figure 13) the correspondence between the system of lotus flowers and the planetary system is indicated. That which the hermetic man represents comprises a vehicle through which the individuality works in the unfolding of its mission. The hermetic man holds the key to the correspondence between the macrocosmic domain of the individuality and the microcosmic world of the human being's psycho-spiritual organism (comprising the system of lotus flowers) via which the individuality works in a given incarnation. The hermetic chart shows the macrocosmic situation, and from it — applying the key indicated by the hermetic man — the corresponding relationship of the lotus flowers to one another in the incarnated human being can be interpreted.

As an example, let us consider the opposition between the Moon and Jupiter at Richard Wagner's birth. From the figure of the hermetic man (*Hermetic Astrology* I, Figure 13), the Moon corresponds to the 4-petalled lotus flower and Jupiter to the 2-petalled lotus flower. Since these two lotus flowers are on opposite sides of the 12-petalled lotus flower (heart center) — which corresponds to the Sun — the opposition between the Moon and Jupiter reflects the «natural relationship» between these two lotus flowers. The opposition between Jupiter and the Moon is therefore beneficial for a cooperation between the 2-petalled and 4-petalled lotus flowers. That Richard Wagner chose to incarnate when the Moon and Jupiter were in opposition (in the hermetic chart) indicates that a working together of the 2-petalled and 4-petalled lotus flowers was important to this individual for the unfolding of his mission. In other words, he sought a cooperation between the organ of higher thought (the 2-petalled lotus flower, corresponding to Jupiter) and the organ of the will (the 4-petalled lotus flower, corresponding to the Moon).

The same can be said of St. Teresa of Avila, who chose to incarnate when the Moon was square to Jupiter (in the hermetic chart — see Chart 3). The square relationship between the Moon and Jupiter — like the opposition — signifies a cooperation between the 2-petalled and 4-petalled lotus flowers. The difference between the square and the opposition, however, is that whereas the opposition is conducive to a continous cooperation between these two lotus flowers, the square indicates a dynamic interaction between them, i.e. an alternation from one lotus flower to the other — with one lotus flower becoming active for a time, and then the other.

Can this help us to grasp the mission of this individuality, who incarnated in the sixteenth century as St. Teresa of Avila and in the nineteenth century as Richard Wagner? If it is possible to gain insight into the mission of this individuality, we shall be in a better position to understand the karmic relationship between Richard Wagner and Friedrich Nietzsche, which started out so promisingly, but which took such a tragic turn. Perhaps Nietzsche's destiny would have taken a different — more happy — course, if his relationship with Richard Wagner had not become so disturbed?

Whatever the answer to this question may be, there is no doubt that it is possible to learn from history, from the examples of our forerunners, and this is sufficient justification for the study of karmic relationships of historical personalities. Much can be learnt — from their mistakes as well as from their positive achievements. The positive achievements of historical personalities can serve as examples to be followed, and their mistakes as warnings, i.e. as examples from which it is possible to learn about life's temptations and trials. With this in mind, let us turn to the individuality Teresa of Avila/Richard Wagner with the question: What mission did this individuality have? (In the sense that the individuality is the eternal entelechy of the human being, this question should be phrased: What mission does this individuality have?)

One way of arriving at a comprehension of the mission of an individuality is to look at various incarnations for common characteristics coming to expression in the different incarnations. This means searching for an *archetypal form* that imprints itself into each incarnation, which becomes discernable through the common characteristics manifesting in each of several incarnations. It is this archetypal form which can reveal something of the individuality's mission.

In some incarnations this archetype may come to expression more strongly than in others. That is, in some incarnations the imprint of the individuality is stronger than in others. It can happen that in a given incarnation the imprint of the individuality is particularly strong, in which case this incarnation itself can serve as an archetype in the light of which later incarnations can be viewed. This is the case, in fact, in the reincarnation example under consideration. An earlier incarnation of the individuality Teresa of Avila/Richard Wagner serves as an archetype for the later incarnations. And it is thanks to Rudolf Steiner's karma research that this earlier incarnation has been brought to the light of day. It is almost certain that Rudolf Steiner himself communicated that an earlier incarnation of Richard Wagner was the magician Merlin; at any rate Rudolf Steiner is generally attributed with the reincarnation statement Merlin/Richard Wagner.[27] It is this earlier incarnation — as Merlin — which serves as an archetype for the later incarnations as St. Teresa of Avila (sixteenth century) and Richard Wagner (nineteenth century).

Who was Merlin? According to Rudolf Steiner, he was the founder of King Arthur's Round Table.[28] The *Historia Britannorum* of Nennius contains the following passage concerning the destiny of the young Merlin:

God allowed Merlin to possess knowledge of the past and to know the mysteries of nature and of the elements. He will search for a balance between heaven, earth and hell. He will cultivate the arts, especially singing and harp music. Prophecy, clairvoyance, divine intuition will come to him. Merlin will be allowed to choose freely whether he wants to apply his gifts to serve heaven or hell.[29]

Merlin rejected the offer of the Roman bishop Gildas to enter his (Gildas') service and to unite with dark magical forces:

I will give my life for the harp of God, for the heavenly light, for the poet's crown. I hear within me harmonies; I hear the voices of the depths, the weeping of mankind and the song of angels. I seek the mystery of the supersensible. I want to unite myself with the power of the Sun spirit.[30]

Inspired through his gift of seership, Merlin sang of past events in a wonderful, prophetically-inspired epic poem, which proclaimed the future in connection with the spiritual mission of King Arthur and the Round Table. Merlin represented the poetic-musical genius and clairvoyance of the Druids, united with the Christ Impulse.[31]

The life of Merlin presents an archetype against which the later incarnations of this individuality as St. Teresa of Avila in the sixteenth century and as Richard Wagner in the nineteenth century can be appraised. Of course, a major difference between these latter two incarnations is determined by the fact that the incarnation in the sixteenth century was as a woman, whilst that of the nineteenth century was as a man. Nevertheless, despite this far-reaching difference of orientation in the two incarnations, certain common traits are discernable.

In both incarnations there was a consciousness of founding something new (just as Merlin founded the Round Table). In the sixteenth century incarnation it was the founding of the Carmelite Reform, whilst in the nineteenth century it was the founding of the «new music» — the «music of the future» and the «artwork of the future» — to which this individuality dedicated himself. In both incarnations, however, the «new» connected onto the existing tradition (just as Merlin connected onto the Druid tradition). This is a very important point, as all genuine spiritual missions are for the sake of bringing that which is positive in the existing order to a higher stage of perfection. As the Master expressed it: «I have come not to abolish the Law and the prophets, but to fulfil them» (*Matthew* v, 17).

Thus, St. Teresa united herself fully with the spiritual tradition of the Catholic Church. Her place in religious history is assured not just on account of her works on the mystical life — which rank as masterpieces of Christian mysticism — but also as the founder of the Discalced Carmelite Reform within the Catholic Church. Similarly, Richard Wagner's point of departure was the music of Beethoven on the one hand, and Shakespeare's dramas on the other hand. Richard Wagner thus connected onto the existing cultural tradition, which at his time attained its high point in the sphere of music in Beethoven's symphonies and in the sphere of drama in Shakespeare's plays. (Goethe's play *Faust* — regarded by some as the greatest drama ever written — was also much studied and admired by Wagner. In the sphere of opera itself, Wagner's model was Carl Maria von Weber.)

Wagner brought together two realms — music and drama — in his operatic compositions. His was a rare accomplishment, achieved through the fusion of poetry and music in the dramatic action of the opera — all the more remarkable considering that he combined two normally separate functions: the writing of poetry (the dramatic material for his operas) and the composition of the operatic music. (Franz Liszt wrote: «He has achieved being a great dramatist and an extraordinary symphonic composer at the same time.»)[32]

In both incarnations — that of St. Teresa and that as Richard Wagner — there was an opening up of supersensible faculties. But this came to expression quite differently in the life of St. Teresa of Avila than it did in the life of Richard Wagner. (Here the life of Merlin serves as an archetype.)

St. Teresa consciously followed a spiritual path, practising prayer and meditation for many years, until — around the age of 40 — she came to have an increasing consciousness of the presence of the Divine. She began to experience the *prayer of quiet* and the *prayer of union*, together with visions and divine locutions. Her relationship to the supersensible world then developed further to a level at which she began to experience raptures, and to meet — in vision, or through divine locution — the risen Jesus Christ. She heard Our Lord say: «I will have thee converse now, not with men, but with angels.»[33] Here we may recall Merlin's words: «I will live my life... for the heavenly light... I hear... the song of angels. I seek the mystery of the supersensible. I want to unite myself with the power of the Sun spirit» (i.e. the resurrected Jesus Christ).

In the case of Richard Wagner, it is not possible to speak of an opening up of supersensible faculties in the same way as with St. Teresa. In fact, he took little interest in the religious life until he began composing *Parsifal* at the age of 63. Nevertheless, his artistic experience — his inner hearing of music and poetry — were also supersensible experiences, even if he did not recognize them as such. Again, it is the life of Merlin which holds the key here: «He will cultivate the arts, especially singing and harp music...» And in Merlin's own words: «I will give my life for the harp of God... for the poet's crown. I hear within me harmonies...»

According to Professor George Balan, the founder of music meditation and the spiritual path known as *Musicosophia*, there is an approach to the spirit to be found in the works of Richard Wagner. After long and intensive meditative study of all of Wagner's operas, Professor Balan came to the following conclusion:

Wagner's creative path of development from RIENZI to PARSIFAL revealed itself to me as an archetype of the modern spiritual path. The message which Wagner brought is not to be understood through any work of his considered on its own — and also not through several works together (which is the case with almost all other composers). It reveals itself only through an all-embracing and holistic view of all the steps he went through. To attain this view is not at all easy. Few love Wagner, and still fewer love him to the extent that they would take the trouble to immerse themselves in his entire work. However, he who devotes himself to such an undertaking will be rewarded with inestimable knowledge and insight into the experience which the modern human being has to go through step by step in order to arrive at illumination. The seven stages of this process of development which the Faustian-split soul — our own soul (that of modern man) — has to ascend through are: THE FLYING DUTCHMAN, TANNHÄUSER, TRISTAN, SIEGFRIED, HANS SACHS, LOHENGRIN (and) PARSIFAL.[34]

The path of development that Richard Wagner followed was not a conscious spiritual path, as was the case with St. Teresa. Rather, he lived through a *life drama* — and the path through this life drama is mirrored in his operatic compositions. It began at the age of 28 with the composition of the *Flying Dutchman*. At that time Wagner wrote: «Now I have entered upon a new path: that of revolution against the artistic public of the present day.»[35] The composition of the *Flying Dutchman* meant the birth of Wagner's genius, which then unfolded through his following compositions and culminated in *Parsifal*. This path of development — from the *Flying Dutchman* to *Parsifal* — reflects the path taken by Richard Wagner himself. At the same time, it serves as an archetype for the path of every human being: from the condemned wanderer (the Flying Dutchman) to the Grail king (Parsifal). (That Wagner's operas reflect his life-path comes to expression most clearly with the opera *Tristan and Isolde*, which Wagner composed at the time of his Platonic love relationship with Mathilde Wesendonck. Wagner saw himself as Tristan, Mathilde as Isolde, and Mathilde's husband as King Mark. He composed the opera *Tristan and Isolde* directly out of — and in response to — his life situation at the time of his relationship with Mathilde Wesendonck.)

The opposition between the Moon and Jupiter in the hermetic chart at Richard Wagner's birth indicates a driving will on the one hand (4-petalled lotus flower, that of the will, corresponding to the Moon) and a thirst for enlightenment on the other hand (2-petalled lotus flower, that of higher thought, corresponding to Jupiter). But this is precisely the Faustian-split soul of modern man! Richard Wagner, who was born at the time of this configuration, could not do otherwise than to follow the restless drive of his will (the Flying Dutchman, condemned to wander restlessly across the seas). As Wagner wrote to his mother (at the age of 28, in the year of composing the *Flying Dutchman*):

> *Every human being who wants to attain true inner and outer independent creative self-realisation should — as long as he can bear the accompanying feeling of being in the right or not being in the right — go the way of his deepest inclinations and follow a certain inner, irresistible drive.*[36]

It was under this sign — Moon opposite Jupiter — that Wagner's life drama unfolded. Like the Flying Dutchman, he followed «a certain inner, irresistible drive» (related to the 4-petalled lotus flower, corresponding to the Moon). But in the course of time — through life itself — he acquired the wisdom of Jupiter (higher thought, the organ for which is the 2-petalled lotus flower). Eventually — like Parsifal — he attained illumination (an aspect of the Grail). All along Jupiter had guided him, for it was his quest for «inner and outer independent creative self-realisation» (Jupiter, 2-petalled lotus-flower) which had led him. The opposition between Jupiter and the Moon in the hermetic chart at Richard Wagner's birth, which — as referred to earlier in this chapter — signifies a cooperation between the 2-petalled and 4-petalled lotus flowers, could not be better expressed than in the words: «Every human being who wants to attain true inner and outer independent creative self-realisation should... go the way of his deepest inclinations and follow a certain inner, irresistible drive.»

At the same time Wagner indicates — with the words «as long as he can bear the accompanying feeling of being in the right or not being in the right» — the dilemma of the modern human being, with his Faustian-split soul, motivated by the thirst for knowledge and enlightenment on the one hand, and by the inner, irresistible drive to experience life on the other hand. For in the opposition between Jupiter and the Moon — and the corresponding cooperation between the 2-petalled and 4-petalled lotus flowers — there is the danger that the thirst for knowledge combined with the dictates of the will becomes all important. Then the danger arises that the human being begins to act regardless of whether he is «in the right or not... in the right», i.e. no longer guided by conscience.

Here a fundamental difference between the incarnation as Richard Wagner and that as St. Teresa is revealed. To a certain extent St. Teresa's destiny also stood under the sign of Jupiter and the Moon, for at her birth there was a square aspect (90 degrees) between the two planets in the hermetic chart. The aspect of square — as discussed in *Hermetic Astrology* I, Chapter 5 — is one of *dynamic interaction*, which reveals itself as an alternation between one pole and the other. The interaction between higher thought (2-petalled lotus, Jupiter) and the will (4-petalled lotus flower, Moon) is exemplified in a remarkable way in the life of St. Teresa. After her spiritual experiences began, she usually undertook action only when it proceeded from divine guidance. Although she is remembered as the founder of a contemplative order, nevertheless she proved to be a woman of action — as her biography reveals. It was precisely out of her contemplation — through the divine locutions she experienced — that her active life was guided. She was thus able to move with great dexterity from the pole of higher thought or contemplation (2-petalled lotus-flower, Jupiter) to the pole of action or will (4-petalled lotus flower, Moon).

The problem of the will

The relationship between mind and will — which is exemplified so well in the biography of St. Teresa, and which is revealed in a rather different light in the life of Richard Wagner — is one of the most crucial problems confronting the modern human being. It is essentially a moral problem. It was this problem which Friedrich Nietzsche had to deal with also. Like Wagner, Nietzsche was born when the Moon was in its node, signifying an openess of the will (Moon, 4-petalled lotus flower) to instreaming cosmic influences. (The Moon's nodes represent gateways or openings to the cosmos.) Both Wagner and Nietzsche (up until his breach with Wagner) were enthusiastic about the philosophy of Schopenhauer, who wrote *The World as Will and Idea*. The dominating thought in this philosophical work is that the will is the primary force of life. It is hardly surprising that Wagner and Nietzsche — both born with the Moon in its node — were captivated by Schopenhauer's philosophy of the will, which helped them to understand what they could actually feel of this «inner, irresistible drive» of the will.

It would go beyond the scope of this study to enter into Schopenhauer's philosophy here. It suffices to say that Nietzsche went on to develop his own philosophy of the will, in which he saw the *will to power* as the basic drive in all life. According to Nietzsche, the goal of mankind is to produce the *superman*, in whom the will to power triumphs and becomes sublimated into creativity. A presentiment of Nietzsche's superman was evoked by Wagner in his version of the character Siegfried in the *Ring of the Nibelungen*. Thus, George Bernard Shaw wrote:

> *Siegfried is a completely amoral creation, the born anarchist, the ideal of Bakunin, a presentiment of Nietzsche's superman. He is incredibly strong, full of life and recklessness, dangerous and destructive in the face of*

everything he does not like, and full of sympathy for everything he likes.[37] However, neither Siegfried nor the superman constitute the goal of mankind, as the twentieth century's experience of the *Third Reich* has shown. Hitler, who was possessed by the will to power, cannot be seriously considered as an example of an ideal human being. Alone Jesus Christ — the Son of man — can be considered as the prototype and goal of mankind.

In service of the Christ Impulse

A key to understanding Wagner's and Nietzsche's destinies is indicated in the following words of Christ, which also shed light on the moral problem of the will referred to above: «I have come in my Father's name, and you do not receive me; if another comes in his own name, him you will receive» (*John* v,43).

Wagner and Nietzsche were two of the most outstanding personalities of the nineteenth century, who — each in his own way — contributed to mankind's cultural life. Yet, whether intentional or not, both «came in their own name», and this gave rise to «Wagnerism» and «Nietzscheanism» — cults surrounding these two individuals during their life-times and after their deaths.

What a contrast between the nineteenth century incarnations and the sixteenth century incarnations of these two individualities! For neither St. Teresa of Avila nor St. Peter of Alcantara came «in their own names», but in the name of the One Master, Jesus Christ, and in service of the Church that He founded. The two saints subordinated their personal wills to the service of the Divine, in devotion to the Master. Both St. Peter of Alcantara and St. Teresa of Avila were blessed with supersensible experiences of a nature which brought them into connection with the Master, out of which St. Peter dedicated himself to the Discalced Franciscan Reform and St. Teresa to the Discalced Carmelite Reform. In their sixteenth century incarnations both connected themselves to the positive karma of the Christ Impulse.

The tragedy of Nietzsche's incarnation — when viewed against the karmic background of his former incarnation as St. Peter of Alcantara — is that a breach occurred. He broke with that to which he had dedicated himself in his former incarnation — the Christ Impulse — and became fervently anti-Christian in his later philosophical writings (e.g. *The Antichrist*). In this respect he turned against his own self, betraying his mission as it had — in part — come to expression in his former incarnation.

The breach in Richard Wagner's case was not so complete, and in his creation of *Parsifal* — the crowning masterpiece of his life's work — he re-united with the Christ Impulse in a truly sublime way. (Nietzsche wrote concerning Wagner's creation of *Parsifal*: «The old magician has again enormous success.»[38])

But, in the light of karma research, the question can be raised: Would not Wagner's work have taken on a new and higher significance if he had composed out of a consciousness of his former incarnation as St. Teresa of Avila? And in Nietzsche's case the question can be put: Would the tragic course of his destiny have been avoided if he had had knowledge of his former incarnation as St. Peter of Alcantara? Might not the relationship between these two great personalities have brought forth magnificent fruits if they had come together with a knowledge of their karmic relationship from the sixteenth century? Could not something truly great have blossomed from a united working together of these two personalities, if they had jointly united their impulses again in the service of the Christ Impulse, in consciousness of their positive karmic relationship?

It is hardly thinkable that these questions could have been put in the context of European culture in the nineteenth century, since at that time there was virtually no consciousness of reincarnation. But now, in the twentieth century, the situation is very different. A new era of mankind is breaking in, and the possibility is now given, through uniting with the Christ Impulse, of arriving at concrete knowledge of reincarnation and karma. Certain preconditions have to be fulfilled, of course, in order to arrive at this knowledge. Of primary importance is that concrete knowledge of reincarnation and karma presupposes a moral development. However, in the latter part of the twentieth century a way has come into existence — the path of Christian hermeticism — which opens up a path of moral development and which, in union with the Christ Impulse, may serve as a basis for the fulfilment of this basic prerequisite for karma research. The possibility is given — through the spiritual paths opened up in the twentieth century (see chapter 9) — of undertaking karma research and arriving at concrete knowledge of reincarnation and karma.

Hermetic astrology, springing from the spiritual impulses discussed in Chapter 9, is a new science of the stars dedicated to the pursuit of karma research — to the study of reincarnation and karmic relationships. It is a new science of the stars — based on the results of astrological karma research — but at the same time it connects onto the astrological tradition, especially the astrology of the hermeticists of antiquity.

Hermetic astrology has its roots in the science of the stars cultivated by the hermeticists of antiquity, and looks back to the founder of the ancient star wisdom — Hermes Trismegistus. At the same time, hermetic astrology looks into the future — to a time when concrete knowledge of reincarnation and karma will, through taking up the Christ Impulse, be a matter of general knowledge. It is in preparation for this time, and as a contribution towards — and hopefully shedding light upon — the problem of human relationships, that this hermetic-astrological study of the karmic relationship between Richard Wagner and Friedrich Nietzsche is presented here. In the next chapter we shall look further at the study of karmic relationships in the light of hermetic astrology.

Chapter 1
Notes and references

1. Reginald John Hollingdale, *Nietzsche: The Man and his Philosophy* (Routledge & Kegan Paul, London, 1965), p.70.
2. Ibid., p.48.
3. Ibid., p.49.
4. Ibid., p.70.
5. Martin Gregor-Dellin, *Richard Wagner* (Piper & Co, Munich, 1980), p.622.
6. Ibid., p.613.
7. Reginald John Hollingdale, op. cit., p.75 (quoted from *Ecce Homo* II,5).
8. Ibid., p.129.
9. Ibid., p.128.
10. Ibid., p.111, «Nietzsche's notebooks dated January of this year (1874) are full of critical comments on Wagner, as a man and as an artist.»
11. Ibid., p.71.
12. Ibid., p.304, quoted from Carl Albrecht Bernoulli, *Franz Overbeck und Friedrich Nietzsche* (2 vols., Jena, 1908), vol. ii, p.370.
13. Rudolf Steiner, *Karmic Relationships* (Rudolf Steiner Press, London, 1972), vol. i, pp. 143-158.
14. Reginald John Hollingdale, op. cit., p.304.
15. Ibid., p.134.
16. Ibid., p.144.
17. *Handausgabe der Werke der hl. Teresa* V,17, chapters 17-18 (ed. Pater Silverio de Santa Teresa, Burgos, 1919).
18. Ibid., V,30, chapter 5.
19. Ibid.
20. *The Life of St. Teresa of Avila* XXIII, i,151-152 (trsl. E. Allison Peers, Burnes Oates, London 1935). Hereafter cited as *Life*.
21. *Life* XXIV, i,155.
22. *Life* XXV, i,162-163.
23. San Pedro de Alcantara, *Tratado de la oracion y meditacion* cited in *Kritische Ausgabe der Werke der hl. Teresa*, ed. Pater Silverio de Santa Teresa, Burgos, 1915, vol.ii, p.507.
24. *The Life of St. Teresa of Avila* (trsl. J.M. Cohen, Penguin, 1958), p.273.
25. *Life* XXX, i,96.
26. Rudolf Steiner, *Life between Death and Rebirth* (trsl. R.M. Querido, Anthroposophic Press, New York, 1975), p.97.
27. Rudolf Steiner is generally attributed with the communication that Richard Wagner was the reincarnation of Merlin, cf. Melitta Reichart, «Merlin — Richard Wagner, eine karmische Betrachtung», *Mitteilungen aus der anthroposophischen Arbeit in Deutschland* 17 (1963), pp.89ff. And according to D.J. van Bemmelen, «Zur Frage Merlin/Richard Wagner», *Mitteilungen aus der anthroposophischen Arbeit in Deutschland* 19 (1965), p.269, this oral communication was made by Rudolf Steiner to Eleonor Merry when he visited the ancient site of King Arthur's castle at Tintagel, England.
28. Rudolf Steiner, *Karmic Relationships* (Rudolf Steiner Press, London, 1957), vol. iv, pp.37-52.

Notes and references

29. Nennius, *Historia Brittanorum* (London, 1838).
30. Quoted from Elisabeth Leu-Schmidt, *Ein Gralsimpuls im Osten* (Rudolf Geering Verlag, Dornach, 1980), pp.53-54.
31. Ibid.
32. Martin Gregor-Dellin, op. cit., p.317.
33. *Life* XXIV, i,55. St. Teresa's spiritual experiences are described in detail throughout her autobiography.
34. George Balan, *Wie ich die Musik als höchste Offenbarung entdeckte* (Musicosophischer Verlag, Bad Heilbrunn, 1984), p.53.
35. Martin Gregor-Dellin, op. cit., p.161.
36. Ibid., p.165.
37. Ibid., p.322.
38. Ibid., p.822.

Chapter 2

Further Aspects of Karmic Relationships

The priority of karmic relationships

The study of *partner relationships* has long played a central role in astrology, both in the East and in the West. In India the comparison of horoscopes of prospective marriage partners is considered so important that marriages there are often decided on the basis of astrological compatibility. In the West, computer «dating bureaus» undertake to find astrologically compatible partners.

The traditional basis of assessing astrological compatibility is the comparison of the horoscopes of the prospective partners for harmonious aspects between the two horoscopes. These harmonious aspects can generally be classified according to astrological domain — as defined in the last chapter, in the comparison of birth and death configurations in reincarnation examples. There, three astrological domains are listed: (i) the houses (the positions of the planets in the houses); (ii) the aspects (the mutual relationships of the planets to one another); and (iii) the zodiac (the locations of the planets in the signs of the zodiac). Similar principles apply in the comparison of partners' horoscopes for astrological compatibility as in the comparison of planetary configurations in reincarnation examples (from death in one incarnation to birth in the next incarnation).

In both kinds of comparison it is a matter of aspect metamorphoses (domain ii) and zodiacal alignments (domain iii). In addition, in the comparison of partners' horoscopes for astrological compatibility usually the positions of the planets in the houses (domain i) are also taken into consideration.

In the normal definition of the houses, the Ascendant and the Midheaven are taken to define the primary division into four house quadrants, where each quadrant is then subdivided into three sectors to arrive at the twelve houses. (The Ascendant is the degree of the zodiac rising on the eastern horizon at the moment of birth, and the Midheaven is the degree of the zodiac culminating overhead at the moment of birth.) The Ascendant axis (the axis across the zodiac from the Ascendant to the opposite point, the Descendant) and the Midheaven axis (the zodiacal axis from the Midheaven to the opposite point, the Nadir) — as the two most important house axes — are therefore attributed with considerable significance in the comparison of prospective partners' horoscopes. In India, for example, prospective marriage partners are considered compatible if the Moon in one horoscope is in conjunction with the Ascendant in the other horoscope, i.e. if there is a zodiacal alignment of the Ascendant and the Moon.

II. Further Aspects of Karmic Relationships

Just as the Moon node axis can be included in the search for zodiacal alignments when comparing two horoscopes, so the Ascendant and Midheaven axes, which provide a «partial representation» of the houses, can also be included. In this way — by including the Ascendant and Midheaven axes in the search for zodiacal alignments — the houses (domain i) are taken into consideration, even if only partially.

In the last chapter the karmic relationship between Richard Wagner and Friedrich Nietzsche was looked at, and it was pointed out that the Ascendant at Wagner's birth (6° Taurus, see Chart 1) was diametrically opposite the Ascendant at Nietzsche's birth (6° Scorpio, see Chart 2). Here it is a matter of a zodiacal alignment of the two Ascendants, aligning on opposite sides of the zodiac. This zodiacal alignment appears to be the main significator of the karmic relationship between Wagner and Nietzsche. In fact, comparing the two birth charts (Charts 1 and 2), the only other zodiacal alignment is h-Mercury at Nietzsche's birth on the opposite side of the zodiac to h-Saturn at Wagner's birth. In terms of aspect metamorphoses, both were born when the Moon was in its node (as mentioned already in the last chapter) and at the time of a geocentric opposition between Mars and Jupiter.

This rather meagre tally of zodiacal alignments and aspect metamorphoses in comparing the birth charts of these two karmically related individuals points to something extremely important, which at the same time reveals the fallacy of assessing partner relationships according to astrological compatibility. For it is a fundamental principle of hermetic astrology that karmic relationships are primary and astrological compatibility (usually defined in terms of aspect metamorphoses and zodiacal alignments) is secondary. People meet and find their way together on account of their karmic relationships, not because of their astrological compatibility. It may happen — and it often does — that a karmic relationship between two people comes to expression in the compatibility of their respective horoscopes, but nevertheless it is not the stars (reflected in their compatible horoscopes) which brings them together; it is their karmic relationship which leads them together.

For example, it is not the fact that there was a zodiacal alignment of their Ascendants which led Richard Wagner and Friedrich Nietzsche together, nor the fact that both were born with a geocentric opposition between Mars and Jupiter (an aspect metamorphosis involving Mars and Jupiter). Rather, what led them together was the fact that they had known each other in the previous incarnation in the sixteenth century. It was this karmic relationship — a relationship carried over from the previous incarnation — which brought them together. Astrologically speaking, their karmic relationship came to expression in the zodiacal alignment of their Ascendants. However, this astrological relationship is secondary — an expression of the karmic relationship, which is primary. If there had been no karmic relationship between Wagner and Nietzsche, then the zodiacal alignment of their Ascendants would not have brought these two individuals together. It was the compelling force of their relationship from the previous incarnation which led them to resume the relationship again in the nineteenth century.

Therefore in hermetic astrology priority is given to karma research, to the finding — through research — of karmic relationships. This is given priority over the comparison of horoscopes for astrological compatibility. The respective horoscopes may serve as a starting point for karma research, but in hermetic astrology the compatibility or incompatibility of two horoscopes is not seen as determinative, in itself, as to the nature of a relationship between two people. It is the karmic relationship between them which counts.

The fallacy of an astrological prognosis of compatibility

It is a serious mistake to believe that two people who want to get married should be counselled about their marriage prospects on the basis of the relationship between their horoscopes. In the light of the priority of karmic relationships over astrological considerations, the arrangement of marriages on the basis of astrological compatibility — as it is practised in India — is not only a fallacious practice, it actually operates against the free will of the people concerned, cutting across karmic relationships which might otherwise become fulfilled if their free will were allowed to come to expression.

Two people who are led together in complete freedom by the working of destiny, who fall in love with one another and genuinely love one another, and who — out of their love for one another — get married, are almost invariably brought together on account of a karmic relationship. The relationship may not be from the immediately preceding incarnation — it can be from a still earlier incarnation — but this does not matter. The important point is that it is the karmic relationship which has led them together again, and this is something largely independent of the relationship between the horoscopes of the couple concerned. An astrologer who sees many negative aspects between their respective horoscopes, and who consequently advises them not to get married, is giving advice based on a false premise (the theory of astrological compatibility) if he overlooks the karmic relationship which led the couple together. The hermetic astrologer, aware of the priority of karmic relationships over astrological considerations, sets himself a different task. Rather than counselling on the basis of the compatibility or incompatibility of the horoscopes of the two people, he seeks through karma research to find the nature of their karmic relationship from earlier incarnations. A couple with astrologically incompatible horoscopes may be destined — out of their karmic relationship — to marry. In this case they should marry in spite of their horoscopes!

Needless to say, the hermetic astrologer is obliged to exercise the utmost caution with regard to the communication of the results of karma research. Very strict rules pertain to communicating the findings of karma research (see «Four principles of karma research» in Chapter 7 of *Hermetic Astrology* I). In fact, in

II. Further Aspects of Karmic Relationships

certain cases it could be positively harmful to a couple's relationship if one or the other partner — or if both partners — knew of their karmic relationship. This is especially the case when a marriage — and this is a not infrequent occurrence — takes place on the basis of a negative karmic relationship in order to make good the negative relationship of a previous incarnation. If the negative relationship from an earlier incarnation were to come to the consciousness of the couple, it could introduce difficulties and complicate the existing relationship, which may be relatively harmonious. On the other hand, if the existing relationship is problematic, the knowledge of a difficult karmic relationship from the past may be the «straw that breaks the camel's back», leading to an irreconcilable breach between the two individuals. Alternatively, it could actually lead them to understand the deeper nature of their difficult relationship, and thereby help them to reconcile themselves to their marriage. These are some of the «pros and cons» which have to be weighed up by the hermetic astrologer before he can take upon himself the deep responsibility attached to the communication of the findings of karma research.

Genuine marriages are «made in heaven», i.e. they are almost invariably the result of a karmic relationship from an earlier incarnation, whereby the respective partners are led together again by the heavenly powers that work in the bringing of karma to fulfilment. In so far as each individual seeks to incarnate at the time of a birth configuration that accords with his destiny, the stellar configuration at his birth relates to — and is an expression of — his destiny. His destiny is literally carried over by the stars. It is not surprising, therefore, that two individuals whose destinies are strongly linked to one another, to the extent that their karmic relationship leads to marriage, may have horoscopes which relate strongly to one another. Since the stellar configuration at the birth of each individual is chosen to reflect his destiny, two individuals whose destinies are strongly linked may choose stellar configurations which bear certain similiarities — coming to expression in terms of aspect metamorphoses and zodiacal alignments. Thus there is some justification to the tradition of comparing horoscopes for astrological compatibility, and it explains why C.G. Jung came up with positive results when he made a statistical investigation comparing the horoscopes of several hundred marriage partners. (Jung found a significant number of zodiacal alignments of the Sun and Moon in the horoscopes of marriage partners.[1])

The manifestation of links between partners' horoscopes — in terms of aspect metamorphoses and zodiacal alignments — can generally be interpreted as an expression of a karmic relationship, since genuine marriages are usually the outcome of a karmic relationship. However, a karmic relationship need not come to expression in links between their respective horoscopes at all, or there may be very few links. For example, as discussed above, in the case of the karmic relationship between Richard Wagner and Friedrich Nietzsche, the links between their horoscopes are very few.

On the other hand, many links between two horoscopes need not necessarily indicate a karmic relationship between the two people concerned. It can happen that two people who have no karmic relationship have numerous links between their horoscopes. If both were to apply to an astrological computer dating bureau, it could happen that they would be selected by the computer to meet one another, on account of the numerous links between the two horoscopes. In this case it would be totally misleading to advise the couple to marry on account of their astrological compatibility, when in fact — in terms of destiny — they may have nothing whatsoever to do with one another!

The karmic basis of marriage

Much confusion has arisen with regard to the question of marriage, owing to lack of understanding. In fact, without a knowledge of karmic relationships it is virtually impossible to grasp the underlying significance of marriage. From a karmic standpoint, the two main underlying motivations for marriage are:

(i) the fulfilment of a positive karmic relationship (leading to a higher stage of perfection); and
(ii) the working out of a negative karmic relationship (making good the negative karma wrought between two people in a past incarnation).

Both motivations are equally valid, and both can lead to happy or unhappy marriages. A marriage based on a positive karmic relationship is assured of a good start, but — as exemplified in the karmic relationship between Richard Wagner and Friedrich Nietzsche (see Chapter 1) — a positive karmic relationship does not ensure life-long friendship. If it is not cultivated in the right way, a positive relationship can develop into a negative relationship.

On the other hand, the impulse to make good — the impulse underlying a marriage based on a negative karmic relationship — can work wonders in a marriage between people brought together on account of a negative karmic relationship. The impulse to make good can heal all the wrongs wrought between them in the past, transforming the negative karmic relationship into a positive relationship.

The question arises: Given that an individual has many karmic relationships, why should one be singled out above all others to become sealed in the life-long bond of marriage?

This question, the answer to which is central to an understanding of marriage, leads to the heart of an esoteric comprehension of life. According to the hermetic initiate who wrote *Meditations on the Tarot*, true love may be comprehended in terms of the esoteric doctrine of *twin souls*.[2] Thus, among all the karmic relationships that an individual may have, one karmic relationship — that with his twin soul — is of supreme importance, as it constitutes his original, primal karmic relationship. To seal this karmic relationship in a life-long bond — in the sacrament of marriage — is to acknowledge the primacy of this karmic

II. Further Aspects of Karmic Relationships

relationship over all others. This is the archetype, the ideal underlying marriage. Looked at in the light of the esoteric teaching concerning twin souls, the institution of marriage corresponds to a higher spiritual reality.

Marriage is for the sake of love, for the realisation of the deepest meaning of existence — which is love. This is the esoteric teaching of the Pythagorean Brotherhood, for whom the institution of marriage played an important role. Pythagoras taught that love operates on three different levels, and that on the deepest level it finds its fulfilment in marriage. The significance of marriage was made evident to the Pythagoreans by way of the esoteric teaching of three levels (spiritual, soul and physical) of love.

1. level On the level of the spirit, love is of the nature of light. On this level every human being can love — i.e. can be united in spiritual light — with every other human being. On this level — that of the spirit — love is universal, embracing the whole of mankind. Each individual is able to love every other human being as a spiritual being.

2. level Love can extend to every human being as a spiritual being, but it is able to extend only to a particular circle of human beings as soul beings, i.e. as beings of soul and spirit. On the level of the soul, love comes to expression as warmth, and this love is able to extend to all human beings with whom the individual has a soul relationship (a karmic relationship, or a relationship of friendship that is newly formed). Spiritual love — which is of the nature of light — can be felt for all human beings; soul love — which is of the nature of warmth — can be felt for those human beings with whom a soul relationship (karmic or new) exists. The human beings with whom an individual has a karmic relationship constitute his *karmic circle*. The individual's karmic circle is the group of human beings with whom he has karmic relationships; and with those belonging to this group, love on the soul level is possible. The human beings belonging to the karmic circle — or who through a new relationship enter this circle — can be loved both on the level of the spirit, where love is of the nature of light, and on the level of the soul, where love is of the nature of warmth. Light and warmth may be felt by the individual for those human beings in his karmic group.

3. level Just as spiritual love (light) can extend to all human beings, and just as soul love (warmth) can be felt for a circle of human beings (the karmic circle), so physical love (life force) is a matter of exchange with one human being, the chosen one from the karmic circle. Ideally this chosen one is the twin soul. For, as referred to above, the karmic relationship between twin souls is the archetypal, primal karmic relationship. However, it is seldom that marriage between twin souls is possible, as many conditions of destiny have to be fulfilled in order for this to take place. (For example, if twin souls do not incarnate at the

same time, i.e. if they incarnate widely separated in time by many years, marriage is generally not possible. Even if they incarnate at the same time, within a few years of one another, they may — in a given incarnation — be of the same sex, in which case marriage is again out of question. Or it may be that twin souls incarnate as brother and sister, or some other close blood relationship, which also precludes marriage.) Often, therefore, the chosen one from the karmic circle is not the twin soul, but is one who — for reasons of destiny — is called to fill the place of the twin soul. This choice is made on a higher level of being — prior to incarnation — so that the later meeting (after incarnation) between two people who are destined to marry often has the quality of a meeting between twin souls. It is a meeting that was «arranged in heaven» between the two individuals concerned, prior to their incarnation. Hence the expression «marriages are made in heaven» is literally true.

The marriage relationship of total love

Marriage — when it is genuine — is almost invariably a matter either of a union of twin souls, or of a union for reasons of destiny (i.e. on account of a positive or negative karmic relationship) of two individuals belonging to the same karmic circle. In the case of a union for reasons of destiny the marriage nevertheless follows the archetype of the union of twin souls. In other words, every genuine marriage has as its archetype the union of twin souls. And the archetype of this union of twin souls is presented in the Bible. This is the union of the first man and the first woman to incarnate on the Earth, the union of Adam and Eve.[3]

The union of Adam and Eve was that of «bone of my bones and flesh of my flesh... therefore a man leaves his father and his mother and cleaves to his wife, and they become one flesh» (*Genesis* ii, 23-24). As it is expressed in the New Testament: «A man shall leave his father and mother and be joined to his wife, and the two shall become one. So they are no longer two but one» (*Matthew* xix, 5-6). Thus, on the third level of love — the physical level — there is a physical union («they become one flesh»). Thereby a transmission of life force takes place. The fulfilment of love — in marriage — is *total love*, which is the fulfilment of love on all three levels: spiritual, soul and physical. Here there is:

light   (spiritual level, extends to all human beings)
plus warmth   (soul level, extends to the karmic circle)
plus life force (physical level, extends to one — ideally the twin soul — chosen from the karmic circle).

LIGHT + WARMTH + LIFE FORCE = TOTAL LOVE (love on the spiritual, soul and physical level).

Having summarized the esoteric teaching of the three levels of love, it is possible to answer the original question: Given that an individual has many karmic relationships, why should one be singled out above all others to become sealed in the life-long bond of marriage?

The answer is: *total love is possible only with one human being*. He who unites with a chosen partner on all three levels — spiritual, soul and physical — where this union, as a genuine marriage, proceeds from his higher being, will do so *totally*, otherwise it would not be total love. He cannot then split part of himself off to unite physically with another human being other than his beloved, his chosen one. Regardless of whether the beloved one is the twin soul or one chosen from the karmic circle, the archetype — that of the union of twin souls — is the same. And to betray the beloved one — the twin soul or the chosen one — is to betray the archetype of total love, the archetype represented in the Old Testament by Adam and Eve.

The significance of marriage is not only evident from the archetype of Adam and Eve presented in the Old Testament. It is also of the highest significance in the New Testament, since the first of Christ's miracles described in the Gospel of St. John is that of the Wedding at Cana. So important is marriage in the eyes of Jesus Christ that his first miracle was to bestow his blessing on the couple married at Cana. Just as the Father — in the Old Testament — bestowed his blessing on the first couple («be fruitful and multiply, and fill the Earth and subdue it» — *Genesis* i, 28) so the Son — in the New Testament — hallowed the institution of marriage with his presence at the wedding at Cana and with the transformation of water into wine. The union of Adam and Eve, and the wedding of the couple at Cana, serve as archetypes for *every* marriage union. The blessing of the Father and the blessing of Jesus Christ rest upon every genuine marriage.

Confusion in the level of relationship

The confusion that has arisen — especially in the twentieth century — with regard to marriage is largely a confusion of the three levels of love: spiritual, soul and physical. Thus, it is right to want to love everybody, every human being, on the spiritual level. But it would be absurd to try and carry this over onto the physical level, to try and enter into a physical relationship wherever possible. Similarly, the warmth of soul which it is possible to experience with one's circle of friends cannot be carried over as genuine warmth with respect to every man, woman and child on this planet, as warmth of soul can be experienced only where there is a soul relationship (i.e. where there is a karmic relationship, or where a new relationship is formed). The warmth of soul that it is possible to experience with members of one's karmic circle can be carried over outside of this circle only through taking up contact with human beings outside of the karmic circle, and it is impossible to take up contact — to make friends — with every man, woman and child on this planet!

Frequently an error of judgement occurs when two karmically related people meet. The experience of the light and warmth of love which both may feel for one another can all too often be interpreted as a mark of true love in the sense of conjugal love. Of course, it *is* true love! And it is only right that members of a karmic circle experience this light and warmth of love for one another, each through the being of the other. An error of judgement may be made, however, if this experience is then immediately identified as true love in need of fulfilment on the physical level, which properly belongs to conjugal love. The wisdom of a period of engagement before a soul relationship becomes consummated as a physical relationship in marriage is precisely in order to circumvent such errors of judgement. (After all, the choice of someone with whom one is to spend the rest of one's life is a matter of no small significance!) Of course, it can happen that twin souls recognize one another immediately, or that the meeting with the chosen one is intuitively experienced so that there is no doubt as to the rightness of marriage, but even in such cases there is wisdom in allowing a period of time to elapse before the soul relationship becomes consummated on the physical level. This lapse of time can help to intensify consciousness of the sacramental nature of physical union in marriage.

The healing remedy — at least, one of the remedies — for the problem of the increasing chaos in marriage relationships, and in human relationships in general, is an awareness of the three levels of love: spiritual, soul and physical. With this awareness it is evident to which realm the human being's different love relationships belong. For example, a married person who becomes conscious of an experience of love — as light and warmth — towards a new aquaintance, may then recognize this as a karmic relationship, as a meeting with someone from his karmic circle. If this person has an awareness of the three levels of love, he or she will be able inwardly to acknowledge the love that is felt, which might be mutual, but will recognize that it belongs to the level of the soul, and will not allow this experience to disturb his or her existing marriage relationship. On the contrary, soul relationships — and also spiritual relationships — need not disturb, but can enrich a marriage (physical) relationship. It is a question of trust between marriage partners, for each to acknowledge the validity and necessity of the other's soul and spiritual relationships, resting secure in the knowledge of faithfulness in the total love that marriage affords. The total love of marriage can actually create the free space in which each marriage partner's soul relationships (karmic relationships) and spiritual relationships can blossom forth. In this way, a true understanding of the esoteric significance of marriage can lead to an immensely enhanced fulfilment of life and of all the varied human relationships that the human being enters into during the course of his life.

St. Teresa of Avila and St. John of the Cross

Marriage is not the only way towards life fulfilment. Moreover, a strong and powerful relationship between two people of the opposite sex need not necessarily be consummated in marriage in order for the individuals concerned to unfold their creative spiritual potential. As an example of a relationship on the soul and spiritual level — between an older woman and a younger man — in which both individuals unfolded their spiritual potential to a remarkable degree, let us consider the friendship and spiritual bond between St. Teresa of Avila and St. John of the Cross. For several years St. John of the Cross, who was twenty-seven years younger, was St. Teresa's spiritual director and «spiritual son». He and another were the first friars to join St. Teresa when she began to extend the Carmelite Reform to include monasteries for men.

> *St. Teresa of Jesus (= St. Teresa of Avila) and St. John of the Cross will always have a double title to fame. Individually, they are known throughout Christendom as authors of works on the mystical life which rank high among other masterpieces of Christian mysticism. Jointly, they are remembered, not only by Carmelites, but by all for whom the history of religion has a meaning, as the founders of the Discalced Carmelite Reform.*[4]

In the course of the twentieth century both saints have become pronounced Doctors of the Church — St. John of the Cross in 1926, and St. Teresa of Avila in 1970 — on account of the inestimable value of their writings as expositions of the mystical life. As «text books» of authentic mysticism, these writings also rank high among the works cited by the renewer in the twentieth century of the hermetic spiritual path.[5] For this reason it is of special interest in hermetic astrology — which is allied with the path of hermeticism — to follow the destiny of these two individuals.

The destiny of St. Teresa of Avila is outlined in Chapter 1, where the results of karmic-astrological research are presented, in which St. Teresa's subsequent incarnation as Richard Wagner is discussed. In this reincarnation example — as is evident from a comparison of the planetary configuration at Wagner's birth with the configuration at St. Teresa's death — both the first «law» of reincarnation and the «law» of h-Mercury/h-Venus zodiacal alignment hold. Similarly, the reincarnation of St. Teresa's friend and spiritual teacher — St. Peter of Alcantara, who reincarnated as Friedrich Nietzsche — is discussed in Chapter 1, but in this case it is only the first «law» of reincarnation which holds (see *Hermetic Astrology* I, Appendix III, Table 18).

The point of departure in Chapter 1 is the karmic relationship between Richard Wagner and Friedrich Nietzsche, which exemplifies the carrying over of a soul and spiritual relationship from one incarnation to the next. Richard Wagner, as the reincarnated St. Teresa of Avila, and Friedrich Nietzsche, as the reincarnated St. Peter of Alcantara, were led together by destiny, to continue their relationship from the previous incarnation in sixteenth-century Spain. These «soul-friends», who had such an intense spiritual relationship — St. Teresa of Avila and St. Peter of Alcantara — were led together in the next incarnation, where their relationship again blossomed with extraordinary intensity. Tragically, after seven years of friendship, the relationship took a negative turn, and later Nietzsche strongly criticized Wagner in his work *The*

Wagner Case (although he had written in *Ecce Homo*: «I name Wagner the greatest benefactor of my life... I loved him, and no one else»[6]).

If we now turn to the relationship between St. Teresa of Avila and St. John of the Cross, we again find a metamorphosis — a carrying over — of this relationship into the next incarnation in the nineteenth century. St. John of the Cross was born at Fontiveros, not far from Avila, on June 24, 1542 (see Chart 5). At the age of 21 he took the habit of the Carmelite Order at Medina. Then, after studying Arts at Salamanca University, he was ordained a priest in 1567. In this same year he first met St. Teresa, and undertook to join her in the Carmelite Reform. When St. Teresa was made prioress at the unreformed Carmelite convent of the Incarnation (in Avila), she requested that John of the Cross — this «very holy Discalced Father»[7] — be appointed confessor of the convent. This was in 1572. Through their collaboration great improvements took place at the Incarnation, which became noticeable in the community's increased amenableness and in the tranquillity and sanctity which began to prevail in the convent. Such was St. Teresa's appreciation of St. John of the Cross — this «divine, heavenly man» — that she later wrote, after he had left:

> I assure you, my daughter, since he left us I have not found another like him in the whole of Castile, nor anyone else who inspires souls with such fervour to journey to Heaven.[8]

St. John of the Cross' stay as confessor at the convent of the Incarnation was brought to an abrupt end in December 1577 when he was abducted by some Calced friars and imprisoned in the priory at Toledo. This abduction was a blow dealt by the Calced Carmelites in their growing hostility and opposition to the Carmelite Reform. During this period of imprisonment, he wrote several stanzas of the *Spiritual Canticle* and also — so it is believed — the poem *Dark Night*. After over eight months' solitary confinement St. John of the Cross was able to escape. For safety he then lived in various remote places in Andalusia, southern Spain, where he wrote several of his poems and mystical works.

Eventually in 1580 the Discalced Reform received independent status, and the strife with the Calced Carmelites came to an end. However, St. John of the Cross remained in the south for several more years, until in 1588 he returned to Castile as prior of the house of Segovia. After a disagreement with the provincial, he was removed from office and sent back to Andalusia, where — attacked by a fever and suffering excruciating agony — he died (at Ubeda) on December 14, 1591 (see Chart 6).

The metamorphosis of the relationship

The last time that St. Teresa saw St. John of the Cross was eleven months before her death. (She died on October 4, 1582 — see Chart 4.) He travelled to Avila to see her at St. Joseph's convent — he was still her confessor — and had a long conversation with her on the evening of November 28, 1581.

II. Further Aspects of Karmic Relationships

Chart 5
*St. John of the Cross
St. John of the Cross *June 24, 1542 at Fontiveros

Chart 6
†St. John of the Cross
St. John of the Cross †00.00 on December 14, 1591 at Ubeda

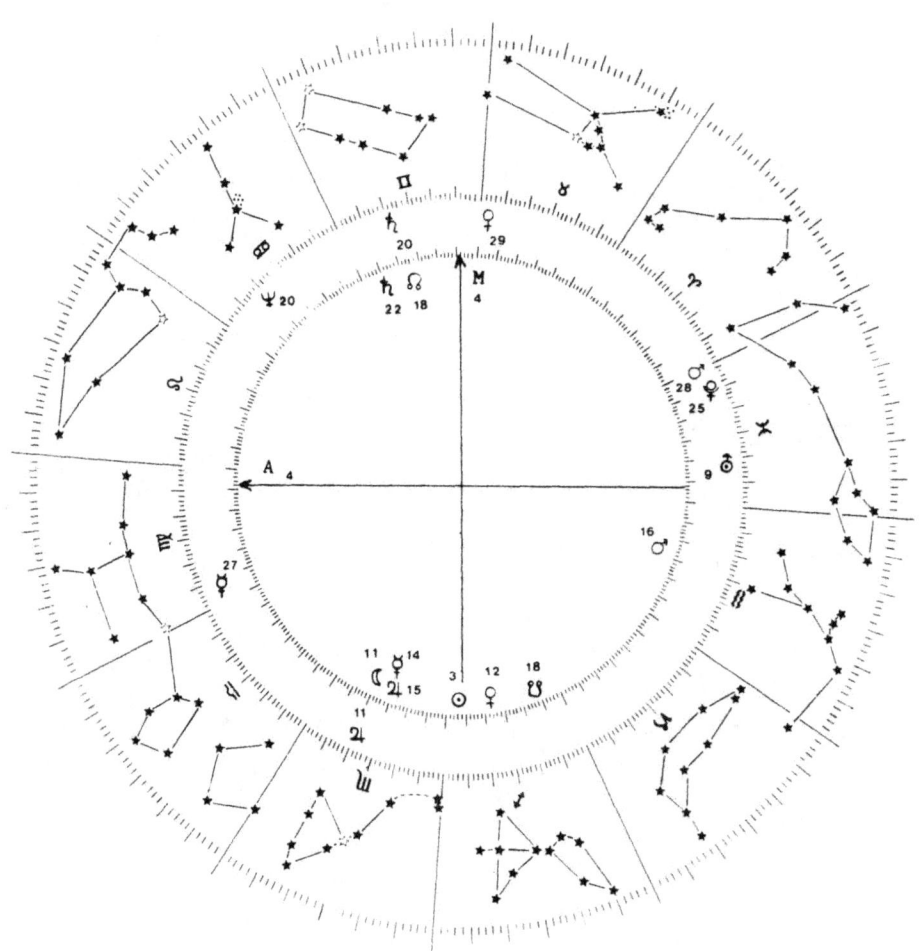

II. Further Aspects of Karmic Relationships

Two hundred and eighty-two years and five months later, the two met again on the earthly plane of existence — this time in very different circumstances. It was at the king's residence in Munich, Germany — at two o'clock on the afternoon of May 4, 1864 — that the meeting took place, the outcome of which was that the two instantly became bosom friends. At this meeting Richard Wagner — the reincarnated St. Teresa of Avila — met his young benefactor, the reincarnated St. John of the Cross, who Wagner later described as his «compassionate guardian angel».[9] At that time Richard Wagner was eighteen days short of being fifty-one, and was in a desperate situation — ill, tired of life, up to his neck in debts, and without a hope of completing his major operatic tetralogy *The Ring of the Nibelungen*. Only a month before the meeting, as Wagner had come to realise the full extent of his desperate plight, he had written: «A light has to shine from somewhere. Somebody has to appear who can help effectively... A truly helpful miracle must occur now, otherwise everything is finished.»[10]

A miracle did indeed take place! No less a person than the newly-crowned king of Bavaria sent an envoy to seek out Richard Wagner and to summon him to their fateful meeting on May 4, 1864 in the king's Munich residence. In the ensuing conversation the king said that Wagner should compose *The Ring of the Nibelungen* to the end, that his debts would be paid, and that all financial worries would be removed from him. At the end of the conversation the young king — not yet nineteen years of age — drew Wagner to him, embraced him, and swore him eternal faithfulness.

This fateful meeting, which signified the turning point in Richard Wagner's life, can be understood against the background of the karmic relationship between St. Teresa of Avila and St. John of the Cross. These two saints — two of the great Christian mystics — had united spiritually in their common espousal of the Carmelite Reform and had formed a deep soul friendship in their sixteenth century incarnation in Spain. A higher power of destiny led them together again in their next incarnation, in Germany in the nineteenth century. The cause which brought them together this time was Wagner's music, his operas, to which the newly-crowned king of Bavaria was devoted with all his passionate, romantic idealism. The young king, since having attended the opera *Lohengrin* at the age of fifteen, looked to Wagner as his «sole true teacher and educator»[11]. A letter of Wagner's, written towards the end of May 1864, describes the idyllic days he spent living close by the king, following on from their first meeting:

> *The king of Bavaria died quite unexpectedly, and my compassionate guardian angel — against all rules of fate — ascends the throne. His earliest care a month thereafter is to send for me: while I am draining the cup of sorrow to its lowest dregs... the envoy already is seeking me in my deserted home... he must bring the king a pen, a pencil from me. Ah! at last a tie that brings with it no pains and tortures! What*

it is for me, to have this glorious youth before me! He is thoroughly aware who I am, and what I need: not a word have I to waste about my situation. He feels that a king's prerogative must assuredly suffice to keep all common cares from me, to give me altogether to my muse, and procure me every means to produce my works when and how I wish. At present he mostly resides in a little castle near to me; in ten minutes the carriage takes me there. Daily he sends either once or twice. Then I fly as to a sweetheart. 'Tis a fascinating interview. This thirst for instruction, this comprehension, this quiver and glow, I have never encountered in such splendid unrestraint. And then this charming care for me, this winning chastity of heart, of every feature, when he assures me of his happiness in possessing me: thus do we often sit for hours together, lost in each other's gaze.[12]

For Richard Wagner it was a fairy-tale come true. Until the end of his life, the king remained his benefactor, the saviour in his need, to whom he owed not only the end of his depressing misery but also the decisive turn towards the realisation of his ideas and plans. Wagner wrote addressing the king as «my most worshipful, angelic friend», and the king wrote back: «O saint, I worship thee.»[13] In these words something of their karmic relationship sounds through — the relationship of the young St. John of the Cross to the older St. Teresa of Avila. (The age difference between the young king and the older composer, which amounted to 32 years, was of approximately the same order as the age between the two saints, which amounted to 27 years.)

Among the appellations used by the king in addressing Wagner — as their relationship developed — are the following: «Most inwardly beloved», «source of the light of my life», «bliss of life», «highest good», «majestic, divine Friend».[14] Often the king referred to Wagner simply as «the Friend» or «the Great Friend». The king later wrote to Cosima von Bülow, who subsequently became Wagner's second wife:

Wagner is a god who has come down from the heights of heaven to proclaim the new, joyful teaching to mankind, to redeem the world! I have been chosen by him to make known his will to our fellow men.[15]

When the king became engaged, he told his fiancée: «The god of my life is, as you know, R. Wagner.» By this time, Wagner was addressing the king as «Parsifal», and the king's fiancée wrote to Wagner: «Parsifal, your truest friend, has initiated me in full trust to his inner union with you.» And Wagner wrote to the king: «O Parsifal! How I must love you, my trusted hero!»[16]

A turn in the relationship

The relationship between Wagner and the king, which initially had been so idyllic, became clouded by the scandal that erupted when it became known that Cosima von Bülow, who was married to the pianist and conductor Hans von Bülow, had become Wagner's mistress. Even before the scandal became public,

II. Further Aspects of Karmic Relationships

such a fierce campaign was waged against Wagner in the press that the king was compelled to request Wagner to leave Munich. Thus Wagner and Cosima had to leave Bavaria, and went to live at Haus Triebschen, near Lucerne. Nevertheless, the king continued to support Wagner, and generously came to the rescue when Wagner's plan to build a Festival House at Bayreuth for the performance of his operas was on the point of being abandoned. In 1876 the Festival House in Bayreuth became opened with the premier performance of the tetralogy of operas *The Ring of the Nibelungen*. After seeing the rehearsals, the king wrote to Wagner: «You are a godman, the true artist of God's grace, who has brought the holy fire from heaven to earth, in order to purify, enoble, and redeem her!»[17] The performance in Bayreuth of the four operas comprising *The Ring of the Nibelungen* marked the crowning — hitherto — of the composer's mighty labours. He was aged sixty-three.

He then went on to his greatest achievement: the composition of the opera *Parsifal*, to which he had been repeatedly urged by the king. (The king wrote to Wagner: «I am forced to think continously of *Parsifal*. I am burning for it,» and later: «Do not forget, I beg you, here's to *Parsifal*.»[18]) In 1877, when Wagner at last sent the completed poem of *Parsifal*, the king wrote:

My mood, when sinking into the wonderfully soulful and elating poetry, can only be compared to the one I was once filled with when I received my first Holy Communion, so sacred, so pure.[19]

In November 1880 the composition of the music to *Parsifal* was sufficiently advanced for Wagner to present the Overture to *Parsifal*. This took place in Munich on November 12.

On November 10 Wagner attended with the king a private performance of LOHENGRIN. This, too, seemed like a significant stroke of destiny, namely that the two were able again to experience LOHENGRIN, which originally had brought them together, for after November 1880 they were not to see one another again on this earth: the circle is closing. On the afternoon of November 12, Wagner conducted the PARSIFAL OVERTURE with the king as the only audience, after having prepared for him a short written explanation in which the inner motives of the Overture — love-belief-hope — are outlined.[20]

Following this, the king wrote in his private diary:

Was present with Richard Wagner at the performance of LOHENGRIN, very successful and beautiful. He present, with Him in the appartment, supped in the Wintergarten, a long time together. On the 11th. at 5 o' clock He came to dine (Wintergarten)... intimate, precious hours... On the 12th. in the afternoon twice heard the miraculous and glorious prelude to PARSIFAL conducted by the creator himself. Profoundly significant. Also the prelude to LOHENGRIN. Present with Him in the evening... magnificent performance, (Saturday the 13th.) happy with Him, about 6.30 o'clock left, with Him via Nymphenburg to the railway station, the beloved lake, looked in the direction of Berg (May)

Staltach departure. Cordial and sad. Happiness and blessings on His beloved head.[21]

In July and August of 1882, the completed opera *Parsifal* was performed sixteen times at Bayreuth, and it was a bitter blow to Wagner that the king did not attend a single performance: «No blow could strike so hard — who encouraged me to this mammoth last effort of all spiritual strength? In retrospect — for whom did I carry all this out?»[22]

The king had been unable to conquer his shyness towards crowds, and in his last letter to the composer he conveyed his wish for a private performance of *Parsifal* in Munich in the spring of 1883. Wagner, who died on February 13, 1883 — before the arrival of spring — wrote in his last letter to the king, after mentioning *Parsifal*: «So I shall close today again the circle of my existence with the memory of the favours, in which noble enjoyment, I am dying.»[23]

The king outlived the composer by only three years and four months. His circle of existence, too, was drawing to a close. A plot was set in motion to have the king declared insane, and in the early hours of Whit Saturday – June 11 – in the year 1886, Dr. Gudden and a group of assistants seized the king in his remote castle Neuschwanstein. Declaring him insane — without an examination — the king was transported to his castle on Lake Starnberg, where he was locked up. On the next day — Whit Sunday — the king, accompanied only by Dr. Gudden, took a walk along the lakeside. It was early evening. When the two men did not return, a search was sent out. Their bodies, lying a short distance apart in shallow water, were then discovered. Thus the king of Bavaria — known as the «fairy-tale king» — died in mysterious circumstances. Aged only forty, King Ludwig II of Bavaria — the reincarnated St. John of the Cross — ended his life in the waters of Lake Starnberg.

At the death of Richard Wagner, Ludwig had said: «The artist whom the entire world is mourning was recognized by me first, was saved for the world by me!»[24] With the composer's death, however, the inner support that Ludwig had experienced through his relationship with Wagner went too. From this point onwards that which he experienced as his real being, which had lit up in his relationship with Wagner, began to sink away. The king became more and more reclusive. And like a strange echo of the abduction and imprisonment in his former incarnation as St. John of the Cross, Ludwig II of Bavaria became «abducted» and suffered the humiliation of being locked up in one of his own castles. However, whereas St. John of the Cross had escaped from captivity, the king met his end in the waters of Lake Starnberg.

Lohengrin, the Swan Knight

That which spiritually united Ludwig II of Bavaria with Richard Wagner was the Grail, especially the knights of the Grail: Parsifal and Lohengrin. The «Swan Knight» (Lohengrin) and the motif of the swan had played an important role for Ludwig, even as a child.

From childhood on, Ludwig lived in a fairy-tale picture world. Fate would have it that he spent a long span of his childhood in Hohenschwangau Castle, in whose close proximity he later had Neuschwanstein Castle built, from where he was arrested in the last days of his life. This, for Ludwig, so fatefully significant south-west corner of Bavaria, was always connected with the motif of the swan. There is a village there called Schwangau and the Lake Schwan. The nobility of Schwanstein had their castle built in the twelfth century. In that time the saga of the Knight of the Swan (Lohengrin) was still alive in the consciousness of the people. Lohengrin was a son of Parsifal. People who spoke about the latter cherished the secret of the Holy Grail; they were a kind of Christian underground movement, who worked... (to) lay the foundations for a future Christendom of the Holy Spirit. It was not without purpose that King Arthur held his Round Table at Whitsun — the festival of the Holy Spirit — and it is said of the Knights of the Holy Grail that they received their orders on the Saturday before Whitsun. It was at Hohenschwangau that the young Ludwig saw the romantic frescoes, which were painted in 1836. There was Lohengrin's farewell from the Grail Castle and the scene where the emperor hears the horn of the approaching Knight of the Swan, and (the scene where) he fights for Elsa, and finally (that of) Lohengrin's wedding. When the young boy was not living at Hohenschwangau, he used to look at these pictures repeatedly in an album he took with him. He loved these pictures passionately. Included on one of his childhood wishing lists is «a picture of the Knight of the Swan.»[25]

Small wonder that the 15-year old Ludwig should have had an overwhelming experience at his first visit to the opera, to hear Wagner's *Lohengrin*. During the performance he shed tears of rapture. After, he learnt the text by heart, and read the remaining operatic dramas that Wagner had written. On February 21, 1864, a little more than two weeks before his father died (Ludwig ascended the throne on March 12, 1864, two days after his father's death), he again heard a performance of *Lohengrin*. It was under the magical influence evoked for him by the «Knight of the Swan» that the young newly-crowned king sent for Richard Wagner. The envoy was given a portrait of the king and a ruby ring to be presented to Wagner, and was instructed to speak the following words in handing over the ring to the composer: «As this ruby glows, so King Ludwig glows passionately with desire to see the poet-musician who wrote *Lohengrin*»[26]

How is the compelling fascination which the Grail theme exerted on Ludwig — and also on Wagner — to be understood? What was the karmic background to this spiritual bond that united the king and the composer?

In their previous incarnations in sixteenth century Spain, these two individuals — two of the greatest mystics of Christendom — were united inwardly in their spiritual striving. Their mystical experiences were centered around inner spiritual meetings with the Risen One, Jesus Christ. Outwardly, both were united in the struggle to establish the Carmelite Reform, but inwardly their souls journeyed «with such fervour... to heaven.»[27]

With poetic talent and theological clarity, St. John of the Cross describes in his works the mystic path through the three stages of purification, illumination, and union — depicting the extraordinary trials that the soul has to pass through to arrive at union with the Divine. The writings of St. Teresa of Avila, too, while lacking the theological clarity of those of St. John of the Cross, vividly describe the depths and heights of the mystic way — her descriptions springing directly from her intimate and personal experiences. Much that St. Teresa describes seems fantastic to modern ears, e.g. her experience of the «transverberation of the heart» (being pierced through the heart by a sword of Divine Love wielded by a Cherubim).[28] Indeed, in the eyes of modern psychiatry both St. Teresa of Avila and St. John of the Cross would rank as «psychiatric cases» on account of their abnormal experiences.

It cannot be denied that their experiences rank as out of the ordinary — since they are beyond the range of experience of the normal human being — but from the Christian-hermetic standpoint the descriptions by the two saints of their mystical experiences are of inestimable value. For their descriptions reveal something of the spiritual experiences that more and more people in future will pass through, in the age of the second coming of Jesus Christ. In this New Age, which has begun in the twentieth century (see *Hermetic Astrology* I, Appendix II), an increasing number of people will begin to have mystical experiences of the kind that St. Teresa and St. John of the Cross had. In this sense, the two saints — and also others, notably St. Peter of Alcantara (see Chapter I) — were forerunners of modern mankind. Their experiences were «abnormal», as — through grace — they experienced something which will become only gradually accessible in the course of time to more and more people. Through the onset of the second coming, however, supersensible meetings with the Risen One are becoming experienced by many people in different countries.[29] In this respect, St. Peter of Alcantara, St. Teresa of Avila and St. John of the Cross lived through something in advance, which is only now becoming more generally accessible. The descriptions of their experiences — written down by St. Teresa and St. John — can be invaluable, therefore, as a help towards orientation in the domain of the inner life.

The quest for the Holy Grail

The central core of the spiritual striving of St. John of the Cross and St. Teresa of Avila — as it comes to expression in their writings — can be designated as the *quest for the Holy Grail*. The Holy Grail symbolizes the spiritual treasure of the inner world, and the quest for this treasure — which is to be found in the inner being of man — is the path of the soul to attain it. In the description of St. Teresa the path taken by the soul leads into the *interior castle*. Her work *The*

Interior Castle describes seven stages of this path of the soul to attain the heavenly peace of union with Christ. In the language of the Grail legends, this interior castle is the *castle of the Grail*, in the innermost sanctuary of which the Holy Grail is to be found. It is here that the deeply mysterious union of the soul with the Divine takes place. The soul must exert itself in order to follow this path, but the reward is that the Divine comes to meet the soul, to unite with it.

In the imagery of St. John of the Cross the path of the soul is described as the *ascent of Mount Carmel*. His works — *The Ascent of Mt. Carmel, The Dark Night of the Soul, The Spiritual Canticle* and *The Living Flame of Love* — describe the soul's ascent to the Divine along the way of purification, illumination and union. Here, as with St. Teresa, a «science of the Grail» emerges — a description of the path of the soul to attain union with the Divine. In the description of St. John of the Cross it is the sacred Mount Carmel — known as *Monsalvaesche* («mount of salvation») in the Grail legend — which the soul ascends on its spiritual quest.

Knowing of St. Teresa's earlier incarnation as Merlin, the founder of the Round Table (see Chapter 1), it is possible to begin to comprehend what was at work in the Carmelite Reform of St. Teresa of Avila and St. John of the Cross. The Order of Carmel, so it is claimed, was founded by Enoch, the father of Methusalah, on Mount Carmel in Palestine. The Order was later renewed by the prophet Elijah. As reported in the *Book of Kings*, Elijah — after defeating the priests of Baal — ascended to the top of Mt. Carmel and from there beheld «a little cloud like a man's hand... rising out of the sea» (I *Kings* xviii, 44). The Carmelites interpret this cloud as a prefiguration of the Virgin Mary, who from that time on floated in the form of a mist over the solitaries who settled on Mt. Carmel, inspiring and protecting them. The Carmelites thus claim the special protection of the Blessed Virgin — as «Our Lady of Mt. Carmel».

Another source reports that Mt. Carmel was regarded from the earliest times as a special sanctuary. Iamblichus writes of it as the most sacred of mountains, whose access was forbidden to the public, and claims that Pythagoras once spent a night in silent prayer on Mt. Carmel.[30]

For the mystic it is the interior ascent of Mt. Carmel which is important, to arrive at the holy sanctuary in which the inner birth of Christ is fulfilled. Thus, the Carmelites can be seen historically as explorers of the inner world — on the quest for the Holy Grail. However, by 1562, when St. Teresa founded her reform, the original strict rule of the Carmelite Order — which had been given in 1209 by St. Albert (Patriarch of Jerusalem) to the community of anchorites living on Mt. Carmel — had become considerably relaxed.

St. Teresa of Avila experienced with full intensity the irresistible call of the Grail. As Merlin in an earlier incarnation, this individuality had called into being the spiritual circle comprising the Round Table, whose knights were enjoined to seek the Holy Grail. In the incarnation as St. Teresa, this individual felt called again to found — through the Carmelite Reform — a «spiritual school» motivated by the search for union with the Divine. In the foundation of the Carmelite Reform she was joined and assisted by St. John of the Cross.

The metamorphosis of the relationship between St. Teresa of Avila and St. John of the Cross in the sixteenth century to that between Richard Wagner and Ludwig II of Bavaria in the nineteenth century exemplifies a significant change of orientation with regard to the mode of collaboration between these two individuals. Although the inner call of the Grail remained the common bond between them, there was a major change in their sphere of activity. Whereas the two saints were active in the sixteenth century in the sphere of the religious life — within the Catholic Church — the impulse represented by Wagner and supported by Ludwig II was a cultural impulse completely separated from the sphere of the religious life.

In his poetic-musical creations Wagner came a long way in succeeding to bring something of the inner experience of the Grail to expression in musical-dramatic form. This was recognized by Ludwig II, and it accorded closely with that which he experienced of his own inner, deeply mystical soul life. Out of their karmic relationship, Ludwig felt called to support Wagner, to help bring his cultural impulse to the world.

Wagner's achievement in his operatic creations — above all in *Parsifal* — is that through the flowing together of poetry and music in dramatic action something of the Christ Impulse may be brought closer to the consciousness of the hearer. The *total work of art* — to use Wagner's term for the fusion of poetry, music and dramatic action — is well-suited to serving the Christ Impulse. It is especially music, however, which has the potential to convey something of the Christ Impulse to the inner being of the hearer. The nature of music in general — when it is genuine music, i.e. when it reflects the heavenly music of the harmonies of the spheres — is that it enables spiritual beings to enter into a relationship with the souls of the people listening to it. In the spatial realm where it is played, music can create a kind of invisible temple into which higher beings are able to descend toward the human beings gathered together. The music of *Parsifal* goes in the direction of creating a temple for the Christ Being, and thus can help to bring about the «Grail experience» — union with Christ — in the inner being of the listener. In the words of George Balan, the founder of the spiritual movement of music meditation (*Musicosophia*):

> Through Wagner I found my way into the realm of the Grail — the realm in which I had recognized quite early on the central core of every genuine spiritual path of European origin. It was the meeting with this powerful and mysterious radiant symbol that set in motion within me the process of becoming spiritually awake. This was possible owing to the fact that I let myself be led through the numerous trials that such a spiritual awakening entails — led by the light that radiates from the spirituality of the Grail. This support I owed above all to the fortunate circumstance that I became acquainted with Richard Wagner's last musical drama (Parsifal) at a

point in my life when I was in desperate need of the revelation communicated by this work. The suffering, the struggles and the redeeming deeds of Parsifal appeared to me as the archetype of every genuine spiritual quest, this archetype being none other than the quest for the Holy Grail.[31]

These words reveal the enormity of Richard Wagner's achievement. That which had lived within this individuality in the former incarnation as St. Teresa of Avila — her rich inner spiritual-mystical life — became metamorphosed and incorporated by Wagner into his musical dramas, above all in *Parsifal*. Thereby he succeeded in leading over the Christ Impulse from the religious life into the cultural life, with the potential — through theatres and opera houses — of reaching a vast number of people. In this respect Richard Wagner was a forerunner — one who helped to pave the way — for the advent of the New Age, the age of the second coming of Christ. For the New Age is one in which Christianity is to become a force in cultural life (in the various arts), in university life (in the sphere of knowledge), and in practical life (especially in connection with the relationship between man and nature) — as well as in the religious life, where a rebirth of religion through genuine mystical experience will take place.

The missions of Wagner, Nietzsche and Ludwig II

The three individuals who had lived as great Spanish mystics (St. Teresa of Avila, St. Peter of Alcantara and St. John of the Cross) had the task — in reincarnating in Germany in the nineteenth century as Nietzsche, Wagner and Ludwig II of Bavaria — of pioneering the way for the New Age of Christianity. Despite the incredible forces of opposition with which Wagner had to battle in order to exist as a composer, he eventually pulled through — thanks to the help of Ludwig II — to bring his impulse to fruition. The crowning fruit of this impulse is *Parsifal*, which — as described by Professor Balan — has the potential to bring the essence of the New Age, i.e. the quest for the Holy Grail, alive as an inner experience. Thus Wagner triumphed in his heroic struggle — out of the strength of his personality, and helped by the powers of destiny.

Alas, in the case of Friedrich Nietzsche it is not possible to speak of a triumph. Great though his philosophical achievements are, he was unable to rise to his true mission. The forces battling against him proved to be too strong for him to deal with. Whereas Wagner's task was to bring a contribution towards a renewal of European cultural life, Nietzsche's mission lay in the sphere of university life — in a renewal in the sphere of knowledge. Here — if he had been able to break through, i.e. if he had been true to his own higher self — he might have become a great philosopher of a new kind of Christianity, a Christianity based on inner knowledge. This «New Age» Christianity, which Nietzsche had the potential to found philosophically, would have included the teaching of reincarnation and of the higher self, the indwelling divine self, to be found on the spiritual path.

That Nietzsche was on the way to the teaching of reincarnation — that he nearly broke through to it — is reflected in his idea of the eternal return. Instead of breaking through to the concept of return by way of reincarnation, however, he postulated a materialistic conception of the return of everything through the recombination of atoms after some unknown, vast period of time. Further, that Nietzsche had an inkling of the higher self is evident in his teaching of the superman. But instead of coming to the realisation of a divine self indwelling every human being, he conceived of a Darwinian kind of evolution which would eventually bring forth the higher human being, the superman.

Nietzsche did not break through to the higher truths. They lit up within him, but the prevailing materialistic conception, combined with his anti-Christian attitude, prevented him from grasping them, and he arrived instead at a caricature of them. The concept of the eternal return is a caricature of the fact of reincarnation. Similarly, the superman is a caricature of the higher divine self indwelling every human being, which is to be found on the path of spiritual development. Eventually Nietzsche succumbed to the subtle temptation of the *will to power*. Having succumbed to this temptation, he inwardly broke with the spiritual striving of his inner being as it had come to expression in his previous incarnation as St. Peter of Alcantara. He turned against the Christ Impulse, as his work *Antichrist* reveals.

The third of these three personalities — Ludwig II of Bavaria — had the unique opportunity, as king of Bavaria, of accomplishing a mission in an altogether different sphere from that of Wagner (cultural sphere) and that of Nietzsche (sphere of knowledge). He might perhaps have achieved a breakthrough in the political sphere. But the mystically-inclined personality of St. John of the Cross — reincarnated as Ludwig II of Bavaria — was ill-equipped to carry out innovations of a political nature. (This is highlighted when Ludwig II is compared with his contemporary Bismarck, a vigorous and energetic politician, who later became chancellor of the German empire.)

In his political conceptions Ludwig II idolized the «Sun king», Louis XIV of France, who had affirmed the absolute power of the monarchy. The Herrenchiemsee Castle, which Ludwig II had constructed on the island of Chiemsee, was modelled after Louis XIV's palace at Versailles. Ludwig II had two other castles built: Linderhof Castle in the Graswang Valley near Oberammergau, and Neuschwanstein Castle near Füssen. The king's intention with Neuschwanstein Castle, which is located in a beautiful spot in mountainous terrain, was that it should be a «Castle of the Grail», along the lines of the Wartburg Castle — the scene of the battle of the Grail minstrels (the subject of Richard Wagner's opera *Tannhäuser*).

Ludwig II's passion for building castles, especially as it comes to expression in Neuschwanstein Castle, is a sign of the impulse that was living within him — metamorphosed from his previous incarnation as St. John of the Cross — of bringing the Grail impulse to external manifestation. But it is above all his recognition and support of Richard Wagner which marks him out in this respect.

He enabled Wagner to compose his later operas and to build the Festival House at Bayreuth. His loyalty towards Wagner – at least, towards the higher aims and ideals of the composer – shows that he remained true to their karmic relationship from the previous incarnation, where they had joined forces to work for the establishing of the Carmelite Reform.

As mentioned earlier in this chapter, the tragic end to the life of Ludwig II of Bavaria appears karmically as a metamorphosis of the abduction and imprisonment suffered by St. John of the Cross on account of his support for the Carmelite Reform. Just as St. John of the Cross' abduction and imprisonment was the result of a deliberate plot to impede and suppress the Carmelite Reform, so the seizure of Ludwig II was the outcome of a deliberate conspiracy to have the king incapacitated by declaring him insane. But whereas St. John of the Cross – through his mystical experiences, above all through his inner relationship with Jesus Christ and with the Virgin Mary* – was able to stand up to the incredible trial of eight months solitary confinement, and was able eventually to escape and continue his activity further, Ludwig II of Bavaria, not having found his way to spiritual heights along the inner path, did not have sufficient inner strength to effectively resist those who conspired against him. Also, the inner support that he had experienced through his relationship with Richard Wagner was – since the composer's death – no longer there. Ludwig II therefore took the line of least resistance, and his life came to an end. Whatever the real cause of his death might have been – shrouded as it is in mystery – it may well have been that if he had been inwardly stronger he would have lived on.

Chart comparison: St. John of the Cross/Ludwig II

Looking now at the relationship between the planetary configuration at the death of St. John of the Cross (Chart 6) with that at the birth of Ludwig II of Bavaria (Chart 7), it is evident that the first "law" of reincarnation is fulfilled, since the angle between the Sun and Saturn at the death of St. John of the Cross amounted to 161 degrees, whilst at the birth of Ludwig II of Bavaria it was 163 degrees. The zodiacal alignments of planets at the birth of Ludwig II with planetary positions at birth/death of St. John of the Cross are listed in Table 3. (Note: there are no aspect metamorphoses between the birth/death configurations of St. John of the Cross and the birth configuration of Ludwig II of Bavaria.)

---

*St. John of the Cross reported that he was assisted by the Virgin Mary in his escape: "One night... the Virgin appeared to him in a vision, filling the cell with her beauty and brilliance, and announced to him that his trials would soon be over and that he would leave prison... (Later) he told the nuns at Toledo of the 'help, consolation and interior impulses' which Christ and the Virgin had given him when he had prayed to them for aid in his escape" (Gerald Brenan, *St. John of the Cross*, Cambridge University Press, 1973, p. 33).

From Table 3 it is apparent that there were numerous zodiacal alignments between Ludwig II's birth configuration and the birth/death configurations of St. John of the Cross, but the "law" of alignment of h-Mercury/h-Venus was not fulfilled.

Chart 7: *Ludwig II of Bavaria
Ludwig II *00.30 a.m. on August 25, 1845 at Nymphenburg

II. Further Aspects of Karmic Relationships

Looking now at the relationship between the horoscopes of Ludwig II of Bavaria and Richard Wagner (Charts 1 and 7), there are only three zodiacal alignments and no aspect metamorphoses between the two charts. (The three zodiacal alignments are: the Moon at the birth of Ludwig II aligned with the Sun at Wagner's birth; Saturn at Ludwig II's birth aligned with the Moon and the Moon's descending node at Wagner's birth; and h-Mercury at Ludwig II's birth aligned with h-Saturn at Wagner's birth.) This paucity of connections between the birth charts of Ludwig II and Richard Wagner indicates the unreliability of horoscope comparison as a means of assessing whether a karmic relationship exists between two individuals. Considering the depth and significance of the karmic relationship between Ludwig II and Richard Wagner – carried over from their incarnations in the sixteenth century as St. John of the Cross and St. Teresa of Avila – the astrological relationship between their horoscopes is remarkably weak. Even without taking account of their karmic relationship from the previous incarnation in the sixteenth century, i.e. looking solely in terms of the relationship between these two individuals in the nineteenth century (for Richard Wagner it was the financial support of Ludwig II which completely changed his life, and for Ludwig II it was the profound inner significance of his relationship with Wagner which supported him inwardly), there is nevertheless a remarkable lack of correspondences between the birth charts of Richard Wagner and Ludwig II of Bavaria. Once again this goes to show – as discussed at the beginning of this chapter – that karmic relationships are primary and astrological considerations are secondary.

This does not mean to say that the comparison of horoscopes of individuals is completely invalid, as often much can be learnt from such a comparison. Rather, the consequence for hermetic astrology is a shift of emphasis – to look beyond the horoscope to the individuality manifesting through the previous incarnation, or from still earlier incarnations. It is the individual and his karmic relationships from earlier incarnations which becomes the central focus of interest for the hermetic astrologer. The main area of research in hermetic astrology is the individuality – the incarnations of the individuality seen in the context of the karmic circle, i.e. the circle of karmic relationships carried over from one incarnation to the next.

The significance of karma research

When a particular individual is studied by way of karma research, his karmic circle may also come into view. It is then the strongest and most significant karmic relationships which are of special interest to the hermetic astrologer.

In the example of a personality of such historical significance as Ri-

Table 3
St. John of the Cross/Ludwig II of Bavaria chart comparison for zodiacal alignments.
See Appendix II for the computation of the planetary positions – geocentric and heliocentric – listed in the following table.

Abbreviations: h = heliocentric sidereal longitude (hermetic chart)
 g = geocentric sidereal longitude (geocentric chart)
 * = birth
 † = death

St. John of the Cross		Ludwig II of Bavaria	
*g-Mercury	(15° Gemini)	*Ascendant	(16° Gemini)
†Moon's node	(18° Gemini)		
*Moon's node	(15° Aquarius)	*Midheaven	(16° Aquarius)
†g-Mars	(17° Aquarius)		
*h-Uranus	(7° Leo)	*Sun	(9° Leo)
		*h-Mars	(7° Aquarius)
†h-Jupiter	(11° Scorpio)	*Moon	(11° Taurus)
†Moon	(11° Scorpio)		
*g-Jupiter	(5° Virgo)	*g-Mercury	(4° Virgo)
†g-Uranus	(6° Pisces)	*g-Venus	(6° Virgo)
*g-Mars	(17° Libra)	*g-Jupiter	(18° Libra)
†g-Neptune	(21° Cancer)	*g-Saturn	(22° Capricorn)
*g-Neptune	(2° Aries)	*g-Pluto	(2° Aries)
*g-Sun	(23° Gemini)	*h-Mercury	(22° Sagittarius)
†h-Saturn	(20° Gemini)		
*h-Jupiter	(16° Virgo)	*h-Uranus	(15° Pisces)

chard Wagner, the karmic circle of such a personality is often very large. Two karmic relationships from this large karmic circle have been looked at so far from the point of view of karma research: in Chapter 1 his karmic relationship with Friedrich Nietzsche, and in this chapter his karmic relationship with Ludwig II of Bavaria. Looking into the karmic background of Wagner's relationship with these two personalities, we are led back to the great Spanish mystics of the sixteenth century: St Peter of Alcantara, St. Teresa of Avila and St. John of the Cross. Richard Wagner himself was the reincarnation of St. Teresa of Avila, the founder of the Carmelite Reform. St. Teresa was supported and encouraged in this reform by the ascetic Franciscan reformer, St. Peter of Alcantara. It is against the background of the relationship between St. Peter of Alcantara and St. Teresa of Avila that the karmic relationship between Friedrich Nietzsche and Richard Wagner can be understood. Later St. Teresa was joined in her reforming activity by the young St. John of the Cross, who helped to pioneer the Carmelite Reform for monks. It is in the collaboration of these two Carmelites that the karmic background to the relationship between Richard Wagner and Ludwig II of Bavaria is to be found. Thus the karmic circle of the individuality St. Teresa of Avila/Richard Wagner can be seen in the sixteenth century in St. Teresa's relationships with St. Peter of Alcantara and St. John of the Cross and in the nineteenth century in Richard Wagner's relationships with Friedrich Nietzsche and Ludwig II of Bavaria.

There is much more still to be uncovered concerning Richard Wagner's karmic circle – regarding other karmic relationships of significance to him – to be discovered by way of karma research. Here only two relationships from his karmic circle have been looked into. Nevertheless, it is to be hoped that on the basis of the example of these two karmic relationships, some insight may be gained into the domain of karmic relationships. Great mysteries are connected with this subject, for it is through the unfolding of karmic relationships that the brotherhood of man – the community of mankind united in Christ – will arise in the far-distant future. This, in turn, will give rise to the "new Heaven and the new Earth" – the future Jerusalem – spoken of in the Apocalypse of St. John (*Revelation* xxi).

Christ is the Being who unites all human beings, and it is he who works invisibly in the guiding together of human beings for the unfolding of their karmic relationships. To participate in this hidden work is the high ideal of hermetic astrology, and the first step in such a participation is to begin to penetrate the mysteries of destiny. This is possible in the light of the Being of Christ, through his second coming. It is against the background of the work of Christ in building up the brotherhood of man that the hermetic astrologer may find a starting point in seeking to understand the mysteries of karmic relationships. By looking at numerous examples of karmic relationships much can be learnt – both from the "happy endings" and from those relationships that end in tragedy. Indeed, that which can be learnt from the latter can often be of inestimable value for the future. Through knowledge of mistakes made in the past, we can learn how to avoid making such mistakes again in the future. In this way hermetic astrology – as a new astrological science of karma (destiny) – may be able to help future mankind, placing itself in the service of the Christ Impulse, in the work of Jesus Christ in uniting all human beings in divine love through the fulfilment of karmic relationships.

Chapter 2: Notes and references

1. Carl Gustav Jung, *Synchronicity* (trsl. R.F.C. Hull, Routledge & Kegan Paul, London, 1972), pp. 60–94, 145–146.
2. *Meditations on the Tarot* (trsl. R. Powell, Amity, Warwick NY, 1985), Chapter 6.
3. Ibid.
4. E. Allison Peers, *Handbook to the Life and Times of St. Teresa and St. John of the Cross* (Burns Oates, London, 1954), p. 3.
5. *Meditations on the Tarot*, Chapter 12 (see ref. 2).
6. Martin Gregor-Dellin, *Richard Wagner* (Piper & Co., Munich, 1980), p. 759.
7. *The Letters of Saint Teresa of Jesus* (2 vols., Burns Oates, London, 1951), 42.
8. Ibid., 261.
9. Desmond Chapman-Huston, *Bavarian Fantasy. The Story of Ludwig II* (John Murray, London, 1955), p. 67.
10. Rudolf Frieling, *King Ludwig II of Bavaria* (ed. and trsl. John Fletcher, privately printed, Ongar, Essex, 1976), p. 4.
11. Desmond Chapman-Huston, op. cit., p. 67.
12. Ibid., pp. 67–68.
13. Martin Gregor-Dellin, op. cit., p. 526.
14. Ibid., p. 525.
15. Ibid., pp. 572–573.
16. Ibid., pp. 576–577.
17. Ibid., pp. 715–716.
18. Rudolf Frieling, op. cit., pp. 10–11.
19. Ibid., p. 11.
20. Ibid.
21. Desmond Chapman-Huston, op. cit., p. 216.
22. Rudolf Frieling, op. cit., p. 11.
23. Ibid.
24. Ibid.
25. Ibid., pp. 2–3.
26. Werner Richter, *Ludwig II* (Verlag Bruckmann, Munich, 1939), p. 32.
27. See ref. 8.
28. *The Life of St. Teresa of Avila* (trsl. J. M. Cohen, Penguin, 1958), p. 210.
29. Cf. G. Hillerdal and B. Gustafsson, *Sie erlebten Christus* (Verlag Die Pforte, Basel, 1979).
30. Iamblichus, *Life of Pythagoras* (trsl. T. Taylor, J. M. Watkins, London, 1965), pp. 7–8.
31. George Balan, *Wie ich die Musik als höchste Offenbarung entdeckte* (Musicosophischer Verlag, Bad Heilbrunn, 1984), p. 67.

Chapter 3

An Example of Astrological Biography

A tribute to Willi Sucher

So far in Volume II of *Hermetic Astrology* we have looked at the complex realm of karmic relationships. From the two examples of karmic relationships looked at in Chapters 1 and 2, it emerges that karmic relationships need not necessarily come to expression – at least, not in an especially noticeable form – in the comparison of horoscopes of karmically related individuals. This raises the question: How is destiny carried over by the stars? If it does not show up particularly in the astrological study of relationships, where does it manifest?

This question has been answered in part through the content of *Hermetic Astrology* I, which to a large extent is concerned with the comparison of horoscopes from death in one incarnation to birth in the next incarnation. From these comparisons it is evident that it is literally true that destiny is carried over by the stars from death in one incarnation to birth in the next incarnation. This finding is part of the hermetic-astrological science of destiny, and it is to the study of this science – known simply as *astrological biography* – that we shall now direct our attention. Through astrological biography the question as to how destiny is carried over via the stars from one incarnation to the next is answered. We shall see that in astrological biography it is not just the moments of birth and death that are important, but also the moment of conception – as determined by the rule of Hermes.

In fact, the hermetic rule (rule of Hermes) holds the key to astrological biography. Therefore it occupies a central place in modern hermetic astrology, just as it did in the hermetic astrology of ancient Egypt at the time of Nechepso and Petosiris, whose writings have been dated to the second century B.C. (The original formulation of the hermetic rule is attributed to Petosiris – see *Hermetic Astrology* I, Appendix I.)

A new application of the hermetic rule in the twentieth century, which has helped to lay the foundation for the development of astrological biography as outlined in this book, was introduced by Willi Sucher in the 1930's. To the best of the author's knowledge, the first time that a discussion of this new application of the hermetic rule by Willi Sucher appeared in print was in an article published in Volume i (1937) of the *Modern Mystic* (discontinued since World War II). This article – entitled "Looking through the Horoscope of Birth: the Significance of the Pre-natal Events among the Stars" – was republished in Volume ii (1976) of the *Mercury Star Journal* (discontinued since 1981). In this article Willi Sucher applied the hermetic rule to an historic example, namely to the horoscope of Richard Wagner.

As a tribute to Willi Sucher for his discovery of the deeper significance of the hermetic rule, we shall turn to his study of Richard Wagner – to look at Wagner's horoscope in the light of Willi Sucher's original research. Having focused our attention on Richard Wagner's karmic circle in Chapters 1 and 2, we shall now look at his destiny in relation to the stars at the time of his incarnation.

The implication of Willi Sucher's discovery of the deeper significance of the hermetic rule is that it is not just the stars at the moment of birth which are important for the destiny of the human being, but also the movements of the planets against the background of the stars throughout the entire period of incarnation between conception and birth. The meaning of this period – the embryonic period – is indicated in *Hermetic Astrology* I, Chapter 10. There it is described how, parallel to the formation of the physical body (embryo) in the womb, the etheric body (life body) is formed in the Moon sphere encircling the Earth. The formation of the physical body and of the etheric body run parallel to one another – the physical body being built up in the womb out of earthly matter, whilst the etheric body is formed in the lunar sphere out of cosmic forces. The formation of the physical body begins at the moment of physical conception (fertilization of the egg), and the formation of the etheric body begins at the moment of etheric conception, when the archetype of the physical body (formed by the image) is released from within the sphere of the Moon to unite with the fertilized egg (see *Hermetic Astrology* I, Chapter 10). The moment of etheric conception, which lies close in time to that of physical conception, is determined by the hermetic rule. Thus the hermetic rule is applied to the birth configuration – assuming that the birth takes place naturally, i.e. at the cosmically appointed time – to calculate back (retrospectively) the moment of etheric conception.

An example of the hermetic rule

As an example of the application of the hermetic rule, let us consider the birth horoscope of Richard Wagner (Chart 1). The hermetic rule – as described in the ancient hermetic writings of Nechepso and Petosiris (see *Hermetic Astrology* I, Appendix I) – specifies the importance of the Ascendant and the Moon, stating that the zodiacal locations of the Ascendant and the Moon at birth become interchanged with the zodiacal locations (or their opposites) of the Ascendant and the Moon at conception. In the hermetic rule, therefore, it is a matter of *zodiacal alignments*, i.e. there is an alignment of the Ascendant - Descendant axis at birth with the zodiacal location of the Moon at conception, and there is an alignment of the Ascendant - Descendant axis at conception with the zodiacal location of the Moon at birth. At Richard Wagner's birth (*), the zodiacal locations of the Ascendant and the Moon were:

III. An Example of Astrological Biography

*Ascendant = 6° Taurus; *Moon = 24° Capricorn.

According to the hermetic rule, therefore, at the conception (∅) of Richard Wagner there was a zodiacal alignment of ∅Moon with *Ascendant, and there was a zodiacal alignment of ∅Ascendant with *Moon. Since alignment means the taking up of the same zodiacal longitude or aligning on the opposite side of the zodiac (diametrically opposite zodiacal longitude), this can be expressed as follows:

∅Moon = 6° Taurus or 6° Scorpio (zodiacal alignment with *Ascendant)
∅Ascendant = 24° Capricorn or 24° Cancer (zodiacal alignment with *Moon)

Knowing that the etheric conception – conception as determined by the hermetic rule – takes place close in time to the physical conception, i.e. roughly nine months prior to birth, it is possible to utilize the hermetic rule to determine the exact moment of etheric conception. In the case of Richard Wagner, we have to go back some nine months prior to his date of birth (May 22, 1813), which leads us back to August 1812. In fact, on August 15, 1812 the Moon was located at 6° Scorpio in the sidereal zodiac, and on August 28, 1812 the Moon was located at 6° Taurus. Both these dates, falling roughly nine months prior to the date of birth, fit the first specification of the hermetic rule, i.e. there is a zodiacal alignment of the Moon at conception with the Ascendant - Descendant axis at birth.

Of course, it could be that Richard Wagner was born prematurely, in which case the date of conception would have been less than nine months prior to the date of birth. For example, the date September 12, 1812, which lies eight months and ten days prior to the date of birth, also fits the hermetic rule, since the Moon was located at 6° Scorpio in the sidereal zodiac on September 12. Alternatively, he may have been born overdue, in which case the date of conception would have been more than nine months prior to the date of birth. For example, the date August 1, 1812, which lies nine months and twenty-one days prior to the date of birth, again fits the hermetic rule, since the Moon was located at 6° Taurus on August 1.

The hermetic rule thus yields several possible conception dates, and in Richard Wagner's case the four most likely conception dates are: August 1, August 15, August 28 and September 12, 1812. On each of these dates there is a zodiacal alignment of the Moon with the Ascendant-Descendant axis at birth.

Of these four dates, the most likely – according to the law of probability – are August 15 and August 28, as these two dates are closest to the normal 9-month duration of the embryonic period. However it is not just the laws of probability which count, but also the planetary positions on these dates. For, as is evident from the application of the hermetic rule to the reincarnation example in *Hermetic Astrology* I, Chapter 10, the planetary positions at the moment of conception may bear a relationship – in terms of zodiacal alignments and aspect metamorphoses – with the planetary positions at birth/death in the last incarnation. Therefore, bearing in mind Richard Wagner's previous incarnation as St. Teresa of Avila, the planetary positions on the various conception dates specified by the hermetic rule can be compared with the birth/death configurations of St. Teresa of Avila. On the basis of a comparison of the planetary positions on the four possible conception dates listed above with the birth/death configurations of St. Teresa of Avila (Charts 3 and 4), it emerges that the planetary configuration on August 15, 1812 relates strongly to the planetary configurations at the birth and death of St. Teresa (see Table 4).

August 15, 1812 is also the date that Willi Sucher – through applying the hermetic rule – determined to be Richard Wagner's date of conception. Moreover, applying his discovery, he was able to confirm that this date can be considered as the correct date of Wagner's conception, since it fits with the major events in Richard Wagner's life. Willi Sucher's discovery – that the events in life are prefigured by the planetary movements during the embryonic period – enables a particular conception date computed by the hermetic rule to be verified (or not) with a high degree of certainty, by comparing the major planetary configurations during the embryonic period with the major events in the human being's biography. In the example of Richard Wagner, taking August 15, 1812 as the date of conception, this date yields a remarkable fit with the events in his life, and this confirms that August 15, 1812 can in all probability be considered as the actual date of conception.

Willi Sucher's discovery

What is Willi Sucher's discovery? How do the planetary movements during the embryonic period prefigure the course of events in life? And how does this form the basis of astrological biography?

Experience itself has shown that the lunar cycles in ... (the embryonic period) are like reflected pictures, as it were foretelling the subsequent rhythms of man's earthly life. Take once again the example of Richard Wagner. In the ... (planetary configuration) of August 15, 1812 the Moon took its start from the ... constellation of Scorpio. Following the Moon (on) its further course through 27⅓ days, we ... come again to the Moon in ... (Scorpio). This first of the prenatal lunar cycles is related to the period in Wagner's earth-life (from birth) ... to seven years (of age) ... The next lunar cycle (orbit of the Moon around the

III. An Example of Astrological Biography

zodiac), leading once more after 27⅓ days to the starting-point in ... (Scorpio), is ... (reflected in) the life period from seven to fourteen years. Each of the subsequent lunar cycles (orbits of the Moon around the zodiac) in this way represents a further period of seven years. In the approximately ten prenatal lunar cycles, ten times seven years, that is about seventy years are prefigured. Seventy years represents a certain ideal average of the length of life. This relation of the prenatal lunar cycles to the septennial periods of subsequent earthly life is a completely new thing in astrology ... This correspondence of the prenatal period with the subsequent time rhythms gives rise to an expressive picture of the drama of human life. In Richard Wagner's case, at the beginning of each new cycle the Moon came once again into the constellation of Scorpio. From this we can surmise that this personality, at the beginning of each new 7-year period of life — at the ages, for example, of 21, 28 and 35 — had to undergo a difficult time in his life; Scorpio is, indeed, difficult. We shall find this confirmed to some extent when we consider his biography. Yet the Moon rhythms by themselves would only give us indications of something that should repeat itself monotonously about ten times — dull and invariable. It is due to the other planets that it is not so. These planets, too, in the whole time (of the embryonic period) before birth, have their dramatic meetings and relationships to one another; thereby the regularly repeated rhythms of the lunar cycles are given a more individual character.[1]

The above description by Willi Sucher characterizes the nature of his discovery — a discovery that forms the foundation for the hermetic science of astrological biography outlined in this book. This discovery implies that destiny unfolds in 7-year periods during life, and that the unfolding of destiny in each 7-year period is prefigured by the planetary movements during the corresponding lunar cycle in the embryonic period.

The first lunar cycle starts at the moment of conception as computed by the hermetic rule. In Richard Wagner's case this was on August 15, 1812, when the Moon was at 6° Scorpio. The orbit of the Moon around the sidereal zodiac is followed — lasting 27⅓ days — until the Moon returns again to 6° Scorpio, and this denotes the end of the first lunar cycle. (At the same time, of course, it denotes the start of the second lunar cycle.) During the first lunar cycle — corresponding to one orbit of the Moon around the sidereal zodiac — the destiny for the first seven years of life is woven into the etheric body, mirrored in the planetary movements during this first lunar cycle. Similarly, during the second lunar cycle, corresponding to the Moon's second orbit of the sidereal zodiac — the destiny for the seven years of life from 7 to 14 is woven into the etheric body, mirrored in the planetary movements during this second lunar cycle. Continuing further, therefore, it is evident that the entire embryonic period is a time of the weaving of destiny for the whole of life. During this period of time between conception and birth the "web of destiny" is woven, which later unfolds between birth and death. This web of destiny is woven into the etheric body, which is formed during the embryonic period of development, parallel to the formation of the physical body (embryo) in the womb.

The weaving of the web of destiny

Just as the formation of the physical body takes place on Earth, within the womb, the formation of the etheric body between conception and birth takes place within the sphere of the Moon, i.e. the sphere extending from the Earth up to the Moon's orbit. Each orbit of the Moon around the zodiac indicates one cycle in the formation of the etheric body. Whereas the physical body exists on Earth in three-dimensional space, the etheric body is a *time organism*, which interpenetrates the physical body in the flow of time. It does not belong to earthly, physical space but acts in from the Moon sphere and comes to manifestation in the unfolding of time – in the rhythm of 7-year periods in earthly life. The etheric body is therefore concealed from normal earthly consciousness, but may become revealed at the level of lunar consciousness (described in *Hermetic Astrology* I, Chapter 4), i.e. when consciousness is raised beyond the physical, earthly realm to the sphere of the Moon.

The manifestation of the etheric body in the unfolding of 7-year periods in human life was known of in antiquity. Various references to the septennial periods (7-year periods) as the basic rhythm underlying man's development through life occur in the writings of Greek authors, e.g. Hippocrates, the earliest reference being Solon (sixth century B.C.), who taught that life comprises ten 7-year periods, each distinguished by a particular quality and phase of development. (See Appendix I for a summary of various references by Greek authors to this teaching, which later came to expression in Shakespeare's "Seven Ages of Man".) The idea that human life follows an archetype of ten 7-year periods is confirmed indirectly in the Old Testament: "*The years of our life are threescore and ten*" (*Psalm 90, 10*).

An analogy can help to make clear the activity of the etheric body as a time organism unfolding archetypally through the 7-year periods of life. A comparison may be drawn with the winding up of a watch. It is wound up a certain number of times, and then winds down – measured by the lapse of hours – in the course of the following day (or days). Similarly, the etheric body is "wound up", as it were, during the ten or so orbits of the Moon around the sidereal zodiac between conception and birth. From the moment of birth it then "winds down" – measured by the unfolding of 7-year periods – between birth and death. (Ten septennial periods is the archetype for this, but in practice deviations from this archetype are the rule rat-

III. An Example of Astrological Biography

her than the exception – see Chapter 6 for a discussion of the significance of major deviations from this archetype.)

The rhythm of 7-year periods is the basic pattern underlying the unfolding of human life. Thus the sequence of ten 7-year periods as the archetype for the course of life is referred to in hermetic astrology as the *spiral of life*. In Chapters 4 and 5 the qualities and astrological characteristics of the different phases (septennial periods) of the spiral of life are looked at more closely.

For astrological biography, however, it is not just the rhythm of the etheric body unfolding through 7-year periods that is of significance. It is the fact that the *web of destiny* is woven into the etheric body and unfolds together with the unfolding of the etheric body – this provides the essential foundation upon which the hermetic science of astrological biography is based. The 7-year rhythm of the etheric body is related to the Moon's orbits of the sidereal zodiac during the embryonic period, where each orbit of the Moon around the sidereal zodiac corresponds to one cycle in the formation of the etheric body. As the etheric body is formed, during the Moon's orbits of the sidereal zodiac, destiny is woven into the etheric body, and this weaving of the web of destiny mirrors the various planetary configurations taking place at this time.

In the following – when we return to look at Richard Wagner's biography – we shall look at a specific example, namely a conjunction between the Sun and Saturn, which took place about halfway through Wagner's embryonic period. This cosmic event, which occurred during a particular phase of formation of the etheric body (the latter measured by the Moon's orbit of the sidereal zodiac),became woven into Richard Wagner's web of destiny, into his etheric organism, in the form of a pictorial image – known in hermetic astrology as a *destiny image,* i.e. a pictorial image of destiny. In the unfolding of his etheric body (time organism) after birth, eventually the point in time was reached – approximately midway through his life – when the image woven into his etheric body at that time, i.e. the destiny image correlating on the cosmic level with the conjunction of the Sun and Saturn, emerged as an actual event of destiny. In the following we shall look more closely at the nature of this event, as to how it may be viewed in connection with the conjunction of the Sun and Saturn, and how the timing of this event in Richard Wagner's biography is correlated with the cosmic event (Sun conjunct Saturn) that occurred roughly midway through his embryonic period.

This example reveals the basic principle of the hermetic science of astrological biography. It is based an the spatial hermetic principle "as above, so below", i.e. cosmic events taking place "above" are correlated with the events of destiny taking place here on Earth "below". Further, astrological biography utilizes the temporal hermetic principle "that which was is as that which shall be", i.e. the destiny images comprising the web of destiny woven during the embryonic period emerge as actual events of destiny in the course of life between birth and death. The basis of astrological biography is that there is a direct correspondence between the embryonic period (viewed from the cosmic perspective of solar, lunar and planetary conjunctions, oppositions, etc.) and the pattern of destiny as it unfolds in 7-year periods during the course of life.

Where possible, therefore, the hermetic astrologer looks at the entire sequence of planetary movements between conception and birth in order to gain an overview of the individual's web of destiny that unfolds in 7-year periods between birth and death. The orbits of the Moon around the sidereal zodiac during the embryonic period indicate the formation of the etheric body (specifying the sequence of 7-year periods) and the various cosmic events (conjunctions, oppositions, etc., of the planets with one another and with the Sun and the Moon) signify the events of destiny – in the form of the destiny images comprising the web of destiny – woven into the etheric organism concurrent with its formation.

Once the correspondences between cosmic events of the embryonic period and the events of destiny in the human being's biography become established, which depends of the successful application of the hermetic rule, the human being may begin to attune to his destiny – initially on a cosmic level. Then, through inward contemplation of the cosmic events corresponding to the destiny images woven into his etheric organism, he may – through grace – be able to raise to consciousness the destiny images corresponding to particular cosmic events that took place during the embryonic period.

The raising to consciousness of destiny images gives rise to the faculty of *karmic clairvoyance,* which is the ability to behold clairvoyantly the elaboration of karma (destiny). Needless to say, the development of this faculty presupposes a high level of moral development and a deep understanding of the higher wisdom of destiny. The development of karmic clairvoyance is one of the ideals of hermetic astrology, and astrological biography is – so to say – a scientific counterpart to this ideal. Through the study of astrological biography – for example, as it applies to the lives of historical personalities – a foundation is provided for understanding the working of destiny, and at the same time an idea can be gained of the nature of karmic clairvoyance, one aspect of which is the beholding of the mysterious correlation between cosmic events in the embryonic period and events of destiny in the course of life. The ideal is to attune to destiny – *to walk in cosmic time,* i.e. to be always at the right place at the right time, for the miracle of the fulfilment of destiny. This calls for a *spiritual awakening to destiny* on the part of the hermetic astrologer – then to be transmitted to others seeking guidance in their destiny, so that order may begin to prevail in the sphere of destiny. The archetype for this order is to be found in the starry heavens. In accordance with the bringing to realisation of "Thy will be done on Earth as it is in heaven", a reflection of the order prevailing in the starry heavens is to be established here on Earth. Hermetic astrology seeks to contribute towards this, to serve Christ Jesus – the Lord of karma – in bringing the kingdom of heaven down to Earth ("Thy kingdom come").

A fundamental principle of astrological biography

Willi Sucher's discovery – one of the most important findings of twentieth century astrological research – is the relationship between the formation of destiny ("weaving of the web of destiny") and the unfolding of destiny between birth and death. The web of destiny is woven during the embryonic period concurrent with planetary events (conjunctions, oppositions, etc.) taking place in this period, and destiny then unfolds between birth and death as an enactment of that which was prefigured on a cosmic level between conception and birth. The fulfilment of destiny is thus a bringing to realisation of heaven on Earth, in the sense that what was "planned" in heaven (on the way into incarnation) actually becomes fulfilled. Astrological biography can be a help towards becoming more conscious of this working of destiny, with a view to contributing towards the divine ideal conveyed by the words "Thy will be done on Earth as it is in heaven."

The key to astrological biography is the correspondence between the sequence of the Moon's orbits around the sidereal zodiac during the embryonic period and the sequence of 7-year periods between birth and death. Since one lunar orbit of the sidereal zodiac lasts $27\ 1/3$ days, then ten lunar orbits of the sidereal zodiac amount to 273 days, which is close to the average length of the gestation period. (The average period from conception to birth is usually reckoned to be ca. 270 days.) During ten lunar sidereal orbits the destiny for ten 7-year periods is woven, prefiguring seventy years of life, which is close to the average length of human life. This serves as an archetype for the *spiral of life* – the unfolding of life through a sequence of ten 7-year periods – which is considered in detail in the next two chapters.

The relationship discovered by Willi Sucher between the weaving of destiny during the embryonic period and the unfolding of destiny in 7-year periods during life is the key in hermetic astrology to the study of destiny. It forms the basis of the hermetic-astrological science of destiny (astrological biography) by indicating how the human being's destiny may be read from the stars, i.e. from the movements of the planets (including the Sun and Moon) against the background of the fixed stars during the embryonic period. The movements of the planets during the embryonic period thus outline and prefigure the human being's biography from birth to death – this is the foundation of astrological biography.

But before looking at Richard Wagner's destiny as an example illustrating the practical approach of astrological biography, let us return to the application of the hermetic rule to determine Wagner's date of conception. The first part of the hermetic rule – which led us back to August 15, 1812 as Wagner's conception date – concerns the zodiacal alignment of the Moon at conception with the Ascendant-Descendant axis at birth. The second part of the hermetic rule concerns the alignment of the Ascendant-Descendant axis at conception with the zodiacal location of the Moon at birth. Just as the first part of the hermetic rule enables us to determine the day of conception, so the second part allows us to determine the time of conception on the specified day. Since the zodiacal location of the Moon at Richard Wagner's birth was 24° Capricorn, then the Ascendant at conception was either 24° Capricorn or 24° Cancer. In fact, at 7 p.m. local time (Leipzig) on August 15, 1812 the Ascendant was 24° Capricorn, and the Moon was located at 6° Scorpio – thus fulfilling both parts of the hermetic rule. The chart computed for 7 p.m. local time (Leipzig) on August 15, 1812 gives the planetary configuration at Richard Wagner's conception (Chart 8).

Comparing the planetary configuration at Richard Wagner's conception with the birth/death configuration of St. Teresa of Avila, several relationships emerge (see Table 4). Firstly, it is interesting to note that the Moon at the conception of Richard Wagner was diametrically opposite its zodiacal location at the death of St. Teresa. Secondly, it is most significant that the angular relationship between the Sun and Saturn at Richard Wagner's conception (129 degrees) is the same as that between the Sun and Saturn at St. Teresa's birth (130 degrees). This is an example – analogous to the first "law" of reincarnation – in which the preservation of the Sun-Saturn angle from birth in one incarnation to conception in the next incarnation is evident.

The first "law" of reincarnation states that the angular relationship between the Sun and Saturn at death in one incarnation is preserved to recur either as the same angle or as the complement (with respect to 180 degrees) between the Sun and Saturn at birth in the next incarnation (see *Hermetic Astrology* I, Appendix III). Thus the first "law" of reincarnation establishes a definite relationship between death in one incarnation and birth in the next incarnation. Hermetic-astrological karma research reveals, however, that there exists also a definite relationship between birth in one incarnation and conception in the next incarnation. This relationship may come to expression in various ways, one of which is the parallel "law" to the first "law" of reincarnation, namely that the angular relationship between the Sun and Saturn at birth in one incarnation is preserved to recur either as the same angle or as the complement (with respect to 180

III. *An Example of Astrological Biography* 73

degrees) between the Sun and Saturn at conception in the next incarnation.

Chart 8: ∅ Richard Wagner
(conception chart computed through applying the hermetic rule)
Richard Wagner ∅ 7.02 p.m. on August 15, 1812 at Leipzig

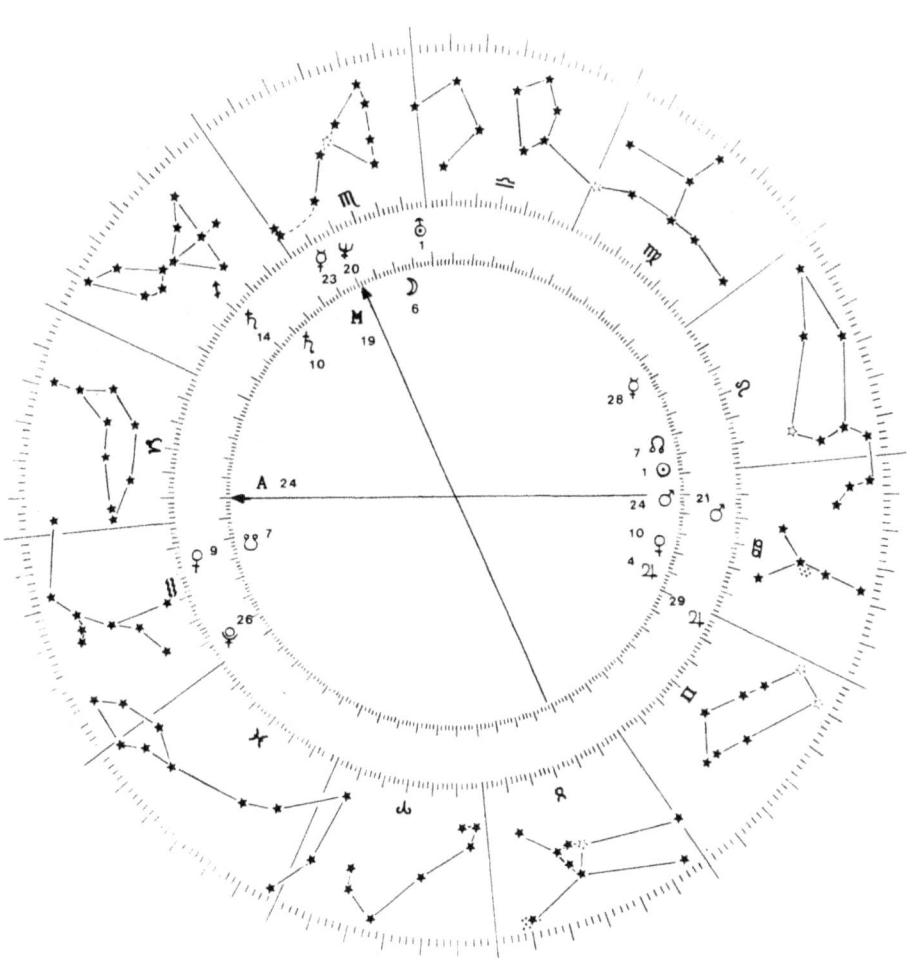

Table 4:
St. Teresa of Avila/Richard Wagner (conception) chart comparison

See Appendix II for the computation of the planetary positions listed in the following table.

zodiacal alignments

St. Teresa of Avila		Richard Wagner (conception)	
†Moon	(6° Taurus)	Moon	(6° Scorpio)
*Moon's node	(2° Leo)	Sun	(1° Leo)
*g-Neptune	(2° Aquarius)		
†g-Uranus	(0° Aquarius)		
†g-Jupiter	(23° Capricorn)	Ascendant	(24° Capricorn)
		g-Mars	(24° Cancer)
*g-Saturn	(19° Scorpio)	Midheaven	(19° Scorpio)
*g-Mars	(21° Taurus)	g-Neptune	(19° Scorpio)
†g-Venus	(27° Leo)	g-Mercury	(28° Leo)
†h-Neptune	(30° Gemini)	h-Jupiter	(29° Gemini)
†g-Neptune	(1° Cancer)	g-Jupiter	(4° Cancer)
*g-Pluto	(12° Sagittarius)	g-Saturn	(10° Sagittarius)
†Moon's node	(16° Sagittarius)	h-Saturn	(14° Sagittarius)

(There are only two aspect metamorphoses, both in the hermetic chart: the opposition between Mercury and Pluto at St. Teresa's death metamorphosed to become a square between the two planets at Richard Wagner's conception, and the square between the Moon and Uranus at St. Teresa's death metamorphosed to become a conjunction between the two planets at Richard Wagner's conception. However, most significant is that the Sun-Saturn angle at Richard Wagner's conception – 129 degrees – is more or less the same as the Sun-Saturn angle of 130 degrees at the birth of St. Teresa)

In the case of Richard Wagner, both the first "law" of reincarnation and the parallel first "law" of reincarnation are fulfilled:

	Sun-Saturn angle
first "law" of reincarnation:	134 degrees †St. Teresa of Avila
	132 degrees *Richard Wagner
parallel first "law" of reincarnation:	130 degrees *St. Teresa of Avila
	129 degrees ⌀ Richard Wagner

As there are many cases in which it does not hold, the parallel first "law" of reincarnation – relating birth in one incarnation to conception in the next incarnation – cannot be regarded as a strict law. As with the first "law" of reincarnation, there is the possibility that it will be fulfilled purely by chance. Therefore great caution must be exercised in applying the "laws" of reincarnation, for even if they hold, this does not prove the validity of a reincarnation example. The reincarnation example St. Teresa of Avila/Richard Wagner is one of those examples in which both the first "law" of reincarnation and its parallel "law" hold. Nevertheless, the main point is that the first "law" of reincarnation (death → birth in the next incarnation) and its parallel "law" (birth → conception in the next incarnation) supply us with the fundamental guiding principle of the hermetic-astrological science of destiny (astrological biography). This principle can be expressed as follows:

Fundamental principle of astrological biography: the destiny experienced between birth and death in one incarnation forms the foundation for the elaboration of the web of destiny between conception and birth in the next incarnation.

According to this fundamental principle of astrological biography there is:

(a) a relationship between birth in one incarnation and conception in the next incarnation;
(b) a relationship between death in one incarnation and birth in the next incarnation; and
(c) the experiences between birth and death in the one incarnation form the foundation for the elaboration of the web of destiny during the embryonic period in the next incarnation.

Taking this fundamental principle together with Willi Sucher's discovery that the web of destiny woven between conception and birth unfolds in 7-year periods between birth and death, we have a remarkable picture as to how the stars carry over destiny from one incarnation to the next (see Figure 1).

Figure 1
The fundamental principle of astrological biography

Abbreviations: Ø = conception; * = birth; † = death.

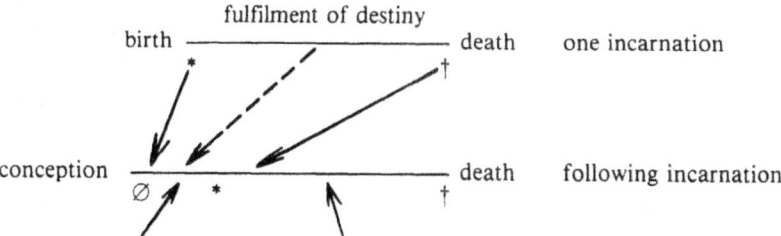

web of destiny reflecting   destiny unfolds in 7-year periods
the movements of the planets corresponding to the lunar cycles
during the embryonic period   of the embryonic period

> The dotted line indicates how destiny fulfilled in one incarnation becomes metamorphosed to become incorporated into the web of destiny woven during the embryonic period of the following incarnation.

The meeting between Richard Wagner and Ludwig II

In order to illustrate the fundamental principle of astrological biography depicted in Figure 1, let us consider the most fateful moment in Richard Wagner's life – his meeting with King Ludwig II of Bavaria. (The karmic background to this meeting is referred to in Chapter 2.) This meeting, which took place on May 4, 1864 – eighteen days prior to his 51st. birthday – was the major turning point in Wagner's whole destiny. Wagner himself highlighted the significance of this meeting by writing his autobiography up to this date, which he concluded with the words (referring to Ludwig II as his "sublime friend"): *"Under the protection of my sublime friend, the burden of the most common pressures of life should never touch me again."*[2]

As referred to in Chapter 2, the karmic background to the meeting between Richard Wagner and Ludwig II of Bavaria is to be found in the relationship between St. Teresa of Avila and St. John of the Cross. St. Teresa's first meeting with St. John of the Cross took place in September 1567, at which St. John of the Cross made his decision to enter and support the Carmelite Reform. At the time of this meeting, St. Teresa was close to the age of 52½. From this time on her relationship with St. John of the Cross lasted until the end of her life. He meant very much to her, as she recognized in him one of the truest supporters of the Carmelite Reform. In the enactment of St. Teresa's destiny, therefore, the last fifteen years of her life – from the age of 52½ until her death at the age of 67½ – were coloured by her relationship with St. John of the Cross.

In the next incarnation as Richard Wagner, the karmic relationship with St. John of the Cross – who reincarnated as Ludwig II of Bavaria – became part of his (Wagner's) web of destiny, woven during the embryonic period. (The same applies, of course, to Ludwig II, but here we are considering the relationship from Wagner's point of view.) It was brought about ("arranged") by the powers of destiny that at a certain point in his life Wagner would meet his benefactor, who had collaborated with him in his previous incarnation. It was arranged that this meeting would approximately reflect their first meeting from the previous incarnation. St. Teresa had been 52½ years old at the time of her first meeting with St. John of the Cross. The powers of destiny arranged – in preparing Wagner's web of destiny (see Figure 1) – that he would meet Ludwig II at around the age of 51*. We can find this prefigured in the movements of the planets during Richard Wagner's embryonic period. There we find the karmic meeting between Wagner and Ludwig II is reflected, prefigured at a particular mo-

---

*This close reflection – almost to the same year of life – of the karmic meeting between Wagner and Ludwig II (reflecting the meeting between St. Teresa of Avila and St. John of the Cross) is unusual. Normally the metamorphosis of situations, meetings, etc. from one life to the next does not follow the same pattern in the next life, but becomes a totally different pattern.

ment in Wagner's incarnation in the time between conception and birth.

In order to find the moment during Wagner's embryonic period prefiguring his karmic meeting with Ludwig II, it is necessary to transform from "earth time" to "embryonic time". As the embryonic period is specified by approximately ten lunar cycles (ten orbits of the Moon around the sidereal zodiac), embryonic time is expressed in terms of the Moon, i.e. in terms of the Moon's longitude in the sidereal zodiac. The equation discovered by Willi Sucher for the transformation from earth time to embryonic time (and *vice versa*) is:

1 orbit of the Moon around the sidereal zodiac = 7 years of life.

Since Wagner's meeting with Ludwig II took place at the age of 51 (less 18 days), this is equivalent – in terms of embryonic time – to seven complete orbits of the Moon around the sidereal zodiac (corresponding to 7 x 7 = 49 years of life) plus two-sevenths of a lunar cycle (corrsponding to 2 years of life). Two-sevenths of the Moon's 360-degree orbit of the sidereal zodiac amounts to 103 degrees. This must then be added to the Moon's sidereal longitude (6° Scorpio) at the completion of the Moon's seventh orbit. Adding 103 degrees to 6° Scorpio yields 19° Aquarius as the longitude of the Moon in the sidereal zodiac. Therefore the zodiacal location of the Moon at the point in time in the embryonic period prefiguring Wagner's 51st. birthday was 19° Aquarius. Since the event under consideration took place almost three weeks before Wagner's 51st. birthday, 3 degrees must be subtracted from the Moon's longitude – for, as we shall see, in converting from embryonic time to earth time, one degree of motion by the Moon in the sidereal zodiac corresponds to one week of life. Subtracting 3 degrees brings the Moon's longitude to 16° Aquarius, which was therefore the sidereal longitude of the Moon at the point in time in the embryonic period prefiguring Wagner's first meeting with Ludwig II, three weeks (actually 18 days) prior to his 51st. birthday.

Looking back to the appropriate point in time in Wagner's embryonic period, the Moon's sidereal longitude was 16° Aquarius on March 2, 1813 at about 3.15 p.m. The Moon had completed seven orbits of the sidereal zodiac on February 22, 1813, and was located at 6° Scorpio (6° Scorpio being the starting sidereal location of the Moon at the time of conception on August 15, 1812). Between August 15, 1812 and February 22, 1813 the Moon made seven orbits of the sidereal zodiac, corresponding to 7 x 7 = 49 years of life. Between February 22 and March 2, 1813 it travelled 100 degrees – corresponding to 2 years of life (less 3 weeks) – to arrive at 16° Aquarius. The planetary configuration on March 2, 1813, 3.13 p.m. GMT – when the sidereal location of the Moon was 16° Aquarius – is shown in Chart 9. This planetary configuration during Richard

Wagner's embryonic period was that which prefigured the destiny which unfolded for him three weeks (actually 18 days) prior to his 51st. birthday.

Looking at the geocentric planetary configuration shown in Chart 9, it is evident that on March 2, 1813 there was a conjunction of the Moon with Mercury, followed by a conjunction of the Sun and the Moon. Also on this day Venus was in conjunction with the Moon's descending node. Moreover, Uranus was at 6° Scorpio, the longitude of the Moon at the start of the embryonic period – this zodiacal location denoting the beginning and the end of each lunar cycle during the embryonic period. (6° Scorpio = the Descendant at Richard Wagner's birth.)

This configuration (Chart 9) – apart from the conjunction of the Venus with the Moon's descending node – relates strongly to the planetary configuration at the death of St. Teresa of Avila, in that at her death g-Saturn = 16° Aquarius, h-Saturn = 20° Aquarius and the Moon = 6° Taurus (see Chart 4). But what is the significance of this? Why should the death configuration from the previous incarnation be so important in the formation of destiny for the new incarnation during the embryonic period?

The shaping of destiny in a given incarnation takes place during the embryonic period between conception and birth, whereby the web of destiny becomes woven into the etheric body during the period of formation of the latter. Thereby the planetary configuration at the moment of birth presents itself as the goal of the incarnating human being, and the entire formation of destiny between conception and birth is directed towards this goal. In this respect the planetary configuration at the moment of birth offers a summary of the web of destiny woven during the whole period between conception and birth. It summarizes the most important prefigurations of karmic events as these are reflected in the planetary movements during the embryonic period.

Similarly, the planetary configuration at the moment of death presents a summary of the destiny lived through in the period between birth and death. It summarizes the most important events of life as these are reflected in the planetary movements during life. (See Willi Sucher's article "The Horoscope of Death", *Modern Mystic* ii (1938), pp. 16 ff., where he shows how the planetary configuration at the moment of death expresses a summary of the most important events as these are indicated by the planetary movements during life.)

Therefore, in the formation of destiny during the embryonic period in the next incarnation, although the entire course of destiny lived through in the previous incarnation serves as the foundation for the formation of destiny in the new incarnation, it is especially the summary of past karma from the previous life presented in the planetary configuration at the moment of death in the past life which is important. We can thus understand why the alignment during Richard Wagner's embryonic period of Sun,

III. An Example of Astrological Biography 79

Moon and Mercury (Chart 9) with the zodiacal location of Saturn at death in the previous incarnation (Chart 4) was of such special significance. At this moment the powers of destiny active in the formation of Richard Wagner's karma decreed that part of his past karma should return in metamorphosed form – in particular, that he should meet with the individual who had been his most outstanding supporter from his previous incarnation as St. Teresa of Avila. Thus it was decreed that he should meet Ludwig II, the reincarnation of St. John of the Cross. This was the destiny image prefigured in the formation of his web of destiny, which became woven into his etheric body at the time of the alignment of Mercury with the Moon and the Sun (= New Moon) on March 2, 1813.

The conjunction of the Moon with Mercury prefigured the event of Ludwig II sending out an envoy to find Richard Wagner, to bring him to meet him. (A conjunction between the Moon and Mercury in itself is not an especially significant event, but the zodiacal alignment of this conjunction with g-Saturn at death in the previous incarnation lends it significance as a cosmic event reflecting a karmic occurrence.) The conjunction between Mercury and the Moon took place at 1.25 p.m. GMT on March 2, 1813. Converting from embryonic time to earth time, this corresponds to four weeks prior to Wagner's 51st. birthday. On this day, exactly four weeks prior to Wagner's birthday – it was April 24, 1864 – Ludwig II sent his cabinet minister off on a mission to find the composer. In this example of astrological biography there is a perfect correspondence between the cosmic event of Moon conjunct Mercury in the embryonic period and the biographical event of the king sending off his cabinet minister to find the composer. (Mercury has always been considered as a "messenger".)

Let us reconstruct this period in Wagner's biography. At Easter – March 1864 – Wagner was in desperate straights. On the Wednesday before Easter he fled from Vienna in order to escape his creditors. He was ill, tired of life, and up to his neck in debts. He travelled to Munich, not really knowing why he was going there. On Good Friday – March 25, 1864 – he made his way under overcast skies through the streets of the city. In a side street he saw a portrait of the newly-crowned king – Ludwig II of Bavaria – and was captured by the "indescribably soulful features" of the 18-year old monarch. He thought to himself: "If he were not king, how I would like to make his acquaintance. But as he is king, he is not able to know anything of me."[3] Silent and sunk in thought, he went further.

Here already, in the fact of having gone to Munich (the city of the king's residence) and seeing a portrait of the young king, it seems that Wagner unconsciously had a presentiment of his impending destiny. One month later the king began actively to seek to make contact with the composer, his cabinet minister Pfistermeister departing on Sunday, April 24 on his mission to find Wagner. (This was the decisive step in Wagner's as-

Chart 9
Embryonic correspondence (Richard Wagner)
Wagner's first meeting with Ludwig II of Bavaria:
e.c. 3.13 p.m. on March 2, 1813 at Leipzig
Abbreviation: e.c. = embryonic correspondence

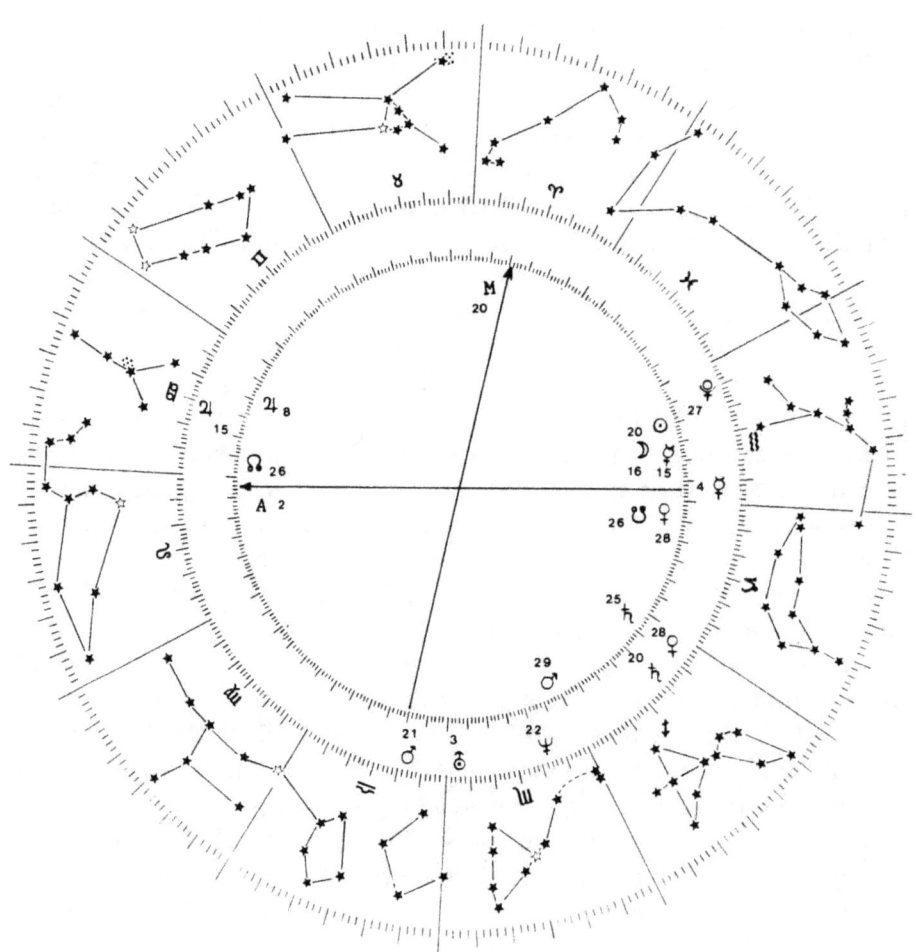

trological biography, corresponding to the conjunction of the Moon and Mercury – described above – in his embryonic period.) Nine days later, on Tuesday, May 3, 1864 the king's envoy (Pfistermeister) eventually found Wagner in Stuttgart and was able to persuade him to come and meet the king.

Having considered the significance in Wagner's astrological biography of the conjunction of Mercury and the Moon in his embryonic period, let us now look further at the conjunction of the Moon with the Sun, which took place on the same day in the embryonic period – on March 2, 1813. The conjunction of the Moon with the Sun – New Moon – signified the beginning of a new phase in Richard Wagner's life. Henceforth he stood under the protection of the king. (The conjunction between the Sun and the Moon in itself is not such an outstanding cosmic event, but the fact that it took place in zodiacal alignment with h-Saturn at death in the previous incarnation is what distinguishes it as a cosmic event prefiguring a significant karmic occurrence.) Converting from embryonic time to earth time, the actual moment of the conjunction of the Sun and Moon (9.43 p.m. GMT on March 2, 1813) corresponds to May 30, 1864, eight days after Wagner's 51st. birthday. This was the time of the blossoming of his idyllic relationship with the king – the time when Wagner lived close by the king at Lake Starnberg and visited him daily. (See Wagner's description of this idyllic time in his letter written at the end of May, 1864, quoted in the last chapter.) It was a kind of "honeymoon", this period of time at the beginning of the relationship between Wagner and the king, when they met daily, each revelling in his delight at the other. This "honeymoon" was prefigured in Wagner's embryonic period by the conjunction of the Sun and the Moon (= New Moon), which signified the beginning of a new phase in his life. Henceforth the financial burdens of existence were lifted from his shoulders, and he was free to resume composing *The Ring of the Nibelungen.*

A new romance: the message of Venus

There was another aspect to this start of a new life for Richard Wagner. This further aspect relates to the romantic side of life, which since time immemorial has been associated astrologically with the planet Venus. That a new development in Richard Wagner's love life was underway at this very time can be "read" from his astrological biography. This new development was prefigured in his embryonic period by the passage of Venus through the Moon's descending node, also on March 2, 1813 (still referring, as in the foregoing, to the geocentric planetary configuration on March 2).

Converting from embryonic time to earth time, we have seen already that this date in the embryonic period corresponds to the time in Wagner's life around his 51st. birthday. (Note: when converting from embryonic time to earth time, as one degree of the Moon's motion equates with one week of life, then one day in the embryonic period prefigures some 12 to 15 weeks of life, since the Moon travels some 12 to 15 degrees in the zodiac on a given date, i.e. the destiny images belonging to a particular date in the embryonic period relate to the fulfilment of destiny over a 3-month period of life.) In terms of Wagner's astrological biography, what destiny image in his embryonic period corresponded to the passage of Venus through the Moon's descending node on March 2, 1813?

In order to answer this question, let us look again at the events in Richard Wagner's biography when he reached the age of 51. The most important event was his meeting with Ludwig II of Bavaria, who provided Wagner with a home and a steady income. Wagner, however, had long been separated from his wife, and even before resuming composing, his immediate concern was to find a female companion in his new life. It seems that the destiny image related to the passage of Venus through the Moon's descending node signified that new love would enter his life. (The Moon's nodes can be conceived of as openings or gateways to the Moon sphere; hence when a planet passes through the Moon's node it works in directly via this gateway as an inspiring influence. In the case of Wagner's astrological biography Venus worked in as a destiny-shaping influence at this critical point in Wagner's life.)

At the commencement of the new phase in Wagner's life, opened up through his meeting with Ludwig II, a desperate longing for a female companion arose within him. All that he was lacking at this new start at the age of 51 was a woman in his life. After becoming established by the king in a house overlooking Lake Starnberg, with no other purpose than to devote himself to composing, he began a frenzied search for someone to join him as his "house keeper". Eventually an answer came: in the shape of the young wife – Cosima – of his devoted assistant, the pianist and conductor Hans von Bülow. Wagner had already for some time felt deeply attracted to Cosima. Hans von Bülow – unaware of the implications of what he was doing, and wanting only to help out his composer-friend – instead of travelling together with her, sent his wife on in advance to join Wagner, delaying his own departure on account of his work committments, and he followed her to Lake Starnberg a week later. Already within this one week together at Lake Starnberg, Cosima and Wagner declared their love for one another, and in the absence of Hans von Bülow sealed their relationship. During this week Cosima conceived a child – her third child, and Wagner's first child – who became christened Isolde. To the end of his life Hans von Bülow maintained that Isolde was his own child. (It was not until six years later that Wagner married Cosima, by which time his relation-

III. An Example of Astrological Biography

ship with Cosima had become known publicly, and Cosima was able to obtain a divorce from Hans von Bülow.)

The passage of Venus through the Moon's descending node on March 2, 1813 – during Wagner's embryonic period – was the cosmic event in his astrological biography which prefigured a new development in his emotional life. Although it was not until some two months after his 51st. birthday that Cosima joined him, already the impulse for their union had lived within him and was called awake again when he found himself in a new life-situation, following on from his 51st. birthday. As is often the case, the cosmic events of the embryonic period prefigure events of destiny by proclaiming them, and the time of fulfilment may be delayed. (In this case the delay amounted to some two months of life, but throughout this time Wagner was seeking a female companion.)

Here it should be noted that although the powers of destiny arrange the events of destiny, the fulfilment of these events is up to the human being. It is a matter of the old saying: "You can lead a horse to water, but you cannot make it drink!" The powers of destiny work to bring about events and circumstances, but ultimately it is the human beings concerned who enact their destiny. For example, the powers of destiny worked to bring about the meeting between Ludwig II and Richard Wagner. This meeting came about as a result of the positive karmic relationship between these two individuals from the previous incarnation. However, once having been brought together, it depended upon them – as individuals – how their relationship would develop.

To begin with they were born along upon the wings of the positive karma that united them, and this endowed the early days of their friendship with an idyllic "honeymoon" quality. Later their relationship became severely strained by the "Cosima affair" – the scandal that erupted when it became known publicly that Cosima was Wagner's mistress. To the credit of Ludwig II, he did not allow Wagner's human failings to cloud his perception of the higher genius of the composer. To the end he maintained a positive attitude towards Wagner, acknowledging the latter's artistic greatness. Thus the relationship between Wagner and Ludwig II – despite all the problems that arose between them – on the whole remained a positive one.

It was different in the case of the relationship between Wagner and Friedrich Nietzsche. Here again – as discussed in Chapter 1 – they were brought together by a positive karmic relationship from the previous incarnation. Again the relationship had an idyllic quality in the beginning, borne along by the positive karma that existed between these two individuals. But gradually the higher vision that united the two became clouded – especially when Wagner's human failings became all too apparent to Friedrich Nietzsche. After seven years of friendship, they became increasingly estranged from one another – Nietzsche eventually launching his bitter attack on Wagner in *The Wagner Case*. This is a clear example of how a positive karmic relationship can degenerate into a negative one, showing how human beings may be brought together by destiny, but that it is up to them what they make of their relationship.

The further question arises as to the nature of the relationship between Cosima and Richard Wagner. As the published diaries of Cosima Wagner reveal, she was tormented for the rest of her life on account of the guilt that she experienced through having left Hans von Bülow to join Wagner. She took this step out of the higher motivation to help Wagner, whom she recognized as a great composer – but one who needed the help of a woman in order to realise his creative potential. Thus she dedicated herself selflessly to fulfilling Wagner's complex needs and to helping to create the right atmosphere in which he could compose. She and Wagner were deeply happy together, but she could not forget the deep wound she had inflicted upon Hans von Bülow through leaving him. The diaries that Cosima wrote until the end of her life indicate the inner conflict that she had to live with, and reveal something of the intricate question as to the interrelationship of karma and morality. There can be little doubt that Cosima was led by destiny (karma) to Wagner. But from a moral point of view she betrayed her husband, Hans von Bülow, through taking the step of uniting herself with Richard Wagner. Consequently she had to bear the negative karma brought about by this step. Such a betrayal, where the moral perspective of a situation becomes over-ridden by the karmic aspect, may give rise to a "karmic knot" (something to be "unravelled" in a future incarnation). It is precisely such karmic knots which hinder the aspirant on the path of spiritual development from attaining higher spiritual stages of consciousness (lunar, solar and zodiacal consciousness) beyond terrestrial consciousness. For one who has made progress on the spiritual path, therefore, the moral perspective of a situation almost invariably takes priority over the karmic aspect.

Astrological biography

Returning to Willi Sucher's original study of Wagner's destiny, let us look more closely at Wagner's biography in the light of Willi Sucher's research. Central to astrological biography is the correspondence between the planetary movements during the embryonic period and the course of events between birth and death. Applying this correspondence, Willi Sucher investigated the major planetary events in Richard Wagner's embryonic period, looking at them in relation to Wagner's biography:

> *We have discovered with the help of the hermetic rule how it is possible to find a certain prenatal configuration (the horoscope of conception)... It will now be our task to bring these cosmic facts (taking*

III. An Example of Astrological Biography

place between conception and birth) into connection with the earthly life of man... Take, for example, the beginning of the sixth Moon-cycle in the prenatal... (embryonic period) of Richard Wagner, namely December 30, 1812. Until this moment – beginning... on August 15, 1812 – the Moon had passed five times completely round the zodiac and was about to commence her sixth cycle. A few days later, on January 2, 1813, it was New Moon – that is, the Moon passed before the Sun... At the same time the Sun was in conjunction with Saturn, so that we have the following picture in the cosmos. Moon, Sun and Saturn were at this moment one behind the other, and all of them were in the ... constellation of Sagittarius. At this moment, therefore, something of individual and unique significance was taking place in the prenatal development, and as it was at the beginning of the sixth lunar cycle... a reflection of events in Richard Wagner's life (took place) about the change from the fifth to the sixth 7-year period.[4].

Here Willi Sucher saw that the significant cosmic event – a conjunction of the Moon and the Sun with Saturn in Sagittarius, which took place near the beginning of the sixth lunar sidereal period in the time between Wagner's conception and birth – prefigured something important in Wagner's destiny at the beginning of the sixth 7-year period in his life, i.e. between the age of 35 and 36 (= the 36th. year of life). This is an example of astrological biography, i.e. of the hermetic science of destiny based on the correspondence between the cosmic events taking place during the embryonic period and the biographical events occurring between birth and death. Transposing from embryonic time to earth time, the start of the sixth lunar orbit of the sidereal zodiac during the embryonic period corresponds to the start of the sixth 7-year period in life, i.e. it corresponds to the 36th. year of life. Therefore, in looking at Wagner's biography, we can expect to find that this cosmic event prefigured something significant in Wagner's life during his 36th. year.

In order to find the exact correspondence in Wagner's life with the cosmic event of the alignment of the Moon, Sun and Saturn in Sagittarius, we need to look more closely at the moment of conjunction of these three heavenly bodies. The conjunction between the Sun and Saturn took place at 1.55 a.m. GMT on January 1, 1813. This was followed on January 2 by the conjunction of the Moon first with Saturn (at 2.38 p.m. GMT) and then with the Sun (at 5.26 p.m. GMT). The key to the transposition from embryonic time to earthly time is the Moon's zodiacal longitude at these three moments"(☌ = conjunction):

cosmic event during embryonic period		Moon's sidereal longitude	
(1) Sun ☌ Saturn:	01.55 on January 1, 1813	29°	Scorpio
(2) Moon ☌ Saturn:	14.38 on January 2, 1813	18½°	Sagittarius
(3) Moon ☌ Sun:	17.26 on January 2, 1813	20°	Sagittarius

How does knowing the Moon's sidereal longitude in the embryonic period enable us to transpose to earthly life? The answer is: as one orbit of the Moon around the sidereal zodiac (through 360 degrees) corresponds to seven years of earthly life, the increment of the Moon's longitude by one-seventh of 360 degrees (i.e. ca. 51½ degrees) corresponds to one year of life. This yields the following approximate equation:

Moon's motion through 360 degrees → 7 years of life
Moon's motion through 51½ degrees → 1 year of life (= 52 weeks)
Moon's motion through 1 degree → 1 week of life.

The approximate equation of one week of life corresponding to one degree of the Moon's motion through the sidereal zodiac during the embryonic period enables a fairly exact correspondence to be established between the embryonic period and the course of life between birth and death. At the start of each lunar cycle – corresponding to the start of a new 7-year period of life – the Moon is located at its starting point, i.e. at its zodiacal location at the moment of conception as determined by the hermetic rule. In Richard Wagner's case, the Moon's starting point at the moment of conception determined by the hermetic rule (7 p.m., August 15, 1812) was at 6° Scorpio (see Chart 8). At the start of each new lunar cycle the Moon was located at 6° Scorpio, prefiguring the start of a new 7-year period in life. Taking the first of the three cosmic events listed above, at (1) – the conjunction of the Sun with Saturn – the Moon's sidereal longitude was 29° Scorpio. The difference in degrees of longitude between 6° Scorpio – corresponding to the start of the sixth 7-year period – and 29° Scorpio amounts to 23 degrees. These 23 degrees of the Moon's motion through the sidereal zodiac correspond approximately to 23 weeks of life. As the start of the sixth 7-year period in Richard Wagner's life was his 35th. birthday on May 22, 1848, the cosmic event of the conjunction of the Sun with Saturn near the beginning of the sixth lunar prenatal cycle is reflected – when transposed to earthly time – to 23 weeks after his 35th. birthday. Adding 23 weeks to May 22, 1848, we arrive at the end of October/beginning of November 1848. In other words, we have to look at Wagner's biography around the beginning of November 1848 – 23 weeks after his 35th. birthday – in order to find the circumstances of destiny prefigured in the embryonic period by the conjunction of the Sun and Saturn in Sagittarius.

Similarly, at event (2) in the embryonic period – the conjunction of the Moon with Saturn – the Moon's sidereal longitude was 18½° Sagittarius. Transposing to Wagner's biography, this equates with the point in time 42½ weeks after his 35th. birthday, since the difference between 6° Scorpio and 18½° Sagittarius amounts to 42½ degrees.

Lastly, at event (3) in the prenatal period – New Moon (the conjunction of the Sun and Moon) – the Moon's sidereal longitude was 20° Sagittarius. As the difference between 6° Scorpio and 20° Sagittarius amounts to 44 degrees, this transposes to the point in time 44 weeks after Wagner's 35th. birthday.

The transposition from the significant zodiacal alignment of Saturn, Sun and Moon on January 1/2, 1813 in Wagner's embryonic period leads us to his 36th. year of life – more specifically, to 23 weeks, 42½ weeks and 44 weeks after his 35th. birthday. As Wagner reached the age of 35 on May 22, 1848, 23 weeks, 42½ weeks and 44 weeks later equate with (1) the beginning of November 1848, (2) the middle of March 1849, and (3) the end of March 1849. Let us look at Wagner's biography to see what was taking place during the period 1848/49 in his 36th. year of life.

Turning point in Wagner's destiny

The year 1849 in fact marked a decisive turning point in Wagner's life. On May 3, 1849 the Dresden revolution broke out, in which Wagner took part. The resistance of the revolutionaries to the approaching Prussian troops collapsed on May 9, and they withdraw from the barricades, fleeing for their lives. For his part in having sided with the revolutionaries a warrant was issued for Wagner's arrest, and he was able to escape arrest only by leaving Germany and living in exile in Switzerland. This marked the culmination of events in his 36th. year of life, which led him to take up a completely new life in Switzerland.

He had lived in Dresden for seven years (1842–49), having held the post of director/conductor of the court orchestra and choir there since February 1843. During this time three of his operas – *Rienzi, The Flying Dutchman* and *Tannhäuser* – had had their premières at the court theatre in Dresden. Through his revolutionary activities Wagner lost his prestigious post and with it the opportunity for directing performances of his operas at a theatre under his direction. Under a cloud of disgrace he had to leave his native country and settle in a foreign land. Yet, as Willi Sucher points out, it was precisely this dramatic turn of events which signified the coming to birth of Wagner's higher being:

In the year 1849 Wagner came into a very difficult situation. He had taken active part in the revolution which then broke out in Dresden. The revolutionaries were defeated and Wagner was obliged to flee to Switzerland, which was for him the beginning of a long and arduous period of exile. In their more outward aspect these events came very near to the destruction of his physical existence, but they were no less important in their spiritual aspect. This was about the middle of Wagner's life, and it is as though at this moment two different beings were meeting and wrestling with one another in his inner life. Wagner was one of those men who are strong enough and brave enough to imprint the higher mystical reality of their true self upon the ordinary lower human nature.

These two – the lower man, and the higher man who belongs to the future – were in this year in a peculiar relation to one another in Wagner's life. His share in revolutionary conflict is a symptom of it. He bore within him the strong will to bring to birth a new form of art – one which should bear the human being upward on to a new and hitherto undivined level of existence. But in the many years of struggle and bitter disappointment until then, he had experienced all the hindrances to which the lower man is subject. In a radical convulsion of the existing social order, he thought he saw the preparing of the ways along which mankind should rise to a higher level, in harmony with the artistic ideals which he felt within himself. The course of events showed this assumption to be wrong, and Richard Wagner had to suffer for it. The year 1849 represents a deep incision in his life. Henceforth he was to work inexorably at the realisation of his artistic ideal, leaving the ordinary, the merely civic man, the 'citizen' behind him. Indeed at this moment the civil community to which he had belonged drove him into banishment and exile. He was pursued for the part which he had played in the revolution, and many years were to elapse before he could again set foot upon his native German soil.

These events, as I said, are reflected in the prenatal conjunction of Saturn and the Sun in the constellation of Sagittarius. How shall we relate this situation in the human being's destiny to the cosmic facts? Old astrological rules will not avail us here, for we are dealing with an altogether new astrological conception. We must look for other ways and methods.

In the first place we shall observe that the conjunction took place in the constellation of Sagittarius for which the symbol ♐ is used. Let us now try to enter rather more deeply into the symbolic language of the zodiacal signs. The Sagittarius arrow indicates something like a movement – a direction leading towards a certain goal. To make the language clearer and more meaningful to us, we may perhaps transform the symbol into: ⤴ (representing) as it were, a steep and winding uphill path.

During the whole of Wagner's embryonic development Saturn was in... Sagittarius. Now Saturn has the character of heaviness; it is indeed related to the metal lead. It is above all the representative of fate – of destiny inexorable as the course of time itself. Saturn in Sagittarius, therefore, indicates a pathway of development towards a certain goal, yet steep and arduous and even painful. Now (at the conjunction of the Sun and Saturn, the Sun passes) before Saturn... coming from *the constellation of Leo... (At Wagner's conception on August 15, 1812 the Sun was at 1° Leo, in conjunction with Mars at 24° Cancer – see Chart 8.) The Sun in conjunction with Mars... is a true picture of the remarkable energy of Wagner's nature. For the conjunction of the Sun and Mars signifies* in this regard *an enhancement of active power, the physiological significance of this conjunction notwithstanding.*

When, therefore, the Sun passes before Saturn in Sagittarius, it is made possible for this great energy in action, directed as it is in Wagner's being to an artistic ideal for the future of mankind, to be purified and transmuted to a higher level. This is what happened in the events of 1849.[5].

Let us now look again at Wagner's biography, to follow the events in 1848/49 – his 36th. year of life – more closely. As referred to above, this 36th. year culminated with the Dresden revolution in May 1849, which took place just two weeks before Wagner's 36th. birthday. In the light of Willi Sucher's analysis, the conjunction of the Moon, Sun and Saturn in Sagittarius prefigured the catastrophic turn of events in Wagner's life signified by his participation in the Dresden uprising.

The exact sequence of events at this point in Wagner's astrological biography – as computed below– is as follows:

(1) the conjunction of the Sun and Saturn, corresponding to the beginning of November 1848;
(2) the conjunction of the Moon and Saturn, corresponding to the middle of March 1849;
(3) the conjunction of the Sun and Moon (= New Moon), corresponding to the end of March 1849.

The event proclaimed by the conjunction of the Sun and Saturn was the death of Wagner's existence as a "normal citizen" – a death which at the same time signified a coming-to-birth, extending over a long period of time, of Wagner's higher being. Transposing to earthly life, the exact conjunction between Saturn and the Sun corresponds to the beginning of November 1848 in Wagner's astrological biography. But just as a conjunction between the Sun and Saturn is not an instaneous cosmic event, but one which lasts – astrologically speaking – for several days, so the corresponding transposition to earthly life cannot be looked at as signifying merely an instant in time, but as relating to a period of time extending over several months before and after November 1848. The "death" proclaimed by the conjunction of the Sun and Saturn – corresponding to November 1848 – became a physical reality six months later, at the Dresden uprising in May 1849. But the spiritual message of this "death" came through in a remarkable way already in November 1848. Between November 12 and 28 of 1848 Wagner wrote the text to his poetic rendition of *Siegfried's Death*, the closing piece to his operatic tetralogy *The Ring of the Nibelungen*. In Siegfried – consciously or unconsciously – Wagner glimpsed something of himself:

Siegfried: this is the living incarnation of Wagner, with his father-complex and his mother-problem, his total naivity, his unabashed drive to climb to the top, with his inclination to self-delusion, pious deception and the semi-conscious betrayal of his friends – from the point of view of society at large, an individual rebel, completely lacking in social morality, upon whom many place their hopes, but precipitously.[6]

Seen in this light, *Siegfried's Death* proclaimed the "death" of Wagner himself. The lower human being has to die in order for the higher human being to be born. "Siegfried" had to die to make way for "Parsifal" – the latter representing the higher human being. (It was only with the completion of the *Ring of the Nibelungen* that Wagner was able to devote himself to the composition of *Parsifal*.) The beginning of this long process of death took place in Wagner's 36th. year of life. It was outlined in poetic-dramatic form in his text for *Siegfried's Death* written in November 1848, and his flight to exile in the wake of the Dresden revolution in May 1849 marked the "death" of his existence as a "normal citizen" up until that time.

The conjunction between the Sun and Saturn on January 1, 1812 in Wagner's embryonic period was the major significator of this process of "death and rebirth" that set in in his 36th. year of life. To this conjunction came the alignment of the Moon with the two planets on January 2, 1812 – corresponding to March 1849 in Wagner's astrological biography. Just as the conjunction of the Sun and Saturn prefigured the writing down of the text of *Siegfried's Death* in November 1848, the conjunction of the Moon with Saturn prefigured a fateful meeting for Wagner in March 1849. This meeting was with one of the most notorious revolutionaries of the day – the Russian anarchist Michail Bakunin.

Already since October 1848 Wagner had been publishing – anonymously – revolutionary articles in the publication of his friend August Roeckel. (Roeckel was an ardent revolutionary.) Bakunin was on the run, and came to stay with August Roeckel, who introduced him to Wagner. Bearded and jovial, Bakunin struck up a warm relationship with Wagner. Bakunin preached the burning of everything in the flames of the revolution, and remarked to Wagner: "Then you won't need so many instruments, and that will be very good!"[7] This curious pair – Bakunin and Wagner – were inseparable during the period leading up to the May revolution. On April 1, 1849 – Palm Sunday – Wagner directed a performance

III. An Example of Astrological Biography

of Beethoven's ninth symphony. Slipping in without being noticed, Bakunin was present at the dress rehearsal. As the last accord died away, he made his way towards the orchestra and called out to Wagner that if all music were to go under in the great fire that was expected to sweep the whole world, the two of them should join forces and – risking death – see to it that this symphony would be spared from the flames. Nothing would be saved but this!

Wagner's meeting with Bakunin – prefigured by the conjunction of the Moon with Saturn at the corresponding time in Wagner's embryonic period – signified the flaring up of lower destructive forces, which filled him with the fire of revolutionary frenzy. (The Moon represents in particular the lower, unpurified will.) His meeting with the "prophet of world fire" – Bakunin – indicated the inner turmoil in which he found himself at this time of his life, in his 36th. year.

Wagner experienced inwardly the onset of the process of "death" of his lower being to give birth to his higher being – this was prefigured by the conjunction of the Sun and Saturn. To this conjunction came the Moon, which prefigured the period March 1849 when Wagner met Bakunin, at which time an intense revolutionary fervour arose within him. Instead of comprehending his inner death experience as a soul event relating to the death of the lower forces within him, Wagner fell prey to the illusion that everything corrupt and tainted outside of him – external to him – would be consumed in the flames of the revolution. He failed to meet the challenge of the inner *trial by fire* – the inner process of purification – entailed in his spiritual death experience, and projected it outwards as the sense for a revolution that would purge and transform everything.

The conjunction of the Sun and Moon – New Moon – in the embryonic period, when transposed into the fulfilment of destiny during life, generally signifies the start of a new phase of life. The alignment of Saturn, Sun and Moon in Wagner's embryonic period meant that here a conjunction between the Sun and Moon took place at the same time that the Sun was in conjunction with Saturn. Transposing from the embryonic period to life, a new phase of life did indeed begin for Wagner, but it meant inwardly a death experience in view of the shattering of his revolutionary ideals in the face of the fiasco of the Dresden uprising. After having fled to safety in Zurich, Switzerland, he later wrote to his wife Minna: "The Dresden revolution and its entire consequences have taught me that I am not at all a revolutionary."[8]

Here it can be seen that the prefiguring of life's events during the embryonic period takes place on the level of soul experiences – reflecting the planetary movements – where the soul experiences become incorporated into the etheric body as destiny images, then to become translated into life experiences of destiny between birth and death. Learning to interpret the meaning of the planetary movements during the embryonic period is a matter of comprehending the language of the soul, of understanding the experiences that the soul goes through. Then it may be possible to grasp from the level of these soul experiences how they become translated into events of destiny. For example, Willi Sucher's interpretation of the conjunction of the Sun and Saturn can be summed up as a soul experience of death, in which the human being "dies" on the level of the personality in order to make way for his higher being or individuality. Expressed in the symbolic language of soul experiences, the conjunction of Saturn and the Sun during the embryonic period signifies *initiation,* in the sense that initiation is the spiritual death experience in which the personality "dies" to make way for the "birth" of the individuality.

In Richard Wagner's case the conjunction of the Sun and Saturn was joined by the Moon. In the symbolic language of the soul, this can be interpreted as a "trial by fire", where the lower, dark will forces (Moon forces) have to be purified and brought under control. For Wagner, however, this soul experience, when it later became translated into destiny, became projected outwards as an impulse to purify the world through revolution. (This serves as an archetype for nearly all revolutionaries, who generally tend to project outwards with great vehemence the impulse of purification which arises within them.)

Lead us not into temptation

In the example of Richard Wagner – and this is typical for all human beings – it is evident that the transposition of soul events experienced during the embryonic period to become events of destiny in the course of life is accompanied by the working in of *temptation.* For Wagner, Bakunin appeared in his life as a Mephistophelian figure who encouraged him in the illusory idea of a transformation of the world for the better through revolution. The experience of the Dresden revolution shattered this illusion, enabling Wagner to see that he was not a revolutionary. It was only then that he became released from the temptation which had taken hold of him in the form of revolutionary fervour.

For the hermetic astrologer it is important to discern the working of temptation, to learn to perceive how it inserts itself into the events of destiny. Temptation almost invariably works as a corruption or perversion of the normal course of destiny. It makes its entrance first of all into the soul, and from there works as a corrupting influence leading the human being astray from his true path of destiny. Just as the forces of the soul may be distinguished as impulses of thinking, feeling or the will, so temptation has three levels of access to the human being's inner life: via thinking, feeling or the will.

The temptation of the will is that of power – the *will to power.* Here the

III. An Example of Astrological Biography

human being allows his sense of egocentricity to assert itself to the extent that he comes to regard himself as being at the center of things, that everything revolves around him, and that his own will is the determining force of his existence. Instead of "Thy will be done" he adopts "my will be done" as his maxim in life. It then becomes all too easy for him to worship the idol of power, as the more power he has, the more it seems that his will is being accomplished. But as Christ replied, when he was offered power over "all the kingdoms of the world": "You shall worship the Lord your God and him only shall you serve" (*Matthew* iv, 10).

Obedience to God, to serve only him ("Thy will be done"), is the answer to the temptation of the will to power that is directed at the human will.

The temptation that is directed at the human being's feeling life is that in which the satisfaction of feelings becomes the highest goal, whereby this satisfaction takes precedence over the dictates of reason and conscience. Just as in the temptation of the will it is the execution of his will that becomes all important to the human being, so in the temptation aimed at the feeling life it is the satisfaction of feelings that acquires precedence. This temptation works in such a way that the human being is impelled via his feelings to blot out reason and conscience altogether. In the language of the New Testament, he is urged "to cast himself down from the pinnacle of the temple" (*Matthew* iv, 6).

In symbolic language the "pinnacle of the temple" signifies the uppermost part of the human being in which the Divine manifests itself. Expressed in terms of the *hermetic man,* the "pinnacle of the temple" relates to the two uppermost lotus flowers – the 8-petalled and the 2-petalled lotus flowers, which are the lotus flowers of conscience and reason, corresponding to the planets Saturn and Jupiter respectively (see *Hermetic Astrology* I, Figure 13). It is via the 8-petalled lotus flower (Saturn) that conscience comes to expression as a revelation of the Divine in man, and this can be carried over – translated into reason – by way of the 2-petalled lotus flower (Jupiter).

An archetypal expression of the temptation directed at the feeling life is shown in the temptation of Adam and Eve in the Garden of Eden. There the Divine revealed itself to Adam and Eve in terms which could be readily translated into the "voice of conscience": "You may freely eat of every tree of the garden; but of the tree of the knowledge of good and evil you shall not eat, for on the day that you eat of it you shall die" (*Genesis* ii, 16). Over and against this revelation of the Divine, temptation presented itself to Eve by way of the feeling life, through desire: "The woman saw that the tree was good for food, and that it was a delight to the eyes, and that the tree was to be desired to make one wise" (*Genesis* iii, 6). In the Biblical account Adam and Eve succumbed to this temptation, and the event known as *the Fall* took place. The Fall indicates in archetypal form the consequences of going against the dictates of reason and conscience. The consequence of "casting oneself down from the pinnacle of the temple" is loss of contact with the Divine, expulsion, becoming an outcast – this was the fate of Adam and Eve.

In contrast to Adam and Eve, Jesus Christ resisted the temptation to cast himself down from the pinnacle of the temple. His response to this temptation was: "You shall not tempt the Lord thy God" (*Matthew* iv, 7). In other words, the Divine – as it comes to manifestation in man via conscience and reason – must remain above temptation. That which is higher within man should not be tempted by that which is lower. The divinely-guided human being – who acts in accordance with his conscience – will not succumb to lower impulses which are against his conscience or against that which he holds to be right. He will remain *chaste* in the face of the temptation directed at the feeling life. Thus, just as *obedience* is the protection against the temptation of the will, so *chastity* (understood in its deeper, spiritual sense) is the safeguard against falling into the temptation of the feeling life.

Lastly, the temptation directed at the human being's thought life comes to expression in terms of the acquisition of knowledge. It is by way of thinking that the human being acquires knowledge. However, knowledge has a quantitative and a qualitative aspect. For example, a quantitative aspect of our knowledge of light is that it travels at 186,000 miles per second. A qualitative aspect of light, which may be discovered through meditation, is that light in its purest form reveals the Divine in existence. All mystics agree on this: that the opening up of the world of spirit is always heralded by a new experience of the purest quality of light, and that this accompanies – in fact enables – spiritual vision. Thus there are different levels of truth on the scale quantitative-qualitative. At one end of the scale it is certainly true that light travels at 186,000 miles per second. But at the other end of the scale it is just as true – and ultimately for the human being it is more meaningfully true – that the pure rays of light reveal that which is Divine in the world.

In the acquisition of quantitative knowledge, which is the main concern of science, there is the danger that the higher qualitative aspect of knowledge becomes obscured. Science proceeds by way of collecting facts and analysing them to discover their underlying meaning. The hard facts ("stones") are the outermost aspect – the purely quantitative aspect – of knowledge. The scientist then seeks to turn these "stones" into "bread" by seeking – through analysis – for their significance. "Bread" is the body of scientific knowledge gained through the transformation of the "stones" – i.e. the hard facts – into something meaningful, which the human being can "digest". It is believed – and it is to a certain extent true – that this "bread" nourishes and sustains the human being. It is true that this "bread" – the body of scientific knowledge – does partially nourish and sustain the human being, insofar as it represents a first level of the qualitative aspect of knowledge.

In fact, it is the qualitative aspect of knowledge which is nourishing and sustaining, but this qualitative side of existence "proceeds from the mouth of God". For this reason, Jesus Christ, when he was assailed by this temptation, answered: "Man shall not live by bread alone, but by every word that proceeds from the mouth of God" (*Matthew* iv, 4).

In this answer it is not denied that man lives on bread, but it is pointed out that on another level – on the spiritual level – man lives by virtue of that which proceeds from the Divine. If the Divine is acknowledged as underlying all existence, then everything in existence is ultimately rooted in the Divine. Knowing this, the seeker for knowledge will not remain satisfied with merely amassing facts (collecting "stones"), but will seek to penetrate through the facts to arrive at their inner, qualitative significance. And he will not remain content with the outermost level of qualitative knowledge ("turning stones into bread"), but will seek further for the revelation of the Divine underlying the "bread" – this revelation being "the word that proceeds from the mouth of God".

The scientific approach to knowledge – that of gathering facts and analysing them – has to be supplemented by *spiritual science,* which looks for the revelation of the Divine beyond the level of natural science. Natural science is characterized by the turning of facts ("stones") into scientific theory ("bread") on the level of the natural world. This has to be supplemented by spiritual science which seeks for "every word that proceeds from the mouth of God" on the level of the supernatural world.
(Rudolf Steiner's motivation in the founding of spiritual science was to complement and supplement existing natural science.[9])

He who practises poverty on the level of knowledge remains open to the revelation of the Divine ("the word that proceeds from the mouth of God") and is protected from the temptation of amassing a fortune on the level of the "wisdom of this world", which in the eyes of God is folly. ("Has not God made foolish the wisdom of the world?" – I *Corinthians* i, 20.) Thus the hermeticist sets more value upon the wisdom of divine revelation – at the purely qualitative end of the scale of knowledge – than he does upon the "wisdom of this world" belonging to the quantitative end of the scale, which is acquired on the scientific path of knowledge through amassing facts and analysing them for theories ("turning stones into bread"). Of course, a hermeticist – insofar as he is scientifically active – may also follow the scientific path of knowledge, but in so doing he recognizes that "man shall not live by bread alone, but by every word that proceeds from the mouth of God". He will acknowledge the priority of divine revelation over the "bread" of the wisdom of this world. Ultimately it is a question of values, of recognizing that the treasures of spiritual wisdom are of infinitely greater value than the treasures of the wisdom of this world.

The three temptations – directed at thinking, feeling and the will (this is their order in the description in the Gospel of St. Matthew) – are combatted on the hermetic spiritual path through the "three vows" of poverty, chastity and obedience (conceived of in their deeper, spiritual sense).[10] The practice of the three vows – poverty, chastity and obedience – equip the human being with that which is necessary to withstand the temptations towards richness, debauchery and power, which assail thinking, feeling and the will. Once they have gained entrance on the level of the soul, they can begin to manifest as forces active in the shaping of the human being's destiny. Thus, for example, the will to power – when it has taken hold of someone's soul – will become an active force in his destiny, leading him again and again into situations where the temptation to gain and exercise power arises. Once a temptation has become an active force in the shaping of a person's destiny, it becomes all the more difficult to resist. For this reason an awareness of the three temptations and how they work on the level of the soul is most helpful, as it is on this level that they can be most effectively resisted. If they are prevented from taking root at all in the soul, then they are powerless to become effective as active forces in a person's destiny.

An astrological perspective of temptation

Having outlined the three temptations, we are now in a position to consider them from an astrological point of view. As referred to in the discussion of the hermetic man in *Hermetic Astrology* I, Chapter 5, the three lotus flowers beneath the level of the heart are the bearers of the soul forces of thinking, feeling and the will. These three lotus flowers – 10-petalled (umbilical center), 6-petalled (pelvic center) and 4-petalled (reproductive center) – correspond to the planets Mercury, Venus and the Moon, respectively. Therefore, on the macrocosmic level the three temptations – directed at thinking, feeling, and the will – are related to the planets Mercury, Venus and the Moon. (They are not the original source of these temptations, however. See Chapter 8 – Uranus, Neptune and Pluto – concerning the macrocosmic source of the forces of temptation directed at thinking, feeling and the will.)

For example, if the will to power takes hold of someone, he is then as if possessed by the dark currents of the will, the negative lunar forces. This was the case with Adolf Hitler, who – consciously or unconsciously – chose the symbol of the swastika as a visible expression of his will to power. The swastika has always served as a symbol of the 4-petalled lotus flower, the lunar center in the human being. (Hitler, in fact, chose the reversed swastika as his symbol, clearly indicating that he was under the influence of the negative lunar forces, the dark currents of the will.)

The 4-petalled lotus flower is normally subservient to the higher lotus flowers, but if it becomes dominant – as in the case of the will to power – the normal relationship between the lotus flowers becomes reversed. Instead of the will being guided by the light of reason (2-petalled lotus flower) and conscience (8-petalled lotus flower), the will itself becomes the guiding power in the human being's soul, and dictates what he thinks and believes. An analogous reversal of the normal functioning of the lotus flowers takes place in the case of someone who succumbs to the temptation directed at the feeling life, in which case it can happen that the 6-petalled lotus flower becomes dominant. Then it is the negative side of Venus which takes possession of the human being. The normal functioning of the lotus flowers is also reversed when the temptation directed at thinking takes hold of someone. Here the 10-petalled flower may become dominant, and the negative Mercury forces are then able to capture the human being's thought life.

It can happen that all three temptations assail someone simultaneously and take hold not only of his soul life but also his self. Here the self becomes the instrument of temptation, i.e. the human being consciously adopts a negative direction in his spiritual development. When the self itself succumbs to temptation, leading the human being in the direction of the "grey" or "black path", it is the heart center (12-petalled lotus flower, corresponding to the Sun) which is the point of attack. The inspiring force on the path of black magic is the so-called *Sun demon* (Antichrist), the negative spirit of the Sun, who gains entrance via the heart center. Here the human being becomes a vehicle of the anti-Christian forces proceeding from the Antichrist – Christ being the spiritual-moral Sun center in existence. This represents a fourth temptation, which is the synthesis of the three temptations described archetypally in the Gospel of St. Matthew that assailed Jesus Christ and were overcome by him. This fourth tempation proceeds directly from the being of Antichrist, whilst the three temptations bring to expression, as it were, the thinking, feeling and the will of Antichrist.

Temptation in Wagner's destiny

Let us now continue with our study of the destiny of Richard Wagner, in order to gain a comprehension of the language of the soul which is needed to understand the soul events that take place during the embryonic period, prefiguring the enactment of the human being's destiny in 7-year periods between birth and death. It is especially the alignment of the Moon, Sun and Saturn in Richard Wagner's embryonic period which interests us. As discussed earlier in this chapter, the alignment of these three planets during Wagner's embryonic period prefigured the dramatic turn of events in his life connected with the Dresden revolution. This finding – originally discovered by Willi Sucher – can now be illuminated in the light of the foregoing discussion concerning the working of temptation.

First came the conjunction of Saturn and the Sun, which found a direct expression in Wagner's life in his writing the text of *Siegfried's Death*. In the language of the soul, the solar being of Siegfried had to die to make way for the Saturnine Parsifal. As George Bernard Shaw wrote: "Siegfried is a completely amoral creation, the born anarchist, the ideal of Bakunin, a presentiment of Nietzsche's 'superman'."[11] This indicates that the self – the solar being in man – when it does not become imbued with the spiritual-moral nature of Christ ("Not I, but Christ in me") can develop in an anti-Christian direction. (It is interesting to note that Siegfried was adopted as the heroic representative ideal of the Third Reich. It should be noted further, however, that in the original *Ring of the Nibelungen* Siegfried represents a solar kind of human being with many characteristics that are deeply Christian.)

Wagner experienced within himself an intense struggle, one which eventually triumphed in the entering in of the Christ impulse, which came to expression above all in his last opera, *Parsifal*. This struggle is summarized in the words: *Christ or Antichrist*. The conjunction between the Sun and Saturn during his embryonic period signified – in the prefiguring of Wagner's life – the turning point in this struggle between Christ and Antichrist in his soul, as this struggle later came to expression in the fulfilment of his destiny.

To this conjunction came the Moon, the bearer of lower, unpurified will forces. It was here that Wagner – instead of directing his energies to the purification of the lower forces within himself – fell into a kind of revolutionary frenzy, where his energies became directed outwards in pursuit of purification of the world through revolution. This became a force of destiny, and – as described earlier in this chapter – his friendship with Michail Bakunin can be seen in this light. The lower forces overpowered the higher ones of reason and conscience, and Wagner allowed himself to become involved in the dangerous revolutionary activity that culminated in the Dresden uprising. It was only through the experience of the catastrophic consequences of this uprising that he became freed from the spell of the lower forces that had taken hold of his soul. He then realised that he was not a revolutionary at all.

Thus the three temptations (and also their synthesis, the fourth temptation) are essential to an understanding of the enactment of destiny, when studying the prefiguring of destiny by the planetary movements during the embryonic period. The simple astronomical fact of an alignment of the Moon, Sun and Saturn during Wagner's embryonic period actually signified a tremendous "soul trial" for Wagner – a battle of lower forces with higher forces, which later came to expression in his destiny, culminating in his participation in the Dresden uprising.

The web of destiny

In his study of Wagner's biography in the light of the planetary movements during the embryonic period, Willi Sucher – in his original study – drew attention to four essential moments, of which the conjunction of the Sun with Saturn is the first. Each of these four moments involves a conjunction with Saturn. When transposed to his life, each marked a decisive point along Wagner's path of destiny. As Willi Sucher expresses it: "All these (conjunctions of the planets – Sun, Mercury, Venus and Mars – with Saturn during the embryonic period) are pictures of successive stages in an arduous and uphill way of destiny, from out of which, however, the outstanding genius of Richard Wagner is able to bring forth his true creative power."[12]

Without going into a discussion of these further cosmic events during Wagner's embryonic period – of their significance to his life's destiny – it is nevertheless appropriate to quote the conclusion of Willi Sucher's study:

In the prenatal (planetary movements between conception and birth)... of a human being, seen in relation to the lunar cycles, we have something like a prefigured and prophetic plan of the Earth-life that is about to begin. It is indeed a highly complex organism, woven out of the spiritual essences of the cosmos, formed in a fully individual way for every single human life and incorporated into the human being's earthly nature. Nor does this delicate and cosmic entity (the etheric body, into which the web of destiny is woven) work in the human being as a mere abstract power or decree of Fate. It is a living reality, helping to form and shape even the physical body itself. In its effects, we can detect this "body of the stars" even in the building of the organs of the body, in illnesses and tendencies to illness. It is itself a "body" answering to the physical body upon a higher level. We may relate it to what is known in occultism as the "etheric body" (into which the web of destiny is woven). Yet this "body", woven as it is out of the forces of the stars, is no more than a prefigured plan of the coming Earth-life. It is like the map of a country. We can map out our journey in a particular direction; we are then bound to some extent by such resolve. Yet for our inner experience of the landscape we are never bound. From the impressions which we receive with our senses as we go upon our way, we can arouse within us all that the inner life and imagination of the soul makes possible. The more alive we are, the more we shall receive. So, too, there cannot be any absolute determination of the course of human life by the world of stars.[13]

Willi Sucher's discovery of the mystery of the web of destiny (karma) woven into the etheric body between conception and birth parallel to the Moon's orbits of the sidereal zodiac, and of the correspondence between this weaving of destiny during the embryonic period and the unfolding of destiny in the sequence of 7-year periods during life, forms the foundation for the hermetic-astrological science of destiny – astrological biography – outlined in this book. Hermeticism applies the law of correspondences – "that which is below is like to that which is above" – and when referring to time this correspondence can be expressed: "That which shall be is like to that which was." This expresses the metamorphosis of karma from one incarnation to the next. That which the human being lives through in the sequence of 7-year periods in one incarnation becomes metamorphosed in the shaping of destiny between conception and birth in the next incarnation. In turn, that which is shaped during the weaving of destiny during the embryonic period then comes to expression in the unfolding of destiny through the sequence of 7-year periods between birth and death. This is the principle underlying the hermetic-astrological science of destiny – astrological biography – discussed in this volume.

In the next chapter we shall look more closely at the sequence of 7-year periods, known in hermetic astrology as the *spiral of life*.

Chapter 3: Notes and references

1. Willi Sucher, "Looking through the Horoscope of Birth: the Significance of the Pre-natal Events among the Stars", *Mercury Star Journal* 2 (1976), pp. 69–70; reprinted from the *Modern Mystic* 1 (1937), pp. 44–46.
2. Hans Mayer, *Wagner* (Rowohlt, Hamburg, 1959), p. 109.
3. Martin Gregor-Dellin, *Richard Wagner* (Piper & Co., Munich, 1980), p. 516.
4. Willi Sucher, op. cit.
5. Ibid., pp. 71–72.
6. Martin Gregor-Dellin, op. cit., p. 252.
7. Ibid., p. 257.
8. Ibid., p. 274.
9. Thus, for example, Rudolf Steiner's book *Occult Science* (Rudolf Steiner Press, London, 1972) is a spiritual-scientific work which complements and supplements the Darwinian theory of evolution.
10. *Meditations on the Tarot*, Chapters 4–6 (trsl. R. Powell, Amity, Warwick NY, 1985).
11. Quoted from Martin Gregor-Dellin, op. cit., p. 322.
12. Willi Sucher, op. cit., p. 72.
13. Ibid., pp. 74–75.

Chapter 4

The Spiral of Life (up to 21)

The life periods

In Chapter 3 the relationship between the weaving of destiny during the embryonic period and the unfolding of destiny in 7-year life periods is outlined, and two examples of the application of this relationship in the life of Richard Wagner are referred to: the dramatic events connected with his participation in the Dresden uprising in his 36th. year, and his meeting with Ludwig II of Bavaria in his 51st. year of life. The turn of events associated with the Dresden revolution took place near the beginning of the sixth 7-year period and was prefigured by the conjunction of the Moon, Sun and Saturn near the beginning of the sixth lunar cycle of the embryonic period. The meeting with Ludwig II fell less than two years after the start of the eighth 7-year period and was prefigured by a conjunction of the Moon, Sun and Mercury during the early part of the eighth lunar cycle of the embryonic period. From these two examples, and also from other examples to be discussed later, it is evident that the human being's destiny for the approaching earthly life is woven during each lunar cycle of the embryonic period and unfolds during the corresponding 7-year period of life. In this relationship it is apparent that the 7-year periods are of significance for a comprehension of the unfolding of life. In fact, the 7-year life periods were known of in antiquity. They were referred to by certain Greek authors (see Appendix I). But the application of this knowledge to astrological biography is something quite new in astrology.

Knowledge of the *spiral of life* – the unfolding of destiny through 7-year life periods – forms an essential part of the hermetic-astrological science of destiny. For this reason we shall now look more closely at the spiral of life, and at the historical background of the transmission of knowledge concerning it – transmitted since the days of ancient Greece.

In his article *The Life Periods*[1] Franz Boll describes the Greek tradition elaborating the life periods, tracing it back to the philosopher Solon (first half of the sixth century B.C.). (See Appendix I for accounts by Solon, Hippocrates, Philo and Shakespeare, relating to the unfolding of life through 7-year periods.) The basic idea, which through various authors – including Shakespeare in his "seven ages of man" – has come to expression repeatedly, is that human life unfolds in distinct stages between birth and death. Further, in the astrological tradition these stages are brought into correspondence with the rulership of the planets, one after the other, in the classical geocentric sequence known to the Babylonians: Moon, Mercury, Venus, Sun, Mars, Jupiter, Saturn. This was the sequence that the Greek astronomer Ptolemy (second century A.D.) adopted as the basis for his astronomical system. (See *Hermetic Astrology* I, Chapter 4, for a discussion of the Babylonian-Ptolemaic astronomical system.)

In his astrological textbook (the *Tetrabiblos*), Ptolemy presents the doctrine that each planet – in the order Moon, Mercury, Venus, Sun, Mars, Jupiter, Saturn – rules a particular life period. However, instead of allotting each planet with a rulership of seven years of life – the length of time assigned to each life period by Solon, Hippocrates and Philo (see Appendix I) – Ptolemy ascribes the Moon with rulership over the first 4 years of life, Mercury with the years from 5 to 14, Venus from 15 to 22, the Sun from 23 to 41, Mars from 42 to 56, Jupiter from 57 to 68, and Saturn from 69 until death.[2] However, the Greek tradition represented by Solon, Hippocrates and Philo emphasizes that the life periods are equal in length, each seven years long. It can be seen that for the Moon, Mercury, Venus and the Sun, Ptolemy's figures are an approximation to the following: Moon (0–7), Mercury (7–14), Venus (14–21), Sun (21–42), where the Sun rules over three 7-year periods, during the period of the "prime of life". As Boll points out in his discussion of Ptolemy's doctrine, the qualities which come to manifestation in these life periods correspond astonishingly well with the astrological attributes of the ruling planets:

It is fitting that the stages of human life receive their character by way of impression from the seven planets in the order from below above, from the Moon to Saturn: their nature does in fact correspond to the quality of the planets brought into connection with them.

During the first four years of life the child is ruled by Selene (the Moon). The Moon changes rapidly and has a short period of revolution of the zodiac; it draws up damp mists from the Earth. Likewise the infant is subject to swift changes, grows rapidly, and needs moist nourishment – as it is the moist element which dominates in him; his body is not at all firm, his limbs are not very formed, his soul forces are undeveloped – all of this corresponds to the weak and inconstant forces of the Moon.

The second period of life, from 5 to 14, is ruled by the planet Mercury. It begins to build and develop the soul and spiritual 'skeleton' in the child, and sows the seeds and foundations of science; through teaching and education it awakens the youthful spirit and initially brings to light individual differences in capacities and strivings.

The third period, from 15 to 22, belongs to the planet Venus, with which the stormy awakening of the sexual life is associated: falling in love at random, the mad illusion of passion, charging forward with closed eyes.

The fourth stage, the first period of adulthood, lasts 19 years, from 23 to 41. It is the middle, solar culmination of human existence, and on this account is assigned to the Sun, which occupies the central place among the seven (planetary) spheres. The Sun god – 'King Helios' – implants in the soul the need to rule, independence of action, the desire for fame and a well-established existence, and turns it away from the playful, unprincipled idiocies of youth towards principles and steadfastness.[3]

Taking 7-year periods as in the classical Greek tradition, instead of the ages listed by Ptolemy, the first four stages of life – Moon (0–7), Mercury (7–14), Venus (14–21) and Sun (21–42) – are nevertheless appropriately characterized by the above description. Continuing the 7-year periods further, after the completion of the Sun period, the planets Mars, Jupiter and Saturn then each rule for seven years: Mars (42–49), Jupiter (49–56), Saturn (56–63). Since in the classical astrological tradition the sphere of the zodiac follows the sequence of the seven planetary spheres, the remaining years of life are ascribed to the rulership of the zodiac (fixed stars). Figure 2 summarizes this basic outline of the spiral of life, giving the cosmic correspondence to the life periods in terms of the classical representation of the Ptolemaic system.

On account of the turbulence of emotions that come to expression during the seventh 7-year life period (the Mars period, 42–49), this period is regarded as a kind of "second adolescence", mirroring the Venus period from 14 to 21. (See *Hermetic Astrology* I, Chapter 9, concerning the symbiotic relationship between Mars and Venus.) Interpreting this in a literal sense, taking the age of 49 to be a mirror image of the age of 14, the occurrence of the menopause at (or around) this age signifies the end of the childbearing capacity, just as the start of menstruation at (or around) 14 signifies the beginning of the capacity to conceive and give birth to children. In terms of these biological facts, the Mars period (42–49) literally mirrors the period of adolescence (the Venus period, 14–21).

Similarly, the Jupiter period from 49 to 56 mirrors the childhood years (Mercury) from 7 to 14 (symbiotic relationship between Jupiter and Mercury), and the period from 56 to 63 (Saturn) mirrors the first seven years of life (Moon, 0–7). After the age of 63, the human being enters his tenth 7-year period. This, and in fact the whole remaining period of life, is ruled by the fixed stars (zodiacal sphere), in accordance with the Babylonian (Ptolemaic) conception of the solar system (see Figure 2).

The weaving of destiny between conception and birth

For astrologers the key question is: What is the cosmic background to the 7-year periods? It is by looking at the embryonic period – the time between conception and birth – that this question is answered. The discovery that the cosmic background to the 7-year life periods is to be found by

Figure 2:
The spiral of life

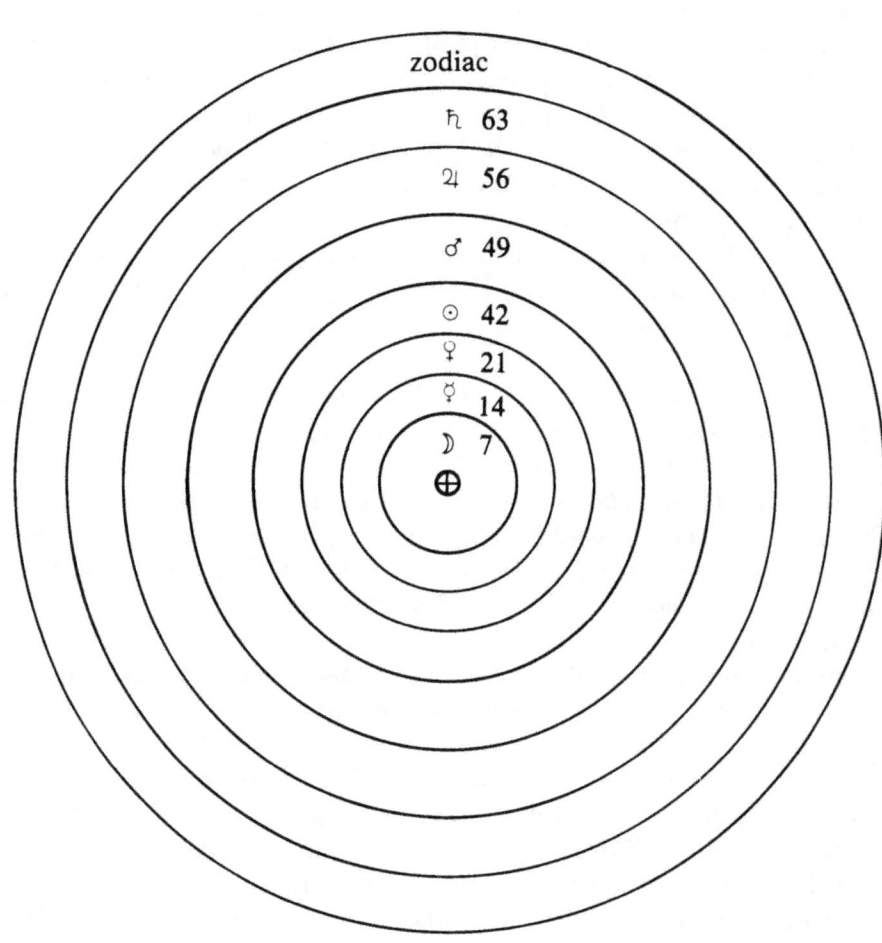

IV. The Spiral of Life (up to 21)

Sucher during the 1930's. Until now, this important discovery has remained unknown to the majority of astrologers.

Willi Sucher's research finding can be summarized as follows: the ten lunar sidereal months of the embryonic period, during which the embryo is formed, prefigure ten 7-year periods of life. ("The years of our life are threescore and ten" – Psalm 90, 10.) This is meant in the sense that the karma (destiny) under which the incarnating soul stands becomes "woven" into the human being's etheric body during the embryonic period in such a way that during each successive lunar sidereal month the karma for each successive 7-year period becomes incorporated into his etheric organism. During the embryonic period, just as on Earth the physical body is formed in the womb over nine months (= ten lunar sidereal months), correspondingly within the sphere of the Moon the etheric body is drawn together from the cosmic ether, and the karma relating to the soul's past becomes woven into the etheric organism during this time. This weaving of karma into the etheric body during the embryonic period takes place in the Moon sphere concurrently with the movements of the planets at this time, mirroring them ("as above, so below"). Looked at astrologically, the weaving of the web of destiny begins with the commencement of the formation of the etheric body. This starts – astrologically speaking – with the horoscope of conception, cast for the moment of conception calculated according to the hermetic rule; and it ends with the horoscope of birth, cast for the moment of birth. In the approximately ten lunar sidereal months between conception and birth there are 273 days (1 sidereal month = 27.32 days, and 10 x 27.32 = 273.2 days), and each lunar sidereal month corresponds to one of the ten 7-year life periods in such a way that the karma woven into the etheric body during one lunar sidereal month becomes fulfilled during the corresponding 7-year life period. (Note that ten lunar sidereal months amount to more or less nine calendar months = 273.9 days. The duration of pregnancy is normally reckoned to be nine calendar months, and in medical textbooks is often given as 270 days.) In practice the moment of conception does not generally lie exactly 273 days before birth, but using the hermetic rule the precise moment of conception – whether lying more than or less than 273 days before birth – can be calculated. (See *Hermetic Astrology* I, Appendix I, for a discussion of the hermetic rule and its transmission from ancient Egypt.)

In this connection it should be emphasized that the moment of conception computed according to the hermetic rule does not necessarily coincide exactly with the moment of physical conception. Here it is a matter of distinguishing between two events taking place not more than a few days apart. These two events, taken together, comprise conception. The first is the fertilization of the egg by the sperm: this is the physical aspect of conception, constituting the commencement of the formation of the physical body. The second event is the uniting of the incarnating soul with the fertilized egg by way of releasing the archetype of the physical body formed by the image. (See *Hermetic Astrology* I, Chapter 10, for a description of the archetype of the physical body formed by the image, prior to incarnation, out of the forces of the twelve signs of the zodiac.) The archetype of the physical body works in from the Moon sphere into the fertilized egg, and it is the moment of the commencement of this working in upon the fertilized egg which is computed by applying the hermetic rule. This moment constitutes conception from the spiritual point of view, and it is from this moment onwards that the formation of the etheric body begins, into which the incarnating soul's karma becomes woven. The provision of a fertilized egg by the parents is the prerequisite for the working in of the image in the formation of the embryo. It is the moment at which the image begins to work in via the archetype of the physical body which constitutes the beginning of the soul's descent into incarnation from the Moon sphere onto the Earth. Therefore it is this moment which is of supreme importance astrologically speaking, and which is the focus of attention in the hermetic rule.

Further, as Willi Sucher points out: "At the time (of conception, calculated by the hermetic rule) the star configuration of the prenatal epoch is present, projecting a mighty tableau of the coming Earth life, right into the physiological make-up."[4] Here the soul experiences, in the form of a tableau, a vision of its karma, its destiny to be unfolded through the sequence of 7-year life periods on Earth. This works down even into the human being's physiological constitution. It can happen that the soul receives such a shock at this moment of prevision of its karma that it holds back, not wanting to go forward with its incarnation, and the building up of the physical body then does not take place with the full cooperation of the soul. (This is one of the causes of mongolism, where the physical body becomes retarded in its development and the soul is not fully incarnated.)

In the case of a normal conception and birth, the physical body (embryo) is built up during the 9-month period of gestation, to become the vehicle through which the incarnating soul is able to fulfil its destiny on Earth. Parallel to the embryonic development of the physical body within the womb, the formation of the etheric body takes its course within the Moon sphere. This is hidden from normal terrestrial consciousness, but is accessible to lunar consciousness (as referred to in *Hermetic Astrology* I, Chapter 4). The formation of the etheric body is directly bound up with the Moon, as is evident from the hermetic rule, which states that this moment in time (when the formation of the etheric body begins) is specified by the Moon's position in the zodiac (being related to the zodiacal location of the Ascendant at the moment of birth). (See *Hermetic Astrology* I, Figure 27 – the hermetic rule – for a diagrammatic representation of the four possible relationships between the Moon and the Ascendant at conception, given the relationship between them at birth.)

Willi Sucher's research finding, relating the 7-year life periods to the ten lunar sidereal months during the embryonic period, opens up a new vista of the background to the stellar configuration at the moment of birth depicted in the birth chart. It shows that the birth configuration is the culmination of a process beginning with the moment of conception which may be calculated by the hermetic rule. The planetary configuration of the birth chart is the goal and destination of the incarnating soul, but the "disembarkation" of the soul from the Moon sphere on its journey into incarnation upon the Earth is indicated by the planetary configuration at the moment of conception. And the journey itself – of the soul's descent into incarnation – is mapped out by the movements of the planets during the embryonic period. This journey prefigures life's journey in such a way that the karma under which the soul stands is inscribed into the etheric body between conception and birth, to become fulfilled in the living out of destiny during the sequence of life periods between birth and death. In the case of correctly applying the hermetic rule, the inscription of karma in the etheric organism may be read from the planetary movements between conception and birth, the planetary movements being the macrocosmic counterpart to the inscription of karma into the etheric body. Thus the entire sequence of planetary configurations between conception and birth – conjunctions, oppositions, etc., between the planets – provides a key to the unfolding of destiny between birth and death. How this works out in detail in an individual's biography – his *astrological biography* – was indicated in the last chapter in relation to Richard Wagner's destiny, based on an original study of Wagner's destiny by Willi Sucher.[5] Before going on to consider further examples of this hermetic-astrological science of destiny, let us look more closely at the *spiral of life* – the sequence of 7-year periods that hold the key to the unfolding of the human being's life on Earth.

The astrological significance of the Babylonian (Ptolemaic) system
As shown in Figure 2, there is an exact correspondence between the sequence of 7-year life periods and the planetary sequence of the ancient geocentric astronomical system of the Babylonians (elaborated by Ptolemy in the second century A.D.). This is the deeper meaning of the Babylonian planetary sequence (Moon, Mercury, Venus, Sun, Mars, Jupiter, Saturn) in contrast to the Egyptian-hermetic planetary sequence (Moon, Venus, Mercury, Sun, Mars, Jupiter, Saturn). *Hermetic Astrology* I is devoted primarily to the Egyptian system, which was formulated scientifically by the Danish astronomer Tycho Brahe towards the end of the sixteenth century A.D. The Egyptian (Tychonic) system holds the key to the "likeness" of the human being – the *hermetic man,* embodying the rela-

tionship between the planets and the lotus flowers (see *Hermetic Astrology* I, Figure 13). This volume (*Hermetic Astrology* II) is concerned essentially with the Babylonian (Ptolemaic) system, which is relevant to the human being's temporal evolution – his astrological biography – described in terms of the planetary rulers of the life periods. It is as if the human being passes through different spheres of influence of the planets ("planetary spheres") during the course of his life. First of all he passes through the sphere of influence of the Moon (0–7), then the Mercury sphere (7–14), then the Venus sphere (14–21), then the Sun sphere (21–42), then the Mars sphere (42–49), then the Jupiter sphere (49–56), then the Saturn sphere (56–63), followed by the zodiacal sphere (63 onwards) – where the spheres are indicated by the sequence of planets given by the Babylonian (Ptolemaic) system. However, what is the basis of this system?

In contrast to the Egyptian system, which relates to man's cosmic nature (the system of lotus flowers mediating the cosmic forces of the planets), the Babylonian system refers to the human being's temporal evolution. As discussed in *Hermetic Astrology* I, Chapter 4, the reality of the Egyptian system is experienced on the level of solar consciousness, at which the human being becomes inwardly attuned to the "center of the sounding light" (the inner reality of the Sun). The Babylonian (Ptolemaic) system, on the other hand, is experienced as a reality on the level of lunar consciousness, which is of a pictoral nature in contrast to the auditory quality of solar consciousness. In rising from normal terrestrial consciousness to lunar consciousness, the spatial-geographical perspective of terrestrial consciousness gives way to a temporal consciousness. On the level of lunar consciousness, time relationships become all important.

From the vantage point of lunar consciousness it is the time-sequential ordering of events that is significant; and this consciousness supersedes the cognition of spatial distribution which is characteristic of terrestrial (Earth) consciousness. For lunar consciousness, therefore, perception of the solar system takes on a temporal character, and the ordering of the planets is a matter of their time-sequential distributions, i.e. it is according to their period of rotation. For lunar consciousness the macrocosmic temporal reality of the solar system is the following planetary sequence, yielded by arranging the planets according to their orbital periods of the sidereal zodiac:

Moon (orbital period of 27.32 days), Mercury (87.97 days), Venus (224.70 days), Sun (one year = 365.26 days), Mars (687 days), Jupiter (11.86 years), Saturn (29.46 years). This sequence is the temporal reality underlying the solar system, extending from the Earth – or rather, from the Moon sphere surrounding the Earth (this being the vantage point of lunar consciousness, via which the orbital periods are beheld sequentially).

In the Ptolemaic system the planets are depicted in this sequence – Moon,

Mercury, Venus, Sun, Mars, Jupiter, Saturn – arranged as a sequence of nested spheres one above the other, with the sphere of the fixed stars (zodiacal sphere) encircling the outermost planetary sphere, that of Saturn. (Here again, for the time being, the more recently discovered planets – Uranus, Neptune, Pluto – are left out of the discussion; in any case, these planets were not known to the Babylonians or to Ptolemy.) The traditional diagrammatic representation of the Ptolemaic system might give a false impression, as it appears diagrammatically as a spatial system, when in fact it relates actually to macrocosmic temporal reality beheld from the vantage point of lunar consciousness. However, the classical diagrammatic representation of the Ptolemaic system may be utilized in order to portray the relationship with the 7-year periods of life, which is a key to understanding the basis of astrological biography (see Figure 2).

In fact, in order to understand astrological biography as it comes to expression in the unfolding of the 7-year life periods, it is not only the Babylonian (Ptolemaic) system which is important, but also the Egyptian (Tychonic) system. In transforming consciousness from the earthly level to the lunar level, the spatially orientated geographical consciousness normal to the Earth gives way to the temporal perception of lunar consciousness, which is orientated towards time phenomena. Here a transition is made from the dimension of space to that of time. In transposing further from lunar consciousness to solar consciousness a transition is made from the dimension of time to that of causality – in attaining the level of solar consciousness, which enables a cognition of causality. It is at this level (solar consciousness) that the validity of the Egyptian (Tychonic) system becomes apparent. At this level consciousness is orientated neither towards space nor time, but towards causality. (The relevance of the various cosmological systems to different levels of consciousness is summarized in Table 5.)*

Table 5:
Cosmological systems relating to different levels of consciousness

level of consciousness	cosmological system	applying to (dimension)
terrestrial consciousness	heliocentric (Copernican)	physical-spatial
lunar consciousness	Babylonian (Ptolemaic)	temporal
solar consciousness	Egyptian (Tychonic)	causal (correspondence between macrocosm and microcosm)

*The next transformation of consciousness – from solar to zodiacal consciousness – entails a transposition from the realm of causality to that of being. Space, time, causality and being are the four realms accessible to four different modes of consciousness – terrestrial, lunar, solar and zodiacal.

Perception in the realm of causality entails direct cognition of the relationships between macrocosm and microcosm. For example, in this realm the *hermetic man* is self-evident, i.e. it is a matter of direct cognition that the system of lotus flowers in the human being corresponds to the planetary system as depicted in *Hermetic Astrology* I, Figure 13 ("hermetic man"). Direct cognition of the relationship between things is the basis of the hermetic law of correspondences – "as above, so below". Thus hermeticism itself, which is based on the application of the law of correspondences, could be described as a "science of the realm of causality".

Just as the heliocentric (Copernican) system offers a cosmology of the physical-spatial dimension, so a cosmology appropriate to the realm of causality is given by the Egyptian (Tychonic) system. (As we shall see, the Egyptian system, when viewed in connection with the hermetic man, is relevant to an understanding of the unfolding of the 7-year life periods.) Similarly, a cosmological system applicable to the dimension of time is offered by the Babylonian (Ptolemaic) system. Moreover, the Babylonian system is also of fundamental importance for a comprehension of the sequence of the 7-year life periods, when viewed in relation to *occult physiology*.

Occult physiology

It was not so long ago that occult physiology was taught in the universities of Europe. For example, in his lectures at the University of Copenhagen – a series of lectures that commenced on September 23, 1574 – Tycho Brahe spoke of

> the great analogy between the parts of the human body and the seven planets. The heart, being the seat of the breath of life, corresponds to the Sun, and the brain to the Moon. As the heart and brain are the most important parts of the body, so the Sun and Moon are the most powerful celestial bodies; and as there is much reciprocal action between the former, so there is much mutual dependence between the latter. In the same way the liver corresponds to Jupiter, the kidneys to Venus, the milt (spleen) to Saturn, the gall (gall-bladder) to Mars, and the lungs to Mercury.[6]

Occult physiology is the science of the hidden life forces in man. Of fundamental significance in occult physiology is the correspondence between the organs of the body and the planets – as indicated above by Tycho Brahe. It is above all during the embryonic period, when the organs of the body are being formed, that occult physiology is important. For it is during this time that the hidden forces can be observed, how they work in from the cosmos in the formation of the various organs. It is during the embryonic period that the organs are built up from the forces radiating in from the various planets – the Moon working in the formation of the brain, the Sun in the formation of the heart, Mercury in the formation of the lungs, etc.

As described earlier in this book, the Moon's orbits of the sidereal zodiac are the main rhythmic phenomenon of the embryonic period. The formation of the etheric body, which takes place in the Moon sphere parallel to the building up of the embryo on Earth, runs concurrently with the Moon's orbits around the zodiac. Although all of the planets work in continously from the cosmos in the shaping of the etheric body and in the formation of the organs of the physical body, during each lunar orbit a particular planet – and correspondingly a particular organ – is emphasized. During the first orbit it is the formation of the brain which is emphasized, the first lunar cycle being ruled by the Moon, and the brain being the organ that is formed by the cosmic forces radiating in from the Moon. Since the processes in question take their course within the Moon sphere during the embryonic period, it is readily understandable that the Moon itself is the predominant cosmic body during the first lunar cycle.

Within the Moon sphere lunar consciousness, which is temporal in nature, holds sway. Out of this lunar consciousness arises a cognition of the temporal sequence of the planets – as given by the Babylonian (Ptolemaic) system. This temporal cosmology holds the key to the rulership of the planets during each lunar cycle of the embryonic period. Thus after the Moon, which rules the first cycle, Mercury rules the second lunar orbital period, and correspondingly the formation of the lungs is emphasized during the second lunar orbit. Similarly, Venus rules the third lunar cycle of the embryonic period, during which the formation of the kidneys becomes more pronounced. In the fourth, fifth and sixth lunar orbital periods – ruled by the Sun – it is the turn of the heart; in the seventh lunar sidereal month (Mars) – the gall-bladder; in the eighth sidereal month (Jupiter) – the liver; in the ninth sidereal month (Saturn) – the spleen; and in the tenth sidereal month (zodiac) the formation of the physical body is "rounded off", as it were, through the impress of the twelve zodiacal signs. (The impress of the twelve zodiacal signs via the Moon on its passage around the zodiac is actually of great significance not just during the tenth lunar sidereal month, but during each lunar orbit of the sidereal zodiac, as discussed in Chapter 7.)

The foregoing outline of occult physiology may seem far-fetched from the point of view of a study of the physical embryo during these ten lunar cycles, since it is readily apparent that *all* the organs develop throughout the whole embryonic period. Nevertheless, it is a matter in occult physiology of *formative forces*, and it is in terms of planetary formative forces associated with the different organs that the predominance of one or the other organ during the embryonic period is to be understood. In other words, the formative force connected with the formation of the brain – the formative force proceeding from the Moon – is emphasized during the first lunar cycle; that connected with the formation of the lungs (the formative force of Mercury) is emphasized in the second lunar cycle; and so on.

Occult physiology thus offers a basis for understanding the development that the human being passes through during the 7-year periods of life. Taking account of the correspondence between the lunar cycles of the embryonic period and the sequence of 7-year life periods, a physiological basis for comprehending this development is opened up. The first 7-year period (corresponding to the first lunar cycle of the embryonic period) is ruled by the Moon, and physiologically it is the brain which is the key organ during this life period. The development of the infant up to the age of seven is centered physically in the brain, but in fact it involves the whole head, and the sign of the termination of this period of development is the emergence of the second teeth to replace the milk teeth. The appearance of the second teeth shows that the forces that were at work in the head throughout the entire first life period have completed their task. This does not mean that the head stops growing at this point, but simply indicates that the main shaping of the head is complete. The head continues to grow along with the growth of the rest of the body, but the configuration of the head – and especially of the brain – is largely accomplished by the time of the emergence of the second teeth around the age of seven.

In the next 7-year period (7–14), ruled by Mercury, the scene of activity shifts – physiologically speaking – to the lungs. In this life period it is the lungs, and in fact the entire chest-rhythmic system, which becomes central to the development of the growing child. The end of this period is signified by the onset of puberty. Adolescence means a new 7-year period (14–21) – ruled by Venus – in which the kidneys play a key role. Moreover, just as during the first 7-year period it is physiologically the head which develops and during the second 7-year period it is the chest system, so in the third 7-year period it is physiologically the limbs (arms and legs) which develop most pronouncedly. In this physiological development of the *threefold human being* (see *Hermetic Astrology* I, Chapter 10, for a discussion of the significance of the threefold human being in relation to the astrological factors: Ascendant, Sun and Moon), the brain, the lungs and the kidneys are the mediating organs – the brain acting as the mediating organ for the Moon forces between 0 and 7, the lungs as the mediating organ of the Mercury forces between 7 and 14, and the kidneys as the mediating organ of the Venus forces between 14 and 21.

However, an understanding of the development of the human being through the 7-year life periods would be incomplete if it were to be looked at solely from the physiological point of view. The physiological perspective is one-sided if it alone is taken into consideration; it needs to be complemented. The perspective offered by occult physiology is gained by way of lunar consciousness directed to the processes taking place within the Moon sphere during the embryonic development, which then become elaborated in the sequence of 7-year periods between birth and death. From the standpoint of lunar consciousness it is the temporal sequence of the planets, as in the Babylonian (Ptolemaic) system, which is true. In the light of occult physiology it is thus the sequence: Moon, Mercury, Venus, Sun, Mars, Jupiter, Saturn which applies to the human being's development through 7-year periods.

The Egyptian (Tychonic) system in astrological biography

The perspective offered by occult physiology (based on lunar consciousness) is complemented by taking the human being's psychic development into consideration. Here it is solar consciousness that is relevant. In the light of solar consciousness the *hermetic man* is revealed – the correspondence between the human being's psychic organism (the system of lotus flowers) and the seven planets of the solar system (see *Hermetic Astrology* I, Figure 13). From the standpoint of solar consciousness, which is able to cognize the causal relationships between things, it is the human being's psychic development that takes its course in the sequence of 7-year periods. The cosmology that applies to the realm of causality is that of the Egyptian (Tychonic) system – discussed in *Hermetic Astrology* I – which yields the planetary sequence: Moon, Venus, Mercury, Sun, Mars, Jupiter, Saturn.

Just as occult physiology opens up the perspective of the correspondence between certain organs and the planets, so the hermetic man holds the key to the correspondence between the lotus flowers and the planets. The first perspective is phyiological, involving the relationship of the planets to the life forces connected with the various organs, whilst the second is psychic, based on a knowledge of man's psychic organism (the system of lotus flowers) and how the various lotus flowers relate to the planets. Both perspectives are equally valid and important, when considering the human being's development through 7-year periods. Having looked briefly at the physiological development of the human being through the first three 7-year periods, from birth up to the age of 21, let us now turn to a consideration of the corresponding psychic development during these three life periods.

Physiologically it is the brain, corresponding to the Moon, which is the mediating organ during the first seven years of life. Psychically, however, it is the 4-petalled lotus flower that mediates the Moon's forces during the first 7-year period. As described in *Hermetic Astrology* I, Chapter 5, the 4-petalled lotus flower is (on the psychic level) the mediator of the lunar forces, and these are brought to realisation inwardly in relation to the physical body of the human being, in connection with the will. This lotus flower is most closely associated with the will, and it is the will that carries over higher impulses to their physical realisation. Observation of the baby or infant reveals that it is indeed the will that comes most directly to expression during the first seven years of life, and that its whole development is concerned with the physical body and its needs.

During the second 7-year period the mediating organ – physiologically – is the lungs, corresponding to Mercury. On the psychic level, however, the 6-petalled lotus flower – corresponding to Venus – is the mediating organ in the system of lotus flowers. Here a difference between the Babylonian system (Mercury) and the Egyptian system (Venus) emerges, in consideration of the planetary rulership of the period between 7 and 14. On the physiological level the Babylonian (Ptolemaic) system applies, and Mercury is the ruler of this life period. But on the psychic level the Egyptian (Tychonic) system holds true, and Venus is the ruler of this period of life. The Venus forces relate to the feeling life, which awakens in the child between 7 and 14, who tends at this age to live strongly in the polarity of sympathy and antipathy. At the same time the Venus forces work via the 6-petalled lotus flower as a mediating impulse in the regulation of the etheric body. Thus in contrast to the physical body, the development of which is emphasized in the first seven years of life, between the ages of 7 and 14 the etheric body undergoes a special development. Correspondingly, children of this age show a remarkable degree of grace and harmony, owing to the harmonious influence of the etheric body during this time.

Coming to the third 7-year period (14–21), again a distinction has to be drawn between the physiological and the psychic levels. Physiologically the kidneys are the key organs, mediating the influence of Venus. Here the whole emphasis of the physiological development shifts to the limb system. On the psychic level, however, the 10-petalled lotus flower – corresponding to Mercury – becomes the mediating organ. This is central to the astral body, which comes to the fore in the development of the human being during adolescence. At the same time there is a pronounced awakening of intelligence – the forces of the thought life – connected with the planet Mercury

Summarizing the human being's psychic development during the first three 7-year periods: the development of the will is foremost in the first period, that of the feeling life in the second period, and that of the thought life in the third period. Running parallel to this is the physiological development: centered in the head in the first period, in the chest (rhythmic) system in the second period, and focusing upon the limb system in the third period. (See Table 6 for a summary of the human being's development during the first three 7-year periods of life.)

Table 6:
The first three 7-year periods of life

physiological development

7-year period	ruling planet	mediating organ	central focus
1	Moon	brain	head
2	Mercury	lungs	chest
3	Venus	kidneys	limbs

psychic development

age	ruling planet	lotus flower	soul forces	related body
0–7	Moon	4-petalled	will	physical
7–14	Venus	6-petalled	feeling	etheric
14–21	Mercury	10-petalled	thinking	astral

From Table 6 it is evident during the first three 7-year life periods that physiologically there is a descending development: first the head, then the chest (rhythmic) system, then the limbs; and that psychically there is an ascending development – via the three lower lotus flowers – of the soul forces of the will, feeling and thinking. It is only by holding both in view – the ascending (psychic) development and descending (physiological) development – that the complex evolution of the human being during the first three 7-year periods of life can be understood. Here it is not possible to go into much detail concerning this evolution up to the age of 21, as our main concern is to gain an overview of the whole course of life, of all the 7-year periods. But with the help of the general background outlined so far (summarized in Table 6), much can be discerned of the deep mystery of human life and how this mystery entails a concrete knowledge of man's relationship to the cosmos.

The first three life periods are connected with the so-called "inferior planets", i.e. those passing between the Earth and the Sun – the planets Moon, Venus and Mercury (Egyptian system), and Moon, Mercury and Venus (Babylonian system). Owing to the importance of the first three life periods as a foundation for the whole of life, it is particularly interesting to consider the location of these three planets in the zodiac at the moment of birth. Here two charts for the moment of birth are relevant: the hermetic chart and the geocentric chart. From the hermetic chart – drawn according to the Egyptian (Tychonic) system – it is more the psychic development of the person concerned that is revealed, whilst the geocentric chart indicates more the physiological development. Both are relevant to an understanding of the person's overall development, especially in the diagnosis of developmental problems.

An example of diagnosis

Very often the onset of a disturbance or illness can be seen directly from either the hermetic or the geocentric birth chart. This the author has experienced many times over in his practice as a curative eurythmist (movement therapist). For example, one adolescent girl who came for curative eurythmy, to receive movement therapy for her short-sightedness, recalled that her vision had been normal up until the onset of puberty. It was only with the commencement of the third 7-year period that she had become short-sighted. This was indicated in her hermetic chart by a conjunction of Mercury and Saturn. As Mercury – when considered in relation to the Egyptian system – is the ruler of the third 7-year period, the conjunction of Mercury and Saturn in the hermetic chart indicated the emergence of a karmic problem in the period of adolescence. (Needless to say, it is not possible to generalize this, as each case must be looked at in the light of karmic considerations.)

As discussed in *Hermetic Astrology* I, the hermetic chart generally indicates future karma – talents and faculties to be developed – but if these are not developed, then that which is potentially positive can actually emerge in a negative sense. A conjunction of Mercury and Saturn in the hermetic chart represents on the psychic level, i.e. on the level of consciousness, a polarity between the 10-petalled lotus flower (Mercury) and the 8-petalled lotus flower (Saturn): the lotus flowers of thinking (rational, combinatorial thinking) and conscience. This is potentially a most favourable configuration for clear and conscientious thinking, which corresponds psychically to "clear-sightedness". It is a typical configuration for a scientifically-minded person. (See, for example, the hermetic chart at Bertrand Russell's birth – Chart 10 in *Hermetic Astrology* I – where Mercury and Saturn are in conjunction. Russell was a pioneer in the field of mathematical logic.) Alongside her scientific capacity for clear thinking, however, the girl in question – for some karmic reason – become short-sighted.

In this case, at the same time as indicating a positive faculty for "clear-sightedness" on the level of consciousness, for karmic reasons the conjunction of Mercury and Saturn in the hermetic chart also pointed to a problem to be worked with, which manifested organically as short-sightedness. This example shows that every astrological aspect has its positive and negative side. Thus the aspects in the hermetic chart, while on the one level, i.e. on the level of consciousness, indicating talents and faculties to be developed, can point at the same time to problems to be dealt with –

problems that are the negative counterpart of the potentially positive faculties indicated, problems which may even emerge organically. Similarly, the aspects in the geocentric chart in general refer to past karma, especially to failings and shortcomings from the previous incarnation(s) needing to be made good. Although the deeper cause underlying such an aspect may be negative, it is precisely such aspects which can indicate positive aptitudes or personality traits. While pertaining essentially to the organic level, geocentric aspects can refer on the level of consciousness to personality traits and on the level of destiny to aspects of life which the person concerned is likely to encounter.

Different levels of astrological significance

In order to clarify the different levels to which the geocentric and hermetic charts refer, it is helpful to consider a diagram. Figure 3 shows four levels of astrological significance: being, consciousness, life and destiny. The level of being is that of the individuality. The individuality, when incarnating upon the Earth, emerges in a given incarnation as a personality. On the way into incarnation the human being becomes equipped with "consciousness" and "life" in order to fulfil a particular destiny. The hermetic chart, which in *Hermetic Astrology* I was termed the *map of the individuality*, is not identical with the individuality. Rather, it is a map of consciousness, i.e. the psychic constitution, chosen by the individuality for the given incarnation. The hermetic chart actually relates to the level of consciousness, and the only justification for referring to it as the "map of individuality" is that the individuality comes to expression primarily via consciousness.

The incarnating human being becomes endowed not only with consciousness (a given psychic constitution) but also with life, i.e. with a given physiological constitution. This takes place within the sphere of the Moon, between conception and birth, in the formation of the etheric body. During this time, also, the human being's destiny for his approaching life becomes woven into his etheric body. At the moment of birth the incarnating human being – equipped with an appropriate psychic constitution and with a suitable physiological (life) organism – enters onto the path of destiny that leads through earthly life between birth and death.

In the sense that the hermetic chart relates to the human being's psychic constitution (the correspondence of the planets with the system of lotus flowers) and the geocentric chart to his physiological organism (the planetary correspondence with the organs: heart, brain, lungs, etc.), the hermetic chart refers to the level of consciousness, while the geocentric chart relates to the level of life. However, both charts are relevant to the sphere of destiny. Destiny comes to expression on the earthly level, to which also the astrological houses apply. (In hermetic astrology the houses are consi-

**Figure 3
Different levels of astrological significance**

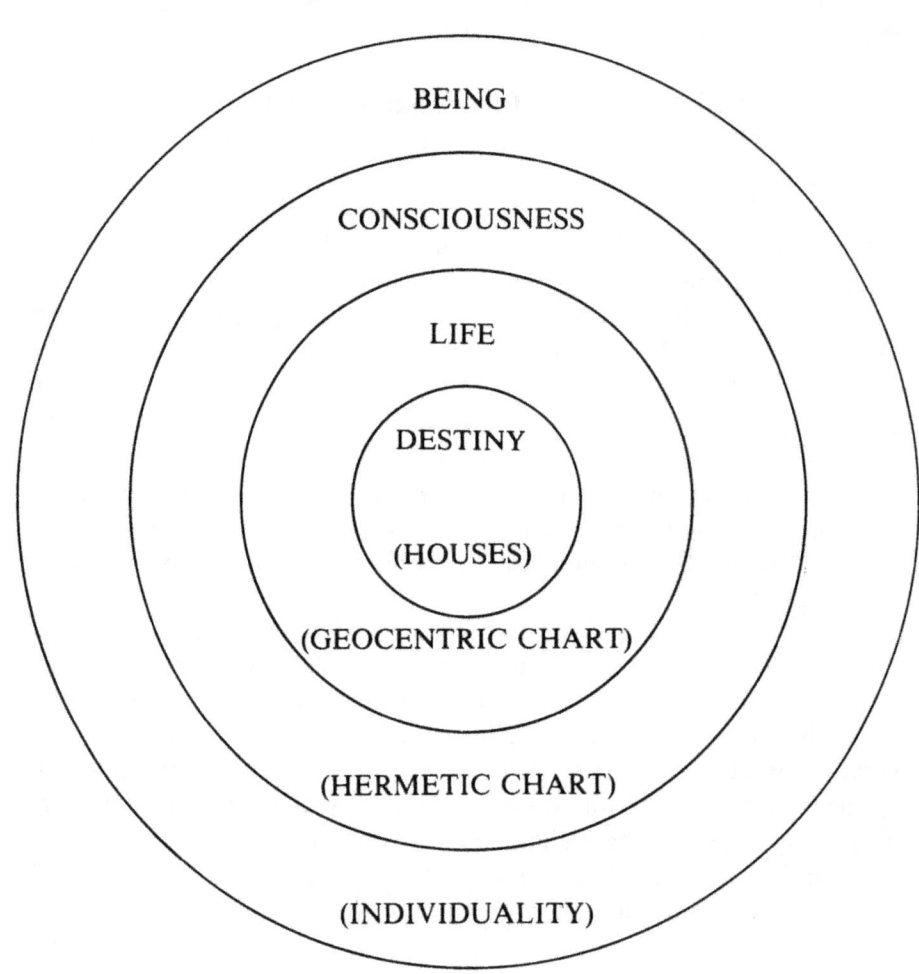

IV. The Spiral of Life (up to 21)

dered separately from the geocentric chart – see Chapter 7.) Destiny is a matter of both consciousness and life – and, ultimately, also of being. Destiny, in fact, brings to manifestation on the earthly level a complex interaction between the levels of being, consciousness and life. Therefore it is not possible to isolate the spheres of influence of the hermetic and geocentric charts merely schematically as in Figure 3. Although, however, if the schematic outline in Figure 3 is pictured dynamically, it can give an indication as to how the different levels interact.

In picturing a dynamic interaction between the levels of being, consciousness, life and destiny, the hermetic and geocentric charts can each be seen in connection with different levels. While referring primarily to the level of consciousness, the hermetic chart also brings to expression the level of being – the individuality – on the one hand, and works into the realms of life and destiny on the other hand. Similarly, the geocentric chart, although relating primarily to the level of life, also reflects the individuality and the consciousness with which the individuality is equipped on the one hand, and works into the realm of destiny on the other hand.

The individuality – on the level of being – is free, in the sense that the realm of being is eternal, and eternal beings are free beings. The process of incarnation onto the Earth, the realm where destiny is enacted, can be likened to the building of a house; and the entering into this house – the destiny shaped for the new incarnation – may be felt as a loss of freedom. Nevertheless, in all hermetic-astrological considerations it should be borne in mind that however constricting the experience of destiny may be – and this constriction may be especially heightened through the experience of hard blows of fate – destiny is the "house" that on a higher level the human being has built for himself. Seen in this light, the hermetic and geocentric charts are indicators of the "implements" that the individuality makes use of in the construction of its "house" (destiny). The hermetic chart refers primarily to the "instrument of consciousness" chosen by the individuality, and the geocentric chart relates essentially to the "instrument of life".

Consciousness is orientated more towards the future (future karma), whilst life flows from the well-springs of the past (past karma), but again this can serve only as a general guideline, for consciousness is also shaped by the past, and life looks with expectation towards the future. Beyond the levels of life and consciousness is the realm of being, the sphere of the individuality, and in hermetic astrology it is the individuality – working through the hermetic and geocentric charts – that is held in view, for ultimately destiny can only be understood as an expression of the interplay between being (individuality), consciousness and life. This is why reincarnation – the passage of the individuality from one incarnation to the next – plays such a central role in hermetic astrology.

Whereas the individuality's "instruments" of consciousness and life are represented astrologically by the hermetic and geocentric charts, the individuality itself is beyond astrological characterization. For true knowledge of the individuality entails penetrating the mystery of reincarnation. Each incarnation comprises a partial revelation of the individuality. Thus by surveying a sequence of incarnations it is possible to gain some idea of the nature of the individuality. Therefore reincarnation is the missing factor in traditional astrology, which – as discussed at length in *Hermetic Astrology* I – has to be taken into consideration in order to arrive at a true knowledge of destiny and a deeper understanding of the being of man.

An example of interpretation

To illustrate the complex interaction of the different levels: being, consciousness, life and destiny, let us look at an example – one in which the 7-year periods come to expression in a remarkably clear way. This example is highly appropriate. For, in connection with the spiral of life, the personality under consideration has done more than any other human being to reawaken a new consciousness of the 7-year periods in life. The personality concerned is Rudolf Steiner, who has pioneered a new method of education (Waldorf Education) based on a knowledge of the three 7-year periods leading up to the age of 21. An understanding of the 7-year periods underlies the curriculum and teaching in the Waldorf schools.

In Waldorf education, the child is not considered to be ready for school, i.e. it is not truly capable of learning (in the sense of exercising mental capacities), until the end of the first 7-year period, the period ruled by the Moon. Prior to the age of 7, usually for the three years from 4 to 7, the child attends a pre-school play-group (kindergarten). It is only upon entering the second 7-year period, the Mercury period, that the child is considered capable of exercising mental faculties in order to learn to read and write, etc. Further, the educational program in Waldorf schools pays special attention to the difference between the development undergone by the child in the second 7-year period, that of Mercury, and in the third 7-year period, that of Venus (where the designations "Mercury" and "Venus" follow the traditional – Babylonian – astrological sequence: Moon, Mercury, Venus, Sun, Mars, Jupiter, Saturn).

This is not the place to enter in detail into the field of Waldorf education developed by Rudolf Steiner, as there already exists a considerable body of literature concerning this subject. Our intention is to look at the 7-year periods – the spiral of life – in the light of hermetic astrology. Having outlined the hermetic-astrological basis of the first three 7-year periods (summarized in Table 6), it is now appropriate to consider how this works out in practice, looking at a concrete example.

In choosing the example of Rudolf Steiner, it is clear that it is a matter

IV. The Spiral of Life (up to 21) 121

of a great individuality. This is evident from a consideration of the former incarnation of Rudolf Steiner, which is referred to in *Hermetic Astrology* I, Chapter 10. This individual was able to make the very best use of the "instruments" placed at his disposal. Looking at the indicators of the "instruments" of consciousness and life – the hermetic and geocentric charts at Rudolf Steiner's birth (see *Hermetic Astrology* I, Charts 13, 16 and 17) – it is especially the planets Moon, Mercury and Venus that are of interest in relation to the first three 7-year periods.

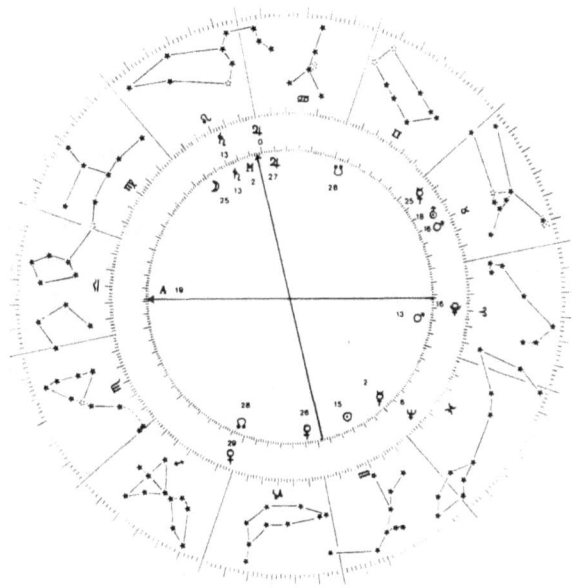

**Rudolf Steiner *11.26 p.m.
on February 25, 1861 at Kraljevec**

The first 7-year period

Firstly, the Moon: it was just past Full Moon at Rudolf Steiner's birth. The Moon was on the tail of the Lion, more or less opposite the Sun in the middle of Aquarius. In fact, the planet Saturn, in the middle of Leo, was almost diametrically opposite the Sun. This meant that during the night preceding his birth Saturn was in conjunction with the Full Moon in the middle of Leo. Thus Rudolf Steiner's birth was heralded by this striking geocentric cosmic configuration – that of the Full Moon together with brightly shining Saturn in the middle of the stars of the Lion.

There is nothing to distinguish, as such, between the Moon in the geocentric configuration and the Moon in the hermetic chart. However, there are two different perspectives concerning the Moon which give rise to a different emphasis in the two charts. In the geocentric chart the phase of the Moon is especially significant, and in the hermetic chart the Moon's location in the sidereal zodiac is most important, Clearly both the Moon's phase and its zodiacal location are *geocentric* phenomena. But if we consider the level to which they apply, then the phase of the Moon relates more to the physiological level (geocentric chart) and the position of the Moon against the background of the sidereal zodiac is a phenomenon pertaining more to the psychic level, that of consciousness (hermetic chart).

Nevertheless — and it is here that the complexity of man's relationship to the cosmos becomes apparent — these two levels interact with one another. The Moon's phase, whilst relating to the ebb and flow (waning and waxing) of life forces, reflects back from the physiological level into the level of consciousness, reflecting into the human being's soul nature, shaping his psychic constitution. Similarly, although the Moon's passage through the signs of the sidereal zodiac depicts a continual transformation of consciousness from sign to sign, this works also upon the level of life and has a corresponding effect upon the human being's life organism.

As referred to in Table 6, physiologically the Moon relates to the brain, whilst on the level of the psyche the organ corresponding to the Moon is the 4-petalled lotus flower. Since, however, the brain is physiologically the organ of consciousness and the 4-petalled lotus flower is psychically the organ of the will (the latter taking its course primarily in the sphere of the subconscious), there is a paradoxical element to the Moon's working into the human being.

In Rudolf Steiners birth chart, the Moon was in the sidereal sign of Leo, and it was close to Full Moon. On the level of the psyche, the Moon was coloured in its working into the 4-petalled lotus by virtue of its location in Leo. Considered purely on this level — that of consciousness — the Moon in Leo signifies a compassionate force of will, i.e. the will, signified in the hermetic chart by the Moon, is imbued with the heart forces of Leo. Someone born with the Moon in Leo has potentially a compassionate will nature, and through acting out of compassion can become ever more free. With Rudolf Steiner this was the case to a very high degree. His compassion appears to have been virtually unlimited. His continual striving was to be increasingly of service to his fellow men, and through his compassionate deeds he was led to ever-higher levels of freedom. In this sense he lived according to the philosophy outlined in his fundamental work *The Philosophy of Freedom*,[7] which characterizes freedom as the consequence of acting out of moral insight. (To love and serve God and to be of service to one's fellow human beings is ultimately the foundation of all morality.)

IV. The Spiral of Life (up to 21)

The configuration of "Moon in Leo", while referring essentially to the level of the psyche, can also indicate physiologically an abundance of life forces, in so far as the level of consciousness also works upon the level of life. This was accentuated in Rudolf Steiner's case by virtue of the Moon being almost full. The 4-petalled lotus flower, as the organ of the psychic organism which borders onto and works into the life organism (etheric body), thus represents a meeting point between the realm of consciousness and the realm of life. (This is brought to expression by the fact that the Moon's location in the sidereal zodiac is the same in both the hermetic and geocentric charts.)

The intensity with which the psychic forces work into the life organism is indicated by the phase of the Moon, i.e. it is at a peak at Full Moon and at a minimum at New Moon. At Rudolf Steiner's birth the Full Moon (actually just past Full Moon) signified a strong penetration of the psychic forces into the life organism. In other words, the compassionate will nature (indicated by the Moon in Leo) impressed itself so as to give rise to a corresponding effect in the life organism — one of powerful life forces. This came to manifestation on the one hand in Rudolf Steiner's remarkable capacity for work (he often worked late into the night, or sometimes even through the whole night), and on the other hand in his artistic creativity.

Following the ebb and flow of the life forces through the phases of the Moon, during the waxing period from New Moon to Full Moon the etheric (life) forces "flow", building up to a peak at Full Moon. Between Full Moon and New Moon, in the waning phase, the etheric forces "ebb", reaching a minimum at New Moon. This, archetypally, is the underlying physiological activity associated with the phases of the Moon. How does this reflect back into the human being's psychic constitution?

In the human psyche a complementary activity takes place during the phases of the Moon — complementary to the Moon's working into the realm of life. (The realm of life and that of consciousness are complementary to one another.) Thus at the lowest ebb of life forces — at New Moon — the Moon works most strongly into the upper pole of human consciousness, the pole associated with the brain and which comes to expression in the activity of thinking. Correspondingly, at the "high tide" of life forces — at Full Moon — it is the opposite pole, that of the subconscious (including the will), that is emphasized, i.e. at Full Moon the pole of the subconscious becomes most active. In between, at the First and Last Quarter of the Moon, it is the feeling life that is accentuated, the realm between the conscious thought life reflected in the brain and the subconscious will life of the lower human being.

Using Jung's definition of the psyche, i.e. psyche = ego-consciousness + unconsciousness,[8] the effect on the psyche of the cycle of the Moon's phases is such that at New Moon the pole of ego-consciousness is emphasized, and at Full Moon the pole of the unconscious (subconscious). Between the depths of the unconscious, which become stirred at Full Moon, and the brain-centered ego-consciousness, which comes to the fore at New Moon, there is the twilight realm of transition from the sphere of ego-consciousness to that of the unconscious. This twilight realm is that of the feelings, which sink down into the unconscious sphere of the will on the one hand (this is more the tendency at First Quarter), and which play up into the conscious life of thought on the other hand (as is more the case at Last Quarter).

For the incarnating human being – during the period from conception up to the moment of birth – the psychic correspondence to the Moon's physiological activity in the forming of the brain throughout the embryonic period can be summarized as follows:

New Moon– thinking (pole of ego-consciousness)
Full Moon– the will (pole of the subconscious)
First and Last Quarter– feeling (in between the pole of ego-consciousness and that of the subconscious).

The period of embryonic formation culminates at the moment of birth, whereby the stellar configuration at this moment is the goal of the incarnating human being. Thus the lunar phase at the moment of birth – denoting the termination of the formation of the etheric body – is of special significance. As well as indicating the physiological (life) phase – mirrored in the etheric body – of the human being's relationship to the Moon, it also colours his psyche by way of reflection back into his psychic constitution.

Returning to the starting point of our considerations, although the Moon's activity in the sphere of life (via the lunar phases) can be distinguished from its activity on the psychic level (via its passage through the signs of the sidereal zodiac), there is always a complementary effect. Thus complementary to the passage of the Moon through the signs of the zodiac there is a corresponding effect in the human being's life organisation (etheric body). This attains a maximum at Full Moon (when the etheric forces build up to a peak), at which time the strongest penetration of the psychic level into the level of life takes place. And complementary to the working of the lunar forces in the etheric body (via the Moon's phases) there is a psychic correspondence that comes to expression in the human soul forces of thinking, feeling and the will.

In Rudolf Steiner's case, as he was born shortly after Full Moon, the vital forces were near their maximum, and the corresponding psychic effect was evident in the will. This highly evolved individual manifested an extraordinary *will to serve*, a will of remarkable purity, that enabled him to accomplish outstanding feats of achievement during his lifetime.

How is the foregoing consideration of the Moon's sidereal location and its phase at Rudolf Steiner's birth relevant to the first seven years of his life?

It is during the first seven years that the psychic and vital qualities associated with the Moon's sidereal location and its phase are developed in seed form, serving as a foundation for the later course of life. However, it is not only the Moon's position in the sidereal zodiac and its relationship to the Sun (expressed by its phase) that are important. Its relationship to the planets (a) in the hermetic chart and (b) in the geocentric chart are also significant. The planetary relationships to the Moon often show the cause of illness or disturbances in the first seven years of life, which can work on into the following 7-year periods.

In Rudolf Steiner's case there are no major aspects (conjunction, opposition or square) to the Moon in his geocentric chart, but in the hermetic chart there is an interesting aspect – that of a square between Mercury and the Moon. The significance of this aspect did not begin to emerge until his third 7-year period, when the 10-petalled lotus flower (corresponding in the hermetic chart to Mercury) undergoes a development. We shall return to consider this when we come to look at the third 7-year period in Rudolf Steiner's life.

The second 7-year period

Turning now to the second 7-year period: this is termed the *Mercury period,* since in traditional geocentric astrology – stemming from the Babylonian (Ptolemaic) tradition – Mercury is the planet following on from the Moon in the geocentric sequence Moon, Mercury, Venus, Sun, Mars, Jupiter, Saturn. In hermetic astrology it could equally well be called the *Venus period,* as the age from 7 to 14 is that of the development of the 6-petalled lotus flower, corresponding to Venus in the hermetic chart. However, for the sake of agreement with the established tradition, we shall continue to refer to it as the *Mercury period* (the designation used by Rudolf Steiner and in the Waldorf schools).

Looking at Rudolf Steiner's geocentric chart, Mercury was in conjunction with Neptune in the sign of Pisces. As an aspect in the geocentric chart, this conjunction refers primarily to the domain of life. In considering the Moon in relation to the domain of life, the correspondence with the brain serves as a point of departure. Similarly, the correspondence of the lungs with Mercury offers a starting point for considering the physiological implications of this conjunction.

The activity of the lungs can be summarized as "breathing in" and "breathing out". This is expressive of the activity of the child between the ages of 7 and 14, which is very much one of "going out" and "coming in"

– going out to school, to learn, to make friends, to play; and coming in, returning home, being with parents, brothers and sisters. A conjunction in the geocentric chart of Mercury with Mars, for example, could mean that the child's activity becomes "martialized", with the child becoming active in sports, games, etc. In the example under consideration, however, the conjunction of Mercury with Neptune points to a more "mystical" activity and this is exactly what is evident in Rudolf Seiner's life at this age. (See Chapter 8 for a description of the significance of Neptune and how this may be viewed in connection with mysticism.)

Rudolf Steiner's deepest experiences in his second 7-year period were on the one hand those that he underwent in church, where he was able to experience the spiritual reality of the Mass, and on the other hand his joy in the discovery of geometry, where he found an inner certainty comparable with his inner certainty of the reality of the spirit.[9] Thus the conjunction of Mercury and Neptune in the geocentric chart at his birth came to expression already in his second 7-year period in mystical experiences and a love for geometry, which in seed form laid the foundation for deeper mystical experiences combined with geometrical clarity that Rudolf Steiner experienced throughout his life.

Looking now at the hermetic chart at Rudolf Steiner's birth, it is the planet Venus which is relevant to an understanding of the domain of consciousness in the second 7-year period. This is the period in which the second lotus flower (ascending from below upwards) – the 6-petalled lotus flower, corresponding to Venus – is the focus in the child's psychic constitution. In Rudolf Steiner's hermetic chart (*Hermetic Astrology* I, Chart 16), it is highly significant that the planet Venus is placed in the Moon's ascending node. The Moon's nodes, where the Moon sphere intersects the ecliptic, can be thought of as "gateways" to the cosmic world, and the location of Venus in the axis of these gateways points to something quite definite. It indicates that the 6-petalled lotus flower – the lotus flower corresponding to Venus – is open to the cosmic world. This lotus flower is the organ in man's psychic constitution which enables him to enter into communion with beings in supersensible realms, e.g. with departed souls.

In the case of Rudolf Steiner, already in his second 7-year period he began to have experiences of departed souls, as indicated by the favourable location of Venus in his hermetic chart. In a lecture that he held in Berlin on February 4, 1913, Rudolf Steiner reported his first experience at the age of 7 of a departed soul, who appeared to him as he sat in the waiting room of the railway station at Pottschach:

(It was as if the door opened)... a woman ... entered by the door, went to middle of the room, made some gestures and also spoke some words which may be rendered as follows: "Try now, and later in life, to help me as much as you can."... She remained in the room for a while

and made gestures...[10]

Throughout this experience the boy (Rudolf Steiner) knew that the woman was not a living person, but he knew also that he could not speak with anyone else about this or similar experiences. A few days later he learnt that at more or less exactly the same time as he had been sitting in the waiting room of the railway station, this woman – a distant relative of the family, living in a far away place – had committed suicide.

This was the first experience in a life full of such experiences, of departed souls, who for Rudolf Steiner were just as real as living human beings. These experiences began already in his second 7-year period, as may be understood on the basis of the relationship of the 6-petalled lotus flower with the planet Venus in the hermetic chart, when viewed against the background knowledge of the development of the various lotus flowers through the 7-year periods of life.

Just as the 4-petalled lotus flower (Moon) assumes a central role in the (very much unconscious) psychic development of the child during the first 7-year period, so the 6-petalled lotus flower (Venus) becomes the central focus in the human being's psychic constitution during the second 7-year period. This is the lotus flower of balance and harmony, and its prominence in the development of the child during the second 7-year period endows the child with an abundance of grace and harmony in this time. It is the lotus flower which is brought to development through the practice of *right standpoint* (see *Hermetic Astrology* I, Chapter 7), attained through the ordering of life in balance between the world of nature and the spiritual world. In the second 7-year period of life the emphasis placed on the 6-petalled lotus flower generally comes to expression on the one hand in the child's deep relationship to nature and on the other hand in its natural religiousness. Both the child's religious nature and its relationship to the world of nature are indicated by the location of Venus in the hermetic chart, taking account also of the sign of the zodiac in which Venus is placed. It is above all the *feeling nature* that is revealed here, which develops in seed form during the second 7-year period, just as the will nature develops in seed form during the first 7-year period.

In Rudolf Steiner's case the planet Venus (relating to the 6-petalled lotus flower) in the hermetic chart at his birth was emphasized by virtue of its location in the Moon's ascending node, where the sign of the sidereal zodiac occupied by h-Venus was Sagittarius (h-Venus at 29° Sagittarius). Sagittarius is traditionally the sign of the hunter, who goes out into nature to search for game. Venus in Sagittarius (in the hermetic chart) thus points to an active, outgoing relationship towards nature, and also towards the spiritual world. As Rudolf Steiner describes in his autobiography, he spent much time as a child wandering through the woods and forests searching for berries, often wandering afar in order to collect mineral water from a spring.[11] His questing feeling nature not only led him again and again into the world of nature, but also prompted him to explore with remarkable intensity the spiritual world. (His ability to follow souls after death into the spiritual world has already been mentioned.) This questing feeling nature – indicated by Venus in Sagittarius – developed in seed form during the second 7-year period of Rudolf Steiner's life.

The third 7-year period

Turning now to the third 7-year period, in the psychic constitution (indicated by the hermetic chart) it is Mercury that comes to the fore, as Mercury is the planet relating to the 10-petalled lotus flower, which becomes emphasized in the development of the human being between 14 and 21. Just as the first two 7-year periods are associated with the development in seed form of the will and the feeling life, so the third 7-year period is a time in which the thought life undergoes a special development. Here the capacity for abstract thinking emerges – the thinking which is characteristic of science. Scientific thinking – clear-sighted, analytical, combinatorial – is precisely the faculty initially acquired through the development of the 10-petalled lotus flower. When this development is taken further, on the spiritual path, it can be led over into clear-sightedness on the psychic level, i.e. to the development of clairvoyance. Here it is the practice of *right judgement* on the eightfold path that is relevant to the development of the 10-petalled lotus flower.

The exercise of judgement which appears in adolescence is on a fairly unconscious level the correlate of the conscious pursuit of right judgement on the spiritual path. Often the judgement of the young person between 14 and 21 can be exceptionally hard, but when seen as a part of a process of psychic development, the sometimes cold and cynical judgement may be better understood.

The nature of the young person's thought life – his scientific thinking and capacity for judgement – is indicated in the hermetic chart by Mercury, taking account of the sign of the zodiac in which it is located as well as the relationship of Mercury to other planets in the hermetic chart. In Rudolf Steiner's case, as already referred to, there was an exact square between the Moon and Mercury in his hermetic chart. Also, Mercury was in loose conjunction with Uranus – both planets were placed in Taurus. Viewed in the light of the indication outlined in *Hermetic Astrology* I, Chapter 5, the square between Mercury and the Moon points to a dynamic relationship between the 10-petalled and 4-petalled lotus flowers, i.e. between the lotus flower of thought and that of the will. In addition, the conjunction of Mercury and Uranus signifies an imaginative mentality. (See Chapter 8 for a description of the significance of Uranus and of the relationship of this planet to the imaginative faculty.) Being placed in

Taurus, however, this imaginative mentality is coloured in such a way that it seeks a solid foundation, just as the Bull in its whole nature is "solid" and in its stance supports itself squarely.

This configuration relating to Mercury in Rudolf Steiner's hermetic chart, which came to the fore in the third 7-year period of his life, indicates a remarkable potential capacity. It refers to a potentially highly imaginative mental capacity fired dynamically by the will, but seeking always a secure foundation in reality. Against this background it is possible to understand Rudolf Steiner's extraordinary mental capacity, which began to come to expression in his third 7-year period. It appeared on the one hand in his study of sciences – primarily mathematics, physics, chemistry and biology – and on the other hand in his study of the philosophers Kant, Fichte, Hegel and Schelling in his search for a thorough foundation in the theory of knowledge. He felt called to seek the truth through the study of philosophy, as he was convinced that he would not find a proper relationship to science until he could consider scientific findings upon the sure foundation of a sound philosophical theory of knowledge.[12] This attitude emerged as an expression of the stellar configuration involving Mercury in the hermetic chart at his birth (Mercury in Taurus in conjunction with Uranus, and square to the Moon).

Looking now at the geocentric chart, it is the planet Venus that is relevant to the third 7-year period. Here it is the physiological correspondence of the kidneys with Venus which offers a key to an understanding of the "life aspect" of the third 7-year period. The kidneys form part of the so-called *urogenital system,* and the activation of the kidneys in the life organism between 14 and 21 generally leads to an increased awareness of sexuality. The psychic counterpart to this emphasis on the kidneys and sexual organs is the awakening of love between the sexes, which from time immemorial has been associated astrologically with the planet Venus. This love was originally on a pure level, coming to expression through word and song, as cultivated in earlier times by minstrels singing ballads to their loved ones. The minstrel cult arose as a reflection of the archetypal, pre-Fall Venus influence. (The emergence of modern pop-music, generally aimed at teenagers, i.e. young people in the Venus period of life, on the whole seems to be a decadent corruption of the minstrel cult.) What was the underlying impulse of the minstrels?

The archetypal love between man and woman is expressed in the Bible in the relationship between Adam and Eve. In Paradise, prior to the Fall, this was a pure love, i.e. a love which existed purely on a soul level. "Adam and Eve" means to say *twin souls* (see Chapter 2). At that time the human being was not physically incarnated on the Earth – the term *Paradise* refers to the spiritual level of existence of the human being prior to earthly incarnation. It was only with the Fall that the human being began to incarnate into a physical body, and started the sequence of reincarnations. Then sexuality – procreation – began, in order to provide a physical body for the incarnating human being.

The paradisiacal love between twin souls – "Adam and Eve" – was an expression of the pre-Fall Venus influence, which at that time was mediated by the kidneys: not the physical kidneys, but the etheric counterpart of the kidneys in the human being's life organism (etheric body). (Man's bodily nature at that time, not yet including a physical-material body, extended down as far as the etheric body.) In this pre-Fall period there was no urogenital system, as such. Rather, the kidneys were etherically bound up with the larynx. Therefore this paradisiacal love between souls came to expression by way of the voice – in word and song. The minstrel cult was a reflection of this original pure love, and so is truly inspired love poetry.

With the Fall the kidneys "fell", as it were, in that man's constitution – now incorporating a physical body – become reconstituted to include the urogenital system, in which the kidneys are linked to the sexual organs. The Venus impulse thus became redirected, in order to help fulfil the task of procreation – the provision of a physical body for the incarnating soul. The Venus influence mediated by the kidneys, which before the Fall was directed towards the larynx, then became directed towards the sexual organs. Becoming subject to the influence of Venus in the third 7-year period of life (14–21), the tremendous longing experienced by the young person in adolescence is a yearning for the pure love that once existed between twin souls, but which now is generally associated with sexual love.

From the geocentric chart, looking especially at Venus' relationship to the other planets, something can be learnt of what comes to expression in the third 7-year life period, the Venus period according to traditional astrology. Rudolf Steiner was born when Venus and Jupiter were almost exactly in opposition to one another. This aspect worked most favourably for Rudolf Steiner's spiritual development, in that the impulse associated with Venus (the planet of love) became raised into connection with the planet Jupiter (the planet of wisdom). Rudolf Steiner's inner longings became directed towards spiritual wisdom, and this became an actual force of destiny, which led him far on the path of initiation already during the third 7-year period of his life. Two most significant meetings took place during this period, which opened up to him the treasures of spiritual wisdom that he sought.

At fifteen years of age, Steiner became acquainted with a herbalist... The remarkable thing about this man was that he knew not only the species, families and life of plants in their minutest details, but also their secret virtues. One would have said that he had spent his life in conversing with the unconscious and fluid soul of herbs and flowers. He had the gift of seeing the vital principle of plants, their etheric

IV. The Spiral of Life (up to 21)   131

body, and what occultists call the elemental beings of the plant world. He talked of it as of a quite ordinary and natural thing. The calm and coolly scientific tone of his conversation still further excited the curiosity and admiration of the youth. Later on, Steiner knew that this strange man was a messenger from the Master, whom as yet he knew not, but who was to be his real initiator, and who was already watching over him from afar...

It was at the age of nineteen that the aspirant to the mysteries met with his guide – the Master – so long anticipated... The Master of Rudolf Steiner was one of those men of power who live, unknown to the world, under cover of some civil state, to carry out a mission unsuspected by any but their fellows in the Brotherhood of self-sacrificing Masters. They take no ostensible part in human events. To remain unknown is the condition of their power, but their action is only all the more efficacious. For they inspire, prepare and direct those who will act in the sight of all. In the present instance the Master had no difficulty in completing the first and spontaneous initiation of his disciple. He had only, so to speak, to point out to him his own nature, to arm him with his needful weapons. Clearly he did show him the connection between the official and the secret sciences; between the religious and the spiritual forces which are now contending for the guidance of humanity; the antiquity of the occult tradition which holds the hidden threads of history, which mingles them, separates, and re-unites them in the course of ages. Swiftly he made him clear the successive stages of inner discipline, in order to attain conscious and intelligent clairvoyance. In a few months the disciple learnt from oral teaching the depth and incomparable splendour of the esoteric synthesis.[13]

Rudolf Steiner's meetings and experiences on the path of initiation during the third 7-year period of his life were indicated in the opposition of Venus and Jupiter in the geocentric chart at his birth. Jupiter was located close to the Midheaven, so that this planet – the planet of wisdom – shone forth high in the night sky at the moment of his birth. The prominence of Jupiter indicated the leading role which the quest for spiritual wisdom (and later its transmission in his work as a spiritual teacher) was to play in his life. The opposition with Venus signified that the Venus forces were yielded up in dedication to this spiritual quest, which took its start in the third 7-year period.

This offers a clear example as to how an astrological aspect – in this case the opposition of Venus and Jupiter in the geocentric chart, referring to the level of life – can become an active force in the shaping of destiny. The quest for spiritual wisdom begun in the Venus life period (14–21) – under the sign of Venus, so to say – led to the meetings described above, meetings with these two elder men, both bearers of spiritual wisdom (the

Jupiter principle). The opposition of Venus and Jupiter thus came to expression in terms of Rudolf Steiner's destiny in that he – representing Venus (during the Venus period) – was led to encounter the representatives of Jupiter, the bearers of spiritual wisdom. The meeting of the young Rudolf Steiner (representing Venus) with his Master (representing Jupiter) is highlighted in the following account:

> *Rudolf Steiner's Master was not in the least like himself. The Master had not that extreme and feminine sensibility which, though not excluding energy, makes every contact an emotion and instantly turns the suffering of others into personal pain. He was masculine in spirit, a born ruler of men, looking only at the species, and for whom individuals hardly existed. He spared not himself, and he did not spare others. His will was like a ball which, once shot from the cannon's mouth, goes straight to its mark, sweeping off everything in its way. To the anxious questioning of his disciple he replied in substance: "If thou wouldst fight the enemy, begin by understanding him. Thou wilt conquer the dragon by penetrating his skin. As to the bull, thou must seize him by the horns. It is in the extremity of distress that thou wilt find thy weapons and thy brothers in the fight. I have shown thee who thou art, now go – and be thyself!"*[14]

Rudolf Steiner followed the guidance of his master and entered the "skin of the dragon". He immersed himself in the study of the sciences and learnt how to apply the scientific method to the path of acquisition of spiritual knowledge. Thereby he evolved *spiritual science*, a science of knowledge of the spiritual realms, supplementing the natural sciences, which are concerned with acquiring knowledge of the material world. Thus Rudolf Steiner himself later became a transmitter of spiritual wisdom, a representative of Jupiter. But this belongs to a later period of his life, which we shall look at in the next chapter.

In this chapter we have looked at the development through the first three 7-year periods of Rudolf Steiner's life, following it according to the summary given in Table 6 of the planetary rulers of these three periods. In this way we have seen how the hermetic and geocentric charts at the moment of birth can be looked at in relation to the *spiral of life*, how the different planets offer a picture of the human being's psychic development and unfolding of life, working even into the shaping of destiny, during the various 7-year periods.

In each period the focus is on a different planet, and it is as if the human being becomes identified with that planet during the period in question. Of course, it is not a matter of identity. Rather, the human being becomes a mediator of the influence of the relevant planet – on the level of consciousness on the one hand, and on the level of life on the other hand (as indicated in the hermetic and in the geocentric chart, respectively – see

IV. The Spiral of Life (up to 21)

Table 6). Thus the unfolding of the spiral of life – the course of life through the sequence of 7-year periods – can be "read" from the birth chart (geocentric and hermetic).

With the exception of the second and third 7-year periods, where the planets Mercury and Venus are interchanged in the hermetic chart, the planetary sequence for the 7-year periods is the same in both the geocentric and hermetic charts. It is the classic geocentric planetary sequence: Moon (0–7), Mercury (7–14), Venus (14–21), Sun (21–42), Mars (42–49), Jupiter (49–56), Saturn (56–63) – followed by the zodiacal sphere of fixed stars beyond the age of 63. So far, in contemplating this unfolding of the spiral of life in relation to Rudolf Steiner's biography, we have looked at the first three 7-year periods, leading up to the age of 21. In the next chapter we shall look at the further unfolding of Rudolf Steiner's life in terms of his birth chart (geocentric and hermetic), from the age of 21 onwards.

Chapter 4: Notes and references

1. Franz Boll, "Die Lebensperiode", *Kleine Schriften zur Sternkunde des Altertums* (ed. V. Stegemann, Leipzig, 1950), pp. 190 ff.
2. Ptolemy, *Tetrabiblos* iv, 10 (ed. and trsl. F.E. Robbins, Loeb Classical Library, 1980, p. 441).
3. Franz Boll, op. cit., pp. 194–195.
4. Willi Sucher, "The Constellation of Cosmic Thought", *Mercury Star Journal* 6 (1980/1981), p. 32.
5. Willi Sucher, "Looking through the Horoscope of Birth: the Significance of the Prenatal Events among the Stars", *Mercury Star Journal* 2 (1976), pp. 64–75; reprinted from the *Modern Mystic* i (1937), pp. 44–46.
6. J.L.E. Dreyer, *Tycho Brahe* (Edinburgh, 1890), pp. 76–77.
7. Rudolf Steiner, *The Philosophy of Freedom* (trsl. M. Wilson, Rudolf Steiner Press, London, 1964).
8. C.G. Jung, *The Practice of Psychotherapy* (trsl. R.F.C. Hull, *The Collected Works of C.G. Jung*, vol. 16, London, 1954), p. 90.
9. Rudolf Steiner, *An Autobiography* (trsl. R. Stebbing, Rudolf Steiner Publications, New York, 1977), pp. 28–34.
10. Ibid., p. 426.
11. Ibid., pp. 25–26.
12. Ibid., pp. 53–55, 59.
13. Eduard Schuré, "The personality of Rudolf Steiner and his development", in: Rudolf Steiner, *The Way of Initiation* (Trismegistus Press, Ferndale MI, 1980), pp. 14–15, 18–20. Eduard Schuré wrote this description on the basis of notes made for him by Rudolf Steiner in 1907. The general content of what Schuré wrote agrees with Rudolf Steiner's autobiographical sketch from his lecture of February 4, 1913, held in Berlin. However, Schuré's account is not entirely accurate, as Rudolf Steiner must have been at least 18 years old when he made the acquaintance of the herb gatherer, as it was only in Autumn 1879 that he began to study at the Vienna Polytechnic. (He met the herb gatherer whilst travelling on the train to Vienna. Therefore Schuré's account has to be corrected in this respect, changing "fifteen years of age" to "at least eighteen years of age".)
14. Ibid., pp. 20–21.

Chapter 5

The Spiral of Life (21 onwards)

The organic and the psychic basis of the 7-year periods

The basic pattern of the spiral of life is outlined in Chapter 4. It can be summarized as follows: man's earthly life unfolds from birth to death through a sequence of 7-year periods, whereby three levels are to be considered, i.e. each ring of the spiral (= 7 years) can be considered from three perspectives – destiny, life, and consciousness (see Figure 3).

The basic structure of the 7-year periods is determined in the embryonic period when, during approximately ten lunar sidereal cycles, the incarnating human being's destiny becomes woven into the etheric organism, where each lunar orbit of the sidereal zodiac corresponds to seven years of life (see Chapter 3). This is the first perspective – that of destiny – of the spiral of life. The plan of destiny woven during the embryonic period determines the pattern underlying the unfolding of the spiral of life.

This plan constitutes the "house" (destiny) into which the human being incarnates. It comprises the basic outline – and embodies the higher significance – of his existence here on Earth.

On the way into incarnation the individual becomes equipped with an "instrument of consciousness" (a particular psychic constitution) and with an "instrument of life" (a particular life organism). By means of these "instruments" of consciousness and life the individuality is active – via the levels of consciousness and life – in shaping the unfolding of its destiny. Moreover, it is in conformity with the underlying pattern of the unfolding of destiny through the spiral of life that the individuality utilizes the "instrument of life" and the "instrument of consciousness". Thus the basic 7-year rhythm also applies to the levels of life and consciousness. On the level of consciousness, i.e. in the human being's psychic constitution, it is a particular lotus flower – ascending from below upwards – which comes to the fore in each 7-year period. On the level of life, i.e. in the human being's physiological (life) organism, it is a particular organ – each organ corresponding to a planet (according to occult physiology) – which becomes the central focus mediating life impulses during a given 7-year period. (See Table 7 for a summary of the relationships involved, extending throughout the entire spiral of life.)

The relationships indicated in Table 7 should not be interpreted as rigid delineations. In fact, as is readily apparent, all the organs (heart, brain, etc.) are active all the time, throughout the entire spiral of life. (No one could live if his heart or lungs were to cease functioning!) Rather, it is a matter of a particular organ becoming emphasized – or in the psychic con-

Table 7:
The spiral of life

	"instrument of life" (life organism)			"instrument of consciousness" (psychic constitution)	
7-year period	ruling planet	mediating organ	age	ruling planet	lotus flower
1	Moon	brain	0– 7	Moon	4-petalled
2	Mercury	lungs	7–14	Venus	6-petalled
3	Venus	kidneys	14–21	Mercury	10-petalled
4			21–28		
5	Sun	heart	28–35	Sun	12-petalled
6			35–42		
7	Mars	gall-bladder	42–49	Mars	16-petalled
8	Jupiter	liver	49–56	Jupiter	2-petalled
9	Saturn	spleen	56–63	Saturn	8-petalled
10→	zodiac	—	63→	zodiac	—

stitution of the activity of a particular lotus flower becoming accentuated – during a given 7-year period. Using the analogy of an orchestra, all the instruments play together, but at any one time a particular instrument may come to the fore, its contribution becoming marked out in relation to the other instruments. So it is with the various formative forces associated with the planets and coming to expression via the various organs, and it is likewise also with the different lotus flowers in the human being's psychic constitution.

For example, the process of breathing – associated with the planet Mercury and coming to expression via the lungs – is continuously active throughout the whole life. Nevertheless, it becomes emphasized during the Mercury period, between the ages of 7 and 14. In this life period the lung-breathing system comes to the fore in relation to all the other organs and associated processes. The child of this age has a deep-seated need to go out and breathe in fresh air. It would be highly unnatural for a child of this age to remain indoors all the time. But prior to the age of 7 (and also after the age of 14) this emphasis on breathing is not so pronounced, and it is not at all out of the ordinary for very young children (in the Moon period, 0–7) or for adolescents (in the Venus period, 14–21) to remain indoors much of the time. (Needless to say, it is not very healthy for the baby or small child to receive insufficient fresh air!)

Similarly, when considering the human being's psychic development, the accentuation of the 10-petalled lotus flower (Mercury) during the third 7-year period (14–21) means that the adolescent's critical-analytical faculty of thought becomes pronounced. (Usually it begins to awaken around

V. The Spiral of Life (21 onwards)

the time of the first Jupiter return at around the age of 12.) This does not signify that it is only during the life period from 14 to 21 that the human being is capable of critical-analytical thinking. Rather, once having emerged it can in all probability be used for most of the remaining period of life. Then the adult human being is in possession of a faculty that emerged in the past (in the period from 14 to 21), which he is able to make use of throughout most of his life.

Or, for example, consider the 8-petalled lotus flower – corresponding to Saturn – which comes to the fore fairly late, i.e. in the ninth 7-year period (56–63). This is the lotus flower of memory and conscience. In between the ages of 56 and 63 the activity of memory and also of conscience become heightened, but the role that memory and conscience play during the preceding life periods cannot be overlooked. Here it is the case that this Saturn principle on the level of consciousness rays into the human being's life from the future (from the Saturn period), acting already in advance in his life prior to the age of 56.

Thus a dynamic picture emerges of the interrelationship on the one hand of psychic faculties (connected with the lotus flowers) and on the other hand of the working of cosmic forces mediated by the various organs. The interaction of cosmic forces mediated by different organs is analogous – on the organic level – to the interplay of planetary impulses relating to the various lotus flowers on the psychic level. The latter come to expression as faculties on the level of consciousness, which become activated during the various rings (7-year periods) of the spiral of life, but which nevertheless work in a conscious or subconscious way throughout the whole life. Each faculty in man's psychic constitution has its rightful time at which it comes to the fore (as in the analogy of the different instruments of an orchestra), so that there is a continual interplay between past and future, between faculties already developed which accompany the human being on his further path, and faculties that become accentuated later in life but which already come to expression beforehand in a less conscious way.

In terms of the "ascent of the tree of consciousness" – the working in of the different lotus flowers into the sequence of 7-year periods (see Table 7) – a distinction can be drawn between the three lotus flowers (corresponding to the Moon, Venus and Mercury) emphasized during the first three 7-year periods (0–21) and those lotus flowers (corresponding to Mars, Jupiter and Saturn) accentuated between the ages of 42 and 63. The three lower lotus flowers are essentially *soul organs* – those of the will (Moon), feeling (Venus) and thinking (Mercury) – whilst the three higher lotus flowers are more *spiritual organs* – those of speech/power (Mars), thought/wisdom (Jupiter) and memory/conscience (Saturn). The middle lotus flower (Sun) – the 12-petalled lotus flower, associated with the heart center – holds a middle position between the upper and lower lotus flowers, and is emphasized in the central life period, from 21 to 42. It is the organ of the self.

The fact of ruling the prime of life (21–42) indicates the central importance of the Sun in the birth chart. Physiologically it is the heart which is the organ of the Sun, and the corresponding process is the circulation of the blood. In the psychic constitution the 12-petalled lotus flower corresponds to the Sun, the central focus of the self. The Sun period of life (21–42) is the time during which the human being finds himself, his identity, after passing through the often turbulent storms of youth. His true identity begins to manifest with the "shining in" of the Sun during this period of life. It is also the time during which tasks of destiny begin to approach the human being.

The Sun period in Rudolf Steiner's life

In Rudolf Steiner's life he was presented with a task of destiny at the age of 21. During the winter 1879/1880 (he reached the age of 19 on February 25, 1880), the young Rudolf Steiner attended a course of lectures entitled "German Literature since Goethe" held by Karl Julius Schröer at Vienna Polytechnic. These lectures made a deep impact on the 19-year old, and awoke his interest in Goethe. Karl Julius Schröer (see *Hermetic Astrology* I, Appendix IV, for a brief biography) was devoted to Goethe's life work, both in his capacity as professor for German Literature at Vienna Polytechnic and as president of the Goethe Society in Vienna. Through Schröer, who took a fatherly interest in his academic striving, the young Rudolf Steiner not only became encouraged to take up an intensive study of Goethe's works but also became recommended to undertake the editing of Goethe's scientific literature. So it came about that at the age of 21 Rudolf Steiner became invited by Joseph Kürschner to edit and write commentaries on Goethe's botanic and zoological writings, for publication in the *German National Literature* edition of Goethe's works.

In the introduction he wrote: "Goethe is the Copernicus and Kepler of the organic world."[1] With this work Rudolf Steiner endeavoured to bring Goethe's contribution to biological science to the light of day, to indicate the importance of Goethe as a scientist. Although Goethe is generally acknowledged as the greatest poet and playwright of German literature, it is often overlooked that he sought for decades to develop a new science of the organic world. Rudolf Steiner did everything within his power to try and bring Goethe's scientific work forward, and his commentaries on Goethe's scientific writings are a major step in this direction. Thereby Goethe – principally "Goethe the scientist" – came to occupy a central position in Rudolf Steiner's destiny during the Sun period (21–42) of his

V. The Spiral of Life (21 onwards)

life. Is it possible to understand this development in Rudolf Steiner's destiny from his birth horoscope (see *Hermetic Astrology* I, Chart 13)?

In the Sun period it is of course the Sun which holds the key to the spiral of life. In fact, unlike the Moon and the planets, which each rule over one ring (7 years) of the spiral, the Sun assumes overwhelming importance in that it rules over three rings (amounting to 21 years) of the spiral of life. The Sun at Rudolf Steiner's birth was located in the middle of Aquarius, in opposition to Saturn in the middle of Leo. As it was just after Full Moon, the Moon – also in Leo – was in loose opposition to the Sun. Comparing this birth configuration with that at Goethe's birth, an interesting polarity emerges. (See *Hermetic Astrology* I, Chart 12, for Goethe's birth horoscope.) Goethe was born when the Sun was in the middle of Leo, and his birth also took place just after Full Moon, i.e. the Moon – in Aquarius – was in loose opposition to the Sun.

Comparing these two geocentric configurations, the Sun at Goethe's birth stands in a direct relationship with the opposition of the Sun and Saturn at Rudolf Steiner's birth. The Sun in the two configurations were located exactly in opposition, at opposite sides of the zodiac, and at the same time Saturn at Rudolf Steiner's birth coincided with the zodiacal location of the Sun at Goethe's birth. Although not the only aspect involving the Sun (we shall return to the other aspects later), the opposition between the Sun and Saturn is the most striking aspect in Rudolf Steiner's birth chart, and at the same time it is related to the zodiacal position of the Sun at Goethe's birth (as described above). This relationship offers an astonishingly exact picture of Rudolf Steiner's destiny during the Sun period of his life.

Upon entering the Sun period, the Sun comes to the fore in a person's horoscope. In Rudolf Steiner's case this meant the coming to birth of his *Aquarian self* (the Sun, representing the self, being in Aquarius), and at the same time the opposition of Saturn to the Sun began to make itself felt especially strongly – as a destiny shaping influence – in the Sun period of his life. On the level of consciousness, Saturn is the planet of the 8-petalled lotus flower, that of memory and conscience. When in opposition to the Sun, Saturn is at its brightest in the night sky. For someone born at this time, the impulse of Saturn is particulary strong. This can signify – at least potentially – a good memory and a high degree of conscientiousness. This is particularly appropriate for scientific work, which demands both these qualities.

It is the same aspect of opposition between Saturn and the Sun in the geocentric chart, which refers more to the level of life, and which also can work into the shaping of destiny. This aspect – Saturn opposite the Sun – came to the fore in Rudolf Steiner's life in the Sun period (21–42), and re-emerged again (but with a different emphasis) in the Saturn period

(56–63). Whereas in the Saturn period, which we shall consider later, this aspect was experienced more from the standpoint of Saturn, in the Sun period it was from the standpoint of the Sun that it came to expression.

With the entrance into the Sun period, as already remarked, Rudolf Steiner's *Aquarian self* came to birth. This inner awakening to his identity brought with it an increasing consciousness of his relationship to the world of spirit. Rudolf Steiner became more and more aware of himself as a spiritual being on Earth – an earthly citizen awake to the beings of the spiritual world. Over and against this inner experience there came to meet him from without the stream of destiny that brought the Goethe work to him (signified by Saturn in Leo – in the same part of the zodiac as the Sun was at Goethe's birth). Rudolf Steiner described this as follows:

> *In my case the inner impulse was directed toward conscious experience of the spiritual; the external spiritual life brought me the Goethe task. These two impulses met in my consciousness, and I had to bring them into harmony.*[2]

It is a measure of the greatness of this individual that he was able to experience his inner life consciously, which makes the study of his horoscope in relation to the spiral of life exceptionally illuminating, especially when studied alongside his autobiography. In conformity with the Saturn-Sun aspect of opposition, during the Sun period of his life there was an ongoing interplay between the outer stream of destiny connected with Goethe (Saturn in Leo) and the inner spiritual impulse that ripened within him (Sun in Aquarius).

In his relationship to Goethe Rudolf Steiner consciously adopted an important maxim of the spiritual life: the *principle of continuity*. This is the principle that every Christian esotericist endeavours to uphold, namely to connect onto the positive stream of tradition and to lead it further. In so doing the esotericist seeks a *forerunner* whose ideal he can identify with, and also has in mind that he will be followed by a *successor* for whom he is to prepare the way. In other words, the Christian esotericist does not come "in his own name", but seeks simply to serve and support the spiritual tradition, the links in which are human beings.

Goethe was the forerunner of Rudolf Steiner. Already in the elaboration of his karma prior to incarnation, Rudolf Steiner's destiny was so prepared that he would be led to Goethe's work, in order to take it up and develop it further. For Rudolf Steiner Goethe was the last (i.e. the foregoing) link in the chain of spiritual-cultural tradition, and much of Rudolf Steiner's endeavour in the Sun period of his life was connected with the question as to whether it would be possible for him to develop his spiritual mission through the Goethe work. In this he went through three phases, closely connected with the three 7-year periods during the Sun period. Subdividing the Sun period into three 7-year stages, these three different phases can be looked at in relation to the opposition between Saturn and the Sun in Rudolf Steiner's horoscope, where this opposition reflected the interplay between the outer stream of destiny connected with Goethe and the inner spiritual impulse that lived within him.

The 7-year periods

During the first seven years of the Sun period (21–28) – corresponding to the years from 1882 to 1889 – Rudolf Steiner lived in or near Vienna. Until 1884 he lived at his parent's home, travelling from there into the city, and from 1884 onwards he lived as a guest in the home of Ladislaus and Pauline Specht, whose four sons received private tuition from him. His work on editing and commenting Goethe's botanic and zoological writings for publication in Kürschner's *German National Literature* occupied him throughout this period. As a fruit of this work he wrote his first book *The Theory of Knowledge Implicit in Goethe's World Conception*, which became published in 1886.

The Vienna period in Rudolf Steiner's life was a time of immersion in Goethe's thought. But at the same time the young Goethe scholar led an active social life, which brought him into contact with such diverse people as the poetess Marie Eugenie delle Grazie, the Catholic theologian Laurenz Müllner, the Cistercian priest Wilhelm Neumann, the writer Fritz Lemmermayer, the poet Fercher von Steinwand, the feminist Rosa Mayreder and the theosophist Friedrich Eckstein.

In 1889, at the start of the the second seven years of the Sun period (28–35), Rudolf Steiner was invited to collaborate in the work of the Goethe Archives at Weimar, Germany. Again his task was to prepare Goethe's scientific writings for publication – this time in the edition sponsored by the Grand Duchess Sophie of Saxony. After visiting Weimar in 1889, he accepted the post, but did not leave Vienna to start work at the Goethe-Archives until 1890. The stay in Weimar lasted seven years, so that the second 7-year period within the Sun period in Rudolf Steiner's life (1889–1896) more or less coincided with the Weimar period (1890–1897).

In Weimar, the town where Goethe had lived and worked, Rudolf Steiner came into a more intense connection with the spirit of Goethe. There he was privileged to have access to manuscripts which supplemented those that he had worked with in Vienna. Whilst pouring over these documents, he was concerned with understanding Goethe's relationship to nature and to the spiritual world, and how he could build further upon the foundation of knowledge laid by Goethe. More and more he focused upon the question:

> *How is one to build further upon the foundation of knowledge laid by Goethe in order to lead thinking over from* his *view over to a view that includes a conscious* experience *of the spirit such as I had gained?*[3]

It is in the light of this question, which correspondingly gave rise to an inner quest for his own theory of knowledge, that Rudolf Steiner's Ph.D. thesis and his book *Philosophy of Freedom* can be seen. The title of his doctoral thesis was *The Fundamentals of a Theory of Knowledge, with special reference to Fichte's Scientific Teaching*, with the subtitle: *How Human Consciousness can come to an Experience of Itself.* In this work, submitted shortly after his thirtieth birthday in 1891, i.e. about one-third of the way through the second 7-year period within the Sun period, Rudolf Steiner tried to show that man can come to understand the true reality of the outer world only by viewing it through and within the reality of his own self. The essential content of this thesis was published in book form one year later (1892), entitled *Truth and Knowledge*.[4]

Truth and Knowledge was published with the subtitle: *Prelude to a Philosophy of Freedom*. Thus at the time of publication of his doctoral thesis Rudolf Steiner was already engaged on his major philosophical work *Philosophy of Freedom*, to which he regarded his thesis as a prelude. The *Philosophy of Freedom*, which became published in 1894, some months after he had reached the age of 33, signified a major extension of his Ph.D. thesis. In the *Philosophy of Freedom* (also known in translation as the *Philosophy of Spiritual Activity*[5]), Rudolf Steiner laid the foundation of the theory of knowledge which served as the basis of his life's work. The subtitle of this work – *Results of Introspective Observations According to the Method of Natural Science* – shows clearly the nature of Rudolf Steiner's main concern, namely to develop a *spiritual science* by extending the method of natural science and applying it to the realm of the spirit.

Rudolf Steiner developed the method of "introspective observation" – interior or soul observation – for arriving at knowledge of the self and of the world. Through interior observation he was able to explore the inner nature of man. Among his many discoveries arrived at in this way, he came to a new knowledge of the spiral of life – the unfolding of life through a sequence of 7-year periods – thus confirming the ancient tradition known to the Greeks of the 7-year periods in human biography (see Appendix I for references, translated from the Greek, to the spiral of life.) Moreover, he was able to identify exactly what takes place in each 7-year life period. For example, he observed that in the first three 7-year periods the various "bodies" undergo their main development – the physical body in the first seven years, the etheric body from 7 to 14, and the astral body in the third 7-year period (see Table 6). On this basis he developed the educational program used in the Waldorf Schools.

In the Sun period – the three 7-year periods (septenaries) from 21 to 42 – he observed that the self comes to birth around 21 and goes through three phases of development, each phase lasting approximately seven years. According to his description, the first phase of development (the fourth septennary, 21–28) takes place more on the feeling level (sentient self), the second phase (28–35) is more on the thought level (intellectual self), and the third phase (35–42) is more on the level of the will, where the higher spiritual will begins to come to consciousness (consciousness self, also known as "spiritual self").[6] In contrast to both the sentient and the intellectual nature of the self, which are already highly developed in the modern human being, the will nature, through the development of which man becomes conscious of himself as a free spirit, is by and large still at a preliminary stage of development. Although it is observable in seed form in modern man, it does not often emerge in a developed way. (How many people in the twentieth century genuinely experience themselves in full consciousness as free spiritual beings at the deepest level of expression of the self, i.e. on the level of the will?)

In Rudolf Steiner's case these three distinct phases of development between the ages of 21 and 42 are clearly recognizable. The first phase (fourth septennary, 21–28) comprised the major part of the Vienna period of his life. Here Rudolf Steiner's sentient self manifested itself clearly in his extensive social life, e.g. in the poetry evenings at the house of Marie Eugenie delle Grazie, and in the endless conversations in the Griensteidl Coffee House. In the second phase (fifth septennary, 28–35) it was the development of his intellectual self that came to the foreground, especially in his occupation with arriving at a well-founded theory of knowledge. The theory of knowledge outlined in preliminary form in his doctoral thesis *Truth and Knowledge* and elaborated in detail in the *Philosophy of Freedom* was Rudolf Steiner's principal achievement in the second septennary within the Sun period, which ran more or less parallel with the Weimar period in his life. After Weimar he moved to Berlin, so that the third septennary in the Sun period (= the sixth septennary, 35–42) coincided largely with the first part of his Berlin period. (He moved to Berlin in 1897, at the age of 36.)

When we come to look at Rudolf Steiner's life as it unfolded in Berlin, we are presented with a good example of the *will self* – referred to here as the *consciousness self* – that develops in the human being between the ages of 35 and 42. This consciousness self can be seen in relationship to the center, the kernel, of the human being:

In the human personality I saw a center where man is altogether at one with the Absolute Primordial Being of the world. This center is the wellspring of man's will. And if the clear light of the spirit is effective in this center, then man's will is free. He acts in harmony with the world's spiritual foundation which becomes creative within him, not out of necessity but purely in fulfilling its own nature. In this inner center are born human ideals to be fulfilled through human deeds, that is, ideas that do not spring from obscure impulses but from moral intuitions,

intuitions as transparent as the clearest thought. Thus, in the contemplation of free will I attempted to discover the spirit that makes man an individuality.[7]

In order to clarify the interrelationship of the three aspects of the self, which develop during the three 7-year periods between 21 and 42, it is helpful to look again at their macrocosmic parallels. Applying the hermetic principle of correspondences – "as above, so below" – each different aspect of man's nature mirrors an aspect of cosmic reality. The center of the self – "this center (which) is the wellspring of man's will" – is macrocosmically the Sun. The self is centered in the Sun, and therefore the Sun is the astrological indicator of the self. But assuming that there are three aspects to the self, how are they to be distinguished?

Occult cosmology

In order to arrive at an understanding of the correspondence between the macrocosm and the three layers (sentient, intellectual, spiritual) of the self, a knowledge of occult cosmology is needed, entailing a comprehension of the origin of the solar system. According to modern scientific conceptions, our solar system was originally a primeval nebula, a disk of spinning gas, in which local condensations occurred leading to agglomerations that formed into planets. In occult cosmology, which is concerned with the spiritual reality underlying the genesis of our cosmos, it is above all the order of the formation of the planets out of the primeval nebula which is important. The clearest description of planetary formation in terms of occult cosmology known to the author is that of Rudolf Steiner, who described how first the planet Saturn was formed, then Jupiter, then Mars, whilst the Earth and Moon, together with the Sun, Mercury and Venus, formed a vast central cosmic body within the primeval nebula.[8] Saturn, Jupiter and Mars orbited around this central body, as shown in Figure 4. (Uranus, Neptune and Pluto are not depicted in Figure 4 as their relationship to the solar system is of a quite different nature than that of the traditional planets – see Chapter 8.)

Then the Earth separated out from the central body, giving rise to the polarity Sun – Earth. In the Biblical account, something of this polarity is indicated in the words: "In the beginning God created Heaven and Earth" (*Genesis* i, 1). In the original polarity Sun – Earth, Mercury and Venus were still part of the Sun, whilst the Moon was still bound up with the Earth. Mercury and Venus subsequently separated out from the Sun, and later the Moon separated out from the Earth. Thus, just as the Moon is a satellite of the Earth, Mercury and Venus can be regarded as satellites of the Sun (see Figure 5).

In the sense of occult cosmology, Mercury and Venus mark the boundaries of "layers" of the Sun that became separated out from it. The outer-

V. The Spiral of Life (21 onwards) 145

Figure 4:
The formation of the solar system

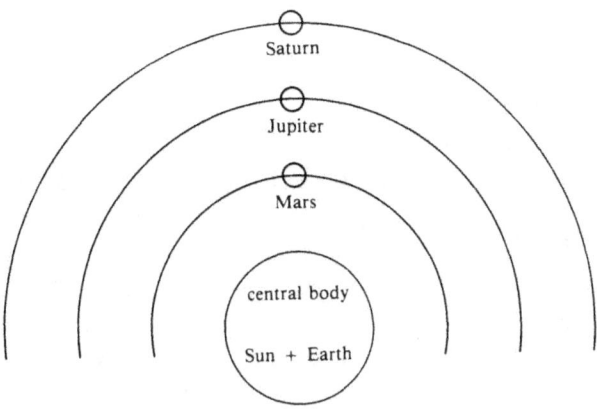

Figure 5
The further formation of the solar system

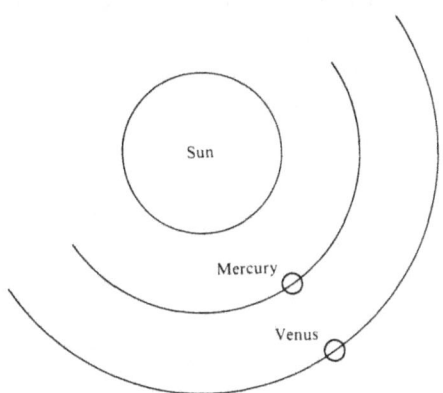

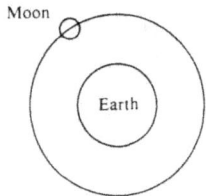

most layer, specified by the orbit of Venus, corresponds to the macrocosmic feeling nature of the original Sun, whilst the orbit of Mercury indicates a middle layer – that of macrocosmic thought nature – which also belonged to the original Sun. The innermost layer, the macrocosmic will nature, remained in the center, united with the Sun. These three layers represent the will, thought and feeling aspects of the cosmic self centered in the Sun (see Figure 5).

Applying the hermetic law of analogy, the self of the human being, which develops in the Sun period (21–42) of life, also has three layers. The outermost layer, the sentient (feeling) self, develops between the ages of 21 and 28. In the light of occult cosmology, this bears a relationship in the hermetic chart with the orbit of Venus around the Sun. Then follows the development of the intellectual (thinking) self (28–35), correspondingly bearing a relationship in the hermetic chart with the orbit of Mercury around the Sun. Lastly the consciousness (will) self unfolds in the 7-year period from 35 to 42. This is bound up with the Sun itself in the hermetic chart.

Although the Sun, the center of the cosmic self, essentially rules the entire period from 21 to 42, it is as if the feeling and thought layers of the self, whose boundaries are signified macrocosmically by the orbits of Venus and Mercury around the Sun, have to be worked through first before penetrating to the kernel of the self, identified macrocosmically with the Sun itself. There are therefore three layers of the self: an outermost layer (sentient self, 21–28), a middle layer (intellectual self, 28–35) and a kernel (consciousness self, 35–42). In this kernel lies "the wellspring of man's will".

Seen macrocosmically, the Sun is the wellspring of man's will. However, this may seem to contradict *Hermetic Astrology* I, Chapter 10, which discusses the zodiacal location of the Moon at the moment of birth as indicating the cosmic orientation of the will of the incarnating human being. This apparent contradiction can be clarified by referring again to a brief outline of occult cosmology. The three layers of the Sun, the cosmic self, extend down to the orbit of Venus, as in the light of occult cosmology Venus, Mercury and the Sun were originally one body. Similarly, the Moon and the Earth were one body, after the separation out of the Earth-plus-Moon from the central body. Prior to this separation, Sun, Mercury, Venus, Moon and Earth were all united together in one central body, around which Mars, Jupiter and Saturn orbited (see Figure 4).

The division of the central body into the Sun (actually Sun-plus-Mercury-plus-Venus) on the one hand and the Earth (actually Earth-plus-Moon) on the other hand is referred to in the first sentence of the Bible in the words: "In the beginning God created Heaven and Earth" (*Genesis* i,1). The separation of the Earth and the Sun is the primal event taken as the point of departure in the Biblical account of the creation. Applying the hermetic axiom – "as above, so below" – the question arises: What did this cosmic event ("above") signify for the human being ("below")?

This separation signified on the archetypal level a potential division of the human being into a higher self and a lower self – the higher self identified with the Sun and the lower self with the Earth. These two selves are referred to in terms of Jungian psychology as the self (higher self) and the ego (earthly self). (See *Hermetic Astrology* I, Chapters 8 and 10, for a discussion of the astrological significators – the Sun and the Ascendant – of the self and the ego, the Ascendant relating to the earthly self as it indicates the cosmic orientation of the Earth at the moment of the human being's birth.)

In consideration of occult cosmology it is evident that the ego (bound up with the Earth) was originally part of the self (centered in the Sun). The separation of the Earth from the Sun signified on the cosmic level the possibility of a division into a higher self and a lower self. This remained only a possibility, however, as long as man did not incarnate on the Earth. The division became a reality through the event of the Fall, when man commenced his series of incarnations upon the Earth, whereby the earthly self (ego) began its development.

The development of the earthly self in the course of reincarnation upon the Earth is described in *Hermetic Astrology* I, Chapter 7, using the analogy of a string of beads to characterize the sequence of incarnations. There it is pointed out that the sense of personality – as an expression of the lower self – has emerged ever more strongly in the course of history, especially in incarnations since the Mystery of Calvary (see *Hermetic Astrology* I, Figure 17).

Thus it can be understood how a separation of the self into a higher self and an earthly self has come about, where the higher self is bound up with the Sun and its satellites (Mercury and Venus) and the earthly self with the Earth and its satellite (the Moon). This has given rise to a higher (solar) will and a lower (lunar/earthly) will, i.e. the Sun can certainly be described as "the wellspring of man's will", but it is also appropriate – as indicated in the last chapter – to view the Moon astrologically as representing the will of the earthly self, denoting the human being's orientation of will in his incarnation upon the Earth. Astrologically speaking, the Moon represents the human being's *natural will*, as opposed to his higher spiritual will.

In the last chapter the development of the natural will is described as taking place primarily in the Moon period of life (0–7). Further, a distinction is drawn between two perspectives of the human being's development during the first three 7-year periods. These two perspectives are: the human being's development on the level of consciousness (indicated more by the hermetic chart) and that on the level of life (indicated more by the geocentric chart). Now, in the light of occult cosmology, it is possible to characterize these two perspectives from another point of view.

From this new viewpoint the hermetic chart indicates more the perspective of the higher (solar) self, centered in the Sun, whilst the geocentric chart is more concerned with the perspective of the lower (earthly) self. With regard to the Sun and the Moon – representing the higher and the lower will – there is no difference between their respective zodiacal positions in the hermetic chart and those in the geocentric chart. But the zodiacal positions of Mercury and Venus are usually quite different in the hermetic chart from those of the geocentric chart. The positions of Mercury and Venus in the sidereal zodiac, as seen from the Sun (hermetic chart), represent astrologically the thinking and feeling layers of the solar self, whilst their positions as seen from the Earth (geocentric chart) relate more to the thinking and feeling layers of the earthly self, and thus may be called *natural thinking* and *natural feeling*. Thus the perspective of the geocentric chart – with respect to the Moon, Mercury and Venus – is that natural will (Moon), natural thinking (Mercury) and natural feeling (Venus) unfold during the first three 7-year periods: Moon (0–7), Mercury (7–14) and Venus (14–21). And the perspective of the hermetic chart is that the feeling (Venus), thought (Mercury) and will (Sun) layers of the self unfold during the next three 7-year periods: Venus (21–28), Mercury (28–35) and Sun (35–42).

This new viewpoint does not contradict that which is described in the last chapter concerning the psychic development indicated by the Moon, Venus and Mercury in the hermetic chart during the first three 7-year periods, i.e. Moon (4-petalled lotus flower, 0–7), Venus (6-petalled lotus flower, 7–14) and Mercury (10-petalled lotus flower, 14–21), since this psychic development takes place on a deeper subconscious level. It is then the Sun (12-petalled lotus flower) which comes into consideration with the regard to the human being's psychic development between the ages of 21 and 42 (see Table 7). However, insofar as the Sun – according to occult cosmology – originally included Venus and Mercury, then during the Sun period of life (21–42) the deeper subconscious psychic development passed through between 7 and 14 (Venus) and between 14 and 21 (Mercury) is reawakened and recapitulated on the level of the self. This recapitulation of an earlier development on the level of the self means that "Venus" and "Mercury" phases are repeated, but this time encompassed within the aura of the emerging self, represented astrologically by the Sun. Thus the recapitulation of the Venus phase within the period of development of the self is from 21 to 28, and the recapitulation of the Mercury phase is from 28 to 35. Expressed in terms of traditional astrological terminology: the Sun "rules" the entire period from 21 to 42, but included within this solar rulership Venus is the "sub-ruler" of the period from 21 to 28 and Mercury is the "sub-ruler" from 28 to 35 – when the planetary periods are looked at in terms of the hermetic chart, i.e. looked at from the perspective of the higher self.

The deeper significance of the Egyptian (Tychonic) system

A knowledge of occult cosmology helps to provide a basis for understanding the complexity of the human being, comprising a higher (solar) self and a lower (earthly) self. However, our survey of occult cosmology would not be complete without contemplating the event signifying the beginning of a reunion of the earthly self with the solar self. Just as "in the beginning God created Heaven and Earth", i.e. the Sun and the Earth became separated, so through the Mystery of Calvary "Heaven and Earth became reunited" (on a spiritual level). At the crucifixion Christ, the Spirit of the Sun, united with the Earth and through his sacrifice there began the overcoming and transformation of the consequences of the Fall. The taking up of the Christ Impulse by the human ego means that the lower self can become infused and permeated by the solar nature of the higher self centered in the Sun, becoming inwardly united with it. Christ, the Being of the Sun, leads the human being back into connection with the higher self.

Christ's deed in uniting with the Earth through the Mystery of Calvary signified the transference of the moral center of the solar system from the Sun to the Earth. Here lies the deeper justification of hermetic astrology, based on the Tychonic system. For, although the heliocentric (Copernican) system appropriately describes physical reality, the hermetic (Tychonic) system relates to moral and astrological reality.

Christ is the Lord of Karma. It is he who guides each human being in the unfolding of destiny through the spiral of life. This destiny is fulfilled on the Earth. From the point of view of Christ's working, the Earth is the center – astrologically and morally – of the solar system.

The Copernican system is certainly appropriate for the computation of the physical movements of the heavenly bodies, e.g. the return of Halley's comet (1985/86) was computed to a remarkable degree of accuracy by applying Kepler's laws in accordance with the Copernican system. Nevertheless, the hermetic system – brought forward scientifically by Tycho Brahe towards the end of the sixteenth century – is valid both from an astrological and a moral point of view. Its astrological validity is considered in *Hermetic Astrology* I, Appendices IV and V, and its moral significance can be seen in connection with the event of the Mystery of Calvary.

Using the analogy of Halley's comet, which returns to orbit around the Sun once every 76 years, the incarnation of the human being upon the Earth can be likened to the return of a comet. But whereas Halley's comet is subject to purely physical laws, and its orbit is orientated around the

Sun, the human being is subject to astrological laws – the "laws" of reincarnation (see *Hermetic Astrology* I, Appendices III and IV) – which relate to the human being's earthly incarnations. (A further difference is that the laws of planetary motion are hard and fast, whereas the "laws" of reincarnation are flexible, adapted according to the human being's requirements in a given incarnation.) The Copernican system applies to the physical aspect of the cosmos, where the movements of the heavenly bodies obey hard and fast laws, whilst the Tychonic system relates to the soul-spiritual reality of the human being's incarnation upon the Earth for the fulfilment of destiny.

Through the Mystery of Calvary Christ became the Lord of Karma, the overseer of human destiny on the Earth. The fundamental pattern underlying the fulfilment of destiny is that of the 7-year periods, the spiral of life. As discussed in Chapter 3, the destiny experienced and lived through in each 7-year period is prepared during the embryonic period in accordance with the Moon's orbits of the zodiac. The position of the Moon in the zodiac at the moment of birth denotes the completion of the weaving of destiny. In this sense the zodiacal position of the Moon at birth shows the orientation of the will that lives in the human being – the will that leads him into incarnation for the fulfilment of his destiny on the Earth. This is the so-called *natural will* belonging to man's lunar nature, residing in the depths of the subconscious.

Mingled with the natural will in subconscious depths is the human being's "astrality", i.e. his negative, unpurified soul nature. The human being's astral body is centered in the Moon (see *Hermetic Astrology* I, Chapter 8). The astral body embodies not only the thought, feeling and will impulses of the soul, but also all the animal-like drives and emotions residing in the human subconscious. These drives and emotions mix in with the human being's natural will, as long as he does not purify and overcome them. They come to expression as "dark currents of the will", and are to be mastered on the spiritual path, i.e. they have to be "paralysed" or rendered ineffective. It is only when the human being has purified and transformed the lower impulses of the astral body that his earthly will (natural will), as it comes to expression in the unfolding of his destiny, can truly reflect his higher will, the will of the higher self, centered in the Sun.

The development of the consciousness self (35–42)

Returning to Figure 5, the wellspring of man's will is to be found in the kernel of the self, centered in the Sun. The self, the solar being of man, works down via the layers of thought and feeling represented in Figure 5 by the orbits of Mercury and Venus around the Sun. Normally the ego, which is bound up with the Earth, is cut off from the self by the astral body, represented in Figure 5 by the Moon's orbit around the Earth. The consequence of the Fall of man was that man began to develop the ego through his series of earthly incarnations and at the same time became subject to the sphere of astrality bounded by the Moon's orbit around the Earth. Man, insofar as he is an ego being incarnated on the Earth, became separated from his higher self, his solar nature, by the enveloping influence of his astral body.

The sacrifice of Christ through the Mystery of Calvary meant that the Spirit of the Sun, embodying the essence of man's solar nature, united with the Earth and with man's destiny on Earth. Through uniting with the Being of Christ and with the Christ Impulse proceeding from the Mystery of Calvary, man can begin to unite inwardly with his solar nature, his higher self. Thereby the chasm separating the higher self from the lower self may be bridged.

In this way the higher self can begin to work on a more conscious level into the enactment of the human being's destiny on Earth, guiding the unfolding of the will through the spiral of life. However, the will, as it initially reveals itself in the fulfilment of destiny (i.e. natural will, before it becomes an expression of the higher self), is bound up with the Moon, in which man's astral body is centered. The human being's "astrality" mingles in with his natural will, so that generally the Moon (i.e. what the Moon represents astrologically in the human being) does not (except in rare cases) reflect the higher will of the self issuing from its center in the Sun. It is only "if the clear light of the spirit is effective in this center, then man's will is free."[9] As long as the "dark currents of the will" mingle in with the human being's natural will, man is not free.

The aim of the Christian-esoteric path of spiritual development is to enable the aspirant to find the moral center in his own being, the kernel of the self, so that the light of the spirit may become effective within him, and at the same time to purify and transform the dark currents of the will residing in subconscious depths, in the astral body. Along this path of development the human being may begin to act "in harmony with the world's spiritual foundation which becomes creative within him."[10] Natural will as it comes to expression in the earthly self of man (belonging to his lunar nature) then harmonizes with the higher will of the self (issuing from his solar nature).

Initially, therefore, the consciousness self of the human being is generally of a lunar nature, but through moral-spiritual development it becomes ever more permeated by solar impulses, to become radiant and sunlike. The deeds of man then take on more and more a moral character as the inner center becomes active. "In this inner center are born human ideals to be fulfilled through human deeds, that is, ideas that do not spring from obscure impulses but from *moral intuitions,* intuitions as transparent as the clearest thought."[11] Instead of acting out of necessity (the sphere of past karma, that of the Moon), the human being begins to act out of freedom (the sphere of future karma, that of the Sun). This is the deep mystery of the consciousness (spiritual) self, the deepest layer of the self, that awakens during the sixth septennary (35–42) of the spiral of life.

As an individual in whom the consciousness self was developed to a high degree, it is illuminating to look at Rudolf Steiner's life in the period from 35 to 42, corresponding to the years 1896 to 1903. Rudolf Steiner himself remarked that he was able to observe the onset of a profound change within him at the age of 35, signifying the birth of the consciousness self:

> *I was thirty-six years of age at the end of my Weimar period. About a year earlier a profound transformation began to take place in my inner life. When I left Weimar (to go to Berlin) this transformation had become a decisive experience. It had nothing to do with the change in my outer circumstances, great though that was. Knowledge and experience of the spiritual world had always been something self-evident to me, whereas to grasp the sense-world through physical perception caused me the greatest difficulty. It was as if my inner soul-experience of sense perceptions did not penetrate sufficiently into the sense-organs to unite fully with what takes place in them. This changed entirely from the beginning of my thirty-sixth year. I became able to observe physical things and events more accurately and completely than before... The more exact and more thorough penetration of sense-observation opened for me the door to an entirely new world. When the sense-world is approached objectively, independent of all subjectivity, it reveals aspects about which spiritual insight can say nothing. This threw light also upon the spiritual sphere. When the true nature of the physical reveals itself purely through sense-observation, then the possibility is also present for cognition to assess the distinct nature of the spiritual, unmingled with any physical impressions.*[12]

From this description, insofar as it is representative for everyone in the sixth septennary of life, it emerges that the awakening of the consciousness self brings with it an enhancement of consciousness – both of the physical and of the spiritual world. In Rudolf Steiner's case – as a highly evolved individual – this enhancement of consciousness was especially marked. In fact, the level of development of the consciousness self is generally not so evolved as in this case. The reason for this is that the consciousness self is something new that is undergoing development in the present historical epoch. In other words, whereas man's feeling and intellectual nature – the sentient self and the intellectual self – are intrinsically part of the human being (having developed already in earlier historical periods), the consciousness self is in the process of development. This process of development has been underway since the beginning of the Piscean cultural epoch, which started in A.D. 1414 (see *Hermetic Astrology* I, Figure 11), and will continue throughout this epoch.

The Renaissance, the Reformation, and the arising of modern science, all of which occurred or began at the start of the Piscean cultural epoch, point to the first emergence of the consciousness self in the history of mankind. At that point in history man began to become conscious of himself in relation to the physical world in a much more intense way. The development of scientific observation and experimentation is symptomatic of this, which has continued unabated right into the present time. However, this development hitherto has been one in which primarly the lunar nature of the consciousness self has come to expression. This side of the consciouness self is reflective, amoral, and readily influenced by the influx of negative astrality.

The deeper solar nature of the consciouness self will emerge in the course of time through taking up the Christ Impulse, which will bring with it an awareness of the spiritual world every bit as intense as the present awareness of the physical world. Just as in the present historical phase of development of the consciousness self the domain of the ego, the Earth, looms large in human consciousness, so in the future course of development of the consciousness self the domain of the self, the Sun, will penetrate ever more into man's inner life. Correspondingly the emphasis will shift from physical, earthly reality to moral-spiritual reality. Cosmologically this will surely signify a wider recognition of the Tychonic system as being valid with respect to moral-spiritual reality, in contrast to the Copernican system, which is appropriate to describe the physical aspect of the solar system.

Hermetic astrology, based on the Tychonic system, represents a step in this direction. It opens up an astrology of the higher self, centered in the Sun, just as traditional astrology has occupied itself more with the lower self, the ego, the domain of which is the Earth. Above all, however, it is by way of the path of moral-spiritual development that the deeper, solar nature of the consciousness self can begin to come to expression. Central to this is the awakening of *conscience*. For in its higher aspect the consciousness self could be called the *conscience self*, the source of moral intuitions. (The connection between conscience and consciousness is exemplified in the French language by the fact that no distinction is drawn between them, i.e. the same word – *conscience* – means both conscience and consciousness.)

Whereas the lunar side of the consciousness self is reflective, amoral and open to the influence of negative astrality, the solar side – the conscience self – is moral and creative (the source of moral intuition), and is able to rise above the sphere of influence of negative astrality. However, it is a matter of a schooling of consciousness in order to arrive at the higher unfolding of the consciousness self, and this schooling is *meditation*. The path of meditation outlined in Rudolf Steiner's work *Knowledge of the Higher Worlds*[13] offers a spiritual training which can bring to expression the kernel of the self, the deeper consciousness self. It constitutes a path of the inner life able to lead man out of his unfree or natural will (lunar nature) to a free and truly moral will (solar nature).

It was at about the age of 35 that Rudolf Steiner discovered the immense significance of meditation:

I came to recognize, through actual experience, the significant part meditation plays in attaining insight into the spiritual world. I had lived a meditative life before this time, but the impulse for doing so had been simply a conceptual recognition of its value for a world-view that acknowledges the spirit. But now a demand for meditation arose within me as an absolute necessity for the soul's existence. The inner life had reached a stage where meditation became a necessity just as at a certain stage in the evolution of an organism, breathing through lungs became a necessity... During such meditation, practised out of inner necessity of spiritual life, one becomes ever more conscious of an "inner spiritual man" who lives, perceives and moves within the spiritual sphere, entirely detached from the physical organism. Through the influence of meditation this self-contained spiritual man entered the field of my experience.[14]

The experience described here is that of the birth of the higher being of man, which took place in Rudolf Steiner's life during the 7-year period from 35 to 42. This 7-year period – the period of the awakening of the consciousness self – can be regarded as a kind of embryonic period leading up to the birth of the "inner spiritual man". The age of 42 – denoting the end of the Sun period and the start of the Mars period in the spiral of life – thus can signify the birth of the spiritual man alongside the physical human being. It can happen, as in Rudolf Steiner's case, that this "second birth" takes place shortly before reaching the age of 42, or it may take place later (for example, Emmanuel Swedenborg's illumination came at the age of 57 – see *Hermetic Astrology* I, Appendix III). Nevertheless, the age of 42 represents an important point of transition in the unfolding of the spiral of life. It is the age at which – following on from the awakening of the consciousness self – the higher being of man (the inner spiritual man) may begin to take an increasing part in the course of the human being's life.

The Mars period (42–49)

In the spiral of life the 7-year period from 42 to 49 is that of Mars, and hence the position of Mars in the horoscope takes on central importance during this life period. In Rudolf Steiner's horoscope the position of Mars

V. The Spiral of Life (21 onwards)

is accentuated both in the hermetic and in the geocentric chart. In the hermetic chart, referring more to the level of consciousness, Mars is located in the middle of Taurus in conjunction with the planet Uranus and it is also square to the planets Saturn and the Sun, the latter two being in opposition to one another. In relation to the hermetic man (see *Hermetic Astrology* I, Figure 13) Mars is connected with the 16-petalled lotus flower (larynx center), the lotus flower of speech. The square relationship of Mars to the opposition of Saturn and the Sun signifies a dynamic interaction between the 16-petalled lotus flower (Mars), the 12-petalled lotus flower (Sun) and the 8-petalled lotus flower (Saturn).

We have already considered the opposition of Saturn and the Sun in relation to the Sun period (21 to 42), pointing out that Saturn (in the middle of Leo) was in the same part of the zodiac as the Sun at Goethe's birth. The first two septennaries of Rudolf Steiner's Sun period were taken up with his work of editing Goethe's scientific writings. But during the third septennary this work came to an end, and at the age of 36 Rudolf Steiner moved from the Goethe-Archives in Weimar to start a completely new way of life in Berlin. Here already Mars – and also Uranus, in conjunction with Mars in the hermetic chart – started to exert an influence, as it were "superseding" the opposition of Saturn and the Sun, which had dominated the first two-thirds of the Sun period. In the last six years of the Sun period, during which time Rudolf Steiner lived in Berlin, the square of Mars and Uranus to the Sun came to the fore, in place of the opposition of Saturn to the Sun, as the main shaping influence in his destiny.

This is evident from a consideration of Rudolf Steiner's new life in Berlin. He would have liked to continue to see the people whom he knew from Weimar, but was prevented from doing so on account of his involvement with a completely new circle of people. It is as if the opposition aspect between the Sun and Saturn ceased to work on in the shaping of his external destiny, becoming superseded by the square aspect between the Sun and Mars-conjunct-Uranus. When an aspect ceases to play a role in the external shaping of destiny, it can nevertheless continue to work on in the inner life. This was certainly the case with Rudolf Steiner: the opposition of the Sun and Saturn, relating to the 8-petalled lotus flower (crown center) and the 12-petalled lotus flower (heart center) came to expression in the tremendous awakening of conscience that took place within him from the time he moved to Berlin – conscience being a matter of the heart and of the spiritual organ of conscience, the 8-petalled lotus flower.

When Rudolf Steiner moved to Berlin, he took on the task of editing the magazine *Review of Literature*. As a result he became associated with the circle of people connected with this magazine, mainly artists and literary types. They claimed his attention completely, which prevented him from seeing his former friends and acquaintances, mainly the people he knew from Weimar. This situation, which caused Rudolf Steiner much pain, he recognized as the working of karma (destiny). Although it would have been perfectly possible for him, in terms of his own inner inclinations, to turn his interest towards both circles of people – the one he knew from Weimar, and the literary circle in Berlin – karma led him out of the one circle into the other. This turn of events, taking place during the last third of the Sun period of his life, is indicated in the hermetic chart by the square aspect between the Sun and Mars, which – as Rudolf Steiner approached the Mars period of life – began to act in the shaping of his destiny, superseding the opposition between the Sun and Saturn.

Whereas the first two-thirds of the Sun period stood under the aspect of "Sun opposite Saturn", the last third was under the aspect of "Sun square Mars" (actually "Sun square Mars-conjunct-Uranus"). The first two thirds were taken up with the more scientifically orientated (saturnine) task of editing Goethe's scientific writings, whilst the last third was a time of activity devoted towards *communication* – an outward-going (martial) activity, i.e. writing and lecturing, to do with the transmission of the word. (Mars is connected with the 16-petalled lotus flower, the larynx center, the organ of the word.)

The fact that Mars was in conjunction with Uranus in the hermetic chart is of significance here, for the majority of people in the literary circle in Berlin with whom he was led into connection through destiny were *avant-garde*, including such visionaries as Paul Scheerbarth, whose writings display an inner cult of the bizarre and fantastic. As discussed in Chapter 8, Uranus, Neptune and Pluto, located beyond the orbit of the planet Saturn (traditionally the outermost planet of our solar system), represent impulses working in from beyond the normal bounds of human faculties. Uranus, as the first planet beyond the orbit of Saturn, is interpreted in astrology as representing a breach with authority (Saturn). The *avant-garde* circle in which Rudolf Steiner found himself was distinctly anti-authoritarian, in contrast to the much respected and culturally honoured circle bound up with the Goethe tradition with which he had been connected in Weimar. The new ring in the spiral of life which opened up with Rudolf Steiner's move from Weimar to Berlin was one which led him out of a time-honoured tradition (Saturn) into an *avant-garde* cult world (Uranus).

This step, however, was only a preliminary one. For as he approached the Mars period – the Sun period nearing its end – Rudolf Steiner's destiny led him into connection with the Theosophical Society. The *avant-garde* literary circle was, in fact, merely a stepping stone to the Theosophical Society, also comprising *"avant-gardists"* – those interested in spiritual ideas, in the spiritual life. This step is indicated by the location of Mars in Rudolf Steiner's hermetic chart, which is in conjunction with Uranus

V. The Spiral of Life (21 onwards)

(both in the middle of Taurus) and the latter, in turn, is in conjunction with Mercury (also in Taurus). The activation of Uranus through Mars signified also a reactivation of Mercury – to become an active agent in his destiny – in the Mars period of Rudolf Steiner's life.

The founding of the German Section of the Theosophical Society, with Rudolf Steiner as general secretary, on October 18, 1902, just four months before his 42nd. birthday, marked the new phase of destiny into which he entered. This new phase stood under the aspect "Mars conjunct Uranus conjunct Mercury" in his hermetic chart, just as the foregoing ring of the spiral of life stood under the aspect "Sun square Mars-conjunct-Uranus". Rudolf Steiner's principal activity continued to be writing and lecturing, but instead of proceeding from and being colored by his personality, from now on he was devoted purely to the transmission of spiritual ideas (the latter signified by the conjunction of Mercury and Uranus). His self, represented by the Sun, went through a development such that he became more and more a herald of the spirit, via the pure transmission of spiritual ideas.

Turning now from the hermetic chart to look at the position of Mars in the geocentric chart, related more to the level of life, Mars was in conjunction with Pluto at Rudolf Steiner's birth. (See Chapter 8 for a discussion of the significance of Pluto.) On the level of life Mars is connected with the gall-bladder, which has much to do with the regulation of the flow of energy within the human being. The conjunction of Mars with Pluto, if mastered by the individual, can signify an extraordinary enhancement of life energy. This appears to be the case in Rudolf Steiner's life from the Mars period onwards. (His manifold accomplishments in different realms – agriculture, medicine, eurythmy, architecture, etc. – entailed a remarkable output of energy, and this activity as a spiritual teacher began with the founding of the German Section of the Theosophical Society just as Rudolf Steiner was approaching the beginning of the Mars period.)

The strong emphasis on the planet Mars – in conjunction with Uranus in the hermetic chart, and in conjunction with Pluto in the geocentric chart – shows the importance of this planet in Rudolf Steiner's destiny. The fact is that during his period of activity in the Theosophical Society (later the Anthroposophical Society) he held over 6000 lectures. (Mars as the planet of the word!) In addition, his activity as a spiritual teacher meant that he conducted a large correspondence and had an enormous number of private conversations with individuals seeking spiritual help and guidance. This activity in the Theosophical Society (later the Anthroposophical Society) can be dated from around the beginning of the Mars period (42–49), corresponding to the years 1903–1910 in his life. The mathematically exact commencement of the Mars period – coinciding with his 42nd. birthday – was on February 25, 1903, but the organic beginning was four months earlier, when Rudolf Steiner became general secretary of the German Section of the Theosophical Society on October 18, 1902. (The organic beginning of a given 7-year period may differ by several months – either way – from the mathematically exact commencement.)

The Mars, Jupiter and Saturn periods

Rudolf Steiner's further destiny can be best understood in connection with the history of the German Section of the Theosophical Society, later the Anthroposophical Society, which became founded when Rudolf Steiner separated from the Theosophical Society. In his case we have a rare and outstanding example of the unfolding of the higher spiritual members latent in man, over and beyond the three aspects of the self (sentient, intellectual and consciousness self). These higher members, which are part of the inner spiritual man, are usually latent, i.e. the human being's development generally does not extend beyond that of the consciousness self (35–42), since the present historical epoch is that of the unfolding of the consciousness self. What takes place after the age of 42 almost invariably depends upon all that the human being has developed up to this time in his life, unless the inner spiritual man begins to come to expression, as in Rudolf Steiner's case.

In his life the "second birth", i.e. the birth of the inner spiritual man, took place shortly before the commencement of the Mars period, and unfolded further during the Mars (42–49), Jupiter (49–56) and Saturn (56–63) periods. Mars, Jupiter and Saturn represent three aspects of the higher being of man, just as there are three aspects – sentient (feeling), intellectual (thought) and consciousness (will) – of the self. These three aspects of the higher being of man arise through the spiritual transformation of the three bodies (physical, etheric and astral) developed during the first three 7-year periods of life (see Table 6). To comprehend this it is helpful to recall the symbiotic relationship between the planets referred to in connection with the planetary rulers of the zodiacal signs (see *Hermetic Astrology* I, Figure 22).

In the astrological doctrine of the planetary rulers of the zodiacal signs a symbiotic relationship between planets ruling opposite zodiacal signs comes to expression. The relationships involved are: Venus – Mars, Mercury – Jupiter, Moon – Saturn. (See *Hermetic Astrology* I, Figure 22, where the relationships between planets ruling opposite signs of the zodiac is given. In addition there is the relationship Sun – Saturn, but this is not of significance as far as the inner connections between the life periods are concerned.)

In view of the symbiotic relationships between the planets, there is an inner connection between the Venus period (14–21) and the Mars period

(42–49), between the Mercury period (7–14) and the Jupiter period (49–56), and between the Moon period (0–7) and the Saturn period (56–63). Applying this to the spiral of life, the Mars period can be regarded as a counterpart to the Venus period – a kind of "second adolescence". The mirror image of the relationship between the two periods is even indicated physiologically in a phenomenon that begins around the age of 14 and ends around the age of 49. This is the phenomenon of menstruation, the onset of which generally occurs at the start of the Venus period and the termination of which (at the menopause) usually takes place towards the end of the Mars period.

However, the Mars period is not simply a second adolescence, for there is a major difference between this period and that of adolescence. The young person experiences the emergence of the astral body in the Venus period (14–21) *without* the presence of the self, which emerges only in the Sun period (21–42). In contrast, the mature person entering the Mars period (42–49) does so equipped with the self, over and beyond the physical, etheric and astral bodies. Through the self, represented by the Sun, the possibility is given of spiritually transforming the various bodies – first the astral body, then the etheric body, and lastly the physical body.

The nature of the Mars period is that the astral body, which first emerged during the Venus period, reasserts itself – but this time in conjunction with the self. And depending upon the extent to which the self is able to spiritually transform the astral body, the Mars period can be a time of heightened spirituality and increased inner activity. On the other hand, the astral body is by nature egotistical, and if little or no spiritual transformation via the self (e.g. through moral development) takes place, the period from 42 to 49 can be a time of intensified egotistical activity accompanied by a corresponding loss of contact with the spiritual world. Already 2500 years ago the Buddha taught the eightfold path for the transformation of the astral body, and this path – for example, as it is practised in hermetic astrology (see *Hermetic Astrology* I, Chapters 7 and 9) – is still relevant now. It constitutes a path of moral development whereby the self is able to work upon the transformation and regeneration of the various centers (lotus flowers) in the astral body.

In Rudolf Steiner's case the conjunction of Mars with Uranus in the hermetic chart (more on the level of consciousness) and that of Mars with Pluto in the geocentric chart (more on the level of life) meant that extremely powerful forces became set in motion in the Mars period of his life. Without having undergone a corresponding transformation of the astral body via the self, these forces would almost certainly have come to expression in a negative way. Instead, however, they emerged as extremely beneficial forces – owing to the path of purification that he had already undergone, a path which led to a deep spiritual experience in the 39th.

year of his life. "This experience culminated in my standing in the spiritual presence of the Mystery of Golgotha in a most profound and solemn festival of knowledge."[15]

Through the experience towards the end of the Sun period of his life, Rudolf Steiner came into a deep inner relationship with the Being of Christ, who henceforth spiritually accompanied him in his life's work. He was able to rise above the egotistical nature of the astral body, becoming inwardly devoted to the Christ Impulse. The cosmic impulses of Uranus and Pluto (referred to above in connection with the Mars period) were able to work in a positive way instead of as forces of hindrance. Thus Uranus (Mars conjunct Uranus) helped Rudolf Steiner forward to new levels of spiritual experience, which he was able to formulate in conceptual terms (Uranus was in conjunction with Mercury in the hermetic chart). On the other hand, Pluto (Mars in conjunction with Pluto in the geocentric chart) opened up new reservoirs of inner creative energy, which he poured into his writing and lecturing activity and into his work as a spiritual teacher.

Rudolf Steiner's development of the spirit self

Rudolf Steiner described three phases of development in the history of the Anthroposophical Society, which he founded at Christmas 1923.[16] (Without going into detail concerning the events which necessitated the breach between Rudolf Steiner and the Theosophical Society, it suffices to say that the German Section of the Theosophical Society formed the nucleus of what later became the Anthroposophical Society.) These three phases equate more or less with three 7-year periods running from October 18, 1902 (the founding of the German Section of the Theosophical Society) to December 25, 1923 (the foundation meeting of the Anthroposophical Society). Just as the human being passes through three 7-year periods of development leading to the birth of the self around the age of 21, it is evident that the Anthroposophical Society also went through three 7-year phases in order to become "born" at the Christmas foundation meeting in 1923.

What is of special interest here in our study of the spiral of life is that the three 7-year phases of development leading up to the birth of the Anthroposophical Society ran more or less parallel with the Mars, Jupiter and Saturn periods in Rudolf Steiner's life. Thus the characteristics of these three phases of development apply also – directly or indirectly – to the Mars, Jupiter and Saturn periods of his life. Summarizing briefly the characteristics of the three periods in question:

(1) 1902–1909: the development of the fundamental teachings of spiritual science in the books *Theosophy, Knowledge of the Higher Worlds* and *Occult Science*, as well as in numerous lectures;

(2) 1909–1916: the cultivation of the arts, especially the development of eurythmy and speech-formation, and the writing of four mystery plays; also the beginning of the building of the Goetheanum as a center for the production and performance of the mystery plays;

(3) 1916–1923: the practical application of spiritual science to the development of new approaches to social-political questions (the so-called "threefold social order"), to religion (the founding of the Christian Community), to therapy (including curative eurythmy and the outline of a medical training in the application of spiritual science to healing), and to education (Waldorf Schools). (Later, in 1924, Rudolf Steiner also developed new approaches – based on spiritual science – to agriculture, known as "bio-dynamic agriculture", and to curative education, such as now exemplified in the Camphill movement.)

These three periods represent three levels of spiritual activity, three phases of unfolding the activity of the inner spiritual man. The first phase, the Mars period, as already described, signifies a new emphasis on the astral body – analogous to that at the time of the emergence of the astral body during adolescence – but this time combined with the activity of the self. In its higher significance this phase could also be described as that of "exploration by the self of the higher planes of existence". It means – potentially – the opening up to higher planes of existence, and a corresponding acquisitation of spiritual wisdom. This is the higher task confronting the human being in the Mars period of life and continuing in the subsequent life periods. This came to expression in a model form in Rudolf Steiner's life, when in phase (1) described above he developed the fundamental teachings of spiritual science, based on his exploration of higher planes of existence.

In order to characterize what is meant here by "exploration by the self of the higher planes of existence" it is necessary first of all to clarify the use of the word *self*. In *Hermetic Astrology* I, Chapter 4, a distinction is drawn between the ego and the self, in the Jungian sense of these words. In this sense the ego is identified with the personality that comes to expression on the Earth, the astrological significator of which is the Ascendant, whilst the self is equated with the higher being of man, the individuality, which is centered in the Sun. (Therefore the astrological significator of the self is the Sun.)

In the sense of occult cosmology, as described earlier in this chapter, the origin of the division of the self into an earthly personality and a cosmic individuality was already implicated by the separation of the Earth from the Sun. But through his sacrifice in coming down from the Sun and uniting with the Earth, Christ has initiated the reintegration of the Earth and the Sun on a spiritual level. It lies within the possibility of each human being to connect himself inwardly with Christ's work of reintegration, which can lead to the establishment of a new relationship between the ego and the self. The stronger this relationship grows, the more the self acts into the ego, and ultimately the ego may become one with and absorbed into the self, i.e. through taking up the Christ Impulse the separation into an earthly and a cosmic self eventually disappears and the ego becomes reintegrated into the self.

At this stage of development, brought about by union with the Christ Impulse, the earthly ego nature of the human being becomes christianized, i.e. "solarized" – to shine like the Sun. This has to be borne in mind when considering the development of an individual such as Rudolf Steiner, who attained an inner connection with the Christ Impulse during the Sun period of his life, which led to the acting in of the solar nature of the self in his life to an unusually high degree. This meant that the solar nature of the self was able to irradiate the astral body to the extent that there arose "an inner spiritual man who lives, perceives and moves within the spiritual sphere, entirely detached from the physical organism."[17] This inner spiritual man – arising from the irradiation and transformation of the astral body by the solar nature of the self – can be called the *spirit self*, over and above the self.

Just as the self begins to come to manifestation (insofar as it comes to manifestation via the ego) during the Sun period (21–42), so there is the possibility – by way of the second birth – of the spirit self beginning to come to expression during the Mars period (42–49), continuing on into the Jupiter period (49–56) and the Saturn period (56–63). The spirit self – the "inner spiritual man who lives, perceives and moves within the spiritual sphere, entirely detached from the physical organism" – is able to explore the higher planes of existence. The spirit self is at home in cosmic realms, just as the human ego is at home on the Earth. Thus the expression "exploration by the self of the higher planes of existence" refers essentially to the spirit self, the self acting via the transformed and purified astral body.

In *Hermetic Astrology* I, Chapter 10, the transformation and purification of the astral body (giving rise to the spirit self) is referred to as the "restoration of the likeness to its divine origin." For the spirit self is none other than the likeness restored to its divine origin, the archetypal form of which is the hermetic man (see *Hermetic Astrology* I, Figure 13). The macrocosmic hermetic man – cosmic man in relation to the seven planetary spheres from the sphere of Saturn down to the sphere of the Moon – reveals the archetypal structure of the spirit self. The self acting through the astral body, when the latter is purified and raised to the level of its cosmic archetype, begins to live into the cosmos. This line of development can be expressed simply as man → hermetic man.

The hermetic man thus portrays the ideal of the stage of evolution going beyond the self, leading to the development of the spirit self. The line of development man → hermetic man is that which widens the human being's experience of himself as an earthly being to embrace an awareness of himself as a cosmic being. Along this line of development the human being begins to "live into" the cosmos. It is the path of experiencing the correspondences between the macrocosm and the microcosm, whereby the hermetic man becomes a reality of inner experience. It then becomes a matter of experience, for example, that speech, which issues from the larynx (16-petalled lotus flower) in the microcosm, proceeds from Mars in the macrocosm. This living into the cosmos is helped by spiritual exercises such as those outlined by Rudolf Steiner in his books *Knowledge of the Higher Worlds* and *Occult Science*.[18]

"Man → hermetic man" is also the deeper meaning of the hermetic chart in hermetic astrology. The hermetic chart reveals the potentiality of the hermetic man in each human being. It points to the line of development leading to the spirit self, over and beyond the self. This line of development, which signifies a living into the cosmos, does not mean losing contact with the Earth. Rather, it opens up the possibility of a new and deeper relationship to the Earth. As exemplified in Rudolf Steiner's life during the Mars period, his exploration of higher planes of existence – his experience of which is described in his works *Theosophy*, *Knowledge of the Higher Worlds* and *Occult Science* – actually brought him into a much more intensive life activity. The conjunction of Mars with Uranus (together with Mercury) in the hermetic chart – all three planets in the sign of Taurus – indicates something of this new life activity, where he became a herald of the spirit, a transmitter of ideas concerning man's relationship to the spiritual world.

The Mars period of life, as the counterpart to the Venus period (14–21), has to do with the renewed activity of the astral body – the difference from adolescence being the presence of the self. What actually emerges during the Mars period in a given person's life depends upon the level of spiritual development, i.e. it depends upon the extent to which the astral body is transformed and purified by the self to give rise to the spirit self. On the highest level, in the case of the full development of the spirit self (as exemplified by Rudolf Steiner), the Mars period is one of living into the cosmos – the blossoming of the hermetic man – and carrying over the cosmic wisdom acquired in this way as spiritual knowledge fruitful for earthly life. At the lowest level it is a time in which the unpurified astral body asserts itself anew – a kind of second adolescence – during which the human being may feel as if he is totally cut off from the spiritual world. Here the spiritual exercises referred to earlier – especially that of the eightfold path – can help to restore an inner connection with the spiritual world, the loss of which often becomes especially apparent during the Mars period of life.

The Jupiter period (49–56)

Just as the Mars period is the counterpart of the Venus period, so the Jupiter period (49–56) is the counterpart of the Mercury period (7–14), in which the etheric body goes through a special development. Again, as with the Venus and Mars periods, the difference between the Mercury and the Jupiter periods is the presence of the self during the latter period. In order to perceive the potential development inherent in the Jupiter period, let us return to a consideration of Rudolf Steiner's life, where the Jupiter period corresponds more or less to phase (2) described above.

During phase (1), coinciding approximately with the Mars period, he explored the higher planes of existence and formulated the fruits of his experiences in terms of spiritual science. Following on from this, in phase (2) – approximately the Jupiter period – he devoted himself increasingly to the cultivation and development of the arts. Here he became more than the spiritual teacher he had been in phase (1). He became a creative artist, creating artisticly out of the spirit. Each year – 1910,1911,1912 and 1913 – he wrote a mystery play, each time produced and performed in August of the same year. These performances took place in Munich, the capital of Bavaria.

Words can hardly begin to describe the immense significance of these mystery plays, which can be likened to dramatic "spiritual happenings". Through the course of the four mystery plays the spiritual development of a group of human beings is followed – including flashbacks into previous incarnations, which illumine the destiny of these people in their present incarnation (set in the twentieth century).

With these plays the need arose for a suitable theatre where they could be performed. This led to the building of the Goetheanum at Dornach, near Basel in Switzerland. The foundation stone of this building was laid on September 20, 1913. Rudolf Steiner designed the Goetheanum as a spiritual work of art, and the whole building (apart from the foundation) was of wood – carved and sculpted, and in places painted with remarkable frescoes. (Unfortunately the building was reduced to ashes in a fire which broke out on New Year's Eve 1922. On the same site there now stands the second Goetheanum, made of concrete.)

Apart from his extraordinary spiritual creations in the realm of drama and architecture, Rudolf Steiner also brought into existence two new art forms: eurythmy and speech-formation. Eurythmy, a new art of movement based on the spiritual qualities inherent in music and language, took its origin in the year 1912 and developed sufficiently to enable a first performance to take place on August 28, 1913. The art of speech-formation was developed by Rudolf Steiner primarily in conjunction with Marie von Sivers (later Marie Steiner), and the greatest impulse towards the development of speech-formation was the mystery plays, in the performance of which Marie Steiner played a leading role.

From this brief outline it is apparent that the Jupiter period in Rudolf Steiner's life was one in which he was active as a spiritually creative artist alongside his work as a spiritual teacher. (He continued to hold lectures throughout this entire period and, in fact, for the rest of his life.) Looking at Jupiter in his horoscope, the most striking aspect is the opposition of Jupiter to Venus in his geocentric chart. This aspect refers more to the level of life, the level of the etheric body, and it is evident that it indicates a remarkable artistic talent (Venus as the "regent of the arts"), which came to full expression in the Jupiter period of his life.

In contrast to spiritual knowledge – acquired through the development of the spirit self, by way of the self acting into and irradiating the astral body – spiritual art, i.e. wisdom-filled artistic creation, is a matter of the self acting transformingly a stage deeper, down into the etheric body. This is the possibility latent in the Jupiter period that became realised in Rudolf Steiner's life, the karmic-astrological indicator of which is the opposition between Jupiter and Venus in the geocentric chart at his birth. Goethe also was born at the time of a geocentric opposition between Jupiter and Venus (see *Hermetic Astrology* I, Chart 12), and he too was gifted with the capacity for spiritual art – wisdom-filled artistic creation – as his drama *Faust* shows. This does not mean that everyone born at the time of an opposition between Jupiter and Venus will have artistic gifts comparable to those of Goethe or Rudolf Steiner, since spiritual art depends upon a working down of the self into the etheric body ("life body"). This denotes a stage of development beyond the spirit self, i.e. beyond the stage at which the self irradiates and transforms the astral body. This higher stage of development is one in which the self – actually the spirit self – is able to work down into the flow of life. Hence the name for this stage of development, when the self works down into the etheric body, thereby being able to shape the flow of life substances, is *life spirit*.[19]

Life spirit is the stage at which the spirit-irradiated self – over and beyond exploration of the higher planes of existence – acquires the capacity to work creatively into the sphere of life. Depending on karmic predisposition, this may come to expression via artistic creation – music, drama, poetry, art, architecture, sculpture, etc. – or it may manifest in a quite different way, for example, as in the lives of certain saints who irradiated life-giving impulses (e.g. St. Elisabeth of Hungary, who founded a hospital in Marburg, Germany, and who accomplished a number of healing miracles there).

At the stage of spirit self the self acts via the purified astral body, whereas at the stage of life spirit it is a matter of activity via the transformed etheric body. This can be grasped by way of considering the art of eurythmy, where the aim is to move the physical body (to the sound of music or poetry) as if it were the etheric body, i.e. in accordance with the laws of movement of the etheric body. This art of movement, which Rudolf Steiner began to develop during the Jupiter period of his life, effectively corresponds to the life spirit stage of evolution – the stage at which the self begins to work shapingly via the etheric body into the flow of life substances.

A study of the unfolding of the spiral of life through 7-year periods, as exemplified in almost model form in Rudolf Steiner's biography, reveals the ever-higher potentialities latent in the human being. After the special phases of development of the three bodies – physical, etheric and astral – in the first three 7-year periods of life, the self comes to birth around the age of 21 and develops through three levels or layers: sentient (feeling), intellectual (thinking) and consciousness (will) in the three 7-year periods up to the age of 42. Over and beyond this, along the moral-spiritual path of development the self is able to take hold of the three bodies, step by step transforming them, to give rise to three levels or layers of the inner spiritual man: *spirit self* (the self acting through the purified astral body), *life spirit* (the self acting into the transformed etheric body) and *spirit man* (the self acting via the spirit-permeated physical body).[20] These three higher levels of development are present – in potentiality – in the Mars, Jupiter and Saturn periods of life.

The Saturn period (56–63)

Turning now to the Saturn period in Rudolf Steiner's life, it is possible to see something of the *spirit man* coming to expression. For in this period of his life, over and above his activity as a spiritual teacher and his ongoing creative activity in the realm of spiritual art, phase (3) described above refers to the spiritual impulses set in motion by Rudolf Steiner on the physical plane of existence, i.e. where the spirit worked right down into the physical world as a destiny-shaping power (spirit man). As with the Mars and Jupiter periods, where it was possible to give only the briefest outline of Rudolf Steiner's accomplishments as a spiritual teacher and in the realm of spiritual art, so also in the Saturn period it is not possible to do justice here to his manifold achievements. The most well-known is the establishment of the Waldorf school in Stuttgart, Germany, which subsequently has served as a model for the numerous Rudolf Steiner schools now spread throughout the world. These schools are truly "model schools", founded upon deep spiritual insight into the needs of the child.

The first Waldorf school proved to be a success, and tens of thousands

V. The Spiral of Life (21 onwards)

of children have since benefitted from the spiritual impulse that was able to bring the idea of such a model school right down to the physical plane of existence, where it has worked in the shaping of destiny of all those human beings who have attended, or who are attending, a Rudolf Steiner school.

Not so successful was the threefold social order movement, a movement that sought – under Rudolf Steiner's guidance – to bring a new social-political order into being, one based on clearly formulated spiritual principles. It was in the wake of World War I that this movement came into being, at which time there was actually a chance – although small – of establishing a new social-political order in Europe. The threefold social order could then have arisen out of the ruins of the past as something completely new in the history of mankind – a social-political order modelled on the trichotomy (spirit, soul, body) of the human being. In the face of intense opposition to it, however, Rudolf Steiner was obliged to disband the movement for a threefold social order which, if it had succeeded, would certainly have brought an incisive change in mankind's political-historical destiny in the twentieth century.

The level of working of spirit man – a level transcending that of spirit self and life spirit – is characterized by the activity of man's higher being right down into the spirit-permeated physical body, acting as a destiny-shaping power on the physical plane. This is the potential inherent in the Saturn period of life (56–63) which – needless to say – rarely comes to manifestation. More often than not, the new awareness of the physical body that arises in this phase of life is accompanied by a feeling of heaviness, i.e. the human being becomes weighed down by the physical body rather than being able to permeate it and elevate it through the power of the spirit.

In Rudolf Steiner's horoscope the planet Saturn is emphasized on account of its opposition to the Sun. (When Saturn is opposite the Sun, it is at its brightest in the night sky, i.e. it is most powerful.) Moreover, Saturn was in the sidereal sign of Leo at Rudolf Steiner's birth. In this sign of the zodiac Saturn endows the human being with the capacity to meet his destiny courageously. For the sign of Leo bestows courage-awakening impulses – impulses that enable the human being to say "yes" to what life brings to him.

Therefore when Saturn is placed in this sign – as Saturn is the planet of karma, in the sense of being the *cosmic memory*, always calling the individual back to his karmic tasks – it endows the human being with special courage in the facing of his destiny. This quality, together with the emphasis on Saturn by virtue of its opposition with the Sun, was indicated in Rudolf Steiner's horoscope. This Saturn aspect was the karmic-astrological indicator of the special destiny that awaited Rudolf Steiner in the Saturn period of his life (considered in relation to the level of his spiritual development).

The Saturn period of life is one in which – depending on the level of spiritual development – *spirit man* may come to expression, albeit only in seed form. This level of development, in which the self takes hold spiritually of the physical body, represents a still higher stage of evolution than life spirit (transformation of the etheric body) and spirit self (purification of the astral body). Just as – potentially – spirit self and life spirit may emerge in seed form in the Mars and Jupiter life periods, respectively, so may spirit man come to manifestation as a seed impulse in the Saturn period of life. Spirit self, life spirit and spirit man should not be identified with Mars, Jupiter and Saturn any more than the self should be identified with the Sun. (Since the self is centered in the Sun, the latter is regarded astrologically as the significator of the self.) However, the working in of each of the planets Mars, Jupiter and Saturn – as the counterparts of Venus, Mercury and the Moon in the first three 7-year life periods – relates to the astral, etheric and physical bodies, respectively, i.e. in passing from the Mars to the Jupiter and then to the Saturn period the emphasis shifts from the astral body to the etheric body and then to the physical body. It is precisely this work of transformation by the self of the three bodies that gives rise to spirit self, life spirit and spirit man. In this sense, therefore, the possibility is presented in the Mars, Jupiter and Saturn periods for these three aspects of the higher being of man to come to expression. Rudolf Steiner's biography is one of the rare examples in which these three higher members – spirit self, life spirit and spirit man – are revealed to a greater or lesser extent in the corresponding life periods.

Summary of the spiral of life

The brief outline of Rudolf Steiner's destiny presented in this chapter and in the last chapter, as it unfolded through the 7-year life periods, shows that the spiral of life can be studied in relation to the planetary positions and aspects in the birth horoscope, where the hermetic chart relates more to the level of consciousness and the geocentric chart to the level of life. At the very least an overview of the unfolding of the spiral of life is revealed through the study of the birth horoscope in this way. Of course, in order to penetrate to a deeper understanding of the unfolding of destiny through 7-year periods, it is necessary to look at the whole embryonic period, at the planetary movements through the sequence of lunar orbits of the sidereal zodiac between conception and birth. But in the sense that the birth configuration is the aim, the goal, of the incarnating human being, whereby this configuration comprises a summary of the planetary movements throughout the embryonic period, the birth horoscope offers an abbreviated summary of the spiral of life. This is of fundamental importance in the hermetic-astrological science of destiny outlined in this book – the science of destiny known as *astrological biography*. For in astrological biography it is not always possible to undertake a detailed investigation of an individual's destiny by looking at the entire embryonic period (e.g. if only the date of birth of a historical personality is known, it is not possible to compute his conception horoscope). In such cases at least an overview of the spiral of life is provided by the analysis of the birth horoscope (similar to the analysis made here with respect to Rudolf Steiner's biography, looking at the 7-year periods in relation to the corresponding planets in his birth horoscope).

Even knowing nothing whatsoever about the casting of horoscopes, a fundamental knowledge of human destiny is conveyed by the spiral of life. For example, a knowledge of the deep change that the individual goes through around the age of 42 – in passing from the Sun period to the Mars period – can be useful in helping to gain an understanding of the inner and outer difficulties that may arise at this point in life. Moreover, the spiral of life indicates the true *plan of life*, and knowledge of this plan can help every human being, regardless of whether he is interested in astrology or not.

For those who are versed in astrology, the spiral of life presents a remarkable key to human biography and to an understanding of its connection with cosmic reality. Thus knowledge of the spiral of life comprises an essential element in astrological biography, providing the foundation for a deeper comprehension of the human being's connection with the cosmos.

In astrological biography other planetary periods are also significant, e.g. the 29½-year Saturn period (see *Hermetic Astrology* I, Chapter 5), but the 7-year period is the most significant rhythm, as it forms the basis for the weaving of destiny into the etheric body during the embryonic period. The destiny woven during the embryonic period then unfolds through the sequence of 7-year periods between birth and death, ascending from one planet to the next in the sequence: Moon, Mercury, Venus, Sun, Mars, Jupiter and Saturn. (As referred to in the last chapter, this sequence applies to the geocentric chart, in ascending the *tree of life*. However, when considering the hermetic chart, where it is a matter of the ascent of the *tree of consciousness*, i.e. the ascent of consciousness via the lotus flowers, Mercury and Venus are reversed, yielding the order: Moon, Venus, Mercury, Sun, Mars, Jupiter and Saturn.)

The zodiacal period (63 onwards)

There still remains the question: What transpires in the spiral of life after the age of 63, following on from the end of the Saturn period? Here the application of the hermetic principle of analogy can help to answer this question. For there is a direct analogy between the unfolding of the spiral of life and the passage of the human being through the planetary spheres in the life after death. The hermetic teaching concerning this journey through the planetary spheres is referred to in the *Corpus Hermeticum*:

At the dissolution of your material body, you yield up the body itself to be changed, and the visible form you bore is no longer seen... And thereupon the man mounts upward through the structure of the heavens. And to the first zone of heaven he gives up the force which works increase and that which works decrease; to the second zone, the machinations of evil cunning; to the third zone, the lust whereby men are deceived; to the fourth zone, domineering arrogance; to the fifth zone, unholy daring and rash audacity; to the sixth zone, evil strivings after wealth; and to the seventh zone, the falsehood which lies in wait to work harm. And thereupon, having been stripped of all that was wrought upon him by the structure of the heavens, he ascends to the substance of the eighth sphere, being now possessed of his own proper power.[21]

According to the hermetic principle – "as above, so below" – there is an exact analogy between the human being's journey through the spiral of life ("below") and the voyage of the soul through the planetary spheres in the life after death ("above"). The hermetic text quoted here refers to the voyage of the soul through the seven planetary spheres. Although the spheres are not named explicitly, it is easy to recognize from the brief description of the negative characteristics yielded up by the human being in each sphere, that the order of the planetary spheres is the classic Babylonian (Ptolemaic) order: Moon ("increase and decrease"), Mercury ("evil cunning"), Venus ("lust"), Sun ("domineering arrogance"), Mars ("rash audacity"), Jupiter ("strivings after wealth"), Saturn ("falsehood"). This sequence of the planetary spheres ("above") is mirrored in the passage of the spiral of life ("below"). The hermetic text then goes on to describe how the human being "having been stripped of all that was wrought upon him by the structure of the heavens... ascends to the substance of the eighth sphere". Having yielded up the negative characteristics bestowed upon him by the seven zones of heaven (planetary spheres), he enters into the eighth sphere – the zodiacal sphere of fixed stars.

Analogously, in the passage through the spiral of life, having passed through seven planetary periods (Moon, Mercury, Venus, Sun, Mars, Jupiter, Saturn) from birth up to the age of 63, the human being then enters the eighth period, the period of the zodiacal sphere of fixed stars. He then enters into the life period corresponding to the zodiac, which circumscribes the planetary spheres, i.e. the *zodiacal period* of life begins (63 onwards). This period is a time of freedom, in the sense that the zodiacal sphere is a realm of freedom lying beyond the planetary spheres (the latter being the spheres into which man's destiny is inscribed). What does this signify?

V. The Spiral of Life (21 onwards)

A conception of the significance of the zodiacal period (63 onwards) in the spiral of life can be gained by way of analogy with the human being's life after death. As indicated in the hermetic text quoted above, when man ascends to the eighth sphere he enters into "his own proper power". At the moment of death the most external element with which the human being is clothed, the physical body, is laid aside on the Earth, and in ascending through the seven planetary spheres further aspects of the human being's "clothing" are laid aside in each successive sphere until, upon entering the zodiacal sphere, man is reduced to his essential being ("stripped of all that was wrought upon him"). He is then free – a pure spirit – unencumbered by all that which was "wrought upon him" when entering into incarnation upon the Earth.

In the sphere of the zodiac, the eighth sphere, man becomes a pure spirit. In this sphere, closest to the Realm of the Father, man is reduced to his essential self; he is absolutely free and unencumbered. But how does the human being exercise his freedom? He surveys his previous incarnations; he beholds also the ongoing evolution of mankind upon the Earth; and he makes the decision – in complete freedom – to incarnate upon the Earth again. He decides to make amends for his mistakes from earlier incarnations (past karma), and to help the Earth and mankind forward on the path of spiritual evolution (future karma). The decision to reincarnate is how man exercises his freedom in the sphere of the zodiac.

The first step is then the choice of a suitable planetary configuration for the next incarnation, one in harmony with the individual's past karma and also in line with his future karma. (See *Hermetic Astrology* I, Chapter 6, for a discussion as to how past karma is indicated more by the geocentric configuration according the Ptolemaic system, and future karma more by the hermetic configuration according to the Tychonic system.) Fundamental to the planetary configuration chosen for the new incarnation is the Ascendant, which brings to expression the human being's orientation within the zodiacal sphere. This orientation acts as a guideline throughout the whole descent into incarnation, aligning with the Moon-Earth zodiacal axis at the moment of conception and with the Ascendant-Descendant axis of the moment of birth – as is brought to expression by the hermetic rule (see *Hermetic Astrology* I, Appendix I).

Whilst indwelling the zodiacal sphere man begins to draw together the forces from the various signs of the sidereal zodiac needed for the building up of the physical body in the next incarnation. Here the Ascendant zodiacal constellation (i.e. the fixed-star sign chosen as the Ascendant in the oncoming incarnation) acts as a kind of focal point in this activity of drawing together the zodiacal forces for the physical body. By analogy, when the human being enters into the zodiacal period of life, although the entire zodiac of twelve signs becomes meaningful to him, the Ascendant sign acquires special significance as a sign of orientation within the circle of twelve. (The Midheaven sign is also of importance – see below.)

The activity of the human being in drawing together the forces of the physical body from the various signs of the zodiac whilst indwelling the zodiacal sphere is inspired by what is known in esotericism as the *temple*. The temple is an image of the perfect human being of the future. In beholding this exalted ideal such a majestic impression is created that it awakens the impulse to reincarnate upon the Earth in order to work towards its realisation. Something of the impulse evoked by beholding the temple lives as a primal motivation within every human being, underlying his will to incarnate upon the Earth. It comes to manifestation, also, in the great works of architecture – from the temples of antiquity to the magnificent churches of more recent times. All truly great works of architecture are inspired by the image of the temple.

The zodiacal period in Rudolf Steiner's life

The ideal of the temple provides us with a key towards understanding the zodiacal period in Rudolf Steiner's life. During the Saturn period (56–63) he suffered a devastating blow of destiny when the Goetheanum was destroyed by fire, which broke out on New Year's Eve 1922, as Rudolf Steiner was approaching the age of 62. For the Goetheanum was truly an artistic architectural creation, a labour of love created by him and erected during a period of some eight or nine years with the assistance of hundreds of selflessly devoted helpers. Just one year after the destruction of the Goetheanum – as he was nearing the age of 63, at the end of the Saturn period – he found the answer to the "lost temple" (referring here to the Goetheanum that was destroyed by fire).

The answer that Rudolf Steiner brought came at the beginning of the zodiacal period in his life, just two months prior to his 63rd. birthday. (The beginning and end of each 7-year period can be thought of as approximately coinciding with the relevant birthdays, but some leeway – a few months either way – has to be allowed.) Rudolf Steiner's answer was in the form of a deed – a completely free deed – corresponding to the nature of the free spirit in the zodiacal sphere in the life after death. Just as in the zodiacal sphere the human being – inspired by the image of the temple – makes a free decision to reincarnate upon the Earth to work upon the building of the temple, so Rudolf Steiner entered the zodiacal period of life with a free deed to "incarnate" anew and rebuild the lost temple of the Goetheanum. His free deed of "reincarnation" was the founding of the Anthroposophical Society – on Christmas Day 1923 – of which he became president. And his rebuilding of the lost temple was not simply to redesign the Goetheanum, but also to outline a *School of Spiritual Science* with the new (to be rebuilt) Goetheanum as its center.

The "temple" that Rudolf Steiner set about building in the zodiacal period of life he conceived of as a *mystery school* – the first to be founded since the mystery centers of antiquity disappeared. This mystery school – the School of Spiritual Science, with its center at the Goetheanum – he envisaged as being open to all those seeking initiation, the only condition to entry being two years' membership of the Anthroposophical Society (implying a thorough acquaintance with spiritual science and a positive attitude towards the School of Spiritual Science). He outlined three grades or classes of initiation in this mystery school, but was able to found only one class before illness and ensuing death interrupted his work on this "temple". (He became seriously ill just nine months after the Christmas foundation meeting, and he died after a further six months of illness.)

In the short space of nine months' activity in establishing this "temple" Rudolf Steiner accomplished an almost superhuman amount of work. This short-lived zodiacal period represented the crowning of his life's labours. It was as if all twelve signs of the zodiac poured their forces of cooperation into his creation of the School of Spiritual Science. But it was above all the signs of Leo and Libra – the Midheaven and Ascendant in his birth horoscope – which came to the fore in this zodiacal period. Leo poured forth courage and boundless enthusiasm for the great task which he undertook. And Libra bestowed its balance and harmony upon him throughout the execution of the manifold tasks that had to be accomplished in connection with the establishing of the School of Spiritual Science.

The significance of the Ascendant and Midheaven

In every individual the Ascendant plays a key role, as the significator on the one hand of the physical body and on the other hand of the ego, the earthly personality of the individual. It brings to expression the way in which the human being orientates himself in the physical world, but – as described in *Hermetic Astrology* I, Chapter 10 – the Ascendant also indicates the orientation taken up by the human being in the zodiacal sphere prior to incarnation. The Ascendant therefore reflects something of this higher aspect of the human being – the *image,* the archetype of which is the *zodiacal man* (see *Hermetic Astrology* I, Figure 23 and Table 16). The Ascendant indicates the "axis of contemplation" of the zodiacal man, the orientation of the image in beholding cosmic reality.

In the case of the image becoming active, a second axis of the zodiacal man – the "axis of initiative" – arises over and above the axis of contemplation. The axis of initiative is indicated in the individual's birth horoscope by the Midheaven. The Midheaven is the highest point in the zodiac above the horizon at the birth of the individual. Similarly, the opposite point – the Nadir – is the lowest point in the zodiac beneath the horizon at the moment of birth. The axis running from the Nadir to the Midheaven (below → above) is the axis of initiative, which generally is more or less perpendicular to the horizontal axis of contemplation running from the Descendant to the Ascendant (see Figure 6).

Figure 6:
The two axes of the zodiacal man

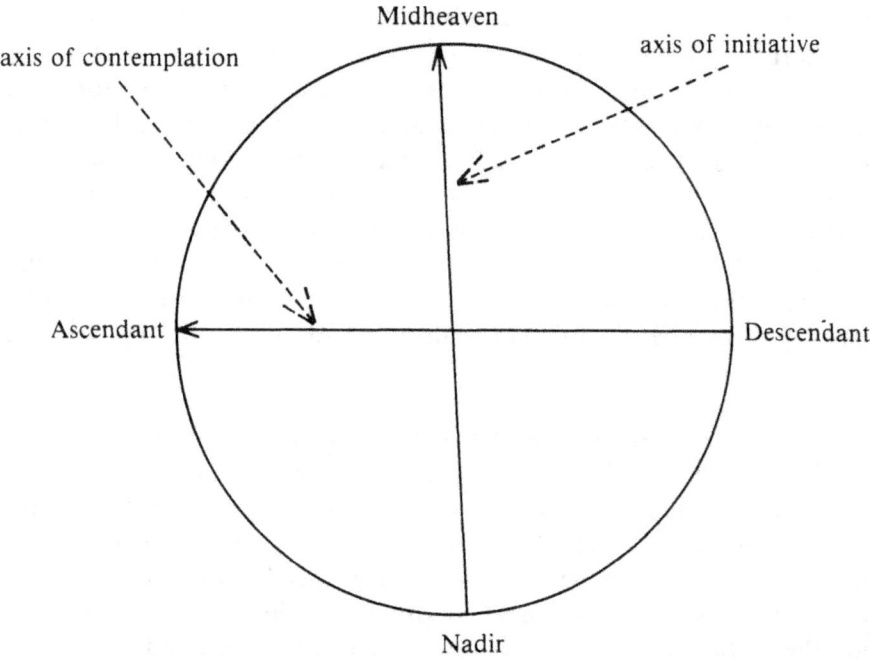

The image is essentially contemplative, until the human being attains the stage of *divine evolution*, at which he begins – like the Father-Creator – to become creative himself. Man as a divine being is then capable of independent creative activity out of his own spiritual initiative. The line of development indicated here is: man → spiritual man → divine man, i.e. (expressed archetypally) man → hermetic man → zodiacal man. In terms of the 7-year periods, the zodiacal man (the archetype of the divine man, the image) may begin to come to expression during the zodiacal period of life. This is analogous, but on a higher level, to the possibility that the hermetic man (the archetype of the inner spiritual man, the likeness) undergoes a development in the Mars, Jupiter and Saturn periods. In turn, this is analogous to the development of the human being as a self during the Sun period of life.

This level of divine evolution, signifying the emergence of the zodiacal man, lies in the far-distant future. But in the case of an evolved individual such as Rudolf Steiner, the zodiacal man may come to expression in seed form already during the zodiacal period in the spiral of life. This stage of development, lying beyond that of the hermetic man, is that at which the human being takes on attributes of the Father-Creator. Man then creates – out of his participation in free-flowing cosmic existence beyond the planetary spheres – as a creator on Earth. He is no longer simply contemplative, but becomes creative – a creator on Earth whose consciousness reaches up towards heaven. Thus over and above the axis of contemplation (the astrological significator of which is the Ascendant), the axis of initiative (signified by the Midheaven) also acquires new significance. This axis passes in the vertical plane up through the Earth, reaching up towards heaven (see Figure 6).

What is described here (concerning the Ascendant and Midheaven axes, with respect to the zodiacal man) comes to expression in the human being already long before the zodiacal period of life begins, but it does so in a much weaker and less far-reaching form. From the moment of birth onwards the human being is a perceiving being, i.e. he looks out into the world. In the sense that the Ascendant specifies the axis of contemplation, the direction of beholding the world, the Ascendant plays a role in the human being's relationship to the Earth right from the moment of birth. Thus it relates to man's earthly personality, his ego. (This is in accordance with the traditional astrological meaning of the Ascendant – considered as the ruler of the first house, the house of the personality.)

Further, from around the age of 21 onwards, with the emergence of the self, the human being becomes increasingly capable of self-initiative, i.e. initiative born out of his self, and not instilled into him from without by others. This usually manifests in the drive towards establishing a position for himself in the world. Here, then, the axis of initiative – signified by the Midheaven – becomes of significance over and beyond the axis of contemplation (perception) indicated by the Ascendant. (This is in accordance with the traditional astrological view of the Midheaven as the ruler of the tenth house, the house of profession or position in the outer world.)

However, what is meant by *initiative* in the sense of the zodiacal man has little to do with the conventional meaning of this word, which is usually connected with ambition. In other words, the higher significance of the axis of initiative indicated by the Midheaven – considered from the standpoint of the zodiacal man – is the realisation of God's will on Earth. "Not my will, but thy will be done" is the keynote of the zodiacal man in taking initiative. The significance of the Midheaven for the zodiacal man is that it is an axis connecting heaven and Earth, whereby the connection is made through initiative taken freely but in accordance with the Being of God the Father. The initiatives taken are free, and they are creative deeds for the good of the Earth and mankind; they are deeds of sacrifice. It is in this light that we may see Rudolf Steiner's foundation of the Anthroposophical Society and the School of Spiritual Science as he was entering the zodiacal period of his life.

The line of development: man → hermetic man → zodiacal man is the path of *restoring the likeness to its divine origin* (hermetic man) and then of attaining to the *realisation of the archetypal image nature (zodiacal man)*. (See *Hermetic Astrology* I, Chapter 10, for a discussion of this, where also the Church teaching concerning the image and the likeness is referred to, namely that although the likeness fell, the archetypal image nature remained intact.)

Potentially the unfolding of the spiral of life – as revealed in Rudolf Steiner's life – can lead along the path from man to hermetic man to zodiacal man. This path summarizes the ideal of human evolution, for it brings to expression that man is made in the image and likeness of God and that the spiritual capacities of the likeness and the divine power of the image are latent in every human being.

Rudolf Steiner's destiny offers a striking example of the latent potentials of the image (zodiacal man) and the likeness (hermetic man), and of what may be accomplished when a human being restores his likeness to its divine origin and unites with his archetypal image nature, allowing it and the restored likeness to come to expression. A study of Rudolf Steiner's destiny through 7-year periods shows that over and above the development as "man" up to the age of 42, an unfolding of the spiritual capacities of the likeness (archetypally the hermetic man) can take place in the Mars, Jupiter and Saturn periods of life, and that this may be followed by the acting in of the divine power of the image (archetypally the zodiacal man) during the zodiacal period.

The spiral of life reveals the sublime plan of life, which can be deciphered in remarkable detail from the birth horoscope, as this hermetic-astrological study of the course of Rudolf Steiner's life shows. The study undertaken here (in this chapter and in the last chapter) could not be more than an outline – one dedicated respectfully to Rudolf Steiner, above all for his new revelation in the twentieth century of the spiral of life, which serves as a basis for a new science of the stars, a new science of destiny, known as *astrological biography*.

Chapter 5: Notes and references

1. *Goethes Naturwissenschaftliche Schriften* (5 vols; ed. R. Steiner, Rudolf Steiner Verlag, Dornach 1975), vol. 1, p. lxxiii.
2. Rudolf Steiner, *An Autobiography* (trsl. R. Stebbing, Rudolf Steiner Publications, New York, 1977), p. 158.
3. Ibid., p. 137.
4. Published in English translation in Rudolf Steiner, *Philosophy of Spiritual Activity* (Rudolf Steiner Publications, New York, 1963).
5. Ibid.
6. Cf. Rudolf Steiner, *The Gospel of St. Luke* (trsl. G. Metaxa, Rudolf Steiner Publishing Co., London, 1935), pp. 135–137.
7. Rudolf Steiner, *An Autobiography*, op. cit., p. 129.
8. Rudolf Steiner, *Spiritual Hierarchies and their Reflection in the Physical World* (Rudolf Steiner Press, London, 1980) describes the occult cosmology.
9. Rudolf Steiner, *An Autobiography*, op. cit., p. 129.
10. Ibid.
11. Ibid.
12. Ibid., pp. 276–277.
13. Rudolf Steiner, *Knowledge of the Higher Worlds* (Rudolf Steiner Press, London, 1977).
14. Rudolf Steiner, *An Autobiography*, op. cit., pp. 282–284.
15. Ibid., p. 319.
16. Rudolf Steiner, *Awakening to Community* (trsl. M. Spock, Anthroposophic Press, Spring Valley NY, 1974), pp. 46 ff.
17. Rudolf Steiner, *An Autobiography*, op. cit., p. 284.
18. Rudolf Steiner, *Knowledge of the Higher Worlds* (London, 1977) and *Occult Science* (London, 1972).
19. Cf. Rudolf Steiner, *Theosophy* (trsl. M. Cotterell and A.P. Shepherd, Rudolf Steiner Press, London, 1970), pp. 71–79 for a description of spirit self, life spirit and spirit man.
20. Ibid.
21. *Corpus Hermeticum* I, 24–26a (trsl. W. Scott, *Hermetica*, Oxford, 1924; repr. Boulder, 1982, pp. 127–129).

Chapter 6

The Hermetic-Astrological Science of Destiny

The human being's development through the spiral of life

The spiral of life forms the basis in hermetic astrology for a new science of destiny in which the horoscope of birth is viewed as expressing an extract summarizing the destiny formed during the embryonic period of development. The law underlying the formation of destiny during the embryonic period, specified by the Moon's orbits of the sidereal zodiac, comes to manifestation in the spiral of life as the rhythm of 7-year periods. In the spiral of life each 7-year period is "ruled" by a planet, and the given planet's position in the birth horoscope indicates something of the nature of life (geocentric chart) and consciousness (hermetic chart) in the relevant period of the individual's life. Thus the birth horoscope (hermetic and geocentric charts) – representing the goal of the individual's descent into incarnation and embodying a condensed summary of the planetary movements between conception and birth – can be read in relation to the unfolding of the spiral of life.

But what is the basis of the planetary sequence of 7-year periods underlying the spiral of life?

The key to this planetary sequence is the hermetic correspondence between the passage of earthly life and the journey of the soul in the life after death. There is an analogy between the course of life on Earth ("below") and the afterlife of the soul in the planetary spheres ("above"). The soul at death departs from the body – and therewith from the Earth – and begins an existence in realms beyond the Earth, in the so-called "planetary spheres". The soul's ascent through the planetary spheres was known of in earlier times, and is described in poetic form by Dante in his work *The Divine Comedy*. There Dante describes the human being's ascent through the spheres: Moon, Mercury, Venus, Sun, Mars, Jupiter, Saturn, to the zodiacal realm of fixed stars. It is exactly this journey of the soul through the planetary spheres to the zodiacal sphere which is mirrored in the spiral of life. When looked at in relation to the birth horoscope, something of the human being's potential development through the sequence of 7-year periods of the spiral of life can be read, as indicated in the last two chapters in the example of Rudolf Steiner's destiny.

The birth horoscope holds the key to the potential development of the human being during the course of life – on the level of life (geocentric chart) and on the level of consciousness (hermetic chart). At the same time

VI. The Hermetic—Astrological Science of Destiny

this development through the spiral of life corresponds to the journey of the soul in the life after death – ascending through the planetary spheres to the zodiacal sphere of fixed stars, the realm closest to the Father (Creator). In this respect the unfolding of the spiral of life can be thought of as a journey through life leading step by step towards the Divine Father. Just as the embryonic period between conception and birth comprises a preview of the journey through life, so the course of life from birth to death constitutes a preview of the soul's journey through the planetary spheres in the life after death. Thus there is a correspondence on the one hand between the embryonic period and the course of life, and on the other hand between the course of life and the journey of the soul in the after-life. The latter correspondence means that the soul's journey through the planetary spheres is mirrored in the human being's journey through life, through the sequence of planetary periods between birth and death. (In fact the journey of the soul through the planetary spheres in the life after death entails a review of the life between birth and death.) And just as in the life after death the soul enters the zodiacal sphere after traversing the planetary spheres, so in the unfolding of the spiral of life the human being enters the zodiacal period (63 onwards) after living through the planetary periods, the last planetary period being that of Saturn (56–63).

In Chapter 5 the archetypal line of development through the spiral of life is summarized as: man → hermetic man → zodiacal man. The unfolding of the first stage – that of "man" – is revealed essentially in the first six 7-year periods of life (up to the age of 42). "Man" comprises the self and three vehicles of expression related to the three spheres: destiny, life and consciousness. These three vehicles – the physical, etheric and astral bodies – undergo their special development (i.e. the development of each is emphasized in turn) in the first three 7-year periods: physical body (0–7), etheric body (7–14), astral body (14–21). Then the self emerges and develops through the next three 7-year periods, unfolding first the sentient self (21–28), then the intellectual self (28–35), and lastly the consciousness self (35–42).

In the next phase – beyond "man" – it is a matter of the inherent potential of the hermetic man unfolding in the Mars (42–49), Jupiter (49–56) and Saturn (56–63) periods of the spiral of life. During these three periods there arises the possibility – depending on the level of spiritual development, and also upon grace – of the likeness or inner spiritual man (archetypally the hermetic man) coming to expression. The three stages of development here relate to the three spheres: consciousness, life and destiny – the consciousness aspect of the spiritual man (spirit self) unfolding in the Mars period, the life aspect (life spirit) in the Jupiter period, and the destiny aspect (spirit man) in the Saturn period.

After the Saturn period comes the zodiacal period (from the age of 63 onwards), where the human being enters into a free-moving cosmic existence – beyond the level of the planetary spheres as these are mirrored in the spiral of life. He enters the sphere of the zodiac as this is mirrored in the spiral of life – the sphere of the archetypal divine image. Thus, following on from the revelation of the likeness during the Mars, Jupiter and Saturn periods, there comes the period of realisation of the divine image, if – through moral development – the human being is able to attain to the level of being at which the image can begin to manifest itself actively. In this event – over and above restoring the likeness to its divine nature – man becomes a co-creator (with the Divine) on Earth, creating "in the image of God". At this highest level of realisation of the potential inherent in the spiral of life, the human being fulfils the word of God: "Let us make man in our image, after our likeness" (*Genesis* i, 26), in that both man's likeness to the Divine and his divine image unfold their latent capacities.

To create "in the image of God", i.e. where man's archetypal divine image comes to expression, is to work at the building of the temple, which is an image of the perfect human being of the future. It is reported that Jesus said: "I am able to destroy the temple of God, and to build it in three days" (*Matthew* xxvi, 61). Here Jesus was referring to his body, his resurrection body, which is the temple. When the divine image (archetypally the zodiacal man) unfolds to the full its latent capacity, the power of all twelve signs of the zodiac become active in the body (Aries in the head, Taurus in the larynx, Gemini in the shoulders and arms, Cancer in the breast region, etc.). This was the case with the resurrection body of Jesus Christ. After the Resurrection he was present and active in the Earth's aura for forty days in his resurrection body, and then came the Ascension, when he ascended to the Father. In these forty days the temple – the resurrection body – was made manifest in the aura of the Earth, but with the Ascension it ascended to the zodiacal sphere, the realm in which the human being approaches closest to the Father in the life after death.

The path of development: man → hermetic man → zodiacal man is the path towards the building up of the resurrection body, when man will become zodiacal man. Then he will overcome death. Instead of dying there will be only "ascension" – ascension towards heaven, towards the Father. The zodiacal period of life therefore embodies the ideal of the realisation of the temple, the building up of the resurrection body, and the consequent overcoming of death.

This ideal cannot be realised in one incarnation, but is something to be worked towards through the sequence of incarnations on the Earth. Therefore reincarnation is not something to be avoided, as it provides the opportunity for work on the "building of the temple". The building of the resurrection body is the ideal to be worked towards, and reincarnation is the means towards this end. Seen in this light, reincarnation is not an

VI. The Hermetic—Astrological Science of Destiny

ideal. Rather, it is a path towards the attainment of the ideal of resurrection.

An example of a stroke of destiny

Knowledge of the ideal of resurrection can be a source of inspiration, especially in the case of problems relating to the physical body. In a therapeutic sense it is the power of the signs of the zodiac – as revealed in the resurrection body of Jesus Christ – which have to be called upon in the case of problems afflicting the physical body. As an example of the kind of problem afflicting the physical body which can arise as a stroke of destiny, consider the following example drawn from the author's practice as a curative eurythmist (movement therapist).

A patient came to the author for treatment of a paralysis of the right side of the body resulting from a stroke. The stroke occurred in the Mars period of his life, at the age of 46 years and 5 months. It left the patient unable to speak anything but "yes" and "no", and the entire right side of his body became more or less rigid. He could do nothing with his right hand, and could walk – or rather limp – only slowly with the help of a stick. Chart 10 shows the birth configuration of the patient. Using the hermetic rule the conception configuration was also found (see Chart 11).

Having drawn the birth and conception charts of the patient, the next step is to undertake research into the cosmic background of the stroke, as indicated by the planetary movements during the embryonic period. As the stroke occurred in the Mars period, the seventh 7-year period in the spiral of life, this means looking at the seventh lunar orbit during the embryonic period. Transforming from earthly time to "embryonic time", the age of 46 years and 5 months lies over halfway through the Mars period (42–49), and therefore during the corresponding (i.e. seventh) lunar cycle the Moon had traversed over half its orbit around the zodiac. Since the Mars period commences at the age of 42, the age of 46 years and 5 months means that 4 years and 5 months had elapsed within this period.

4 years and 5 months = 0.6309523 of a 7-year period,
and 0.6309523 of a lunar orbit = 227 degrees
(since 0.6309523 x 360 = 227).

Thus the Moon had passed 227 degrees around the zodiac in its seventh lunar sidereal cycle during the embryonic period. Since the Moon's longitude in the sidereal zodiac at the moment of conception was 23° Gemini (see Chart 11), then – adding 227 degrees to 23° Gemini – the Moon's longitude at the moment in the embryonic period corresponding to the stroke was 10° Aquarius. Looking at an ephemeris, the Moon's sidereal longitude was 10° Aquarius (during the seventh lunar cycle of the embryonic period) at ca. 6.30 a.m. GMT on June 11, 1936. The planetary configuration for this moment of time is shown in Chart 12. It indicates an exact conjunction of the Sun and Mars at 26° Taurus! Moreover, the conjunction of the Sun and Mars is in opposition to the planet Jupiter, which in turn was exactly conjunct the sidereal longitude of the Sun at the moment of conception (26° Scorpio). In addition the Moon was in conjunction with the sidereal longitude of Saturn at the moment of conception (10° Aquarius).

All in all, a most striking cosmic background is indicated by the planetary configuration at the moment in the embryonic period corresponding to the stroke. This planetary configuration bears a relationship primarily to the conception configuration rather than to the birth configuration. As discussed in *Hermetic Astrology* I, Chapter 10, the conception configuration embodies more the image of the human being, whereas the birth configuration relates more to the likeness. For it is the image which forms the archetype of the physical body in the zodiacal sphere, and which works upon the building up of the physical body from the moment of conception. The conception configuration thus refers primarily to the image, to the cosmic archetype of the physical body.

In the case of the patient under consideration, the conjunction of the Sun and Mars (at the same time both planets in opposition to Jupiter), which took place during the embryonic period, was related to the conception configuration (in particular to the position of the Sun in the conception configuration). The relationship was such that Jupiter was in conjunction with the Sun's sidereal position in the conception configuration and correspondingly Mars and the Sun were in opposition. At the same time the Moon was in conjunction with Saturn's sidereal position in the conception configuration (see Figure 7).

As a picture (see Figure 7), the configuration during the embryonic period relating to the stroke shows a "striking in" of cosmic forces with respect to the conception configuration. It presents a picture of an incisive event of destiny taking its effect in relation to the physical body. But could it have been foreseen that this would signify a stroke, which would paralyse the entire right-hand side of the body?

As indicated in Figure 1, the weaving of destiny during the embryonic period not only reflects the planetary movements but also reviews, i.e. looks back to, the experiences of destiny between birth and death in the previous incarnations, particularly in the immediately preceding incarnation. The destiny lived through in the former incarnation forms the foundation for the weaving of destiny during the embryonic period in the present incarnation. It is only by looking back into the former incarnation (in this case the previous incarnation of the patient) that the deeper significance of a particular planetary configuration during the embryonic period

VI. The Hermetic—Astrological Science of Destiny

**Chart 10:
*Stroke patient**

Stroke patient *0.30 a.m. MET on September 10, 1936 at Stuttgart

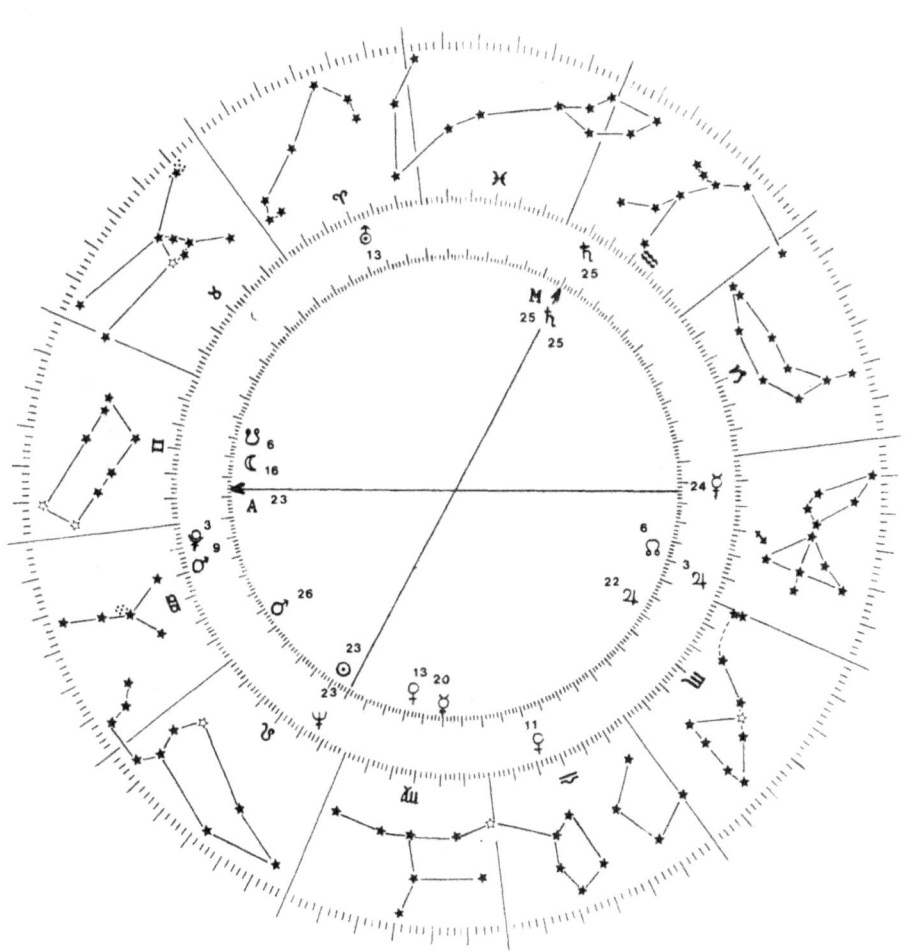

Chart 11:
⌀ Stroke patient

Stroke patient ⌀ 8.44 a.m. GMT on December 12, 1935 at Stuttgart

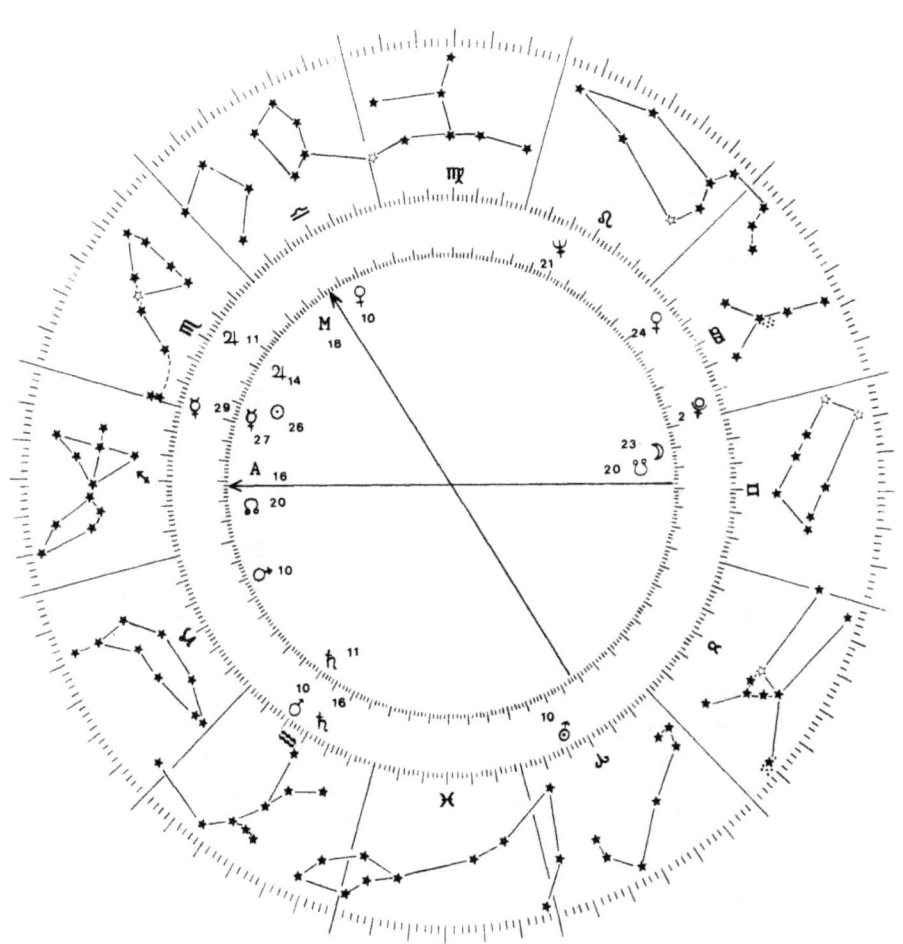

Chart 12:
Embryonic correspondence (Stroke patient)
Event of stroke at 46 years 5 months of age
e.c. 6.30 a.m. GMT on June 11, 1936 at Stuttgart

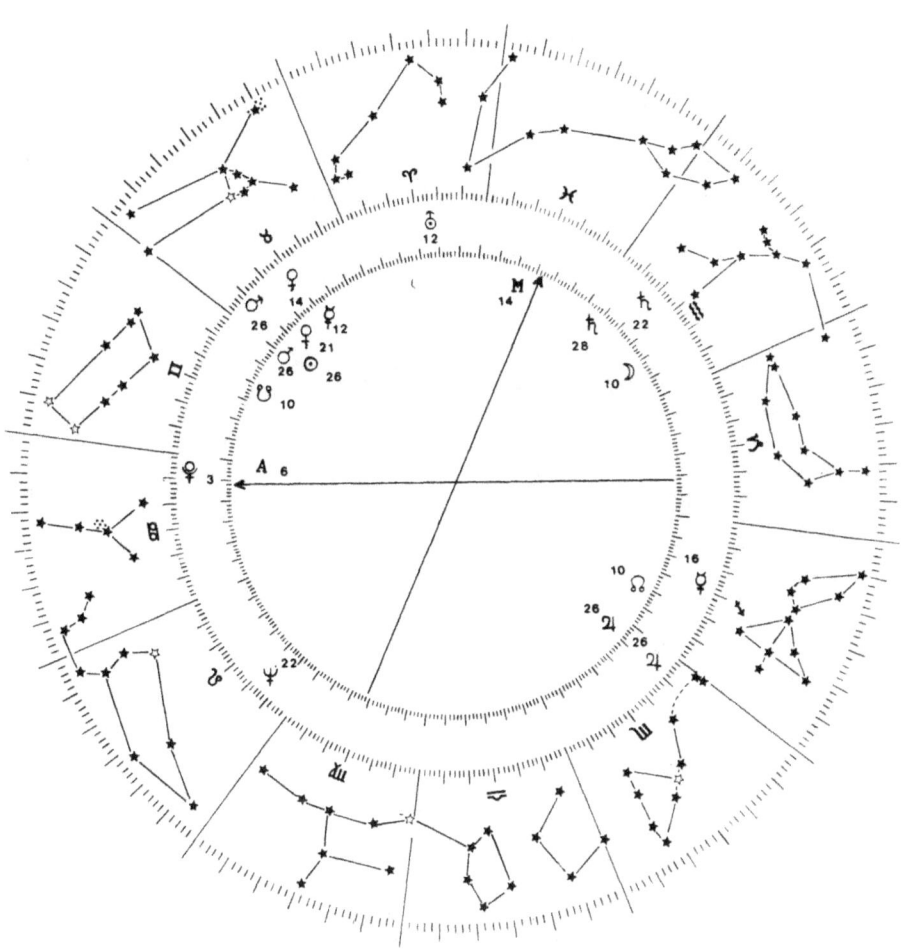

can be assessed. In the case of the patient, the conjunction of the Sun and Mars in opposition to Jupiter points back to some event in the previous incarnation (or possibly in some earlier incarnation), the consequences of which returned as a stroke in the Mars period of his present incarnation.

An event such as this – terrible though it may be – can have the deeper

Figure 7:
The destiny image of the stroke

Embryonic stroke configuration seen in relation to the conception configuration

The outer circle shows the positions of the Sun and Moon, Mars and Jupiter at the moment in the embryonic period corresponding to the destiny image of the stroke. The inner circle shows the positions of the Sun and Saturn at conception, i.e. at the start of the embryonic period. (See Charts 11 and 12.)

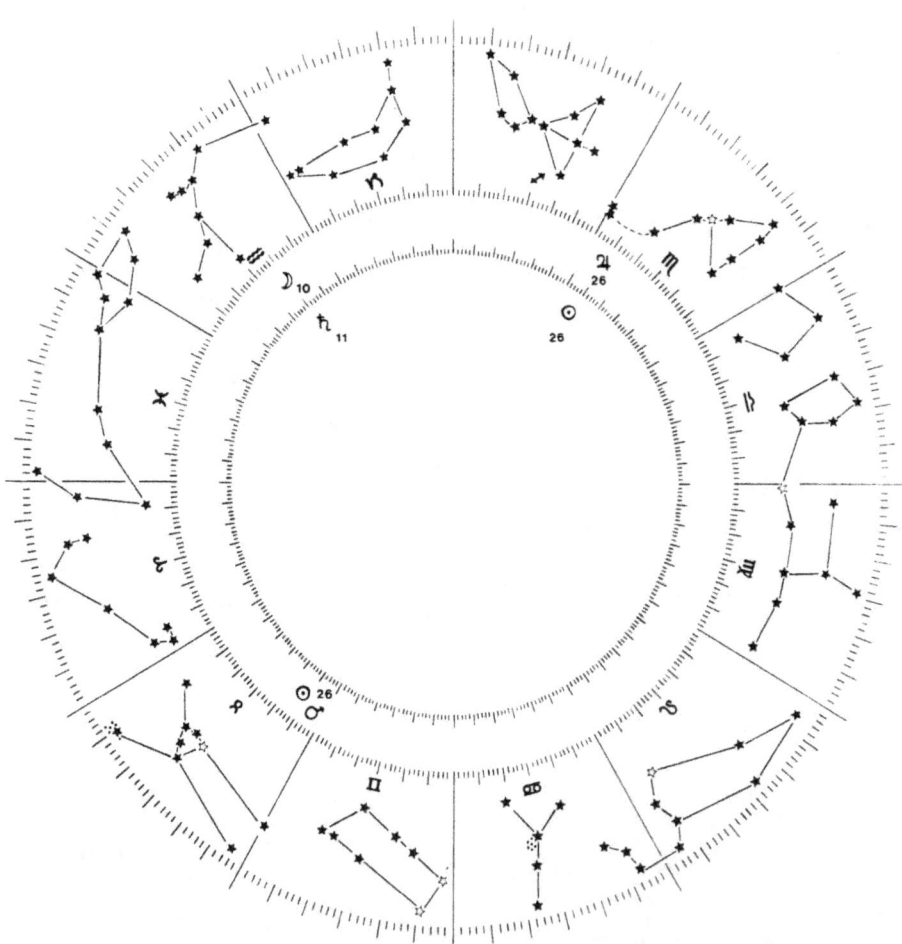

meaning of awakening the person concerned to the spiritual world. A stroke is essentially a meeting with death. It need not result in death, however. In this sense it can be regarded as a kind of parallel to *initiation*. The parallel to initiation comes to expression in the Biblical account of the initiation of the Old Testament patriarch Jacob, who experienced one night the meeting with death.

> *A man (= the angel of death) wrestled with him until the break of day. When the man saw that he did not prevail against Jacob, he touched the hollow of his thigh; and Jacob's thigh was put out of joint as he wrestled with him. Then he said, "Let me go, for the day is breaking." But Jacob said, "I will not let you go, unless you bless me." And he said to him, "What is your name?" And he said, "Jacob." Then he said, "Your name shall no more be called Jacob, but Israel, for you have striven with God and with men, and have prevailed." Then Jacob asked him, "Tell me, I pray, your name." But he said, "Why is it that you ask my name?" And there he blessed him. So Jacob called the name of the place Penuel, saying, "For I have seen God face to face, and yet my life is preserved." The Sun rose upon him as he passed Penuel, limping because of his thigh.*
>
> (Genesis xxxii, 24–31)

Here the meeting with death resulted in initiation, a second birth, whereby Jacob received the name Israel. In the language of the Bible, initiation means: to encounter God face to face and yet not to die. In this case Jacob did not pass through this shattering experience completely unscathed, for his thigh was put out of joint, resulting in a limp.

Someone who has a stroke and yet does not die also has a kind of initiation experience, a meeting with the spiritual world, but generally is not conscious of this direct encounter with higher beings. And usually the consequences are much more severe than a thigh being put out of joint. In the case of the patient concerned, whose entire right side became paralysed, the meeting with death meant that he "half died", as it were. A stroke is not so much a "wrestling with death", as depicted in the initiation experience of Jacob, rather, it is more akin to being struck down by a bolt of lightening from the angel of death. The karmic reasons for a stroke obviously vary in the case of each individual, but its cosmic significance is that it represents a striking in of the spiritual world into the human being's earthly existence. An appropriate attitude towards it, therefore, would be a turning of consciousness towards the spiritual world on the part of the person afflicted. Drastic though it may seem, this may even be a reason for its occurrence, i.e. in order to call a human being out of a materialistic way of life and to remind him of his divine-spiritual origin.

In the case of an affliction affecting the physical body, it is a matter of directing consciousness towards the divine image, the archetype of the physical body. In hermetic astrology this is reflected especially in the conception configuration, which is determined by means of the hermetic rule. According to the hermetic rule, the Ascendant in the birth horoscope is indicated by the zodiacal position of the Moon or its opposite in the conception horoscope (see *Hermetic Astrology* I, Appendix I). Thus the divine image is reflected also in the Ascendant of the birth horoscope. As referred to in the last chapter, the Ascendant represents the *axis of contemplation* of the divine image in the zodiacal sphere. Moreover, insofar as the image nature comes to expression in human initiative, there arises an *axis of initiative* within the zodiacal sphere – more or less perpendicular to the axis of contemplation. The axis of initiative is indicated by the Midheaven in the birth horoscope. These two axes in the birth configuration – that of the Ascendant and that of the Midheaven – are therefore also related to the divine image, over and above the conception configuration.

In contrast to an affliction of the physical body, the astrological background to which can often be found in relation to the conception configuration, in the case of an affliction of the soul or psyche – e.g. a psychological disturbance – it is a question of the likeness, which comes to expression primarily in the birth configuration. On the other hand, the image, the archetype of the physical body, is revealed more in the conception configuration. Since the ideal of the physical body is the resurrection body, it is the resurrection body of Jesus Christ which has to be called upon in bringing in the forces of healing in the case of an affliction of the physical body. Then it may happen that even such a devastating affliction as paralysis can be turned to good account.

A second example of a stroke of destiny

As a second example of someone struck down in the prime of life – becoming partially paralysed – but who turned this stroke of destiny to good account, let us consider the British astrologer John Addey. In John Addey we have an example of a higher destiny at work. He himself – as emerges from the following biographical sketch by his friend and colleague Charles Harvey – viewed the affliction which struck him down as an intervention of destiny which led him to reflect on the meaning of life, especially by way of philosophy and astrology. Thereby he arrived at his true calling as an innovator in the field of astrology.

John Addey was arguably the greatest astrologer of whom we have record. For next to those ancients, who actually articulated our great tradition in the first place, no one has ever done more to uncover the basic laws and principles on which astrology is based.

John was drawn to the mysteries of astrology from childhood. He was born in Barnsley, Yorkshire on June 15, 1920 at 8.15 a.m., the descendant of amongst others an archbishop of York and an horologist.

The youngest in the family by 19 years, he was sent at the age of ten as a boarder to the fine Quaker school, Ackworth in Pontefract, becoming its head boy before he left in 1939. There, and later at St. John's College, Cambridge, where he read literature, he excelled not only academically, especially in English, but at all forms of sport and athletics, notably cricket, football, and long jump, at which he set up several records, some of which still remain unbroken.

At the outbreak of World War II, as a convinced pacifist, he joined the Friends Ambulance Unit in Cambridge. Here, in 1942, he was to meet Betty, his future wife and loyal and devoted helpmate, whom he married in 1946 and who was to do so much to make his work possible. But shortly after their meeting, tragedy struck. Working non-stop, with his characteristic zeal, to clear a delivery of coal which was obstructing the ambulance yard, he was suddenly struck down by ankolysing spondilitis, *an acute form of rheumatism, which within 24 hours held him rigid on his back unable to move for the pain. He was to remain on his back, unable even to read for the next 18 months. Despite an acutely painful hip operation later, he never did regain the use of his legs or back.*

In later years, with a characteristic twinkle in his eye, John was wont to remark that if he had not thus been forced to stay still for a moment and reflect on life, that he would have probably been all too happy to spend his days between golf and horses! In all events he did begin to reflect on the two areas which had attracted him intermittantly since childhood: philosophy and astrology. For John these two were always to go hand in hand, growing and flowering simultaneously in the ensuing years.

Thus it was that as a true philosopher and loyal devotee of Urania, that John's great motivation became the desire to discover and unfold that final and integral astrology, which must ultimately subsist over and above all the particular ideas we may have about astrology, that astrology which is securely rooted in the vision of spiritual realities, in fully intelligible principles. And so it was, inspired and motivated by this vision, that he worked unceasingly and systematically, against the enormous odds of illness and physical handicap, to reveal the deepest insight and understanding we yet have of astrology.[1]

The application of the hermetic rule

The time of John Addey's birth – presumably stated by his parents – is given in the foregoing account as 8.15 a.m. As it was summer time, this equates with 7.15 a.m. GMT. Applying the hermetic rule to find the moment of conception, it is evident that a correction has to be applied to the time of birth, i.e. the time of birth should have been a quarter of an hour later. Such discrepancies either can be due to a lack of exactness in recording the birth time, e.g. when it is later stated from memory, or they may be genuine discrepancies. (A genuine discrepancy occurs when the physical time of birth diverges from the cosmically appointed time of birth.)

Normally the actual birth time coincides to within a few minutes with the cosmically appointed time specified by the hermetic rule. Given the actual birth time – assuming that the birth was not induced – the rule of Hermes can be applied to find the moment of conception and then, having found the moment of conception, the hermetic rule can be re-applied to yield the cosmically appointed time of birth. Through this procedure, applied to John Addey's stated time of birth of 8.15 a.m. (= 7.15 GMT), the hermetic rule yields the rectified birth time of 8.31 a.m. (= 7.31 GMT).

The following outlines the procedure in detail:
Zodiacal location (sidereal zodiac) of the Moon (MO) and the Ascendant (AS) at stated time of John Addey's birth: MO = 12°11' Taurus; AS = 12°05' Cancer. According to the hermetic rule (see *Hermetic Astrology* I, Appendix I) the Moon's sidereal longitude at conception was 12°05' Cancer (or Capricorn) and the sidereal longitude of the Ascendant at conception was 12°11' Taurus (or Scorpio).

Thus, possible dates of conception, when the Moon was at 12°05' Cancer (or Capricorn), were: (1) September 7, 1919; (2) September 19, 1919; (3) October 4, 1919; and (4) October 17, 1919.

The actual date of conception, as will later become apparent, was October 17, 1919, i.e. John Addey was born one month premature. On this day, the Moon was located at 12°05' Cancer in the sidereal zodiac at 5.44 a.m. GMT. By computation for this time on October 17, 1919 – assuming that the conception took place in Barnsley (the place of birth) – the Ascendant (sidereal zodiac) was 19° Virgo (to the nearest degree). However, since the hermetic rule specifies that the Ascendant was 12°11' Taurus or Scorpio, either the conception took place 11 hours 8 minutes earlier (Ascendant 12°11' Taurus) or 5 hours 6 minutes later (Ascendant 12°11' Scorpio).

As will become evident in the following, the conception did in fact take place later, at 10.51 a.m. GMT, when the Ascendant was 12°21' Scorpio (having advanced from 19° Virgo). At this time the Moon's sidereal longitude was 14°54' Cancer. According to the hermetic rule, therefore, the conception took place at 10.51 a.m. GMT on October 17, 1919, when the sidereal location of the Moon and the Ascendant were: MO = 14°54'; AS = 12°21' Scorpio.

From this information, re-applying the hermetic rule, the cosmically appointed sidereal locations of the Ascendant and the Moon at birth were: AS = 14°54' Cancer; MO = 12°21' Taurus. (Note that the direct interchange of the Ascendant at birth with the Moon at conception and the complementary interchange of the Moon at birth with the Ascendant at conception corresponds to case (b) in Figure 27, *Hermetic Astrology* I.) Taking the Ascendant at John Addey's birth to be 14°54' Cancer implies that he was born 16 minutes later than the stated time, i.e. he was born at 8.31 a.m. (= 7.31 GMT).

Through the double application of the hermetic rule, a rectified birth time is yielded, 16 minutes later than the stated birth time. Whether or not this rectified birth time was the actual time of birth is of purely academic interest, as it is the cosmically appointed birth time that is decisive for hermetic-astrological considerations. In other words, what is of significance in hermetic astrology is the Ascendant chosen by the incarnating soul – chosen already long before the moment of birth – and not the Ascendant computed for the exact moment of birth.

In ideal circumstances, the two will coincide, but usually the actual moment of birth is an approximation to the cosmically appointed time, and correspondingly the Ascendant computed for the given time of birth is usually an approximation to the soul's choice of Ascendant. However, through the above procedure, applying the hermetic rule, the cosmically appointed time (and correspondingly the soul's chosen Ascendant) can be derived from the given time of birth. In John Addey's case, the chosen Ascendant was 15° Cancer in the sidereal zodiac (expressed to the nearest degree).

Confirmation of the conception horoscope by way of karma research

How is it possible to be certain that the above line of reasoning is correct, not only in view of the multiple choice of the day of conception, but also considering the twofold choice (on the given day) regarding the Ascendant at conception? It is sometimes possible by way of karma research to arrive at a high degree of certainty, and to become sure of the day and time of conception. When through karma research the previous incarnation is found, and the planetary sidereal zodiacal positions at birth/death in the previous incarnation can be computed, these sidereal zodiacal positions may then be compared with the various possible planetary configurations at conception. Often, through the comparison, it is then possible to arrive with a high degree of certainty at the actual conception configuration. By way of illustration, let us again consider the example of John Addey.

Through karma research it was possible to trace the previous incarnation of John Addey, which took place in Germany in the latter half of the sixteenth century and the first third of the seventeenth century. In the former incarnation of this individuality, he lived a life in which he was active in the sciences of mathematics and astronomy. Historically the personality in question is remembered for his contribution to astronomy. The following incarnation – as John Addey, in which he is remembered for his contribution to astrology – can be regarded as a metamorphosis from the previous one. The metamorphosis of this individual's sphere of interest from astronomy to astrology represents a metamorphosis from an interest in the physical aspect of the surrounding universe to one in the soul aspect – as to how the cosmos comes to manifestation through the human soul. In the sense of cosmic evolution, the activity of this individuality represents an advance from the one incarnation as an astronomer (i.e. a "scientist of the physical realm") to the next incarnation as an astrologer (i.e. a "scientist of the soul realm"). For John Addey was an astrologer who brought scientific discipline – as a fruit of his former incarnation – into the realm of astrology. As such he will be remembered in the future, when true astrology will emerge from the mass of superstitious beliefs surrounding it today.

John Addey's former incarnation

In his former incarnation as the astronomer Michael Maestlin, this individual is most remembered as the scientist who brought the Copernican heliocentric system to the attention of the young mathematician Johannes Kepler. Kepler entered the evangelical theological seminary of Tübingen in September 1588, and at that time Maestlin was professor of mathematics at the University of Tübingen, from 1584 until his death in 1631, i.e. for 47 years.[2] The young student attended Maestlin's lectures and heard him expound on the superiority of the Copernican system over the Ptolemaic. The pupil-teacher relationship between Maestlin and Kepler developed into one of friendship, which was to last a lifetime, where they shared not only a common interest in astronomy, but also in astrology.

Kepler's discovery of the planetary laws of motion would not have been possible without his conversion to the Copernican system, the introduction to which he owed to Maestlin's championing of the Copernican cause. (Maestlin announced in 1578 his "adoption of the cosmology of Copernicus, truly the foremost astronomer since Ptolemy."[3]) Despite his acknowledgement of Copernicus, Maestlin's introductory textbook on astronomy (*Epitome Astronomiae*, Heidelberg, 1582), which was so popular that seven editions appeared between 1582 and 1624, outlined the traditional Ptolemaic system, as easier for beginners to understand. (Maestlin's first acquaintance with the Copernican system had been as a student at Tübingen University, 19 or 20 years of age, when he had acquired a copy of Copernicus' book *De revolutionibus*.)

After receiving an M.A. from the University of Tübingen in 1571, Maestlin entered the theological course, and in 1576, at the age of 26, he became appointed Lutheran pastor at Backnang. In April 1577, aged 26½, he married his first wife, Margaret, who bore him six children (three daughters and three sons). In 1580, at the age of 30, Maestlin returned to

VI. The Hermetic—Astrological Science of Destiny

academic life, becoming professor of mathematics at Heidelberg University, and within less than four years he entered his professorship at Tübingen University, where he remained until the end of his life.

His first marriage lasted less than eleven years, owing to the death of his wife on February 15, 1588. However, within a year he remarried, and his second wife – also called Margaret – brought nine children into the world.

Michael Maestlin was a man of slight build (for a reproduction of an oil portrait painted in 1619, see Edward Rosen's book.[4]) He was much respected by his students and colleagues, and is noted in the history of astronomy not only as an early champion of the Copernican cause, but also as the first scientist to correctly explain the phenomenon of earthshine.

What is of interest, from the point of view of hermetic astrology, is that Michael Maestlin's birth and death dates are known, i.e. he was born on September 30, 1550 (Julian calendar) at Göppingen, east of Stuttgart, Germany, and he died on October 30, 1631 (Gregorian calendar) at Tübingen, Germany. From these dates the planetary configurations at Michael Maestlin's birth and death have been computed (see Charts 13 and 14). These charts may be compared with the conception, birth and death charts of John Addey (see Charts 15, 16 and 17).

The planet Neptune emerges prominently in these charts. At Maestlin's birth Neptune was close to perihelion, its closest position to the Sun (h-Neptune 19° Aries; perihelion of Neptune 22° Aries). At the death of Michael Maestlin Neptune was in conjunction with the Sun (Neptune 16° Libra; Sun 17° Libra). At John Addey's conception Neptune (16° Cancer) was approaching its ascending node to arrive at exact conjunction with it at his birth (h-Neptune 17° Cancer; ascending node of Neptune 17° Cancer). At his conception h-Neptune and h-Mars were in conjunction (see hermetic chart 15) and the Moon was conjoined with g-Neptune (see geocentric chart 15). At John Addey's birth g-Neptune (16° Cancer) was in conjunction with the Ascendant (15° Cancer), i.e. Neptune was rising at John Addey's birth (see Chart 16).

It has already been outlined in Volume I – as a fundamental principle of hermetic astrology – that the birth chart of one incarnation usually displays a similarity with the birth/death charts of the previous incarnation, in terms of alignments of the planets in the sidereal zodiac from one incarnation to the next. In addition, the first "law" of reincarnation – which, however, does not apply in every reincarnation example – yields a direct relationship between the death chart in one incarnation and the birth chart of the following incarnation, coming to expression in the angular aspect between the Sun and Saturn (see *Hermetic Astrology* I, Appendix III). Thus a special relationship often exists between the birth chart in one incarnation and the death chart of the previous incarnation. Similarly, as a further research finding of hermetic astrology, the conception chart often displays a close connection – again in terms of planetary alignments in the sidereal zodiac – with the birth chart of the foregoing incarnation (see Figure 1).

These two relationships emerge as a part of a larger relationship existing between the course of life in one incarnation and the embryonic period in the next incarnation. This may be expressed as follows: the consequences of the life between birth and death in one incarnation become karmically elaborated in the period between conception and birth in the next incarnation. That is, the karmic consequences of the course of life between birth and death in one incarnation are elaborated in the weaving of karma during the embryonic period between conception and birth in the next incarnation. Here the starting point of the embryonic period (conception) corresponds to the starting point of the former incarnation (birth). Similarly, the end of the embryonic period (birth) corresponds to the end of the former incarnation (death). This correspondence between the elaboration of karma during the embryonic period in one incarnation and the course of life in the previous incarnation (see Figure 1) is a major key in hermetic astrology towards the understanding of destiny. This will become evident in the case of John Addey's destiny, looked at against the karmic background of his former incarnation as Michael Maestlin.

Chart comparison: Michael Maestlin/John Addey

Before looking at John Addey's life and endeavouring to understand his karma, let us compare the birth/death charts of Michael Maestlin with the conception/birth charts of John Addey, looking firstly at John Addey's birth chart. (Note: an alignment between planetary positions in two charts means that either the planets line up on the same side of the sidereal zodiac, or on opposite sides; these alignments are listed in Table 8.)

From Table 8 it is evident that a considerable number of zodiacal alignments occurred between John Addey's birth chart and Michael Maestlin's birth/death charts. However, the first "law" of reincarnation is not fulfilled, as the Sun-Saturn angle at Michael Maestlin's death was 12° and that at John Addey's birth was 72°. Nor is the second "law" of reincarnation fulfilled, i.e. there is no alignment of h-Mercury and/or h-Venus between Michael Maestlin's death chart and John Addey's birth chart. (See *Hermetic Astrology* I, Appendix IV, concerning the "law" of alignment of h-Mercury/h-Venus.) This reincarnation example is therefore one in which neither the first nor the second "laws" of reincarnation hold. What does come to expression, however, is an alignment of the Ascendant at John Addey's birth with g-Saturn at Michael Maestlin's birth. (This is a not infrequent alignment to be found in the comparison of birth horoscopes from one incarnation to the next.) Let us now go a stage further

VI. The Hermetic—Astrological Science of Destiny 195

Chart 13:
*Michael Maestlin
Michael Maestlin *September 30, 1550 at Göppingen

Chart 14:
†Michael Maestlin
Michael Maestlin †October 30, 1631 at Tübingen

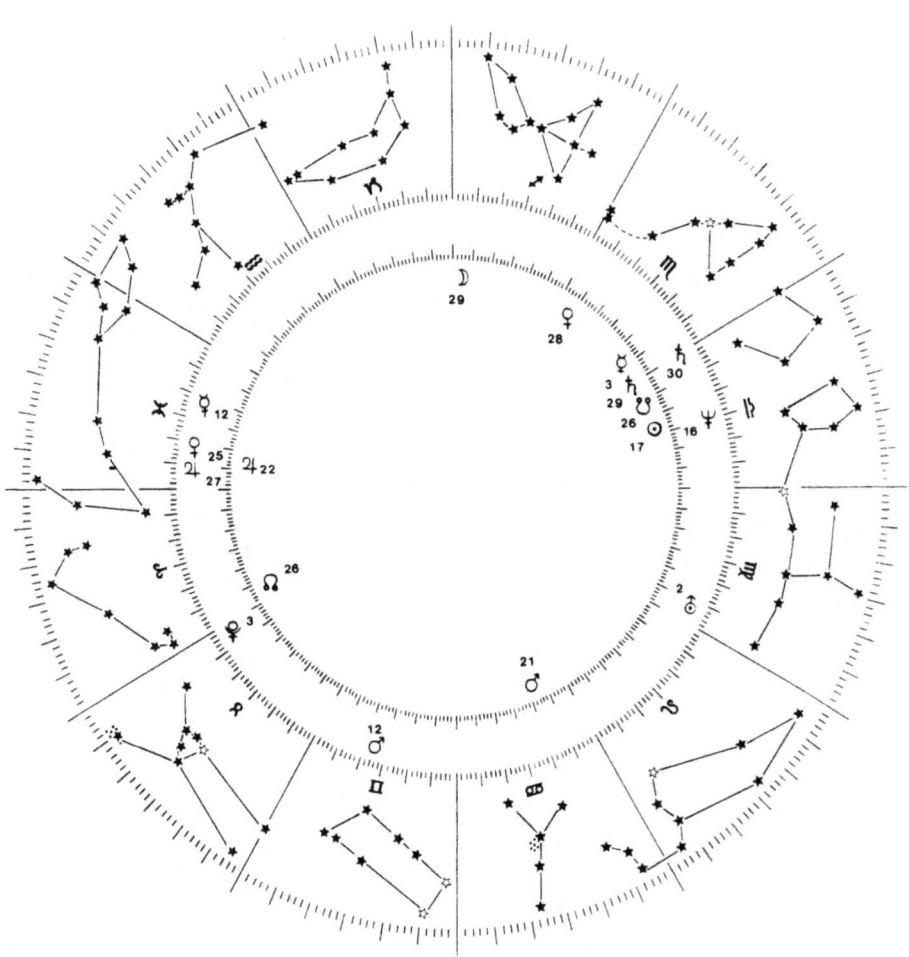

Chart 15
⌀ John Addey
John Addey ⌀ 10.51 a.m. GMT on October 17, 1919 at Barnsley

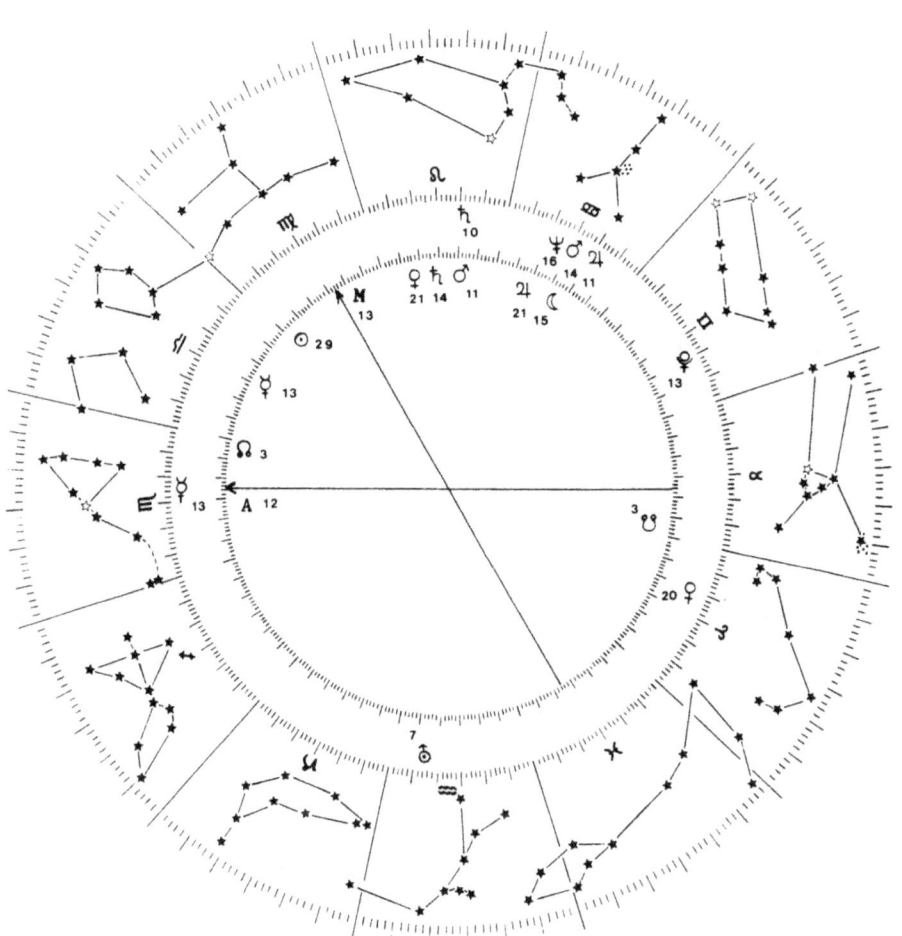

Chart 16:
*John Addey
John Addey *8.31 a.m. BST on June 15, 1920 at Barnsley

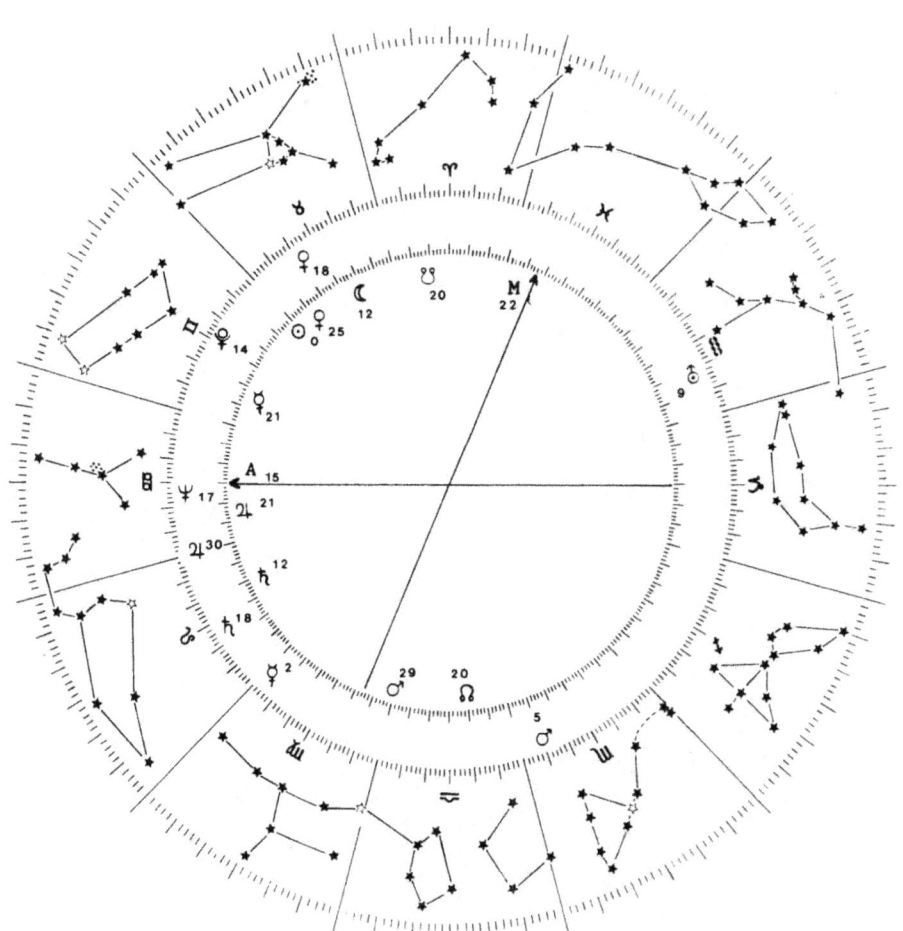

Table 8:
Michael Maestlin/John Addey zodiacal alignments at John Addey's birth

See Appendix II for the computation of the planetary positions – geocentric and heliocentric – listed in the following table.

Abbreviations: h = heliocentric sidereal longitude (hermetic chart)
g = geocentric sidereal longitude (geocentric chart)
* = birth
† = death

Michael Maestlin (*/†)

†Sun	17° Libra
*h-Jupiter	1° Gemini
*h-Mars	10° Taurus
*g-Mars	20° Gemini
†g-Venus	28° Scorpio
*Sun	28° Virgo
*h-Saturn	21° Capricorn
†g-Mars	21° Cancer
*g-Saturn	15° Capricorn
*g-Jupiter	12° Gemini
†h-Uranus	2° Virgo
*Moon**	20° Taurus
†g-Mercury	3° Scorpio
†g-Pluto	4° Taurus
*g-Venus	21° Leo
*h-Pluto	9° Aquarius

John Addey (*)

*Moon's node	20° Libra
*Sun	0° Gemini
*Moon	12° Taurus
*g-Mercury	21° Gemini
*g-Venus	25° Taurus
*g-Mars	29° Virgo
*g-Jupiter	21° Cancer
*g-Neptune	16° Cancer
*Ascendant	15° Cancer
*g-Pluto	13° Gemini
*h-Mercury	2° Virgo
*h-Venus	18° Taurus
*h-Mars	5° Scorpio
*h-Saturn	18° Leo
*h-Uranus	9° Aquarius

(** Note that as the exact time of Michael Maestlin's birth is not known, the midday Moon position listed here is only approximate, and the actual position could differ by up to 7 degrees from the value computed here.)

and look at John Addey's conception chart in relation to the birth/death charts of Michael Maestlin (see Table 9).

From Table 9 a strong relationship between John Addey's conception chart and the birth chart of Michael Maestlin is evident. Especially striking is the alignment of the Sun between the two charts, and also that of g-Venus. Further, the Moon at conception lined up on the opposite side of the zodiac to g-Saturn at Maestlin's birth.

It is these striking alignments – above all of the Sun and g-Venus between the two charts – which leads to the conclusion, with a high degree of certainty, that October 17, 1919 was (among the various possibilities yielded by the hermetic rule) the actual date of conception. And the align-

Table 9:
Michael Maestlin/John Addey zodiacal alignments at John Addeys conception

See Appendix II for the computation of the planetary positions – geocentric and heliocentric – listed in the following table.

Abbreviations: h = heliocentric sidereal longitude (hermetic chart)
  g = geocentric sidereal longitude (geocentric chart)
  Ø = conception
  * = birth
  † = death

Michael Maestlin (*/†)		John Addey (Ø)	
*Sun	28° Virgo	ØSun	29° Virgo
*g-Saturn	15° Capricorn	Øh-Mars	14°Cancer
		ØMoon	15° Cancer
*g-Venus	21° Leo	Øg-Venus	21° Leo
*h-Pluto	9° Aquarius	Øg-Mars	11° Leo
		Øh-Saturn	10° Leo
†g-Mars	21° Cancer	Øg-Jupiter	21° Cancer
*h-Saturn	21° Capricorn		
*h-Neptune	19° Aries	Øh-Venus	20° Aries
†Sun	17° Libra		

ment of the Moon on the opposite side of the zodiac to g-Saturn led then to the determination of the time of conception on this day, at which time the Moon was exactly opposite to the sidereal zodiacal location of g-Saturn at Michael Maestlin's birth.

Correspondence between the embryonic period and the course of life

Further support leading to the conclusion that October 17, 1919 was the actual conception date of John Addey arises from the following consideration of his destiny, relating to Willi Sucher's finding that the destiny lived through during each 7-year period of life corresponds to the elaboration of karma during the relevant lunar sidereal month of the embryonic period. In the light of this finding, let us look at the death of John Addey, which took place in London at 5.17 p.m. on March 27, 1982 (see Chart 17).

John Addey died at the age of 61 years 10 months 12 days and 10 hours (= 61.867328 years). He died during the 7-year period of Saturn (56–63). As each orbit of the Moon around the sidereal zodiac during the embryonic period corresponds to seven years of life, the karmic background to the moment of death occurred during the ninth lunar sidereal month of the embryonic period, corresponding to the ninth 7-year life period (that of Saturn). That is, the first eight lunar sidereal months relate to the first

56 years of life (8 x 7 = 56), so that the ninth lunar sidereal month corresponds to the age from 56 to 63, i.e. the period of Saturn towards the end of which death occurred. Since in one lunar sidereal month the Moon orbits 360 degrees of the sidereal zodiac corresponding to seven years of life, its orbit through 301.75 degrees of the zodiac corresponds to 5.867328 years of life (age at death = 61.867328 = 56 + 5.867328, where 5.867328/7 x 360 degrees = 301.75 degrees). Adding 301.75 degrees (= 302 degrees to the nearest degree) to the Moon's starting point in the conception chart (15° Cancer), we find that during the embryonic period the sidereal longitude of the Moon at the karmic background to the moment of death was 15° Cancer + 302 degrees = 17° Taurus. This is represented diagrammatically in Figure 8.

From Figure 8 the striking fact emerges that there is an almost perfect correspondence between the elaboration of karma during the embryonic period of development and the fulfilment of John Addey's destiny between birth and death, where the closing date of the embryonic period (= the day of birth: June 15, 1920) corresponds to the closing date of his life (= the day of death: March 27, 1982). In other words, the karmic background to the moment of death, to be sought for during the embryonic period, coincided with the date of birth. This coincidence would have been exact – not only to the day, but also to the hour – if the Moon's sidereal longitude at the karmic background to the moment of death (= destiny image of death) had been 12° Taurus, where the Moon was located at the hour of his birth. But as the Moon's sidereal longitude at the destiny image of death was 17° Taurus, this moment fell 6 hours 55 minutes later, i.e. it occurred at 2.26 p.m. on June 15, 1920 and thus overshot the moment of birth by 6 hours 55 minutes.

Correspondingly the Moon overshot its birth position by 5 degrees (actually closer to 4½ degrees). Since the passage of the Moon through 360 degrees corresponds to seven years of life, its passage through one-seventh of 360 degrees (= 51.43 degrees) corresponds to one year of life (= 52 weeks), i.e. one degree of the Moon's movement through the zodiac during the embryonic period corresponds to approximately one week of life. This means that the passage of the Moon through 5 degrees (actually 4° 21') during the embryonic period corresponds to approximately five weeks of life (actually 31 days). Going back this period of time prior to John Addey's date of death (31 days prior to March 27) leads back to February 24, 1982, when he was already in hospital, seriously ill, with the illness which led to his death (cancer of the lungs) – having entered hospital towards the end of January 1982.

Thus the karmic background to John Addey's death can be seen to lie in the fact that he had completed the elaboration of his past karma. Applying the correspondence between the elaboration of karma during the em-

Chart 17:
†John Addey
John Addey †5.17 p.m. GMT on March 27, 1982 at London

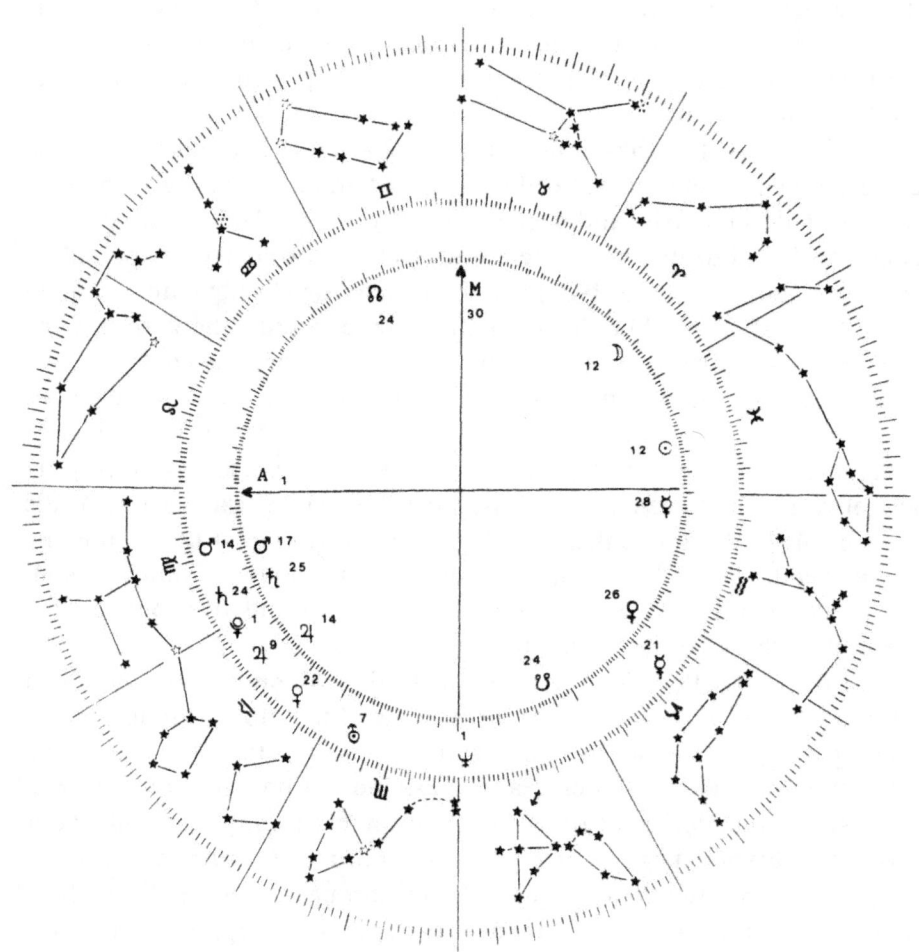

VI. The Hermetic—Astrological Science of Destiny   203

Figure 8:
Karmic background of the moment of death during John Addey's embryonic period

Above the line: the lunar sidereal months of the embryonic period
Below the line: the corresponding 7-year life periods

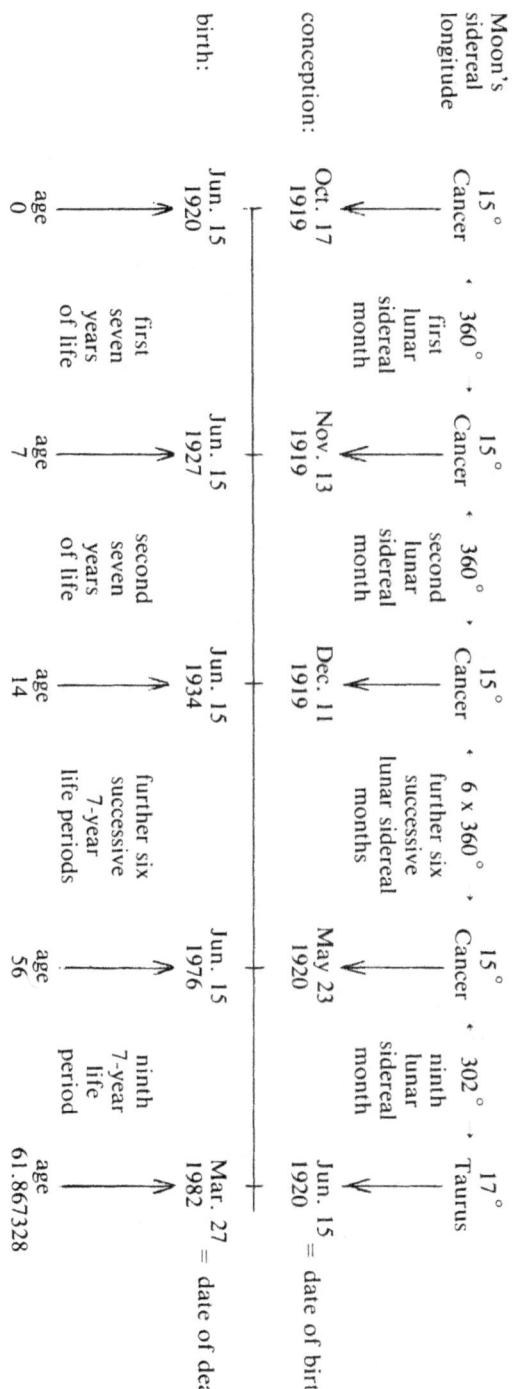

bryonic period and the living out of destiny during the course of life (see Figure 8), it is evident that John Addey, when he was lying in hospital seriously ill with lung cancer, had arrived at the closing date in the sequence of 7-year periods – the closing date corresponding to the cut-off date (= birth date) of the embryonic period. (The exact closing date fell on February 24, 1982, one month prior to his actual date of death.) The illness leading to his death became acute as the closing point in the elaboration of his karma was reached, in February 1982. There was then a brief period of time of about one month during which the question existed as to whether he would live further – by virtue of grace – or whether he would move on to other, spiritual realms of activity. But as the decision to move on was arrived at, it was then a matter of passing on under an appropriate configuration of stars. The right stellar configuration for this event came at 5.17 p.m. GMT on March 27, 1982, when John Addey's soul took leave of this world. (See Chart 17 for the stellar configuration at this moment of his death.)

This example of how – astrologically – karma works out, as it did in the termination of John Addey's life, is particularly striking, since the event of death is indicated by the cut-off point of the elaboration of karma. (The cut-off point is the moment of birth, which terminates the embryonic period.) However, it would be a mistake to assume that it is always the case that the cut-off point of the embryonic period corresponds to the occurrence of death. This would mean that all overdue births would result in longevity (living beyond the age of 70), and that all prematurely-born people would die before reaching the age of 70 (= 10 x 7, since the embryonic period lasts on average ten lunar sidereal months = 10 x 27.32 = 273.2 days, where each sidereal month correspond to seven years of life.)

Just to mention one example which disproves this: Winston Churchill was born 228 days (= 7½ calendar months) after the marriage of his parents, indicating that he was a 7½-month child. (Even if he was conceived before the marriage, the length of the embryonic period could hardly have been 11½ calendar months, which would be the length of an embryonic period required to correspond to 90 years of life.) Assuming that the length of Winston Churchill's embryonic period was 7½ calendar months (228 days), this equates with 8.35 lunar sidereal months. Since one lunar sidereal month of the embryonic period corresponds to seven years of life, then an embryonic period of 8.35 lunar sidereal months equates with 58½ years of life (8.35 x 7 = 58.45). This implies that the cut-off point of the elaboration of Winston Churchill's karma corresponds approximately to the age of 58½ years. Yet Winston Churchill (1874–1965) lived to the age of 90! By virtue of grace he lived a further 31½ years after the cut-off point of the elaboration of his karma.

According to the strict laws of karma, Winston Churchill's life would have ended at approximately 58½ years of age, corresponding to the cut-off date of the elaboration of karma from his previous incarnation, assuming an embryonic period of 7½ calendar months. But he was granted a further 31½ years, during which came the most important years of his life – as leader of the British people in the defence against the Nazi onslaught. This example shows that human life is also a matter of grace, and not just a strict living out of destiny. Life lived after the cut-off date is bestowed by grace of the spiritual powers working for the future of the Earth and mankind. It is out of gratitude to higher beings, and in a spirit of service towards the Earth and mankind, that the "years of grace" – the period of life corresponding to the time following the cut-off date of the embryonic period – can be regarded.*

In the case of John Addey, however, his life did not extend beyond the cut-off date for the elaboration of karma. Instead he was released from this planet, to enter into a life of grace in cosmic spheres. Having fulfilled the elaboration of past karma, having arrived at the cut-off date, he became released from the heavy load of destiny which he had borne since the age of 23½, at which age he had lost the use of his legs. Looking back to the embryonic period, is it possible to gain insight into the karmic background to this difficult destiny, whereby as a young man in the prime of life he had lost the use of his legs?

The karmic-astrological background to John Addey's paralysis

To find the karmic background to this stroke of destiny in John Addey's life, first the sidereal zodiac position of the Moon during the embryonic period at the time corresponding to the age of 23½ has to be found. The "embryonic age" corresponding to the age of 23½ may be expressed in terms of the sidereal location of the Moon. This can be computed as follows: the completion of three lunar sidereal revolutions leads up to the age of 21, and since $2½/7 \times 360$ degrees = 129 degrees, then the Moon's orbit traversed a further 129 degrees of the sidereal zodiac corresponding to an additional 2½ years ($21 + 2½ = 23½$ years of age).

The embryonic age corresponding to the age of 23½ therefore equals three lunar sidereal orbits plus 129 degrees (expressed in terms of the Moon's sidereal motion). Since the Moon started out at conception at 15° Cancer in the sidereal zodiac (see Chart 15), the Moon's location in the sidereal zodiac after three orbits plus 129 degrees was 15° Cancer + 129 degrees = 24° Scorpio. Starting from the conception date (October 17,

---

*Note: assuming a normal-length embryonic period of ten lunar sidereal months (ca. 273 days), the cut-off date normally corresponds to 70 years of age ($10 \times 7 = 70$). In the case of a premature birth, after nine lunar sidereal months (246 days), the cut-off date would correspond to 63 years ($9 \times 7 = 63$). And in the case of an overdue birth, after eleven lunar sidereal months (301 days), the cut-off date would correspond to 77 years ($11 \times 7 = 77$).

1919), following the Moon's orbit through three sidereal revolutions plus 129 degrees to reach 24° Scorpio, the date arrived at during the embryonic period coincides with January 17, 1920. On this date the Moon was at 24° Scorpio in the sidereal zodiac at ca. 6.00 p.m. GMT. The planetary configuration at 6.00 p.m. GMT on January 17, 1920 (computed for Barnsley, the place of birth) is shown in Chart 18. This configuration indicates the destiny image (woven in the elaboration of John Addey's karma) corresponding to the stroke of destiny that took place at the age of 23½. At this age John Addey became partially paralysed, losing the use of both legs.

The striking in of destiny from the previous incarnation

The striking in of the destiny of the former life as Michael Maestlin is evident in the planetary configuration on January 17, 1920 during the embryonic period — the point in the embryonic period when the destiny image became woven in corresponding to the sudden affliction of partial paralysis at the age of 23½. Most prominent in this configuration (see Chart 18) is the position of Mars, in the same part of the zodiac as the Sun and Mercury at Michael Maestlin's birth and as the Sun at John Addey's conception. Mercury in this embryonic configuration was aligned opposite Mars at Michael Maestlin's birth and Jupiter was aligned opposite Mars at his death (referring here throughout to the geocentric chart). Also, the Moon's ascending node in this embryonic configuration was conjunct Saturn at Michael Maestlin's death (see Chart 14). Here it was as if a door (the nodal axis) opened to the previous incarnation, the destiny of which was summarized in the position of Saturn at the moment of Michael Maestlin's death.

Even without a knowledge of the planetary configurations at birth/death in the previous incarnation, the conjunction of Mars in the embryonic period with the Sun's position at conception shows the possibility of a karmic event with its consequences taking effect in the physical body. (The divine image, the archetype of the physical body, is reflected in the conception configuration.)

John Addey's courage in facing the major affliction which beset him in the prime of life indicates something of the power of the Christ Impulse, especially that which lives in the resurrection body of Jesus Christ, which is able to transmute the forces of the physical body. The forces that otherwise would come to expression in the physical body become released in the case of an illness or accident affecting the physical body, and through the Christ Impulse become capable of being directed into spiritual activity. The loss of use of any part of the physical body signifies, of course, an enormous sacrifice — one which, however, as is evident in John Addey's case, may yield extraordinary fruits if the transmuting power of the Christ Impulse is able to enter in.

VI. The Hermetic—Astrological Science of Destiny

Chart 18:
Embryonic correspondence (John Addey)
Event of paralysis at age 23 years 6 months
e.c. 6 p.m. GMT on January 17, 1920 at Barnsley

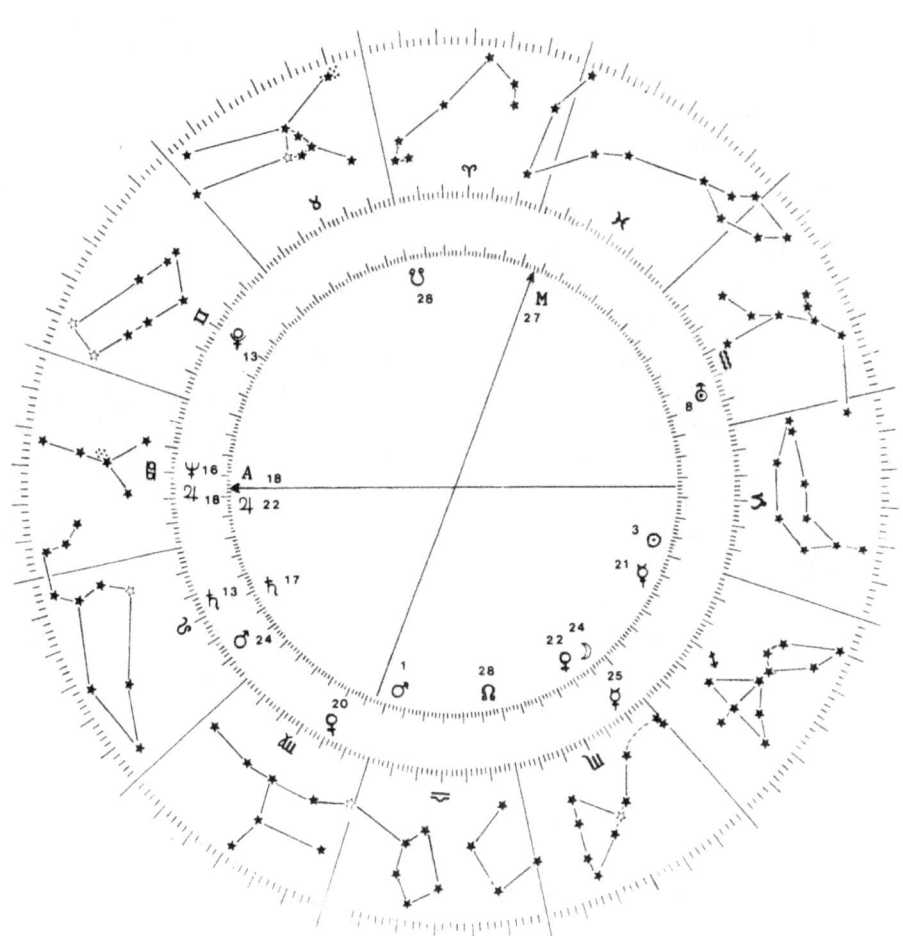

A letter that John Addey wrote to the author on July 7, 1977 reveals something of the higher impulse that motivated him in the latter half of his life.

In 1955 I set out to find a secure scientific basis for astrology and have worked at this for twenty-two years since then... My driving force has been a deep love of and reverence for astrology and a burning belief that it has a vital role to play in bridging the gap between science and religion, and in revealing to an atheistic age the glory of God.

Thus the motivation underlying John Addey's endeavour to reform astrology can be seen in the spirit of the Christ Impulse, which works to bring about the reintegration of man and the Earth with the Divine.

It was the very fact that a terrible stroke of destiny befell him in his twenty-fourth year of life which awoke John Addey to his karmic mission. The former life of Michael Maestlin "broke through", as it were, into his present life, and gave it a new direction, imbuing it with spiritual ideals and motivation. But instead of becoming – as he had been in his former incarnation – a champion of heliocentric astronomy (for which Michael Maestlin is most remembered in the history of science), John Addey devoted himself to the development of a new astrology. What appears outwardly as a terrible blow of destiny in his twenty-fourth year of life was the start of bringing to birth a new astrology. And like every other birth, such a birth can be accomplished only through pain, effort and enormous sacrifice. The blow of destiny he received as a young man meant that he had to sacrifice his physically active life and his interest in sport, to become mentally and spiritually active. Here manifested the call of the previous incarnation for him to be true to his karmic mission, to be true to that which he had set in motion in his foregoing incarnation as a champion of the new astronomy. And with tremendous perseverance and endeavour he devoted himself to his karmic task: that of laying the foundations of a new astrology.

The use in hermetic astrology of the correspondence between embryonic age and age of life opens up a perspective of the karmic background to the events of life, especially when combined with karma research. Each life is a metamorphosis of the preceding one, and often certain parallels between successive incarnations can be seen. In the case of the individuality who incarnated in the sixteenth/seventeenth centuries as the astronomer Michael Maestlin and who reincarnated in the twentieth century as the astrologer John Addey, some of the parallels are quite striking.

For example, Michael Maestlin married in the twenty-seventh year of life; John Addey in his twenty-sixth year. At the age of 38 Maestlin was elected dean of the Tübingen Arts Faculty,[5] and at the age of 38 John Addey founded the Astrological Association, of which he became president three years later.[6] Maestlin was at the forefront of the scientific-astronomical revolution of the sixteenth/seventeenth centuries. John Addey was a pioneer of the scientific-astrological revolution of the twentieth century. In the light of hermetic astrology, the karmic consequences of the incarnation as Michael Maestlin became woven into the elaboration of karma during John Addey's embryonic period of development. By way of the correspondence between embryonic age and age of life, this karmic background can be looked at in detail.

The passage of the Sun during the embryonic period

The correspondence between the embryonic period and the course of life is fundamental to hermetic astrology, as the basis of astrological biography. Moreover, it introduces a dynamic element into astrology. For, instead of becoming fixed solely upon the birth configuration, the planetary positions at birth can be viewed as the culmination of the course of development between conception and birth, where the birth configuration is the goal towards which the incarnating human being aims. However, it is not the goal alone which is important, but also the journey made between conception and birth to arrive there. In John Addey's life we have seen how significant a moment of time it was when during the embryonic period of development Mars transited the zodiacal position of the Sun at the conception, which in turn was located in the same part of the zodiac as the Sun (and also Mercury) at birth in his former incarnation as Michael Maestlin. At this moment of time the destiny image relating to the affliction which beset him as paralysis at the age of 23½ became woven into the elaboration of his destiny.

The planetary configuration for this moment of time during the embryonic period is given in Chart 18. Here it may be seen that the Sun at this point in time was located at 3° Capricorn. Therefore during the corresponding age of life (i.e. in the twenty-fourth year of life) it was especially the sign of Capricorn which provided the zodiacal background to the unfolding of his destiny. But some years later, at the age of 38, when John Addey founded the Astrological Association (of which he subsequently became president), the zodiacal background coincided with the Sun's entrance into the sidereal zodiacal sign of Pisces during the embryonic period. (During this part of the embryonic period, in 1920, the Sun entered the sidereal sign of Pisces on March 14, corresponding in the spiral of life to John Addey's attaining the age of 38 – see Table 10.) Here a new phase of life began, corresponding karmically to the zodiacal background of Pisces. Furthermore, in the seven preceding years, from 1951 to 1958 (i.e. from the age of 31 to 38) – corresponding embryonically to the Sun's passage through the sidereal sign of Aquarius – John Addey had been vice-president of the Astrological Lodge of the Theosophical Society.

In fact, the passage of the Sun through each sign of the sidereal zodiac during the embryonic period of development gives rise to corresponding 7½- or 8-year periods (on average 7.8 years long) during the course of life, which correlate not only with new epochs in life, but also with the human being's spiritual development through different religious/philosophical outlooks. The passage of the Sun through the various signs of the sidereal zodiac during the embryonic period thus gives rise to a phenomenon of considerable importance in hermetic astrology. Let us look at this more closely in relation to John Addey's path of development.

From the age of 38 to the age of 45½, the years during which he founded and became president of the Astrological Association, the zodiacal background to John Addey's spiritual development had its source in the sidereal sign of Pisces, through which the Sun passed during the corresponding time in the embryonic period. During the 7½ years prior to this, from 30½ to 38, when he was vice-president of the Astrological Lodge of the Theosophical Society, the embryonic zodiacal background to his spiritual development was that of the sidereal sign of Aquarius. (See Table 10, where the embryonic zodiacal periods are summarized in relation to the corresponding 7.8-year periods of life.)

Although John Addey was born with the Sun at 0° Gemini, which was the goal for the zodiacal location of the Sun on the journey into incarnation, also important for his spiritual development was the whole passage of the Sun through the various signs of the zodiac during the embryonic period. Following this passage in detail: the Sun started out at 29° Virgo at conception, and passed through the sidereal signs of Libra, Scorpio, Sagittarius, Capricorn, Aquarius, Pisces, Aries and Taurus in order to reach the goal of birth (Sun at the beginning of the sign of Gemini). Correspondingly, John Addey's path of spiritual development passed through eight 7.8-year periods to reach this goal, each period associated with the Sun's passage through eight complete zodiacal signs during the embryonic period, as listed in Table 10.

From Table 10 the zodiacal phases can be seen corresponding to successive stages of spiritual development through which John Addey passed during his life. Here a dynamic element is introduced into astrology in that the passage of the Sun through the signs of the zodiac during the embryonic period gives rise to 7.8-year zodiacal periods of spiritual development during life. These 7.8-year periods of spiritual development each relate to successive signs of the zodiac, so that the human being passes through a development corresponding to the passage through (on average) nine zodiacal signs during the course of a normal-length life of seventy years (9 x 7.8 = 70.2 years). Important changes in life and in outlook often occur in accordance with the unfolding of this sequence of 7.8-year zodia-

Table 10:
The zodiacal periods in John Addey's life

Sun at John Addey's conception on October 17, 1919: 29°24' Virgo
Sun at John Addey's birth on June 15, 1920: 0°15' Gemini
Between conception and birth the Sun passed through the last ½-degree of Virgo, and then through Libra, Scorpio, Sagittarius, Capricorn, Aquarius, Pisces, Aries and Taurus, and then through the first ¼-degree of Gemini. Transposing from embryonic time to the spiral of life, this means that the zodiacal background influence for the first two months of John Addey's life corresponded to the Sun's passage through the last ½-degree of Virgo. Then began the zodiacal background of Libra, lasting 7 years and 8 months, followed by Scorpio, lasting 7 years 7 months, etc., as listed in the following tabulation:

Monthly zodiacal divisions within the embryonic period 1919/1920

Sun in:	dates	corresponding age	corresponding life period
Libra	Oct. 18 – Nov. 17	$0^y\ 2^m - 7^y 10^m$	Aug. 1920 – Apr. 1928
Scorpio	Nov. 17 – Dec. 16	$7^y 10^m - 15^y\ 5^m$	Apr. 1928 – Nov. 1935
Sagittarius	Dec. 16 – Jan. 15	$15^y\ 5^m - 22^y 11^m$	Nov. 1935 – May 1943
Capricorn	Jan. 15 – Feb. 13	$22^y 11^m - 30^y\ 5^m$	May 1943 – Nov. 1950
Aquarius	Feb. 13 – Mar. 14	$30^y\ 5^m - 38^y\ 0^m$	Nov. 1950 – Jun. 1958
Pisces	Mar. 14 – Apr. 13	$38^y\ 0^m - 45^y\ 9^m$	Jun. 1958 – Mar. 1966
Aries	Apr. 13 – May 14	$45^y\ 9^m - 53^y\ 8^m$	Mar. 1966 – Feb. 1974
Taurus	May 14 – Jun. 15	$53^y\ 8^m - 61^y\ 9^m$	Feb. 1974 – Mar. 1982

cal periods, where each period is coloured by the corresponding zodiacal background.

In John Addey's life, as has already been mentioned, the start of the Pisces period at the age of 38 coincided with the founding of the Astrological Association, which owed much to his guiding genius. (The founding meeting of the Astrological Association took place on June 21, 1958, six days after John Addey's thirty-eighth birthday.) It was during the Pisces zodiacal period that he became president of the Astrological Association. (He assumed the presidency in 1961) In the next period of spiritual development, the Aries period, he set up the Urania Trust for astrological research. After enormous legal tussles the Urania Trust was set up in 1970 as an educational charity recognised by the Ministry of Education and Science. This was about midway through the Aries period, which extended from March 1966 to February 1974 (see Table 10).

In the Taurean phase, the last zodiacal period of development in John Addey's life, his book *Harmonics in Astrology* (1976), the fruit of twenty years of astrological research, became published.[7] With this book John Addey's spiritual insights and research findings were brought onto the wider intellectual horizon of the western astrological world. Through the publication of this book during the last 7.8-year zodiacal period of his life, he was brought much more into the limelight, and this entailed an increase in his lecturing activity and teaching work.

With the entrance during the embryonic period of the Sun into the sidereal sign of Gemini on June 15, 1920 (John Addey's date of birth), the goal of his incarnation (between conception and birth) was reached. The corresponding zodiacal life period of Gemini commenced on March 3, 1982, i.e. 24½ days prior to his date of death. Shortly before this date he had entered hospital, seriously ill. Thus the commencement of the Gemini zodiacal period (corresponding embryonically to the arrival of the Sun at its location at birth) really did signify the end (embrionically the zodiacal goal) of this incarnation. The further development of this individuality is now taking place in spiritual realms, released from the "confines of the body",[8] having completed the span of life allotted to him for the absolvement of the karmic consequences of his former incarnation as Michael Maestlin – a life during which he devoted himself to the renewal of astrology for "the glory of God" (see letter quoted earlier).

Astrological biography

In this chapter concerning the hermetic-astrological science of destiny, in which we have been looking – in the example of John Addey's life – at the correspondences between the embryonic period and the course of life, it is evident that two distinct rhythms are to be distinguished during the embryonic period: the lunar rhythm of the sidereal months, and the solar rhythm of the Sun's passage through the signs of the sidereal zodiac. These two rhythms are of fundamental significance to the human being's astrological biography. They present a key to the unfolding of the human being's destiny on the one hand, and to his spiritual development on the other hand.

The lunar rhythm of the sidereal month (lasting 27.32 days, measured by the orbit of the Moon around the sidereal zodiac), starting from the Moon's location in the sidereal zodiac at the moment of conception (= the Ascendant at birth or its opposite, the Descendant), corresponds to seven years of life. During a normal-length embryonic period of 273 days there are ten lunar sidereal months (10 x 27.32 = 273.2 days). This gives rise correspondingly to a normal life-span of seventy years, comprising ten 7-year periods (10 x 7 = 70), during which the human being's destiny becomes fulfilled. This is the spiral of life, amounting (on average) to ten 7-year periods, each corresponding to a particular planet. Thus a normal

VI. The Hermetic—Astrological Science of Destiny

life consists of ten 7-year planetary periods connected with the unfolding of the human being's destiny.

On the other hand the planetary periods are also connected with the human being's development. Thus, in line with our consideration of Rudolf Steiner's life in the last two chapters, the planetary periods are associated with a definite development which can be summarized as man → hermetic man → zodiacal man. As Rudolf Steiner expressed it:

Together with the Earth we exist within seven interpenetrating (planetary) spheres, and we grow into them, enter into connection with them in the course of life (as indicated in Table 11, the seven planetary periods extend from birth to the age of 63). Our life from birth to death is unfolded out of its original inherent tendencies, inasmuch as the star (i.e. planetary) spheres draw us from birth to death. When we have reached the Saturn sphere (56–63) we have passed through all that the beings of the various planetary spheres in grace accomplish for us and then, speaking in the occult sense, we enter into a free-moving cosmic existence of our own.[9]

The seven planetary spheres – as given in the classical (Babylonian-Ptolemaic) geocentric sequence – are: Moon, Mercury, Venus, Sun, Mars, Jupiter and Saturn. The human being enters into connection with these planetary spheres, one after the other, from birth until the age of 63. Then, from 63 onwards, he enters into a "free-moving cosmic existence". In accordance with the classical geocentric conception, this "free-moving cosmic existence" corresponds to the realm of the zodiac, beyond the planetary spheres. This division of life into 7-year periods, together with an indication of the development that the human being passes through during these periods, is listed in Table 11.

The lunar rhythm during the embryonic period, giving rise to 7-year periods of development in life, works right down into the human being's physical constitution. For example, the start of the second 7-year period, that of Mercury, is indicated in the physical constitution by the change of teeth, i.e. the acquisition of new teeth to replace the milk teeth. The start of the third period, that of Venus, is signified on the physical level by the bodily changes that take place at the onset of puberty. The changes associated with later succeeding 7-year periods are much more subtle – inner changes in soul development – but nevertheless they can be observed. For example, the turbulent emotions which often come to expression during the Mars period of life (42 – 49) are well known.

Every human being passes through the stages of soul development connected with the planetary spheres (at least the earlier stages of development), but few people pay attention to the corresponding 7-year periods. In hermetic astrology consciousness is directed towards the 7-year periods of soul development, through which the human being can begin to experi-

Table 11:
The human being's development through the 7-year periods
(shown in relation to the classical geocentric planetary sequence)

7-year period	planet	development	
0– 7	Moon	physical body	
7–14	Mercury	etheric body	man
14–21	Venus	astral body	
21–42	Sun	self	
42–49	Mars	spirit self	hermetic man
49–56	Jupiter	life spirit	(likeness)
56–63	Saturn	spirit man	
63→	Zodiac		zodiacal man (image)

ence a relationship between his inner soul life and the planetary spheres. Further, through a study of the hermetic correspondence between the 7-year life periods and the sidereal lunar months of the embryonic period, a new understanding as to how destiny unfolds through the cycle of 7-year periods is made possible. But for this possibility to become realised, the hermetic rule must be applied to the birth information, calculating back from the date of birth to the date of conception. Here it is a help if knowledge is available as to whether the birth took place on time, or whether it was premature or overdue; if this information is known, it helps to locate the correct date of conception among the various possible solutions offered by the hermetic rule.

In the case of applying the hermetic rule successfully to determine the correct date of conception, not only the sequence of lunar sidereal months between conception and birth can be followed, but also the passage of the Sun through the signs of the zodiac during this time. The solar rhythm of the Sun's passage through the zodiacal signs, each sign being traversed in ca. 30½ days of the embryonic period, when transposed to the spiral of life gives rise to 7.8-year *zodiacal periods* – periods of spiritual development in contrast to the 7-year periods of soul development associated with the planetary spheres (the latter arising through the lunar rhythm of the sidereal month). Both rhythms are of fundamental significance to the human being's development, but they operate on different levels: the solar rhythm on the level of the zodiac (the passage through the various signs giving rise to phases of spiritual development), and the lunar rhythm on the level of the planetary spheres (giving rise to phases of soul development).

Knowledge of these two rhythms can help to give a completely new relationship to life and to the cosmos. Through the 7-year periods of soul development a living connection with the successive planetary spheres can be established, and at the same time a new security in the unfolding of life's destiny can be found. On the other hand, through the 7.8-year periods of spiritual development the signs of the zodiac become spiritually tangible, and progress through these zodiacal life periods opens up new possibilities of a conscious spiritual development.

In astrological biography there are two fundamental rhythms established during the embryonic period which manifest in the human being's biography: the lunar rhythm of 7-year periods and the solar rhythm of 7.8-year periods. To illustrate this, let us look again at the main events in John Addey's life. From Table 10 it can be seen that fairly early during the Sun period (21–42, corresponding to the years 1941–1962) on the one hand he suffered the blow of destiny which resulted in him losing the use of his legs, and on the other hand he got married – all during the Capricorn zodiacal period (1943–1950). The following zodiacal period, that of Aquarius (1950–1958) – towards the end of the Sun period – denoted a time of increased activity in astrological affairs: on the one hand as vice-president of the Astrological Lodge of the Theosophical Society, and on the other hand as a full-time astrological consultant for a short period of time (ca. 1953–1955).

He founded the Astrological Association (at the age of 38), coinciding with the start of the Pisces zodiacal life period (1958–1966). Later during the Pisces period he became president of the Astrological Association, and retained this post until 1973, almost to the end of the Aries period (1966–1974). The main work on his book *Harmonics in Astrology* he accomplished during the Jupiter period of his life (49–56, coinciding with the years 1969–1976), and the book became published at the end of this period (1976). By the time of publication he had already entered his last zodiacal period – that of Taurus (1974–1982) – and the Saturn 7-year period was beginning (starting 1976). It was during the Saturn period that he became ill and died, his death occuring just after the Gemini zodiacal period had commenced. With the occurrence of death, John Addey departed from earthly life to begin his journey through the planetary spheres, commencing with the passage through the Moon sphere. Life in the planetary spheres and in the realm of the zodiac will continue for this individuality – Michael Maestlin/John Addey – until the time comes when a new decision to reincarnate upon the Earth is made.

Juxtaposition of the lunar and solar rhythms

From the foregoing brief survey of John Addey's astrological biography in relation to the lunar and solar rhythms, it is evident that the unfolding of the spiral of life through 7-year periods, which is a consequence of the lunar rhythm during the embryonic period, is complemented by the zodiacal phases arising through the solar rhythm during the embryonic period. The spiral of life – which is of general validity, applying to everyone – becomes *individualized* when viewed in relationship to the zodiacal periods stemming from the solar rhythm. This is illustrated by the tabulation in Table 12, which shows the juxtaposition of the two rhythms in John Addey's life, yielding a detailed astrological biography comprising planetary and zodiacal periods.

The juxtaposition of the two rhythms – that of the spiral of life and that of the zodiacal periods – gives rise to phases of life each specified by a planet and a sign of the zodiac. For example, from Table 12, the period in John Addey's life from November 1950 to June 1958 was the Sun/Aquarius period. During this time John Addey was vice-president of the Astrological Lodge of the Theosophical Society. This was followed by the Sun/Pisces period (June 1958 – June 1962), and for much of this time he was secretary of the Astrological Association, becoming president in 1961.

Table 12:
Juxtaposition of the lunar and solar rhythms in John Addey's life
(detailed astrological biography comprising planetary and zodiacal periods)

age	lunar rhythm/ ↓ planet	solar rhythm ↓ zodiacal sign	Corresponding life period
birth – $0^y\ 2^m$	Moon	Virgo	June 15 – Aug. 1920
$0^y\ 2^m - 7^y\ 0^m$	Moon	Libra	Aug. 1920 – Jun. 1927
$7^y\ 0^m - 7^y 10^m$	Mercury	Libra	Jun. 1927 – Apr. 1928
$7^y 10^m - 14^y\ 0^m$	Mercury	Scorpio	Apr. 1928 – Jun. 1934
$14^y\ 0^m - 15^y\ 5^m$	Venus	Scorpio	Jun. 1934 – Nov. 1935
$15^y\ 5^m - 21^y\ 0^m$	Venus	Sagittarius	Nov. 1935 – Jun. 1941
$21^y\ 0^m - 22^y 11^m$	Sun	Sagittarius	Jun. 1941 – May 1943
$22^y 11^m - 30^y\ 5^m$	Sun	Capricorn	May 1943 – Nov. 1950
$30^y\ 5^m - 38^y\ 0^m$	Sun	Aquarius	Nov. 1950 – Jun. 1958
$38^y\ 0^m - 42^y\ 0^m$	Sun	Pisces	Jun. 1958 – Jun. 1962
$42^y\ 0^m - 45^y\ 9^m$	Mars	Pisces	Jun. 1962 – Mar. 1966
$45^y\ 9^m - 49^y\ 0^m$	Mars	Aries	Mar. 1966 – Jun. 1969
$49^y\ 0^m - 53^y\ 8^m$	Jupiter	Aries	Jun. 1969 – Feb. 1974
$53^y\ 8^m - 56^y\ 0^m$	Jupiter	Taurus	Feb. 1974 – Jun. 1976
$56^y\ 0^m - 61^y\ 9^m$	Saturn	Taurus	Jun. 1976 – Mar. 1982
$61^y\ 9^m$ – death	Saturn	Gemini	Mar. 1982 – March 27

Everyone's life can be looked at in terms of the spiral of life, which gives a general overview of life through the sequence of 7-year planetary periods. Moreover, as indicated in the last two chapters, the spiral of life can be viewed in relation to the birth horoscope – in terms of the planetary positions and relationships between the planets – to gain more detailed insight into the human being's development on the levels of life and consciousness through the 7-year planetary periods. If the hermetic rule is then utilized to determine the horoscope of conception from the birth horoscope, the zodiacal periods can be determined by following the passage of the Sun through the signs of the zodiac during the embryonic period. (The lengths of the zodiacal periods thus arising are listed in Table 13.)

Table 13:
Lengths of the zodiacal periods in life

zodiacal sign	length of zodiacal period	
	years	years and months
Aries	7.91288	$7^y 11^m$
Taurus	8.01536	$8^y\ 0^m$
Gemini	8.05895	$8^y\ 1^m$
Cancer	8.03013	$8^y\ 0^m$
Leo	7.93779	$7^y 11^m$
Virgo	7.80933	$7^y 10^m$
Libra	7.67998	$7^y\ 8^m$
Scorpio	7.58373	$7^y\ 7^m$
Sagittarius	7.54423	$7^y\ 7^m$
Capricorn	7.57038	$7^y\ 7^m$
Aquarius	7.65650	$7^y\ 8^m$
Pisces	7.78104	$7^y\ 9^m$

Utilizing Table 13 to determine the sequence of zodiacal periods arising in connection with the Sun's passage through the zodiacal signs during the embryonic period, the zodiacal periods may then be juxtaposed with the 7-year planetary periods to give an individualized overview of the course of life, one that is unique to each individual. This overview constitutes a basic *astrological biography* of the individual's life, one that brings to consciousness in any given period of life the planet and the zodiacal sign that provides the cosmic background to the individual's soul/spiritual development in that particular phase of life.

Reading the signs from the embryonic period

Returning to the question as to whether a blow of destiny such as that of paralysis can be foreseen from the birth/conception horoscopes, let us look once again at John Addey's conception chart – the chart which relates archetypally to the image, indicating the starting point of the weaving of destiny during the embryonic period. The hermetic chart of the conception configuration shows that Mercury was rising, in conjunction with the Ascendant, and that the Moon was in conjunction with Mars, Jupiter and Neptune (see Chart 15). Mercury and the Moon, as the planets corresponding to the 10-petalled and 4-petalled lotus flowers, relate primarily to the impulses of movement and the will. These two planets are therefore of key significance in connection with paralysis.

Looking now at the planetary configuration during John Addey's embryonic period, at the moment corresponding to the point in life (age 23½) at the onset of the paralysis, in the hermetic chart Mercury is in conjunction with the Moon, with both planets square to Mars (see Chart 18). As a picture this does not necessarily mean "paralysis", but it is interesting that h-Mercury and the Moon are in conjunction with one another at this moment in time. (Moreover, g-Mars at this point in time is more or less exactly conjunct the zodiacal location of g-Mercury at birth in the previous incarnation as Michael Maestlin.)

Turning now to the other example of paralysis considered earlier in this chapter, Mercury in the hermetic chart at birth was setting, in conjunction with the Descendant, opposite to the point in the zodiac occupied by the Moon at the moment of conception (see Charts 10 and 11). And at the moment in the embryonic period corresponding to the stroke (age 46½), when the paralysis set in, h-Mercury was conjunct the place of the Ascendant at conception and opposite the place occupied by the Moon at birth (see Chart 12). Again, as in John Addey's case, Mercury and the Moon – the planets of movement and the will – were implicated in the stroke of destiny that took place here.

It goes beyond the bounds of human judgement to foresee the precise nature of the events of destiny that befall a person, on the basis of studying the planetary movements between conception and birth. Human intelligence can do no more than "read the signs" of the manifestation via the planetary movements of the weaving of destiny between conception and birth. It would require the higher faculty of *karmic clairvoyance* (referred to in Chapter 3), which ultimately is a matter of grace, in order to behold the exact nature of the destiny images woven into the etheric body during the embryonic period. In fact, it is a blessing in disguise not to be able to behold directly the actual weaving of destiny itself, and only retrospectively to survey the reflection of the weaving of destiny as it manifests in the planetary movements. For if anyone were able to behold the destiny woven into the etheric body between conception and birth, he might be tempted to avoid any difficult blows of destiny lying ahead of him, which would inevitably result in chaos instead of order in destiny. Thus karmic clairvoyance entails a very high level of moral development and a total acceptance of the higher wisdom of karma.

In the absence of the development of the faculty of karmic clairvoyance, all that can be learnt from a study of the planetary movements between conception and birth is that at certain points in life (determined by converting from embryonic time to age in life) events of destiny will occur, indicated by the conjunctions and oppositions of the planets – among themselves and also in relation to the planetary positions at conception and birth. (Of particular importance here, as evident in the two examples discussed in this chapter, are the zodiacal locations of the Sun at conception and birth, and of the Moon at conception and birth – the latter related via the hermetic rule to the Ascendant at birth and conception).

Important phases in life are revealed through a study of the planetary movements between conception and birth, e.g. the 7-year periods indicated by the periodic return of the Moon to its zodiacal location at conception, and the 7.8-year periods arising in connection with the Sun's passage through the signs of the zodiac between conception and birth. A consciousness of these rhythms and of their correspondences with the phases of life can help to open up a new inner connection with the cosmic world.

In hermetic astrology consciousness is directed towards the embryonic period as the time of preparation of destiny, which takes place within the sphere bounded by the orbit of the Moon. It is within the Moon sphere, hidden from normal human consciousness, that an individual's destiny becomes elaborated. The significance of acquiring a general consciousness of the embryonic period and its associated rhythms, even if the nature of events of destiny prepared during the embryonic period cannot be directly known in detail, is that thereby the individual can gain access to deeper levels of his being. He may become led inwardly into connection with the Being of Christ. For Christ is the Lord of karma. It is he who can be described as the "guardian" of the weaving of destiny during the embryonic period. In this way, consciousness of the spiral of life – which constitutes the general form of the plan of destiny outlined in detail during the embryonic period – can be a step on the way towards consciousness of Christ, the Lord of karma. The hermetic-astrological science of destiny is thus a science rooted not only in the reality of cosmic rhythms, but also in the higher reality of the working of the Being of Christ in the elaboration of karma during the embryonic period. Moreover, through the grace of Christ the faculty of karmic clairvoyance may begin to develop, so that the direction of consciousness towards the embryonic period – as outlined above – can serve as a preparatory stage leading to the development of karmic clairvoyance.

Soul development/spiritual development

The hermetic-astrological science of destiny looks at the embryonic period between conception and birth as the time during which the human being's destiny becomes elaborated, when his destiny for the new life on Earth is prepared. Through a study of various examples it is apparent that the entire course of planetary movements taking place during the embryonic period is of significance for the elaboration of the human being's karma, but the conception and birth configurations – denoting the start and the culmination of the weaving of destiny – are especially important. For the weaving of destiny during the embryonic period comprises a review of the course of life between birth and death in the previous incarnation – a review in which the moment of conception corresponds to birth in the former incarnation (conception → birth) and where birth (signifying the culmination of the embryonic period) corresponds to death in the last incarnation (birth → death). (See Figure 1 for a summary of these correspondences, which constitute the fundamental principle of astrological biography.)

The correspondences (conception → birth, and birth → death) between the embryonic period and the course of life are then carried over to the present incarnation. In the weaving of destiny between conception and birth, the destiny for the coming incarnation is prepared such that the moment of conception corresponds to the start of the unfolding of destiny at birth. And the termination of the weaving of destiny at the moment of birth corresponds archetypally to the moment of death, i.e. to the completion of the course of life. (In practice, the human being may – through grace – live further, or he may – on account of his karma – be called out of life prematurely, prior to the completion of the unfolding of the web of destiny woven during the embryonic period.) Moreover, in looking at the course of planetary movements between conception and birth, the movements of the Sun and Moon hold the key to the human being's spiritual and soul development during the course of life. This spiritual and soul development – arising through the solar and lunar rhythms during the embryonic period – needs now to be examined more closely, and as will become apparent, the terms "spiritual development" and "soul development" are inadequate, or even misleading.

In the preceding chapters we have looked in depth at the lunar rhythm – the sequence of approximately ten lunar sidereal months during the embryonic period – as the basis for the spiral of life. The spiral of life denotes the unfolding of the human being's destiny through a sequence of approximately ten 7-year periods between birth and death. Further, it indicates the soul (psychic) development of man during the sequence of 7-year periods, in the sense that it bears an analogy with the journey of the soul through the planetary spheres in the life after death. Thus each 7-year period up to the age of 63 corresponds to a planetary sphere: the first period (0–7) to the Moon sphere, and on through the remaining planetary periods up to the period between 56 and 63 (Saturn sphere), with the period beyond the age of 63 corresponding to the sphere of the zodiac (see Table 11).

The term *soul development* is not really appropriate to characterize the human being's evolution through the 7-year periods of the spiral of life, and it is applied here essentially to distinguish it from the *spiritual development* (again an inadequate term) arising through the solar rhythm of zodiacal phases each approximately 7.8 years long. Although there is a definite soul development through the spiral of life, which can be characterized as Moon phase (infancy), Mercury phase (childhood), Venus phase (youth), Sun phase (adulthood), etc., the early life phases are connected more with the human being's physical development, whilst the later phases are related essentially to the human being's spiritual development (i.e. to the potential unfolding of the latent capacities of the inner spiritual man – the likeness – through the Mars, Jupiter and Saturn life periods, and of the image during the zodiacal period). It is only during the Sun phase that, strictly speaking, the term soul development is applicable in a pure sense – during which time the three layers or levels of the self (feeling, thinking and will) emerge and develop.

The first three 7-year periods

The first three 7-year periods of the spiral of life are phases in which the development of one of the three "bodies" – physical, etheric and astral – is emphasized. The development of the will, thinking and feeling that takes place in the first three 7-year periods (those of the Moon, Mercury and Venus) arises primarily as a consequence of the development of the physical, etheric and astral bodies during these three periods. The first three periods can thus be characterized as phases of development of *natural will, thinking and feeling*.

Here, however, it is necessary to distinguish between two developments occurring during the first three 7-year periods. The significance of these two developments was referred to earlier in connection with interpreting the difference between the hermetic chart and the geocentric chart. The former refers more to the level of consciousness, and the latter to the level of life, although there is a reciprocal interaction between these two levels. In terms of the spiral of life, it is primarily the geocentric sequence which applies: Moon, Mercury, Venus. In Chapter 4 it was indicated that this development is bound up with the emphasis on certain organs. During the Moon, Mercury and Venus periods the emphasis is on the brain (Moon), the lungs (Mercury) and the kidneys (Venus). Here it is a matter of a descending organic sequence. Corresponding to this organic-physiological development during the first three 7-year periods, however, there is a reciprocal soul (psychic) development of the faculties of natural will (Moon), natural thinking (Mercury) and natural feeling (Venus). These faculties emerge as the counterpart or correlate to the respective organic development.

Thus during the Moon period (0–7) the brain is the organ which receives the most pronounced emphasis in connection with the development of the physical body in the first period of life. At the same time, as is evident from the vigorous movements of its arms and legs by the baby or infant, the Moon forces are active in the limbs. These movements are an expression of natural will, which emerges as the soul (psychic) counterpart to the organic development of the physical body between the age of 0 and 7. Just as the Moon reflects light from the surrounding cosmos, so the baby or small child reflects everything taking place around it, e.g. if it is smiled at, it smiles back.

During the Mercury period (7–14) the etheric body undergoes a special development. The etheric body manifests itself above all in the various rhythmic processes taking place in the organism, the most important of which are the beating of the heart and the breathing of the lungs. The psychic correlate to this organic-physiological development involving the lungs is the awakening of questions (natural thinking) in the child. From around the age of 7 onwards it wants to know everything about the world around it. This natural thinking is the counterpart to the development of the etheric body. At the same time the child of this age becomes a social being, going out and interacting with other children (corresponding to "breathing out") and returning home to the security of its family (corresponding to "breathing in"). In this way the child between 7 and 14 reveals the working of the Mercury forces, when considered from the standpoint of the spiral of life.

Similarly, the adolescent – between the ages of 14 and 21 – reveals the working of the Venus forces, when looked at in terms of the spiral of life. In this Venus period the astral body emerges, which has a special relationship with – streaming into – the kidneys. The soul (psychic) correlate to this is the experience of a flood of feelings (natural feeling). Deep emotions and longings, also tender feelings of love, arise in the adolescent as the counterpart to the emergence of the astral body during this period of life.

In consideration of the spiral of life, the geocentric sequence: Moon, Mercury, Venus is relevant to an understanding of the first three periods. The zodiacal locations of the Moon, Mercury and Venus in the geocentric chart, as well as the geocentric planetary aspects involving these three planets, are of significance in understanding the human being's development in life up to the age of 21. This life development, which correlates with that of natural will, thinking and feeling, tends to overshadow the more subtle development of consciousness, which is indicated by the Moon, Venus and Mercury in the hermetic chart. Contrary to the *de-*

scending organic development (geocentric sequence: Moon, Mercury, Venus), this more subtle development on the level of consciousness (hermetic sequence: Moon, Venus, Mercury) is an *ascending psychic development*. It is connected with the ascending unfolding of the various lotus flowers (4-petalled – Moon; 6-petalled – Venus; 10-petalled – Mercury), whereby the 4-petalled lotus flower is the organ of the will, the 6-petalled lotus flower that of feeling (balance and harmony) and the 10-petalled lotus flower that of thinking (rational, analytical, combinatorial). Nevertheless, the unfolding of these three lower lotus flowers during the first three 7-year periods is also bound up with the development of the physical, etheric and astral bodies. It is only later, through the emergence of the self (its organ being the 12-petalled lotus flower, that of the Sun), that the lower lotus flowers can be developed consciously. Prior to this, the capacities of will, feeling and thought bound up with the three lower lotus flowers are also "natural", i.e. a consequence of the natural development of the physical, etheric and astral bodies, rather than arising from a conscious soul-spiritual development. (See *Hermetic Astrology* I, Chapter 5, for a description of the relationship of the three lower lotus flowers to the forces of the physical, etheric and astral bodies.)

For example, the zodiacal location of Venus in the hermetic chart is indicative of the child's feeling life – oscillating between sympathy and antipathy – which emerges between the ages of 7 and 14, whilst the zodiacal position of Mercury in the hermetic chart indicates the emergence of the adolescent's rational, analytical thinking capacity between the ages of 14 and 21. The capacities of the will, feeling and thinking – arising through the subtle development of the lower three lotus flowers during the first three 7-year periods – become the foundation for the human being's inner soul life and gain in significance the further he advances along the path of spiritual development. For the stronger the development of consciousness becomes, the more the lotus flowers and their associated faculties become activated. Thus the hermetic chart essentially shows latent capacities to be unfolded by the human being on the path of moral-spiritual development, and it is only insofar as a natural unfolding of the lotus flowers also takes place during the 7-year periods that the hermetic chart is relevant to every human being regardless of his spiritual development. Moreover, owing to the interaction between the level of consciousness and that of life, the planetary positions in the hermetic chart may also reveal organic problems. (An example of this was discussed in Chapter 4, where the conjunction between Saturn and Mercury in the hermetic chart of an adolescent girl indicated the onset of short-sightedness at the age of 14.)

The Sun period onwards

Following on from the first three life periods comes the Sun period

(21–42). In the Sun period the self emerges and passes through three stages of development – sentient self (21–28), intellectual self (28–35) and consciousness self (35–42) – which can be designated as phases of soul development, in the pure sense of this expression. For the feeling, thinking and will which come to expression in the Sun period of life are no longer "natural", i.e. no longer simply a consequence of the development of the physical, etheric and astral bodies, but are truly a matter of soul or inner development. Here feeling, thinking and will develop inwardly in connection with the evolution of the self. Thus there is a world of difference between the natural thinking of a child and the thinking directed by the self of which the adult is capable. Even though Friedrich Nietzsche became a professor of philology at the early age of 24 (see Chapter 1), the real power of his thought – self-directed thought – emerged later. And although the transition from the natural feeling of the adolescent to the feeling life of the adult is not so marked, there is generally a depth and maturity to the adult's feeling life which the young person lacks. Similarly, the true will of the self is free in relation to the natural will. The latter is the source of unconscious impulses, and when the human being acts out of these impulses he is not free. Whereas the deeper core of the consciousness self – the inner center of the self – is the source of moral impulses (moral intuitions), according to which the individual acts in freedom.

When man acts from instincts, urges, passions and so on, he is unfree. The impulses that determine his actions reach his consciousness in the same way as do sense impressions. In this his true self is not active. He is acting on a level at which his true self does not come to expression at all. His true selfhood discloses itself no more on this level than the physical world discloses its true inner reality to mere sense observation. However, the sense world is not in truth an illusion; it is man who turns it into an illusion. But the urges, cravings and so on, resembling sense impressions, can through deeds become actual illusions; this happens when man allows the illusions within him to act; he is not himself acting. He allows the non-spiritual in him to act. It is only his own spirit that acts when the impulse to action originates, as a moral intuition, in the sphere of sense-free thinking. Then it is he himself, and he alone, who acts. Then he is free, he acts out of his true self.[10]

The soul development of the Sun period stands between the natural development during the first three 7-year periods and the spiritual development which may unfold in the life periods beyond that of the Sun. These later phases of development were characterized in Chapter 5. Here it is a matter of distinguishing between this higher development, which may take place in the later 7-year periods of life, and the development arising through the solar rhythm of the zodiacal phases each approximately 7.8 years in length.

In Chapter 5 man's potential development during the 7-year periods of the spiral of life was summarized as man → hermetic man → zodiacal man, or alternatively as man → likeness (inner spiritual man) → image (divine man), where the likeness is restored to its higher spiritual nature. The development of "man" in the Sun period, between the ages of 21 and 42, is that of the self, which is centered cosmically in the Sun. The development over and beyond the level of the self – the coming to expression of the likeness and the image – corresponds cosmically to the planetary spheres beyond that of the Sun, i.e. the spheres of Mars, Jupiter and Saturn, followed by the zodiacal sphere. Here lies the difference from the development arising through the solar rhythm of the zodiacal phases, for the latter is bound up with the Sun. It does not go beyond the level of the Sun (corresponding to the self), and hence a more appropriate term for it is *self development*.

The path of self development

The path of self development through 7.8-year zodiacal periods is unique to each individual and is specified by the passage of the Sun through the signs of the zodiac between conception and birth. However, the term *self development* is not wholly accurate, for in the early zodiacal phases of life the self is not fully incarnated. It emerges primarily during the Sun period of life, usually coming to birth around the age of 21. After the age of 21, therefore, it is possible to speak of a development of the self. The term self development can then be applied to the 7.8-year periods arising in connection with the Sun's passage through the zodiacal signs during the embryonic period. (Prior to the age of 21 these 7.8-year zodiacal phases are not periods of self or inner development, but are epochs of "outer development" – see below.)

From approximately the age of 21 onwards, each zodiacal sign colours the impulse of the "inner Sun", the self, on its course of development through life. Here the goal of this journey through life of the self is indicated by the Sun's location in the zodiac at the moment of birth. This sign of the zodiac radiates into the human being's inner life of the self, beckoning the self onwards, as it were, towards self-realisation.

In the example under consideration – that of John Addey – the Sun's zodiacal location at the moment of birth was 0° Gemini. It was this zodiacal location of the Sun which signified the goal of the journey of the self through life. As emerged in the foregoing, upon reaching this goal in his sixty-second year, John Addey completed his life journey and passed on to higher realms of existence. In this case there was an almost perfect correspondence between the course of the embryonic period and the course of life, i.e. the correspondences: conception → birth, and birth → death were both fulfilled.

Given that birth takes place, the correspondence conception → birth is always fulfilled. However, it is by no means a frequent occurrence that the correspondence: birth → death is also fulfilled. In general it can happen that either the human being dies before the destiny woven during the embryonic period has unfolded completely, or that he lives on beyond the cut-off date (= the date in life corresponding to the embryonic age reached at the moment of birth, since the moment of birth signifies the "cut-off" point in the embryonic period).

The occurrence of death prior to the cut-off date can occur for a variety of reasons, usually bound up with the future karma of the individual concerned. For example, it may be that he is called out of life prematurely in order to begin preparation already for his next incarnation. In this case the "unused destiny", i.e. the destiny woven in the last part of the embryonic period but not lived through in life, may become rewoven in metamorphosed form into the web of destiny of the next incarnation.

On the other hand, if the individual lives beyond the cut-off date, it is a matter of grace. He lives further in a "karma-free existence", having absolved his allotted karma through the unfolding of the web of destiny. There is then no possibility of his going astray from his path of destiny. For this reason Rudolf Steiner made a practice of communicating to someone knowledge of his previous incarnation(s) only when they had attained their seventieth birthday. (He made exceptions to this rule, however.)

On average the embryonic period, during which the human being's destiny is woven, lasts ten lunar sidereal months, which means that destiny is unfolded through a sequence of ten 7-year periods – normally signifying its completion, i.e. arrival at the cut-off date, by the time of the seventieth birthday. Rudolf Steiner was aware of the danger of communicating to someone his previous incarnation prior to the cut-off date of his destiny, the danger being that this knowledge could lead the person concerned to become too preoccupied with the past, or could influence him to act in the illusion that he would be fulfilling a "karmic task", which in fact could be completely at variance with his actual chosen destiny in the new (present) incarnation. This is in accordance with the saying: "A little knowledge is dangerous." Thus, the communication of a little genuine knowledge concerning previous incarnation(s) to someone is sufficient to be instrumental in possibly leading the person astray with regard to his chosen destiny in the present incarnation, if the person concerned were to apply this knowledge misguidedly. To avoid this possibility, Rudolf Steiner waited until there was no further likelihood of a person straying from the chosen path of destiny. Rudolf Steiner was well aware of the deep karmic responsibility which is bound up with the communication of knowledge of previous incarnations. He knew full well that this knowledge lead may lead to errors of judgement along the path of human destiny. (This karmic responsibility was discussed from another aspect in *Hermetic Astrology* I, Chapter 7, in connection with the related dangers of ego inflation and self annihilation, which also may result from the communication of the "little knowledge" concerning previous incarnations.) There is also the possibility that when someone arrives at "knowledge" of previous incarnations, it may be wrong. This could have serious consequences, especially if this false knowledge were to be communicated. This danger should be avoided at all costs, by applying the guidelines for karma research outlined in *Hermetic Astrology* I, Chapter 7, and above all by resisting the initial desire to inform people of previous incarnations.

On an archetypal level, the development of the self (the "inner Sun") during the course of life is signified by the journey of the Sun through the zodiacal signs between conception and birth. Applying the correspondence between the embryonic period and the spiral of life, there is a corresponding journey along the path of self development, which leads through the zodiacal periods in life. The zodiacal periods may be juxtaposed with the 7-year planetary periods, as in the example of John Addey (see Table 12), to give rise to an outline of the individual's astrological biography.

As remarked above, the zodiacal periods – as epochs of self development – acquire full significance only after the emergence of the self during the Sun period of life, commencing around the age of 21. From this age onwards it is possible to speak of an inner development of the self. Prior to this age the zodiacal periods are indicative of "outer developments" taking place in the person's environment. As an example, consider the difference between an event in a child's biography and one in the biography of an adult. In the case of a child, for example, whose family moves from one town or country to another, the change is not initiated from within himself, but approaches him as an "outer development" – one which nevertheless affects him deeply. The adult, however, chooses out of himself to move, even if the reasons for him doing so are compelling, and in his case the self is involved in bringing about the change in his life.

In both instances – in the life of the child and in that of the adult – it can be the case that such changes coincide with the beginning of new zodiacal periods, in which case the outer changes simultaneously denote inner changes. Usually, however, the succession of zodiacal periods denote purely inner changes. For this reason they are difficult to detect in the human being's life prior to the age of 21. (Outer changes in an individual's life are often correlated with the occurrences of New and Full Moon during the embryonic period, i.e. new phases in life are frequently prefigured in the embryonic period by the transition from one lunar phase to the next.)

The inner changes that the individual undergoes along the path of self development are usually philosophical or religious in nature, generally involving a change in world outlook, e.g. coming to expression in a religious deepening, or the discovery of a new spiritual orientation in life. An example was indicated earlier in the life of John Addey, whose Aquarian zodiacal period coincided with the time when he was vice-president of the Astrological Lodge of the Theosophical Society. A new spiritual orientation showed itself in the following zodiacal period in his life – that of Pisces – from the beginning of which he was secretary (later becoming president) of the Astrological Association (see Table 10 for dates). The change in orientation from the Aquarian to the Piscean zodiacal period signified turning towards a more scientifically-based kind of astrology, one that could make its way in the present scientific-intellectual climate of the western world. (The Astrological Association has since acquired such a reputation on account of its support of scientific research in astrology.) In this case the transition from one zodiacal period to the next signified not only an inner change in spiritual orientation, but also an outer change, since the Astrological Association came into being then as something new in the world, and John Addey carried a large share of responsibility for this "new birth".

The passage of the Sun through the signs of the sidereal zodiac between conception and birth thus holds the key to an outline of the individual's self development. But how may a deeper understanding of the zodiacal periods in the course of an individual's self development be acquired?

The arcana of the Tarot

Spiritual comprehension of the nature of self development in relation to the zodiacal periods of life can be gained through a study of the major arcana of the Tarot, as given in the book *Meditations on the Tarot*[11]. The twenty-two major arcana of the Tarot form a circle, just as the twelve signs of the zodiac comprise a circle. The zodiacal signs are the so-called "animal circle". (The German word for zodiac – *Tierkreis* – means literally *animal circle*.) However, the circle of the twenty-two arcana forms a circle which embraces not only the the twelve signs of the zodiac, but also the seven planets, and the three forces of hindrance (connected astrologically with Uranus, Neptune and Pluto – see Chapter 8). The seeker on this spiritual path has to acquire knowledge and experience through meditation of the entire circle of existence, as to how these twenty-two macrocosmic forces work within him.

The twenty-two major arcana of the Tarot represent in pictorial form on the human, microcosmic level the twenty-two macrocosmic forces – the forces of the twelve signs of the zodiac and the seven planets, and the three forces of hindrance mediated by the planets Uranus, Neptune and Pluto.

VI. The Hermetic—Astrological Science of Destiny

Applying the hermetic principle "as above, so below", first the correspondences between the arcana (on the microcosmic level) and the signs of the zodiac (on the macrocosmic level) have to be found. Then it is possible to turn to the *Meditations on the Tarot* in order to acquire an understanding of the nature of the self development called for in a particular zodiacal period of life. For the *Meditations on the Tarot* are concerned with the path of spiritual development, i.e. development of the self.

For example, for someone in the zodiacal period of life corresponding to the Sun's passage through Virgo during the embryonic period, the nature of the development of the self called for in this period of life is indicated by the eleventh arcanum (*Force*). The eleventh arcanum portrays microcosmically the working of the forces of Virgo in the human being, in the sense of spiritual development. On passing to the next zodiacal period of life (Libra), the relevant arcanum is *Justice*, which corresponds on the microcosmic level with the sign of Libra.

Thus a new arcanum becomes relevant to the development of the self during each new zodiacal period of life. This development proceeds from one sign to the next, aiming always towards the zodiacal sign in which the Sun was placed at the moment of birth. Hence the arcanum corresponding to the birth sign of the Sun is especially important as an indicator of the tasks and trials connected with the goal of the individual in his spiritual development.

The vehicle of the self

The zodiacal location of the Sun at birth represents the culmination of the development of the self – the goal of the incarnating self – but it is only the "tip of the iceberg", so to speak. The submerged part of the iceberg, represented by the Sun's passage around the zodiac from conception up to the time of birth, is also of major significance with respect to the self. It signifies the *vehicle of the self*. This expression is accurate in view of the fact that the self is centered in the Sun. The passage of the Sun through the signs of the zodiac between conception and birth traces out a form which indicates the spiralling in of the self into incarnation. This form, then, constitutes the vehicle of the self on its passage into incarnation. The form of the vehicle of the self is determined by the zodiacal starting point of the Sun at conception ("origin") and by the zodiacal finishing point of the Sun at birth ("goal"). The *zodiacal origin* and the *zodiacal goal* of the self are thus of key significance in understanding the nature of the vehicle of the self.

In traditional astrology only the culminating point (goal), the outermost expression of the vehicle of the self, is taken into consideration – this being the zodiacal location of the Sun at the moment of birth. In hermetic astrology, however, the entire form of the vehicle of the self is taken into consideration (if it is possible to do so, i.e. if the hermetic rule can be applied to calculate the date of conception). This form usually comprises three-quarters of the zodiacal circle. For example, in the case of a conception on April 15, when the Sun is at 0° Aries, if the embryonic period is of normal length, then the birth may well take place on January 15, when the Sun is at 0° Capricorn – having traversed exactly three-quarters of the zodiac. This example is indicated in Figure 9a.

Figure 9 (a and b):
Normal length embryonic period
conception on April 15, when the Sun is at 0° Aries (0°♈)
birth on January 15, when the Sun is at 0° Capricorn (0°♑)

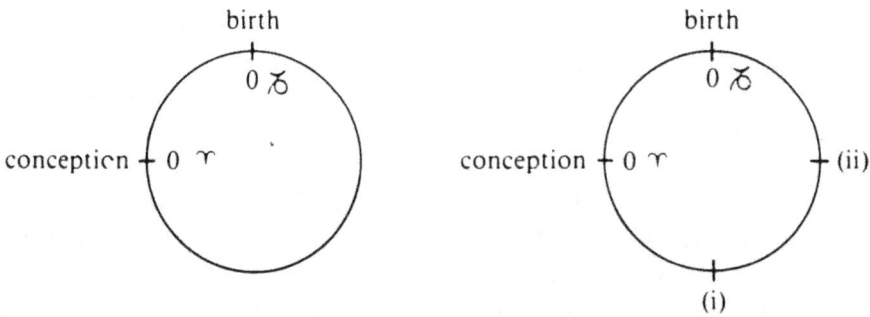

In an example such as that shown in Figure 9a, the length of the embryonic period is three-quarters of a year. This period of time amounts to nine calendar months or ten lunar sidereal months. These ten lunar sidereal months equate with seventy years of life, where the starting point of the Sun at conception corresponds to the age of 0 and the finishing point of the Sun at birth corresponds to the age of 70.

Looking at the form traced out by the Sun during the embryonic period, two points of special interest are: (i) when the Sun is opposite the position at birth, and (ii) when it is opposite its position at conception (see Figure 9b). When transforming from embryonic time to the course of life, what ages in life do (i) and (ii) correspond to?

VI. The Hermetic—Astrological Science of Destiny

Since three-quarters of the zodiac is traversed by the Sun between conception and birth, and one-quarter of the zodiac between conception and (i), then the ratio one-quarter/three-quarters equates with one-third, i.e. correspondingly point (i) is one-third of the way through life, at the age of $23\frac{1}{3}$ ($\frac{1}{3} \times 70 = 23\frac{1}{3}$). Similarly, point (ii) is reached – correspondingly – two-thirds of the way through life, at the age of $46\frac{2}{3}$, assuming a life of 70 years. What do these two moments in life signify, in terms of the development of the self?

The call of the image and of the likeness

As described earlier in this chapter, the zodiacal location of the Sun at birth radiates into the inner life of the self, beckoning the self onwards towards self-realisation. With regard to this inner call of the self, point (i) is especially significant, corresponding to the time in life when the individual begins to be drawn strongly towards self-realisation. A kind of awakening of the self on a deeper level takes place, and an active search for the realisation of the goals of the self in this incarnation commences. From this point in life onwards, the self begins to work towards its goal in incarnation. In the case of a full-term (10 lunar sidereal months) embryonic development, this point corresponds to the age of $23\frac{1}{3}$. (It is somewhat different when the birth is premature or overdue – see below.)

In order to grasp more fully what takes place at this age, corresponding to the point in the embryonic development when the Sun is opposite its position at birth, it is helpful to refer again to the image and the likeness, cosmically represented in hermetic astrology by the planetary configurations at conception and birth. The image, which is active in the formation of the physical body – that the latter is shaped to become a vehicle of the self – is reflected more in the conception configuration (although it is also indicated by the orientation within the zodiacal circle at birth, i.e. by the Ascendant and Midheaven axes). The likeness, on the other hand, works formatively in the configuration of the soul as a vehicle of the self, and comes to expression primarily in the birth horoscope. At the starting point (origin) of its journey from conception to birth, the self is turned more towards the image, and at the culmination (goal) it is the likeness which is the central focus of the self.

This can help us to grasp what takes place at or around the age of $23\frac{1}{3}$ (in the case of a full-term embryonic period), when the Sun reaches the point in the zodiac opposite its location at birth. Here the *call of the likeness* is experienced by the self. The inner spiritual man, or likeness, which embodies the true mission of the incarnated human being, calls the self forward on its journey through life – awakening an impulse to creativity in the individual, towards the fulfilment of his mission. This is the significance of point (i) in Figure 9b, corresponding (in a normal-length pregnancy) to the age of 23⅓. But what is the significance of point (ii) in Figure 9b, corresponding to the age of 46⅔ in life?

Point (ii) is reached during the embryonic period when the Sun is opposite the origin from which it started out in the zodiac at conception. Here the *call of the image* is experienced by the self, and the self becomes directed towards the divine, the eternal being of man. It is a call which inwardly leads the human being back towards his divine origin, orientating him beyond death towards the realm of the Father, the Creator. This is indicated schematically in Figure 10, where the call of the image leads beyond the end of life towards the journey into the afterlife. It is a call which leads to the *completion of the circle* (see Figure 10).

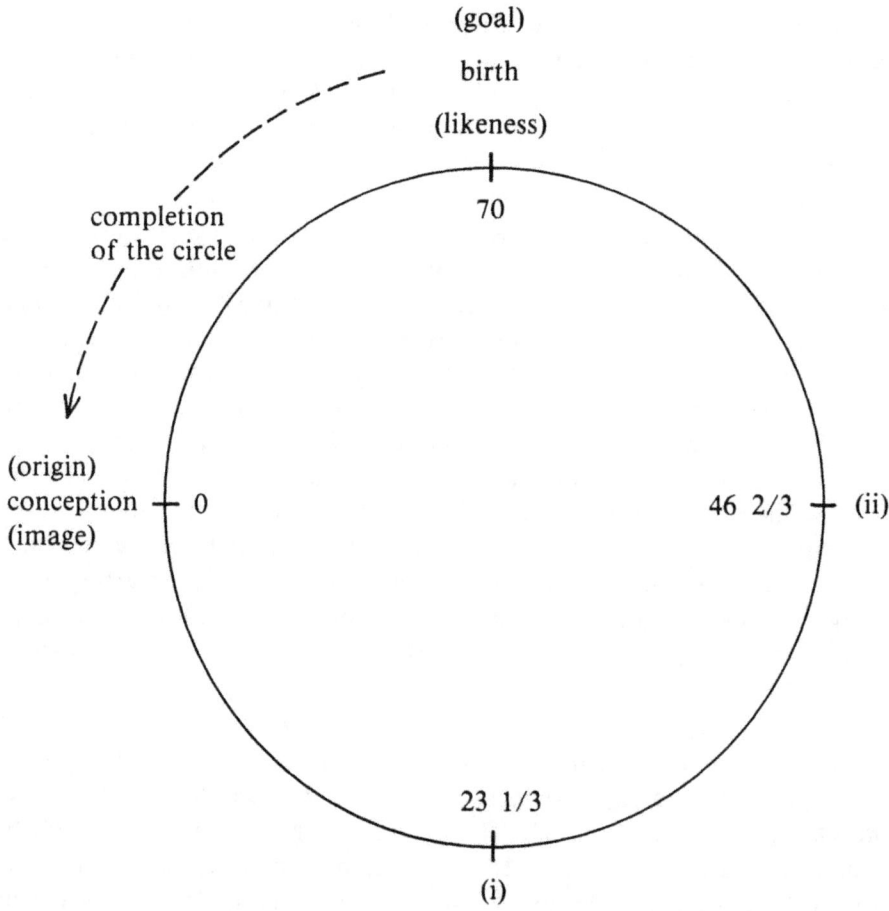

**Figure 10:
The completion of the circle**

The full circle of existence is completed by the human being only when he goes beyond himself. The form of the vehicle of the self is generally three-quarters of the circle. The full circle is formed only by going beyond the self, as indicated by the evolution: man → hermetic man (likeness) → zodiacal man (image). In Chapter 5 it was discussed that the likeness unfolds in three stages, and that – over and above these – the image itself may come more fully to expression in the life of the individual. The completion of the circle of existence comprises an evolution going beyond the self, where the impulse of the likeness leads back through three stages to the image (see Figure 11).

The call for the individual to go beyond himself takes place at the age of $46^{2}/_{3}$. It is a call for the unfolding of the inner spiritual man, the likeness, to ascend beyond the threshold of death to the image, to return to the Divine, and thereby to complete the circle of existence. This inner call is indicated in archetypal form in the parable of the prodigal son, who, after squandering everything which had been bestowed upon him by his father, returned home and said: "Father, I have sinned against heaven and before you; I am no longer worthy to be called your son" (*Luke* xv, 21). In this sense the age of $46^{2}/_{3}$ indicates the "end of the road" for the incarnated human being; having squandered his natural gifts and talents, having reached the deepest point on the path of life, the path now can only lead further if it leads back towards the Father – a path leading beyond the self, towards the origin of the self in the realm of the Father. (The zodiacal realm – the domain of the image – is the sphere in which the human being approaches closest to the Father in the life after death.)

The archetypal experience of the call of the image, which takes place at about the age of $46^{2}/_{3}$, occurs at this age regardless of the length of the embryonic period (assuming that this age is reached at all). In the case of a six-month embryonic period, which is more or less the minimum possible duration of pregnancy, the conversion from the embryonic age to the cut-off point in life yields the age of $46^{2}/_{3}$. (The cut-off point is the age in life corresponding to birth, this being the cut-off point of the embryonic period.) That is, since six months is two-thirds of a normal embryonic period of nine months, and since the latter yields a cut-off date of 70 years, the cut-off date arising from a six-month embryonic period amounts to two-thirds of 70, equating with the age of $46^{2}/_{3}$. In this extreme case point (i) is identical with conception (corresponding to birth), and point (ii) is identical with birth (corresponding to the cut-off date). This extreme example of a six-month embryonic period is listed in Figure 12, together with examples of eight-, nine- and ten-month embryonic periods.

In each case shown in Figure 12, regardless of the length of the embryonic period, the age corresponding to (ii) remains constant, i.e. $46^{2}/_{3}$ years. In a normal length embryonic period of nine months, the cut-off date is 70 years, and the age corresponding to (i) is $70 - 46.67 = 23.33$ years. In the

Figure 11
Return to the image

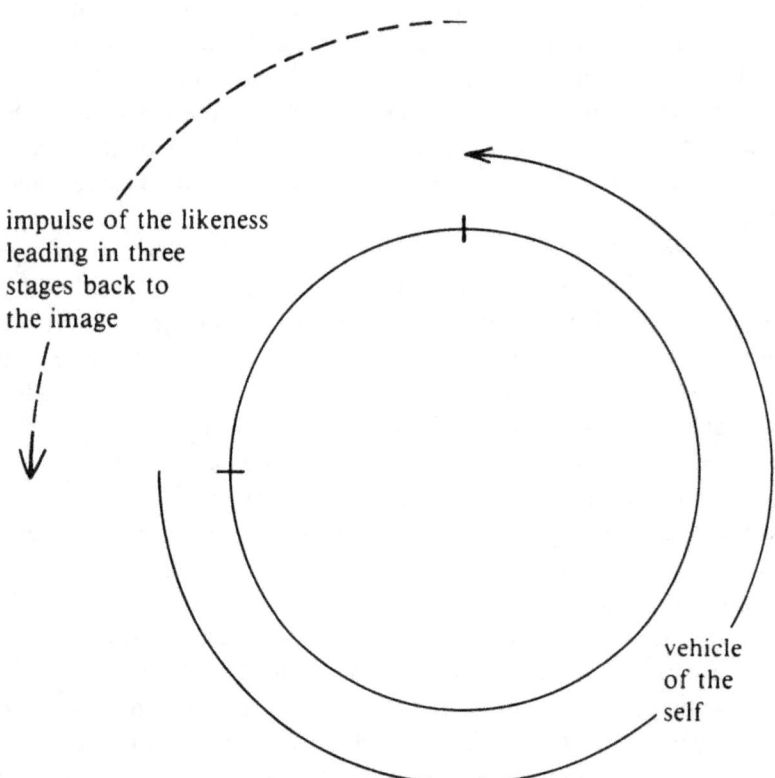

case of a longer embryonic period, e.g. 10 months, the cut-off date is later, i.e. 77.78 years, and so the age corresponding to (i) is correspondingly later: 77.78 − 46.67 = 31.11 years. Here the calling of the self towards its mission takes place relatively late in life.

On the other hand, the call of the self towards its mission occurs relatively early in life in the case of a premature birth. For example, with an eight-month embryonic period, the cut-off date is 62.22 years, and therefore the age corresponding to (i) is: 62.22 − 46.67 = 15.56 years. In such cases, where this call takes place prior to the age of 21, it generally works on a more or less unconscious level, although often it is possible for the prematurely born person to recall an awakening experience stemming from such a relatively early age.

In the extreme case of a sixth-month embryonic period, the incarnating human being appears to proceed at express pace in order to reach his goal! Right from the moment of birth onwards it is as if a higher impulse manifests itself in such a person, calling him towards the fulfilment of his

Figure 12:
Different length embryonic periods
together with life ages corresponding to (i) and (ii)

(i) indicates the call of the likeness, when the Sun during the embryonic period is opposite the position it takes up at birth;
(ii) indicates the call of the image, when the Sun during the embryonic period is opposite its position at conception.

the cut-off date is the age at which the karma woven between conception and birth becomes absolved (70 = 10×7 years in the case of a normal embryonic period of 9 calendar months = 10 lunar sidereal months).

Abbreviations: Ø conception; * birth; co = cut-off date

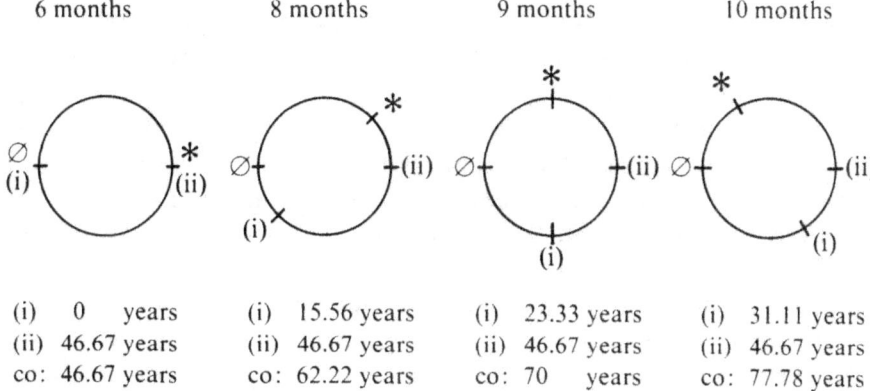

6 months	8 months	9 months	10 months
(i) 0 years	(i) 15.56 years	(i) 23.33 years	(i) 31.11 years
(ii) 46.67 years	(ii) 46.67 years	(ii) 46.67 years	(ii) 46.67 years
co: 46.67 years	co: 62.22 years	co: 70 years	co: 77.78 years

mission in life. Here there is a polarity between the impulse of the image, manifesting at conception, and that of the likeness, coming to expression at birth. The nature of the image is usually contemplative, whilst the likeness is creative in nature. However, when – through initiation – it is possible to complete the circle, leading beyond the threshold of death even during life, then the image may reveal itself as creative in the highest degree. A kind of "godliness" then emerges. Something of this quality of godliness may also appear to surround an individual born after only six months, if he survives at all. For in his case there is a polarity between the image and the likeness, which calls forth the quality of godliness.

The normal relationship between the image and the likeness, as reflected in the zodiacal positions of the Sun in the planetary configurations at conception and birth, is not one of polarity (aspect of opposition), but one of *dynamic interaction* (aspect of square). The self normally lives in a kind of dynamic interaction between the image and the likeness. The inherent impulse of the self is forwards, whereby on the one hand it receives the support of the image (from the past), and on the other hand it is called towards unfolding creativity, the impulse of the likeness, in the future. For the non-initiated person the image acts from the past, from his divine origin, whilst the likeness draws him into the future, towards his goal. The initiate, however, seeks to complete the circle – through the likeness – to return to the image, whereby the image becomes creative also. The initiate is one who transforms the dynamic interaction between the image and the likeness, going beyond the self to complete the circle of existence.

In traditional astrology only the pole of manifestation of the self, that indicated by the the zodiacal location of the Sun at the moment of birth, is usually taken into consideration. This is the active, creative, outermost revelation of the self called forth by the likeness. In hermetic astrology, however, the other pole of manifestation of the self, that indicated by the zodiacal location of the Sun at the moment of conception, is also taken into account. This is – initially – the passive, contemplative, innermost revelation of the self related to the image; but which, later, on the path of initiation, when the individual's divine nature begins to come to expression, can become creative also.

A practical application of this hermetic-astrological knowledge concerning the form of the vehicle of the self traced out by the Sun between conception and birth can be achieved by way of bringing this form to consciousness each year. Normally the individual celebrates his birthday each year. The cosmic significance of this day is that it denotes the return of the Sun to its starting point in the zodiac. The Sun takes one year (365¼ days) to complete its orbit of the 360 degrees of the zodiac, travelling approximately one degree per day. Owing to the precession of the equinoxes, taking account of the precession rate of one degree in 72 years, when a person reaches the age of 70 or so the Sun returns to its starting point in the sidereal zodiac one day later each year. This should be taken into account in the celebration of the birthday. Nevertheless, it is generally true to say that around the time of the birthday the Sun is in that part of the zodiac where it was located at birth. This means that especially the goal of the individual's incarnation can light up each year in his inner being on or around the day of his birthday. For the location of the Sun in this part of the zodiac represents the goal of his incarnation, the culmination of the embryonic period between conception and birth.

Thus it can happen that an individual around the time of his birthday may receive a flash of insight into the course of his life during the next year (or even years). Bearing this in mind, it can sometimes be of value for him to wait until his birthday before making any significant decision about his future. In this way he can then be led to make the right decision in accordance with the higher goal that he set himself for his incarnation.

Just as the yearly occurrence of the birthday may be significant with regard to gaining insight into the goal of incarnation, so the yearly occurrence of the *day of conception* can be of significance to the individual with respect to acquiring a comprehension of his *origin*. As discussed in Chapter 3, the conception configuration has an inner relationship with the birth configuration of the previous incarnation. Especially important is the Sun in the conception configuration, which may help to convey something inwardly bound up with the individual's identity in his foregoing incarnation. The return each year of the Sun to that part of the zodiac where it was located at the time of conception can be "celebrated" (as a private, inner celebration) by the individual as a time when something concerning his origin – in particular his self carried over from his past life – may be brought to consciousness.

In between the celebration of the *origin* on or around the day of conception and celebrating the *goal* on or around the day of birth, there is the yearly recurrence of the journey of incarnation of the self, made between conception and birth. To consciously follow this yearly passage of the Sun around the zodiac – on its course through the zodiacal signs between its zodiacal location at conception and that at birth – can be a help to support the inner development of the self along its journey from the origin to the goal of the present incarnation. And then to follow the passage of the Sun through the reminder of the zodiac – between its zodiacal location at birth and that at conception – lends inner support to the *completion of the circle* which is initiation, going beyond the self, returning to the image by way of unfolding the inner spiritual man, the likeness.

Between the manifestation of the image, through the conception configuration, and that of the likeness, which manifests through and takes its point of departure from the birth configuration, the form traced out by the Sun on its passage through the signs of the zodiac comprises the vehicle of the self. This entire form is of significance for following the development of the self during the course of life, in making the transformation from embryonic time to the spiral of life. Apart from the changing background zodiacal influence of the Sun during the embryonic period, corresponding to changes in outlook (philosophical, religious, etc.) during life, and apart from the two points (i) and (ii) referred to above – indicating the *call of the likeness* and the *call of the image* – over and above these important stages of self-development there are the conjunctions and oppositions of the Sun with the various planets during the embryonic period, which also need to be taken into consideration in relation to the development of the self during the course of life. Moreover, lastly, the Sun's crossing not only of the Ascendant and Midheaven axes, but also of the Moon's nodal axis, are important moments during the embryonic period, which often correlate with incisive changes in the destiny of the human being on his path of development.

In order to gain a clear overview of this complex sequence of cosmic events during the embryonic period, is is helpful to return to the hermetic-astrological perspective of the threefold human being. This was developed in Volume I, especially in Chapter 10, in relation to the application in hermetic astrology of Rudolf Steiner's karma exercises. There it was described how the threefold human being is related in hermetic astrology to the Ascendant (head), Sun (chest) and Moon (limbs). An understanding of this is especially valuable, as it provides a basic outline for a comprehension of the formation of the human being and his destiny during the embryonic period.

Firstly, let us consider the head, which is "ruled" in hermetic astrology by the Ascendant. What exactly does this mean?

The Ascendant and Midheaven axes

The Ascendant is the significator of the entire physical body, but especially of the head, which itself constitutes a microcosm within the macrocosm of the physical body. For the Ascendant shows the human being's orientation within the sphere of the zodiac during the building up of the archetype of the physical body (as an imprint of the image) out of the forces of the twelve signs of the zodiac. The circle of the zodiac is revealed in the human being in the spherical form of the head. And just as the orientation of the head is determined by the direction in which the eyes look, so the Ascendant axis coincides with the "direction" in which the human being "looks" whilst indwelling the sphere of the zodiac, beyond the planetary spheres, in the life after death. (In this sphere, where the human being is a pure spirit, the words "direction" and "look" bear only a faint analogy with their meaning in the earthly world.)

Figure 13 shows on the archetypal level the relationship of the human head to the zodiacal sphere, where the Ascendant axis corresponds to the human being's line of vision, the Ascendant itself denoting the eyes, where the human being looks out into the world. Similarly, the Midheaven axis corresponds to the vertical axis extending from the base of the neck through the top of the head. Above, the Ascendant axis was described as the "axis of contemplation" and the Midheaven axis as the "axis of initiative". This can be understood in the sense that the axis of contemplation of the zodiacal man (the human being in the sphere of the zodiac) coincides with the *line of vision*. Moreover, over and above the orientation of the human being (as zodiacal man) in the sphere of the zodiac, denoted by the Ascendant (the line of vision), there arises, when the human being incarnates upon the Earth, the line of uprightness.

Initially, in the first few months (usually the first year) of life, the human being is aligned in the axis of vision. He remains subject to this horizontal axis until the miraculous moment comes when the infant stands up for the first time by himself. In this moment, over and above the horizon-

Figure 13:
Archetypal relationship of the head to the zodiacal sphere

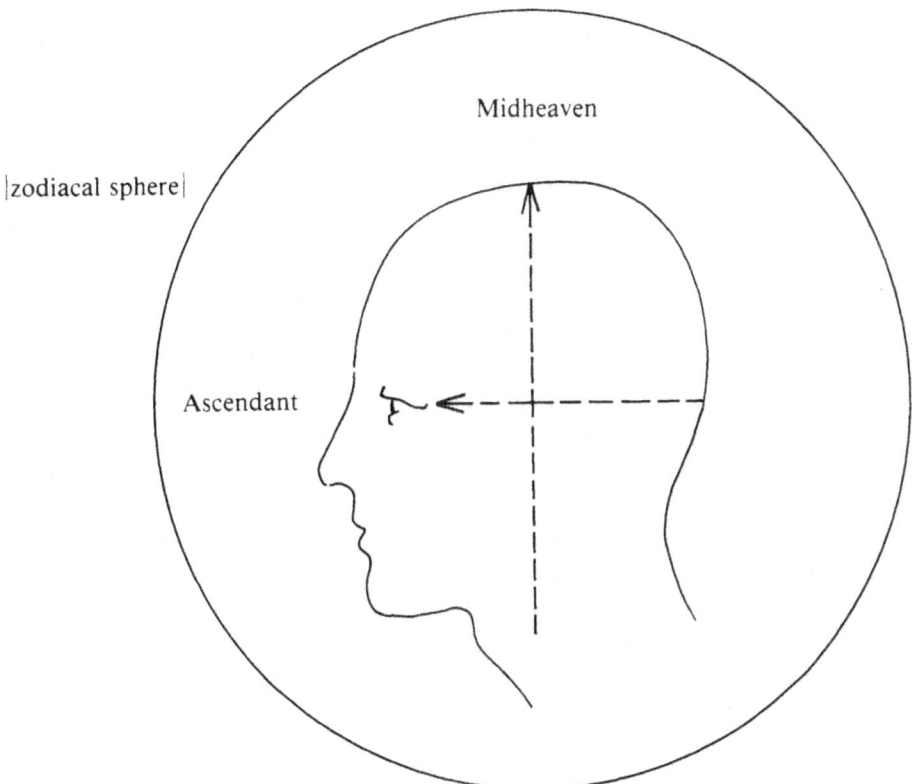

tal axis of the line of vision, he finds for the first time the vertical axis of the line of uprightness. It is in this vertical axis that man finds himself *as a human being on Earth* and is able to carry out initiatives. Each night, however, when he lies down to sleep, he returns to the horizontal axis and gives up his impulse towards initiative. He renounces his status as an active human being on Earth and becomes passive, giving himself over to the upbuilding cosmic forces again, from whence he came prior to incarnation, in order to become regenerated.

It is on the basis of the line of uprightness, in contrast to the line of vision, that the whole problem of freedom can be understood. Man would not be free at all if the line of vision were the sole axis, i.e. if he was a being of perception alone, without initiative. In the upright posture he can take the initiative to act. The young child's act of standing upright for the first time is his first step to freedom; it is his first act of initiative.

The initiate is a human being who follows the line of uprightness further and further, pressing on to ever new spiritual levels. He need not necessarily take initiative in the sense of action (the sphere of initiative on Earth). For example, it is an act of initiative on a spiritual level to put questions to the spiritual world (the sphere of initiative beyond the Earth). The spiritual seeker who becomes initiated is bold enough to put questions concerning the deeper aspects of existence, and this upward-striving tendency is rewarded, according to the words: "Ask, and ye shall receive; seek, and ye shall find; knock, and it shall be opened unto you." (*Matthew* vii, 7).

This Gospel saying expresses the essence of initiative towards the spiritual world. The "opening of the door" to the higher realms of existence is the answer from above to the human being's upward striving, if it is truly a morally upright striving.

The first step into the line of uprightness is the act of standing up, which the young child makes early in the Moon period of the spiral of life. The next step, early in the Mercury period, is the asking of questions. The child around the age of 7 usually begins to ask questions about the world and all that is surrounding him. This is the "initiative" of the schoolchild, the beginning of the search for truth.

In the Venus period the adolescent takes initiative a stage further in that he embarks on a quest for reciprocal recognition, usually in the form of love – even if it remains on an idealized level. On each of these levels of the spiral of life, new steps in the taking of initiative are made. Each time a new step is made, it is a further step towards freedom, along the upward-striving path of man towards the Divine.

In the Sun sphere of life true initiative becomes possible. Through the emergence of the self around the age of 21 the human being becomes capable of acting out of his own inner being: first guided by his feelings (sentient self, 21–28), then more in accordance with his understanding (intellectual self, 28–35), and then primarily out of his true inner will, the source of moral intuition (consciousness self, 35–42). Needless to say, these three different levels of the self are interrelated and may interact with one another beyond the delineations of the 7-year periods described here. (However, this delineation indicates when a given level is emphasized during a particular 7-year period.)

Through the development of the self during these three 7-year periods within the Sun-period (21–42), in each period a new step in the taking of initiative may be made, whereby the human being can become increasingly independent. However, each step entails a small-scale "death", a dying with respect to that which was attained at the previous level. For example, the adult – after the age of 21 – acquires independence and maturity in comparison with the adolescent. However, this step into maturity, into a mature feeling life, entails the subsidence and dying away of the un-

VI. The Hermetic—Astrological Science of Destiny

trammelled emotions of adolescence. The entry into each new planetary sphere through the unfolding of the spiral of life signifies a step along the line of uprightness – a step towards freedom – and at the same time a "death" with respect to the preceding planetary sphere. This "dying" with respect to that which was in the previous ring of the spiral of life becomes increasingly difficult the older the human being becomes. It becomes necessary to develop the ability to "let go" consciously, to become inwardly "empty" in order to create an inner space into which the new – that which seeks to come to birth in a new planetary sphere – is able to enter in.

The transition from the Sun period to the Mars period demands going beyond the self, creating a space for the inner spiritual man, the likeness. The three phases of development of the inner spiritual man – through the Mars, Jupiter and Saturn periods – are likewise made possible through a "dying" from one planetary sphere to the next. Lastly, in passing from the Saturn period to the zodiacal period even the likeness has to make way for the image, if the archetypal line of development: man → hermetic man (likeness) → zodiacal man (image) is to be fulfilled.

The journey through the spiral of life is thus a stepwise bringing to realisation of the line of uprightness, the vertical axis of orientation of the human being on Earth with respect to the sphere of the zodiac. This line is followed throughout life, from the moment of standing upright (in the Moon period) until the moment of death (archetypally in the zodiacal period, around the age of 70). The following of this line of uprightness is the path of man towards God, whereby the degree of moral uprightness is the most important criterion of the human being's development. The journey through the spiral of life prepares – on an earthly level – the voyage of the soul towards God, through the planetary spheres in the life after death.

With each step from one planetary sphere to the next along the spiral of life (and, analogously, in the voyage of the soul in the life after death), there is an "ascent" of the line of uprightness, until the zodiacal period (zodiacal sphere) is attained, where it is a matter primarily of the human being's moral uprightness. The line of uprightness within the zodiacal sphere is indicated by the Midheaven axis in the zodiac, the vertical zodiacal axis at the moment of birth (in contrast to the horizontal Ascendant axis). This vertical axis – the axis of initiative – indicates the upward striving of the human being towards freedom, this at the same time being his path of approach towards the Divine.

In each new period (planetary sphere) of life, along the ascent of the vertical axis, a new mode of perception is opened up. This is connected with the line of vision, indicated by the Ascendant axis. The infant in the Moon period of life has a quite different perception of the world than the adult in the Sun period. The difference in perception between one planetary period and the next become less and less noticeable during the course of life, but nevertheless subtle differences in outlook do occur.

Just as the fulfilment of the line of uprightness is attained in the zodiacal sphere of life, so the culmination of perception is reached in the zodiacal period. For the initiate, this is the time when the image may come to manifestation – not just as a being of perception, but also as a creative being. The Ascendant axis then signifies the mode of outlook of the zodiacal man, and the Midheaven his moral uprightness.

The Sun's crossing the Ascendant and Midheaven axis

The Ascendant and Midheaven axes within the sphere of the zodiac are thus of key significance, referring during the embryonic period especially to the orientation of the head, which in its spherical form is an image of the zodiacal sphere (see Figure 13). The passage of the Sun, Moon and planets across these two axes during the embryonic period therefore often correspond with important points of development in life. With regard to the Moon's return to the Ascendant (or, in some cases, to the opposite point, the Descendant), the meaning of this as the significator of the 7-year periods in life has already been discussed. On the other hand, the Sun's crossing of the Midheaven or of the Ascendant occurs only once in the embryonic period, and this usually corresponds with a major turning point in life. For example, in the case of a woman, the Sun's crossing of the Ascendant (transposed from the embryonic period into the spiral of life) could correlate with her giving birth to a child. (This could also apply to a man, in the sense of his becoming a father.)

In relation to the archetype of the threefold human being, where the Ascendant is the astrological significator of the head, the Sun is the significator of the heart and of the entire chest region. The heart is microcosmically the center of the self, whilst the head is the directing center of consciousness. Thus the transition of the Sun across the Ascendant during the embryonic period usually indicates an interaction between the self (macrocosmically centered in the Sun) and the outlook of the human being in relation to the world (line of vision). It frequently corresponds to a far-reaching change of outlook, bound up with the self, which may come to expression in some event of destiny.

Similarly, the passage of the Sun across the Midheaven during the embryonic period again often points to a major transition in the life of the self, with respect to the line of uprightness, the axis of initiative. Transposing from the embryonic period to the spiral of life, the Sun's crossing of the Midheaven may correspond with the attainment of a goal, or with the taking of a new initiative in life. Again this may be connected with some major change in destiny.

As mentioned above, not only is the Sun's crossing of the Ascendant

VI. The Hermetic—Astrological Science of Destiny

and Midheaven axes during the embryonic period of significance for the self, but also the passage of the Sun across the axis of the Moon's nodes. The lunar nodal axis could be termed the "axis of inspiration", since the Moon's nodes represent gateways to the cosmic world through which inspiration can stream in. Thus, just as *outlook* is connected with the Ascendant axis and *initiative* with the Midheaven axis, so *inspiration* is associated with the axis of the Moon's nodes. The moment in the embryonic period when the Sun is crossing the nodal axis, when transposed to the spiral of life, often correlates with a period of inspiration in which the human being's higher cosmic nature is able to work into his earthly life. More often than not, however, it relates to karmic occurrences – journeys or significant meetings (bound up with earlier incarnations), or possibly illness (usually having a karmic reason) – which may result in new life inspiration.

In addition to the Sun's crossing of these three zodiacal axes, having to do very much with development of consciousness (head) in relation to the self (heart), there are also the manifold meetings during the embryonic period of the Sun with the various planets. A study of examples shows that these meetings – especially with the slower-moving planets: Mars, Jupiter, Saturn, Uranus, Neptune and Pluto – often indicate events of destiny, when transposed to the spiral of life. An example was discussed earlier, where the conjunction of the Sun and Mars – both in opposition to Jupiter – during the embryonic period correlated with a stroke in the life of the person concerned. Further examples need to be looked at in order to gain a better understanding of the way in which destiny works out in such cases.

Of special interest are the conjunctions and oppositions of the Sun and Moon during the embryonic period. For it is here that the third level of the threefold human being – of which the Moon is the significator – has to be taken into consideration. As described in *Hermetic Astrology* I, Chapter 10, this third level (the first two levels being that of the head and that of the heart) comprises the limbs of the human being. It is by way of the limbs that impulses of will are enacted. A picture of the activity of the lunar forces in the limbs can be formed in contemplating the movements of a baby, during the Moon period of life. Its typical mode of expression is through vigorous movements of the arms and kicking of the feet. This is a more or less pure manifestation of the Moon forces – cosmic will impulses – acting in the limbs.

Since the human being's destiny is enacted by way of his limbs, the meetings (conjunctions) of the Moon with the Ascendant, the Sun and the various planets during the embryonic period are generally indicative of the sphere of destiny. For example, the conjunctions of the Sun and Moon (= New Moon), signifying the commencement of new cycles of the lunar phases, when transposed from embryonic time to the spiral of life often point to the beginning of new phases in life, e.g. a change of employment, or moving house (moving from one town to another).

Moreover, just as following the passage of the Sun through the zodiacal signs during the embryonic period holds the key to the development of the self through various world outlooks, so the embryonic course of the Moon through the signs of the zodiac is bound up with the various *spheres of destiny* relevant to the human being. In traditional astrology these twelve spheres are the twelve houses. But what are the houses in reality? This question is examined in the next chapter, dealing with the hermetic house system.

Chapter 6: Notes and references

1. Charles Harvey, "John M. Addey", *Astrological Journal* 24 (1982), pp. 136–139.
2. Cf. Edward Rosen, "Michael Maestlin", *Dictionary of Scientific Biography* 9 (1974), pp. 167–170.
3. Michael Maestlin, *Observatio et demonstratio cometae aetherei, qui anno 1577 et 1578 apparuit* (Tübingen, 1578).
4. Edward Rosen, *Kepler's Somnium* (Madison WI, 1967), p. xvi.
5. Edward Rosen, op. cit. (ref. 2), p. 168.
6. The founding meeting of the Astrological Association took place on June 21, 1958, six days after John Addey's thirty-eighth birthday.
7. John Addey, *Harmonics in Astrology* (Fowler: London, 1976).
8. Cf. Joyce Collin Smith, "John Addey: in memoriam", *Astrological Journal* 24 (1982), p. 144.
9. Rudolf Steiner, *True and False Paths of Spiritual Investigation* (Rudolf Steiner Press: London, 1969), p. 131.
10. Rudolf Steiner, *An Autobiography* (trsl. R. Stebbing, Rudolf Steiner Publications, New York, 1977), pp. 148–149.
11. *Meditations on the Tarot* (trsl. R. Powell, Amity, Warwick NY, 1985).

Chapter 7

The Hermetic House System

The house system of Porphyry

In traditional astrology there is no general consensus of opinion as to how exactly the houses are defined. There are numerous different house systems, each yielding different definitions of the boundaries of the houses, although these differences are generally slight. The central idea underlying most of these definitions is that the Ascendant and Midheaven axes divide the horoscope into four sectors, and that these four sectors may each be further subdivided into three, to yield twelve sectors of houses (see Figure 14).

Figure 14:
The house system of Porphyry

The twelve houses according to the system of Porphyry, where each of the four sectors is trisected. (The four sectors are specified by the Ascendant and Midheaven axes.)

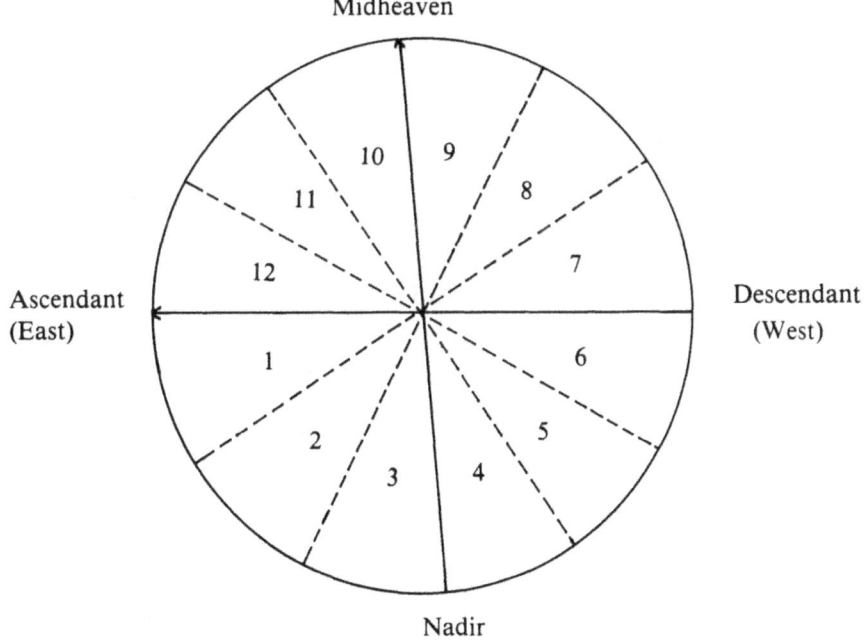

Figure 14 shows one of the simplest – also one of the oldest – house divisions: that of the Neoplatonist Porphyry (A.D. 234 – ca. 304). Porphyry specified that each of the four sectors (given by the Ascendant and Midheaven axes) be simply trisected, to yield the twelve houses. (The house system of Porphyry is given here merely as an example – one that is easy to comprehend – and is not in any way being advocated.) The houses are then numbered from 1 to 12, taking the first house as the first sector beneath the Ascendant, the second house as the second sector beneath the Ascendant, and so on around the horoscope.

What is actually yielded here is a geographical division of space into twelve sectors, where the center from which the division is made is the geographical location of the place of the individual's birth, whereby the division is computed at the moment of his birth. The geographical coordinates: East-West are given by the Ascendant (East) and the Descendant (West). For births in the northern hemisphere the Midheaven, the highest point (overhead) of the zodiac at the moment of birth, is in the direction South of the place of birth. Similarly, the Nadir, the lowest point of the zodiac (beneath the Earth), is geographically North of the place of birth. The house division (in this case that of Porphyry) simply trisects the spatial sectors defined at the place of birth by the Ascendant and Midheaven axes for the moment of birth (see Figure 14).

The original house division

In order to arrive at the real meaning of the houses, it is helpful to return historically to the earliest mention of the houses. As discussed in the introduction to *Hermetic Astrology* I, the division into houses is attributed to Hermes. In the history of astrology again and again Hermes is named as the originator of the astrological teaching concerning the twelve houses.[1] The underlying idea of the houses appears to have been derived from the application of the hermetic principle of correspondences, i.e. that just as there is a twelvefold division of the heavenly world into twelve zodiacal signs, so there is a corresponding division of the earthly world – geographically considered – into twelve. However, further considerations reveals that there is a deeper underlying basis to the houses, which becomes apparent only when the rule of Hermes is taken into account. (The rule of Hermes, the hermetic rule, is applied to the birth horoscope to find the horoscope of conception – see *Hermetic Astrology* I, Appendix I.)

One of the earliest historical references to the houses is that found on four demotic horoscopes, drawn up on four ostraca from Medinet Habu in Egypt. The horoscopes are dated A.D. 13, 17, 18 and 35.[2] These horoscopes reveal the primal definition of the houses, as originated in Egypt in the hermetic astrology of antiquity. In this primal definition each house is simply equated with a sign of the sidereal zodiac: the first house with the

VII. The Hermetic House System

sign in which the Ascendant is located, the second house with the next sign, and so on. The houses in this original definition were therefore each 30 degrees long, identical with the zodiacal signs.

The first house in this original definition of the houses was the house of the Ascendant, i.e. the zodiacal sign rising on the eastern horizon at the moment of birth. The names listed on the four demotic horoscopes of the remaining houses, each house identified with successive zodiacal signs following the sign of the Ascendant, are listed in Table 14.

Table 14
The names of the houses (from four demotic horoscopes)

2. The house of the provision of life
2. The part of the brother
4. The part of the father
5. The part of the child
6. The part of (?)
7. The part of fate
8. The house of the provision of death
9. The part of god
10. The house of the goddess
11. Psais
12. The evil spirit

In addition to the names of the houses listed in Table 14, the Midheaven is termed "the lake of the sky" and the Nadir is designated as "the lake of Duat". These terms are fairly obvious – Duat being the Egyptian name for the underworld. But the designations for the houses listed in Table 14 require further explanation.

In the astrological tradition the first house, i.e. the house of the Ascendant, is that of *life and character*. The second house is that of *estate and fortune*, which accords more or less to the term "house of the provision of life". Traditionally the third house is that of *brothers and sisters*, whilst the fourth is that of *parents*, and the fifth is that of *children* –again agreeing in principle with the terms given on these ancient demotic horoscopes. The sixth house is traditionally the house of *health*, the seventh house that of *marriage* and the eighth house that of *death*. (The term on these demotic horoscopes for the seventh house is *fate*; as a sphere of destiny, marriage is included under the heading "fate", but certainly cannot be identified as fate itself, i.e. here there seems to be a point of divergence between these old Egyptian horoscopes and the later astrological tradition.)

The expression "part of god" used in the demotic horoscopes to refer to the ninth house accords with the term *Deus* ("God") given by Manilius in his account of the twelve houses: "This region is called by the Greek word signifying God."³ Manilius wrote his work *Astronomica* during the reigns of Augustus and Tiberius, round about the time of the demotic horoscopes that we are considering here. (The later astrological tradition designated the ninth house as that of *religion and travels*.)

However, the term "house of goddess", appearing on the demotic horoscopes at the tenth house, is assigned by Manilius to the third house: "Goddess is the name in Roman speech given to this region."⁴ Nevertheless, Manilius' description of the tenth house does bear somewhat upon the term "house of the goddess", for he places the abode of Venus in the citadel of the sky. Here does the Cytherean (Venus) claim her abode among the stars, placing in the very face of heaven, as it were, her beauteous features, wherewith she rules the affairs of men."⁵ Manilius named the tenth house *fortune*, and the later astrological tradition called it the house of *honours*.

There is agreement between the astrological tradition and the demotic horoscopes with regard to the eleventh and twelfth houses, if "Psais" is equated with the *good spirit*. Manilius describes the eleventh house as that of "happy fortune" and the twelfth house as that of "ill fortune", which corresponds with the traditional designations of the eleventh and twelfth houses as the houses of *bonus daemon* ("good spirit") and *malus daemon* ("evil spirit"), respectively.⁶ The astrological tradition assigns *friendships* to the eleventh house and *enemies and misfortune* to the twelfth house.

The houses originate in the embryonic period

Before considering the meanings traditionally associated with the twelve houses, it is important to grasp the origin of the houses. As referred to above, a clue is offered by the reference to Hermes. The origin of the house system, in fact, can only be understood against the background of the horoscope of conception, as determined by the rule of Hermes. The hermetic rule specifies that the Moon at the moment of conception indicates the place of the Ascendant – or its opposite, the Descendant – at birth. As discussed at length in the preceding chapters, during the Moon's orbits of the zodiac between conception and birth the entire course of destiny for the spiral of life is elaborated, whereby each lunar orbit of the sidereal zodiac corresponds to seven years of life.

Considering the formation of karma during each 7-year period in detail, a pattern emerges, whereby each year within a 7-year period acquires a special significance. Thus, life can be looked upon as unfolding in a series of 7-year spiralic rings, where each ring of the spiral realizes on a higher level the preceding one. Each ring of the spiral has seven "steps", corresponding to the seven years of life in a given spiralic ring. Looked at from above, the series of spiralic rings appears in the form of a circle, divided

Figure 15:
Seven steps in each ring of the spiral of life
(a ring comprises seven years, and each step corresponds to one year of life)

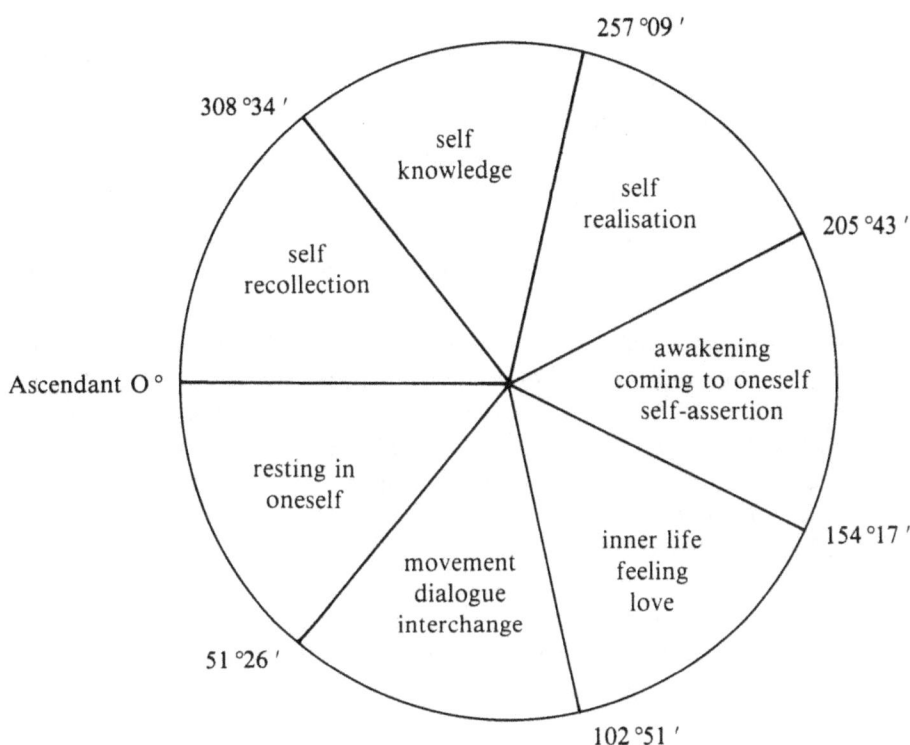

into seven steps, as depicted in Figure 15, where it is assumed that the Moon starts out from the Ascendant at the moment of conception.

Each step within a given 7-year period (see Figure 15) corresponds to the Moon's motion through one-seventh of the zodiac, starting from the Ascendant. (The case in which the Moon starts from the Descendant at conception will be considered later.) As the Moon's movement through the 360 degrees of the sidereal zodiac corresponds to seven years of life, its movement through one-seventh of the zodiacal circle (= 51 degrees 26 minutes) corresponds to one year of life. Hence the seven years of life in a given 7-year period unfold through seven steps, each corresponding to the Moon's movement through one-seventh of the zodiac (= 51°26').

Each 7-year period signifies the beginning of a new cycle of life, the unfolding of some new aspect of life; but within each 7-year period the pattern remains the same. It begins with "resting in oneself" – this is the prime note of a new 7-year cycle. This takes place in the first year of life, the eighth year, the fifteenth year, the twenty-second year, the twenty-ninth year, etc. Then, in the second year of a 7-year life period, there is an opening towards the world; there is a movement leading outwards to enter into dialogue with others, to exchange with others. This occurs in the second year of life, the ninth year, the sixteenth year, the twenty-third year, the thirtieth year, etc. In the third year of a 7-year period an awakening of inner life, the stirring of feeling and love (devotion) takes place. This belongs to the third year of life, the tenth year, the seventeenth year, the twenty-fourth year, the thirty-first year, etc. In the fourth year of a 7-year period – the middle of the period – there is an awakening of self-consciousness, where a corresponding self-assertion takes place. This happens in the fourth year of life, the eleventh year, the eighteenth year, the twenty-fifth year, the thirty-second year, etc. Subsequently, in the fifth, sixth and seventh years of a 7-year period, the human being passes through successive stages of interrelationship with the world, which can be designated as self-realisation, self-knowledge, and self-recollection, although these terms apply, properly speaking, only after the emergence of the self takes place around the age of 21. The seventh step, that of self-recollection, is simultaneously a looking back over the 7-year period and a preparation for the next 7-year period; it is a review and at the same time, on the basis of this review, a preview of the next 7-year period. It is the "sabbath", the seventh year, of the 7-year period.

Just as the sabbath in antiquity was related to the planet Saturn, so does the seventh year in the cycle of 7-year periods – in the sense of it being a time of recollection – correspond with Saturn, the planet whose activity in the cosmos is that of memory. Similarly, each year within a 7-year period corresponds to one of the planets, in the Babylonian (Ptolemaic) order: (1) Moon, (2) Mercury, (3) Venus, (4) Sun, (5) Mars, (6) Jupiter, (7) Saturn. And here, extending the principle of correspondences, it can be seen that the seven steps of a 7-year spiralic ring may be brought into correspondence with the 7-year periods themselves (see Figure 16). By analogy, each 7-year period is a small-scale reflection of the whole spiral of life – or, at least, of the planetary periods up to the age of 63: Moon, Mercury, Venus, Sun, Mars, Jupiter and Saturn. Each 7-year period reflects on a small scale the evolution of the human being through the planetary periods of life.

Just as during the first seven years of life, the Moon period, the infant is contained within itself as a being of will, so during the first year of a 7-year period there is a kind of "resting in oneself" and a coming to expression of will. (The term "resting") is not meant in an outer sense, for this may be a period of intense activity.)

During the Mercury life period from 7 to 14 the child turns more towards the outer world, and through movement (activity) and the unfolding of in-

Figure 16:
Planetary correspondences between the steps in each 7-year period and the sequence of 7-year periods (0–63) themselves

The steps depicted in Figure 15 are shown here in relation to the 7-year planetary periods extending from birth to the age of 63.

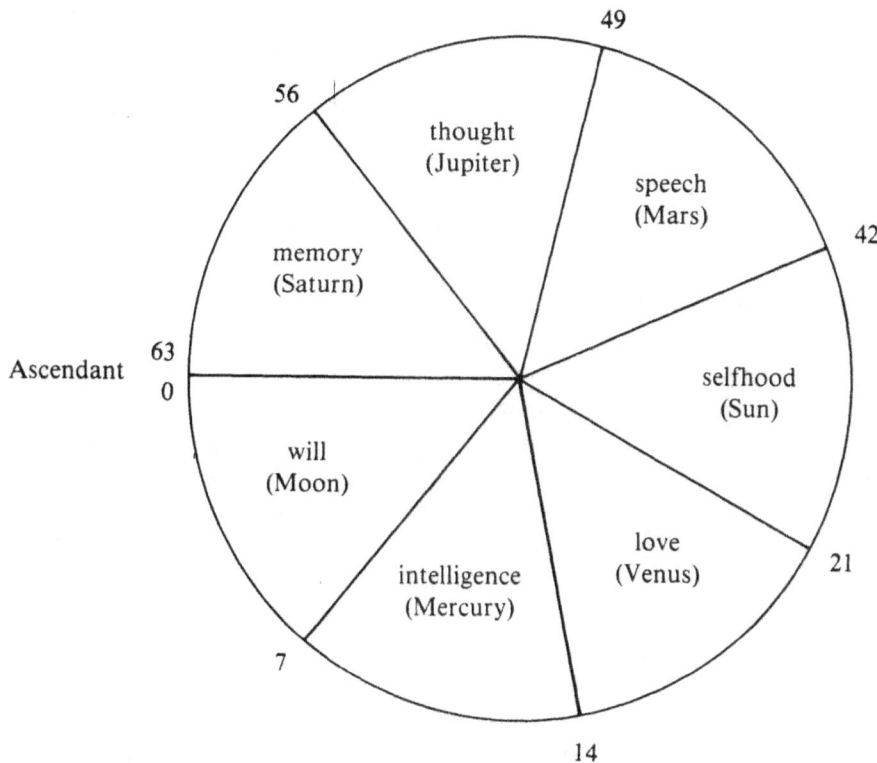

telligence enters into relationship with others. Something analogous takes place during the second year of a 7-year period in that there is a turning towards the outer world, often questioningly, and therefore the second year of a 7-year period is a "Mercury year", corresponding to the Mercury period of life.

The period of adolescence from 14 to 21 – the Venus period – is one in which the inner life of soul awakens; the life of feeling stirs within, and the human being experiences love, as has always been associated with the planet Venus. Similarly, an inner deepening may be observed during the third year of a 7-year period, the Venus year according to the principle of correspondences.

In the Sun period of life, which extends from the age of 21 to 42 – the prime of life – it is the self that comes to expression. Here there is an awakening of self-consciousness, and a channelling of impulses (e.g. in the taking up of a profession). Correspondingly, the fourth year (the Sun year) of a 7-year life period is one of awakening and self-assertion.

The Mars period of life, from 42 to 49, is characterized by the impulse of self-realisation – the carrying over of spiritual impulses towards their realisation. Archetypally this corresponds to the activity of speech – where a purely spiritual impulse is formed and projected outwards to take effect in the outer world. Within a 7-year life period this corresponds to the fifth year, where the self works actively towards bringing its impulses to realisation in the world.

Between 49 and 56, the Jupiter period of life, an inner deepening takes place through the endeavour of the self to understand life. On the archetypal level it is the activity of thought which is the motivating impulse here. Rather than external realisation of the self, it is self-knowledge which becomes the primary motivation of the human being during this life period. This generally works on a very deep level, and may not be consciously realised at all. Analogously, the sixth year (the Jupiter year) of a 7-year period is one in which the human being opens up to the world in a search for understanding, seeking self-knowledge.

Lastly, the Saturn period of life, from 56 to 63, is one of looking back. Archetypally memory is the activating impulse here. Wisdom is gleaned from this reviewing activity, by way of recollection. In the same way, the seventh year of a 7-year period is one of looking back – and also coming to realisations about the future, in the light of the experience of the past. Again, this generally takes place on a subconscious level.

Knowledge of the 7-year periods of life, as the basic rhythm underlying the unfolding of life's destiny, can be an immense help towards comprehending life. Astrologically, the unfolding of destiny – in the sense of the elaboration of past karma – can be studied in detail by looking at the planetary movements during the ten lunar sidereal months of the embryonic period. The knowledge of the 7-year periods is deepened still further by a consideration of the individual years – Moon, Mercury, Venus, Sun, Mars, Jupiter and Saturn years – within a given 7-year period.[7] Any particular year within a given 7-year period may be looked at by finding firstly the lunar sidereal month corresponding to the given 7-year period, and then locating the sector corresponding to the year in question, and then finding when during the relevant lunar sidereal month the Moon was placed in that sector. (See Figure 15 for the seven sectors.)

Since a lunar sidereal month lasts for $27\frac{1}{3}$ days, the Moon is in a given sector for one-seventh of this time, i.e. ca. 4 days, and moves through this sector at a rate such that one degree of the Moon's motion corresponds approximately to one week of life. Thus the past karma relating to a particular year of life is elaborated during a 4-day period in the time of embryonic development, when the Moon is located in a particular sector of the horoscope (in relation to the Ascendant – or the Descendant, if the Moon's starting point at conception is determined by the hermetic rule to be the zodiacal location of the Descendant rather than that of the Ascendant).

In this fact an indication concerning the origin of the houses or departments of life is to be found. Although the traditional astrological doctrine of houses is quite different – involving a division of the horoscope circle (starting with the Ascendant) into twelve, rather than seven houses – the deeper background to the traditional doctrine is nevertheless rooted in the phenomenon connected with the formation of karma during the embryonic period.

The inscription of karma in the planetary spheres

Past karma relating to a particular incarnation is inscribed in the various planetary spheres – Moon, Mercury, Venus, Sun, Mars, Jupiter and Saturn – during the voyage of the soul in the life after death. By the time the human being has traversed these planetary spheres in the life after death, he has completed a review of the entire course of his foregoing life. He then enters the zodiacal sphere, free of the karmic effects of the life lived through on Earth, whereby – as he traverses them – these karmic effects are inscribed into the various planetary spheres.[8] In the sphere of the zodiac preparation is made for a new incarnation upon the Earth. Here, while the physical body of the human being is prepared in archetypal form, the human being is in the "image of God" (zodiacal man), as this comes to expression through the twelve signs of the zodiac. The image finds its impress above all in the horoscope of conception, as the planetary configuration denoting the commencement of the building up of the physical body, the embryo.

When descending to incarnation, firstly the human being leaves the zodiacal sphere and then passes once again through the planetary spheres in reverse order. In the planetary spheres the human being is in the "likeness of God" (hermetic man), as this comes to expression through the planetary spheres. The focus of the human being in his descent through the planetary spheres is the horoscope of birth, which thus receives the imprint of the likeness.

The goal of the incarnating human being is the birth configuration, whereby the moment of conception is an important point of transition on the way towards this goal. For at the moment of conception, as determined by the hermetic rule, the imprint of the image begins to work into the building up of the physical body (embryo), and at the same time the etheric body begins to be formed through the orbits of the Moon around the sidereal zodiac. Simultaneously, parallel to the formation of the etheric body, the karma for the coming life on Earth is woven into the etheric body, reflecting the planetary movements taking place during the embryonic period. Thus the planetary movements between conception and birth indicate the weaving of destiny into the etheric body, and the formation of the etheric body itself – concurrent with the Moon's orbits of the zodiac – occurs in such a way that one lunar orbit of the sidereal zodiac corresponds to seven years of life. The etheric body may be likened to a kind of "time organism", which is wound up between conception and birth and which begins to unwind from the moment of birth, up to the moment of death – through which the unfolding of the human being's destiny in 7-year periods takes place during the course of life.

The weaving of destiny during the lunar orbits of the zodiac takes place on the one hand out of a review of the previous incarnation(s) on the Earth, and on the other hand through a beholding of the inscriptions in the various planetary spheres of the karmic effects of the foregoing incarnation. Thus during the first lunar orbit it is especially from the Moon sphere that the karmic inscriptions are taken up in the weaving of destiny. Hence the first 7-year period in the spiral of life is the Moon period. Similarly, the karmic effects inscribed in the Mercury sphere are taken into account in the elaboration of karma during the second lunar orbit, and correspondingly the second 7-year period is the Mercury period in the spiral of life. Further, the karmic inscriptions from the Venus sphere play into the weaving of destiny during the third lunar sidereal orbit, corresponding to the third 7-year period, that of Venus, in the spiral of life. During the fourth, fifth and sixth lunar sidereal revolutions of the embryonic period it is the Sun sphere which becomes relevant as the planetary sphere from which the karmic inscriptions are "read" in the weaving of destiny into the etheric body. The fourth, fifth and sixth 7-year periods comprise the Sun period in the spiral of life. In the seventh, eighth and ninth lunar orbits the karmic inscriptions from the spheres of Mars, Jupiter and Saturn are incorporated into the weaving of destiny. Thus the seventh, eighth and ninth 7-year periods are those of Mars, Jupiter and Saturn. After this the human being is free of the karmic inscriptions from the various planetary spheres, although his destiny is usually elaborated further (on average up to the age of seventy, corresponding to ten orbits of the Moon around the sidereal zodiac). In the case of a full-term pregnancy, therefore, the tenth lunar orbit is a time in which that which works in from beyond the planetary spheres is able to come to expression. Correspondingly, during the last period of the spiral of life, beyond the age of 63, it is the zodiacal sphere which provides the cosmic background to the elaboration of the human being's destiny, and from this sphere the image (zodiacal man) is able to radiate in, if the circumstances are appropriate (depending on the human being's level of spiritual development).

The hermetic house system

The description earlier in this chapter of the subdivision of each lunar orbit into seven steps, each step corresponding to one year of life within a particular 7-year period, is of a schematic nature, as there is no actual sevenfold division of the zodiac traced out by the Moon in its orbit of the sidereal zodiac. Nevertheless, something of the dynamic of the formation of the etheric body and the weaving in of destiny is conveyed by this sevenfold division (see Figures 15 and 16). For the sevenfold division corresponds to the earthly reality of the sevenfoldness of the seven years comprising one ring in the spiral of life. The cosmic reality, however, is the division of the zodiac into twelve signs – this provides the cosmic background to each orbit of the Moon around the zodiac during the embryonic period. The cosmic reality yields a twelvefold division into houses, rather than a sevenfold division.

Here we have the archetypal, original house division, as given in the four demotic horoscopes from Medinet Habu in Egypt. Taking the Ascendant as the indicator of the zodiacal sign occupied by the Moon at the moment of conception (calculated according to the hermetic rule), this sign of the zodiac is that from which the start of the formation of the etheric body is made. The etheric body is also known as the *life body*, and is built up parallel to the Moon's orbits of the sidereal zodiac during the embryonic period. As the Moon passes through the twelve zodiacal signs in its orbit, the cosmic reality underlying the formation of the etheric body is the Moon's passage through the twelve signs, where the starting point is a particular sign – indicated by the Ascendant at birth (or by the Descendant – see below). In this formation of the etheric body – the *wheel of life* – the starting point is the first sign, the next sign is the second sign, and so on. This is exactly the house system given in the four demotic horoscopes from Medinet Habu.

For example, the third horoscope, cast for February 25, A.D. 18 at "4 o' clock in the evening", gives the first house as Libra, since this is the sign of the Ascendant. The second house ("the house of the provision of life") is Scorpio; the third house ("the part of the brother") is Sagittarius; and so on, continuing around the zodiacal circle to the twelfth house ("the evil spirit"), which is Virgo (see Figure 17).

Let us now consider an application of this hermetic house division to the example of John Addey, discussed in the last chapter. At John Addey's birth the sign of Cancer was rising on the eastern horizon. Through application of the hermetic rule we found that the Moon was in Cancer at the moment of conception, more or less in the exact center (15 degrees) of the sign of Cancer. Thus, the Ascendant at the moment of John Addey's birth was 15° Cancer.

Figure 17:
Hermetic house system (third demotic horoscope)
See Appendix II for chart computation of this horoscope.
The Ascendant is in the sidereal sign of Libra, and therefore
Libra is the first house, Scorpio the second house, etc.

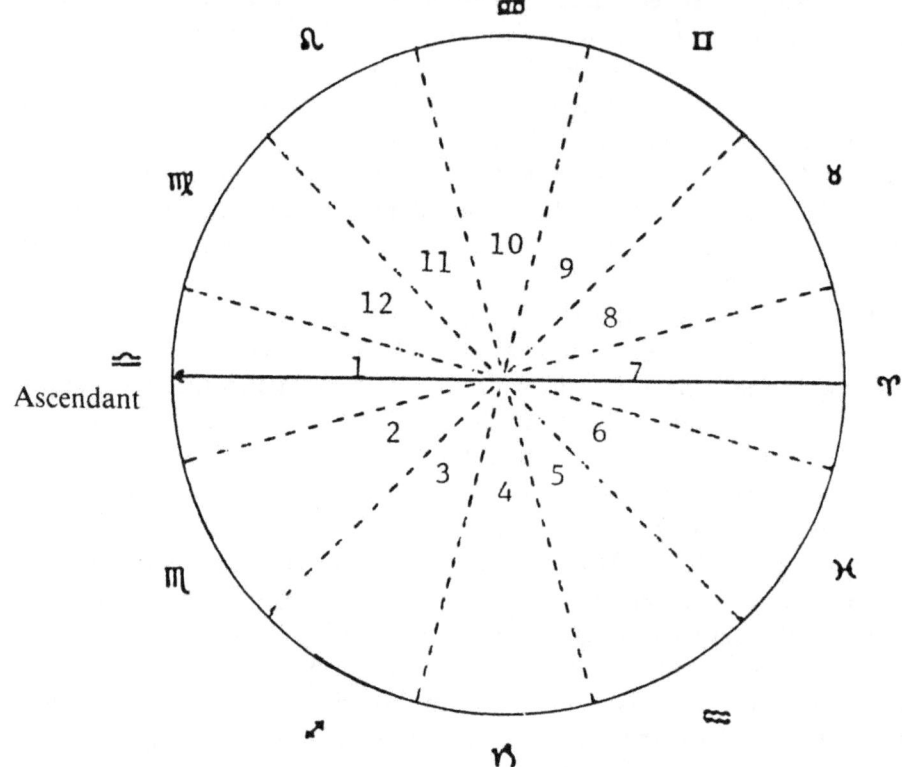

In the light of the hermetic rule, the Moon was in Cancer at the start of the embryonic period, i.e. at the commencement of the formation of the etheric body. According to the division of the houses in the hermetic house system, therefore, Cancer is the first house, Leo the second house, Virgo the third house, and so on (see Figure 18).

The hermetic house system expresses the cosmic reality of the Moon's orbit through the twelve signs of the zodiac during each revolution around the zodiac between conception and birth. Each orbit corresponds to seven years of life. Thus, from the point of view of the earthly reality of the sevenfoldness of the seven years comprising one spiral in the spiral of life, a sevenfold division of the zodiac – starting from the Ascendant – provides a picture of the dynamic unfolding of each 7-year period (see Figure 15). However, from the point of view of cosmic reality the house division is not sevenfold, but twelvefold – corresponding to the twelve signs of the zodiac.

Figure 18:
Hermetic house system (example John Addey)

See Chart 16 (*Ascendant 15° Cancer) and Chart 15 (∅ Moon 15° Cancer); since the Moon at conception was in the sidereal sign of Cancer, this means that in the hermetic house system the first house is the sign of Cancer, the second house is the sign of Leo, etc.

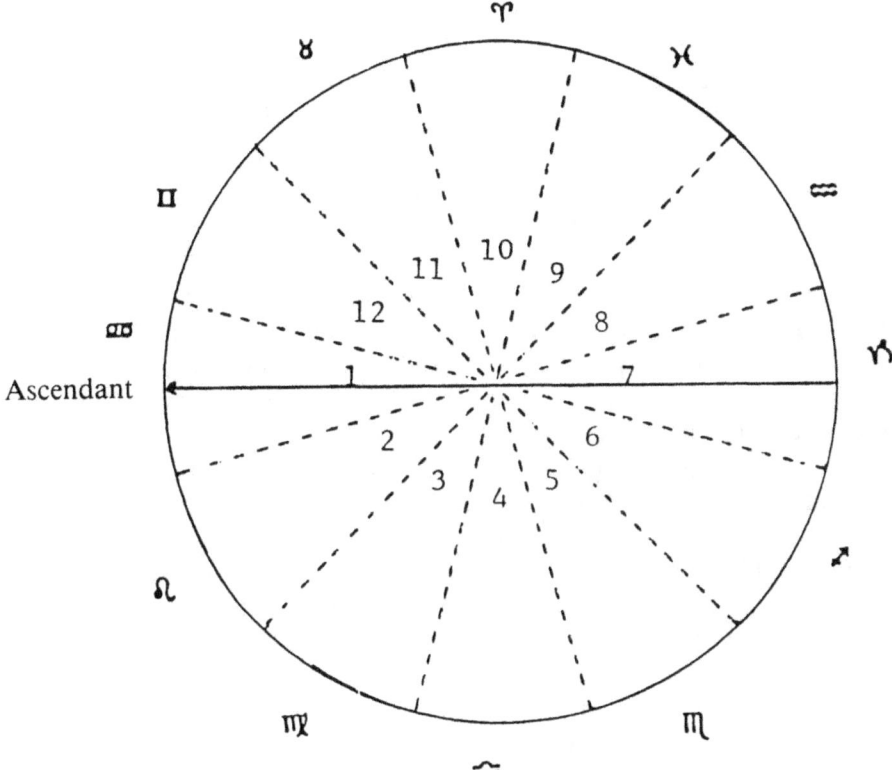

The Moon's orbit through the twelve signs of the zodiac equates with seven years of life, and therefore the passage of the Moon through one zodiacal sign corresponds to seven months in the spiral of life (= one-twelfth of seven years). Thus, analogous to the Sun's passage through the zodiacal signs between conception and birth, giving rise to 7.8-year zodiacal periods in life (i.e. solar zodiacal periods), the Moon's passage through the zodiacal signs between conception and birth gives rise to 7-month zodiacal periods in life (i.e. lunar zodiacal periods). This is the reality underlying the houses as originally conceived of in hermetic astrology.

The hermetic houses as time divisions in the spiral of life

As an example of how the lunar zodiacal periods can be determined in relation to the spiral of life, let us consider once again John Addey's biography. As depicted in Figure 18, according to the hermetic house system the first house was Cancer. Applying the hermetic rule, since the Ascendant at birth was located in the middle of this sign, at 15° Cancer, the Moon at conception was determined to be also at 15° Cancer. The zodiacal location of the Moon at conception denotes the starting point of the formation of the etheric body. It is therefore the house of *life* (etheric body = life body).

After conception, the Moon traversed the second half of the sign of Cancer, and then entered Leo. Leo here was the second house, that of *estate and fortune* in traditional astrology. As referred to above, the Moon's passage through one zodiacal sign corresponds to seven months in the spiral of life.Thus, the passage through half of the sign of Cancer equates with the first 3½ months in John Addey's life. The next lunar zodiacal period, that of Leo, coincided with the 7-month period from the age of 3½ months to 10½ months. Then followed the lunar zodiacal period of Virgo, equating with the 7-month period from the age of 10½ months to 17½ months. The lunar zodiacal periods, each seven months long, can thus be followed further through the course of life, once the duration of the first zodiacal period has been determined.

Whereas the zodiacal periods arising through the Sun's passage through the zodiacal signs are connected with the development of the self (through different religious and philosophical outlooks, etc.), the lunar zodiacal periods (i.e. the houses) are bound up with the various spheres of destiny by means of which man's will manifests itself. For the Moon is the regent of the third level of being in the threefold man – the level of the will, which comes to expression via the limbs. In the formation of destiny during the embryonic period parallel to the Moon's orbits of the zodiac, the cosmic background provided by the Moon's passage through each successive sign yields a subtle differentiation of the way in which the will comes to expression in the unfolding of destiny. The "plan" as to how this takes place was conceived of originally by the division of destiny into twelve spheres, characterized by the traditional astrological designations listed in Table 15.

Let us consider an example, again drawn from John Addey's biography, as to how the hermetic houses may be applied in relation to the traditional astrological scheme of the meaning of the twelve houses, as given in Table 15. For example, John Addey became engaged on February 28, 1945 – his age on this day being 24 years 8 months and 13 days. As this was during the fourth 7-year period in the spiral of life, converting back to embryonic time it corresponds to a moment in the fourth lunar orbit of the zodiac (starting the first orbit at conception). Since 21 years equates with three complete lunar orbits (each 360 degrees), the extra 3 years 8 months and 13 days equates with 190 degrees of the Moon's motion around the zodiac.

VII. The Hermetic House System

Adding 190 degrees to the Moon's starting point at the moment of conception (= Ascendant at birth), yields 15° Cancer + 190 degrees = 25° Capricorn. Since Cancer is the first house (in this example of John Addey), Capricorn is the seventh house, the house of marriage in traditional astrology. Here the Moon's passage through Capricorn is related to the seventh house in the hermetic house system, and as this house is traditionally that of marriage it was the sphere of destiny which became emphasized at this period of time in John Addey's life. His engagement on February 28, 1945 in fact corresponds with a lunar zodiacal period in which (converting to embryonic time) the Moon was traversing the sign of Capricorn. (It is interesting to note that the Sun, also, was in Capricorn in the embryonic period at this time – see Table 10 for the zodiacal periods in John Addey's life. Moreover, h-Venus was at 28° Virgo in the embryonic configuration at this moment in time corresponding to John Addey's engagement, and therefore h-Venus was conjunct the Sun's zodiacal location at his conception and conjunct the Sun's zodiacal location at birth in his previous incarnation – see Charts 13 and 15.)

Table 15:
Traditional one-word designations for the twelve spheres of destiny, the twelve houses.
In the hermetic house system the twelve houses are identified with the twelve signs of the zodiac, such that the first house is the sign occupied by the Ascendant, the second house is the sign following that of the Ascendant, etc.

house	traditional designation	hermetic house system
1	life	1st house = sign of the Ascendant
2	estate	2nd house = sign after that of the Ascendant
3	brothers	3rd house = 3rd sign from the Ascendant
4	parents	4th house = 4th sign from the Ascendant
5	children	5th house = 5th sign from the Ascendant
6	health	6th house = 6th sign from the Ascendant
7	marriage	7th house = 7th sign from the Ascendant
8	death	8th house = 8th sign from the Ascendant
9	religion	9th house = 9th sign from the Ascendant
10	honours	10th house = 10th sign from the Ascendant
11	friends	11th house = 11th sign from the Ascendant
12	enemies	12th house = sign preceding that of the Ascendant

Obviously it would be wrong to conclude that the passage of the Moon through the various signs (corresponding to the different houses) signifies an exclusive focusing upon a particular sphere of destiny during the corresponding 7-month period in life. It can only be a matter of a tendency of the relevant sphere of destiny becoming emphasized in a given 7-month period, for it would be absurd to think that every seven months the human being is concerned solely with one aspect of his destiny, be it "estate" (2nd. house) or "marriage" (7th. house) or "friends" (11th. house) or any other house. Also, there remains the question as to whether the traditional astrological designations (as given in Table 15) of these various spheres of destiny are entirely appropriate for the modern human being.

Before looking further at this question, let us summarize the main principle underlying the hermetic house system and also consider the anomalies associated with this system.

Discussion of the hermetic house system

The hermetic house system is the oldest and simplest house system of all. In this system the first house is the sign of the Ascendant, and the subsequent houses are identical with the subsequent zodiacal signs, counted off around the zodiac from the Ascendant. However, this system applies only when the application of the hermetic rule to the birth horoscope yields the result that the Moon at conception was in the zodiacal sign occupied by the Ascendant at birth. In the event that the application of the hermetic rule leads to the result that the Moon at conception was in the sign opposite to that occupied by the Ascendant at birth, then the houses in the hermetic system are defined in relation to the Descendant. In this case Table 15 has to be modified accordingly, so that, for example, the first house = the sign of the Descendant, the second house = the sign following that of the Descendant, etc.

This surprising reversal of the houses in the hermetic house system – whenever the hermetic rule determines the Moon's starting point at conception to be the place of the Descendant – is not so difficult to comprehend when it is borne in mind that the opposite houses have a reciprocal relationship with one another. In some cases this is easier to see than in others. For example, the house of life (1st. house) and the house of marriage (7th. house) clearly have a reciprocal relationship, in that the marriage partner is, so to say, the counterpart of the individual's own life. Similarly, the house of children (5th. house) and the house of friends (11th. house) are reciprocal, in the sense that children are essentially "friends" within the individual's own household. (The reciprocal nature of opposite houses is looked at further in the example considered below.)

Thus in hermetic astrology a distinction is drawn between the zodiacal location of the Ascendant, and the zodiacal location of the Moon at conception. In the sense of the threefold division of man – head, chest, limbs – the zodiacal location of the Ascendant indicates cosmically the axis of vision of the head, as taken up by the human being in the zodiacal sphere prior to incarnation. The zodiacal location of the Moon at conception is

VII. The Hermetic House System

connected with the will sphere, coming to expression via the limbs. It denotes the starting point of the formation of the etheric body (wheel of life), and the zodiacal sign in which the Moon is located at conception indicates the cosmic background to the first house or first department in the wheel of life (known traditionally as the "house of life", indicative of the individual's character).

According to the hermetic rule, the zodiacal sign of the Moon at conception is either that of the Ascendant at birth, or it is the opposite sign (that of the Descendant). In the event that the Moon at conception is in the sign of the Ascendant, the starting point of formation of the etheric body coincides with the axis of vision of the head (Ascendant). But when the Moon at conception is in the sign of the Descendant, the starting point of the formation of the etheric body lies on the opposite side of the zodiac to the orientation of the axis of vision.

There are therefore two possibilities in the hermetic house system:
(1) When the Moon at conception is in the sign of the Ascendant, the first house in the wheel of life is the sign of the Ascendant, the second house is the sign following that of the Ascendant, the third house is the next sign, and so on.
(2) When the Moon at conception is in the sign of the Descendant, the first house in the wheel of life is the sign of the Descendant, the second house is the sign following that of the Descendant, the third house is the next sign, and so on.

An example of (1) was mentioned above: that of John Addey. The Moon at his conception was in the sign of Cancer, which was the Ascendant at his birth. In his case, therefore, the first house in the hermetic house system equated with the sign of Cancer. Thus, according to the traditional astrological meaning attributed to the first house, John Addey's *life and character* were signified by the sign of Cancer. Similarly, his *estate and fortune* were signified by the sign of Leo, the second sign in the wheel of life (= the sign following the sign of Cancer in the formation of the etheric body between conception and birth). *Brothers and sisters* were indicated by the sign of Virgo, the third sign from the Ascendant in the wheel of life; and *parents* (fourth house) by the sign of Libra. The domain of *children* (fifth house) was under the sign of Scorpio, and that of *work and health* (sixth house) under the sign of Sagittarius. Further, the affairs of the seventh house (*marriage/partners*) were "ruled" by Capricorn, whilst those of the eighth house (*death*) were "ruled" by Aquarius. *Religion and travels* (ninth house) came under Pisces, and *honours* (tenth house) under Aries. Lastly, *friends* were signified by Taurus and *enemies and misfortune* by Gemini.

Without denying that there may be some validity in the traditional astrological designation of the houses – as the human being's twelve *spheres of destiny* on the Earth – it is evident that for the modern human being the houses need to be conceived of in a wider sense than the meanings with which they have been endowed by tradition. The most accessible method open to us for acquiring a new understanding of the houses in modern hermetic astrology is that of research. In the following example, which exemplifies the second possibility of the hermetic house system referred to above (2), a mode of research is outlined whereby the nature of the houses can be investigated. The example chosen here is that of Richard Wagner, whose destiny has already been considered in some detail in the first three chapters. His life, owing to the detail with which his biography has been documented, provides a good example for the more extensive research required in order to investigate the spheres of destiny (houses).

The key to the method of research into the houses, as developed in hermetic astrology, is held by the Moon. For the Moon is the regent of the "limbs" of the threefold human being, i.e. the Moon holds sway over the sphere of the will. If the hermetic rule is applied successfully to determine the true date of conception, the passage of the Moon through the signs of the zodiac in the period between conception and birth can be followed. By converting from embryonic time to the spiral of life, it is possible to follow the main events of life – correlating them with the zodiacal location of the Moon at the corresponding time during the embryonic period. Given a well-documented biography – such as that of Richard Wagner – it is possible to tabulate the main events in his life in relation to the signs of the zodiac occupied by the Moon during the embryonic period. In this way, as we shall see below, the houses become objectified in relation to events in life.

In Richard Wagner's case the Ascendant at his birth was $5^{1}/_{2}°$ Taurus (see Chart 1), and the Moon's location at his conception, according to the hermetic rule, was $5^{1}/_{2}°$ Scorpio (see Chart 8). The first house, therefore, equates with Scorpio – the sign opposite to that of the Ascendant. According to traditional astrology the first house signifies *life and character*, i.e. Richard Wagner was a Scorpionic character, and his life came under the sign of Scorpio. How is this to be understood in the light of hermetic astrology?

The Ascendant at birth and the Moon's zodiacal location at conception

Firstly, it is helpful to contrast the two signs of Scorpio and Taurus in this example, where Scorpio was the sign of the first house (in the hermetic house system) and Taurus was the sign of the Ascendant. In the first place it is a matter of contrasting the physical body and the etheric body. The Ascendant indicates the human being's orientation in the sphere of the zodiac during the formation of the archetype of the physical body according to the image. The Ascendant thus indicates the physical appearance, which comes to expression especially in the face, where the Ascendant axis coincides with the axis of vision (the eyes being the "windows of the soul"). The zodiacal location of the Moon at conception, however, denotes the commencement of building up the etheric body; it is therefore the significator of the etheric body, indicating the starting point of the wheel of life.

Hitherto we have considered only the case where the zodiacal location of the Moon at conception coincides with the Ascendant, where there is a concordance between "life" (etheric body) and "form" (physical body). However, now we have to correct the impression given hitherto, to arrive at a more exact understanding. Now it is necessary to look at the second possibility, in which – as in Richard Wagner's case – the Moon at conception is located in the sign of the Descendant (opposite the sign of the Ascendant). In this instance there is a polarity between the human being's "form" (physical body) and "life" (etheric body). In Richard Wagner's case the physical body was signified by Taurus, whilst the life body came under Scorpio

There is in any case a natural polarity between the physical and etheric bodies. For if the physical body is male in a given incarnation, then the etheric body is female – and *vice versa*. The implications of this inner polarity coming to expression on a cosmic level, as in the case of Richard Wagner, is often a natural inner duality with respect to maleness and femaleness. In his case it is possible to understand this against the background of his previous incarnation as St. Teresa of Avila. The karmic indicator of the Ascendant of $5^1/2°$ Taurus at Richard Wagner's birth was given by the zodiacal location (at $5^1/2°$ Taurus) of the Moon at the death of St. Teresa. In the zodiacal sphere between the two incarnations, having completed the "voyage of the soul" through the planetary spheres, this individuality looked towards entering into a new incarnation upon the Earth again. As the decision to reincarnate was made, a point in time was chosen at which to be reborn upon the Earth. The planetary configuration for this point in time was chosen to be in harmony with the planetary configuration at death in the incarnation as St. Teresa, in order to represent a continuation from the one incarnation to the next, a "carrying over" of destiny via the stars. And the Moon's exact zodiacal location ($5^1/2°$ Taurus) at the moment of death in the last incarnation was chosen to be the Ascendant at birth in the new incarnation. This zodiacal location ($5^1/2°$ Taurus) thus specified the orientation of this individuality in the zodiacal sphere during the time of the weaving together of the zodiacal forces – in the image of the zodiacal man – for the archetype of the physical body for the next incarnation on Earth (as Richard Wagner). The Ascendant ($5^1/2°$

Taurus) thus indicated the imprint of the image in the formation of the embryo.

However, at the moment of conception the Moon was located at 5½° Scorpio, and it was therefore this zodiacal degree which signified the start of formation of the etheric body, the wheel of life. Here a polarity is indicated between the physical body (considered as formed by way of the imprint of the image) and the etheric body, which bears the human being's life forces. The imprint of the image in forming the physical body connected onto the moment of death in the previous incarnation, when the Moon was located at exactly this point in the zodiac. But at the commencement of the formation of the etheric body the Moon was at the polar opposite point in the zodiac.

It would lead beyond the scope of this study to examine in detail how this inner polarity in Wagner's being manifested itself. Here it is simply a matter of separating out the two factors: the Ascendant (5½° Taurus) and the Moon's position at conception (5½° Scorpio). Considered on one level, the Ascendant indicates more the physical appearance, whilst the Moon's position at conception relates more to how the life impulses work into the physical organism. However, there is a further level to take into consideration, since – as referred to in *Hermetic Astrology* I, Chapter 8 – the Ascendant is not only the astrological significator of physical appearance, but also of the personality and outlook of the incarnated human being.

Firstly, let us consider how the human being's outlook, his direction of thought, is coloured by the Ascendant. This can be grasped readily from Figure 13, which shows how the imprint of the image comes to expression in the spherical form of the head, where the Ascendant coincides with the axis of vision. In the sense that the eyes are the "windows of the soul", the way in which the human being looks out into the world is directly linked with the orientation of his axis of vision – and on the cosmic level, i.e. with respect to the individual's orientation within the sphere of the zodiac, this is indicated by the Ascendant. The inner reality of this can be characterized by the term *direction of thought*, so that the Ascendant signifies at one and the same time the human being's outlook and his direction of thought. Both are connected with the head, which – in the sense of the threefold human being – relates to the Ascendant.

The Ascendant is therefore of significance with respect to physical appearance, outlook and direction of thought, and insofar as these factors play a role in determining the human personality, the Ascendant is also indicative of personality. By "personality" is meant the earthly reflection of the individuality, i.e. how the individuality manifests itself in a given incarnation, in a given physical body on Earth. This is obviously a very complex issue, in which the physical appearance does play a role, as also do outlook and direction of thought, in the shaping of the personality.

The issue is further complicated, however, when the Moon's position at conception is also taken into account. For, as discussed in *Hermetic Astrology* I, Chapter 7, the sense of personality – although it arises essentially as a result of incarnation into a physical body – also sets in via the etheric body, insofar as the human being incarnates into the etheric body between conception and birth, and the latter works into the physical body. Thus the Moon's zodiacal location at conception, as the astrological significator of the etheric body, not only denotes *life* but also *character*. When the Moon's position at conception coincides with the Ascendant, life and character on the one hand, and physical appearance, outlook and direction of thought on the other hand, all have the same astrological significator – and this entire complex plays a significant role with respect to the nature of the personality. However, when the Moon's conception position is opposite in the zodiac to the Ascendant, life and character are signified by the sign occupied by the Descendant, in contrast to physical appearance, outlook and direction of thought, which are denoted by the sign of the Ascendant. In this case the personality is not clearly described by one sign (that of the Ascendant), for the sign of the Descendant also plays in. This has to be taken account of when considering the personality of the individual in question.

In Richard Wagner's case, it is a matter of an individual who in his appearance, outlook and direction of thought was Taurean, whilst having a Scorpionic character and life impulse. Earlier in this book his personality was characterized as Taurean in nature, in contrast to the Scorpionic personality of Friedrich Nietzsche. (Nietzsche's Ascendant was 6° Scorpio, identical with the zodiacal location of the Moon at Wagner's conception.) Yet in the light of the more exact study undertaken in this chapter, it is evident that Wagner's personality – with respect to his life and character – had Scorpionic traits, which partly explains why initially Nietzsche was able to identify himself so totally with Wagner.

The hermetic house system applied to Richard Wagner

Having clarified the difference in hermetic astrology between the Ascendant and the Moon's zodiacal location at conception, let us return to consider the twelve houses, as defined in the hermetic house system, in relation to the biography of Richard Wagner. The sign occupied by the Moon at conception is the first house, where the first house in this example equates with the sign of Scorpio. In converting from embryonic time to the spiral of life, the Moon's position at conception relates to the age of 0, i.e. it corresponds to birth. Thus the first house in the hermetic house system is the house of birth, the starting point of life, which for Richard

Wagner was 5½° Scorpio (= Moon at conception). In tabulating the main events in Richard Wagner's life – tabulating them in terms of the Moon's zodiacal location at the corresponding moment during the embryonic period – the tabulation commences with the event of birth (Moon = 5½° Scorpio).

The tabulation of events concludes with the death of Richard Wagner on February 13, 1883 at the age of 69 years, 8 months and 21 days. In order to transpose from the spiral of life to find the Moon's zodiacal location in the embryonic period corresponding to the event of death, Richard Wagner's age at death has to be looked at in terms of the 7-year periods, where each 7-year period corresponds to one orbit of the Moon around the zodiac during the embryonic period. The age of 69 years, 8 months and 21 days lies close to the end of the tenth 7-year period. In fact, death occurred when 6 years, 8 months and 21 days of the tenth 7-year period had elapsed. Since seven years corresponds to the Moon's orbit through 360 degrees of the zodiac, then 6 years, 8 months and 21 days corresponds to 346 degrees of the Moon's orbit around the zodiac. As the starting point of each lunar orbit is given by the Moon's location at conception, these 346 degrees have to be added to the starting point of 5½° Scorpio. Through this addition (5½° Scorpio + 346 degrees = 21½° Libra) the Moon's zodiacal position in the embryonic period at the moment corresponding to Wagner's death is determined to be 21½° Libra. This concludes the tabulation of events in Richard Wagner's life, i.e. the tabulation starts with birth (5½° Scorpio) in the first house (= sign of Scorpio) and concludes with death (21½° Libra) in the twelfth house (= sign of Libra in the hermetic house system as applied in this example).

The tabulation of events between birth and death according to the Moon's corresponding zodiacal location during the embryonic period is determined exactly by means of the procedure outlined here for the event of death. For each event in Richard Wagner's life, his age at the time of the event is assessed in terms of the 7-year periods of the spiral of life, and is then converted to embryonic age (measured by the Moon's orbit around the zodiac). In this way a tabulation of events in his life is determined in relation to the Moon's embryonic passage through the various zodiacal signs during the embryonic period (= the twelve houses – see Table 16).

Table 16 gives an overview of Richard Wagner's life in relation to the twelve houses in the hermetic house system, where the first house – in this example equating with the sign of Scorpio – is the sign in which the Moon was located at conception. The first house is therefore the house of birth, denoting the start of life. It is the house to which the Moon returns (when converting to the spiral of life) at the beginning of each new 7-year period.

Table 16:
The twelve houses in relation to Richard Wagner's biography

The first house equates with the sign of Scorpio, since the Moon at conception was located at 5½° Scorpio (in the tabulation rounded down to 5° Scorpio). This corresponds to birth, which starts the tabulation of events in his biography. The tabulation is completed by the occurrence of death, where the Moon's corresponding zodiacal longitude in the embryonic period was 21½° Libra (rounded down to 21° Libra in the tabulation). In the hermetic house system as applied in this example, the sign of Libra equates with the twelfth house.

(Note: In the tabulation, events are identified with a specific degree of the zodiac, which pinpoints a given week in life, as the Moon's motion through one degree of the zodiac during the embryonic period equates with one week of life. However, many of the events in this tabulation, e.g. the premiere of the *Ring*, took place over a period of several weeks. In such cases the identification of the event with a particular degree of the zodiac is an approximation, since it should stretch over several degrees, if it lasted several weeks.)

1st house
(Scorpio)

5°:	birth on May 22, 1813
5°:	wrote text of *Flying Dutchman* May 1841 (start of career to success)
5°:	Nietzsche's first visit to Wagner at Triebschen on May 17, 1869
7°:	birth of Wagner's son, Siegfried, on June 6, 1869
15°:	first meeting with his first wife, Mina, in late July 1834
18°:	premiere of the *Ring*, August 1876 (crowning point of whole career)
19°:	completed orchestra sketch of *Flying Dutchman* in August 1841
23°:	premiere of *Rheingold* on September 22, 1869
24°:	first draft of text of the *Ring* completed on October 4, 1848

2nd house
(Sagittarius)

11°:	engagement to first wife, Mina, at beginning of February, 1835
20°:	left Paris on April 7, 1842, to go to Dresden
23°:	completed text of *Parsifal* on April 19, 1877
25°:	fled Dresden on May 10, 1849, after the fiasco of the Dresden revolt

3rd house
(Capricorn)

1°:	premiere of *Walküre* on June 26, 1870
5°:	first sight of Bayreuth on July 26, 1835
9°:	nervous tension and illness, August 1856
14°:	stepfather died on September 9, 1821
15°:	began art-theoretical writings on September 16, 1849

23°: fateful meeting with Cosima in Berlin on November 28, 1863
29°: premiere of the *Flying Dutchman* on January 2, 1843

4th house
(Aquarius)

2°: appointed as director of the orchestra in Dresden on Feb. 2, 1843
10°: fled from Vienna on March 23, 1864
13°: visited Bayreuth with Cosima on April 17, 1871
15°: moved into "Asyl" on April 28, 1857; first conceived of *Parsifal*
16°: first meeting with King Ludwig II of Bavaria on May 4, 1864
18°: completed text of *Tannhäuser* on May 22, 1843
24°: relationship started with Cosima on June 29, 1864

5th house
(Pisces)

1°: began composition of *Tristan* on August 20, 1857; start of relationship with Mathilde Wesendonck
2°: premiere of *Lohengrin* on August 28, 1850
13°: received permission to build Festspielhaus in Bayreuth (Nov. 17, 1871)

6th house
(Aries)

6°: moved to Bayreuth on April 22, 1872
8°: first draft of *Siegfried* written in May, 1851
12°: premiere of *Tristan* on June 10, 1865
18°: commenced dictation of autobiography on July 17, 1865
22°: left "Asyl" on August 17, 1858
23°: first draft of *Parsifal* written end of August 1865

7th house
(Taurus)

8°: left Munich for Switzerland on December 12, 1865
14°: death of first wife, Mina, on January 25, 1866
24°: found Triebschen together with Cosima on March 30, 1866
26°: completed orchestration of *Tannhäuser* on April 13, 1845

8th house
(Gemini)

0°: Cosima first came to live at Triebschen on May 12, 1866
9°: completed orchestra sketch of *Tristan* on July 16, 1859
9°: first draft of *Meistersinger* completed on July 16, 1845
12°: text of *Lohengrin* completed on August 3, 1845
17°: arrived in Paris, mid-September 1859
22°: premiere of *Tannhäuser* on October 19, 1845
30°: text of *Ring* completed on December 12, 1852

9th house
(Cancer)

5°:	Ludwig II donated money for Bayreuth Festspielhaus on Jan. 25, 1874
16°:	directed Beethoven's 9th symphony (great success) on April 5, 1846
23°:	Richard Wagner Festspiel in Zürich: May 18–22, 1853

10th house
(Leo)

0°:	left Riga on July 9, 1839
10°:	arrived in Paris on September 17, 1839
12°:	first meeting with Cosima (15 years old) on October 10, 1853
14°:	completed *Meistersinger* on October 24, 1867
15°:	began composition of the *Ring* on November 1, 1853
18°:	completion of the *Ring* on November 21, 1874
23°:	completion of *Parsifal* on December 25, 1881

11th house
(Virgo)

5°:	disastrous performance of *Tannhäuser* in Paris, March 1861
18°:	premiere of *Meistersinger* on June 21, 1868
23°:	premiere of *Parsifal* on July 26, 1882
23°:	left Paris on July 30, 1861, after two disappointing years there
27°:	completed orchestra sketch of *Lohengrin* on August 28, 1847

12th house
(Libra)

3°:	first read (October 1854) Schopenhauer's work *The World as Will*
8°:	first meeting with Nietzsche on November 8, 1868
8°:	began to re-write text of *Meistersinger* on November 12, 1861
13°:	*Tristan* composition inspired by Mathilde Wesendonck, December 1854
21°:	death in Venice on February 13, 1883

The first house

From Table 16 it is evident that this is the most eventful house in Richard Wagner's biography, containing the following major events:
physical birth;
"birth" as a successful operatic composer, with the writing of the text of the *Flying Dutchman* (the first opera for which Wagner is famous);
the "birth" of his relationship with Friedrich Nietzsche;
the birth of his son Siegfried.

These four major events in Richard Wagner's life all fell in the first house (Scorpio), close to the zodiacal degree at which the Moon was located at his conception. In addition, the first house contains the event of his first meeting with his first wife, Mina, which proved decisive for the subsequent course of his life. It also contains the event of the premiere of the *Ring of the Nibelungen*, with which the Bayreuth Festspielhaus became opened for the first time to the public. This event was the crowning point of Wagner's entire career.

How is it possible to understand the remaining houses? Are there any noticeable groupings of events in any particular house?

Research into the meaning of the houses

Surveying Table 16, it can be seen that it presents a breakdown of Richard Wagner's biography in 7-year periods, where each zodiacal degree equates with one week of life. Thus, in the second house (Sagittarius) the event of his fleeing from Dresden on May 10, 1849 (after the Dresden uprising) occurred seven years and five weeks after the event of his leaving Paris on April 7, 1842. Lying seven years apart, these events fell in the same house. If they had been *exactly* seven years apart, they would have fallen at exactly the same degree in Sagittarius, but as there is a five-week difference from the exact period of seven years, they are separated by five degrees in the sign of Sagittarius. This pattern holds true not just for events seven years apart, but also for events fourteen years apart, twenty-one years apart, or any multiple of seven years apart.

Looking at the groupings of events through the twelve houses of the hermetic house system in Table 16, some interesting polarities emerge with respect to houses opposite to one another. For example, as mentioned above Wagner left Paris (for the first time) on April 7, 1842 – this event being located in the second house, at 20° Sagittarius. Some seventeen years later he returned to live in Paris again, and this event is located opposite – in the eighth house, at 17° Gemini.

As another example of a polarity, Wagner first caught sight of Bayreuth on a journey when he was 22 years old. This event fell in the third house, at 5° Capricorn. Over thirty-eight years later, his plans for the building of the Bayreuth Festspielhaus – which had become unrealisable owing to lack of funds – were rescued by the generous intervention of King Ludwig II of Bavaria, who donated a large sum of money for the project. This latter event fell opposite – in the ninth house, at 5° Cancer.

This event (generosity of a benefactor) – falling in the ninth house of the hermetic house system – is more characteristic of the traditional astrological meaning attributed to the tenth house, traditionally known as the house of *honours*. The same can be said with respect to the two other events listed in the ninth house: the emergence of Wagner as a "star director" at the age of (almost) 33, owing to his inspired direction of Beethoven's ninth symphony, through which he received widespread acclaim; and the first Richard Wagner Festspiel in Zürich, which also was a significant occasion of public acclaim for the young composer (he was just 40 years old).

Another interesting polarity is that of his first meeting with his first wife, Mina, in the first house, at 15° Scorpio, and her death opposite in the seventh house, at 14° Taurus. This latter event fits well into the traditional astrological meaning of "partner" attached to the seventh house, as do two other events listed in the seventh house. Namely, the event of Wagner's leaving Munich to live in Switzerland was brought about largely through the scandal aroused on account of his relationship with Cosima, the wife of the conductor Hans von Bülow. This contributed to the public opposition to Wagner, which eventually grew so strong that the king (Ludwig II, Wagner's benefactor) was obliged to request Wagner to leave Bavaria. Shortly after this (still in the seventh house, as referred to above), Wagner's first wife died. He was then joined in Switzerland by Cosima, together with whom he found the house Triebschen, where they later lived together – constituting the happiest period of his life. Cosima actually came to live at Triebschen only after (always referring back to the embryonic period) the Moon had entered the next (i.e. eighth) house, the sign of Gemini, and it was some time later that they married (as Cosima first had to obtain a divorce from Hans von Bülow).

Yet another polarity is that of Wagner's first meeting with Cosima, when she was only fifteen years old, and his first visit to Bayreuth with Cosima. This latter event led to the founding of the Festspielhaus in Bayreuth, representing the culmination of Wagner's life-long ambition to have his own theatre for the production of his operas. Bayreuth became the home of Cosima and Richard Wagner for the latter years of their life together. The first visit to Bayreuth fell in the fourth house, at 13° Aquarius, whilst the first meeting between Wagner and Cosima fell in the tenth house, at 12° Leo.

There is a striking grouping of three events in the tenth house: namely, the completion of three of Wagner's major operatic works: *Meistersinger, Ring of the Nibelungen* and *Parsifal*. Just as the first house is the house of birth, in this example the tenth house seems to represent the house of completion. However, clearly further research is necessary – investigating other examples, applying the same method utilized here – before it is possible to arrive at a new understanding of the nature of the houses. The value of the method of research developed in hermetic astrology in relation to the hermetic house system is that it objectifies the houses in terms of events in the individual's life. The events speak for themselves, and the task is to discern whether there seems to be some underlying pattern to the events in terms of a twelve-fold division into different spheres of destiny (houses).

Comparison of the twelvefold and sevenfold divisions

One way in which it is possible to gain some idea of the nature of the houses in hermetic astrology is to consider the hermetic house system in relation to the sevenfold division described earlier in this chapter. Unlike the twelvefold division into houses, which relates to the cosmic reality of the Moon's passage through the signs of the zodiac during the embryonic period, the sevenfold division does not correspond to a cosmic reality. Rather, it arises through the earthly reality of the seven "life steps" of the seven years comprising a 7-year period in the spiral of life. As already described, there is an analogy between the seven steps within a 7-year period and the seven "steps" through the seven planetary periods – Moon, Mercury, Venus, Sun, Mars, Jupiter and Saturn – during the course of life. Again the Moon's position at conception signifies the starting point for the sevenfold division, where – depending upon the outcome of the application of the hermetic rule – this coincides either with the Ascendant or with the Descendant. (The description earlier in this chapter assumed the Ascendant to be the starting point – see Figures 15 and 16 – and in the case of the Descendant being the starting point, Figures 15 and 16 have to be reversed, as in Figure 19b.)

If the traditional astrological attributes of the houses – although specified in terms of a twelvefold division – are considered in relation to the sevenfold division into life steps, a relationship can be discerned between the houses and the life steps. For example, the sixth house (work) and the seventh house (marriage) more or less coincide with the Sun sector (see Figure 19), which corresponds to the age between 21 and 42, during which period the primary concerns are usually the search for a marriage partner and the finding of the right vocation. Similarly, the tenth house, belonging to the Jupiter sector (see Figure 19), is traditionally associated with success or failure in the outer world, which depends upon thought-initiative (Jupiter) and which generally shows itself by the time the human being attains the Jupiter period of life (between the ages 49 and 56). These three houses may serve here, by way of example, as a stimulus to the reader to explore further the relationship between the life steps and the houses. Despite the intrinsic incompatibility between the sevenfold and the twelvefold divisions, nevertheless it appears that some kind of relationship between the life steps and the houses does exist.

These two divisions are compared in Figure 19 (a and b). The seven life steps comprise a time sequence of one-year steps. They unfold one after the other in the course of a 7-year period. By way of analogy, they correspond to the planetary sequence: Moon, Mercury, Venus, Sun, Mars, Jupiter and Saturn. Similarly, the twelve houses of life also stem from a time sequence traced out by the Moon during the course of a lunar sidereal month. This twelvefold division relates to the Moon's passage through the twelve signs of the zodiac – the passage of the Moon through the various zodiacal signs indicating "shifts" in the enactment of destiny. These shifts from one domain (house) of destiny to the next take place during the weaving of destiny into the etheric body in the embryonic period – there being twelve shifts given by the twelve zodiacal signs through which the Moon passes in the course of one revolution of the sidereal zodiac. The Moon's orbit of the sidereal zodiac during the embryonic period thus gives rise to the houses as departments of destiny. When transposed from embryonic time to the spiral of life, each house, i.e. each lunar sidereal period, lasts for seven months of life, and recurs again seven years later, regularly recurring at 7-year intervals.

Figure 19a:
The sevenfold and the twelvefold divisions
The seven planetary sectors and the twelve houses (hermetic house system) taken from the Ascendant as starting point.

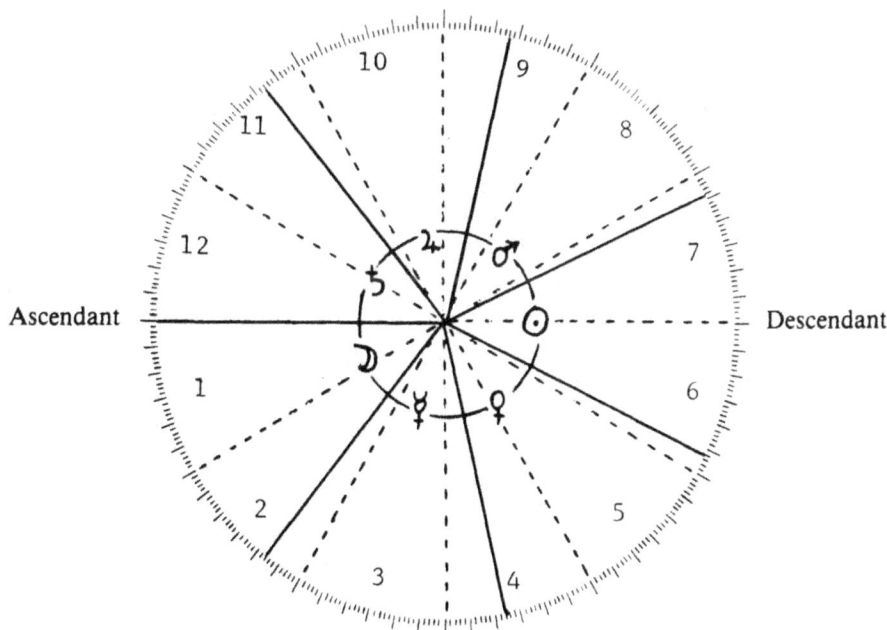

Figure 19b:
The sevenfold and twelvefold divisions

The seven planetary sectors and the twelve houses (hermetic house system) taken from the Descendant as starting point.

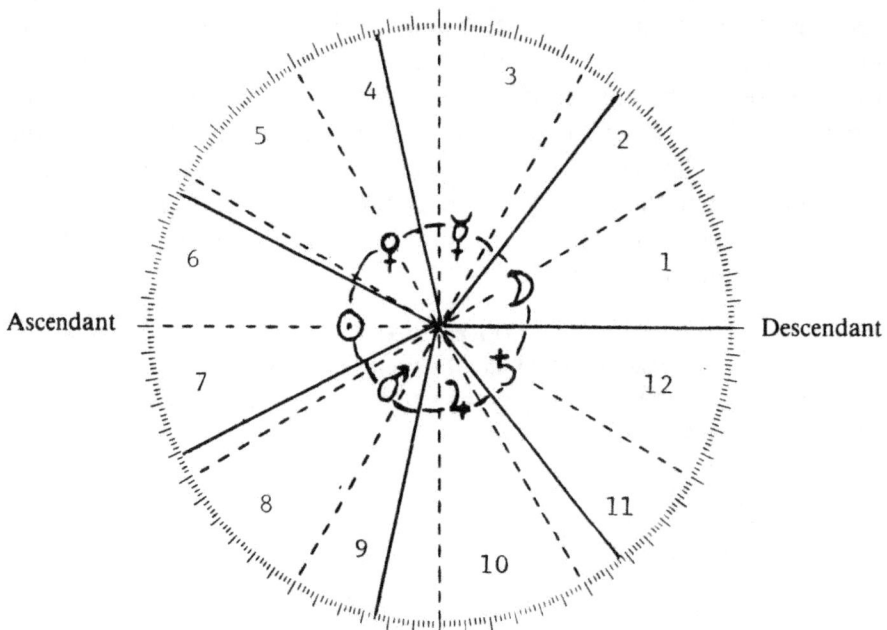

The first house traditionally represents *birth*, i.e. birth into a physical body. The first aspect of life that the human being experiences is the physical body itself. Here the human being "rests", as it were, in his physical body, where the word "resting" is not meant in an outer sense, as the first few months of life (and of each new 7-year period) may be a time of intense activity. What is meant is that the human being experiences a primal relationship to his physical body at birth (first house) and that this recurs – but always at a different level – every seven years, at the start of each new 7-year period.

The second aspect of life experienced by the human being in his relationship to the world is summarized by the designation for the second house; i.e. *estate*. This comprises property and belongings – and for the small baby also its mother. Next to the physical body itself are the clothes that clothe it and the house in which the human being lives and sleeps. This can be extended, for example, to the car in which the human being travels, etc. All of this belongs to the domain of the second house.

The first house, and part of the second house, belong to the Moon sector – assuming that the first house starts with the Ascendant or Descendant, as shown in Figure 19. (As each house in the hermetic house system is identical with a particular sign of the zodiac, the situation depicted in Figure 19 occurs only when the Ascendant – or, if the case may be, the Descendant – is located at the beginning of the zodiacal sign in question. If it is not at the beginning, Figure 19 has to be adjusted accordingly, e.g. if it is in the middle of the relevant zodiacal sign, then the Ascendant – or, if the case may be, the Descendant – lies in the middle of the first house, and each of the twelve houses then has to be rotated through 15 degrees in Figure 19. In the following, however, for the sake of simplicity it will be assumed that the situation shown in Figure 19 holds true, and the entire discussion will refer to the twelve houses in relation to the seven planetary sectors as shown in Figure 19.) Assuming that the first house and part of the second house belong to the Moon sector (see Figure 19), this means that they belong to the sphere of the self considered as a being of will. This certainly holds true – fully and completely – for the first house, as the domain of the physical body, since the physical body can be regarded as an instrument of will. Moreover, the physical body is clearly intimately connected with oneself. But belongings are not necessarily a matter purely to do with oneself; they may be shared (e.g. more than one person living in a house). So, whilst the first house is strictly a matter of oneself, the second house (estate) is no longer necessarily a purely personal matter, but may involve other people. Thus part of the second house extends into the Mercury sector, where there is a turning out towards the world around in a gesture of exchange.

The third house lies entirely in the Mercury sector. This is traditionally the house of *brothers and sisters.* Here there is interchange, dialogue and relationship – on a brotherly/sisterly level. All of this belongs to the sphere of Mercury, where the self comes to expression in relationship to the outer world.

The fourth house lies partly within the Mercury sector and partly in the Venus sector. This is traditionally the house of *parents and home.* This is the fourth relationship of the human being to the world: the relationship to his parents and to his home. This has a mercurial quality insofar as the human being is able to learn from his parents. With them he feels at home. At the same time, the Venus element – the bond of love between the parents – is of significance for the bringing together of the parents and, therewith, for the very creation of the physical body into which the human being incarnates.

The fifth house, lying fully within the Venus sphere, is the house of *pleasure,* i.e. where the inner life of feeling comes to expression in the human being's finding satisfaction in the physical world. It is above all in love relationships that this is the case, and a natural consequence thereof is that children are brought into the world – *children* being a traditional department of life belonging to the fifth house.

The sixth relationship to the world experienced by the human being is that which belongs to the sphere of *work*. The sixth house lies almost entirely in the Sun sector of the horoscope, in accordance with the universal character of work as a matter of the self. A small part of this house belongs to the Venus sector (pleasure may also be derived from work!). But, on the whole, work – engagement in a profession – is an objective task. Here the human being comes to himself as an individual with a position in the community at large, through which he is able to be of service to the community. (*Service* is a traditional attribute of the sixth house.) Another attribute of the sixth house is *health*, which is connected with work in a direct way, since the human being's ability to work depends upon his health.

Like the sixth house, the seventh house – that of marriage – is connected with the human being's position in the community at large, since marriage is the very foundation of civilization. Marriage, therefore, also belongs to the Sun sector, as the objective expression of the human being's self in relationship to another. (This other is the "neighbour" in the sense of Christ's saying: "Love thy neighbour as thyself" – *Mark* xii, 31.) The seventh house is the polar opposite of the first house, i.e. instead of the self in relation to the physical body (first house), it is to do with the self in relation to another self (seventh house). Part of the seventh house extends into the Mars sector of the horoscope, i.e. marriage can go beyond the realm of a relationship between one self and another, to enter the realm of self-realisation – Mars sector. This comes to expression in communication – speech (Mars) as a higher, creative faculty in the human being. One of the tasks of marriage partners is to develop a higher level of communication (extending from the physical level to that of the highest spiritual communion).

The eighth house lies entirely within the Mars sector of the horoscope. Here the self comes into relationship to the world through creative impulses. Creative activity in general, leading to self realisation, belongs to this domain. In the past the aggressive (Mars) side of the human being was associated with this house, which was therefore the house of war and death. But in recent times, through the transformation of the Mars impulse from one of aggression to one of morality – from pugnacity to moral courage – the eighth house has come increasingly to represent the sphere of *rights*, where causes are fought for rather than wars, e.g. tne civil rights movement, the campaign for nuclear disarmament, women's liberation, etc. In all these cases it is a matter of the *power of the word*, as a moral force, whereby the cause in question is fought for.

The ninth house, as the next department of life, belongs partly to the

Mars sector and partly to the Jupiter sector of the horoscope. Here the ninth aspect of the human being's relationship to the world comes to expression. This is traditionally the house of ideals. On the one hand the source of ideals lies in the realm of thought (Jupiter), and on the other hand the bringing of ideals to expression depends upon speech (Mars).

The tenth house, lying wholly within the Jupiter sector of the horoscope, is the realm of thought-initiative. This may be purely on an inner level, in relation to the spiritual world, or it may become translated into designs relating to the outer world. This house is the polar opposite department of life to that of the fourth house (parents and home).

The eleventh house lies partly in the Jupiter sector and partly in the Saturn sector. Here thought-initiative (Jupiter), insofar as this concerns the human being's relationship to the world, is carried over into the realm of memory (Saturn). This is traditionally the house of the *guardian Angel* and of the spiritual impulses leading human beings together to *community*. The memory element (Saturn), when carried over from previous incarnations, is that which leads human beings together (generally unconsciously). The thought element (Jupiter), insofar as this relates to the fulfilling of designs in the outer world, is that which helps a community or group of friends to find a common purpose together.

The twelfth house, lying wholly within the Saturn sector, has to do with memory and the review of life. As such, it is known traditionally as the house of imprisonment, insofar as living in memories and recollections can become a kind of imprisonment. But if permeated with spiritual light, this department of life can be truly spirit-filled, through which insights relating to the past can be gained, which can then serve as a basis for a deeper understanding of life.

The foregoing brief description of the twelve houses in relation to the seven life steps may help to serve as a stimulus to further research and investigation into the nature of the houses. Moreover, in the above description the correspondence between the life steps and the planetary periods, as shown in Figure 16, has not been taken into consideration. This correspondence implies that each of the seven planetary sectors in the horoscope correlates archetypally with a 7-year period, progressing around the horoscope through successive phases of life, i.e. the Moon sector with infancy (0–7), the Mercury sector with childhood (7–14), the Venus sector with youth (14–21), the Sun sector with adulthood (21–42), the Mars, Jupiter and Saturn sectors with maturity (42–49, 49–56, 56–63). Taking account of this correspondence can help to lead to a qualitative deepening of understanding of the twelve houses, when the houses, in turn, are considered in relation to the seven planetary sectors of the horoscope. However, it should be noted that in the case of this correspondence – as with most correspondences – it is simply a matter of a qualitative analogy.

To summarize: despite the basic incompatibility between the seven life steps and the twelve houses, something of the dynamic of the elaboration of karma during each 7-year period is indicated by the planetary pattern of the seven life steps when superimposed on the twelve houses as in Figure 19. Again it must be emphasized, however, that the life steps do not arise out of a cosmic reality, whereas the twelve houses do. For the seven life steps are simply an expression of the earthly reality of the sevenfoldness of each 7-year period, whereas the twelve houses arise through the cosmic reality of the Moon's passage through the twelve zodiacal signs during each orbit of the Moon around the zodiac in the embryonic period.

On the one hand the seven life steps, when viewed in the context of the spiral of life, are the years (first year, second year, third year, etc.) of each 7-year period. On the other hand the twelve houses (in the hermetic house system) equate with 7-month lunar zodiacal periods recurring at 7-year intervals in the spiral of life. That is, each 7-year period in the spiral of life comprises twelve 7-month lunar zodiacal periods, during which a particular sphere of destiny (house) is emphasized, one after the other, through the twelve houses. The lunar zodiacal periods, as epochs of destiny relating to the level of the will (Moon), may be contrasted with the 7.8-year solar zodiacal periods, which are periods of development of the self (Sun, heart center), and which come to expression in changes in philosophical/religious outlook, etc.

Interrelationship of solar and lunar zodiacal periods

During each solar zodiacal period, there takes place a complete cycle of twelve lunar zodiacal periods, since each solar zodiacal period lasts on average 7.8 years, and a complete cycle of twelve lunar zodiacal periods – each seven months long – lasts seven years. For example, returning again to Richard Wagner's biography, the high-point of his life was the Aries solar zodiacal period, lasting from the age of 61 years 5 months to 69 years 4 months (see Table 17). This corresponds to the period in his life from October 1874 to September 1882. Shortly after the start of the Aries solar zodiacal period, in November 1874, he finally completed the tetralogy of operas *Ring of the Nibelungen*, the premiere of which in August 1876 signified the crowning of his life's work. Following this he composed his final opera – *Parsifal* – the premiere of which took place in Bayreuth on July 26, 1882, shortly before the end of the Aries solar zodiacal period. Then – at the commencement of the Taurus solar zodiacal period in September 1882 (see Table 17) – he left Bayreuth together with his family (on September 14) and travelled to Venice. There, five months later, on February 13, 1883, he died. Thus the Taurus period (Taurus being the zodiacal sign in which the Sun was located at his birth) was nothing more than a kind of brief epilogue to this dramatic, highly creative life.

VII. The Hermetic House System 279

Within a particular solar zodiacal period, the passage of a complete cycle of twelve lunar zodiacal periods can be followed, which provides a cosmic differentiation within a given solar zodiacal period. Here it is simply a matter of tabulating the 7-month lunar zodiacal periods in relation to the given solar zodiacal period, as shown in Table 18 with respect to the Aries solar period (October 1874 to September 1882) in Richard Wagner's life.

Table 17:
Solar zodiacal periods in Richard Wagner's life

Sun at Richard Wagner's conception on August 15, 1812: 0°34' Leo
Sun at Richard Wagner's birth on May 22, 1813: 8°28' Taurus
Between conception and birth the Sun passed through almost the entire sign of Leo, and then through the signs Virgo, Libra, Scorpio, Sagittarius, Capricorn, Aquarius, Pisces and Aries, and then through the first 8½ degrees of Taurus. Converting from embryonic time to the spiral of life, this means that the zodiacal background influence for the first 7 years 9½ months of Richard Wagner's life corresponded to the Sun's passage through 29½ degrees of Leo. Then began the solar zodiacal period of Virgo, lasting 7 years 10 months, followed by Libra, lasting 7 years 8 months, etc. (see Table 13), as listed in the following tabulation:

monthly zodiacal divisions within the embryonic period 1812/1813

Sun in:	dates*	corresponding age	corresponding life period
Leo	Aug. 15 – Sep. 15	$0^y\ 0^m$ – $7^y\ 9½^m$	May 1813 – Mar. 1821
Virgo	Sept. 15 – Oct. 15	$7^y\ 9½^m$ – $15^y\ 7^m$	Mar. 1821 – Dec. 1828
Libra	Oct. 15 – Nov. 14	$15^y\ 7^m$ – $23^y\ 3^m$	Dec. 1828 – Aug. 1836
Scorpio	Nov. 14 – Dec. 14	$23^y\ 3^m$ – 30^y10^m	Aug. 1836 – Mar. 1844
Sagittarius	Dec. 14 – Jan. 12	30^y10^m – $38^y\ 5^m$	Mar. 1844 – Oct. 1851
Capricorn	Jan. 12 – Feb. 11	$38^y\ 5^m$ – $45^y11½^m$	Oct. 1851 – May 1859
Aquarius	Feb. 11 – Mar. 13	$45^y11½^m$ – $53^y\ 7½^m$	May 1859 – Jan. 1867
Pisces	Mar. 13 – Apr. 12	$53^y\ 7½^m$ – $61^y\ 5^m$	Jan. 1867 – Oct. 1874
Aries	Apr. 12 – May 13	$61^y\ 5^m$ – $69^y\ 4^m$	Oct. 1874 – Sep. 1882
Taurus	May 13 – Jun. 13	$69^y\ 4^m$ – $71^y\ 8½^m$	Sep. 1882 – Feb. 1885+

---

*Allowing a precession rate of one degree in 72 years, in the 180 years between 1812 and 1992 precession amounts to 2½ degrees (2½ x 72 = 180). Therefore the dates of the Sun's entrance into the sidereal signs of the zodiac occurred on average 2½ days earlier in 1812/1813 than at the present time.

+The Taurus solar zodiacal period in Richard Wagner's life corresponded to the Sun's passage through the first 8½ degrees of the sign of Taurus in the last part of the embryonic period,

Table 18:
Lunar zodiacal periods in Richard Wagner's life during the Aries solar zodiacal period (between October 1874 and September 1882).

At the age of 63 (start of a new 7-year period), the lunar zodiacal period is specified by the Moon's location at conception (= 6° Scorpio at Richard Wagner's conception at 7 p.m. local time, Leipzig, on August 15, 1812). Since the Moon's motion through one degree of the zodiac during the embryonic period equates with one week of life, the lunar zodiacal period of Scorpio began six weeks prior to Wagner's 63rd birthday, i.e. 6 weeks before May 22, 1876. Thus the lunar zodiacal period of Scorpio began on April 10, 1876 and lasted seven months, until November 10, 1876. Then followed the lunar zodiacal period of Sagittarius, which also lasted for seven months. The entire sequence of lunar zodiacal periods (each seven months long) during the Aries solar zodiacal period (October 1874 to September 1882) is tabulated in the following table, where also the houses are numbered according to the hermetic house system, i.e. the first house equates with the sign of Scorpio in which the Moon was located at conception, and the remaining houses are numbered accordingly:

house	zodiacal sign	lunar zodiacal period in the spiral of life corresponding to the Moon's passage through the zodiacal signs during the embryonic period
10	Leo	August 10, 1874 – March 10, 1875
11	Virgo	March 10, 1875 – September 10, 1875
12	Libra	September 10, 1875 – April 10, 1876
1	Scorpio	April 10, 1876 – November 10, 1876
2	Sagittarius	November 10, 1876 – June 10, 1877
3	Capricorn	June 10, 1877 – January 10, 1878
4	Aquarius	January 10, 1878 – August 10, 1878
5	Pisces	August 10, 1878 – March 10, 1879
6	Aries	March 10, 1879 – October 10, 1879
7	Taurus	October 10, 1879 – May 10, 1880
8	Gemini	May 10, 1880 – December 10, 1880
9	Cancer	December 10, 1880 – July 10, 1881
10	Leo	July 10, 1881 – February 10, 1882
11	Virgo	February 10, 1882 – September 10, 1882

leading up to the cut-off date at the moment of birth, when the Sun was located at 8½° Taurus. Converted to the spiral of life, the Taurus zodiacal period began in September 1882 and would have ended at the cut-off date in February 1885. However, since Wagner died on February 13, 1883, he died actually two years before the cut-off date of the embryonic period. Thus Wagner died two years ahead of the date for the completion of the unfolding of his destiny woven in the embryonic period between conception and birth.

VII. The Hermetic House System

Referring to the tabulation of lunar zodiacal periods in Table 18, as the Aries solar zodiacal period in Richard Wagner's life began, the corresponding lunar zodiacal period was Leo, and it was within Leo (tenth house) that the completion of the *Ring of the Nibelungen* on November 21, 1874 took place. Still within the Aries solar zodiacal period, as mentioned above, the premiere of the *Ring* was performed during August 1876. This was within the lunar zodiacal period of Scorpio (first house).

Following on from this, still within the Aries solar zodiacal period, Wagner set to work on re-writing his original draft of *Parsifal* and completed this on April 19, 1877 – in the next lunar zodiacal period, that of Sagittarius (second house). Then began the work of orchestration, which continued through the following lunar zodiacal periods (still within the Aries solar zodiacal period) until work on *Parsifal* was completed at Christmas 1881, in the lunar zodiacal period of Leo (tenth house). The premiere followed on July 26, 1882 in the lunar zodiacal period of Virgo (eleventh house), still within the solar zodiacal period of Aries (referring all the time to Table 18).

Here we have followed a complete cycle of the lunar zodiacal periods within a particular solar zodiacal period (that of Aries) in Richard Wagner's life. In so doing we have penetrated into the mysterious realm of the weaving of destiny during the embryonic period, whereby the Sun and Moon are the two main cosmic "regents of karma" to take account of in this weaving of destiny. For the passage of the Sun through the signs of the zodiac during the embryonic period traces out the vehicle of the self, i.e. it indicates the cosmic path of development of the self. And the passage of the Moon through the signs of the zodiac during the embryonic period delineates the various spheres of destiny (houses), i.e. the spheres of realisation of the self in its incarnation upon the Earth.

To take account of the lunar zodiacal periods (houses) in relation to the spiral of life is to introduce a finely differentiated outline of the realisation of destiny into the individual's astrological biography. Hitherto we have considered astrological biography essentially in relation to the planetary periods (7-year periods in the spiral of life) and the solar zodiacal periods, as in the example of John Addey's astrological biography (see Chapter 6, Table 12). A much more profound and detailed astrological biography is yielded when the lunar zodiacal periods (houses) are also taken into account. The significance for the individual of this is that he is able to gain a deeper inner contact with cosmic reality, as it works into his life.

Thus, if Wagner had been aware of this – of his astrological biography – he could perhaps have raised to consciousness the activity of the self ("inner Sun"), which drew its impulses from the sign of Aries during the period of his life from the age of 61 years 5 months to 69 years 4 months (to consider only one zodiacal period). Over and above the cosmic background of Aries irradiating the impulses of his self during this period, he could also have followed the fine differentiation yielded by the Moon in the working out of his destiny. For example, he might have been able to feel the tenth house (Moon in Leo) in the culmination of his work on completing the *Ring* at the beginning of the Aries solar zodiacal period. And later, towards the end of his Aries solar zodiacal period, perhaps he could have brought to consciousness "Moon in Leo" (tenth house) once again – in the culmination of his work in finishing the composition of *Parsifal*. In this way it might have been possible for Wagner to attune to the cosmic reality underlying the unfolding of his destiny, to find the cosmic impulses of the Sun and Moon forces active within him – as woven already during the embryonic period on his descent into incarnation.

To work out the astrological biography in this sense – over and above the solar zodiacal periods, to include the lunar zodiacal periods arising from the hermetic house system – can thus be a source of strength to the individual. Through his astrological biography he can find an inner connection with cosmic reality, especially with the cosmic differentiation of the Sun and Moon forces active within him in the shaping of his destiny. This is one approach in hermetic astrology to helping the individual to find again an inner connection with cosmic reality.

The twelve labours of Hercules

In this chapter an outline of the aspect of the hermetic-astrological science of destiny which deals with the hermetic house system has been sketched. Underlying this new science of destiny are the planetary movements between conception and birth, which map out the unfolding of destiny through the course of life. Of central importance here are the movements of the Sun and Moon. During each orbit of the Moon around the zodiac in the embryonic period the destiny for a 7-year period in the spiral of life becomes mapped out. In the course of one orbit the Moon passes through the twelve signs of the zodiac, giving rise to twelve *spheres of destiny* (houses). These houses in the hermetic house system are numbered from 1 to 12, where the first house is the sign of the zodiac occupied by the Moon at the moment of conception, the second house is the next zodiacal sign, and so on.

In an average length embryonic period of ca. 270 days, the passage of the Moon through the zodiacal signs is mirrored in the course of life, giving rise to lunar zodiacal periods, each seven months long, recurring at 7-year intervals. In this way the houses are projected into the spiral of life, each house lasting seven months, during which time the affairs of the house in question come to the fore. (By *affairs* is meant all that which belongs to a particular house – considered as a sphere of destiny– whereby the significance attributed to the twelve houses in traditional astrology

VII. The Hermetic House System

possibly stands in need of modification with respect to the modern human being.)

The Moon, which maps out the houses during the embryonic period, is the regent of the will, in the sense that the houses – as spheres of destiny – are the different realms in which the will comes to expression during the course of earthly life. Over and above the sphere of the will governed by the Moon is the self, related to the Sun. Just as the passage of the Moon through the signs of the zodiac during the embryonic period gives rise to the houses, on the level of the will, so the passage of the Sun through the zodiacal signs between conception and birth relates to the path of development of the self. Transposing from the embryonic period to the spiral of life, the Sun's passage through each zodiacal sign gives rise to solar zodiacal periods in life, each approximately 7.8 years long.

As referred to in Chapter 6, the bringing to consciousness of the path of development of the self in the sequence of solar zodiacal periods can be helped by referring to the *Meditations on the Tarot,* especially to the twelve arcana corresponding to the twelve signs of the zodiac. Of these twelve arcana, each arcanum outlines the various tasks and trials connected with a particular sign of the zodiac, which can then be referred to the given solar zodiacal period in which the individual finds himself at the present point in his life. In addition to these twelve arcana relating to the twelve signs of the zodiac, a further seven arcana correspond to the seven planets (Moon, Mercury, Venus, Sun, Mars, Jupiter and Saturn), whilst the remaining three arcana relate to the three forces of hindrance connected with the outermost planets Uranus, Neptune and Pluto. It is especially the three outermost planets which will occupy our attention in the next chapter, but beforehand let us consider the twelve houses again, this time from the point of view of the path of initiation.

Just as the solar zodiacal periods can be brought to consciousness on the path of self development, so the lunar zodiacal periods (houses) can also be raised to consciousness along the path of initiation. The particular task of becoming conscious of the realm of the will and of gaining mastery over the twelve modes of expression of the will through the twelve houses was designated in antiquity by the *twelve labours of Hercules*. The path of self development leads over into the path of initiation when the self is able to gain mastery over the will. The self ("inner Sun") has to penetrate and illumine the lunar sphere of the will, with its twelve domains or houses, corresponding to the twelve signs of the zodiac. The twelve labours of Hercules describe the trials connected with the gaining mastery over the twelve domains of the will, where each labour depicts the mastering of one aspect of the will, i.e. each labour relates to a particular "house", belonging to one of the zodiacal signs.

In the light of modern hermetic astrology, the individual lives through a particular house in the course of seven months. To bring this to consciousness is a first step, whereby during the course of seven months an awareness of the relevant lunar zodiacal period may be acquired, and this consciousness may be enhanced by the regular repetition of each lunar zodiacal period every seven years. (This is not a mere repetition, however, as after seven years usually the human being has entered into a new solar zodiacal period, and is correspondingly at a new stage of development of the self.) The next step is for the self to take hold of the will out of inner strength, which signifies a "labour" during a given lunar zodiacal period. "Hercules" is the strengthened self of the aspirant to initiation, and the twelve labours are the trials confronting the self in acquiring mastery over the twelve aspects of the will, manifesting by way of the twelve houses.

Thus in modern hermetic astrology a 7-year period can be looked upon as a period during which the opportunity is given to experience the twelve aspects of the will, whereby a new aspect ("house") comes to the fore every seven months. Each 7-month period presents a new "labour", to use the terminology of the ancient mysteries of initiation. For example, in the 7-month period corresponding to Leo, the relevant labour – referring back to the original twelve labours of Hercules – is the conquering of the *Nemean lion*. In this period it is especially the "lion in the will" which has to be mastered. The description of the Nemean lion – a raging creature that spread death and destruction – shows the nature of the "lion in the will" if it is not controlled by the self. In modern terms, the "lion in the will" could be described as *rampant egotism*, and in hermetic astrology it is through the practice of *compassion* that this aspect of the will is overcome and transformed. Compassion is the virtue of Leo.[9] It is the practice of this virtue which overcomes and transforms the "lion in the will", which, if left to its own devices, would tend constantly to assert its kingly nature, to lord it over others, even to become a tyrant (as depicted by the Nemean lion).

Similarly, in the 7-month period belonging to Taurus the corresponding labour (from the twelve labours of Hercules) is that of the taming of the Cretan bull. Here the "bull in the will" has to be mastered by the self. From the description of the Cretan bull it is evident that the "bull in the will" – if left uncontrolled – has the tendency to become *enraged*, i.e. to become a relentless driving force that on the level of the will expresses rage or even mania. The virtue of Taurus is *equilibrium*, and it is the practice of this virtue during the relevant 7-month period which can transform and master the "bull in the will". Here it is a matter of harnessing the will, through the practice of equilibrium, such that it never becomes an expression of rage.

Similarly, in the 7-month period belonging to Scorpio, the corresponding trial (from the twelve labours of Hercules) is that of mastering the "scorpion in the will", i.e. the overcoming of the Lernean hydra. The hydra in the swamp of Lerna is described as having nine heads, and with each head that Hercules severed, two grew in its place. Here the struggle with the "scorpion in the will" is evident in relation to consequences for the life of thought, whereby the blotting out of one thought only provokes the emergence of two other thoughts in its place. The virtue which masters the "scorpion in the will" is *patience*. For example, by not allowing a thought to gain control as soon as it arises, but instead subjecting it to patient scrutiny, insight can be gained into the correctness of the thought. Through patience, the self thereby acquires mastery over the "scorpion in the will".

From the foregoing brief description of the three labours of Hercules corresponding to Taurus (the Cretan bull), Leo (the Nemean lion) and Scorpio (the Lernean hydra), and also of the three virtues relating to these three signs – virtues by means of which the self accomplishes the relevant labours, i.e. masters these different aspects of the will – it is evident that knowledge of the 7-month lunar zodiacal periods in life can be of significance on the path of initiation. The key here is the practice of the virtues connected with the twelve zodiacal signs. These virtues are: devotion (Aries), equilibrium (Taurus), perseverance (Gemini), selflessness (Cancer), compassion (Leo), courtesy (Virgo), contentment (Libra), patience (Scorpio), self-control (Sagittarius), courage (Capricorn), discretion (Aquarius) and magnanimity (Pisces).[10]

These twelve virtues can be practised during the twelve months of the year, as referred to in Chapter 10, where they are described in connection with the hermetic calendar. Then it is more on the level of the heart, and the virtues relate to the *beatitudes* (blessings) of Christ. They can also be practised on the level of the will, through the sequence of 7-month lunar zodiacal periods. This can be considered as a metamorphosis of the twelve labours of Hercules, whereby each "labour" is encountered during the corresponding 7-month lunar zodiacal period. Here the virtues – on the level of the will – represent the positive spiritual forces required for the execution of the various trials or labours associated with the twelve houses (spheres of destiny), each lasting seven months, extending over a 7-year period.

This latter cycle arises from a practical application of the hermetic house system, in which the twelve labours of Hercules relate to the twelve houses in hermetic astrology, where the houses – when transposed to the spiral of life – become 7-month lunar zodiacal periods. Of course, the twelve labours have to be conceived of in a modern form, as a metamorphosis from the original twelve labours of Hercules. Three of the labours have been described above, translated into modern form, as the trials of encountering the "bull in the will", the "lion in the will", and the "scorpion in the will". The remaining nine labours of Hercules can be looked at in exactly the same way, also transformed into modern terms and adapted to the modern human being. Thereby the astrological houses receive a completely new meaning, one that is relevant to the modern human being on the path of initiation.

Chapter 7: Notes and references

1. Cf. Wilhelm Gundel, *Neue astrologische Texte des Hermes Trismegistos* (Hildesheim, 1978), pp. 306–313.
2. Otto Neugebauer, "Demotic Horoscopes", *Journal of the American Oriental Society* 63 (1943), pp. 115–126.
3. Manilius, *Astronomica* ii, 909–910 (trsl. P. Goold, Loeb Classical Library, 1977, p. 155).
4. Ibid., ii, 916.
5. Ibid., ii, 922–924.
6. Cf. Ptolemy, *Tetrabiblos* iii, 10 (trsl. F. Robbins, Loeb Classical Library, 1980, p. 273).
7. Cf. Beredyne Jocelyn, *Citizens of the Cosmos* (Crossroads, New York, 1982) for a detailed discussion of the individual years within each 7-year period.
8. Cf. Rudolf Steiner, *Karmic Relationships* V, lectures 5, 6 and 7 (Rudolf Steiner Press, London, 1966, pp. 69–108) for a description of the inscription of the karmic effects of the human being's earthly life in the various planetary spheres during the voyage through these spheres in the life after death.
9. Cf. Rudolf Steiner, *Anweisung für eine esoterische Schulung* (Rudolf Steiner Verlag, Dornach, Switzerland, 1979), p. 31 for a list of the twelve virtues related to the twelve signs of the zodiac. Cf., also, Paul Platt, *The Qualities of Time* (Philmont NY, 1986).
10. Ibid.

Chapter 8

Uranus, Neptune and Pluto

The confrontation with evil

In this outline of hermetic astrology so far the planets Uranus, Neptune and Pluto have been left out of consideration. But as mentioned in the last chapter and in the preceding chapter, Uranus, Neptune and Pluto also belong to the circle of existence represented by the twenty-two major arcana of the Tarot. The circle of the twenty-two arcana is made up of the zodiac (the *animal circle,* comprising the twelve signs of the zodiac), plus the seven planets (Moon, Mercury, Venus, Sun, Mars, Jupiter and Saturn), plus three forces of hindrance. These three forces of hindrance are signified macrocosmically by the planets Uranus, Neptune and Pluto. At the same time, the three forces of hindrance, when inwardly transformed, can become the highest spiritual faculties. It would therefore be one-sided to regard Uranus, Neptune and Pluto as purely negative, for they can also be looked upon as planets of transformation, which can help the human being to go beyond himself and develop higher spiritual faculties.

In Uranus, Neptune and Pluto we encounter the problem of evil. The very discovery of these planets during the last two hundred years or so indicates that mankind has entered a period of evolution in which it is necessary to face up to the existence of evil. Each of these planets was discovered at a crucial historical moment: Uranus in 1781, Neptune in 1846, and Pluto in 1930. From history itself it is possible to read the signs as to the nature of the impulses – primarily in their negative aspect – which arose in the wake of the discovery of each of these three planets.

(1) following the discovery of Uranus: the French revolution, which started in 1789.
(2) following the discovery of Neptune: the socialist revolution in 1848, which spread throughout most of Europe; this paved the way for the communist revolution in Russia (1917) – here it is interesting to note that the Communist Manifesto was first published by Marx and Engels in the year 1848.
(3) following the discovery of Pluto: the rise of the Nazi movement; Hitler came to power in 1933.

The doctrines underlying the French revolution, communism and fascism are connected with the impulses mediated by Uranus, Neptune and Pluto, respectively, as will be elaborated in this chapter. In each case these social movements and their associated doctrines have brought untold misery into the world (and in the case of communism continues to do so, influencing the lives of a large part of the world's population). As will be discussed later in this chapter, it is a matter here of a confrontation with evil. How is this to be understood?

A foundation is given in Chapter 3 for understanding the working of evil. This can help to provide a basis for comprehending the impulses mediated by the planets Uranus, Neptune and Pluto. In Chapter 3 the archetypal three temptations are discussed:

the temptation directed at thinking ("turning stones into bread");

the temptation directed at feeling ("casting oneself down from the pinnacle of the temple");

the temptation directed at the will ("the will to power" over "all the kingdoms of this world").

As will emerge in the following, the macrocosmic source of these three temptations is connected with the impulses mediated by the planets Uranus, Neptune and Pluto, which work on the levels of thinking, feeling and the will, respectively. Thus consideration of these three planets – in their negative sense – means taking account of the problem of evil.

For this reason Uranus, Neptune and Pluto were left out of consideration in *Hermetic Astrology* I, with regard to the interpretation of the hermetic chart. These three planets work in as forces of hindrance, as long as the human being is not in a position through spiritual development to inwardly transform these forces. Moreover, Uranus, Neptune and Pluto do not correspond to any of the lotus flowers comprising man's psycho-spiritual organism. They are not part of the hermetic man (see *Hermetic Astrology* I, Figure 13), and do not belong in the hermetic chart as such. Nevertheless, as we shall see in the examples presented in this chapter, they work in from outside the hermetic man, and therefore they have to be taken account of in the hermetic chart.

Similarly, unlike the other planets, Uranus, Neptune and Pluto do not correspond to any of the human being's organs, in the sense of occult physiology. Moreover, whereas each of the other planets "rules" a 7-year period in the spiral of life (the Sun actually "ruling" three 7-year periods), Uranus, Neptune and Pluto do not have anything to do with the unfolding of the spiral of life. Thus, so far they have been left out of account in *Hermetic Astrology* II with regard to the interpretation of the geocentric chart in relation to the spiral of life. Although the planets Uranus, Neptune and Pluto are not included in the sequence of 7-year periods, nevertheless they do play a role in the shaping of destiny. In order to understand the astrological nature of Uranus, Neptune and Pluto, it is a help to consider mythology, for here is a source which sheds light upon these three planets.

Uranus, Neptune and Pluto in the light of mythology

It would be a mistake simply to look at the characteristics of the figures Uranus, Neptune and Pluto as these are depicted in Greek mythology, without first coming to an understanding of the naming of these three planets. In other words, whereas the names of the planets in antiquity – Saturn, Jupiter, Mars, Sun, Venus, Mercury, Moon – were named in accordance with their spiritual nature and their position in the cosmos (in terms of cosmic evolution), the naming of the more recently discovered planets is to a certain extent arbitrary. To be more precise, the name *Uranus* is not arbitrary in terms of Greek mythology, but the names *Neptune* and *Pluto* do not fit into Greek cosmological mythology in quite the same way. Therefore in astrology associations tend to be made with the planets Neptune and Pluto which, although not completely false, need to be qualified.

The most profound Greek cosmology is that of Orpheus.[1] Orpheus described the sequence of cosmic evolution in terms of the planetary gods. As this has been handed down to us, the Orphic cosmology describes the divine rule of six generations of gods: Phanes, Night, Ouranos, Kronos, Zeus and Dionysos.

Dionysos was the son of Zeus and Persephone. Whilst he was but still an infant, Zeus handed over his power to him. Going backwards in time, the reign of Zeus (Jupiter) was preceded by that of Kronos (Saturn), which, in turn, was preceded by the reign of Ouranos (Uranus). Ouranos (Heaven) was married to his sister Gaia (Earth), and from this union Kronos and Rhea were born. (Zeus was the offspring of the union of Kronos and Rhea.)

Looking at each of the planets as a "marker" in the unfolding of cosmic evolution, the orbit of Jupiter denotes the orb of the reign of Zeus. This is encircled by the orbit of Saturn, which represents an earlier stage of evolution than that of Jupiter, and this earlier stage of evolution corresponds to the reign of Kronos. Similarly, the orbit of Uranus encircles that of Saturn, and therefore Uranus marks a still earlier stage of evolution than Saturn. Thus, the orbit of Uranus delineates the reign of the god of Heaven (Ouranos). Extending this analogy further, Neptune marks the stage of cosmic evolution preceding that of Uranus, and Pluto is the marker of the evolutionary stage preceding that of Neptune.

Since Orpheus described two stages of cosmic evolution prior to that of Ouranos – namely, that of the reign of Night, and prior to this, that of the reign of Phanes – these correspondingly relate to the orbits of the planets Neptune and Pluto, respectively.

Firstly, Neptune: immediately preceding the reign of Ouranos – according to Orpheus – was the reign of the goddess Night (Nyx), the being of supreme wisdom in the cosmos. She corresponds to the Egyptian goddess

Nût. The ancient Egyptian depictions of this goddess show her arched across the vault of heaven. She presents the background against which the stars appear and the Sun, Moon and planets move. Night is the mother goddess from whom Ouranos was born, just as the night sky provides the background against which the stars of heaven (Ouranos) appear. Little is known about the goddess Night, but towards the end of the eighteenth century the poet Novalis wrote his deeply mystical *Hymns to the Night*, which capture something of this mysterious being:

> *Aside I turn to the holy, ineffable, mysterious Night... Dost thou take pleasure in us also, dark Night? What dost thou hold underneath thy mantle that with unseen power affects my soul?... More heavenly than these flashing stars seem to us the infinite eyes which the Night has opened within us. They see further than the palest of those countless hosts; without need of the Light they penetrate the depths of a loving heart, a feat which fills a higher realm with unutterable delight. Praise be unto the world's queen, the high herald of sacred worlds, the fostering nurse of blessed love! She sends thee to me, tender Beloved, lovely Sun of the Night.[2]*

Elsewhere Night is simply referred to as the great goddess: *"The great goddess, the mother of all the gods, the queen of heaven, ruler over all the gods – in the beginning she entered into existence."*[3]

The reign of the goddess Night, preceding that of Ouranos, was delineated in the planetary system by the orbit of the planet that is now called Neptune. Thus, in the light of Orphic cosmology, *Night* (Egyptian *Nût*, Greek *Nyx*) would have been an appropriate name for the planet Neptune. The result of naming this planet *Neptune* is that in astrology the attributes of the Greek mythological figure Neptune have become associated with the planet instead of the attributes of the goddess Night, the mother of all. Some of the attributes of Neptune, the sea god in Greek mythology, overlap with those of Night, e.g. the black depths of the subconscious can be represented by the depths of the ocean as well as by the infinite darkness of outer space beyond the light of the stars. Therefore the astrological associations connected with Neptune are not completely false, but they need to be qualified in the light of the correspondence of this planet with the mythological figure of *Night*. (Neptune is a more appropriate name for the negative side of the working of this planet, as will be shown later in this chapter.)

Secondly, Pluto: in the cosmology of Orpheus – prior to the reign of the goddess Night – there took place, originally, the reign of the god Phanes. Orpheus described Phanes as an androgynous creator god, the source of the primal will, the fire of love that underlies the whole of existence.

> *Phanes is the creator of all, from whom the world has its first origin... He is imagined as marvellously beautiful, a figure of shining*

> light... He is of both sexes, since he is to create the race of gods unaided, "bearing within himself the honoured seed of the gods" (Orphic Fragment 85)... He made an eternal home for the gods and was their first king... Phanes bore a daughter, Night, whom he took as his partner and to whom he gave great power. She assisted him in the work of creation, and he finally handed over his sceptre to her, so that she became the next in order of the rulers of the universe... Night bore to Phanes Gaia and Ouranos (Earth and Heaven)... To Ouranos Night handed over the supreme power.[4]

Phanes and Night thus represent, respectively, the father and mother of the gods, and their attributes bear comparison with those of the Father and Mother in the Christian-Gnostic tradition. In the Christian tradition, according to the Book of Genesis, since the seventh day of creation the Father is at rest. References to the Mother are scanty in the Bible, although the Book of *Proverbs* contains the following allusion: *"The Lord created me at the beginning of his work, before his works of old. I was set up from everlasting, from the beginning, or ever the Earth was... When he marked out the foundations of the Earth, then I was at work beside him"* (*Proverbs* viii, 22–30). Here, through Solomon, the voice of Wisdom (Greek *Sophia*) speaks. Indeed, the Mother can be considered as the supreme wisdom underlying the "seven pillars" of creation. ("Wisdom has built her house, she has set up her seven pillars" – *Proverbs* ix, 1.) As we shall see in the following, the "seven pillars" refer to the seven stages of human evolution.

Thus Phanes and Night represent attributes of the Father and Mother of existence, of the Primal Being whose nature is love, and of the World Soul whose being is wisdom. Similarly, Ouranos represents an aspect of the Intelligence of the Cosmos, whose outer aspect comes to manifestation in the light of the starry heavens.

The domain of Phanes, as the antecedent of Night, corresponds to the realm delineated by the planet that is now called Pluto. In the light of Orphic cosmology, an appropriate name for the planet Pluto would be *Phanes*. As this planet is called Pluto, it has acquired astrological attributes ascribed in Greek mythology to Pluto, the god of the underworld. But as some of the attributes of Pluto overlap with those of Phanes, the astrological associations attributed to Pluto are not entirely wrong. For example, the force of *eros* (primal love-will) is an attribute of Phanes, as well as being associated with Pluto. Nevertheless, the conception of this planet as *Phanes* gives a truer image of the real astrological nature of the planet than the conception of Pluto, god of the underworld. (Pluto is an appropriate name for the negative side of the working of this planet, as will be discussed later in this chapter.)

Cosmic stages of evolution

According to Orphic cosmogony, a divine dynasty of six generations are said to have held in turn the rule of the universe. These six generations of gods are: Phanes, Night, Ouranos, Kronos, Zeus and Dionysos. Each god ruled over a certain stage of evolution. How are the different stages of evolution in Orphic cosmology associated with the planets?

Figure 20:
The heliocentric system

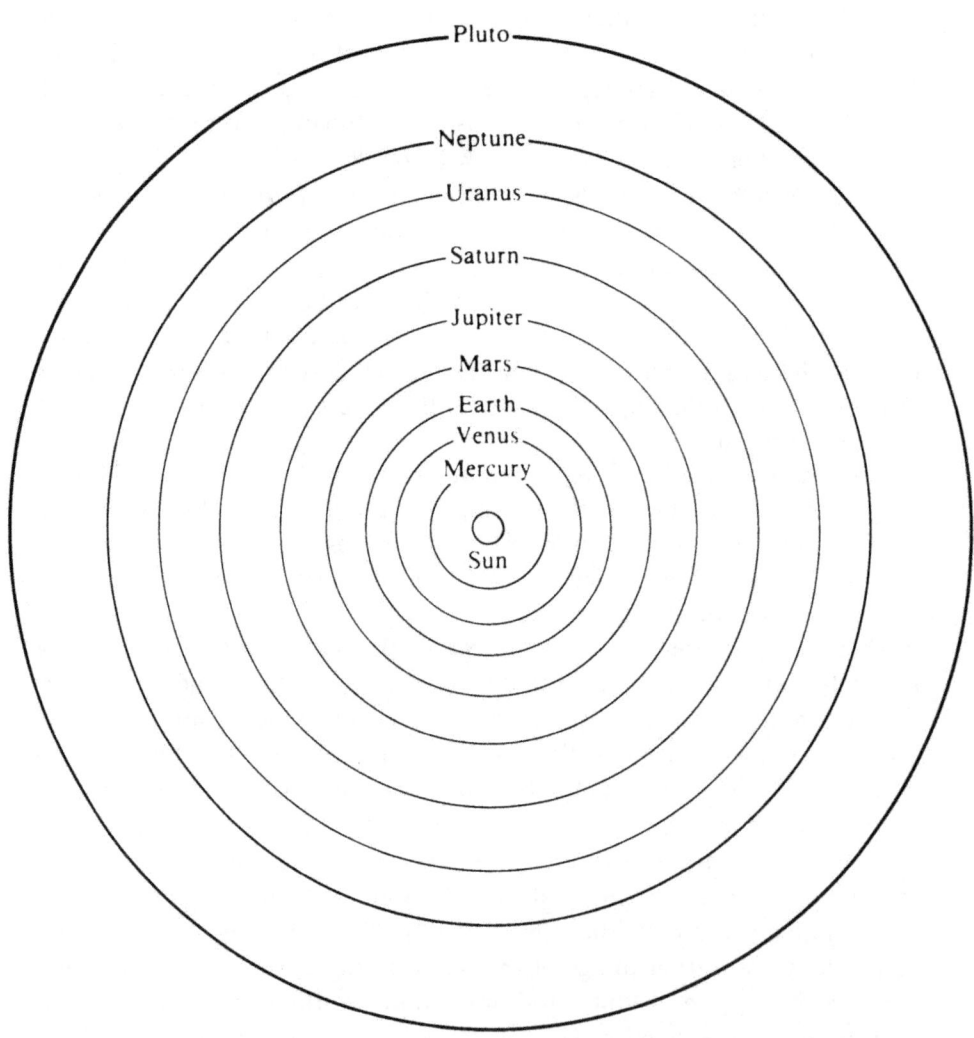

Here the heliocentric conception of the solar system is relevant (see Figure 20). For, in the light of Orphic cosmology, the orbits of the planets are markers of the various stages of evolution. To borrow a Hindu term, cosmic evolution proceeds by way of a series of *manvantaras*, or planetary periods, each drawing successively closer towards the Sun. The first manvantara in the Orphic cosmology, that of Phanes, took place within the orbit of Pluto. During the first manvantara the foundation of life in the cosmos became laid through the all-pervasive primal cosmic will.

The second manvantara, that of Night, took place within the orbit of Neptune. Here a new element became added to the foundation of life. Out of the primal will there arose the cosmic harmony of the World Soul. During the reign of the goddess Night the harmonies of the world sounded forth, of which Orpheus sang to his disciples.

A contraction took place from the first to the second stage of cosmic evolution, which is marked in our present solar system by the difference in tho orbits of Pluto and Neptune. In between these two manvantaras, there took place a *pralaya* (again using a Hindu term), i.e. a rest period, during which the contraction took place. After a second pralaya and a further contraction, the manvantara of Ouranos took place, the third period of cosmic evolution according to the cosmology of Orpheus. During this period the cosmos became endowed with Intelligence. To the Life (primal love-will) laid down during the first manvantara and the Sound (cosmic harmony) laid down in the second manvantara, the element of Light (cosmic intelligence) became woven into the foundations of existence during the manvantara that took place within the orbit of the planet Uranus. With the third manvantara, the cosmos arrived at a threefold foundation of Life, Sound and Light, each laid down successively during the manvantaras taking place within the orbits of the planets Pluto, Neptune and Uranus.

During these three manvantaras, however, the human being did not exist – not even in a rudimentary form. For this reason, the planets Uranus, Neptune and Pluto represent qualities that are superhuman, lying beyond the human being, but which nevertheless pervade the cosmic existence in which man is embedded. Cosmic life, cosmic sound and cosmic light pervade all existence, but it is only when the human being develops higher stages of consciousness that he is able to be illuminated by the light of the cosmos, inspired by the sound of the harmonies of the cosmos, and united with the life (love-will) of the cosmos. These three higher stages of consciousness have been described in *Hermetic Astrology* I, Chapter 4, as *lunar consciousness* (Illumination), *solar consciousness* (Inspiration) and *zodiacal consciousness* (Union). Thus, Uranus, Neptune and Pluto relate to the higher faculties of Illumination, Inspiration and Union, respectively. Without the development of these higher faculties, the forces of cosmic life, cosmic sound and cosmic light continue to work in the subconscious depths of the human being. Through the path of meditation they can become raised into consciousness; but otherwise Uranus, Neptune and Pluto work at a level transcending the sphere of normal human evolution.

The cosmology of Orpheus describes the cosmic reign of Kronos (Saturn) as following on from that of Ouranos. Accordingly, a further contraction took place, in which cosmic evolution became circumscribed by the sphere of Saturn. In the light of Orphic cosmology, the Saturn period of cosmic evolution is the fourth manvantara, but there are grounds, as we shall see, for regarding this as the *first* stage of cosmic evolution – in the sense that *human evolution* began during the Saturn manvantara. In the Orphic cosmology, the Earth manvantara (= the present period of cosmic evolution, associated with the planet Earth) is the seventh period of cosmic evolution, but in terms of human evolution, the Earth period is the fourth stage of evolution (see Table 19).

Looking at the heliocentric planetary system, successive manvantaras are indicated by the orbits of the planets around the Sun, each stage of cosmic evolution – by a process of contraction – drawing nearer towards the Sun. In the Orphic cosmology there are ten manvantaras, identified with the planetary orbits as follows (see Table 19): Pluto, Neptune, Uranus, Saturn, Jupiter, Mars, the Earth, Venus, Mercury and the Sun. Here the Earth is the seventh stage of cosmic evolution, i.e. at present we are in the seventh manvantara, with three manvantaras yet to come. From the standpoint of the evolution of the human being, however, we are now at the fourth of seven stages of evolution, identified with the planetary orbits as follows: Saturn, Jupiter, Mars, the Earth, Venus, Mercury, the Sun (see Table 19).

As indicated in *Hermetic Astrology* I, Chapter 10, Rudolf Steiner had perfect recall not only of his previous incarnations, but also of earlier stages of cosmic evolution, and these seven stages of evolution through which the human being evolves are described by Rudolf Steiner in his book *Occult Science: An Outline*.[5] Thus, by means of his spiritual faculties of perception, he was able to behold and describe not only the history of Earth evolution going back through various cultural epochs (see *Hermetic Astrology* I, Chapter 3) to Atlantis and even earlier, but also the history of each of the preceding stages of evolution, identified with the orbits of Saturn, Jupiter and Mars. He named these stages of evolution according to his clairvoyant perception. For example, he described the stage of evolution which took place within the orbit of the planet Jupiter as the *Sun* period, because the entire sphere bounded by the planet Jupiter was like a giant Sun.[6] Similarly, the stage of evolution which took place within the orbit of the planet Mars he described as the *Moon* period of evolution, because of the moonlike globe that revolved around the orbit which is now

Table 19:
The manvantaras of Orphic cosmology and the stages of human evolution

1 manvantara: orbit of Pluto (Phanes)
2 manvantara: orbit of Neptune (Night)
3 manvantara: orbit of Uranus (Ouranos)
4 manvantara: orbit of Saturn (Kronos)   1 stage: orbit of Saturn *(Saturn)*
5 manvantara: orbit of Jupiter (Zeus)   2 stage: orbit of Jupiter *(Sun)*
6 manvantara: orbit of Mars (Dionysos)   3 stage: orbit of Mars *(Moon)*
7 manvantara: orbit of the Earth   4 stage: orbit of the Earth *(Earth)**
8 manvantara: orbit of Venus   5 stage: orbit of Venus *(Jupiter)*
9 manvantara: orbit of Mercury   6 stage: orbit of Mercury *(Venus)*
10 manvantara: orbit of the Sun   7 stage: orbit of the Sun *(Vulcan)*

* The stages of human evolution are indicated by the names for the days of the week, where the present Earth evolution is divided into two halves: Mars (prior to the Mystery of Golgotha) and Mercury (post-Christian era). Saturday (Saturn), Sunday (Sun), Monday (Moon), Tuesday (Mars), Wednesday (Mercury), Thursday (Jupiter), Friday (Venus), and lastly Saturday (Vulcan) being the "higher octave" of the Saturn stage. The Anglo-Saxon names for the days of the week are partly derived from the names of the Germanic gods: Tiw = Mars, Wotan = Mercury, Thor = Jupiter, Freya = Venus. It should be noted that in the heliocentric system the orbit of the Earth lies between that of Mars and Venus, where Mars represents a continuation from the past Moon stage and Venus leads into the future Jupiter stage of human evolution. According to Rudolf Steiner's esoteric cosmology, the names of the planets Venus and Mercury became interchanged, so that esoterically considered the orbit of the Earth lies between that of Mars and Mercury. In the light of this consideration the validity of the designation of the two halves of Earth evolution as "Mars" and "Mercury" can be seen.

occupied by Mars. These four stages of evolution – the three former evolutionary periods and the present Earth period – were therefore named by Rudolf Steiner: *Saturn, Sun, Moon* and *Earth.* These are to be followed by three evolutionary periods, which Rudolf Steiner named: *Jupiter, Venus* and *Vulcan.* Thus, according to Rudolf Steiner's cosmology, these seven stages of evolution relating to the development of the human being are:

Saturn (which took place within the orbit of the planet Saturn);
Sun (which took place within the orbit of the planet Jupiter);
Moon (which took place within the orbit of the planet Mars);
Earth (which is taking place in the orbit of the Earth around the Sun);
Jupiter (which will take place within the orbit of the planet Venus);
Venus (which will take place within the orbit of the planet Mercury);
Vulcan (which will take place in the sphere of the Sun).

These seven stages of the human being's evolution, together with the names given to them by Rudolf Steiner, are listed in Table 19 alongside the manvantaras of Orphic cosmology.

Human evolution in relation to cosmic evolution

In his book *Occult Science* Rudolf Steiner describes how the rudiments of the physical body of the human being were elaborated during *Saturn* evolution. Analogous to this stage of evolution is the formation of the spiritual archetype of the physical body during the zodiacal sphere of existence between incarnations. For the human being this is a kind of recapitulation – between each incarnation – of the *Saturn* period of evolution. In fact, the entire incarnation process of the human being – from the formation of the spiritual archetype of the physical body in the sphere of the zodiac, to incarnation in a physical body on the Earth – is a kind of recapitulation of the stages of evolution. That is, the *Saturn* period of evolution is recapitulated in the sphere of the zodiac, when the archetype of the physical body is formed according to the image (zodiacal man); the *Sun* period of evolution is recapitulated during the descent through the planetary spheres – the Sun being the central sphere (Saturn, Jupiter, Mars, Sun, Venus, Mercury, Moon) – whereby the astral body is built up from the various planetary spheres according to the likeness (hermetic man); the *Moon* period of evolution is recapitulated between conception and birth, when the etheric body is formed in accordance with the Moon's revolutions of the zodiac through ten lunar sidereal months; and the *Earth* period of evolution corresponds to existence in a physical body between birth and death.

In these four stages of incarnation the human being experiences *Saturn, Sun, Moon* and *Earth* stages of existence. This mirrors on the microcosmic level the fact that the whole of evolution has passed through *Saturn, Sun, Moon* and *Earth* stages, in a series of contractions from Saturn's orbit around the Sun down to the present orbit of the Earth, during which the physical body, etheric body, astral body and self became cosmically formed and bestowed upon man.[7]

However, according to Rudolf Steiner's cosmology, there are three stages of evolution to follow the *Earth* stage. What is the significance of these three future stages of evolution – *Jupiter* (orbit of Venus), *Venus* (orbit of Mercury) and *Vulcan* (sphere of the Sun)?

These three stages of evolution are connected with the goals of mankind. These goals have already been described in Chapter 6 in connection with the higher levels of unfolding of the spiral of life. There reference is made to the task to be accomplished by the human being of developing three further stages, beyond the self. These higher levels of being beyond the self are termed *spirit self, life spirit* and *spirit man* (see Table 11). Spirit self, the first level of development of the inner spiritual man, is attained by way of purification of the astral body. Life spirit, the second level, is arrived at through the transformation of the etheric body. Lastly, at the third level, the human being's higher goal is the spiritual permeation (transubstantiation) of the physical body.

The work of the human being in transforming his three vehicles – astral, etheric and physical bodies – comprise the next three stages of evolution. That is, the purification of the astral body is the goal of *Jupiter* evolution; the transformation of the etheric body is the goal of *Venus* evolution; and the transubstantiation of the physical body is the goal of *Vulcan* evolution.

These stages were all passed through by Jesus Christ in his life on Earth, whereby the last – and highest – stage of evolution was attained by Jesus Christ at the Resurrection. The appearance of Jesus Christ in his resurrection body – the transformed physical body – signifies the accomplishment of the highest goal of mankind, the goal to be accomplished during *Vulcan* evolution. This stage of evolution will take place within the sphere of the Sun, and the presence of Christ's resurrection body on Earth – or rather in the sphere surrounding the Earth – means that already a "piece of Sun" is at present active among mankind. And from within his resurrection body Jesus Christ continues to work in the guidance of mankind towards the attainment of the distant goal of resurrection, that of the transubstantiation of the physical body. (This mystery of transubstantiation is celebrated daily throughout the world in the sacrament of the Mass, where the host – representing Christ (Sun)-permeated matter – is taken into the human being in an act of union with the Resurrected One.)

Similarly, Buddha attained several centuries before Christ the goal of *Jupiter* evolution, namely the purification of the astral body. Therefore Buddha no longer needed to incarnate upon the Earth. But this does not mean that Buddha then ceased his spiritual activity. Working from higher spiritual realms, Buddha continued (and continues) to help mankind towards the attainment of the goal of *Jupiter* evolution. (The purification of the astral body is described in *Hermetic Astrology* I, Chapter 10, as the restoration of the likeness to its divine origin, the hermetic man.) The eightfold path inaugurated by Buddha, referred to in *Hermetic Astrology* I, Chapters 7 and 9, is as effective as ever in the work of purifying the astral body, and is a potent means of accomplishing this spiritual work.

Outlined in general terms, in Rudolf Steiner's cosmology the mission of the first four stages of evolution – *Saturn, Sun, Moon,* and *Earth* – has been the establishment of man as a being incarnated on the Earth: incarnated in physical, etheric and astral bodies.[8] The goal of the next three stages of human evolution – to be attained during the *Jupiter, Venus* and *Vulcan* stages of evolution – is the transformation by the human being of his three vehicles: astral, etheric and physical bodies.

Since the orbits of the planets Uranus, Neptune and Pluto lie beyond the sphere of human evolution, which extends by way of contraction from the orbit of Saturn to the sphere of the Sun, these outermost planets are not present in the structure of the human being's psycho-spiritual organism. Also, they lie beyond the spheres of destiny within which human destiny becomes inscribed, and thus – unlike the other planets – Uranus, Neptune and Pluto do not "rule" any of the planetary periods of the spiral of life. Therefore the question can be raised as to whether Uranus, Neptune and Pluto have anything – in a karmic-astrological sense – to do with the human being? As they lie beyond the seven stages of evolution described in Rudolf Steiner's cosmology, perhaps they are not at all significant in an astrological sense?

The astrological validity of Uranus, Neptune and Pluto

As will be outlined below, research in the domain of hermetic astrology shows that the positions of the planets Uranus, Neptune and Pluto, when compared from one incarnation to the next, *are* astrologically significant. Again, as with the other planets, the soul, when incarnating, seeks to be born when these planets align in the sidereal zodiac with their positions in earlier incarnations, or when they align with the zodiacal positions of other planets at birth or death in earlier incarnations. For example, according to Rudolf Steiner's karma reserch, Mu'awiya (ruled 661 to 680), the fifth caliph after Mohammed, reincarnated as Woodrow Wilson, who was president of the United States from 1912 to 1920.[9] (See *Hermetic Astrology* I, Appendix IV, for brief biographies of Mu'awiya and Woodrow Wilson.) The Moon at President Wilson's birth aligned with Neptune's position in the sidereal zodiac at Mu'awiya's death. (Another example of this is the alignment of the Moon at Friedrich Nietzsche's birth on the opposite side of the zodiac to Neptune at St. Peter of Alcantara's death – see *Hermetic Astrology* I, Table 20.) Further, Uranus at the birth of Woodrow Wilson aligned with its position in the sidereal zodiac at the death of Mu'awiya, as indicated in Table 20.

From Table 20 it can be seen that the sidereal alignments (*Moon with †Neptune, and *Uranus with †Uranus) are more or less exact, and that there is no alignment with respect to the tropical zodiac, i.e. as shown in *Hermetic Astrology* I, Appendix IV, it is the sidereal zodiac which is the astrologically valid zodiac for the incarnating soul. Thus it is evident that both Neptune and Uranus at the death of Mu'awiya were astrologically significant, as their sidereal positions were taken up again at birth in a later incarnation by the Moon and Uranus, respectively.

Another example of an exact alignment in the sidereal zodiac of Uranus at birth with its position at the preceding death is that of Novalis, where Uranus at his birth aligned with its position in the sidereal zodiac at death in the previous incarnation as Raphael. (See *Hermetic Astrology* I, Appendix VII, for the computations of the planetary positions at the death of Raphael and at the birth of Novalis.) Here again the astrological signifi-

Table 20:
Mu'awiya/Woodrow Wilson chart comparison

Geocentrical zodiacal positions are listed, where both the tropical and sidereal positions are given for the sake of comparison. For the computations, see *Hermetic Astrology I*, Appendix VII. Abbreviations: * = birth; † = death.

	planet	tropical	sidereal	vernal point
*Woodrow Wilson	Moon	0°13' Aquarius	7°28' Capricorn	7°15' Pisces
†Mu'awiya	g-Neptune	13°35' Capricorn	7°11' Capricorn	23°36' Pisces
*Woodrow Wilson	g-Uranus	21°27' Taurus	28°42' Aries	7°15' Pisces
†Mu'awiya	g-Uranus	5°31' Taurus	29°07' Aries	23°36' Pisces

Note: As the time of Woodrow Wilson's birth is known, the zodiacal position of the Moon at his birth is accurate. However, several alternative dates have been put forward for Mu'awiya's death, all early in the year A.D. 680. In the computation of the positions of Uranus and Neptune at Mu'awiya's death, the usual date of death has been taken (April 4, 680). Owing to the slow rate of motion of both Uranus and Neptune, their zodiacal longitudes change only very slowly. Thus their longitudes on April 4, 680 also serve fairly accurately for the alternative dates of Mu'awiya's death in the early part of the year 680.

cance of the planet Uranus is confirmed, in the sense that the incarnating soul of Novalis followed the movement of Uranus through the sidereal zodiac to incarnate at a time when Uranus was aligned with its zodiacal position at death in the previous incarnation. (There is also an alignment of Uranus at birth with its sidereal position at death in the preceding incarnation in the reincarnation example given in *Hermetic Astrology* I, Table 19.)

Another example, but this time with respect to Pluto rather than Uranus, is apparent in the case of the incarnation of Wallenstein. Wallenstein, as "chief over all imperial troops in the Holy Roman Empire",[10] was the central figure in the Thirty Years War (1618–1648). A brilliant military strategist, who also utilized astrology in his military undertakings, Wallenstein twice consulted the astronomer Kepler – in 1608 and in 1624 – regarding his horoscope. Wallenstein's horoscope as calculated by Kepler – but converted to the sidereal zodiac, and based on modern computations – is shown in Chart 19.

When Kepler cast the horoscope, he reminded Wallenstein that the stars "are but the father of a man's fate, whereof the mother is his own soul".[11] In other words, Kepler sought to make it clear to Wallenstein that astrology can only depict one side of human destiny. In terms of modern hermetic astrology, the other side of human destiny is indicated by reincarnation. The human being is constituted as he is on account of what has taken place in the previous incarnations that he has lived through upon the Earth. Reincarnation shapes the soul – this is the "mother aspect" according to Kepler (interpreted in the light of modern hermetic astrology). On the other hand, destiny is carried over by the stars – in that the planetary positions taken up at a person's birth bear a relationship with those at birth/death in the previous incarnation; this is the "father aspect" according to Kepler (again interpreted in the light of the basic research finding of hermetic astrology).

Wallenstein "acknowledged the existence of some great, unknown and all-ruling Power that watched over him; believed himself reserved for extraordinary achievements; and... made it the study of his life to penetrate the future and to discover the high destiny that awaited him."[12] Thus Wallenstein had a fundamentally astrological outlook on life, and began at an early age to make a serious study of astrology. But without a knowledge of reincarnation and karma, astrology can give only an incomplete picture of the working of human destiny. However much insight into Wallenstein's character and destiny may be gained from his horoscope, the horoscope alone can never explain why he rose to such heights of power, why it was that his name exerted such a magical appeal, where men streamed to his service in such numbers that he was able to build up an army of between 50,000 and 100,000 men. Wallenstein's ascent from humble origins to the heights of European power can be understood, however, against the background of his previous incarnation.

In hermetic astrology, therefore, karma research – spiritual research through the development of higher states of consciousness – is essential. Through karma research – whereby former incarnations may become disclosed to spiritual investigation – the missing element is provided to enable a more complete understanding as to how destiny works. To use Kepler's expression once again, astrology – as it has developed hitherto – is concerned with the stars, which are "the father of man's fate", but "the mother is his own soul", i.e. the mother of the human being's fate is his own soul as it has been formed through previous incarnations upon the Earth. It is this latter aspect that is the subject of concern in karma research, which belongs intrinsically to modern hermetic astrology. The introduction of the hermetic chart in hermetic astrology – as an aid to karma research – therefore forms an indispensable adjunct to the traditional geocentric chart.

Through karma research it was possible to identify Wallenstein's previous incarnation as the Carolingian Emperor Louis the Pious. Louis (778–840) was the third son of Charlemagne, and at Charlemagne's death in 814 Louis succeeded him as Holy Roman Emperor. Louis is remembered for his pious nature, which also manifested strongly in the next incarnation as Wallenstein. And if Wallenstein is remembered not just as a

VIII. Uranus, Neptune and Pluto

Chart 19:
***Wallenstein**
Wallenstein *4.36 p.m. on September 24, 1583 at Hermanitz

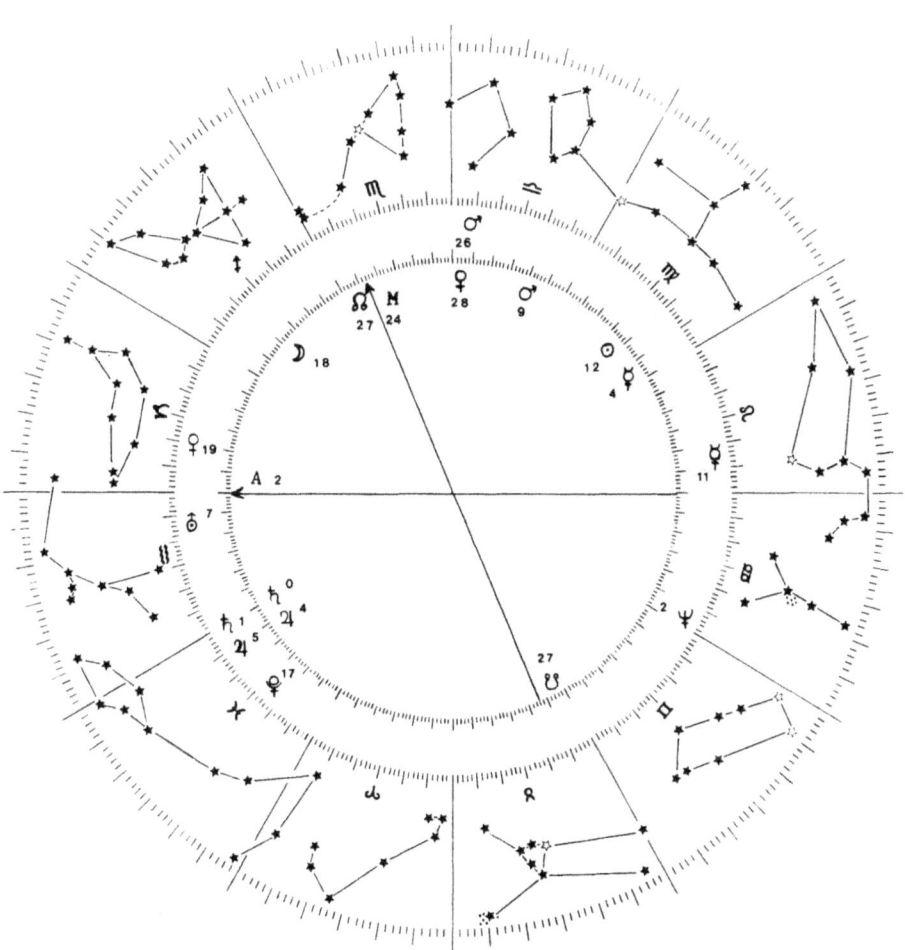

Chart 20
†Louis the Pious
Louis the Pious †10 a.m. (approx. time) on June 20, 840 at Ingelheim

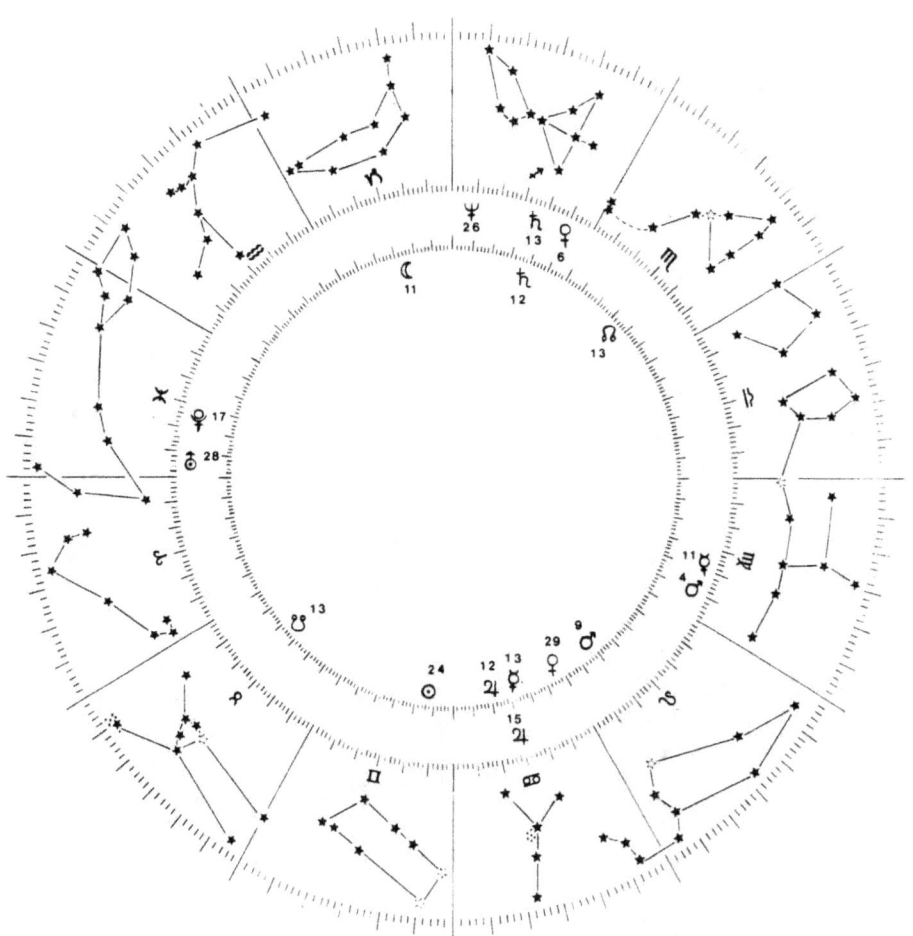

VIII. Uranus, Neptune and Pluto

soldier, but as "a statesman, with a finger constantly on the pulse of European politics",[13] it is out of his former incarnation as Holy Roman Emperor that this can be understood. There lived in Wallenstein's soul the experience of his former incarnation as an emperor, and this guided him unerringly in his sense of statemanship within European political life.

Chart 20 shows the planetary configuration (geocentric and hermetic) at the death of Louis the Pious on June 20, 840. The angular relationship between the Sun and Saturn amounts to 168°. At Wallenstein's birth on September 24, 1583 the angle between the Sun and Saturn was 169°, i.e. it was the same as that at death in the previous incarnation. Here the first "law" of reincarnation is fulfilled, since the angular relationship between the Sun and Saturn is the same at birth as it was at death in the previous incarnation. Planetary alignments between the two charts are given in Table 21.

Table 21:
Louis the Pious/Wallenstein chart comparison

As only the year (and not the date) of the birth of Louis the Pious is known, the chart comparison Louis the Pious/Wallenstein is restricted to that between the death of Louis the Pious and the birth of Wallenstein.

See Appendix II for the computation of the planetary positions – geocentric and heliocentric – listed in the following table.

Abbreviations: h = heliocentric sidereal longitude (hermetic chart)
g = geocentric sidereal longitude (geocentric chart)
* = birth
† = death

Louis the Pious (†)		Wallenstein (*)	
g-Venus	29° Cancer	Ascendant	28° Capricorn
h-Mercury	11° Virgo	Sun	12° Virgo
g-Mars	9° Leo	h-Mercury	9° Leo
h-Mars	4° Virgo	g-Mercury	4° Virgo
		g-Jupiter	4° Pisces
g-Pluto	18° Pisces	g-Pluto	17° Pisces

Most striking in Table 21 is the line-up of Pluto at Wallenstein's birth (17° Pisces) with its position at the death of Louis the Pious (18° Pisces), showing that the planet Pluto is also of astrological significance with respect to the soul's choice of planetary configuration upon entering into incarnation.

The sub-earthly forces

From the foregoing reincarnation examples, assuming that the alignments involving the planets Uranus, Neptune and Pluto are not due to pure chance, it seems that these planets have an objective significance for the incarnating soul, just as the traditional astrological planets do. But whereas the Sun, Moon and five planets (Saturn, Jupiter, Mars, Venus, Mercury) act within the human being, incorporated into his astral body (via the lotus flowers) and acting down into his etheric body (via the corresponding organs: heart, brain, spleen, etc.), Uranus, Neptune and Pluto work from beyond – at a level transcending normal human evolution. (How the Sun, Moon and five planets work in the astral body via the lotus flowers and in the etheric body via certain organs is summarized in Table 7, in relation to the 7-year periods of the spiral of life.)

Uranus, Neptune and Pluto call the human being towards cosmic intelligence (Uranus), cosmic harmony (Neptune) and cosmic life (Pluto), but at the same time they represent forces of hindrance to be overcome by the human being. For, during the course of evolution remnants of cosmic light (Uranus), cosmic sound (Neptune) and cosmic life (Pluto) have become "trapped" as negative forces within the interior of the Earth. These negative forces now – in the apocalyptic age ushered in through modern science – are becoming released in tremendous quantities into human civilization. The releasing of these trapped forces through technology has brought with it immense possibilities for the harnessing of power, which can be utilized for the purpose of technological progress. At the same time, however, grave dangers are presented to the future of mankind and to the planet Earth through the release of these sub-earthly forces.

The discoveries of the planets Uranus, Neptune and Pluto are linked in a remarkable way with the discoveries of the forces connected with them. For, on March 13, 1781 Uranus was discovered by the astronomer William Herschel. Shortly before, late in 1780, Galvani had begun his experiments with frogs' legs, which led to the discovery of electricity. Electricity is essentially *trapped light,* and the release of electricity has brought the negative Uranus forces into the world. It is as if the discovery of the planet Uranus signified that the time had arrived for the trapped light connected with this planet to be found also.

In the case of Neptune, this planet was discovered in 1846 through the calculations of Urbain Leverrier, which led the astronomer Johann Gottfried Galle of the Royal Observatory in Berlin to locate the planet Neptune on September 24, 1846. (In 1841, four years before Leverrier published his calculations giving the position of the unknown planet, an undergraduate at Cambridge University, John Couch Adams, had already embarked upon calculating Neptune's position, but his results were not taken seriously by astronomers.) Already in 1831 Michael Faraday had discovered electromagnetic induction, which was then given a quantitative formulation by James Clerk Maxwell in 1861. And in the very year that Neptune was discovered, Faraday formulated (in his *Thoughts on Ray Vibrations*) the electromagnetic theory of light, later developed further by Maxwell. In due course the principle of electromagnetism became applied, leading to the development of radio and television. Faraday concluded (in 1845) that magnetism must be present in all matter. Magnetism is essentially *trapped sound,* and the release of this force, connected with the planet Neptune, has been utilized, in connection with electricity, in the development of technology during the last 100 years or so.

Lastly, Pluto: this planet was discovered by the astronomer Clyde W. Tombaugh of the Lowell Observatory, Arizona, on March 12, 1930. Early in 1932 – on April 13 – came the event of the artificial splitting of the lithium nucleus by neutron bombardment, carried out by John Cockcroft and E.T.S. Walton at the Cavendish Laboratory, Cambridge, England. This was the crucial step leading to the development of atomic power, and since then atomic power has become increasingly harnessed, as well as being utilized for war purposes in the construction of nuclear weapons. Atomic power is essentially *trapped life,* which becomes released through the chain reaction. The release of this sub-earthly force, connected with the planet Pluto, has signified a new era for mankind – where the possibility of global destruction has become a very real one.

Just as the classical planets (including Sun and Moon) are connected with cosmic forces which have densified in the Earth to become metals: lead corresponding to Saturn, tin to Jupiter, iron to Mars, copper to Venus, quicksilver to Mercury, gold to the Sun and silver to the Moon,[14] so the transcendental planets Uranus, Neptune and Pluto are connected with forces – cosmic light, cosmic sound and cosmic life – which have "densified" to become trapped within the interior of the Earth, as electricity, magnetism and atomic power. And from a study of the working of these sub-earthly forces, an idea can be gained – by way of analogy – as to how Uranus, Neptune and Pluto act within the human being.

The working of Uranus can be compared with the functioning of electricity, which flows between two poles. This can be utilized, by way of setting up a resistance in the connecting wire, to produce light. Analogously, illumination occurs in the human being when the "current of thought" becomes raised to a high degree of intensity such that a "discharge", i.e. a flash of illumination, occurs. In this way, for example, numerous scientific discoveries and inventions have been made. Uranus is thus connected on the highest level with the faculty of Illumination, but there are lower levels of spiritual seeing or clairvoyance, and the entire range may be related to Uranus.

The way in which Neptune acts within the human being is manifested externally in the phenomenon of magnetism, which is a matter of attraction or repulsion – or, on the level of the soul, sympathy and antipathy. Through sympathy the human being is able to enter into spiritual communication with non-incarnated beings, and through inwardly distancing himself from them he is able to close off communication again. Inspiration, or spiritual communication, is thereby enabled through sympathy/antipathy on a soul-spiritual level. This spiritual hearing can take place on a very high level – that of Inspiration – with beings far above man, or on a low level, in which case it becomes mediumism.

The phenomenon of atomic power, which can burst forth like a volcanic eruption, gives an external picture of the way in which Pluto works within the human being. Here the primal life-will is at work: cosmic love within the human being can become released, drawing him into union – oneness – with higher beings. On a lower level it can manifest as erotic sexuality, and even as violence (uncontrolled will impulses). The obsession with sex and violence in modern civilization is a negative aspect on the cultural level of the release of Pluto forces in our time, just as the atomic age is a manifestation of these forces on the technological level. On its highest level the planet Pluto can lead to Union – the spiritual focusing of cosmic love, thereby entering into a relationship of union with higher beings.

In the working of Uranus, Neptune and Pluto the human being is confronted with the task of channelling cosmic forces in the right way. When successfully accomplished, this leads to the development of higher (transcendental) spiritual faculties: Illumination, Inspiration, Union. (Illumination corresponds to lunar consciousness, Inspiration to solar consciousness, and Union to zodiacal consciousness, the three higher levels of consciousness beyond normal Earth consciousness – see *Hermetic Astrology* I, Chapter 4.)

The development of Illumination, Inspiration and Union depends essentially upon the unfolding of moral forces inherent in cosmic light, cosmic sound and cosmic life. But the release of these same forces which have been "densified" (condensed) within the interior of the Earth – electricity (condensed light), magnetism (condensed sound) and atomic power (condensed life) – when not accompanied by moral development, are capable of leading to destruction. The very fact of the worldwide release of these sub-earthly forces in modern times on the one hand points to the commencement of an apocalyptic era (the unleashment of powerful forces of destruction), and on the other hand signifies a call to the whole of mankind to take up the path of spiritual development. The development of new moral qualities – in freedom, by a number of people – is the sole hope for the future of the Earth. The right handling of the sub-earthly forces of electricity, magnetism and atomic power calls for a new morality, which takes account of the whole of mankind (the *brotherhood of man*). Only through the development of a spiritual morality – in the sense of the new commandment brought by Christ* – can the danger of a global catastrophe be avoided.

The Antichrist

The greatest fight is yet to come. This is the fight against Antichrist, which has been described by the Russian author Vladimir Soloviev. In his prophetically inspired work *A short tale of the Antichrist*,[15] Soloviev depicts how the Eastern Orthodox Church and the Protestant Church unite together with the Roman Catholic Church in the struggle to combat the Antichrist, who establishes a world empire. According to Soloviev's account, the united forces of Christianity are able to overcome the tyranny of Antichrist, the world emperor. This would be a prophetic fulfilment of the words spoken by Christ: "The gates of hell shall not prevail against thee." In Soloviev's depiction the Churches which became separated – the Roman Catholic Church, the Eastern Orthodox Church and the Protestant Church – reunite, and the combined forces of Christianity, united in the founding will of Christ and the apostles, are able to withstand the might of Antichrist.

One of the names given to Antichrist in the Apocalypse – the *beast 666* – gives an indication as to when the coming of Antichrist is to be expected. Many have prophecied the end of the twentieth century as the time when Antichrist will manifest, and the arising of the "Nazi beast" during the first half of the twentieth century was a kind of foreshadowing of the coming of Antichrist at the end of the century. According to numerological considerations, 3 x 666 = 1998 may be considered as the year of the beast 666, i.e. two years prior to the end of the twentieth century, around which time – possibly – the manifestation of Antichrist may take place.

The negative forces of Uranus, Neptune and Pluto – arising from the interior of the Earth – are, basically, manifestations of the thought, feeling and will impulses of the Antichrist, who embodies the *false self* – just as Christ bestows the true self upon man. Just as Christ came 2000 years ago as the bearer of the true self of man – in the words of St. Paul: "Not I, but Christ in me" ("It is no longer I who live, but Christ who lives in me") –

---

*John xiii, 34–35: "A new commandment I give to you, that you love one another; even as I have loved you, that you also love one another. By this all men will know that you are my disciples, if you have love for one another."

Galatians ii, 20) – so Antichrist is coming now as the bearer of the false self. Christianity is therefore the prime target which Antichrist seeks to eradicate from the world.

Nothing less than the total eradication of Christianity from the world is the aim of Antichrist, in order to establish a world in which egotism alone is the motivating impulse of existence, for the nature of the false self is egotism. A world of banks, universities, factories and clubs, in which egotism holds sway – a world without churches, and where there is no devotion to Christ, no love of neighbour (except for selfish ends), no praise of God, no church bells to sound forth the worship of God, no charitable deeds, no prayer, and no religion.

The year 1984 – only 14 years (= two 7-year periods) short of 1998 – has already passed by, and in the light of the foregoing it is evident that the intentions of Antichrist have become realised to a certain extent, especially in the communist block. The world in 1984 as depicted by George Orwell – which could be interpreted as portraying a picture of the world as Antichrist intends it to become – is already partly realised in the reality of daily life within most communist countries. But Christianity is still a force to be reckoned with. And as long as it continues to exist, and provided it does not capitulate to the world empire of Antichrist, a source of spiritual power stemming directly from the founding will of Christ has a foothold in this world, whereby mankind has access to a source of spiritual power able to combat the thinking, feeling and will impulses of Antichrist.

These impulses of thought, feeling and will emanating from Antichrist, although also active in earlier historical epochs, are now making their entrance into the world ever more strongly – parallel to the release of the forces of electricity, magnetism and atomic power. This is what is meant by the "opening of the gates of hell". Hitler came as a forerunner of Antichrist, through whom these forces of thought, feeling and will (the negative side of Uranus, Neptune and Pluto) were able to act. The discovery of Pluto in 1930 was the macrocosmic signal that the will of Antichrist would begin to manifest openly in the world – on the one hand externally through the manifestation of atomic power, and on the other hand as the internal driving force active through the "Nazi beast". Here the gates of hell were opened and the will (together with the thought and feeling) of Antichrist emanated forth via the Nazi menace. The Age of the Apocalypse began – this being the shadow side of the Age of the Second Coming, the New Age.

The thought-life of Antichrist is electrical in nature. It can be discerned in Hitler's thinking: electrifying, polemical, discharging "lightning bolts" to distort truth. This is the counterpole to Illumination (the higher aspect of Uranus), where – in perfect clarity of light-illumined thought – truth presents itself in the form of clearly-formed pictorial mental images ("imaginations") to the inner eye. In Illumination human thinking gains access to Cosmic Intelligence, the primal sphere of Ouranos (Uranus), representing the eternal Divine Mind.

The feeling-life of Antichrist is magnetic in nature: a wall of hatred (antipathy) for all that is good, noble, charitable, loving and kind, and a sucking absorption (sympathy) for all that is egotistical in human nature. The magnetic attraction (sympathy) of Antichrist is towards all that comes to expression in cruelty and the "survival of the fittest" – the triumph of the strong over the weak, and the trampling underfoot of the sick, needy and helpless. Hitler's hatred of Jews and gypsies, and his love of the "blond beast" (the Aryan "superman") reflected this aspect of the feeling-life of Antichrist. This is the negative side of Neptune. The positive side comes to expression in the faculty of Inspiration, where the Cosmic Soul is able to inspire the human soul. In its highest form this is the experience of the *harmony of the spheres,* where the human being's personal feeling life makes way to receive and become filled with the primal Cosmic Harmony of the sphere of Night (Neptune), representing the Eternal Mother.

Lastly, the will life of Antichrist comes to expression in the diffusion of "atomic power" in the will – not the actual force of atomic power, but that which inwardly corresponds to atomic power in the human being. This is the *will to power,* which was evident in an unprecedented form in Hitler, in whom its highly destructive nature was also manifest. Here the will to power can go so far that even if it results in wholesale destruction it will seek to have its way. The present madness in the escalating nuclear arms race is also a manifestation of this tendency. Everyone knows that it is wrong to allow the unbridled spread of nuclear weapons, threatening global catastrophe, but few of those in power are able to resist the will to power of the negative Pluto impulse. Consequently, it is difficult for the leaders of those nations that have developed atomic weapons to resist the temptation to go on stockpiling more and more. This is an outer expression of the will of the Antichrist, the negative side of Pluto. The positive side lies in the development of the faculty of Union, where the human being becomes united in spiritual union with the primal Love of the sphere of Phanes (Pluto), representing the Heavenly Father.

The penetration of Antichrist's thinking, feeling and will into the human being – in preparation for the manifestation of Antichrist himself – signifies the electrification of thinking, the magnetization of feeling, and the atomizing of the will. This leads the human being on the opposite path to that of the uplifting of thinking, feeling and will through the Christ Impulse. The transformation of thought, feeling and will through the Christ Impulse leads to their reintegration with cosmic thinking, cosmic feeling and cosmic will. This gives rise to Illumination, Inspiration and Union, whereby thinking becomes the vehicle of cosmic light, feeling the vehicle of cosmic harmony, and will the vehicle of cosmic love.

Thus Uranus, Neptune and Pluto represent at one and the same time both the challenge towards the development of transcendental spiritual faculties, and the confrontation with evil. It is precisely through overcoming the negative impulses in thinking, feeling and will that higher faculties are developed. And when the human being seeks out a birth configuration in which one or more of the three transcendental planets are prominently featured, this often signifies that he has chosen a conflict with a particular element of evil in order to transform this into a higher faculty.

An example of Illumination

For example, the Swedish scientist Emmanuel Swedenborg (1688–1772) was born with the Moon in conjunction with the planet Uranus (see Chart 21). Swedenborg, who was the reincarnation of a significant historical personality (see *Hermetic Astrology* I, Appendix III), grappled for most of his life with the task of uplifting thought to become a vehicle of divine truth. As a young man "he was an enthusiastic scientist and technologist, and published a number of articles in various fields."[16] At the age of 22 Swedenborg went to England and stayed there for three years.

> *During this time he was captivated by what he learned of science. He read Newton. He met Flamsteed, Halley, and John Woodward. He considered the universe to be a problem in mathematics and, filled with youthful self-confidence, he tried to realize grandiose technical inventions, among them flying machines and submarines.*[17]

Through his scientific pursuits he believed that he would arrive at the ultimate truths of existence. He became increasingly concerned with the body-soul problem, and began to make the soul his field of scientific inquiry. During the latter half of the eighth 7-year period (the Jupiter period, 49–56),

> *he wrestled with the greatest problem in metaphysics. Wishing to find words for the ineffable, he experimented with a logical-mathematical universal language... This theory taught that existence was made up of three reciprocal levels – the natural, the psychic, and the divine... The final vision came upon him in the spring of 1745: God revealed himself to Swedenborg and ordered him to interpret the meaning of the Bible; on the same night the world of spirits, Heaven and Hell, were opened to him. At the age of 57 Swedenborg abandoned his scientific investigations. For the rest of his life he was purely a visionary and prophet. In a...gigantic commentary on the books of Moses,* Arcana coelestia *(8 vols; London, 1749–1756), he developed his theory of the spiritual world, which was to be the beginning of a new universal religion, represented on Earth by the Swedenborgian New*

VIII. Uranus, Neptune and Pluto

Chart 21:
*Emmanuel Swedenborg
Swedenborg *5.15 a.m. on January 29, 1688 at Uppsala

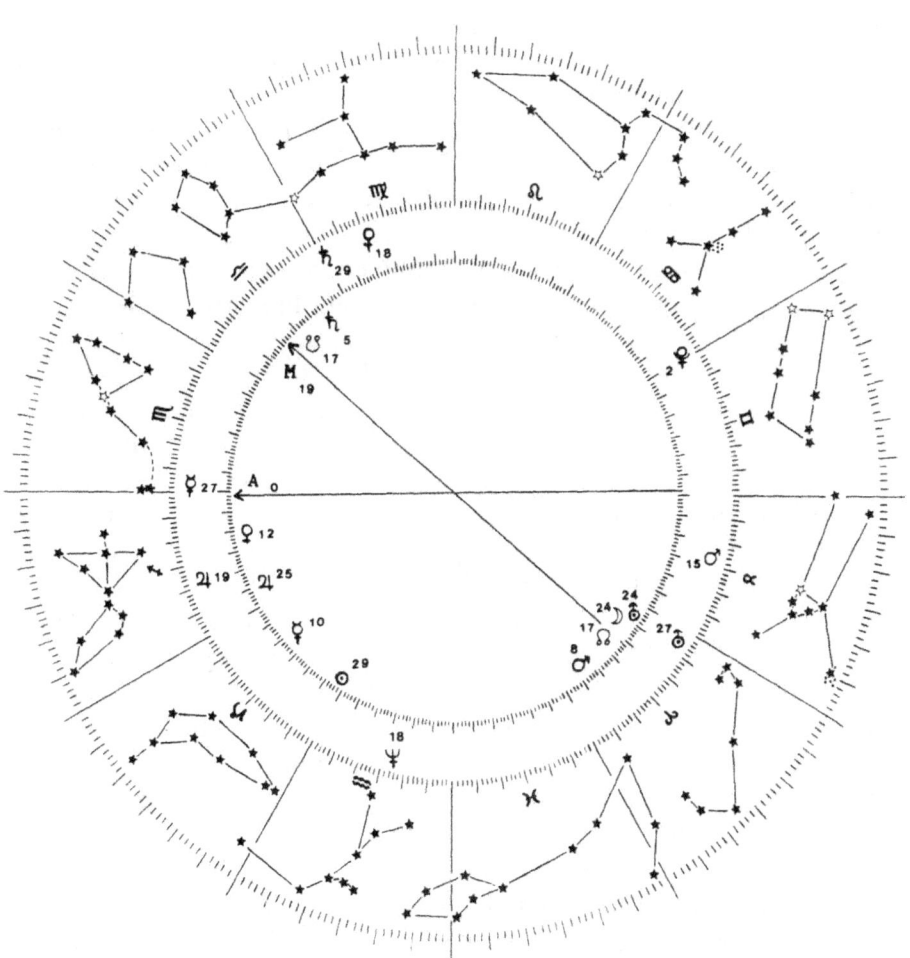

> Church. But despite its bizarre aspects, Swedenborg's theology is by no means a chaos of whims and visions. It is characterized by rigorous logic and obviously is rooted in his previous concern with the physical sciences.[18]

Thus Swedenborg, through his scientific training, had prepared himself for Illumination, which came to him at the age of 57. From this time on he applied himself – by way of the faculty of Illumination (corresponding to Uranus) – to the discovery of spiritual truths, which he then presented in numerous volumes, among them the 8-volume *Arcana coelestia*, which have proved to be a source of spiritual sustenance for many.

Nevertheless, in order to arrive at Illumination, a subtle temptation has to be met with. Instead of thinking becoming a vehicle for divine truth, it can become "brilliant" and then "electrified". And there is a world of difference between an illumined person and a brilliant thinker. The brilliant thinker is able to combine thoughts to his own pleasing, to make everything conform to the way in which he wants to see things, whilst an illumined person is interested solely in divine truth, for which he sacrifices his personal viewpoints. The brilliant thinker is in danger that his thinking becomes "electrified", whilst the illumined person has overcome this "earthly charged" thinking, so that his thought life is membered into the Cosmic Intelligence, which is beyond all electrical, polemical thinking.

The scientist is able to discipline his thinking to become more objective, and thereby to overcome the brilliance of thought as a source of self-assertion, but only when his thinking has become immersed in cosmic light, illumined by the Cosmic Intelligence, is it uplifted beyond the sphere of temptation. The path from "scientist" to "seer" is the step that Swedenborg made, and in so doing the Uranus element chosen by him at birth (the conjunction with the Moon) became fulfilled through his Illumination. His creative will (focused via the 4-petalled lotus, corresponding to the Moon) became lifted up towards the cosmic light and he received the gift of Illumination (corresponding to Uranus). Without spiritual-moral discipline, this astrological aspect chosen by Swedenborg at his birth (Moon conjunct Uranus) could signify the channelling of creative will into brilliance and fantasy, which can be cultivated in an unhealthy way, even leading to a bizarre and fantastic thought life.

An example of this latter tendency is evident in the development of film, television and video technology. The higher faculty of Illumination (corresponding to Uranus) is developed spiritually by transforming the thinking capacities into seership, as Swedenborg did. Cinema, television and video technology simulate "seership" mechanically, externally to the human being, and rob him of the inner impulse to "see" for himself, with his mind's eye. The effort to see with the mind's eye gives the impetus necessary for the initial development of Illumination. But with the spread of television and cinema the striving towards inner seeing is more and more becoming replaced by a passive beholding of technologically created pictures produced externally. Often a tremendous amount of creative will and fantasy go into producing that which is shown on television and at the cinema. On the whole, however, it represents a degeneration and corruption of the human being's spiritual potential for seership. The products of film and television are thus representative of the negative side of Illumination, the faculty which is associated macrocosmically with the planet Uranus.

An example of Inspiration

As a second example, this time related to the planet Neptune, let us consider the birth horoscope of the German astronomer Kepler (see Chart 22).

As in the example of John Addey (discussed in Chapter 6) – who was in his previous incarnation Michael Maestlin, the teacher of Kepler – Kepler was born with Neptune rising, i.e. Neptune in conjunction with the Ascendant. As the Ascendant signifies the orientation of the human being in the zodiacal sphere of fixed stars, the appearance of a planet at the moment of birth on the Ascendant means that this planet makes its presence strongly felt within the individual's horizon of consciousness. Like Swedenborg, Kepler devoted himself to the pursuit of science: mathematics, astronomy, optics and even astrology. But his motivation was, from the outset of his scientific career, the search for the "harmonies of the world".[19]

Kepler pursued a kind of "astral mysticism",[20] and sought the relationships, the cosmic harmonies, between the human soul and the World Soul. This is an expression of the transcendental impulse of Neptune, which was active in his horizon of consciousness. His world outlook was permeated with the call of the all-pervasive cosmic harmony, associated with Neptune (laid down during the second manvantara, that of the goddess Night, according to the cosmology of Orpheus). Kepler's inner life was raised up to become blessed with the Inspiration (corresponding to Neptune) of the World Soul, which led him to discover deep truths about the harmonies of the universe. His inner striving was orientated towards Inspiration – the harmonies of the spheres – as comes to expression again and again throughout his book *Harmonice Mundi*: "Now, Urania, a more majestic sound is needed, while through the harmonic ladder of celestial movements I ascend yet higher, where the true Archetype of the world's structure lies hidden."[21]

Just as the development of thinking depends on overcoming the temptation of the brilliance of "electrified thinking" in order to arrive at Illumination, so does the uplifting of feeling depend on the overcoming of a particular temptation to arrive at Inspiration. This temptation, leading to *magnetized feeling*, occurs when the human being allows his feelings to dictate his life, in the sense of his becoming a slave of sympathy and antipathy. In its extreme form this leads to hedonism – a life orientated towards the pursuit of pleasure – and the modern practices of drug-taking, drinking alcohol, etc., reflect this.

Chart 22:
*Johannes Kepler
Kepler *2.30 p.m. on December 27, 1571 at Weil der Stadt

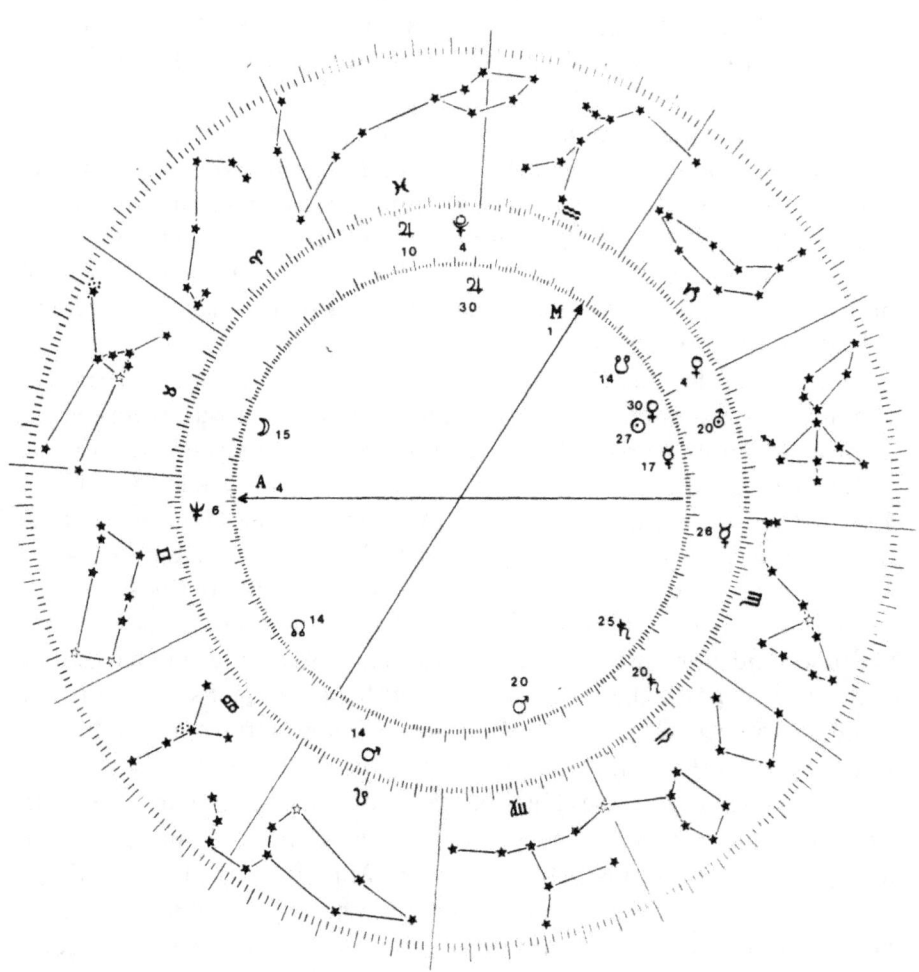

A drug is taken in order to induce a feeling of well-being, which, when it wears off, leads to a negative feeling, that in turn must be made positive by taking the drug again. Here the feeling life becomes magnetized through the taking of drugs: positive, negative, positive, negative... In milder forms the magnetization of the feeling life occurs through numerous channels within modern civilization, e.g. in the phenomenon of pop music. Here the sub-earthly counterpart of the harmonies of the spheres bombards the soul life as a kind of opiate of the senses. True music is composed as a striving to render something of the harmonies of the spheres audible to earthly ears, and some composers of classical music, e.g. Bach and Mozart, were truly blessed with divine Inspiration (corresponding to the higher aspect of Neptune). The "densified sound" of the sub-earthly spheres (the negative aspect of Neptune) is a caricature of the harmonies of the spheres – it is a cacophony sounding forth from the depths of the underworld, as the counterpart to the heavenly music resounding in spiritual realms. Via the spread of pop music* this cacophany is penetrating more and more into the modern world, signifying the progressive magnetization of the feeling life. The growth of pop music parallels the spread of film and television. Just as the latter has a negative influence on the development of Illumination, so the former works to hinder the development of the spiritual faculty of Inspiration. The visual phenomena presented by television and cinema represent a temptation directed towards human thought life which can paralyse and hinder the development of Illumination. Similarly, the auditory phenomenon of pop music embodies a temptation aimed at the feeling life. Instead of the feeling life becoming transformed from within, to become raised up to the harmonies of the cosmic spheres, pop music works externally as a caricature (or negative mirror) of the celestial harmonies. This brings the negative side of Neptune to expression, in contrast to the positive side (Inspiration) evident, for example, in Kepler's life work.

In Kepler's time, of course, the temptation of the feeling life came to expression in different forms than those of the twentieth century. In general, this temptation can be characterized as taking place whenever the human being foresakes the guidance of reason and conscience and allows his instinctual urges to dictate his life. He then becomes a slave of his sympathies and antipathies. On the other hand, the overcoming of this temptation, accompanied by the elevation of the feeling life, leads to Inspiration (the higher aspect of Neptune).

---

*Pop music is not this cacophany itself, but reflects it. Not all pop music is necessarily a reflection of the cacophany of the sub-earthly spheres, but among pop musicians there is generally a lack of consciousness of the divine source of music, whereas classical composers, generally speaking, composed their music to the "glory of God".

An example of the negative working of Pluto

A third example, relating this time to the planet Pluto, is presented by the birth horoscope of the Roman emperor Nero (A.D. 37 to 68, emperor from 54 to 68). In this example the negative aspect of Pluto prevailed, i.e. Nero fell prey to the temptation connected with the negative aspect of Pluto. At Nero's birth the Sun was in conjunction with Pluto (see Chart 23). As the Sun's zodiacal position is chosen by the incarnating human being as a source of cosmic forces supporting and strengthening the self, a conjunction of the Sun with Pluto can signify that the human being seeks to connect himself with the primal cosmic will impulse, laid down during the first manvantara (that of Phanes, according to the cosmology of Orpheus).

A conjunction between the Sun and Pluto may therefore signify very powerful will impulses, which, if channelled in the right way, could lead to the development of the faculty of Union, where the human will becomes lifted up through love to unite with the Divine. But for this to take place, the temptation of the will has to be overcome, just as the temptation of thinking has to be overcome to attain Illumination, and the temptation of feeling to arrive at Inspiration. The temptation of the will is summarized in the words: *will to power.* Falling prey to this temptation can lead to the atomizing of the will, i.e. to the diffusion of destructive impulses in the will, which can erupt forth explosively. (The explosion of an atom bomb is an external analogy to this.)

In Nero's case, instead of overcoming the will to power, he fell prey to it and became a tyrant. The atomizing of the will set in, and destructive impulses soon gained the upper hand in Nero's being, coming to expression above all in two events: the murder of his mother, and the burning of the city of Rome. Murder and destruction are signs of an atomized will. The human being becomes swept along by the tide of the will to power, and ruthlessly disposes of any opposition, e.g. by way of murder, and then destroys – sometimes quite arbitrarily and sometimes as a demonstration of power – when the atomizing forces surge up overpoweringly. The example of Nero, and also of Hitler, present a warning concerning the terrible forces residing in the interior of the Earth which can gain entrance to the human will (negative aspect of Pluto). On the other hand, the very highest faculty – that of Union – is connected with Pluto, and is attained by the elevation of the will to the primal sphere of Phanes (representing the Divine Father), thereby to become a vehicle of divine love.

The three temptations

The discovery of the planets Uranus, Neptune and Pluto signifies the discovery of cosmic forces lying beyond man, and thereby denotes the task

VIII. Uranus, Neptune and Pluto

Chart 23:
*Nero
Nero *7.28 a.m. on December 15, 37 at Anzio

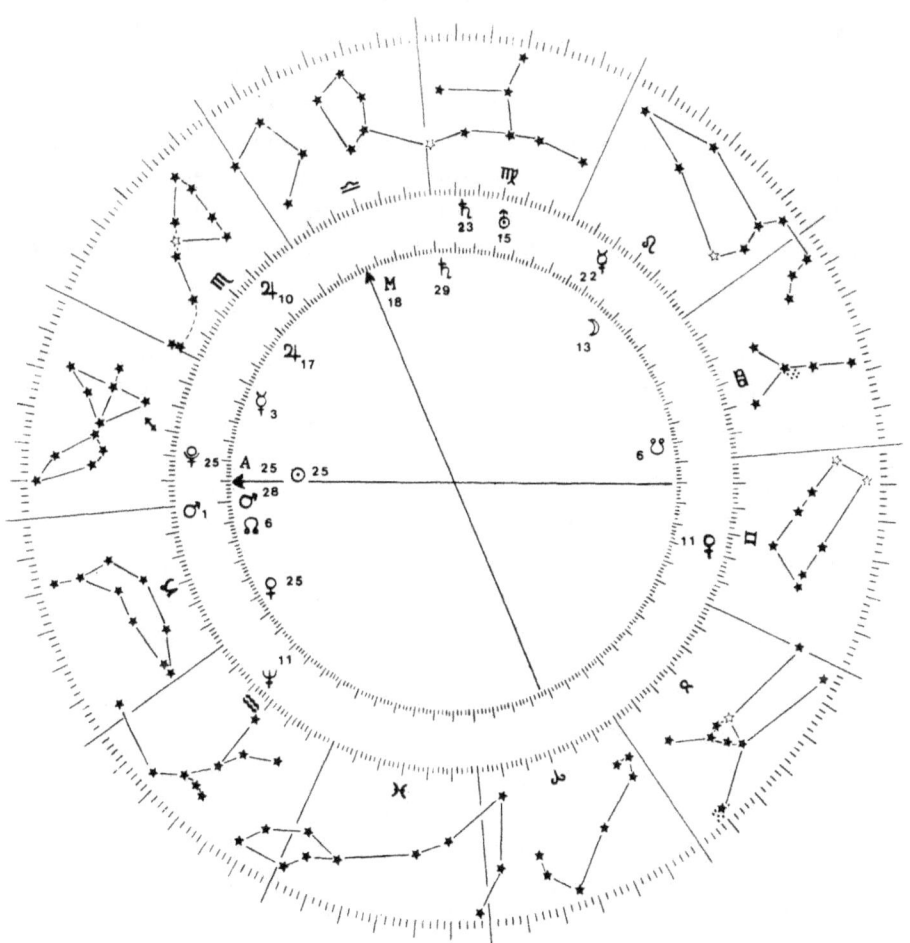

facing man: to bring these forces into consciousness, which formerly worked in subconscious depths. On the one hand, in their cosmic origin these forces of life, sound and light – laid down in the manvantaras of Phanes (Pluto), Night (Neptune) and Ouranos (Uranus) – transcend the human being, having been established in cosmic aeons prior to the origin of man. On the other hand, in so far as remnants of these forces have densified and become trapped in the interior of the Earth, they lie beneath man and work in a negative, dehumanising way into the human being. Through the transformation of thinking, feeling and the will, the higher aspect of these forces can be brought into human consciousness, in the sense that thinking becomes a vehicle for cosmic light (Illumination – Uranus), feeling becomes permeated with cosmic sound (Inspiration – Neptune), and the will becomes united with cosmic love (Union – Pluto). But this transformation entails the overcoming of the three temptations which present themselves to thinking, feeling and the will. When not overcome, the consequence of succumbing to these temptations is that the sub-earthly counterparts of cosmic light, sound and love are able to work from the interior of the Earth into the human being. The consequences are: the electrification of thinking, the magnetization of feeling and the atomizing of the will.

Some 2000 years ago Jesus Christ – as a forerunner, on behalf of the whole of mankind – confronted the three temptations in the wilderness and overcame them. Now, as the coming of Antichrist approaches, the three temptations – or, rather, modern forms of the three temptations – are to be confronted, in some form or other, by every human being. From the birth horoscope chosen by the incarnating human being, insight into the nature of the temptations confronting the person in question can generally be gained by looking at the zodiacal positions of Uranus, Neptune and Pluto in relation to other elements of the horoscope. At the same time, the confrontation with these temptations – when they are successfully overcome – may signify the development of the higher spiritual faculties of Illumination, Inspiration and Union. This way of looking at the birth horoscope in relation to Uranus, Neptune and Pluto is exemplified in the case of the three historical examples considered in'this chapter: Swedenborg (positive side of Uranus: Illumination), Kepler (positive side of Neptune: Inspiration), and Nero (negative side of Pluto: will to power).

Knowledge of the technique of the three temptations is already a help towards successfully resisting them, and the temptations of Jesus Christ in the wilderness serve as an archetype of the three temptations – just as his overcoming of them serves as the archetype for meeting and resisting them. It is through uniting with Jesus Christ that the individual finds the power to overcome the three temptations, and to transform his thinking.

feeling and will into the spiritual faculties of Illumination, Inspiration and Union.

Over and against Jesus Christ, the Perfect Good, stands Antichrist, the embodiment of total evil, who is the source of the three temptations. Man in the twentieth century stands between the choice: Jesus Christ, or Antichrist. This choice is relevant to every human being, to the very core of his being. For it signifies the choice between the path leading to Illumination, Inspiration and Union – cosmic light, cosmic harmony, and cosmic love – on the one hand, and the path leading to electrified thinking, magnetized feeling, and atomized will, on the other hand.

The choice between Jesus Christ and Antichrist is the ultimate choice with which every human being in the twentieth century will be faced. This choice will present itself by way of the three temptations – in some form or other – to everyone. And the modern path of hermeticism offers a means of overcoming the three temptations and embarking on the path leading towards Illumination, Inspiration and Union.[22]

Uranus, Neptune and Pluto in the Tarot

The teaching of modern hermeticism concerning the three temptations is of central importance in hermetic astrology for an understanding of the forces of hindrance embodied in the negative working of the planets Uranus, Neptune and Pluto. This teaching is outlined in the book *Meditations on the Tarot*, where the author describes the practice of the three holy vows – poverty, chastity and obedience (understood in a modern, spiritual form) – as the means of overcoming the temptations directed at thinking, feeling and the will. Through the practice of poverty (on the level of thinking) the temptation presented by way of the negative working of Uranus, i.e. the temptation to develop the false illumination of electrified thinking, is guarded against.

Almost at the same time as the discovery of Uranus in 1781, there came the discovery of electricity by Galvani. In the following years there then took place on a widespread level the "electrification of thinking" which produced the false illumination that led to the French revolution. The doctrines which underlay the French revolution were the product of electrified thinking, whereby on a large scale human minds became closed off from Divine Illumination and became instead the victims of false illumination. This worked so powerfully that some of the most enlightened individuals of that time fell prey to this false illumination. The safeguard against this temptation is *poverty of thought*, for then – as spoken of in the first beatitude – the kingdom of heaven can open itself to the human being to bestow upon him the light of divine truth (Illumination):

> *Blessed are the poor in spirit, for theirs is the kingdom of heaven.*
> *(Matthew v, 3)*

Poverty of thought ("poor in spirit") means not building up a system, not erecting a "tower of Babel", which tries to seize hold of higher truth. The warning to all system builders, who succumb to this temptation directed at human thinking, is portrayed in the sixteenth arcanum of the Tarot "The Tower of Destruction". The destiny of those whose thinking becomes electrified is to become "blasted by a thunderbolt", which destroys the system built up. The sixteenth arcanum reveals the mystery of electricity, connected with the planet Uranus, and teaches the consequence of succumbing to the temptation which the negative side of this planet presents.

Just as poverty (on the level of thought) safeguards against the temptation presented by electrified thought, so chastity (on the level of feeling) protects the human being from succumbing to the temptation of magnetized feeling. Almost at the same time as the discovery of Neptune in 1846, Faraday came to the conclusion that magnetism must be present in all matter. In the wake of Neptune's discovery a wave of magnetized feeling swept Europe, leading to the revolution of the year 1848, which spread to all large European countries (with the exception of Britain and Russia). Moreover, in this very year Marx and Engels published the Communist Manifesto, which opens with the words:

> *A spectre is haunting Europe – the spectre of communism. All the powers of old Europe have entered into a holy alliance to exorcise this spectre: Pope and Czar, Metternich and Guizot, French radicals and German police-spies.*[23]

This spectre was that of magnetized feeling, the negative side of the working of the planet Neptune. It was the force of magnetized feeling which kindled hatred in the breast of millions, hatred directed against the "ruling classes". Here a definite polarization of the feeling life took place, which led to the revolution in Europe in 1848 and which later erupted with terrible power in Russia in the communist revolution of 1917.

A key to understanding the magnetization of the feeling life is presented in the twenty-second arcanum of the Tarot "The World", which depicts a woman holding a wand in her left hand and a philtre in the right. She is the personification of *maya*, the illusion presented by the appearance of the world, which bewitches the human being. The spell that she casts creates the outlook that "The World" is the real world, and that the spiritual world is an illusion. This underlies communist ideology, which teaches that all religion, spiritual philosophy, belief, etc., is merely an illusion, a "spiritual superstructure" superimposed upon the "real world". The personification of *maya* depicted on the Tarot card "The World" holds forth a philtre which, if the human being drinks from it, intoxicates him. It was this intoxicating fervour which gripped Mikhail Bakunin, who took part with Richard Wagner in the Dresden uprising of 1849 (see Chapter 3). Again it was the same intoxicating fervour which gripped

Vladimir Lenin, who led the Bolshevist revolution of 1917 to a triumphant success for communism. It is the illusion presented by "The World" which underlies communist ideology, and a considerable part of the world's population has become subject to the compelling power of this illusion, the power of which derives from magnetized feeling, the negative side of the working of the planet Neptune.

This power can be resisted through the holy vow of chastity (understood in its deeper, spiritual sense), which endows the human being with the means to withstand the tempting allure of *maya* (the illusion of "The World"). For instead of the feeling life becoming filled with the magnetic power of attraction and repulsion as it operates in the earthly world, spiritual chastity helps to keep this false inspiration at bay, and furthers an atmosphere of purity which allows the higher, true inspiration of the spiritual world to flow in. This higher inspiration is that for the Good, and it is in essence itself goodness.

In contrast, Lenin lived under the illusion that he was working for the good, for the betterment of mankind. That this was an illusion is evident from the fact that he allowed the perpetration of monstrous and inhuman deeds to be executed in the accomplishing of his aims. The true Good, on the other hand, cannot do otherwise than spread goodness, for it is in its very essence good (and not an illusion of the good). St. Francis of Assisi, for example, who was inspired by the Good, also accomplished far-reaching aims – without in any way hurting or destroying anybody or anything, which he could *not* do, for he "breathed" goodness. It was the holy vow of chastity (alongside the vow of poverty) which protected St. Francis from the false inspiration of the intoxication of *maya,* and which allowed the higher inspiration of the spiritual world – the inspiration of the Good – to flow into him and permeate him.

Lastly it is the holy vow of obedience (understood in its spiritual sense), which protects the human being from becoming a victim of the temptation of the atomizing of the will. A public manifestation of this temptation – shortly after the discovery of Pluto in 1930 – presented itself dramatically in Nazi Germany in the 1930's. Hitler exemplified the atomized will, ruthlessly bent on the acquisition of power, through tyranny and destruction. This impulse he was able to kindle also in large numbers of his fellow countrymen, leading to a large-scale atomizing of the will.

The atomizing of the will is represented in the fifteenth arcanum of the Tarot „The Devil", which teaches concerning *negative union,* i.e. not union with the Good, but with evil. In the latter case the will becomes an instrument of dark powers, instead of becoming united with the Divine. The path of Union, in its positive sense, depends on the practice of obedience, whereby the human being acts in accordance with the dictates of his conscience, guided by the light of reason. The atomizing of the will occurs by way of the banishment of conscience and reason, where the will is accorded with supreme jurisdiction, i.e. the human being becomes possessed by the *will to power,* the seed of which lies in everyone. Obedience to that which is higher than man safeguards against the will to power. "You shall worship the Lord thy God, and him only shall you serve" (*Matthew* iv, 10). These words express the keynote of obedience, with which Christ overcame the temptation of the will to power.

Spiritual alchemy

These three temptations – directed at thinking, feeling and the will – are not something new, as they were met with and resisted some 2000 years ago by Jesus Christ in the wilderness. These temptations have always approached human beings in some form or other. What is new, since the discovery of Uranus, Neptune and Pluto, is the emergence of these temptations on a large scale and as actual forces at work in the shaping of modern civilization. The *confrontation with evil* is a reality in modern civilization, whereby the task facing modern man is to harness and master evil and thereby to render it impotent, or even to place it in the service of the Good. The release of the sub-earthly forces of electricity ("densified light" – Uranus), magnetism ("densified sound" – Neptune) and atomic power ("densified life" – Pluto) has brought with it the external challenge of harnessing and mastering potentially destructive forces. No less significant, however, are the inner challenges corresponding to the release of these forces – the challenges presented by the electrification of thinking, the magnetization of feeling and the atomizing of the will.

A new kind of spiritual alchemy is called for in the modern scientific age. In antiquity the connection between the seven planets and seven principal metals was known. The usual list of correspondences between the planets and the metals is as follows: Saturn – lead; Jupiter – tin; Mars – iron; Sun – gold; Venus – copper; Mercury – quicksilver; Moon – silver. This list is the standard one found in Arabic alchemical texts. It is also referred to by the Christian astrologer Theophilus of Edessa, who lived in Baghdad in the eighth century A.D.[24] This list is almost identical to the earliest known lists of the planetary metals, those of the Greek astrologers Teucer and Vettius Valens. Vettius Valens lived in the second century A.D., and in his great astrological work *The Anthology* he gives exactly the above list, with the exception that he lists electrum (an alloy of gold and silver) as the metal corresponding to Mercury, instead of quicksilver.[25] It seems likely that the Arabic alchemical tradition adopted these correspondences between the planets and metals from the Greek astrological tradition, and substituted quicksilver for electrum. (It is not surprising that quicksilver is not mentioned by Vettius Valens, as its distillation became established only later – at some time around the fourth century A.D.)

VIII. Uranus, Neptune and Pluto

Alchemy in its deeper sense is concerned with the transmutation of the inner forces connected with the seven planets. The transmutation into gold is nothing other than the christianization of the seven inner planetary forces – to "shine like the Sun" (*Matthew* xiii, 43). A path towards the accomplishment of this alchemical aim is described in *Hermetic Astrology* I, Chapters 7 and 9 (see Chapter 7 – "the eightfold path in hermetic astrology"). There mention is made of the Christian mantrams relating to the christianisation of the seven inner forces of the seven planets. How these inner forces are awoken and harnessed by the human being on the spiritual path of hermeticism is described in the first seven chapters of the work *Meditations of the Tarot*, where these seven chapters are devoted to the first seven arcana of the Tarot. Each arcanum of the first seven arcana is concerned with the inner working of one of the seven planets, and the author outlines in this work how each arcanum can be entered into inwardly through meditation. Each of the first seven arcana thus communicates a teaching relating to the alchemical work of awakening and harnessing the seven planetary forces inwardly.

The first seven arcana deal with the spiritual-alchemical teaching relating to the seven planets. Of the remaining fifteen arcana (of the total of twenty-two), twelve bring forward the teaching concerning the inner awakening of the spiritual forces of the twelve signs of the zodiac, and three arcana relate to the mystery of evil. It is these three arcana which come into consideration here, in our study of the confrontation with evil in the form of the electrification of thinking, the magnetization of feeling and the atomizing of the will. These three arcana – "The Tower of Destruction", "The World" and "The Devil" – teach concerning the overcoming of the negative working of the planets Uranus, Neptune and Pluto. (Those readers already familiar with the twenty-two major arcana of the Tarot may wonder why the thirteenth arcanum "Death" is not included here in connection with the working of evil. *Death* is not evil, however. It is an aspect of existence which actually accomplishes something supremely good, namely it reunites the human being with the spiritual world. *Death* in fact belongs to the circle of the twelve signs of the zodiac, to the sign of Scorpio.)

In modern spiritual alchemy, the transmutation of the forces connected with Uranus, Neptune and Pluto (electricity, magnetism and atomic power) – understood in an inner, spiritual sense – has to be included together with the traditional alchemical work of transforming the seven metals into gold (= the Christianisation of the seven inner planetary forces).

The transmutation of the inner aspects of electricity, magnetism and atomic power belongs to modern spiritual alchemy. The successful confrontation with evil, resulting in the transmutation of the negative forces connected with Uranus, Neptune and Pluto, leads to the development of spiritual faculties: Illumination (Uranus), Inspiration (Neptune) and Union (Pluto). Through Illumination, Inspiration and Union the human being enters into a new relationship with the cosmic forces of light, sound and life (love) laid down in the three primal manvantaras before human evolution began – in the manvantaras of Ouranos, Night and Phanes (in terms of Orphic cosmology). In the subsequent course of evolution some of the primal forces of light, sound and life became "trapped" in the interior of the Earth – life trapped at the deepest level of the Earth's interior (as atomic power), sound in the middle region of the interior of the Earth (as magnetism) and light in the uppermost region of the sub-earthly spheres (as electricity).

With the discovery of Uranus, Neptune and Pluto during the last two hundred years or so, layer by layer the forces trapped in the interior of the Earth have become harnessed and released – first electricity, then magnetism (in the form of electromagnetism), then atomic power. In the language of Christian esoterism, "the gates of hell have become opened." The external manifestation of the opening of the gates of hell is evident in the release of electricity, magnetism and atomic power. The inner aspect of this is the confrontation with evil, in the form of the electrification of thinking, the magnetization of feeling and the atomizing of the will.

A force which potentially has the power to meet and resist the upsurge of evil is indicated in the words of Christ: *"And the gates of hell shall not prevail against it" (Matthew* xvi, 18). Despite the flood of evil surging up from sub-earthly realms into the world, threatening to sweep mankind to destruction, the united forces of Christianity have the potential to withstand all the storms of evil. This is in accordance with the promise of Christ, whose words have eternal value. ("Heaven and Earth will pass away, but my words will not pass away" – *Matthew* xxiv, 35.)

Ouranos, Night and Phanes

Through Christ the three temptations – electrification of thinking, magnetization of feeling and atomizing of the will – may be resisted and overcome. More than this, on the path of moral-spiritual development the negative forces of Uranus, Neptune and Pluto underlying these temptations may become transmuted into the higher forces connected with these three planets, yielding the spiritual faculties of Illumination, Inspiration and Union. In this way the human being enters into a relationship with the primal forces of cosmic light, cosmic sound and cosmic life laid down in the manvantaras of Ouranos, Night and Phanes. Ouranos, Night and Phanes thus represent the positive side of that which is portrayed negatively in the three arcana "The Tower of Destruction", "The World" and "The Devil". For example, the Prince of Hades ("The Devil") embodies the negative side of the working of Pluto; the positive side is Phanes – "marvellously beautiful, a figure of shining light"[26] – representing the Father, bestowing the faculty of Union through divine love. *Maya* is represented in the arcanum "The World" as the negative side of the working of Neptune; the positive side is Night – representing the Mother, bestowing the faculty of Inspiration. Lastly, the "Tower of Destruction" is the arcanum which portrays the negative side of the working of Uranus; the positive side is Ouranos, the regent of the starry heavens, whose light is the sum-total of the radiation of millions of stars, representing the Divine Mind, bestowing the faculty of Illumination.

In so far as the name *Pluto* refers to the Prince of Hades ruling in the underworld, it is an appropriate designation for the negative aspect of this planet, referring to the domain of trapped life at the core of the interior of the Earth; but the name *Phanes* relates to the positive aspect of this planet – the source of creative life-will (cosmic life/love). Similarly, in so far as the name *Neptune* might be thought of as referring to the underworld region of the domain of trapped sound within the Earth, it is a fitting term for the negative aspect of this planet; whereas the name *Night* indicates the positive aspect of this planet – the source of cosmic harmony. The name *Uranus*, in so far as it is conceived of as referring to the regent of the starry heavens, representing the Divine Mind, indicates the positive aspect of this planet – the source of cosmic intelligence. The negative aspect, however, is appropriately indicated by the name *Lucifer*, the Prince of Light in the underworld, the regent of the sub-earthly domain of trapped light. The names *Lucifer-Ouranos, Neptune-Night* and *Pluto-Phanes* thus convey something of the nature of the planets Uranus, Neptune and Pluto, seen in the light of hermetic astrology.

Chapter 8: Notes and references

1. W.K.C. Guthrie, *Orpheus and Greek Religion* (London, 1952), pp. 80–82, describes the cosmogony of Orpheus.
2. Novalis, *Hymns to the Night*, (trsl. C.E. Passage, Liberal Arts Press, Indianapolis-New York, 1960, pp. 3–4).
3. Josefine Schreier, *Göttinnen, Ihr Einfluß von der Urzeit bis zur Gegenwart* (Verlag Frauenoffensive, Munich, 1977), p.12.
4. W.K.C. Guthrie, op. cit. pp. 80–81.
5. Rudolf Steiner, *Occult Science – An Outline* (Rudolf Steiner Press, London, 1979).
6. Rudolf Steiner, *Spiritual Hierarchies and their Reflection in the Physical World* (Rudolf Steiner Press, London, 1980). According to Rudolf Steiner's description, in the Sun period of evolution a giant Sun filled the orbit that is now traced out by the planet Jupiter. At that time, however, Jupiter as a planetary body did not exist.

7. Cf. Rudolf Steiner, *Occult Science – An Outline* (Rudolf Steiner Press, London, 1979).
8. Ibid.
9. Rudolf Steiner, *Karmic Relationships*, vol. i (Rudolf Steiner Press, London, 1972), pp. 169–172 describes the reincarnation of Mu'awiya as President Woodrow Wilson.
10. Francis L. Watson, *Wallenstein, Soldier under Saturn* (London, 1938), p. 132.
11. Ibid., p. 20.
12. Ibid., p. 26 – cited from Wallenstein's first biographer, the Italian Gualdo Priorato, writing in 1643, nine years after Wallenstein's death.
13. Ibid., p. 187.
14. Cf. E.J. Holmyard, *Alchemy* (Penguin, London, 1957), pp. 18–19.
15. Paul M. Allen, *Vladimir Soloviev: Russian Mystic* (Rudolf Steiner Publications, New York, 1978), pp. 366–410 is a recent English translation of Soloviev's *A Short Narrative about Antichrist*.
16. Sten Lindroth, "Emmanuel Swedenborg", *Dictionary of Scientific Biography*, vol. xiii (New York, 1976), pp. 178–181.
17. Ibid.
18. Ibid.
19. *Harmonice Mundi* ("The Harmony of the World") is the title of the book that Kepler wrote and published in 1619, at the age of 47, outlining his astronomical-harmonic researches.
20. Arthur Beer, "Kepler's Astrology and Mysticism", *Vistas in Astronomy*, vol. 18 (1975), pp. 399–426.
21. Johannes Kepler, *Harmonice Mundi*, book V. Cf. D.P. Walker, "Kepler's celestial music", *Journal of the Warburg and Courtauld Institutes* 30 (1967), pp. 228–250.
22. The modern path of hermeticism is outlined in the book *Meditations on the Tarot* (trsl. R. Powell, Amity, Warwick NY, 1985). See Chapters 4, 5 and 6 for the overcoming of the three temptations.
23. Karl Marx and Friedrich Engels, *Manifesto of the Communist Party* (trsl. S. Moore, London, 1932, p. 8).
24. Cf. Arthur Ludwich, *Anecdota astrologica* (Leipzig, 1877), p. 121.
25. Vettius Valens, *Anthologiarum* i, 1 (ed. W. Kroll, Berlin, 1908).
26. W.K.C. Guthrie, op. cit., p. 80.

Chapter 9

The Second Coming and the New Age

In Chapter 8 certain preparatory stages for the coming of Antichrist are outlined in connection with the forces unleashed through the discoveries of Uranus (1781), Neptune (1846) and Pluto (1930), bringing with them the confrontation with evil for modern mankind. The coming of Antichrist, however, may be regarded as the shadow side of the greatest spiritual event of modern times: the second coming of Christ. The second coming – which is not in a physical form, but in a form of light, in the etheric aura of the Earth – is giving birth to a New Age. The basis of the New Age is the return, taking place in accordance with the unfolding of certain rhythms, of Jesus Christ to the etheric realm of the Earth. The "wave" of Christ's etheric return repeats itself rhythmically every $33\frac{1}{3}$ years, mirroring His earthly life, and dividing each century into three parts. In this respect, the $33\frac{1}{3}$-year rhythm is a key rhythm underlying the New Age, the age of the second coming.

It was on Ascension Day in the year AD 33 (Thursday, May 14) that Jesus Christ, in His resurrection body, departed from the earthly realm to begin His ascent to the realm of the Father, entering on the path of this ascent first of all into the cosmic realm of the Angels (Moon sphere) bordering onto the human realm. On this day the Risen One, accompanied by His disciples, proceeded to the summit of the Mount of Olives, becoming ever more resplendent with light as He made His way. Upon reaching the summit He shone with a light more radiant than the midday Sun. Then He raised His right hand and laid His left hand across His breast; turning slowly He blessed the whole world. The glory of the light emanating from Jesus Christ became greater and greater until He disappeared into the cloud of light. From this light two Angels then appeared and addressed the apostles and disciples left behind on the Mount of Olives, saying in resounding tones: "Men of Galilee, why do you stand looking up into heaven? This Jesus, who was taken up from you into heaven, will come in the same way as you saw him go into heaven" (*Acts* i,11). The Angels then vanished into the receding cloud of light, returning to the Angelic realm, the cosmic sphere bounded by the orbit of the Moon.

The return of Christ to the etheric aura of the Earth signifies a fulfilment of the words spoken by the Angels to the disciples on Ascension Day in the year AD 33. As will be outlined in the following, the fulfilment of the promise that Jesus "will come in the same way as you saw him go into heaven" has begun in the twentieth century. But how may this be recognized?

To begin with it is essential to realise that just as the first coming of

Christ was prepared for by the prophets of Israel – culminating with John the Baptist – so the second coming was also prepared for. This was outlined in Appendix II ("The second coming") of *Hermetic Astrology* I, where it was pointed out that Rudolf Steiner (1861–1925) acted as a kind of "John the Baptist" with regard to the second coming. Hence the deeper significance of studying Rudolf Steiner's biography, as undertaken in Chapters 4 and 5 of the present volume. In the following we shall look at Rudolf Steiner's biography in relation to the cosmic background of the second coming, from which it will emerge that his teaching can be regarded essentially as a revelation through which Jesus Christ spoke to mankind as He was descending towards the Earth in His second coming. In this respect Rudolf Steiner's teaching, which he named *Anthroposophy* or *spiritual science*, is of deep significance to the human race, and for the future of the Earth itself. As indicated in *Hermetic Astrology* I, Appendix II, Rudolf Steiner came as a messenger of the Self of Christianity – Jesus Christ, in His second coming – as opposed to the will, feeling and thinking aspects of Christianity represented by the three main Christian confessions. In Rudolf Steiner's own words: "Let us try to imprint the truths of Anthroposophy into our souls as a message of Christ Himself..."[1] How could Rudolf Steiner make such a statement, in which the implication is that Anthroposophy is a "message of Christ Himself"?

Returning to Rudolf Steiner's birth horoscope (February 25, 1861), we find that Jupiter heliocentrically had just entered sidereal Leo (h-Jupiter at 0° Leo in the hermetic chart). According to research presented elsewhere,[2] which will be summarized in the following, it was this configuration which cosmically indicated the onset of Christ's descent from the Sun towards the Earth in His second coming. As described in the preceding chapter, the heliocentric orbit of Jupiter denotes the boundary of the stage of cosmic evolution known as *Ancient Sun*.[3] It was during this stage of evolution, according to Rudolf Steiner's description in his book *Occult Science*, that the etheric body ("life body") of the human being was formed.[4] But how does this bear upon our consideration of the second coming of Christ?

In the forty days following the Resurrection – up to Ascension Day – the Risen One appeared to the disciples on numerous occasions, as described in the Gospels. During this time He manifested Himself not in a physical body, as He could appear and disappear at will, but in His resurrection body – essentially a "body of life" like the etheric body. However, the resurrection body is far more radiant and of a more intensive quality of life than the etheric body of human beings. It is, so to say, a "piece of Sun", and its rhythm seems to accord with that of Jupiter, carried over as a memory from Ancient Sun. This rhythm, which in the following will be described from the heliocentric ("Sun-centered") point of view, is such

IX. The Second Coming and the New Age

that Jupiter requires almost twelve years to make one orbit of the sidereal zodiac, thus spending about one year in each zodiacal sign. It was evidently in accordance with this rhythm that the descent of Christ from cosmic realms, in His resurrection body, took place. Moreover, it appears that the onset of this descent from the realm of the Sun coincided with Rudolf Steiner's birth on Earth, at which time heliocentric Jupiter entered sidereal Leo. From this moment in time onwards the descent of Christ through the ranks of the spiritual hierarchies – from the Sun sphere down to the Moon sphere (realm of the Angels) – took place, such that the passage through each spiritual hierarchy lasted twelve years, in accordance with Jupiter's orbit of the sidereal zodiac. At the end of this descent, around Ascension Day (May 5) in 1932 or somewhat later, Jesus Christ was born into the Earth's etheric aura, encircling the Earth, denoting the commencement of the New Age.

This descent could be called the *Descension*, being the reverse of that which took place at the Ascension. Whereas on Ascension Day in AD 33 the Risen One departed from the Earth on His ascent towards heaven, at the end of His Descension in 1932 He returned "in the same way". In AD 33 the disciples "saw him go into heaven", and in 1932, according to the account printed at the end of Appendix II in *Hermetic Astrology* I, He completed His descent from heaven back to the earthly realm, passing through the ranks of the spiritual hierarchies. Since 1932/1933 the second coming *within the earthly realm* has been underway, signifying that we are living in a time comparable to the forty days from the Resurrection to the Ascension. But just as at that time it was only a small group of people who were aware of the presence of the Risen One, whilst most of mankind had no idea of Him and His appearances to the disciples, so in our time only relatively few people have had a direct experience of Him in His resurrection body. Nevertheless, there are "witnesses", as will be discussed later in this chapter. Before turning to the accounts of these witnesses, however, let us consider more closely the Descension, as the counterpart to the Ascension.

The Ascension, which began historically on Ascension Day in AD 33, was an ascent of Jesus Christ in His resurrection body through the ranks of the spiritual hierarchies. First He entered into the realm of the Angels, the sphere bounded by the orbit of the Moon. Then He passed successively through the ranks of the Archangels (Folk Spirits) and of the Archai (Principalities, Time Spirits). After this, He entered the Sun sphere, where three ranks of spiritual hierarchies dwell. These are, in ascending order, the Exusiai (Powers, Spirits of Form), Dynamis (Mights, Spirits of Movement), and Kyriotetes (Dominions, Spirits of Wisdom). The Descension, which culminated historically around Ascension Day in 1932, was the reverse of the Ascension. It was a descent of Jesus Christ in His resurrection body through the ranks of the spiritual hierarchies. On His descent from the Sun sphere towards the Earth He passed through the spiritual hierarchies in the reverse order: Kyriotetes, Dynamis, Exusiai, Archai, Archangels, Angels. This descent evidently took place in accordance with the heliocentric orbit of Jupiter around the sidereal zodiac, the passage through each hierarchy taking place during one orbit of Jupiter, starting with Jupiter's entrance into sidereal Leo. But why should the ingress of Jupiter into sidereal Leo signify the starting point of this rhythm (with respect to Christ), rather than, say, its entrance into sidereal Aries?

Here it is a matter of a mystery connected with the human heart, for the heart is formed out of the zodiacal forces emanating from sidereal Leo. And the heart – macrocosmically Leo – is the starting point for the development of the Christ Impulse, which is implanted in the heart of every human being. Rudolf Steiner referred to the heart as the center into which the Foundation Stone of love is to become implanted in order to unfold its spiritual potential. The ingress of Jupiter, heliocentrically, into sidereal Leo corresponds macrocosmically to the unfolding of the new cycle of the Christ Impulse, which may be taken up initially in the heart. In this light the designation of Christ as the *Lion of Judah* – obviously referring to the zodiacal sign of Leo – is highly appropriate.

Starting out at Rudolf Steiner's birth on February 25, 1861, with the entrance of heliocentric Jupiter into sidereal Leo,* during Jupiter's orbit of the sidereal zodiac the passage of Christ through the hierarchy of the Kyriotetes (within the Sun sphere) took place. This lasted until Jupiter (heliocentrically) returned to enter sidereal Leo on January 1, 1873. The passage through the realm of the Kyriotetes took place without hindrance. In 1873 the descent (still in the Sun sphere) through the hierarchy of the Dynamis began, lasting until heliocentric Jupiter arrived back at the start of sidereal Leo on November 11, 1884. According to the description of this descent, published for the first time in English translation at the end of Appendix II of *Hermetic Astrology* I, here in the realm of the Dynamis Christ encountered resistance, which became mirrored on the Earth in the Russo-Turkish war (1877–1878). From the end of 1884 until Jupiter heliocentrically entered sidereal Leo on September 21, 1896, there took place the passage of Christ (still within the sphere of the Sun) through the hierarchy of the Exusiai, which occurred without hindrance.

It was during the latter part of this period that Rudolf Steiner wrote his major philosophical work *The Philosophy of Freedom* (1894), but at this point in his life he had not yet had the decisive inner experience of Christ

---

*The exact date of Jupiter's heliocentric ingress into sidereal Leo was February 20, 1861, so that by the time of Rudolf Steiner's birth on February 25 Jupiter had progressed about ½ degree into Leo.

which led him to become the proclaimer of the second coming. This experience came during the next orbit of Jupiter (heliocentric) around the sidereal zodiac, from its entrance into sidereal Leo in 1896 to its return to this part of the zodiac on August 4, 1908. This was the time of Christ's descent, in His resurrection body, through the hierarchy of the Archai, where again He encountered no resistance.

The profound experience that Rudolf Steiner had at that time, shortly before the year 1900, he described in his autobiography as follows: "This experience culminated in my standing in the spiritual presence of the Mystery of Golgotha in a most profound and solemn festival of knowledge."[5] Through this experience there began a process of development through which Rudolf Steiner increasingly became a vehicle for the new revelation of Christ which began through His descent towards the Earth – that is, Rudolf Steiner became the prophet of the second coming. Just as "the word of God came to John in the wilderness" (*Luke* iii, 2), from which point in time onwards John the Baptist began preaching and baptizing in preparation for the coming of the Messiah, so from the turn of the century onwards Rudolf Steiner's activity became increasingly devoted to preparing the way for the second coming of Christ. It was during this time that Rudolf Steiner wrote his basic works *Theosophy* (1904) and *Knowledge of the Higher Worlds and its Attainment* (1904/1905).

The next period in the descent of Christ towards the Earth lasted from August 1908 to the heliocentric ingress of Jupiter into sidereal Leo on June 15, 1920. Not long after the start of this period – during which Christ's descent through the hierarchy of Archangels (Folk Spirits) took place – Rudolf Steiner held a cycle of lectures in Oslo, from June 7 to June 17, 1910, entitled *The Mission of Folk Souls*. These lectures, in which he described the activity and mission of the Archangels of various countries and peoples, may be seen directly in connection with the passage at that time of Christ through the sphere of the Archangels. In the last lecture of this cycle he then spoke of Anthroposophy (spiritual science) as a preparation for the approaching new manifestation of Christ.

> *Those who are open to the stimulus of spiritual science will, from the middle of the twentieth century on, gradually experience a renewal of that which St. Paul saw in etheric clairvoyance as a mystery to come, the "Mystery of the Living Christ". There will be a new manifestation of Christ... It is extremely important to realise that spiritual science is a preparation for the new Christ revelation.*[6]

By this point in time Rudolf Steiner had become conscious, through his highly developed spiritual faculties, of Christ's approach towards the Earth. For, five months previously, in Stockholm, on the evening of January 12, 1910, he had proclaimed for the first time the imminent return to the Earth's aura of the Risen One in etheric form. On this day in January

1910 the Sun had been in conjunction with the planet Uranus, the planet which is often associated with the bringing in of new impulses. Rudolf Steiner's deed at this special cosmic moment made him a prophet of the second coming – a kind of twentieth century "John the Baptist". And just as John the Baptist had not only preached but also acted, in that he baptized those who came to him, so Rudolf Steiner not only held lectures but also set about building a "temple" – the Goetheanum – for Anthroposophy. People from all over Europe came to Dornach, Switzerland, to work together at building the Goetheanum, at the time of the war. (It was at the time of World War I, 1914-1918, which arose during the passage of Christ through the hierarchy of the Archangels on account of the resistance He encountered there.) The peaceful cooperation of people from different countries, working together to build a "temple" in preparation for the new Christ revelation, was a true reflection on Earth of the passage of Christ through the sphere of the Archangels, whereas the war was a terrible counter image.

The final stage of Christ's descent towards the Earth began in 1920 with Christ's entrance into the realm of the Angels, the Moon sphere, and lasted until Jupiter's heliocentric ingress into sidereal Leo on April 25, 1932. It was close to the beginning of this period, on September 26, 1920, that the ceremonial opening of the Goetheanum took place. Here there was now a temple on Earth – a kind of twentieth century "temple of Solomon" – which could serve as a center from which the impulse of Anthroposophy could radiate out into the world. But on the night of December 31, 1922 the Goetheanum became raised to the ground by fire. What did this signify?

Just as the new-born child Jesus became threatened with death at the hands of Herod the Great, so in the twentieth century, with the preparation – through Anthroposophy – for the new Christ revelation, powerful forces of opposition were at work to destroy it. And the nearer Christ drew towards the Earth, the stronger the opposition became. The following words from the twelfth chapter of the *Book of Revelation* are relevant here:

> *And a great portent appeared in heaven, a woman clothed with the Sun, with the Moon under her feet, and on her head a crown of twelve stars. She was with child and she cried out in her pangs of birth, in anguish for delivery. And another portent appeared in heaven; behold, a great red dragon...and the dragon stood before the woman who was about to bear a child, that he might devour her child when she brought it forth.*   *(Revelation xii, 1-4)*

As will be discussed later, the heavenly woman in this vision of St. John is one aspect of Sophia, the divine wisdom. The entire foregoing description of St. John can be seen here in relation to Sophia manifesting as *Anthro-*

pos-Sophia, where Sophia – in resurrected form through the human being (*anthropos*) – sought to "give birth", to prepare the way for the Son of man in His second coming. The temple of Anthroposophy – the Goetheanum at Dornach – was a manifestation of the "birth pangs" in preparation for the second coming of the Messiah. But the powers of evil – portrayed in the vision of St. John in the form of "a great red dragon" – set to work to destroy the temple that had been built as a labour of love and devotion towards Anthroposophy. This can be "read" from the stars at the time of the fire that reduced the Goetheanum to ashes. (It must be borne in mind that the entire building, apart from the foundations, was of wood, much of which had been sculpted in wonderful esoteric forms and also painted with profound wisdom-filled frescoes.)

At the time of the fire – New Year's eve 1922/1923 – the Sun stood in opposition to Pluto, with the Sun at 16° Sagittarius and Pluto at 16½° Gemini in the sidereal zodiac. As outlined in the previous chapter, Pluto may be seen in relation to the evil will of Antichrist. But as an opposition between the Sun and Pluto takes place once every year, what was special about this opposition at the turn of the year 1922/1923?

The degree area in the sidereal zodiac of this opposition was of special significance. For, as discussed in Volume III of this series, *Christian Hermetic Astrology: The Star of the Magi and the Life of Christ,* and also in the companion volume *The Horoscopes of Jesus Christ and the Blessed Virgin Mary,* at the birth of Jesus the Sun's position in the sidereal zodiac was 16° Sagittarius. The return of the Sun to this position each year (in the early twentieth century this was on New Year's eve; now it is one day later) commemorates the divine birth in Bethlehem. And on New Year's eve 1922/1923 this was "commemorated" in a magnificent way at the Goetheanum with a eurythmy performance of the "Prologue in Heaven" from Goethe's *Faust* followed by a lecture by Rudolf Steiner. This lecture – entitled "Spiritual Knowledge is a True Communion, the Beginning of a Cosmic Cult suitable for Human Beings of the Present Age" – was the closing lecture in the cycle *Man and the World of Stars.*[7] This crowning lecture, held at the time when the heavenly commemoration of the birth of Jesus was taking place, and when He Himself on His descent through the hierarchy of the Angels was drawing ever nearer to the Earth, culminated with a meditation on spiritual communion. We can form a mental picture of Rudolf Steiner in the temple below giving a meditation to help lead human beings into the temple above, the temple of the cosmos, in which the Risen One was close at the moment of heavenly commemoration.

But the powers of evil struck from below, at this time of opposition between the Sun and Pluto, and a fire broke out in the basement of the Goetheanum, which was discovered just one hour after Rudolf Steiner had spoken the closing words of meditation ("spiritual communion"). By then it was too late to extinguish the flames, and that night – as the bells were ringing out the change of year – the temple of Anthroposophy went up in flames. Already the next morning, Rudolf Steiner announced the decision to rebuild the Goetheanum, and now there stands a new Goetheanum, made of concrete, in the place of the original temple sculpted in wood.

At that time (1922/1923) atomic power had not yet been discovered. This subterrean force, connected with Pluto, was harnessed by human beings only after Pluto's discovery in 1930. Just as the powers of evil struck from below, from subterrenean depths, at the opposition between the Sun and Pluto at the burning of the Goetheanum, so they struck again on the night April 25/26, 1986 at the atomic plant in Chernobyl, where fire broke out, leading to the worst civilian nuclear catastrophe that the world has yet experienced. It was shortly after 1 a.m. on Saturday, April 26 that the catastrophe occurred. The Sun was at 11° Aries and Pluto was opposite at 11° Libra. This was close to the Sun-Moon (Full Moon) axis at the death of Jesus Christ on the cross on the afternoon of Good Friday, April 3, AD 33. At 12.30 p.m. on Good Friday, as the crucifixion began, the Moon was at 11° Libra, and at 3 p.m., the moment of death, the Moon was at 12° Libra opposite the Sun at 14° Aries. The opposition between the Sun and Pluto at the time of the Chernobyl catastrophe cosmically echoed something of the memory of the death of Jesus Christ on the cross, just as the opposition between the Sun and Pluto at the burning of the Goetheanum recalled His divine birth.

These two events – the divine birth, and the death on the cross – are events which, in the age of the second coming, may be celebrated in their cosmic aspect, when the Sun returns to the same degree in the sidereal zodiac. That is, 16° Sagittarius at the divine birth (at the present time the Sun reaches 16° Sagittarius on January 1 each year), and 14° Aries at the death on the cross/16° Aries at the resurrection (at the present time the Sun arrives at 14° Aries on April 29 and at 16° Aries on May 1). Now, at the end of the twentieth century, the heavenly commemoration of the divine birth takes place at the beginning of January and the heavenly commemoration of the Mystery of Golgotha occurs at the end of April/beginning of May. (The corresponding dates for the major events in the life of Christ are given in *The Star of the Magi and the Life of Christ.*) Of course, this in no way replaces the traditional festivals of Christmas and Easter, but simply adds the cosmic aspect, as appropriate for the New Age. But, insofar as there is a lack of consciousness of the cosmic awakening to Christ signified by the New Age, correspondingly a "vacuum" is present into which the powers of evil may work. Then it is precisely these times of heavenly commemoration that are chosen by the forces of evil to launch their attacks. Through the awakening of consciousness, however, there need no longer be a vacuum into which evil is able to strike. As Rudolf Steiner indicated, when he was asked how was it possible for the Goetheanum to have become burnt down, it was a lack of wakefulness on the part of those around him that had opened up the possibility for the occurrence of this terrible blow.[8] (Here there comes to mind the image of the sleeping disciples in the Garden of Gethsemane, when Christ had asked them to "watch and pray" – *Mark* xiv, 38.)

The burning of the Goetheanum was a blow which adversely affected Rudolf Steiner's physical constitution. As described in Chapter 5, Rudolf Steiner went on to found a "spiritual temple" (School of Spiritual Science) at Christmas 1923, but at Michaelmas 1924 he fell seriously ill and became confined to bed. He never recovered. At his death on the morning of March 30, 1925, the Moon was at 24° Taurus, close to its position (20° Taurus) at the burning of the Goetheanum. Perhaps this was a sign of the inner connection between the two events, in that with the burning of the Goetheanum Rudolf Steiner's physical constitution suffered a blow which led 2¼ years later to his death? Be that as it may, his death in 1925 precluded him from being a witness to that which he had foretold: Christ's entrance into the Earth's etheric aura one-third of the way through this century, signifying the onset of the New Age.

Rudolf Steiner generally spoke of the New Age, which he termed the *Age of Light*, as having begun in the year 1900.[9] Since the year 1900 denoted the start of the first 33⅓-year period of the twentieth century, which culminated with the entrance of Christ into the Earth's etheric aura one-third of the way through this century, it is certainly true to regard 1900 as the cosmically initiated commencement of the New Age. From an earthly standpoint, the end of the first 33⅓-year period after this cosmic commencement signified the onset of the second coming – and therewith the start of the New Age – for the Earth and mankind. This is connected with the 33⅓-year rhythm of the life of Jesus Christ (from birth to the crucifixion/resurrection), which is the key rhythm underlying the New Age.

Following the 12-year Jupiter rhythm through the period from Rudolf Steiner's birth (1861) to the onset of the second coming (1932), the Descension of Christ through the ranks of the spiritual hierarchies – Kyriotetes, Dynamis, Exusiai, Archai, Archangels, and Angels – may be followed.[10] The last phase of the Descension – through the Moon sphere, that of the Angels – saw an increasing opposition to His coming. This opposition gained a focal point in the political sphere when Hitler became leader of the Nazi party in April 1921. Through the Nazi party the ideal of a "counterfeit" New Age or Kingdom, the Third Reich, became promulgated.[11] And just at the time when the New Age through the second coming of Christ was breaking in, at the completion of the Descension in 1932, the Nazi party achieved a phenomenal success at the elections in Germany, with the consequence that Hitler became chancellor on January 30,

1933. At that time Jupiter (heliocentric) was in sidereal Leo, the ingress having taken place on April 25, 1932, shortly before Ascension Day (May 5). And during the twelve years of Jupiter's orbit around the sidereal zodiac the evil will of Antichrist was able to work through Hitler and the Nazi party. Jupiter (heliocentric) re-entered sidereal Leo in March 1944 and remained in Leo for one year, until March 1945. Shortly after leaving Leo, Hitler died on April 30, 1945.

At the very time of the onset of the greatest blessing for mankind and the Earth, through the second coming, the forces of evil were able to break through and wreak havoc and destruction, thus clouding the dawning of the New Age during the first Jupiter cycle of the second coming. In terms of the vision of St. John in the twelfth chapter of the Apocalypse, the Nazi scourge was a manifestation of the demonic power of the dragon.

"Woe to you, O earth and sea, for the devil has come down to you in great wrath, because he knows that his time is short!" And when the dragon saw that he had been thrown down to the earth, he pursued the woman who had borne the male child. (Revelation xii, 12–13)

In this great vision, St. John, who was gifted with a power of clairvoyance that penetrated into the far-distant future, beheld clairvoyantly, whilst on the island of Patmos, the onslaught of the dragon that would take place at the time of the second coming. He saw in vision the birth of the Risen One taking place out of – or with the help of – the cosmic wisdom (as an aspect of Sophia), and how the powers of evil would launch an attack against the woman and her child. The "Nazi beast" was a manifestation of these evil powers, and it almost succeeded in dominating Europe before it finally became overcome some twelve years later after the onset of the second coming in the Earth's aura.

This onset of the New Age – the "birth" of Christ into the Earth's etheric aura – took place at the culmination of the Descension. Indeed, it would be possible to cast a horoscope for the New Age at the time of this "birth" in 1932/1933. Analogously, the event of "solar conception" could be regarded as having taken place at the time of Rudolf Steiner's birth, when Christ's descent from the Sun sphere commenced. Seen in this light, Rudolf Steiner's birth horoscope acquires a profound significance, and his entire biography can be viewed against the cosmic background of the Descension. In fact, there are indications that, if he had not become physically weakened through the burning of the Goetheanum (and also other blows he suffered), he might have lived to the age of seventy-two (1861 + 72 = 1933). In this case, he would have lived to the completion of the Descension and the onset of the second coming in the earthly realm. (Seventy-two years is the length of time required by the vernal point to retrograde

IX. The Second Coming and the New Age

through one degree of the sidereal zodiac, during which time six revolutions of Jupiter around the sidereal zodiac are completed.)

In order to arrive at an exact date for the onset of the second coming in the Earth's etheric aura, it is necessary to take account not only of the rhythm of Jupiter's heliocentric orbit around the sidereal zodiac but also of the $33\frac{1}{3}$-year rhythm. For, the $33\frac{1}{3}$-year rhythm is that of Christ's life on Earth, and it is this rhythm which is of overriding importance for the earthly realm. Whereas following the Descension in relation to the heliocentric ingresses of Jupiter into sidereal Leo leads us to the time around Ascension Day in 1932 for the completion of Christ's descent from the Sun, following the $33\frac{1}{3}$-year rhythm through history from the time of the Mystery of Golgotha leads us to another date, slightly later in time. Bearing in mind that the heavenly commemoration of the divine birth in Bethlehem takes place in the twentieth century around New Year, a natural point in time to think of in connection with the onset of the second coming in the earthly realm would be New Year's eve 1932/1933. However, as will be discussed at length in the next chapter, in the age of the second coming it is the Full Moon which acquires special significance, each Full Moon serving to commemorate the Mystery of Golgotha (recalling the crucifixion, which took place at the time of Full Moon). Thus, the first Full Moon after New Year's eve 1932/1933 can be regarded as the date of commencement of the New Age. This was on January 11, 1933, when the Sun was at $27\frac{1}{2}°$ Sagittarius and the Moon at $27\frac{1}{2}°$ Gemini.

Furthermore, January 11, 1933 denoted the exact completion of fifty-seven $33\frac{1}{3}$-year cycles since the Mystery of Golgotha, dated from the resurrection on Easter Sunday morning. Thus, on January 11, 1933 a new $33\frac{1}{3}$-year cycle of Christ's life began, which lasted until May 11, 1966. This was the fifty-eighth cycle since the Mystery of Golgotha, or the fifty-ninth cycle from the divine birth in Bethlehem. At present we are living in the sixtieth cycle (taking the first cycle to have been the life of Jesus Christ from the moment of His birth in Bethlehem to the hour of the resurrection on Easter Sunday morning). This sixtieth cycle commenced on May 11, 1966 and will last until September 8, 1999. (For the precise computation concerning the $33\frac{1}{3}$-year rhythm of the life of Jesus Christ see *The Star of the Magi and the Life of Christ* and also *The Horoscopes of Jesus Christ and the Blessed Virgin Mary.*)

The New Age, which commenced with the onset of the second coming in the Earth's etheric aura, can be regarded as having begun on January 11, 1933. It is interesting that at that time – as at the burning of the Goetheanum on New Year's eve ten years previously – the Sun was in opposition to Pluto, for the Full Moon at $27\frac{1}{2}°$ Gemini was in conjunction with Pluto ($28\frac{1}{2}°$ Gemini). Shortly after, on January 30, 1933, Hitler became chancellor of Germany, ushering in a "counterfeit" New Age, the Third

Reich. This was a master stroke on the part of the evil powers opposing the second coming of Christ. Yet, judging from St. John's clairvoyant vision of the second coming, as narrated in the twelfth chapter of the Apocalypse, it would seem that this opposition was foreseen. And the onset of the New Age at this time of an opposition between the Sun and Pluto would seem to indicate – taken as a "cosmic sign" – that the confrontation with evil is something intrinsic to the second coming of Christ.

Just as Jesus Christ at His first coming did not shy away from confrontation with Herod or with the Pharisees, so in the second coming it would seem that He is not only the Bringer of Good (being the Good Itself), but also is engaged in the struggle against evil. The twentieth century is evidently a time of an apocalyptic battle between the powers of good and evil, and as referred to in the last chapter this may culminate around the end of the century, possibly with the manifestation of Antichrist. Thus, knowledge of the second coming – of the birth of a New Age through the renewed presence of Jesus Christ in the Earth's etheric aura – is of vital significance in order to be able to withstand the coming trials.

Obviously there can be no "proof" of the second coming in the sense of a scientific demonstration, but nevertheless some evidence of this event has been provided by witnesses of the second coming who have reported their experiences. For example, there is the witness of 1933 referred to in Appendix II ("The second coming") of *Hermetic Astrology* I, who spoke of Christ beginning to move "from the West to the East in wave-like lines. He will begin in America and will continue through Europe to the northeast of Europe." Then again, there is the witness borne by David Spangler in his book *Revelation: The Birth of a New Age:*

> Like most great events, the birth of the New Age occurred quietly...the Cosmic Christ descended and entered the life of Earth on all its levels...now Christ walks amongst us again, through clothed in etheric energy, and His Presence quickens the etheric and spiritual life of all who can open in love and peace and, responding, arise to His level...the true Second Coming has occurred and is this revelation and release of Christ Life within the inner planes of Earth...by Christmas 1967 the initiation was complete...the New Age had been born.[12]

This can be interpreted to mean that the first 33⅓-year period of Christ's etheric return *within* the Earth's etheric aura was completed by Christmas 1967. Thus, although at present we are living in the third 33⅓-year period measured from the cosmic commencement of the New Age in 1900, from the standpoint of the Earth and mankind we are now living in the second 33⅓-year period of the second coming, which will culminate at the end of this century. David Spangler's words, whilst indicating a fulfilment of Rudolf Steiner's prophecy concerning the second coming, point to a some-

IX. The Second Coming and the New Age

what different conception of the New Age than that of Rudolf Steiner.

But, apart from Rudolf Steiner, who was a herald of the New Age in its cosmic perspective, who already in 1910 prophesied the onset of the second coming in the 1930's, and apart from the witness of 1933, who described the beginning of the second coming within the Earth's etheric aura, and apart from David Spangler, who bore witness to the culmination of the first $33^1/_3$-year period in 1967, are there others who have experienced the Risen One in the twentieth century?

A remarkable book published in Stockholm in 1973 confirms the truth of Rudolf Steiner's prophecy first made in Stockholm in the year 1910. Bearing in mind the words of the witness of 1933 concerning the Etheric Christ: "He will begin in America and will continue through Europe to the north-east of Europe," it seems appropriate – shortly after the culmination of the first $33^1/_3$-year period of the wave of the etheric return – that a number of testimonies of experiences of the Risen One from people in Scandinavia have been recorded and presented in book form. It should be added that these testimonies, as far as can be judged, are from people who have no connection either with Anthroposophy or the "New Age" movement, people from all walks of life who have nothing in common apart from the Christian faith.

The book, entitled *They experienced Christ*, was published as a report, compiled by Gunnar Hillerdal and Berndt Gustafsson of the Religious-sociological Institute of Stockholm. The first edition was published in Stockholm by Verbum in 1973 and a second edition in 1979. Also in 1979 a German translation, *Sie erlebten Christus*, translated from the Swedish by Dr. Boris Tullander, was published by Verlag Die Pforte in Basel, Switzerland. From the Foreword it appears that the book came about seemingly by chance. Some letters received by Gunnar Hillerdal, which reported unusual experiences ("meetings with Christ"), led Hillerdal, after consultation with Berndt Gustafsson, to place an advertisement in a large Swedish daily newspaper. This was on December 24, 1972. The response went far beyond the expectations of Hillerdal and Gustafsson. The wealth of reports they received, many deeply impressive and detailed descriptions of profound personal experiences, induced them to edit a selection of the accounts and present them in the form of a book.

Before considering the material published by Hillerdal and Gustafsson, it may be helpful to review some points made by Rudolf Steiner with respect to the second coming. On numerous occasions (from 1910 onwards) he spoke of the onset – in the course of the twentieth century – of a new "Christ revelation", the outcome of which would be such that a number of people would be able to perceive Christ in His etheric form. He called this the "greatest mystery of the twentieth century", but warned of dire consequences if it were not to be heeded by mankind. He emphasized that

Christ would come in the etheric world, and would be active from there for the good of mankind and the Earth, independently of whether or not He would be recognized by human beings. In his descriptions as to how people would experience the Etheric Christ, he pointed to Him as a helper and comforter of needy, sick, and despairing human beings. Rudolf Steiner indicated how it would be possible for all human beings to draw near to Him in what he characterized as *the way to the Christ through thinking*:

> *Instead of taking an interest merely in my own way of thinking, and in what I consider right, I must develop a selfless interest in every opinion I encounter, however strongly I may hold it to be mistaken. The more a man prides himself on his own dogmatic opinions and is interested only in them, the further he removes himself, at this moment of world-evolution, from the Christ. The more he develops a social interest in the opinions of other men, even though he considers them erronous – the more light he receives into his own thinking from the opinions of others – the more he does to fulfil in his inmost soul a saying of Christ, which today must be interpreted in the sense of the new Christ-language. Christ said: "Inasmuch as ye have done it unto one of the least of these my brethren, ye have done it unto me." The Christ never ceases to reveal Himself anew to men – even unto the end of earthly time. And thus He speaks today to those willing to listen: "In whatever the least of your brethren thinks, you must recognise that I am thinking in him; and that I enter into your feeling, whenever you bring another's thought into relation with your own, and whenever you feel a fraternal interest for what is passing in another's soul. Whatever opinion, whatever outlook on life, you discover in the least of your brethren, therein you are seeking Myself." So does the Christ speak to our life of thought – the Christ Who desires to reveal Himself in a new way – the time for it is drawing near – to the men of the twentieth century... This is the way which today must be characterised as the way to the Christ through thinking.[13]*

Since experience of Christ in His second coming is on the whole an intimate subjective encounter with the Divine, most people who have had such an experience do not usually speak about it, except perhaps to their husbands or wives or close friends. For this reason these spiritual experiences, of a deep and profound nature, do not generally become communicated to a wider public. It is therefore something quite out of the ordinary that over one hundred people in Scandinavia reported their "Christ encounters" in writing, and that a selection of these reports have been published in book form. In a clear and remarkable way, these reports confirm Rudolf Steiner's prophetic announcement of the second coming.[14]

Many of the appearances of Christ described in the book *They experi-*

enced Christ are to people in need, and to the sick. Of these, the following, related by a pregnant woman from Denmark, who had become ill with malaria after visiting Thailand, gives an indication of the comforting presence of the Risen One to people in despair:

> *On Christmas Eve my temperature soared rapidly again. I was brought to the maternity ward of the hospital, received pain-killers, and came into a room where I was quite alone. The doctors and nurses encouraged me to be brave and not to be afraid. A nurse brought a bowl of red soup, and I ate it. Strange that I could do this. After the operation I was brought back to the room. A young doctor entered and said words to the effect that our child would not live. At these words everything went* black, *totally dark. Beyond time and space. Death. This I did not know. But suddenly He was there. I saw Him coming, but did not know who He was. With His left hand He took hold of my right and filled me with a joy that cannot be described with words; I felt blessedness, peace, joy, thankfulness. Words are unable to describe it.*

A second account by a Norwegian woman relates her experience in hospital after she had had an accident in which her leg became bored through with steel wire. She lay in bed and suffered much pain. She said she felt herself abandoned by God. Then she heard someone coming. A figure drew near:

> *He wore a long white garment, was tall and majestic, with a radiant golden crown on his head. In spite of the kingly appearance and sublime dignity, unending compassion streamed forth from him. He said: "Today you have seen many doctors here, and you know that there is one who calls himself the head physician. You should know, however, that I am the one who is the head physician in this house, and this is my visiting time. When evening comes, when the lights are dimmed and the noise dies down, I make my rounds; for then I have a chance to speak to the hearts of those here. And I say to you: You thirst, I thirsted also; you feel yourself abandoned by God, so it was with me also; you have hard, cold iron in your flesh and blood, so had I also." He did not say more; he turned and disappeared. But I felt such joy that I could have lept out of bed... And I was allowed to feel in my own body something of that which He had suffered for all of us.*

In this appearance the words of Christ from the Cross are called to mind: "I thirst" and "My God, my God, why hast thou foresaken me", as well as the fact of the hands and feet of Christ having been pierced through by nails at the Crucifixion.

Also frequently reported are appearances of Christ during the holy communion such as the following account, by a Swedish woman, of an experience she underwent in 1966 or 1967 in a church in Onsala:

> As the congregation went up to the altar to receive communion, I remained sitting. I thought I would not go alone today, but would wait for another occasion. I sat to the right in the church, one or two rows under the gallery. I believe that another person also sat beside me. As I was sitting and thinking this, I saw a brilliant appearance in the aisle, just in front of the row where I was sitting, approximately the height of a man. To my left I heard a voice which spoke the single word "Christ". It was as if someone was referring to this appearance in order to say who it was. A moment later I heard from this appearance the words: "Whosoever does not eat and drink with me has no part of me." Then the whole disappeared instantaneously. I do not know if this formulation is in the Bible, whether it was spoken by Jesus, but I recall the words exactly. I stood up immediately to go to the altar...

In this appearance the words of Jesus Christ from the sixth chapter of the *Gospel of St. John* are recalled: "Truly, truly, I say to you, unless you eat the flesh of the Son of man and drink his blood, you have no life in you... He who eats my flesh and drinks my blood abides in me, and I in him."

Apart from appearances to the sick and needy, and apart from experiences in connection with the holy communion, several artists report in *They experienced Christ* of their encounters with Christ. One example of this is that of an artist who was painting a picture depicting Christ in the garden of Gethsemane:

> The whole time that I was painting the picture I regretted that I had agreed to sell it. When the painting was finished, I put it in front of the door to my balcony. I sat down on the sofa on the opposite side of the room. Then it seemed to me as if Christ's eyes and also His hands moved. The flowers in the garden began to come alive. They turned into human beings surrounding Christ. Then I saw Christ moving from one side of the painting to the other. O, how he spoke! But I recall only the word "Gethsemane". In a flash of lightning Christ disappeared, clothed in a light blue cloak. In his place sat Mary, clothed with a red cloak, and holding a baby in her arms. She moved and so did the child. A voice spoke, "Christ is born again." Then I saw a flash of lightning and Christ stood there as before. He spoke the whole time; I saw how his lips moved, but now I heard no words. All this repeated itself several times. First it was Christ, then again Mary with the child.

Not all the encounters described in *They experienced Christ* are of a visual nature. Several refer to the experience of the presence of Christ, a strong and unmistakable sensation of His nearness as a silent, comforting, guiding strength. Others describe inner auditory experiences of Christ in which words of help and consolation spoken by Him are received quietly and inwardly. Almost all those who have had this latter kind of experience, as well as others who both saw Him and heard Him, convey their impression of His soft and gentle voice, full of love. Those who have seen Him often describe the power of His loving gaze, His all-penetrating look. And many refer to the radiant light in which He is bathed, such as in the following account:

> *Suddenly the room became indescribably full of light. It became so bright that the eyes hurt. The light radiated out from the middle of the room. An unparalleled radiance came from the lamp on the ceiling and spread forth in all possible kinds of beautiful rays, as if emitted by a star. In the midst of these rays stood Jesus, vibrantly alive, before me.*

As far as it is possible to judge from the selection of reports in *They experienced Christ*, a large proportion of the appearances of Christ took place at night, with midnight often being referred to. One account describes that it was the night of the Full Moon:

> *It was a strange evening, Full Moon, and a tremendous storm. I stood at the window and looked at the clouds chasing across the heavens, and thought of a poem by Hjalmar Gullberg. After I had spoken the poem, someone came into my room. I knew instantly Who it was, and sank upon my knees at the window-sill, and did not dare to turn my head to look at Him. Light and peace radiated from Him, transcending all understanding. I distinctly felt the touch of His hand as He bent towards me and took away my burden – the burden that I am not fit to be His servant. How long I knelt at the window-sill, I do not know. But outside, looking through the window, there appeared out of the dark cross* another Cross, which was bright and reached up to heaven. His voice explained to me the Mystery of the Cross. I did not hear a voice, but the meaning of the Cross became clear to me in a miraculous way. The whole question of sacrifice had been so difficult for me to grasp; now I suddenly understood, so I believe, the profound sense of Christ's deed of sacrifice and its significance for every single human being. A tremendously great perspective opened up. I saw the Cross between heaven and earth as an axis about which everything revolves, the innermost mystery of creation... Divine Love.*

(*She had been looking at the shadow of the cross formed by the wood in the window.)

This account calls to mind that Christ's death on the Cross on Good Friday took place at the time of the Full Moon.

The foregoing descriptions translated from *They experienced Christ* reveal that a number of people have had experiences of Jesus Christ in His second coming, since the onset of this event in the twentieth century. From these descriptions it is evident that Rudolf Steiner's prophecy is confirmed: appearances of the Etheric Christ can take place unexpectedly – anywhere, at any time, to anyone. Who can tell just how many people in our time may have had such experiences? Common to all these appearances is the experience of Him as a comforter, helper, and source of healing strength. This profound, personal experience is unforgettable, a sacred memory, generally signifying not only a breakthrough to the religious dimension of existence but also being accompanied by a great strengthening of the soul and of the life forces. To use Rudolf Steiner's words, this is the "greatest mystery of the twentieth century", betokening the arising of a New Age, an Age of Light.

Some readers, after reading the above descriptions of Christ experiences in the twentieth century, may raise the question as to what distinguishes these spiritual experiences from those of certain saints, e.g. St. Teresa of Avila, who described at length her various encounters with the Risen One.[15] In view of the Christ experiences of St. Teresa and others, already in earlier centuries, is it valid to speak at all of a second coming? And of a Descension of the Risen One from cosmic realms?

Let us recall the words of Jesus Christ to Mary Magdalene in the Garden of the Holy Sepulchre on Easter Sunday morning. In the morning twilight Mary Magdalene at first thought that He was the gardener, but then she recognized Him, beholding that He had risen from the dead. She cast herself down on her knees before Him and stretched out her hands towards His feet. Jesus said: "Do not touch me, for I have not yet ascended to the Father; but go to my brethren and say to them, I am ascending to my Father and your Father, to my God and your God" (*John* xx, 17). Here the Risen One proclaimed that He would ascend to the Father, foretelling His Ascension, which commenced forty days later. But if, at the Ascension, Christ ascended to the Father, how was it possible for St. Teresa of Avila and other saints, in the historical period prior to the Descension, to experience Him?

Through the Mystery of Golgotha, Christ united Himself for all time with the Earth and mankind ("Lo, I am with you always, to the end of time" – *Matthew* xxviii, 20). Since then He has been connected with the Earth. Indeed, it could be said – drawing an analogy with the human being – that through the Mystery of Golgotha the Earth became His body. This can be likened to the physical birth of a new-born child. Yet just as in the unfolding of the life of the human being the birth of the self takes place at the coming of age, approximately twenty-one years after the physical birth, so the Birth of the Self – Jesus Christ – of the Earth is entering into a new phase now, through the second coming, nineteen centuries after the Mystery of Golgotha. The dating of the stages of this development since the Mystery of Golgotha, through the "infancy", "childhood" and "youth" of Christianity – each in 700-year stages – is indicated

IX. The Second Coming and the New Age

in *Hermetic Astrology* I, Appendix II, Figure 25 (see also Figure 26 for the "lightening up" of the Self of Christianity through the second coming, from 1933 onwards). The age of the second coming – extending over 2 500 years from 1933 to 4433 – is the historical period during which the Self of Christianity is coming to birth, analogous in the life of the human being to the Sun-period (21-42) in the course of life. This analogy is discussed at length in *Hermetic Astrology* I, Appendix II.

On the basis of this analogy with the life of a human being, just as the human being is united with his physical body from the moment of birth but the self is only really incarnated from around the age of twenty-one onwards, so Christ has been united with the Earth since the time of the Mystery of Golgotha but it is only now, from 1933 onwards, that He is more "fully" here as the Self of Christianity. Nevertheless, prior to His Descension it was possible for certain people – through grace, and on account of their spiritual striving – to spiritually encounter the Risen One. How may this be understood?

With the Ascension, the Risen One, Jesus Christ, withdrew in His resurrection body to a higher plane of existence (the realm of the Father). From this higher realm His gaze was directed down to mankind and the Earth, beholding the ongoing course of evolution, awaiting the time when He would begin His descent to return "in the same way" as He departed on Ascension Day. A crucial date was 1861, the year of Rudolf Steiner's birth, which – as discussed in *Hermetic Astrology* I, Appendix II – may be thought of as the first "Moon node return" in the history of Christianity. (In the life of the human being this takes place at the age of 18.61 years.) And, as referred to in the foregoing, at a certain point in his biography Rudolf Steiner had an encounter with the Risen One in spiritual realms, at that time on His path of descent towards the Earth. This was possible for Rudolf Steiner on account of the spiritual faculties he had developed along the path of esoteric training. He was able to raise his consciousness beyond the earthly realm to cosmic spheres of existence, where He beheld the Risen One descending from above. It was thus that in 1910 he was able to proclaim the second coming, even to the extent of being able to date the onset of this event to begin one-third of the way through this century.

What made Rudolf Steiner's encounter with Jesus Christ possible was on the one hand his development on the spiritual path and on the other hand the grace of Christ coming to meet him. An earlier Christ experience, which Rudolf Steiner called "the meeting with the Greater Guardian of the threshold", he described in his book *Knowledge of the Higher Worlds and its Attainment,* written in 1904/1905. In this description, however, there is no mention of Christ's descent towards the Earth or of the approaching second coming, and it is quite possible that Rudolf Steiner became aware of this descent only later.

Just as this spiritual encounter with Jesus Christ, described as "the meeting with the Greater Guardian of the threshold", was made possible for Rudolf Steiner at a certain point on his path of spiritual development, so has this experience always been possible to human beings since the Mystery of Golgotha. In the case of St. Teresa of Avila, as well as with others who have had Christ experiences in past centuries, their meetings with Christ were made possible on the one hand through spiritual development and on the other hand through grace. The difference between St. Teresa and Rudolf Steiner – with regard to their encounters with Christ – is that the latter followed a conscious path of spiritual development leading first to the encounter with the Lesser Guardian of the threshold and then to the meeting with Jesus Christ (the Greater Guardian). With the Christian mystics such as St. Teresa, their spiritual path generally led them unconsciously past the Lesser Guardian to the meeting with the Greater Guardian. (Here the reader should refer to Rudolf Steiner's book *Knowledge of the Higher Worlds and its Attainment* for a detailed description of the Lesser and the Greater Guardians and the meetings with them.[16])

Thus, although Christ experiences have always been possible for certain human beings since the Mystery of Golgotha, since 1933 we have entered a historical period in which the encounter with Christ has become more accessible to everyone, as is evident from the accounts presented in the book *They experienced Christ*. It is the historical period of the "coming of age" of Christianity, ushered in as a consequence of the Descension, through which Jesus Christ has drawn into a closer relationship with mankind in the earthly realm. Active preparation for this New Age was undertaken by Rudolf Steiner from 1900 onwards through his teaching the truths of Anthroposophy, and as referred to earlier this may be seen in connection with the vision of St. John, in the twelfth chapter of the *Book of Revelation*, of the "woman clothed with the Sun, with the Moon under her feet, and on her head a crown of twelve stars; she was with child and cried out in her pangs of birth, in anguish for delivery..."

The heavenly woman of St. John's vision is one aspect of Sophia, i.e. the *cosmic* wisdom. It was Sophia who spoke through Solomon, "I, wisdom, dwell in prudence, and I find knowledge and discretion...I love those who love me, and those who seek me diligently find me" (*Proverbs* viii, 12, 17). Through the historical event of Whitsun, Sophia united with the Virgin Mary,[17] and in the post-Christian era it is possible to speak of "Mary Sophia". And just as in the New Age, since 1933, numerous people have had experiences of encounters with Jesus Christ, the Risen One, so many people have also had experiences of "appearances" of Mary Sophia. Indeed, these appearances of Mary Sophia are, alongside the mani-

IX. The Second Coming and the New Age

festations of Jesus Christ, one of the most important phenomena of the New Age. On account of their profound significance, we shall now turn our attention to these appearances. Like the Christ experiences described in this chapter, the appearances of Mary Sophia are usually beheld in the form of a radiant body of light. Hence, they are not manifestations on the physical plane, but are within the Earth's etheric aura, which interpenetrates the physical world. As an example, let us consider an appearance of Mary Sophia to a young woman, Bärbel Ruess, at Marienfried, near Ulm, Germany, on June 25, 1946, when the Blessed Virgin spoke the following words:

I am the mediator of grace. The Father wants the world to acknowledge this role of his servant. Human beings should believe that as the ever-lasting Bride of the Holy Spirit, I am the mediator of all grace... Tell all that I have a new message for the world.

Bärbel described this manifestation of Mary-Sophia further:

After the Mother of God stopped speaking, there appeared a vast choir of Angels around her. I saw innumerable figures in white, as far as the eye could see... They prayed a remarkable prayer, a song of praise to the Father, the Son and the Holy Spirit... The Mother always said "Amen" and prayed quite alone: "Glory be to the Father, the Son, and the Holy Spirit." In so doing, she bowed low. She did the same when the name "Jesus" was spoken out. And so did the figures in white who were present... Afterwards the Mother bestowed her blessings as she had done in May. She spread out her hands for the blessing, and spoke a prayer to the Most Holy Trinity. She prayed for the Church, that her role be acknowledged and that the will of the Father be heeded. She prayed to the Trinity that the Church be blessed through her and be the mediator of peace. From the start the Mother was much more beautiful and more radiant than in May. She was so good and so friendly, though something of great suffering lay in her face. She complained that her children had left her and that on this account she could not lead the way to the Saviour. This was the cause of her great suffering. As the choir of Angels began to pray, she became still more beautiful, quite radiant and light. The threefold crown of rays upon her head was so bright and so great that it covered the entire heaven. As she gave the blessing, she stretched out her hands as does the priest before the transubstantiation, and I saw many rays radiate out from her hands, which went through the figures (around her) and also through us. The rays came from above into her hands. The figures and also we became quite radiant from them. Rays also proceeded from her body and permeated everything around. She became wholly transparent and bathed in a radiant splendour which one cannot begin to describe. She was so beautiful and pure, so light – words cannot de-

scribe it. I was as if blinded. I forgot everything around and knew only one thing: that this was the Mother of Our Saviour. Then my eyes hurt from the radiance. I looked away, and she and all with her – all that was bright and beautiful – disappeared before my eyes.[18]

The appearance at Marienfried, as described above, is a typical example of the numerous manifestations of Mary Sophia in our time. This appearance, which was on the day after St. John's day in 1946, was not the first manifestation at Marienfried. The first took place on the day after the Festival of the Holy Spirit, on Whit-Monday, May 13, 1940, at which time Bärbel Ruess was sixteen years old. It was at the time when the "Nazi beast" was seeking to dominate Europe. The invasion of the Low Countries had begun on May 10, 1940, and the capitulation of the Netherlands took place on May 15. It was at this dark hour in the history of mankind that Mary Sophia appeared at Marienfried and indicated a prayer to be prayed for a person, a community, or a nation. She requested that Bärbel and those with her pray this prayer for the spirit of Germany, by which we may understand it to have been a prayer for the true spirit (Archangel) of Germany to return, after having been driven out by a "counterfeit spirit", that of the Third Reich.[19] In the words of Bishop Dr. Rudolf Graber: "If one only closely examines the revelation at Marienfried, it is an interpretation of the twelfth chapter of the Apocalypse, where the great dragon makes war upon the woman clothed with the Sun, seeking to destroy her and her child."[20]

Here again we find that the twelfth chapter of the Apocalypse is indicated as presenting a key to understanding the spiritual background to events in the twentieth century. The central image is that of Sophia bringing to birth the child "who is to rule all nations" – Jesus Christ in His second coming. Thus, it is not surprising to find in this New Age, appearances of Mary Sophia taking place as well as those of Jesus Christ.

A study of the appearances of Mary Sophia that have been made publicly known reveals that – in their present form – they commenced about hundred years prior to the onset of the second coming. In terms of the vision of St. John, these hundred years represented historically the "time of delivery". ("She was with child and she cried out in her pangs of birth, in anguish for delivery.") The first manifestation of Mary Sophia of this kind was in the year 1830, when (on November 27) she appeared to 24-year-old Catherine Labouré, who was a noviciate in Paris of the Daughters of Charity, founded by St. Vincent de Paul. At this appearance the Blessed Virgin expressed her wish to the young Catherine that a medallion with her image on it – the Virgin Mary and a symbol, surrounded by twelve stars – should be coined and worn as an amulet. With the permission of the Archbishop of Paris, the medallion became produced, and on account of a number of miraculous healings that occurred with people wearing it, it soon became known as the "miraculous medallion" or the "miracle-working medallion".

The appearance in 1858 of the Blessed Virgin to 14-year-old Bernadette Soubirous at Lourdes in the Pyrenees, southern France, is perhaps the most well-known of all the manifestations of Mary Sophia. During five months, from February 11 to July 16, the Virgin Mary appeared to Bernadette eighteen times in a grotto known as Massabielle. At the appearance on February 25, the Blessed Virgin instructed Bernadette to make known that the waters of a fountain in the grotto would possess miraculous healing powers. She pointed to the ground to indicate the spot where the fountain would arise, and as Bernadette scraped away some earth, crystal-clear water began to issue forth from this spot. The flow of water increased from day to day, becoming a fountain. Shortly thereafter a blind man washed his eyes with the water and his sight was restored to him. Other miraculous healings followed. Soon the name Lourdes became known far and wide on account of the healing power of the water.

The appearance of Mary Sophia at Lourdes reveals something of the special relationship between the Blessed Virgin and Mother Earth, as indicated also in the vision of St. John ("the Earth came to the help of the woman" – *Revelation* xii, 16). In earlier times the Earth and Nature were revered as the *Great Mother*, for example, as Demeter in the Mysteries of Eleusis in ancient Greece. There the myth of the descent of the Cosmic Virgin, Persephone, the daughter of Demeter, was celebrated. Similarly, in our time something of the mysterious relationship between Mary Sophia and Mother Earth is becoming revealed, a relationship analogous to that between Persephone and Demeter, of the nature of a mother-daughter relationship. This is something of deep significance; for, as discussed in the next chapter, the second coming is not taking place solely for the sake of mankind but also for Nature and Mother Earth. The widespread awakening to Nature and the Earth as a living being, taking place at the present time, is a sign of a fundamental difference between the second coming and the coming of Christ two thousand years ago. Whereas at the first coming Christ came in the name of the Father and opened up the path to the Kingdom of the Father ("No one comes to the Father, but by me" – *John* xiv, 6), with the second coming Christ is awakening (or re-awakening) a consciousness of the Mysteries of the Mother, that have been dormant since the days of ancient Greece. And Mary Sophia, through her deep relationship with Mother Earth, has a special role to play in this re-awakening of a consciousness for Mother Earth, alongside her role as a "mediator of grace" who intercedes on behalf of human beings on Earth.

Another much publicized revelation of Mary is that which occurred in the little village of Fatima in the valley Cova da Iria, Portugal, in 1917. Here Mary appeared six times on the thirteenth day of each month, from

May 13 to October 13, 1917, to three young shepherd children: Jacinta, Francesco and Lucia. At the third appearance, on July 13, the children received a vision of the opening of the gates of hell. Mary spoke of the war drawing to a close, but prophesied that if mankind would continue to "insult God", a second, much worse war would begin. In addition to this prophecy concerning World War II, Mary requested the consecration of Russia to her Immaculate Heart. "If my wish is heard, Russia will amend her ways and there will be peace. If not, she will spread her false teaching throughout the world, bringing about wars and the persecution of the Church. The good will be martyred; the Holy Father will suffer greatly; and various nations will be destroyed." Just three months later in St. Petersburg, the Bolshevik revolution began. On October 25 Lenin is reported to have expressed to his inner circle his deeper intention concerning the revolution. "With the revolution I don't have my eye only on Russia. I spit on Russia. Russia is simply a stage of transition to taking up the world revolution, to rulership over the whole world...I prefer a millionaire or a capitalist who denies God to a peasant or a worker who believes in God... From now on we shall be merciless and destroy the existing order, in order to build our temple upon these ruins."[21] Further, Lenin described himself as a "personal enemy of God". Seen in the light of the revelation in Fatima, the Bolshevik revolution was a rebellion, led by Lenin, of man against God. In the meantime, the Virgin Mary's predictions at Fatima have been fulfilled in many ways, and it is believed by some that the assassination attempt on Pope John Paul II, which took place on "Fatima day", May 13, 1981, was also connected with the prediction in 1917 that "the Holy Father will suffer greatly".[22]

At the present time a revelation of Mary is taking place in Medjugorje, Yugoslavia. This revelation began on June 24, 1981, when Mary appeared to six young people and identified herself with the words: "I am the Queen of Peace." Since then the revelation has been continuing with regular appearances, during the course of which the Virgin Mary has revealed ten mysteries concerning the future (not yet made known publicly). Several million people have since visited Medjugorje. At the first of these appearances, on St. John's day in 1981, Mary spoke the words: "On account of its conflicts, the world is taking a path towards destruction. It needs peace, if it is to be saved. Yet peace can be found only through finding God. Those who find God will discover in their hearts a sense of joy through which peace arises." The central message of the Virgin Mary at Medjugorje is that a renewal of the religious life – a new turning towards God – is necessary, to be attained above all through prayer.

From indications made by Rudolf Steiner it is evident that Sophia ("Wisdom"), who spoke to the people of Israel through Solomon, was worshipped by the ancient Egyptians as Isis. He indicated that with the

IX. The Second Coming and the New Age

decline of the ancient Egyptian culture the cosmic wisdom, Isis-Sophia, became "buried" or "killed", but that now in our time she may be found again. She may be sought in cosmic realms as the Cosmic Virgin, and if she is found there, she communicates to us a new wisdom of the stars – Astro-Sophia. But in the New Age, the age of the second coming, Mary Sophia may be sought also here on Earth, manifesting from within the Earth's etheric aura. She may reveal herself to human beings not only in churches and cathedrals, such as the great cathedral at Chartres, but also in the stillness of Nature, in harmonious union with Mother Earth. She manifests herself as the bearer of peace into our troubled civilization. And, as Rudolf Steiner describes, it is with the help of Mary Sophia that the Risen One is able to appear in spiritual form in our time.

It is not on account of something happening by itself from without that Christ will be able to appear again in His spiritual form in the course of the twentieth century, but rather through human beings finding the force represented by the Holy Sophia. The tendency in recent times has been to lose precisely this Isis force, this Mary force, which has become stamped out through that which has arisen within the modern consciousness of humanity. And the more recent Confessions have partly obliterated a perspective concerning Mary. To a certain extent this is the mystery of modern mankind, that basically Mary-Isis has been killed, and that she must be sought again, sought in the widespread heavenly realms with the power which Christ is able to kindle within us when we devote ourselves to Him in the right way.[23]

Hermetic astrology may be taken up as a seed impulse towards the development of a new wisdom of the stars (Astro-Sophia = "star wisdom"), in which case it can be regarded as being placed in the service of Sophia, who comes to meet inwardly each human being striving to bring Christ to birth within himself. Christ and Sophia are central to the arising of a new star wisdom, and the New Age provides a unique opportunity for each human being to find a new relationship with these Divine Beings. In the next chapter some indications are given as to how a deeper relationship with Christ and Sophia may be enhanced through following the lunar rhythm with the help of the hermetic calendar and with the help of two meditations: the *Sanctification of the New Moon* and the *Sanctification of the Full Moon*.

Chapter 9: Notes and references

1. Rudolf Steiner, *Die tieferen Geheimnisse des Menschheitswerdens im Lichte der Evangelien* (GA 117; Rudolf Steiner Verlag, Dornach, Switzerland, 1966), p. 206.
2. Robert Powell, "The Grail and the Stars", *Shoreline* i (1988), pp. 34-40. *Shoreline* is available from: 1 Tanrhiw, Penmorfa, Porthmadog, Gwynedd, Wales/Britain.
3. Rudolf Steiner, *The Spiritual Hierarchies* (trsl. R. M. Querido, Anthroposophic Press, New York, 1970), lecture 8.
4. Rudolf Steiner, *Occult Science* (trsl. G. and M. Adams, Rudolf Steiner Press, London, 1972), pp. 129ff.
5. Rudolf Steiner, *An Autobiography* (trsl. R. Stebbing, Rudolf Steiner Publications, New York, 1977), p. 319.
6. Rudolf Steiner, *The Mission of Individual Folk Souls* (trsl. A. H. Parker, Rudolf Steiner Press, London, 1970), pp. 173-174.
7. Rudolf Steiner, *Man and the World of Stars* (trsl. D. S. Osmond, Anthroposophic Press, New York, 1963).
8. "They want to see and hear everything and to be present at everything, but they do not awaken. So they have to be awakened through catastrophes and personal suffering. Here it is not a matter of destiny, but purely the lack of wakefulness of the members..." Reported by Count Ludwig Polzer-Hoditz from a conversation with Rudolf Steiner on January 1, 1923; German text printed on p. 73 of the February 26, 1989 issue of the *Goetheanum* 68 (1989), No. 9.
9. Rudolf Steiner, *The True Nature of the Second Coming* (trsl. D. S. Osmond, Rudolf Steiner Press, London, 1971), pp. 49ff.
10. Cf. Robert Powell, op. cit., for a description of the Descension and of the significance of the further dates of ingress of heliocentric Jupiter into sidereal Leo during the twentieth century.
11. Cf. Robert Powell, "Mary Sophia and the New Age", *Shoreline* ii (1989), pp. 16-36, for an account of the counterfeit impulse that was active in the Third Reich.
12. David Spangler, *Revelation: The Birth of a New Age* (Findhorn Publications, Scotland, 1974), pp. 34ff.
13. Rudolf Steiner, *The Inner Aspect of the Social Question* (trsl. C. Davy, Rudolf Steiner Press, London, 1974), pp. 40-41.
14. Cf. Robert Powell, "Reflections on the Second Coming", *Shoreline* ii (1989), pp. 40-45.
15. *The Life of St. Teresa* (trsl. J. M. Cohen, Penguin, 1958), Chapter 27.
16. Rudolf Steiner, *Knowledge of the Higher Worlds and its Attainment* (trsl. D. S. Osmond & C. Davy, Rudolf Steiner Press, London, 1977), Chapters 10 and 11.
17. Cf. Valentin Tomberg, *Anthroposophical Studies of the New Testament* (trsl. R. H. Bruce, Candeur Manuscripts, New York, 1981), Chapter 12.
18. Josef Künzli, *Die Erscheinung in Marienfried* (Miriam Verlag, Jestetten, Germany, 1976), pp. 27, 33-34.
19. See footnote 11.
20. Josef Künzli, op. cit., p. 2.
21. Antonio Signoretti, *Morire a Mosca* (Milan, 1967), p. 54.

22. Vendelin Slugenov, *The Drama of St. Peter's Square on May 13, 1981 in the Light of Fatima* (Pro Fratribus, Rome-Coblenz, 1982).
23. Rudolf Steiner, *The Search for the New Isis, the Divine Sophia* (GA 202; Rudolf Steiner Verlag, Dornach, Switzerland, 1980), lecture of December 24, 1920.

Chapter 10

The Hermetic Calendar

The cosmic self and the earthly self

Hermetic astrology may be considered – at least in part – as a resurrection of the ancient Egyptian mystery wisdom of the stars. Belonging to this, the hermetic calendar may be followed as a means for entering into a new relationship with the Being of Christ and with the Being of Sophia. This is a calendar which enables a meditative approach towards experiencing the activity of Christ and Sophia during the course of the year. For, through the hermetic calendar, the times of the year at which Christ and Sophia draw especially near to the human being may be followed. At the same time, following the hermetic calendar through the course of the year can help to awaken a new consciousness of the cosmic forces active in nature.

The hermetic calendar is an aid in the main task of hermetic astrology: that of developing a new wisdom of the stars (*astrosophy* – "star wisdom"). It opens up a pathway towards Christ and Sophia, towards a Christian experience of the personified wisdom of the cosmos (Sophia). Out of this experience a new, Christian wisdom of the stars can arise. This pathway to *Astro-Sophia* has become possible in the twentieth century through the second coming of Christ, through whom the human being may become inwardly raised up to an inner union with the cosmos. But at the same time, this mystical elevation of the human being towards his cosmic self – bringing with it an experience of himself as a cosmic being – can be balanced by his finding a new relationship to the realm of nature, towards the world in which the earthly self is at home, where man experiences himself as a being on the Earth, surrounded by the kingdoms of nature.

The task of modern man – at the same time as bringing the cosmic self more strongly to consciousness – is to establish a new relationship between the cosmic self and the earthly self. And it is precisely this that is made possible through the most important event of this century: the onset of the second coming of Jesus Christ. If the human being were to live with his consciousness directed solely towards his earthly surroundings, he would be in danger of becoming one-sided and forgetting his higher, cosmic self. On the other hand, if he were to take refuge from the Earth and its problems by directing his consciousness solely towards the cosmos, he would again become one-sided and, correspondingly, his earthly self, and his effectiveness in accomplishing tasks on Earth, would become weaker and weaker. However, the Christ Impulse enables a harmonious working together of the cosmic and earthly selves. How is this to be understood?

The Christ Impulse stemming from the first coming, through the death and resurrection of Jesus Christ, has worked on the one hand to streng-

Figure 21
The cosmic self and the earthly self

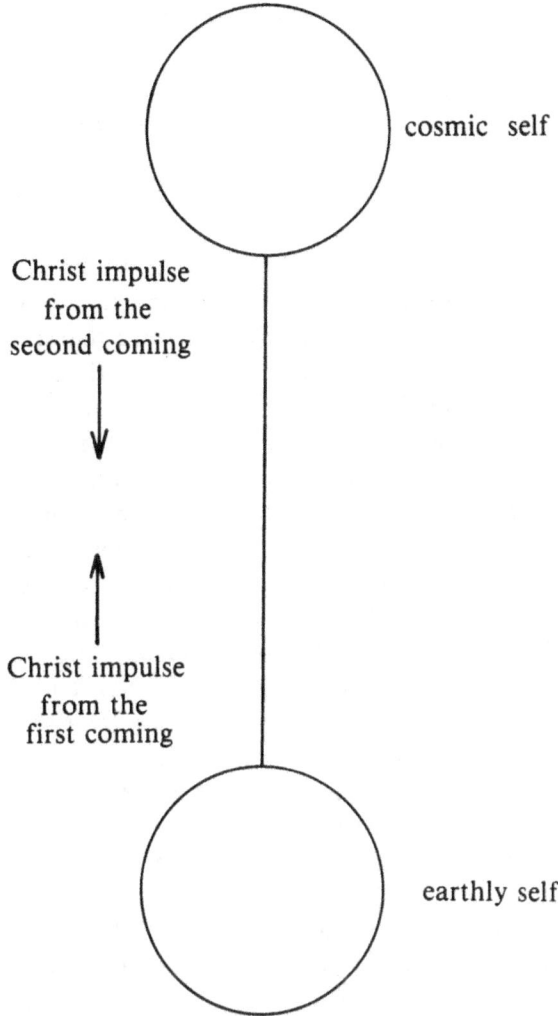

then the earthly self of man, and on the other hand to direct the human being's consciousness towards his higher self, belonging to the kingdom of heaven. The central message of Christianity, that the God-Man (Jesus Christ) lived on Earth for three years and then sacrificed himself for mankind, has directed man's consciousness towards earthly reality, which has become hallowed through the Incarnation and the earthly life of Christ. But, through his death and resurrection, Christ pointed the way to the overcoming of the forces that bind man to earthly life, pointing to the kingdom of heaven, the existence beyond death. Thus the first coming brought divine reality to the earthly self, and implanted a seed impulse in the earthly self to seek the immortal, higher self.

However, with the Christ Impulse stemming from the second coming the situation is different. Through the second coming Christ is bringing divine reality to the cosmic self, whilst at the same time awakening the earthly self to the spiritual side of nature. The emergence of hermetic astrology in the twentieth century, and of the hermetic chart, which is a "map" of the cosmic self, can thus be seen in connection with the second coming of Christ and the corresponding endowment of the cosmic self with divine reality.

The full reality of the Christ Impulse — as it may at present be experienced by man on the Earth — is to be found in the meeting of the two Christ Impulses: stemming from the first and the second coming. This may be sought on the one hand by uniting with the living tradition of Christianity, extending back to the first coming, and on the other hand by uniting with the cosmic activity of Jesus Christ, the Risen One — for example, as it comes to expression in the course of the year in relation to cosmic rhythms. The Christ Impulse then works harmonizingly between the cosmic and earthly selves, which may be represented schematically as two selves ("I's") one above the other, joined by an axis (see Figure 21).[1]

The Christ Impulse works to harmonize the cosmic self, centered in the Sun, with the earthly personality — bound up with man's experience of himself on Earth. It is along the axis joining the cosmic and the earthly selves that the Christ Impulse works, focusing the two "I's", so that man does not become one-sided (in one direction or the other). With the second coming it is especially the sphere of the Moon — between the Earth and the sphere of the Sun — where the center of gravity of the Christ Impulse is located. In fact, since the onset of the second coming, both Christ and Sophia are active in the sphere of the Moon: Christ as the harmonizer of the relationship between the cosmic and earthly selves, and Sophia, the Cosmic Virgin, as the bearer of harmony itself into the human soul and as the mediator of the Holy Spirit to mankind. How is it possible to enter into a relationship with the cosmic activity of Christ and Sophia?

Living with cosmic rhythms

A first step is to begin to observe cosmic events, to follow the movements of the planets — from day to day, month to month, year to year. Thus, with the help of the *American Sidereal Ephemeris*,[2] the daily movements of the planets through the sidereal signs of the zodiac may be followed; here it is the geocentric perspective — the perspective of the earthly self — that comes to expression. The planetary movements according to the perspective of the cosmic self, which — in so far as the human being continues to incarnate upon the Earth — is conveyed by the Egyptian-Tychonic system un-

X. The Hermetic Calendar

derlying the hermetic chart, can be followed with the help of the *American Heliocentric Ephemeris*,[3] where the planetary longitudes have to be converted by subtracting about 24½ degrees (= the amount of precession in 1983) in order to arrive at their longitudes in the sidereal zodiac. (The Egyptian-Tychonic system is essentially equivalent to the heliocentric system, except that it is the zodiacal location of the Sun in the Egyptian-Tychonic system – and not that of the Earth – which is of interest. But since the zodiacal location of the Sun is always diametrically opposite that of the Earth, the Sun's zodiacal location can be read from the heliocentric ephemeris by taking it to be exactly opposite that of the Earth.) Hence, these two ephemerides enable the planetary movements to be followed from day to day – following them simultaneously from the perspective of the cosmic self and from that of the earthly self.

A second step on the path towards *Astro-Sophia* is to participate meditatively in cosmic events – endeavouring to discern their moral significance. A striking historical example of this is provided by the three magi from the East. After beholding the conjunction of Jupiter and Saturn in the middle of the sidereal sign of Pisces in the year 7 B.C., they realised through meditative-spiritual insight the significance of this conjunction: that it heralded the birth of a high spiritual individuality.[4] Acting out of this insight, they undertook the journey to greet him and bestow their blessings on his earthly mission. (Recognizing the significance of cosmic events does not necessarily entail undertaking external action; often the challenge presented by a cosmic event is the development of some moral-spiritual quality, or the finding of the right moral standpoint to meet a given situation.) To be able to arrive at a level of contact with cosmic events so as to be able to comprehend their significance – as exemplified by the magi – entails a living into the events taking place in the cosmos. How is this possible? How can consciousness become raised "above"? And how may it come to recognize the significance of events "above" for mankind here on Earth "below"? (The Lord's prayer is relevant here: "Thy will be done on Earth, as it is in heaven," i.e. there should be a correspondence between heavenly events and events here on Earth, whereby the latter – ideally – should be a fulfilment of divine will.)

A start can be made towards the development of consciousness of macrocosmic events by following certain cosmic rhythms, and the simplest – the one fundamental to the hermetic calendar – is the monthly rhythm of New Moon and Full Moon. The rhythm of the Moon – from New Moon to Full Moon, and from Full Moon to New Moon – forms the basis of the hermetic calendar. It was this very rhythm, also, that played such an important role in the cultures of ancient Egypt and Babylon, and also Israel. Out of an understanding of the significance of this rhythm for the ancient Egyptians, something of its meaning for man in the twentieth century – at this time of the second coming – can be grasped. It is the hermetic principle of analogy that may be applied here: "That which was, is as that which shall be." That which was a living reality for the ancient Egyptians may become – through the second coming – an inner experience for man in the twentieth century, albeit in metamorphosed form (metamorphosed from the days of ancient Egypt).

Isis and Osiris

In ancient Egypt the priests of Hermes taught that Osiris and Isis were active from the sphere of the Moon, and that the activity of Osiris reached a high-point at Full-Moon, whilst that of Isis attained a culmination at New Moon. Osiris was therefore worshipped during the waxing phase of the Moon, culminating with the Full Moon. Here the Moon was seen to pass through fourteen stages, i.e. the fourteen phases during the fourteen days from New Moon to Full Moon. The first appearance of the New Moon on the western horizon at sunset – at the start of the lunar month – was greeted as the re-emergence of Osiris from the underworld, or from the Nile, into which his dismembered body had been cast by his evil brother Seth. Each day after the reappearance of the new crescent, the growth of the waxing Moon from day to day was seen as a rememberment of Osiris, to become whole at the Full Moon. The Full Moon was therefore worshipped as the holy day of Osiris, and especially the rising of the Full Moon on the eastern horizon was celebrated as a most sacred event.

But following this event the day of Full Moon was also experienced as the day of death of Osiris, the day on which – through the jealousy of Seth – he became slain. In the days following the Full Moon there then took place the gradual dismemberment of Osiris. Each day, through the fourteen days of the waning Moon, part of Osiris became dismembered and cast into the Nile – much to the sorrow of Isis, who was associated with the eastern horizon towards which the waning sickle of the Moon made its approach, drawing closer each day towards the end of the lunar month. Finally, the disappearance of the thin crescent Moon at the end of the month into the arms of Isis (on the eastern horizon) signified the climax of Isis' search for the dismembered parts of the body of Osiris, and the reappearance of the waxing sickle on the western horizon at the start of the next lunar month signified the rebirth of Osiris and the start of his gradual rememberment, to become whole again at Full Moon. Just as the waxing phase of the Moon, from New Moon to Full Moon, was associated with Osiris, so the waning phase of the Moon was seen in connection with Isis, who had to look on whilst the body of Osiris became dismembered, but who noted where each dismembered organ became cast into the Nile, in order that she could re-assemble Osiris again, starting at the New Moon.[5]

The rhythmic alternation of the Osiris and Isis phases of the month permeated the whole Egyptian culture with a deeply religious mood of reverence, whereby everyone participated in the cosmic drama of Osiris and Isis each month. Through this hermetic teaching, which reflected a cosmic reality, the Egyptians had a deep connection with the phases of the Moon, celebrating especially the sacred festivals of Full Moon, dedicated to Osiris, and New Moon (disappearance of the Moon), dedicated to Isis. This was an important aspect of the star wisdom of ancient Egypt, which continued to be cultivated until the time came when the Being of Osiris could no longer be experienced in the sphere of the Moon. For the Being whom the Egyptians knew as Osiris is the same as the Being who is known as Christ.

The Incarnation of Christ

Christ, in his gradual approach towards incarnation upon the Earth, dwelt for a time in the Moon sphere – analogous to the time spent in the Moon sphere by the human being during the embryonic period of development prior to incarnation upon the Earth. But whereas the human being spends approximately nine months in the Moon sphere, the Cosmic Being of Christ – known to the Egyptians as Osiris – indwelt the Moon sphere over a considerable period of pre-Christian history (starting in 3102 B.C., the beginning of Kali Yuga, the Dark Age). And prior to this, the Being of Christ had indwelt the sphere of the Sun, where – according to the teaching of the Persian initiate Zarathustra – Christ was worshipped under the name of Ormuzd or Ahura Mazdao.

Thus the initiates of antiquity followed the gradual approach of Christ descending from the cosmos towards the Earth: Zarathustra, in Persia, beholding him in the sphere of the Sun; and Hermes, in Egypt, beholding him in the sphere of the Moon. They beheld the gradual birth – through incarnation – of the Christ Being out of the Cosmic Soul, whom the Egyptians called Isis. (The relationship of Isis, the Cosmic Soul, to Nût, the World Soul, was as daughter to mother. Astrologically this corresponds to the relationship between the planets Venus and Neptune. For, in terms of astrological qualities, Nût = Night is related in Chapter 8 to the planet Neptune, and the Egyptians thought of Venus as the "star of Isis".)

In the pre-Christian era the Christ Being descended gradually from cosmic realms towards the Earth. Prior to Kali Yuga, which started in 3102 B.C., Christ was beheld in the sphere of the Sun (e.g. as Ahura Mazdao in the teaching of the Persian initiate Zarathustra). Later he was beheld in the sphere of the Moon, and was worshipped in connection with the phases of the Moon (e.g. as Osiris in the teaching of the Egyptian initiate Hermes). Then came a time when Christ (Osiris) could no longer be found in the sphere of the Moon – as the Christ Being approached his "birth" on the Earth, through the Baptism in the Jordan, whereby the incarnation and union of Christ with Jesus took place. The cult of Isis and Osiris, and the celebration of their festivals at New and Full Moon, consequently died out. In place of the cosmic image of the birth of Osiris (or the rememberment of Osiris) out of the Cosmic Soul (Isis), mankind now has the image of the birth of the Messiah from the Virgin Mary. And in place of the slaying of Osiris by Seth, mankind has the image of the Crucifixion. The images of the Crucifixion and of the Virgin and Child have come to replace the images concerning Isis and Osiris that lived in the souls of the ancient Egyptians.

With the beginning of the twentieth century the Dark Age (Kali Yuga) came to an end. Already in the year 1900, the dawn of a New Age – the age of the second coming – began. The period between 1900 and 1933 was the dawn of the New Age (known in the East as the Satya Yuga = the "Age of Light"), following on from Kali Yuga (the Dark Age), where 1900 corresponds to "dawn" and 1933 to "sunrise", when the Risen One began to ascend across the horizon of mankind's consciousness. In this New Age – the age of the second coming – the activity of the Risen One is again to be found in relation to the Moon, this time mirroring the period during pre-Christian history when Christ was worshipped in the sphere of the Moon as Osiris. And again the Risen One is born out of the Cosmic Soul (Isis = Sophia).

The New Age, the age of the second coming – mirroring the period of pre-Christian history when Christ was worshipped in the sphere of the Moon as Osiris – will last about 2500 years, until A.D. 4443, when a conjunction between Jupiter and Saturn will take place at the end of the sidereal sign of Pisces. This time more or less coincides with the end of the Age of Aquarius, i.e. with the passage of the vernal point from Aquarius into Capricorn in A.D. 4535 (see *Hermetic Astrology* I, Chapter 3). Thus the age of the second coming extends over the last fifth of the Age of Pisces and through virtually the whole of the Age of Aquarius. Then a new Christ Revelation will begin, mirroring the Persian period of ancient history prior to the start of Kali Yuga in 3102 B.C., when Christ was worshipped as Ormuzd (Ahura Mazdao) in the Sun sphere. This new Christ Revelation – to be heralded by the incarnation of the Maitreya Buddha at the end of the Age of Aquarius/start of the Age of Capricorn – will be a time in which Christ will work directly from the Sun sphere. As referred to in *Hermetic Astrology* I, Appendix II, just as the present Christ Revelation (second coming) is a working from the sphere of the Moon into the Earth's etheric aura bounded by the Moon's orbit, so the next Revelation of Christ will be a working from the sphere of the Sun into the Earth's astral aura bounded by the orbit of the Sun. The present Christ Revelation – from the Moon sphere – was proclaimed in the words: "Then they will see the Son of man coming in the clouds with great power and glory" (*Mark* xiii, 26). In contrast, an intimation of the future Christ Revelation – directly from the Sun sphere – is indicated by the words: "As the lightning comes from the east and shines as far as the west, so will be the coming of the Son of man" (*Matthew* xxiv, 27). This future Christ Revelation will reflect the pre-Christian epoch (prior to 3102 B.C.) when Christ was worshipped in Persia as Ahura Mazdao, the "Aura of the Sun". On the other hand, the present Revelation of Christ, during the age of the second coming, reflects the pre-Christian period (after 3102 B.C.) when Christ was worshipped in Egypt as Osiris, in connection with the phases of the Moon.

A new experience of the lunar phases

Through the second coming of Christ, mankind in the twentieth century can acquire a new relationship to the phases of the Moon; and the hermetic calendar is a means of helping this new relationship to develop. The hermetic calendar represents a metamorphosis of the hermetic teaching of the priests of ancient Egypt, who taught that the Full Moon is sacred to Osiris and the New Moon is sacred to Isis. In the hermetic calendar the Full Moon is sacred to Christ and the New Moon is sacred to Sophia. For through the second coming the activity of Christ in relation to mankind and the Earth is strongest at Full Moon, whilst the Sophia Impulse is most powerful at New Moon. Christ and Sophia are both active during the whole cycle of the lunar month, but their holy mysteries can be experienced anew each month most especially at the times of New Moon and Full Moon: the Sophia mystery at New Moon, and the Christ mystery at Full Moon.

However, there is a metamorphosis from the Osiris-Isis mysteries of ancient Egypt to the Christ-Sophia mysteries of the age of the second coming. The Egyptians experienced the activity of Osiris and Isis as coming from without, proceeding from the visible phases of the Moon. In contrast, modern man experiences the activity of Christ and Sophia in his inner being during the course of each lunar month.

The Cosmic Soul (Sophia), from whom the Risen One is reborn, is experienced most strongly in the human soul at the time of the New Moon, whilst the Risen One is experienced in the inner being of man most intensively at Full Moon. These two experiences each reflect a cosmic mystery, taking shape inwardly in the form of two archetypal images. The cosmic mystery that takes place each month at the time of Full Moon is analogous to the Mystery of Golgotha, and the image which brings this to expression in the inner being of man is that of the Crucifixion. At New Moon, the cosmic mystery of the Sophia Being comes to expression inwardly in the form of the image beheld by John, described in the twelfth chapter of the *Book of Revelation*: "A woman clothed with the Sun, with the

Moon under her feet, and on her head a crown of twelve stars" (*Revelation* xii, 1). John goes on to describe the birth of the Risen One from the Cosmic Soul (Sophia): "She was with child and she cried out in her pangs of birth, in anguish for delivery... She brought forth a male child, one who is to rule all the nations with a rod of iron" (*Revelation* xii, 2, 5). Let us now consider these two archetypal images more closely.

Firstly, the Christ mystery: How is this connected with the phases of the Moon? The waning and waxing of the Moon correspond to the ebb and flow of life forces in the aura of the Earth. This aura extends from the Earth to the sphere of the Moon, i.e. it reaches as far as the orbit of the Moon around the Earth. It is within this sphere that the Risen One, since the year 1933, is active. In contrast to the first coming, where Christ came in a physical form, the second coming of Jesus Christ is in a non-physical (etheric, or life) form. In this form he has been referred to as *Jesus of the Light*.[6] Correspondingly, the plane of activity of Jesus Christ in his second coming is not the physical world, as it was at the first coming, but the etheric (life) realm bordering onto the physical. This is the realm in which the hidden forces of nature are active: the forces of growth and decay in the plant kingdom are etheric forces, which "wax" and "wane" during the course of the year and of the month. It is in this sphere – membered into this sphere – that the Being of Jesus Christ is to be found, since the onset of the second coming, indwelling this sphere in an etheric form, in which he appears in the form of radiant light (hence the name *Jesus of the Light*). The world of nature is receiving his blessing. And through living into the cycle of nature during the course of the year, the human being may enter into – through Jesus Christ – a new relationship with the world of nature. How this may be helped by way of the hermetic calendar will be discussed later in this chapter.

The beatitudes

The mystery of the second coming of Christ is at the same time the mystery of the Comforter (*Paraclete*, in Greek). In the age of the second coming the Greater Guardian of the Threshold – Jesus Christ – is sending the Comforter, the Holy Spirit, to bestow blessings upon mankind. The blessings of Christ at his first coming were spoken at the Sermon on the Mount, where Jesus Christ pronounced nine blessings (beatitudes) upon man (*Matthew* v, 3–12). The passages in the Sermon on the Mount immediately following the beatitudes also contain implicit blessings. In all, three additional blessings can be discerned, which can be formulated approximately as follows:

> "Blessed are those who serve through morally awakened will, for they shall be the salt of the Earth" (cf. *Matthew* v, 13).

"Blessed are those who do good works and give glory to the Father, for they shall be the light of the world" (cf. *Matthew* v, 14–16).

"Blessed are those who keep the commandments, for they shall partake of the tree of life" – this last blessing is from the *Book of Revelation* (xxii, 14) but is in harmony with the reference in *Matthew* v, 17 to "fulfilling the law" (i.e. "keeping the commandments").

The nine beatitudes in the *Gospel of St. Matthew* together with the above three additional blessings yield a total of twelve beatitudes, which can be placed in correspondence with the twelve signs of the zodiac as follows:

Aries:	Blessed are the seekers of the spirit, for theirs is the kingdom of heaven.
Taurus:	Blessed are those who bear suffering, for they shall be comforted.
Gemini:	Blessed are the meek, for they shall inherit the Earth.
Cancer:	Blessed are those who hunger and thirst after righteousness, for they shall be filled.
Leo:	Blessed are the merciful, for they shall receive mercy.
Virgo:	Blessed are the pure in heart, for they shall see God.
Libra:	Blessed are the peacemakers, for they shall be called sons of God.
Scorpio:	Blessed are those who are persecuted for righteousness' sake, for theirs is the kingdom of heaven.
Sagittarius:	Blessed are ye when men revile you and persecute you and utter all kinds of evil against you falsely on my account, rejoice and be glad, for great is your reward in heaven.
Capricorn:	Blessed are those who serve through morally awakened will, for they shall be the salt of the Earth.
Aquarius:	Blessed are those who do good works and give glory to the Father, for they shall be the light of the world.
Pisces:	Blessed are those who keep the commandments, for they shall partake of the tree of life.

Each beatitude relates to a sign of the zodiac and speaks of the reward promised by Christ to those who develop the spiritual quality (virtue) associated with the zodiacal sign in question. For example, the virtue of Leo is the heart quality of *compassion* (the quality of mercy), and those who become compassionate will also receive compassion. Similarly, the virtue of Virgo is *purity* ("pure of heart"), and those who develop this virtue will behold the spirit ("see God"). Further, the morally awakened will (Capricorn) is the virtue of *courage*, which can act in a redeeming way for the

Earth ("salt of the Earth"). And the highest commandment is "Love thy neighbour", so that the "keeping of the commandments" (Pisces) amounts – on the highest level – to the virtue of *love,* the reward for the development of which is the tree of life.

The blessings (beatitudes) spoken by Christ at the Sermon on the Mount may be held in consciousness in connection with the twelve signs of the zodiac. They acquire a special significance each lunar month at the time of the Christ mystery, at Full Moon. For example, when the Full Moon appears in the sidereal sign of Aries, it is the blessing of the first beatitude which may be brought to consciousness: "Blessed are the seekers of the spirit, for theirs is the kingdom of heaven." Or when the Moon becomes full in the sign of Libra, then the seventh beatitude can be thought of as a power of blessing: "Blessed are the peacemakers, for theirs is the kingdom of heaven." Thus each Full Moon provides an opportunity to draw inwardly into a relationship with the Being of Christ, to open oneself to receive the power of the blessing from the sign of the zodiac in which the Moon becomes full. Mindfulness of the beatitudes spoken at the Sermon on the Mount – meditated upon in connection with the twelve signs of the zodiac – can help to awaken a new awareness of the Christ mystery at Full Moon. No less significant, however, is the experience of the Sophia mystery at New Moon, which is the counterpart to the Full Moon mystery.

The speaking out of the beatitudes by Jesus Christ at the Sermon on the Mount was the historical archetype preceding the sending of the Comforter. The Comforter, the Holy Spirit, was sent to the apostles on Whit Sunday via the mediation of the Sophia Being, through the union of Sophia with the Virgin Mary. Now, in the age of the second coming, the Comforter is being sent – again via the mediation of Sophia – upon the whole of mankind. This is an aspect of the Sophia mystery, which is the counterpart to the Christ mystery in each lunar month (where the Sophia mystery can be brought to consciousness especially at New Moon and the Christ mystery at Full Moon). Through the Sophia mystery again a mediation is found for the blessings spoken by Jesus Christ in the age of the second coming – blessings which the Comforter is to bestow on human beings through the development of certain virtues. These blessings can be brought to awareness especially at the time of the culmination of the Sophia mystery, at New Moon.

The virtues

In all, twelve virtues are to be developed – corresponding to the twelve signs of the zodiac. These virtues are mentioned in Chapter 7, in connection with following the passage of the Moon through the zodiacal signs considered as "houses", i.e. transposed from the embryonic period as

7-month lunar zodiacal periods lived through in the unfolding of the spiral of life. Every seven years the human being lives through twelve 7-month periods or "houses" corresponding to the twelve signs of the zodiac. The houses are spheres of destiny, relating to the level of the will. As described in Chapter 7, they can be raised to consciousness on the modern path of hermetic astrology. As a metamorphosis of the twelve labours of Hercules, the human being can bring to consciousness the relevant "zodiacal trial" connected with each 7-month period. Thus each 7-month period – comprising the experience of a particular sphere of destiny (house) – entails the mastery by the self of a certain aspect of the will that comes to the fore in the given period. The mastery of the relevant aspect of the will is attained by way of the practice of the virtue belonging to the zodiacal sign relating to the house in question. The practice of the virtues of the twelve zodiacal signs during the twelve 7-month lunar zodiacal periods in each 7-year period of the spiral of life takes place on the level of the will.

This practice is carried over to the level of the heart, corresponding to the Sun, when the virtues are practised during the Sun's passage through the twelve sidereal signs in the course of one year, i.e. the virtue of each sign of the zodiac is practised for the month during which the Sun traverses the relevant sign (Aries from April 15 to May 15, Taurus from May 15 to June 16, Gemini from June 16 to July 17, etc. – see *Hermetic Astrology* I, Figure 2).

The development of these twelve virtues during the Sun's passage through the twelve sidereal signs is an aspect of the Christ-Sophia mystery in the age of the second coming. The twelve virtues are: devotion (Aries), equilibrium (Taurus), endurance (Gemini), selflessness (Cancer), compassion (Leo), courtesy (Virgo), contentment (Libra), patience (Scorpio), self-control (Sagittarius), courage (Capricorn), discretion (Aquarius), and magnanimity (Pisces).[7] The associated blessings spoken out by Christ through his second coming – bestowed by the Comforter through the mediation of Sophia – may be brought to consciousness especially at the time of the culmination of the Sophia mystery (at New Moon). These blessings, arising from the practice of the virtues, have the following approximate formulation:

Aries:	Blessed are the devoted, for they shall have the power of self-sacrifice.
Taurus:	Blessed are the balanced, for they shall make progress.
Gemini:	Blessed are those who endure, for they shall have faith.
Cancer:	Blessed are the selfless, for they shall undergo catharsis.
Leo:	Blessed are the compassionate, for they shall be free.
Virgo	Blessed are the courteous, for they shall have tact of heart.
Libra:	Blessed are the contented, for they shall have equanimity.

Scorpio: Blessed are the patient, for they shall be enlightened.
Sagittarius: Blessed are the self-disciplined, for they shall know the truth.
Capricorn: Blessed are the courageous, for they shall have the power to redeem.
Aquarius Blessed are the discreet, for they shall have strength of mind.
Pisces: Blessed are the magnanimous, for they shall be filled with love.

These twelve blessings connected with the zodiacal virtues are a metamorphosis in the age of the second coming of the beatitudes spoken by Christ at the Sermon on the Mount. In some cases a metamorphosis can be seen fairly directly. For example, the fifth and the sixth beatitudes ("Blessed are the merciful" and "Blessed are the pure of heart") clearly correspond to the fifth and sixth blessings – those of Leo and Virgo, respectively.

These twelve blessings spoken by the Risen One in the age of the second coming may be thought of in connection with the "twelve stars" that crown the head of Mary Sophia, as referred to in the twelfth chapter of the *Book of Revelation*. How may this passage in the *Book of Revelation* be understood?

Sophia, the Cosmic Soul, represents the archetype of the cosmic soul of man – "clothed with the Sun, with the Moon under her feet, and on her head a crown of twelve stars." Thus the cosmic soul or self of man is of the nature of the Sun; it holds the lower forces (represented by the Moon) underfoot; and it is "crowned" with the twelve signs of the zodiac. Through the second coming, Jesus Christ is bestowing divine reality upon the cosmic self, bringing the cosmic nature of the self to consciousness, i.e. "clothing it with the Sun". At the same time, man is called upon to tread the lower forces underfoot, e.g. by way of the practice of the virtues. Thereby he may unite himself with the cosmic forces represented by the twelve fixed-star signs of the zodiac. Through the practice of the twelve virtues a way is opened up for the human being to unite himself with the twelve signs of the zodiac, and to receive the blessings of Jesus Christ in the sending of the Comforter, mediated by Sophia. In this way, during the course of the year the human being is able to participate in the Christ-Sophia mystery: to draw near to the blessing activity of Christ, which becomes strongest at Full Moon, and to receive the Holy Spirit mediated by Sophia, which is the cosmic mystery celebrated at New Moon.

Each New Moon takes place in a given sidereal sign of the zodiac, at which time the Sun and Moon are together, and the background "star" – one of the "twelve stars" in the crown of Sophia – radiates in its special power. For example, at the New Moon in Aries it is the power of self-sacrifice which radiates in, in answer to the practice of devotion: "Blessed are the devoted, for they shall have the power of self-sacrifice." As the Sun is in the sidereal sign of Aries from April 15 to May 15 (see *Hermetic Astrology* I, Table 2), this is the period of time during which the virtue of devotion is to be practised. The practice of a given virtue during the Sun's passage through a particular zodiacal sign opens up the possibility of becoming "clothed with the Sun". And the blessing at the time of New Moon within this zodiacal sign means that the possibility is given of receiving the "crown of twelve stars", i.e. receiving a "star" from that zodiacal sign (and from each of the zodiacal signs in turn). Thus the "star" which may be received at the time of New Moon within the zodiacal sign of Aries is the power of self-sacrifice. This means to say, when the New Moon (Moon conjunct Sun) falls in Aries – occurring at some time between April 15 and May 15 – this signifies the "Moon under the feet" and being "clothed with the Sun", whilst at the same time the blessing takes effect by way of the radiating in of the "star" of Aries (power of self-sacrifice) as the cosmic answer to the human being's practice of devotion.

Following on from the New Moon in Aries, the next Full Moon occurs some fifteen days later. At this Full Moon, which takes place either in the sign of Libra or in the sign of Scorpio, it is as if – through the Christ mystery – a response from the Being of Christ takes place, whereby the relevant beatitude may be thought of as being echoed back: "Blessed are the peacemakers, for they shall be called sons of God" (Libra), or "Blessed are those who are persecuted for righteousness' sake, for theirs is the kingdom of heaven" (Scorpio).

Thus at each Full Moon the beatitude corresponding to the sign of the zodiac in which the Moon becomes full can be held in consciousness as an aspect of the Christ mystery taking place in the middle of each lunar month. This is the counterpart – the response on the opposite side of the zodiac – to the Sophia mystery at the beginning of each lunar month, at which the blessing related to the virtue of the zodiacal sign in which the New Moon takes place may be brought to consciousness.

The sanctification of the Full Moon

Each lunar month the activity of Christ radiates in, building up with the growth of etheric forces between New Moon and Full Moon, to reach a climax at the Full Moon. Then the Christ mystery takes place: a recurrence of the Mystery of Golgotha, but in the Moon sphere – in the etheric aura of the Earth – and not on the physical plane. This is a cosmic crucifixion, where the Being of Christ may be visualized upon a cosmic cross extending through the whole solar system, down from Saturn to the Moon, conceived in terms of the Egyptian-Tychonic system.

The original crucifixion took place at Full Moon on Friday, April 3, A.D. 33;[8] and now, in the age of the second coming, a recurrence of this event takes place every Full Moon, taking place in the Earth's etheric aura. In contrast to the physical crucifixion of Jesus Christ upon the cross of Golgotha at the first coming, the age of the second coming is characterized by the monthly recurring etheric crucifixion of *Jesus of the Light* on the cosmic cross of the solar system. Each month he draws near to mankind in this mysterious occurrence at Full Moon. And just as he spoke seven sayings from the cross on Golgotha as he was being crucificed, so in the age of the second coming the seven sayings from the cross – in their cosmic aspect – may serve as a meditation to enable the human being to draw near to the Christ mystery enacted at Full Moon. This Christian-hermetic meditation is known as the *sanctification of the Full Moon,* whereby the cosmic crucifixion of Jesus Christ is visualized upon the cross of the solar system, extending down from Saturn to the Moon. The seven marking stars of this cross are the seven planets: Saturn, Jupiter, Mars, Sun, Mercury, Venus, Moon. (This is the order of the planets in the Egyptian-Tychonic system; this order actually occurs when a conjunction of the Sun and Moon with the five visible planets takes place, where Mercury and Venus are in inferior conjunction, i.e. when Mercury and Venus are beneath the Sun.) And the seven sayings from the cross are related to the seven planets of the cosmic cross as follows:

Sanctification of the Full Moon

Saturn: Father, into thy hands I commend my spirit
Jupiter: My God, my God, why hast thou foresaken me?
Mars: I thirst
Sun: Today you will be with me in paradise
Mercury: Father, forgive them, for they know not what they do
Venus: Woman, behold thy son; son, behold thy mother
Moon: It is fulfilled

The Christian-hermetic meditation of the sanctification of the Full Moon is a possible source of help – in the age of the second coming – to enter into the Christ mystery taking place each lunar month. It may be meditated upon not only on the day of the Full Moon, but also throughout the entire first half of the lunar month – from New Moon to Full Moon – in preparation for the actual Full Moon. Thus the sanctification of the Full Moon can be prepared for during the first half of the lunar month. Similarly, the *sanctification of the New Moon* can be prepared for during the second half of the lunar month, from Full Moon to New Moon. Just as the sanctification of the Full Moon is directed towards the Christ mystery, the sanctification of the New Moon is dedicated to the Sophia mystery, culminating at the New Moon. What is the essence of this mystery?

The sanctification of the New Moon

Just as the flow of etheric forces builds up towards Full Moon, so that the Earth's etheric aura densifies, leading to the cosmic crucifixion of Christ ("Jesus of the Light") at Full Moon, so the ebb of etheric forces after Full Moon leads to the resurrection and ascension of the Risen One during the waning phase. In the Christian-hermetic meditation of the sanctification of the Full Moon (especially when carried out actually at Full Moon), the last words from the cross – "It is fulfilled" – point already to the resurrection. Death and resurrection are the two sides of the Christ mystery at the Full Moon. The densification of etheric forces in the Earth's etheric aura leading up to Full Moon culminates with the cosmic crucifixion of Jesus Christ in his etheric form, which is followed by an event analogous to the resurrection. Correspondingly, the ebbing of the etheric forces during the waning Moon signifies the ascent of the Risen One, analogous to the ascension. (The original ascension took place on May 14, A.D. 33, just four days prior to New Moon.)

During the Moon's waning phase the Risen One begins to manifest more and more as the cosmic I AM – ascending, raising up with him mankind and the whole of creation. And just as at the original ascension the ascent of the Risen One was followed by the descent of the Holy Spirit at Whitsun, so the ascent of the Risen One during the Moon's waning phase culminates in the Sophia mystery – the descent of the Holy Spirit – at New Moon.

The archetype of the Sophia mystery is the original Whitsun event, the descent of the Holy Spirit, which took place on May 24, A.D. 33. As seen from the Earth, through the embodiment of Sophia in the Virgin Mary, who at Whitsun was in the midst of the apostles, the Holy Spirit, the Comforter, descended via the mediation of Mary Sophia to fill the hearts and inner being of the apostles. In the age of the second coming, the cosmic counterpart to the Whitsun event is the descent of the Holy Spirit upon the whole of mankind, again via the mediation of Sophia. The prayer given by Mary Sophia in Amsterdam on February 11, 1951, brings this event to expression:

> Lord Jesus Christ, Son of the Father,
> Send now your Spirit over the Earth.
> Let the Holy Spirit live in the hearts of all peoples,
> That they may be preserved from degeneration, disaster and war.
> May the Lady of All Nations, who once was Mary,
> Be our Advocate. Amen.

Here, Jesus Christ as the Risen One, the cosmic I AM, is adressed: to send his Spirit, the Comforter, into the hearts of people all over the Earth, via the mediation – as Advocate – of the Lady of All Nations (= Archangel Sophia), who once was embodied in Mary. Although to be prayed every day, this Sophia prayer can be brought into the Christian-hermetic meditation known as the *sanctification of the New Moon,* which can help to enable the human being to draw near to the Sophia mystery, the culmination of which takes place at New Moon. In this meditation again the Risen One can be visualized against the background of the seven marking stars of the cosmic cross – this time not as the Crucified One, but rather as the Ascended One, the cosmic I AM, who speaks the seven I AM sayings, addressed to the cosmic self of man, represented in the cosmos by Sophia, the Cosmic Soul. In the Christian-hermetic meditation of the sanctification of the New Moon, the I AM sayings – in their cosmic aspect* – are related to the seven planets ("marking stars") as follows:

Sanctification of the New Moon

Saturn: I AM the resurrection and the life
Jupiter: I AM the light of the world
Mars: I AM the good shepherd
Sun: I AM the bread of life
Mercury: I AM the door
Venus: I AM the way, the truth, and the life
Moon: I AM the true vine

---

*On the microcosmic level the significance of the seven I AM sayings for the human being is outlined in *Meditations on the Tarot,* Chapter 9. Taken together with the "hermetic man" (*Hermetic Astrology* I, Figure 13), the macrocosmic aspect of the seven I AM sayings, as given above ("Sanctification of the New Moon"), is plainly evident. It is exactly the same with respect to the seven "sayings from the cross"; for the microcosmic correspondences the source is the author of *Meditations on the Tarot,* and taken together with the "hermetic man", the macrocosmic correspondences with the planets ("Sanctification of the Full Moon") follow. It is necessary to point this out here, in order that a clear idea may be gained concerning these two meditations. For, before doing a meditation, it is important to know where it comes from and what is intended through it. There is a further aspect to these two meditations, and this is that they may be carried through purely in a spirit of commemoration – the Sanctification of the Full Moon in commemoration of the Mystery of Golgotha (which took place at Full Moon), and the Sanctification of the New Moon in commemoration of the Raising of Lazarus (which took place at New Moon, as discussed in *The Star of the Magi and the Life of Christ* and also in *Chronicle of the Life of Christ*). The Raising of Lazarus, in connection with which Jesus Christ spoke the words: "I AM the resurrection and the life" (see *The Gospel of St. John,* Chapter 11), represented the culmination of all the miracles performed by Christ, and to a certain extent all the other I AM sayings "resonated" with this I AM saying spoken by Christ at the time of the Raising of Lazarus. Thus, just as historically the "sayings from the cross" were spoken by Christ at the Full Moon, so the I AM sayings may be brought into relationship with the New Moon, as historically Christ spoke the words "I AM the resurrection and the life" at the time of New Moon, in connection with the Raising of Lazarus.

With the seven I AM sayings the Ascended One sends his Spirit, the Comforter, via Sophia – the Bride of the Holy Spirit – into the hearts of human beings (the heart being the organ corresponding to the Sun, where the cosmic self is centered). On the cosmic level, this event, which takes place at New Moon, signifies the *coronation of the Virgin,* the crowning of Mary Sophia in heaven. At the New Moon the cosmic image of Sophia – "clothed with the Sun, with the Moon under her feet, and on her head a crown of twelve stars" – becomes manifest. For at New Moon the lunar forces are at a minimum – they are held underfoot by the Sun – and the stellar background shines through as a crowning (coronation). Then the Ascended One speaks the seven I AM sayings, and Sophia becomes crowned with one of the twelve stars representing the twelve sidereal signs of the zodiac, where each star corresponds to one of the twelve signs (the "star" being the blessing of the sign bestowed on the human being who practises the virtue of that sign). The Christian-hermetic meditation on the sanctification of the New Moon can help to bring the Sophia mystery, the culmination of which takes place at New Moon, closer to the human being. It may be meditated upon not only on the day of the New Moon, but also throughout the entire second half of the lunar month – from Full Moon to New Moon – in preparation for the actual New Moon. Thus the sanctification of the New Moon can be prepared for during the second half of the lunar month.

These two Christian-hermetic meditations – the sanctification of the Full Moon (which also may be carried out during the entire first half of the lunar month) and the sanctification of the New Moon (which also may be meditated upon during the entire second half of the lunar month) – help to prepare the way for an experience of the Christ-Sophia mystery taking place each month. They may serve as a contribution on the path towards *Astro-Sophia,* towards experiencing the cosmic mysteries in a new way, in a Christian way. As such, they represent a Christian metamorphosis – or resurrection – of the ancient Egyptian hermetic wisdom concerning the mysteries of Isis and Osiris. Just as the ancient Egyptians entered into a relationship with Osiris and Isis during the two halves of the lunar month, so it is possible for modern human beings – in the New Age, the age of the second coming – through taking up these Christian-hermetic meditations to be helped to enter into a relationship with Christ and Sophia during the waxing and waning phases of the Moon, where this entails the practice of the two meditations outlined above: the sanctifiction of the Full Moon and the sanctification of the New Moon.

The twelve lunar months of the year

The hermetic calendar comprises a division of the cycle of the year into twelve or thirteen lunar months. The concept *month* was originally defined in relation to the Moon and its phases, and the hermetic calendar represents a return to the basic concept on account of the new significance that the phases of the Moon have for mankind in the New Age, the age of the second coming. In so far as the age of the second coming mirrors the period of ancient Egyptian civilization during which Christ was worshipped (in connection with the lunar phases) as Osiris, the hermetic calendar represents a metamorphosis of the ancient lunar calendar of the Egyptians.

According to the hermetic principle of correspondences, which was applied by star-gazers in pre-Christian centuries, each lunar month corresponds to one of the twelve signs of the zodiac. This is evident from the Babylonian lunar calendar, which offers the most complete description as to the form and structure of the ancient lunar calendar. Thus, in a Babylonian text referring to the month of Nisan, the first month of the yearly cycle of the Babylonian lunar calendar (Nisan) is brought into correspondence with the constellation of Aries:

> *Nisan is the month of the constellation Ikû (Aries), which is the throne-room of Anu. The king is lifted up, the king is installed. The blessed springing forth of vegetation of (by) Anu and Enlil.*[9]

In the lunar calendar, the first lunar month of the year is the month of Aries. Similarly, the second lunar month is the month of Taurus, the third is the month of Gemini, and so on, until the twelfth lunar month, which corresponds to Pisces. What, however, is the basis for this correspondence between the lunar months and the signs of the zodiac?

It is the principle of analogy: "As above, so below." Since the cycle of lunar months divides the year into twelve (or thirteen – see below), and since there are twelve signs of the zodiac through which the Sun, Moon and planets orbit, each month "here below" must correspond to a sign of the zodiac visible in the starry heavens "above". The next question is: How is the sequence of twelve lunar months, looked at in relation to the yearly cycle of nature, brought into correspondence with the twelve signs of the zodiac comprising the zodiacal belt of fixed stars?

Since the sign of Aries has always been regarded as the first of the twelve signs of the zodiac,* this question can be reduced to: Which lunar month is the first lunar month of the year? For, once a particular lunar month is identified as the first in the yearly sequence, the remaining months follow sequentially.

Looking at the cycle of nature as it was experienced by the Babylonians, the first lunar month of the year started with the New Moon falling after

---

*Aries is the first sign of the zodiac in the zodiacal melothesia, i.e. where the signs of the zodiac are brought into relationship with the parts of the human body (see *Hermetic Astrology* I, Table 16). Since the head, as the first part of the body, corresponds to Aries, Aries is the first sign of the zodiac – so runs the hermetic line of reasoning: "That which is above is like that which is below, and that which is below is like that which is above."

the vernal equinox, since this was regarded by them as the beginning of spring. (For the people of ancient Israel, however, it was the New Moon falling closest to the vernal equinox which designated the start of the lunar year – see Appendix III.) The first New Moon was known in antiquity as the *Neomenia* ("New Moon of the year"), and signified the start of the lunar month of Aries. The occurrence of the Neomenia heralded spring: the awakening of nature – the blossoming forth of new vegetation, new plant life. The celebration of the Neomenia was therefore the great New Year festival in the cultural life of the Babylonians. From their experience of nature, the lunar month starting with the Neomenia – the New Moon falling after the vernal equinox – was the first month of the year. In their application of the hermetic principle of correspondences, the lunar month starting with the Neomenia was the lunar month of Aries. Similarly, the following lunar month was that of Taurus; the next was that of Gemini; and so on. This principle of applying hermetic correspondences underlay the Babylonian lunar calendar, where the first lunar month (Nisan) was sacred to Aries, the second lunar month (Ayar) was sacred to Taurus, etc.

The cycle of the Sun's steps

The application of the hermetic principle of analogy is not simply an abstract principle; it has a justification. As we shall see, there is a genuine parallel between the cycle of the twelve signs of the zodiac and the sequence of lunar months during the course of the year. In *Hermetic Astrology* I, Chapter 1 (see Figure 5), attention was drawn to the fact that the Sun's motion in declination during the course of the year gives rise to a secondary zodiac – the tropical zodiac – which is of vital significance for the cycle of nature. Here, instead of looking at the Sun's passage (in longitude) through the twelve sidereal signs, which is the primary solar astrological phenomenon for the human being, attention is focused upon the Sun's motion in declination during the course of the year. The motion of the Sun in declination is the primary cosmic phenomenon as far as nature is concerned (this motion in the southern hemisphere being the reverse of that in the northern hemisphere, with a corresponding reversal of the seasons).

From the winter solstice to the summer solstice (in the northern hemisphere), the Sun ascends in declination through six steps, and from the summer solstice to the winter solstice the Sun descends through six steps, each step corresponding to the Sun's passage through 30 degrees longitude. (See *Hermetic Astrology* I, Figures 5 and 7, which indicate this, and Table 9, which shows that the course of nature in the southern hemisphere is the reverse of that in the northern hemisphere, since the twelve steps of the Sun in declination in the southern hemisphere are the reverse of the twelve steps in the northern hemisphere.) These twelve steps of the Sun in declination may be placed in correspondence with the signs of the sidereal zodiac, but here again the question is raised: Where does the circle of steps start, i.e. which step – the step which is placed in correspondence with the sign of Aries – can be regarded as the first?

The Sun's step beginning with the vernal equinox is the first step, for it is here that the hours of daylight begin to be longer than the hours of darkness. (See *Hermetic Astrology* I, Table 9, where the first step in the northern hemisphere starts at the vernal equinox on March 21 and in the southern hemisphere on September 23.) The whole plant world is attuned to the light and the warmth of the Sun, so the balance of light and darkness at the equinox is a "zero point" for the plant world. Following on from the spring equinox (in the northern hemisphere), the lengthening of the hours of daylight in relation to those of darkness signifies a "plus" (+) for the plant world. This attains a maximum at the summer solstice, and then descends again to the "zero point" (balance between light and darkness) at the autumnal equinox (see Figure 22).

Figure 22:
The cycle of sunlight in the course of the year
(Note: this figure also applies to the southern hemisphere, if the dates of vernal equinox and autumnal equinox and those of summer solstice and winter solstice are reversed.)

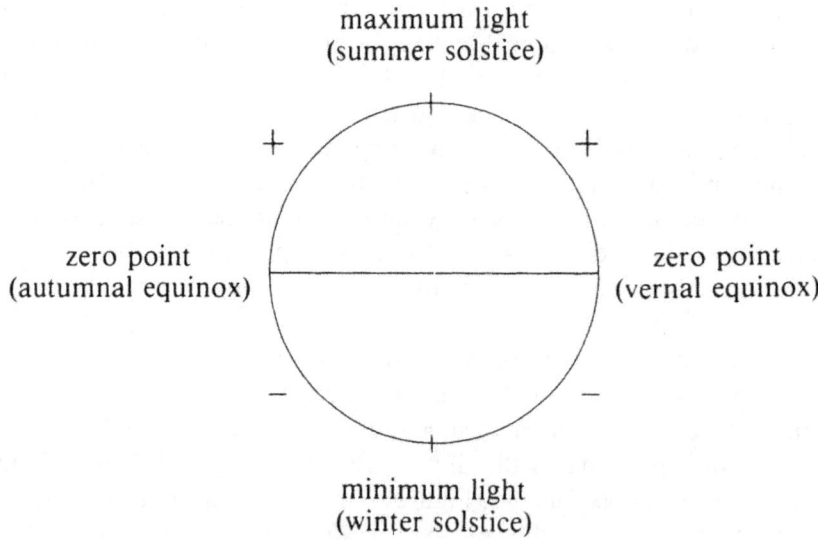

Following the autumnal equinox, the diminishing hours of daylight in relation to those of darkness signify a "minus" (–) for the plant world. The hours of light then reach a minimum at the winter solstice and then return to the "zero point" at the vernal equinox. (See Figure 22 for the complete cycle). From this consideration – the relationship between light and darkness, which is of such vital importance to the plant world – it is clear that the cycle of the Sun's steps in declination begins with the vernal equinox, which is the natural "zero point". This holds for the northern hemisphere. (In the southern hemisphere the reverse holds true, i.e. the first step in the southern hemisphere – as far as the world of nature is concerned – begins on or about September 23.)

It is not only the Sun's light which is of significance for the world of nature, but also the warmth of the Sun. The light of the Sun follows exactly the cycle of steps in declination, attaining a maximum at maximum declination (summer solstice). In the case of the Sun's warmth, however, the maximum is attained not at maximum declination, but midway between the summer solstice and the autumnal equinox. With the warmth of the Sun there is a shift of one-eight of the cycle of steps, which amounts to a time-shift of 1½ months.

This time-shift is exactly analogous to the parallel phenomena taking place in the course of one day. If the cycle of steps of the Sun is followed during the course of the day, maximum light is attained when the Sun is highest in the sky, at midday (12 noon). Maximum warmth, however, is attained one-eighth of the cycle later, amounting to a time-shift of three hours, i.e. maximum warmth occurs (theoretically) mid-afternoon, at 3 p.m.

Returning to the cycle of the year considered in relation to the steps of the Sun, the cycle of the Sun's warmth runs parallel to that of the Sun's light, but is subject to a time-shift of one-eighth of the cycle. Maximum warmth occurs one-eighth of the cycle after maximum light, and minimum warmth occurs one-eighth of the cycle after minimum light. Hence the cycle of the Sun's warmth also can be expressed in terms of the steps of the Sun, by allowing for the time-shift of one-eighth of the yearly cycle (= 1½ months). Therefore the steps indicate both the phenomenon of the Sun's light and that of its warmth, as will be elaborated in more detail later.

The entire world of nature responds to the light and the warmth of the Sun, related to and indicated by the Sun's yearly cycle of steps in declination. In *Hermetic Astrology* I, Table 9, the Sun's cycle of steps is listed in relation to the astrological months of the tropical zodiac, where these months are reversed in the southern hemisphere. The astrological months, given by the Sun's steps in declination, are named after the sidereal signs of the zodiac, according to the principle "as above, so below".

Applying the hermetic principle of correspondences to the cycle of the

Sun's steps in the northern hemisphere, the first step during the first month after the vernal equinox corresponds to the sign of Aries, the second step corresponds to the sign of Taurus, the third to Gemini, and so on. The hermetic principle of correspondences also applies to the cycle of the Sun's steps in the southern hemisphere, where the steps are the reverse of those in the northern hemisphere. This yields a secondary zodiac – the tropical zodiac – analogous to the sidereal zodiac of twelve fixed-star signs. The tropical zodiac thus consists of twelve astrological months: March 21 – April 20 (Aries in the northern hemisphere, Libra in the southern hemisphere), April 20 – May 21 (Taurus in the northern hemisphere, Scorpio in the southern hemisphere), etc., as listed in *Hermetic Astrology* I, Table 9. Here the question arises: Is the tropical zodiac purely the result of applying an abstract principle, or does it correspond to a definite reality?

As is evident from an observation of the cycle of nature in both the northern and southern hemispheres during the course of the year, the tropical zodiac does correspond to a reality: growth during spring (steps of Aries, Taurus, Gemini); expansion during summer (steps of Cancer, Leo, Virgo); decay during autumn (steps of Libra, Scorpio, Sagittarius); and contraction during winter (steps of Capricorn, Aquarius, Pisces). And as indicated in Figure 22, the underlying significance of these four phases in nature's cycle – growth, expansion, decay and contraction – is connected with the Sun, with the changing relationship between light and darkness on the one hand, and with the related changing relationship between warmth and cold on the other hand. But is there any deeper reason for associating Aries with the first step, Taurus with the second step, Gemini with the third step, and so on?

Correspondence of the Sun's steps with the zodiacal melothesia

Again the hermetic teaching concerning the zodiacal melothesia is a help towards answering the question of the naming of the steps after the sidereal signs of the zodiac. The zodiacal melothesia derives from the spiritual perception that during the period between incarnations, whilst indwelling the zodiacal sphere of fixed stars, the human being builds up the spiritual archetype of the physical body for his next incarnation, drawing the forces making up this archetype from the twelve sidereal signs of the zodiac: head (Aries), throat and larynx (Taurus), shoulders and arms (Gemini),..., feet (Pisces) (see *Hermetic Astrology* I, Table 16). Here, as is evident from the correspondence between the sidereal signs and the parts of the body, Aries is the first sign and Pisces the last, corresponding respectively to the head and to the feet.

The first six signs (Aries to Virgo) correspond to the upper half of the human being ("above the belt"), whilst the last six signs (Libra to Pisces) correspond to the lower half of the human being ("below the belt"). The first six signs relate to the realm of the light, since the upper human being is more orientated towards the light; and the lower six signs relate more to the realm of darkness, since the lower human being is more bound up with the Earth (darkness). In this sense, the Sun's steps, yielding the tropical zodiac, are analogous to the zodiacal melothesia: the six steps of (+)light corresponding to the upper half of the human being, and the six steps of (−)light corresponding to the lower half of the human being (see Figure 22). Although referring to quite different phenomena, nevertheless a real parallel exists, and this justifies the application of the principle of analogy, even to the extent of carrying over the names of the zodiacal signs to the names of the steps in the tropical zodiac.

Everything has its archetype, and the archetype of the steps or stages of nature, as they unfold in relation to the changing light and warmth of the Sun during its motion in declination, is to be found in the zodiacal sphere. In this sphere, also, the human body has its archetype. Having the same archetype, it is not surprising to find a parallel between the steps of nature's yearly cycle and the light and dark poles in the human bodily organisation. Again, the cycle of the day also has the same archetype, so that a direct parallel can be seen between the cycle of the day and the cycle of the year: sunrise (spring equinox), midday (summer solstice), sunset (autumnal equinox), and midnight (winter solstice). Correspondingly, the first few hours after sunrise are "Aries hours", which are followed by "Taurus hours" and "Gemini hours", leading up to the "Cancer hours" at midday, and so on.

Wheels within wheels – the cycle of the day within the cycle of the year, and the cycle of the year within the greater cycle of incarnations of the soul in different sidereal signs of the zodiac – such is the nature of God's creation. And based on the understanding that everywhere in divine creation an archetype exists, hermeticism is the science of applying the principle of analogy to discover the divine archetypes underlying creation.

The cycle of the year (and also of the day) and the structure of the human body have the same archetype: the zodiacal sphere of fixed stars. Thus there is a higher reality underlying the correspondence between the archetypal sidereal zodiac and the tropical zodiac of the year of nature: namely, the forces active in the steps of nature during the cycle of the year are analogous to the forces active in the corresponding sidereal signs of the zodiac.The springing up of nature in the time following the vernal equinox, i.e. during the step of Aries, is analogous to the springing, buoyant cosmic impulse of the fixed-star sign of Aries, which works in the shaping and moulding of the human head. Similarly, the deep contraction of nature in the time following the winter solstice, during the step of Capricorn, is analogous to the spiritual inwardness of the fixed-star sign of Capricorn, which is active in the forming of the spiritual archetype of the knees. The forces active in nature (in this case the forces of light and warmth from the Sun) are analogous – on the level at which they work – to the cosmic archetypal forces active in the zodiacal sphere of fixed stars.

Just as the first zodiacal sign is Aries (which is evident from the fact that it is the first in the zodiacal melothesia, as it forms the human head), so the first step in the Sun's cycle of declination (taking effect in nature) is called the *astrological month of Aries*. In the northern hemisphere the astrological month of Aries extends from March 21 to April 20, and in the southern hemisphere the astrological month of Aries extends from September 23 to October 23 (see *Hermetic Astrology* I, Table 9). During these periods the impulse of Aries – the springing up of vegetation – is active in the world of nature, directly in response to the light and warmth of the Sun.

The impulse active in nature at these (respective) times in the northern and southern hemispheres is analogous to that which is active on the cosmic-spiritual level in the fixed-star sign of Aries, e.g. someone born between April 15 and May 15 – when the Sun is in the sidereal sign of Aries – receives on the cosmic-spiritual level the quality of Aries (springing-up forces in the soul, i.e. inner forces of initiative) in connection with the cosmic impulse of his self, centered in the Sun. (Here the direction of hermetic analogy is applied from below above – "as below, so above", i.e. from the realm of nature to the cosmic-spiritual realm – in drawing an analogy between the quality of nature forces and the inner being of man.)

Once having established the astrological month of Aries as the starting month of the twelve steps of the Sun's declination during the course of the year, the names of the remaining months follow, i.e. Taurus is the second astrological month, Gemini is the month determined by the Sun's third step in declination, and so on, bearing in mind that the months are the reverse in the southern hemisphere owing to the reversal of the Sun's steps there. The qualities in nature observable in the twelve astrological months – in the northern and southern hemispheres – are hermetically analogous to the cosmic-spiritual qualities of the twelve fixed-star zodiacal signs with the same names.

Above it was mentioned that there is a time-shift of one-eighth of a cycle between the Sun's light and the Sun's warmth during the course of the year. Expressed in terms of the astrological months, maximum sunlight is attained at the end of the astrological month of Gemini/start of the astrological month of Cancer. Since maximum warmth (in terms of the Sun alone) is arrived at one-eighth of a cycle later, this is attained in the middle of the astrological month of Leo. Similarly, minimum sunlight is reached at the end of the astrological month of Sagittarius/start of the astrological month of Capricorn. Therefore minimum warmth follows one-eighth of a cycle later, in the middle of the astrological month of Aquarius, which is the coldest time of the year in terms of the Sun's steps in declination.

The cycle of warmth/cold in the course of the year is not quite as clear-cut as that of the Sun's light. If the Sun alone played a role in the determination of nature, then the hottest time of the year would always be the middle of the astrological month of Leo and the coldest period would be the middle of the astrological month of Aquarius.

The modification of the Sun's steps effected by the Moon's phases

Nature does not only respond to the Sun, but also to the other heavenly bodies, especially to the Moon. After the Sun, the Moon is the next most important celestial body to take into consideration with regard to effects taking place in the realm of nature. On the one hand the Sun works directly into the world of nature through the sequence of the Sun's steps, and on the other hand it works indirectly by the way of reflection from the Moon, through the phases of the Moon. In other words, a differentiation of the Sun's activity in the world of nature is effected by the phases of the Moon. To use a musical analogy, the steps of the Sun indicate the main theme in the unfolding of nature during the year, whilst the phases of the Moon denote an underlying recurring motif which continually works in (building up to Full Moon) and then recedes again (fading away towards New Moon). This waning and waxing of the Moon signifies the ebb and flow of etheric forces (hidden life forces) active in the world of nature, and these forces play an important role in the growth and decay of plant life during the course of the year, as well as in the variations in weather conditions, etc.

Whereas the most noticeable influence of the Sun in nature is by way of its light and warmth, there is evidently an influence of the Moon with regard to the element of water. The Moon's influence is obvious, for example, in the working of the tides, where it is known that the alignments of the Sun, Moon and Earth at New Moon and Full Moon produces effects in the tides. Another connection of the Moon with the element of water is in the precipitation of rainfall.

> *Precipitation activity over broad areas appears to be closely associated with the monthly lunisolar cycle. Indexes of precipitation in the continental United States over a continuous 50-year period... reveal that heavy rains occur most frequently in the first and third weeks of the synodical months... especially on the third to fifth days after the configurations of both New and Full Moon.*[10]

This statistical finding concerning the precipitation of rainfall shortly after the New or Full Moon has also been independently observed in the southern hemisphere, using data from New Zealand.[11] In an extraordinary way modern statistics confirm an ancient Babylonian observation of the Moon's influence on the weather.

> *The influence of the Moon upon the weather was known to them (the Babylonians). Their rule is as follows: a certain weather condition may change noticeably only at New or Full Moon, in which case the weather changes within five days. If the weather has not changed by the fifth day after the New or Full Moon, it remains unchanged for another two weeks (until the next New or Full Moon).*[12]

This Babylonian rule for guaging the weather can also be taken into consideration when following the lunar months of the hermetic calendar during the course of the year, as will be described below. However, the Moon's influence on the element of water is not limited to the weather, i.e. to the precipitation of rainfall, but extends also into the domain of life forces, especially in the activity of the sap of trees and plants. There is an "ebb" of life forces between Full Moon and New Moon (reaching a minimum at New Moon), and a "flow" of life forces between New Moon and Full Moon (reaching a maximum at Full Moon). This means that the sap – as an expression of the life forces active in nature – rises during the waxing phase and declines during the waning phase of the Moon. The cycle of life forces in nature is therefore directly bound up with the lunar phases, reaching a maximum at Full Moon and a minimum at New Moon.

As referred to above, the Moon's influence on the element of water is also connected with the lunar phases. There is, however, a time-shift of one-eighth of a cycle (ca. 3½ days) – in that, e.g., precipitation of rainfall occurs on average some 3½ days after the New or Full Moon. This timeshift in the cycle of the lunar month – with respect to the Moon's influence on the element of water – parallels that in the cycle of the Sun's steps during the course of the year. The parallel can be expressed as follows:

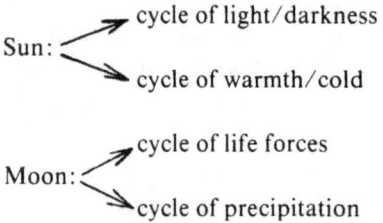

Sun:
- cycle of light/darkness   directly corresponds to the cycle of the Sun's steps in declination
- cycle of warmth/cold   corresponds with a one-eighth shift in the cycle of the Sun's steps in declination

Moon:
- cycle of life forces   ebb and flow corresponds directly to the waning and waxing lunar phases
- cycle of precipitation   corresponds to a one-eighth shift in the cycle of the lunar phases

Whereas the Sun's influences in nature take effect directly by way of light and warmth, the Moon works in as a modifying influence – together with the Sun via the lunar phases – taking effect in the domain of life forces and in the water element, so that a complex interaction between warmth, light, water and life forces take place each lunar month. This complex interaction is largely responsible for the varying conditions in nature (weather, etc.) during the course of the year. (It is not wholly responsible, as other celestial bodies and cosmic factors also play a role.)

The determination of the hermetic calendar

In order to gain a more complete understanding of the cycle of nature during the course of the year, the differentiation of the solar steps effected by the playing in of the Moon's phases needs to be taken into consideration. And it is precisely the lunar calendar – the modern hermetic calendar – which describes this differentiation.

The hermetic calendar may be thought of as a modern adaptation of the ancient lunar calendar. Such a calendar was used by the Babylonians and also by the people of Israel, but with one minor difference in their definition of the starting point. As referred to earlier, the Babylonian calendar started with the New Moon falling *after* the vernal equinox, whereas the Jewish calendar (still in use to the present day – see Appendix III) starts with the New Moon falling *closest* to the vernal equinox. This difference in definition means that although the two calendars are often identical, they may also diverge by one month with respect to their starting points. Since the celebration of Easter is determined in relation to the vernal equinox such that it generally falls in the first month of the Jewish calendar, it is the latter calendar which is important (albeit implicitly) in Christian civilization. For this reason the principle adhered to in the Jewish calendar is taken here as the point of departure for the definition of the modern hermetic calendar. (However, as will become evident below, the hermetic calendar actually represents a synthesis of the Jewish and Babylonian lunar calendars.) In the following discussion, therefore, the months of the lunar calendar will be assumed to commence with the New Moon falling closest to the vernal equinox – this being the Neomenia ("New Moon of the year") for the people of Israel.

In the northern hemisphere the sequence of lunar months starts with the New Moon falling nearest the vernal equinox (Neomenia), so that a modification of the solar steps is given – one in which the Moon's phases are accounted for. Instead of starting with the vernal equinox, which would be appropriate if the Sun alone were active in the cycle of nature, the month of Aries starts with the New Moon falling nearest to the vernal equinox. Here the playing in of the Moon is incorporated with the solar steps. The hermetic calendar thus gives a more accurate representation of the cycle of nature. For example, if the onset of spring is observed from year to year, it soon becomes apparent that it does not start at exactly the same time each year, but shifts in relation to the vernal equinox according to whether the Neomenia (= the New Moon signifying the start of the lunar month of Aries) falls before or after the equinox (March 21). Generally speaking, it may be observed that spring sets in early when the Neomenia falls early (before the equinox) and that it sets in correspondingly late when the Neomenia falls late in relation to the equinox (after the equinox).

Exactly the same principle applies in the southern hemisphere, except that there it is the equinox on September 23 which is decisive. The hermetic calendar in the southern hemisphere is the reverse of the hermetic calendar in the northern hemisphere, just as the cycle of the Sun's steps in the southern heminsphere is the reverse of that in the northern hemisphere. The solar astrological month of Aries ("Aries step") in the southern hemisphere is the month following the equinox (September 23 – October 23). In this astrological month – that of Aries (applying the hermetic principle of correspondences) – the quality of Aries can be experienced in nature, i.e. an impulse of springing up and buoyancy in nature's forces. When the modifying influence of the Moon is taken into consideration, it can be observed that the "Aries mood" in nature sets in with the New Moon falling nearest to the equinox (September 23). When this New Moon falls early in relation to the equinox, then the impulse of Aries in nature ("spring") sets in correspondingly early. Likewise, if the New Moon occurs long after the equinox, the spring impulse of Aries is correspondingly late in coming in the southern hemisphere.

As the hermetic calendar in the southern hemisphere is the reverse of that in the northern hemisphere, the lunar month of Aries (denoting the onset of spring) in the southern hemisphere equates with the lunar month of Libra (denoting the onset of autumn) in the northern hemisphere. Thus, the New Moon at the start of the month of Libra in the hermetic calendar of the northern hemisphere is specified as the New Moon falling nearest to the autumn equinox (September 23). Similarly, the Neomenia ("New Moon of the year") at the start of the lunar month of Aries ("spring") in the northern hemisphere indicates the beginning of the lunar month of Libra ("autumn") in the southern hemisphere. The Neomenia – signifying the start of nature's yearly cycle – is the New Moon falling nearest the equinox of March 21 in the northern hemisphere, and in the southern hemisphere it is the New Moon falling nearest the equinox of September 23. The Neomenia of the northern hemisphere and the Neomenia of the southern hemisphere are the two marking points determining the structure of the hermetic calendar.

Before looking in detail at the structure of the hermetic calendar, let us consider once again the basis of this calendar. It comprises twelve (or sometimes thirteen) lunar months, which run parallel to the astrological (solar) months of the Sun's steps in declination during the course of the year. The solar months (Aries, Taurus, Gemini, etc.) describe the cosmic influence of the Sun's direct working – through light and warmth – in the cycle of nature. This direct working is modified by the indirect working of the Sun via the Moon, as this comes to expression in the lunar phases, where the cycle of the lunar phases takes effect upon the element of water, and also upon the life forces active in nature. The lunar phases – constituting the lunar month – are thus a modifying factor superimposed upon the corresponding solar month. The astrological months therefore provide a kind of archetypal division of the yearly cycle of nature into twelve solar months, whilst the lunar months indicate more closely the real, effective division of the cycle of nature.

The lunar months run parallel to the solar months, but are generally shifted in time by a matter of days according to the occurrence of the New Moon signifying the start of the lunar month. For example, if the Neomenia (the New Moon with which the lunar month of Aries commences) falls on March 21 in the northern hemisphere – as in the year 1985 – then the lunar month of Aries runs almost exactly parallel to the astrological (solar) month of Aries (March 21 – April 20). (In fact, in 1985 the vernal equinox fell on March 20, so that the solar month of Aries extended from March 20 to April 20 in the northern hemisphere and the corresponding lunar month from March 21 to April 19 – see Table 22.) If, however, the Neomenia occurs on March 14, one week before the vernal equinox in the northern hemisphere, then the lunar month of Aries starts one week ahead of the astrological (solar) month of Aries, and likewise subsequent lunar months are shifted ahead in relation to the corresponding solar months. If, on the other hand, the Neomenia takes place on March 28, one week after the vernal equinox in the northern hemisphere, then the lunar month of Aries starts one week after the solar month of Aries, and the lunar month of Taurus is shifted correspondingly in relation to the solar month of Taurus, etc.

The lunar months simply modify the solar months, effecting a time-shift forwards or backwards, which makes itself noticeable in the whole of nature. The key to the determination of this shift is given by the Neomenia, which signifies the actual start of a new cycle of seasons (whereas the equinox indicates the start on a more archetypal level). The Neomenia in the northern hemisphere is the New Moon falling nearest the equinox on March 21, and in the southern hemisphere it is the New Moon closest to the equinox on September 23. Through these two events the hermetic calendar may be determined each year.

The Easter festival in relation to the hermetic calendar

If the Neomenia falls early in relation to the equinox, then – in general – so does the onset of spring; and if it occurs late, then spring is usually correspondingly late in coming. In other words, the hermetic calendar generally yields a direct correspondence between the passage of time and the phenomena of nature, whilst the tropical zodiac based on the steps of the Sun, which does not take the modification effected by the Moon's phases into account, yields only an approximate correspondence. The cycle of lunar months (Aries, Taurus, Gemini, etc.) usually relates more directly to the phenomena occurring in nature (weather, rainfall, etc.) during the course of the year, whilst the steps of the tropical zodiac (Aries, Taurus, Gemini, etc.) only approximate to the actual occurrences.

By living consciously with the hermetic calendar, which expresses the division of the year into lunar months in relation to the cycle of nature, a closer relationship with nature is made possible. For example, the variations in the weather occurring at or after New or Full Moon can be observed with a new consciousness, along the lines of the ancient Babylonian weather rule described earlier in this chapter. Moreover, by becoming aware of the activity of Christ ("Jesus of the Light") – through the second coming – within the etheric aura of the Earth (extending up to the orbit of the Moon), a perception of the spiritual side of nature can begin to develop. For Christ in his resurrection body – like a "piece of Sun" upon Earth – is active in the blessing of nature through the cycle of the lunar months, where the forces active in the various months are analogous to those of the corresponding fixed-star signs of the zodiac.

For example, it is as the fixed-star sign of Aries, i.e. as the *Mystical Lamb,* that Christ comes to manifestation during the first lunar month of the year, the month of Aries. This is the month (in the northern hemisphere) in which Easter takes place each year (with infrequent exceptions – see below). In the celebration of Easter on the first Sunday after the first Full Moon after the vernal equinox, something of the nature of Christ as the Mystical Lamb – "the Lamb of God who bears the sins of the world" (*John* i, 29) – is conveyed. And in the age of the second coming the celebration of Easter acquires a new meaning, through the activity of Christ – as the Mystical Lamb – during the lunar month of Aries. (This is the month in which – during the second half, i.e. after Full Moon – Easter takes place.) This activity builds up from Neomenia to Full Moon, reaching a climax at Full Moon, when the Christ mystery takes place. Nevertheless, the celebration of Easter Sunday as the first Sunday following this is of significance in so far as the day on which the resurrection took place historically is thereby commemorated. Now, in the age of the second coming, it is not simply that the historical occurrence of the resurrection is commemorated on Easter Sunday each year, but that at the Full Moon preceding Easter Sunday – the Full Moon in the lunar month of Aries – something of the Christ mystery may be experienced, as described above in connection with the Christian-hermetic meditation known as the *sanctification of the Full Moon.*

In the northern hemisphere, therefore, the first lunar month of the year (Aries) in the hermetic calendar is the lunar month in which the festival of Easter is celebrated (with rare exceptions – see below). In the southern hemisphere, however, the Easter festival takes place in the lunar month of Libra, as the hermetic calendar in the southern hemisphere is the reverse of that of the northern hemisphere. Since the original Easter, the death and resurrection of Jesus Christ is commemorated as a historical event. This is sufficient justification for its celebration on the same date in both hemispheres, even if in the southern hemisphere the quality of the Being of Christ active in nature is then not that of the Mystical Lamb (Aries), but more that of the *Guardian of the Threshold* holding the scales (Libra).

Intercalation in the hermetic calendar

Turning now to the details concerning the specification of the hermetic calendar each year, a difference between the northern and the southern hemispheres is apparent. This arises by virtue of the fact that the interval between the vernal and autumnal equinoxes (186 days 10 hours) is about one week longer than the period between the autumnal and vernal equinoxes (178 days 20 hours). The period "spring plus summer" is therefore one week longer in the northern hemisphere than it is in the southern hemisphere. This discrepancy is balanced out in the hermetic calendar by way of *intercalation*. How does this work in practice?

Firstly, what is intercalation? This is necessitated by the disparity between the solar year of $356\frac{1}{4}$ days (= 186 days 10 hours + 178 days 20 hours) and the lunar year of $354\frac{1}{3}$ days (= twelve lunar months, each $29\frac{1}{2}$ days long). After completing a lunar year of twelve months (= $354\frac{1}{3}$ days), some eleven days have to elapse before the solar year of twelve astrological (solar) months is also completed ($365\frac{1}{4}$ days). For example, if the Neomenia (start of the lunar year) coincides with the equinox (start of the solar year), then after twelve lunar months the next Neomenia takes place about eleven days prior to the equinox. After a further twelve lunar months the interval would become twenty-two days (prior to the equinox), which is too large – in view of the fact that the Neomenia cannot take place more than fifteen days earlier than the equinox. Therefore a thirteenth lunar month has to be inserted, yielding a lunar year of thirteen lunar months, which brings the occurrence of the Neomenia forward to take place (in this example) some seven or eight days after the equinox. The insertion of an extra lunar month is known as *intercalation*. By means of intercalation the lunar year is regulated, so that it remains in step with the solar year.

Approximately every three years an extra lunar month has to be intercalated, i.e. after two normal years each containing twelve lunar months, the third is an *intercalary year* containing thirteen lunar months. However, the pattern of intercalary years is not exactly once every three years, but follows, in fact, a pattern that recurs every nineteen years. Thus the hermetic calendar follows a 19-year intercalation cycle in which seven of the years – meaning always a lunar year (from Neomenia to Neomenia) – are intercalary years. The 19-year cycle of the hermetic calendar therefore comprises twelve normal years (a normal year contains twelve lunar months) and seven intercalary years (an intercalary year has thirteen lunar months). What is the pattern of the 19-year intercalation cycle of the hermetic calendar?

The pattern of intercalations in the hermetic calendar can best be illustrated by way of considering a particular 19-year period. Let us look at the present 19-year period, extending to the year 2000, i.e. the period 1981–2000.

The present 19-year period in the hermetic calendar

The Neomenia in the northern hemisphere in 1981 is specified by the New Moon that fell closest to the vernal equinox in that year. This took place very early in relation to the vernal equinox; it occurred on March 6, some two weeks before the equinox. Searching for the Neomenia in the southern hemisphere in 1981, we find that the New Moon closest to the autumnal equinox fell on September 28, i.e. five days after the equinox. Here is indicated that nature's year – beginning with the Neomenia (= the start of the lunar month of Aries) – started two weeks early in the northern hemisphere and five days late in the southern hemisphere, in both cases measured with respect to the relevant equinox.

Owing to the early start of the natural year in the northern hemisphere in 1981, combined with the fact that in 1981 the natural year started a few days late in the southern hemisphere, an extra lunar month had to be intercalated in the hermetic calendar between the two Neomenias. Moreover, as mentioned above, since the interval between the vernal equinox and the autumnal equinox is in any case approximately one week longer than the period between the autumnal equinox and the vernal equinox, this discrepancy is balanced out in the hermetic calendar by way of intercalation. The question is: Where is the extra lunar month intercalated?

This question also confronted Babylonian astronomers, who already from the sixth century B.C. onwards utilized a 19-year intercalation cycle to regulate their lunar calendar.[13] In the Babylonian 19-year intercalation cycle an extra lunar month was inserted (in intercalary years) either as a second month of Virgo starting prior to the autumnal equinox, or as a second month of Pisces starting prior to the vernal equinox.

The solution to this problem in the modern hermetic calendar is somewhat simpler than that of the Babylonians. In the hermetic calendar, all intercalated months are inserted – when necessary – prior to the autumnal equinox, in order to balance out the discrepancy that "spring plus summer" in the northern hemisphere is one week longer than "spring plus summer" in the southern hemisphere. Thus in the hermetic calendar of the northern hemisphere an intercalated month is always a second month of Virgo, inserted prior to the autumnal equinox when necessary. As the hermetic calendar of the southern hemisphere is the reverse of that of the northern hemisphere, this means that in the southern hemisphere the intercalated month is always a second month of Pisces.

For example, looking again at the year 1981, the Neomenia in the northern hemisphere fell on March 6, signifying the start of the lunar month of Aries (southern hemisphere: Libra). The following New Moon fell on April 4 – denoting the beginning of the lunar month of Taurus (southern hemisphere: Scorpio). The lunar month of Gemini (southern hemisphere: Sagittarius) began with the New Moon on May 4, whilst the lunar month of Cancer (southern hemisphere: Capricorn) started with the New Moon on June 2. Then followed the lunar month of Leo (southern hemisphere: Aquarius), which commenced with the New Moon on July 1. The New Moon starting the month of Virgo (southern hemisphere: Pisces) thus occurred very early, falling on July 31, which meant that a second lunar month of Virgo (southern hemisphere: Pisces) had to be inserted – starting with the New Moon that came on August 29. This intercalated month of Virgo filled in the period up to the autumnal equinox, so that the New Moon on September 28, five days after the equinox, signified the onset of the lunar month of Libra (southern hemisphere: the Neomenia, start of Aries). These dates are summarized in Table 22.

Regarding the lunar year 1981/1982 as the first year (= year 1) in the 19-year intercalation cycle of the hermetic calendar, this was an intercalary year in which a second month of Virgo (southern hemisphere: Pisces) was inserted, beginning with the New Moon on August 29. Following the dates of the New Moons occurring in the 19-year period from 1981 to 2000 (see Table 22) – looking at them in relation to the dates of the equinoxes – the following intercalation cycle emerges, where intercalary years are marked with an asterisk:

1* 2 3* 4 5 6* 7 8 9* 10 11* 12 13 14* 15 16 17* 18 19

The above sequence gives the pattern of the 19-year intercalation cycle used in the hermetic calendar. Of the nineteen years, twelve are normal lunar years (each containing twelve lunar months) and seven are intercalary years (each containing thirteen lunar months, where the intercalated month is a second month of Virgo in the northern hemisphere and a second month of Pisces in the southern hemisphere). The seven intercalary years are the years 1, 3, 6, 9, 11, 14, 17, where year 1 in the present cycle is the lunar year 1981/1982 in the northern hemisphere (1980/1981 in the southern hemisphere). Year 1 of the next 19-year cycle is the lunar year 2000/2001 in the northern hemisphere (1999/2000 in the southern hemisphere). The 19-year cycle then repeats itself, with the above pattern of intercalary years. (See Table 22 for a summary of the dates of the present 19-year intercalation cycle of the hermetic calendar.)

In year 1 of the 19-year intercalation cycle of the hermetic calendar – e.g. the lunar years 1981/1982 and 2000/2001 – the Easter festival does not fall in the lunar month of Aries (referring to the northern hemisphere). This is an exception, since Easter Sunday is specified as the first Sunday after the Full Moon following the vernal equinox, which normally means that Easter Sunday follows the Full Moon in the lunar month of Aries in the northern hemisphere – as indeed it does in all the remaining years (2 to 19) in the hermetic calendar. But since the lunar month of Aries in the northern hemisphere is defined to begin with the New Moon falling nearest the vernal equinox (Neomenia), it can happen – in rare cases – that the subsequent Full Moon occurs before, and not after, the vernal equinox. In the case of this rare event, the Full Moon is disqualified from the Easter rule, even if it falls only a matter of minutes prior to the vernal equinox.

For example, in 1981 (year 1 of the present cycle of the hermetic calendar), the Full Moon following the Neomenia fell 1 hour 41 minutes *before* the occurrence of the vernal equinox. This Full Moon, although actually the Full Moon in the month dedicated to the sacrifice of the Mystical Lamb (= lunar month of Aries in the northern hemisphere), did not qualify as the Full Moon preceding Easter, since it fell just before the equinox. This meant that the subsequent Full Moon – that of the lunar month of Taurus – became the Full Moon preceding Easter Sunday. Consequently, in 1981 the Easter festival became shifted into the month of Taurus (northern hemisphere).

The same again will take place in year 1 of the next cycle, the lunar year 2000/2001 (northern hemisphere). For the Full Moon following the Neomenia in the year 2000 falls 2 hours and 51 minutes *before* the vernal equinox, and hence is disqualified from the Easter rule, which means that the subsequent Full Moon – that of the lunar month of Taurus – is specified as the Full Moon preceding Easter Sunday. In a spiritual sense the Easter festival belongs to Aries, as expressed in the words of John the Baptist: "Behold the Lamb of God, who bears the sins of the world" (*John* i, 29) – referring to Christ as the Mystical Lamb (Aries).

An analogy with the spiral of life

The hermetic calendar can be a help in following the cycle of the seasons, where the lunar months of Aries, Taurus and Gemini correspond to spring; Cancer, Leo and Virgo to summer; Libra, Scorpio and Sagittarius

Table 22:
19-year intercalation cycle, 1981–2000 (New Moon dates)
hermetic calendar: cycle of the lunar months (intercalated month = 2VI)

No.	lunar year	AR	TA	GE	CN	LE	VI	2VI	LI	SC	SG	CP	AQ	PI
1*	1981–1982	6.MR	4.AP	4.MY	2.JN	1.JL	31.JL	29.AU	28.SE	27.OC	26.NO	25.DE	25.JA	23.FE
2	1982–1983	25MR	23.AP	21.MY	20.JN	19.JL			17.SE	17.OC	15.NO	14.DE	14.JA	13.FE
3*	1983–1984	14.MR	13.AP	12.MY	11.JN	10.JL	8.AU	7.SE	6.OC	4.NO	4.DE	3.JA	1.FE	2.MR
4	1984–1985	1.AP	1.MY	30.MY	29.JN	28.JL	26.AU		25.SE	24.OC	22.NO	22.DE	21.JA	19.FE
5	1985–1986	21.AP	20.AP	19.MY	19.JN	17.JL	16.AU		14.SE	14.OC	12.NO	12.DE	10.JA	9.FE
6*	1986–1987	10.MR	9.AP	8.MY	7.JN	7.JL	5.AU	4.SE	3.OC	2.NO	1.DE	31.DE	29.JA	28.FE
7	1987–1988	29.MR	28.AP	27.MY	26.JN	25.JL	24.AU		23.SE	22.OC	21.NO	20.DE	19.JA	17.FE
8	1988–1989	18.MR	16.AP	15.MY	14.JN	13.JL	12.AU		11.SE	10.OC	9.NO	9.DE	7.JA	6.FE
9*	1989–1990	7.MR	6.AP	5.MY	3.JN	3.JL	1.AU	31.AU	29.SE	28.OC	28.NO	26.DE	26.JA	25.FE
10	1990–1991	26.MR	25.AP	24.MY	22.JN	22.JL	20.AU		19.SE	18.OC	17.NO	17.DE	15.JA	14.FE
11*	1991–1992	16.MR	14.AP	14.MY	12.JN	11.JL	10.AU	8.SE	7.OC	6.NO	6.DE	4.JA	3.FE	4.MR
12	1992–1993	3.AP	2.MY	1.JN	30.JN	29.JL	28.AU		26.SE	25.OC	24.NO	24.DE	22.JA	21.FE
13	1993–1994	23.MR	21.AP	21.MY	20.JN	19.JL	17.AU		16.SE	15.OC	13.NO	13.DE	11.JA	10.FE
14*	1994–1995	12.MR	11.AP	10.MY	9.JN	8.JL	7.AU	5.SE	5.OC	3.NO	2.DE	1.JA	30.JA	1.MR
15	1995–1996	31.MR	29.AP	29.MY	28.JN	27.JL	26.AU		24.SE	24.OC	22.NO	22.DE	20.JA	18.FE
16	1996–1997	19.MR	17.AP	17.MY	16.JN	15.JL	14.AU		12.SE	12.OC	11.NO	10.DE	9.JA	7.FE
17*	1997–1998	9.MR	7.AP	6.MY	5.JN	4.JL	3.AU	1.SE	1.OC	31.OC	29.NO	29.DE	28.JA	26.FE
18	1998–1999	28.MR	26.AP	25.MY	24.JN	22.JL	22.AU		20.SE	20.OC	19.NO	18.DE	17.JA	16.FE
19	1999–2000	17.MR	16.AP	15.MY	13.JN	13.JL	11.AU		9.SE	9.OC	8.NO	7.DE	6.JA	5.FE
1*	2000–2001	6.MR	4.AP	4.MY	2.JN	1.JL	31.JL	29.AU	27.SE	27.OC	25.NO	25.DE	24.JA	22.FE

Footnote to Table 22

The definition of the hermetic calendar underlying Table 22 is such that the Easter festival is always celebrated in the lunar month of Aries (with the exception of year 1 in the 19-year cycle), and the relationship between the lunar months in the northern hemisphere and the southern hemisphere is such that the latter are simply the reverse of the former, whereby the principle is adhered to in both hemispheres that the Neomenia is the New Moon falling closest to the equinox. In the northern hemisphere this principle corresponds by and large to the specification of the Jewish lunar calendar, which is still in use to the present day (see Appendix III). On the other hand, as already referred to, the Babylonian lunar calendar adopted the New Moon *after* the vernal equinox as the Neomenia. In actual fact, it seems to the author that the true hermetic calendar — that which fits the cycle of nature most closely — is somewhere in between the specification of the Jewish and Babylonian lunar calendars, representing a synthesis of these two ancient lunar calendars. Thus, it appears that nature's yearly cycle neither follows the rigid specification of beginning always with the New Moon closest to the equinox (Jewish calendar) nor always with the New Moon falling after the equinox (Babylonian calendar). On the basis of following what actually takes place in nature from year to year (in the northern hemisphere, observation restricted to Western Europe), the author is led to conclude that Table 22 holds good for non-intercalary years, but that in the intercalary years the Neomenia equates with the New Moon listed under Taurus. This means that in intercalary years, as listed in Table 22, the entries in the first seven columns should be modified as follows:

		2PI	AR	TA	GE	CN	LE	VI
1*	1981–1982	6.MR	4.AP	4.MY	2.JN	1.JL	31.JL	29.AU
3*	1983–1984	14.MR	13.AP	12.MY	11.JN	10.JL	8.AU	7.SE
6*	1986–1987	10.MR	9.AP	8.MY	7.JN	7.JL	5.AU	4.SE
9*	1989–1990	7.MR	6.AP	5.MY	3.JN	3.JL	1.AU	31.AU
11*	1991–1992	16.MR	14.AP	14.MY	12.JN	11.JL	10.AU	8.SE
14*	1994–1995	12.MR	11.AP	10.MY	9.JN	8.JL	7.AU	5.SE
17*	1997–1998	9.MR	7.AP	6.MY	5.JN	4.JL	3.AU	1.SE
1*	2000–2001	6.MR	4.AP	4.MY	2.JN	1.JL	31.JL	29.AU

To summarize: this modification signifies that the intercalary month of Virgo (2VI) disappears, and each preceding month in an intercalary year is shifted back, yielding an intercalary month of Pisces (2PI), which actually belongs to the foregoing lunar year.

Notes concerning Table 22

In this table New Moon dates are listed, each date signifying the start of a lunar month. The dates are tabulated according to the 19-year intercalation cycle of the hermetic calendar, where year 1 of the present cycle is the lunar year 1981–1982 and of the next cycle is the lunar year 2000–2001 (in the northern hemisphere). Intercalary years are marked with an asterisk. Normal years contain twelve lunar months, whereas an intercalary year has an extra (thirteenth) month. In the northern hemisphere the intercalated (extra) month is a second (lunar) month of Virgo, and in the southern hemisphere it is a second (lunar) month of Pisces. The headings for the lunar months in the following table are according to the sequence of the lunar months in the northern hemisphere: Aries (AR), Taurus (TA), Gemini (GE), Cancer (CN), Leo (LE), Virgo (VI), 2 Virgo (2VI) – in intercalary years, Libra (LI), Scorpio (SC), Sagittarius (SG), Capricorn (CP), Aquarius (AQ), Pisces (PI). For the southern hemisphere the names of the lunar months have to be reversed in this table, in which case the sequence of lunar months at the heading

X. The Hermetic Calendar

to autumn; and Capricorn, Aquarius and Pisces to winter. Thereby the cycle of growth (spring), expansion (summer), decay (autumn) and contraction (winter) can be followed.

To draw an analogy with the spiral of life in the human biography, spring – the period of growth – is divided into three periods (Aries, Taurus, Gemini) just as the period of growth of the human being is divided into three 7-year periods (infancy from 0 to 7, childhood from 7 to 14, and youth from 14 to 21). According to the principle of correspondences, the month of Aries in the hermetic calendar is the period of infancy in nature's yearly cycle, the month of Taurus is childhood, and the month of Gemini is youth. Similarly, for the human being the first three 7-year periods comprise the *springtime of life*.

Continuing the analogy further, the lunar months of Cancer, Leo and Virgo – the period of expansion and ripening – equate with the three 7-year periods of the *summer of life* (21–28, 28–35, 35–42) in the biography. These periods in nature, and also in the human being's biography, constitute not so much a time of growth as one of maturing (ripening).

If the analogy is continued still further, the lunar months of Libra, Scorpio and Sagittarius – the period of decay in nature's forces – correspond in the spiral of life to the three 7-year periods of 42–49, 49–56 and 56–63 (= the *autumn of life*). Lastly, the lunar months of Capricorn, Aquarius and Pisces – the time of contraction in nature – bear an analogy with the *winter of life*, which sets in around the age of 63.

Here the hermetic principle of analogy allows a glimpse into the manifestation of the spiritual law of the cycle of growth, expansion, decay, contraction, as this comes to expression on the one hand in the four seasons of nature and on the other hand in the spiral of life, whereby man's life can be viewed as comprising four seasons: spring (0–21), summer (21–42), autumn (42–63), and winter (63 onwards).

A path towards Astro-Sophia

As described earlier in this chapter, the hermetic calendar can be a help not only in following the year of nature, but also in allowing a meditative approach towards following the activity of Christ and Sophia throughout

---

should read: Libra (LI), Scorpio (SC), Sagittarius (SG), Capricorn (CP), Aquarius (AQ), Pisces (PI), 2 Pisces (2PI) – in intercalary years, Aries (AR), Taurus (TA), Gemini (GE), Cancer (CN), Leo (LE), Virgo (VI).

Each New Moon date is recorded as a calendar date (day.month), where the following abbreviations for the twelve calendar months are used: January (JA), February (FE), March (MR), April (AP), May (MY), June (JN), July (JL), August (AU), September (SE), October (OC), November (NO), December (DE). The calendar date on which the New Moon falls is specified by the time of occurrence of the New Moon in GMT (Greenwich Mean Time) = UT (Universal Time).

the year. For through the hermetic calendar the times are indicated (New Moon and Full Moon) at which the activity of Sophia and Christ – in relation to man on Earth – can be experienced most strongly. And the two Christian-hermetic meditations – the sanctification of the New Moon, and the sanctification of the Full Moon – can help the Sophia mystery and the Christ mystery, which take place at these times, to become, in the course of time, a matter of experience. In this sense, the hermetic calendar is part of hermetic astrology's contribution towards the task of developing a living experience of the world of stars, on the path towards *Astro-Sophia*.

To bring the Being of Sophia to consciousness each New Moon – through the Christian-hermetic meditation of the sanctification of the New Moon – is to enter into a relationship with the Cosmic Virgin, spoken of in the twelfth chapter of the *Apocalypse of St. John*. This chapter of the *Apocalypse* holds the key to the deeper significance of the lunar months in the age of the second coming. For, just as at the first coming Jesus Christ was born from the Virgin Mary, so at the second coming the Risen One is coming to birth through the Cosmic Virgin, Mary Sophia, to be born into the hearts and minds of men.

And a great sign appeared in heaven: a woman clothed with the Sun, with the Moon under her feet, and on her head a crown of twelve stars. She was with child and she cried out in her pangs of birth, in anguish for delivery... She brought forth a male child, one who is to rule all nations with a rod of iron. (Relevation xii, 1–2, 5)

Each lunar month – at New Moon – the "birth" of the Risen One takes place out of the cosmos, a "birth" into the etheric aura of the Earth, reaching up to the orbit of the Moon. The ascended cosmic I AM bears the cosmic power of the New Moon into the Earth's etheric aura. This birth takes place out of the Cosmic Virgin, who embodies the soul of the cosmos. She is "clothed with the Sun, with the Moon under her feet, and on her head she wears a crown of twelve stars." This is an image of the Cosmic Virgin at New Moon, pictured in the alignment of the Sun and Moon in one of the twelve fixed-star signs of the zodiac ("twelve stars"). That which she bestows upon the human soul – considered as a cosmic being – is drawn from the sidereal sign in which the New Moon takes place.

For example, the northern hemisphere's Neomenia – the first New Moon of the year, signifying the start of the lunar month of Aries – generally falls in the sidereal sign of Pisces, as the Neomenia is the New Moon falling closest to the vernal equinox, and the current location of the vernal point is at $5\frac{1}{2}°$ Pisces. It is then the *power of Pisces* which the Cosmic Virgin bestows upon the human soul at the sanctification of the first New Moon of the year, and the corresponding blessing is: "Blessed are the magnanimous, for they shall be filled with love" (blessing of Pisces). The power of Pisces – "to be filled with love" – is that which is bestowed upon the human being who practises magnanimity. "To be filled with love" is the gift of the soul that radiates as the "star" of Pisces from the twelve stars in the crown of Mary Sophia, the Cosmic Virgin.

However, the human being – when he is incarnated upon the Earth – is bound up with and is part of nature, and for nature the Neomenia signifies the start of the *lunar month of Aries*. In following the lunar months through the course of the year, the human being therefore has to distinguish between that which is bestowed upon him on a cosmic level, on the level of cosmic being as a gift for the soul, and that which flows into nature, to which he – as an earthly being – belongs. In the example under consideration, he receives the blessing of Pisces when the New Moon at the start of the lunar year (Neomenia) takes place in the sidereal sign of Pisces – this is of significance to him as a cosmic being – but as an earthly being it is the impulse of Aries ("spring") which begins to take effect in the whole of nature at the Neomenia.

The human being is both a cosmic and an earthly being. As an earthly being he participates in the course of nature, in the cycle of growth, expansion, decay and contraction, which unfolds through the twelve lunar months of the year (Aries, Taurus, Gemini – growth; Cancer, Leo, Virgo – expansion; Libra, Scorpio, Sagittarius – decay; Capricorn, Aquarius, Pisces – contraction). But in the New Age, the age of the second coming, man is in the process of awakening to himself as a cosmic being. And here again the lunar months are of significance to him, but this time on a cosmic level, in relation to the passage of the Moon through the twelve signs of the sidereal zodiac. That which is of significance to him in awakening to himself as a cosmic being in the age of the second coming is the location in the sidereal zodiac of the New Moon, and also the passage of the Moon through the various signs of the zodiac leading up to Full Moon – the Full Moon "culminating", as it were, in a particular sign of the zodiac – and then again the passage of the Moon through the signs of the zodiac from Full Moon back to New Moon in the course of a lunar month. When brought into relation with the sanctification of the New Moon and the sanctification of the Full Moon, the sidereal sign in which the New Moon is located (together with the Sun) at New Moon acquires special significance, as also does the sidereal sign in which the Moon is located (opposite the Sun) at Full Moon. In the New Age these two configurations – the sidereal signs in which the New Moon and Full Moon are located each lunar month – have acquired a profound meaning for the human being on the path of awakening to his higher, cosmic nature.

At the New Moon the Cosmic Virgin bestows the power of the background sidereal sign upon the human being on the spiritual path, and the Risen One – who, as it were, becomes "born out" of the Cosmic Virgin at the New Moon – bears this power into the Earth's aura. The path of the

Risen One – from New Moon to Full Moon – follows the way of the Passion, culminating with the etheric crucifixion at Full Moon, repeating on the etheric level the physical crucifixion which took place at the Full Moon in Libra on the original Good Friday (April 3, A.D. 33). At Full Moon each month the Crucified One pours forth cosmic love into the human being, pouring it forth from against the background sidereal sign in which the Full Moon is located.

Through the sanctification of the New Moon, therefore, the human being may receive through the blessing of Sophia the power of the zodiacal sign in which the New Moon takes place. Here the twelve blessings, listed earlier in this chapter in connection with the twelve virtues of the twelve zodiacal signs, become relevant. Further, at the sanctification of the Full Moon the spiritually striving human being may receive through the blessing of Christ the power of the zodiacal sign in which the Full Moon takes place. Here the twelve beatitudes listed earlier in this chapter become relevant – each beatitude being a blessing of Christ connected with a particular sign of the sidereal zodiac (that in which the Full Moon occurs). Thereby these two signs – that of the New Moon and that of the Full Moon – acquire special significance for the human being each lunar month in the age of the second coming.

However, at the same time as the awakening of the cosmic self takes place, inevitably a new sense of responsibility towards nature starts to grow. This is the other aspect of the hermetic calendar: its significance to man in his relationship to nature – that this relationship becomes a matter of the heart. For through the hermetic calendar the human being can be helped to enter into a deeper relationship with the second coming of Christ, which is a matter not just for mankind, but for the whole Earth.

The etheric return of Christ will signify a restoration of hope in nature; it will mean her resurrection. Christ will be active throughout the horizontal realm in space. He will visit all the regions of the Earth and this will mean a meeting with the beings of nature and a working as a moral force in the world of nature... How can one picture the effect of Christ on nature? His moving through space in (the realm of) nature? There are many things taking place which anyone who attentively watches and experiences has observed – in nature, every year, much happens which increasingly contradicts the whole traditional process of nature in the past. Springtimes are different from what they used to be. Summer, autumn and winter are becoming different too. In March, there are sultry summer days. People speak of inexplicable manifestations: the whole divine revelation of spring, summer, autumn and winter is mixed up. Chaos is setting in, and this comes not from heaven, but from the interior of the Earth. People think that these are merely changes of climate, but this is not so. When orderly changes again take place in nature – these will manifest the outward signs of the etheric return of Christ. And then new springtimes will come which will not be evil and sultry, but will breathe forth warmth and healing power. Summers will come in which there will be two harvests. Nature will breathe forth goodness and will offer her fruits – as if making a gift of them... Nature will radiate goodness. For example, man will find remarkable consolation in trees when he is in despair. Then goodness will stream forth from plants into human souls. Man will experience that trees will bend before him in goodness, and in generosity. Such goodness will be felt in nature that men will never forget it, they will remember it as a natural marvel. Nothing external, such as thunder and lightning will happen. A breath of goodness will stream forth from the world of nature and human nature will feel this as a regeneration, as a healing. The movement of Christ will progress in concentric circles in the realm of space, and there will be phenomena which will be designated by science as "ozone streams". Tubercular patients will feel better or, in whole regions, will be cured simultaneously. People will speak of lines of ozone in the atmosphere. But it will actually be the breath of Christ *moving in a definite direction over the surface of the Earth... There will be a reconciliation between mankind and the world of nature... which will take place for nature in connection with the coming of the Etheric Christ.*[14]

It is the renewed activity of Christ in the world of nature, beginning with his second coming in the course of the twentieth century, that bestows deeper meaning and significance upon the hermetic calendar. Through the hermetic calendar man is able to enter into connection with Christ's work of redemption in the kingdoms of nature, and may open himself – through the sanctification of the New Moon and the Full Moon – to receive the blessings bestowed upon the inner being of man at these times in each lunar month. In this way the hermetic calendar can become a contribution to helping to re-establish a harmonious relationship between man and nature, one which is blessed from above.

In view of the tragic conditions arising on Earth through man's unbridled egotistical abuse of nature – one need only think of the decay of vast numbers of trees in the forests – the time has come when a new, spiritual relationship between man and nature is called for. This is only possible for each human being to establish himself, but help is offered – by way of the hermetic calendar – in making this step, in that the hermetic calendar offers a key to the activity of cosmic forces in nature through the course of the year, including the activity of the cosmic Being of Christ in nature. On the one hand the hermetic calendar can help to bring to realisation a new, spiritual relationship between man and nature. On the other hand the sanctification of the New Moon and Full Moon each lunar month can open up a new connection with the activity of Christ and Sophia on a cosmic level.

In so far as this connection is actualized, a step is made from astrology to astrosophy – to *Astro-Sophia* ("wisdom of the stars"). This step is the goal of hermetic astrology, as referred to in the introduction to *Hermetic Astrology* I.

Hermetic astrology comprises a new science of destiny, an outline of which has been given in Volume I: *Astrology and Reincarnation* and in Volume II: *Astrological Biography*. This science can help to give a deeper understanding of:

(1) the nature of birth and death (the mystery of reincarnation); and
(2) the course of life (how karma comes to expression in biography).

In this respect hermetic astrology can help to give an orientation to the deeper nature and meaning of existence here on Earth. A true fulfilment of earthly existence, however, is to be found in the attainment of a living connection with Jesus Christ and Mary Sophia. It is the search for Christ and Sophia which is the higher goal of hermetic astrology, leading it over to become astrosophy. In the words of Novalis:

Christ and Sophia.[15]
The star-world melts, dissolving
To golden living wine,
Which we shall drink, resolving
Ourselves as stars will shine.[16]
Established is the empire of eternity,
In love and peace concluded is all enmity,
The long-drawn dream of dreary suffering departs,
Sophia is forever Priestess in our hearts.[17]

Chapter 10: Notes and references

1. Cf. Valentin Tomberg, *The Four Sacrifices of Christ and the Appearance of Christ in the Etheric* (Candeur Manuscripts: Spring Valley NY, 1983), p. 76.
2. Neil Michelsen, *The American Sidereal Ephemeris, 1976–2000* (ACS Publications, San Diego, 1981).
3. Neil Michelsen, *The American Heliocentric Ephemeris, 1901–2000* (ACS Publications, San Diego, 1982). Note that whereas the *American Heliocentric Ephemeris* lists the daily heliocentric aspects between the planets, the *American Sidereal Ephemeris* does not list the daily geocentric aspects between the planets, so that an extra ephemeris, such as *The American Ephemeris* (ACS Publications, San Diego) is required for the geocentric aspects.
4. Cf. Robert Powell, *Christian Hermetic Astrology: The Star of the Magi and the Life of Christ,* for a further discussion concerning the journey of the three kings.
5. Cf. Plutarch, *De Iside et Osiride* (ed. and trsl. J. Gwyn Griffiths, Wales, 1970).
6. Cf. Sister L.L., *Supremo Appello* (Rome, 1969; German trsl. *Höchster Ruf,* Parvis, Hauteville, Switzerland, 1975).
7. Cf. Rudolf Steiner, *Anweisung für eine esoterische Schulung* (Rudolf Steiner Verlag, Dornach, Switzerland, 1979), p. 31, for a list of the twelve virtues related to the twelve signs of the zodiac.
8. Cf. J.K. Fotheringham, "The Evidence of Astronomy and Technical Chronology for the Date of Crucifixion," *Journal of Theological Studies* 35 (1934), pp. 146–162; also, Robert Powell, *Chronicle of the Life of Christ,* Appendix I, and *Christian Hermetic Astrology: The Star of the Magi and the Life of Christ.*
9. Stephen Langdon, *Babylonian Menologies and the Semitic Calendars* (London, 1935), p. 68.
10. D.A. Bradley, M.A. Woodbury, G.W. Brier, "Lunar Synodical Period and Widespread Precipitation," *Science* NS 137 (1962), pp. 748–749.
11. E.E. Adderley and E.G. Bowen, "Lunar Component in Precipitation Data," *Science* NS 137 (1962), pp. 749–750.
12. Balogh Barna, "Relations between Astronomy and Ancient Astrology," *Kapitoly z Vedeckej Astrologie* (Bratislava, 1969), p. 85.
13. Cf. Richard A. Parker – Waldo H. Dubberstein, *Babylonian Chronology, 626 B.C. – A.D. 75* (Brown University Press, Providence, 1956).
14. Valentin Tomberg, op. cit., pp. 80–81.
15. Friedrich Hiebel, *Novalis* (University of North Carolina Press, Chapel Hill, 1954), p. 27 – diary entry by Novalis for June 31, 1797.
16. Novalis, *Hymns to the Night,* 5 (trsl. C.E. Passage, except for the last line, which is given here in the form of a free rendition by the author, Library of Liberal Arts, Indianapolis-New York, 1960, p. 13).
17. Novalis, "Klingsohr's Fairy Tale" in: *Hymns to the Night and Other Selected Writings* (trsl. C.E. Passage, Library of Liberal Arts, Indianapolis-New York, 1960, p. 44).

Appendix I

The 7-year Periods (Septennaries)

The rhythm of 7-year periods – as the fundamental rhythm underlying human biography – was known of in antiquity. Thus according to Philo, who lived in Alexandria and was a contemporary of Christ, the Greek sage Solon (sixth century B.C.) taught the following:

The boy, yet an infant, puts forth his teeth in the first seven years of his age.
When heaven shall have granted him another seven years, he arrives at puberty.
In his third age, his limbs now increasing, the beard of changing colour grows upon his chin.
Every one in his fourth septennary arrives at full strength, and gives proof of manly valour.
In the fifth the man, now mature, is led to think of a wife and his future posterity.
In the sixth the mind of the man is fit for all things, and is no longer pleased with trivial matters.
In the seventh and eighth the understanding and speech are at their best, and continue so through these fourteen years.
In the ninth he still has some powers left, but his eloquence and wisdom are no longer capable of great efforts.
And now let him who shall attain his tenth septennary prepare for a not untimely death.[1]

In the above teaching attributed to Solon, human life unfolds archetypally through ten 7-year periods, whereby the human being develops on various levels (physical, mental, etc.) during the course of his seventy years of life, in such a way that in each 7-year period a particular level of development is emphasized. During the first three periods it is more the physical development that is emphasized; in later periods it is more the intellectual development that comes to the fore. Philo himself wrote a brief account summarizing the above teaching that human life unfolds in a sequence of ten 7-year periods:

Moreover the ages of man from infancy to old age, which are measured by periods of seven years, show very clearly the perfective force implanted in the number seven. For in the first septennary the teeth come forth. In the second we arrive at puberty. In the third we show signs of a beard. In the fourth we acquire increase of strength. In the fifth is the period for marrying. In the sixth the intellect is matured. In the seventh both mind and speech are matured. In the eighth both become perfect. In the ninth we acquire equity and gentleness, the passions being greatly calmed. In the tenth the end of life is to be desired, while all the faculties are sound.[2]

Julian Pollux, writing in the second century A.D., attributed the Greek physician Hippocrates (fifth/fourth centuries B.C.) with teaching that human life consists of seven ages, each age comprising seven years or some multiple of seven years:

Hippocrates says there are seven ages. His words are, "In the nature of man there are seven periods which are called ages: the infant; the boy; the youth; the young man; the man; the elderly man; the aged man. The infant is within seven years, until he puts forth his teeth. The boy until puberty, at twice seven years. The youth until the growth of his beard, at thrice seven years. The young man up to four sevens, until the whole body is grown. The man up to forty-nine. The elderly man to fifty-six, or eight sevens. Whatever is beyond this belongs to old age."[3]

This teaching of the *seven ages of man*, which was later taken up by Shakespeare (see below), is evidently a simple adaptation of the teaching that life consists archetypally of ten 7-year periods. In both cases it is assumed that the basic rhythm underlying human biography is the 7-year rhythm. Moreover, virtually the same text as the above from Julius Pollux's *Onomasticon* is also given by Philo in his work *De opificio mundi* ("On the creation of the world"), directly following on from the text attributed to Solon. This would seem to indicate, as far as Philo was concerned, that the teaching of Hippocrates concerning the seven ages of man was simply an adaptation of Solon's teaching that life comprises ten septennaries.

In his play *As you like it*, Shakespeare gave a poetic rendition of the teaching of the seven ages of man. He used the simile that the world is a stage upon which each human being plays out his life in a series of seven acts (the seven ages of man). In this simile, birth corresponds to the human being's entrance upon the stage and death to his exit. The seven ages of man are termed by Shakespeare: the infant, the schoolboy, the lover, the soldier, the justice, the pantaloon, and second childhood. This corresponds more or less with the seven ages listed by Hippocrates: the infant, the boy, the youth, the young man, the man, the elderly man, and the aged man.

Shakespeare, **The seven ages of man** *(As you like it,* II, 7)
All the world's a stage,
And all the men and women merely players:
They have their exits and their entrances;

And one man in his time plays many parts,
His acts being seven ages. At first the infant,
Mewling and puking in the nurse's arms.
Then the whining schoolboy, with his satchel
And shining morning face, creeping like a snail
Unwillingly to school. And then the lover,
Sighing like a furnace, with a woeful ballad
Made to his mistress' eyebrow. Then a soldier,
Full of strange oaths, and bearded like the pard,
Jealous in honour, sudden and quick in quarrel,
Seeking the bubble reputation
Even in the cannon's mouth. And then the justice,
In fair round belly with good capon lined,
With eyes severe and beard of formal cut,
Full of wise saws and modern instances;
And so he plays his part. The sixth age shifts
Into the lean and slipper'd pantaloon,
With spectacles on nose and pouch on side,
His youthful hose, well saved, a world too wide
For his shrunk shank; and his big manly voice,
Turning again toward childish treble, pipes
And whistles in his sound. Last scene of all,
That ends this strange eventful history,
Is second childishness and mere oblivion,
Sans teeth, sans eyes, sans taste, sans everything.

For hermetic astrology Shakespeare's text is of special interest in view of its obvious astrological allusions. In Chapters 4 and 5 of this book the *spiral of life* is discussed, in which the relationship between the planets and the 7-year periods is outlined (see Table 7 for a summary). Shakespeare partially incorporated these planetary-astrological correspondences into his text. Thus the first three periods described by Shakespeare (infant, schoolboy, lover) are related astrologically to the Moon, Mercury and Venus – the astrological relationship being especially clear in the third 7-year period, that of Venus (traditionally the planet of love). However, Shakespeare omits altogether the Sun period of life, comprising the three 7-year periods from 21 to 42 in the spiral of life, and goes on to the Mars period, which he calls that of a soldier. Here the astrological allusion to Mars is direct, as Mars is traditionally referred to as the planet of war.

Following on from the soldier (Mars) comes the justice. Shakespeare's characterization of the justice ("full of wise saws") fits well astrologically to Jupiter, the planet of wisdom. Then comes the pantaloon, who is fully under the sway of the process of aging. Here astrologically, the influence of Saturn fits, in so far as the astrological tradition attributes Saturn with the rigidifying influence of old age. Lastly, the seventh age, the seventh of life's "acts" in Shakespeare's text, is that of second childhood. Here the human being is beyond the planetary influences and is on his way towards a new life (second childhood), i.e. he has entered the zodiacal period of life (63 onwards in the spiral of life).

In terms of the spiral of life, therefore, Shakespeare's seven ages of man are as follows: infant (Moon, 0–7); schoolboy (Mercury, 7–14); lover (Venus, 14–21); soldier (Mars, 42–49); justice (Jupiter, 49–56); pantaloon (Saturn, 56–63); second childhood (zodiac, 63 onwards).

Returning to Hippocrates' description of the seven ages of man, which might have served as the basis for Shakespeare's poetic version, it can be seen – when compared with the foregoing – that Shakespeare allowed himself considerable poetic licence. In adapting the teaching of the seven ages of man, however, Shakespeare succeeded in bringing in – in poetic form – the planetary-astrological correspondences, with the exception of omitting the Sun period of life, which should come between that of Venus (the lover) and that of Mars (the soldier).

Only in the twentieth century – through Rudolf Steiner – has the complete teaching of the 7-year periods in relation to the planetary correspondences come to the light of day. In 1924 Rudolf Steiner spoke of this – the basis of the spiral of life – as follows:

Together with the Earth we exist within seven interpenetrating spheres, and we grow into them, enter into connection with them in the course of life. Our life from birth to death is unfolded out of its original inherent tendencies, inasmuch as the star (i.e. planetary) spheres draw us from birth to death. When we have reached the Saturn sphere we have passed through all that the beings of the various planetary spheres in grace accomplish for us and then, speaking in the occult sense, we enter into a free-moving cosmic existence of our own.[4]

In the same lecture (as the above quotation) Rudolf Steiner indicated that the human being enters into connection with the seven interpenetrating planetary spheres in the course of the unfolding of the 7-year periods as follows: Moon (0–7), Mercury (7–14), Venus (14–21), Sun (21–42), Mars (42–49), Jupiter (49–56), Saturn (56–63).

This teaching of Rudolf Steiner's was explained further by Willi Sucher's discovery in the 1930's that the archetypal ten 7-year periods of life arise through the (on average) ten lunar orbits of the sidereal zodiac between conception and birth. In the embryonic period the Moon passes on average ten times around the sidereal zodiac, during which time the human being's etheric body is formed. Thus the etheric body – as the human being's *time organism* – is "wound up" between conception and birth. From the moment of birth onwards it "winds down", unfolding in the archetypal series of ten 7-year periods comprising the spiral of life, each 7-year period corresponding to one lunar orbit of the sidereal zodiac during the embryonic period. The teaching of the spiral of life – first described more fully by Rudolf Steiner in 1924 – together with the subsequent discovery of its astronomical basis by Willi Sucher, forms the basis for the hermetic astrological science of destiny *(astrological biography)* outlined in this book.

Appendix I: Notes and references

1. Philo, *De opificio mundi*, 104 (trsl. F.H. Colson and G.H. Whitaker, "On the creation", 10 vols., Loeb Classical Library, vol. i, London-New York, 1929, p.85).
2. Ibid., trsl. pp. 83–85.
3. Julius Pollux, *Onomasticon* II, 4 (ed. T. Hemsterhuis, Amsterdam, 1706, p. 153). Virtually the same text is given by Philo, *De opificio mundi,* 105 (trsl. F.H. Colson and G.H. Whitaker, op. cit., pp. 85–87).
4. Rudolf Steiner, *True and False Paths of Spiritual Investigation* (trsl. A.H. Parker, Rudolf Steiner Press, London, 1969, p. 131).

Appendix II

Computations

The following tabulation lists the computations of the conception, birth and death horoscopes referred to in this book. The tabulation is in alphabetical order of the personalities concerned. The author owes an inexpressible debt of gratitude for assistance he received with these computations – assistance that has made possible the research work presented in this book.

Presentation of the data

First are listed the name, place and date (of conception, birth or death) of the personality concerned, together with an indication as to whether the date referred to is in terms of the old Julian calendar or the modern Gregorian calendar introduced by Pope Gregory XIII in 1582.

Then follow brief comments concerning the personality and the source of the data, which may be a biographical or an astrological source. Here certain abbreviations are used:

DSB: Dictionary of Scientific Biography
CBC: Circle Book of Charts, compiled by Stephen Erlewine
LIFE: Life (=biography) of the personality concerned

The classification refers to the Chapter in which the chart is referred to, and in the case of drawn-up charts lists the Chart number (see Index for page number of the Chart).

In the right-hand column, under the heading "sid.", several items of data are listed:

Time: If no time is known, then the computation is made for midday on the given date, indicated by the entry 12. If the actual time was midday, the entry is 12.00. In the first case, the entry indicates an approximation, whilst in the second case a more exact entry is indicated. This principle is adhered to throughout, e.g. the difference between the entries 10 and 10.00 is that the first indicates an approximate time, whilst the second refers to a more exact time. The time in each case is either Local Time or Zone Standard Time (ZT). In the latter case an indication is made as to the number of hours difference of ZT from Greenwich Mean Time (GMT), where (-) denotes East of Greenwich. DST denotes the number of hours of daylight saving time.

Further items: ST = sidereal time; LO = longitude; LA = latitude.
Astrological items: AS = Ascendant; MC = Medium Coeli (Midheaven); MN = Moon's ascending (north) node; MP = Moon's perigee. In each

case of these four astrological items, first the longitude in the sidereal zodiac is given (heading "sid."), and then the longitude in the tropical zodiac (heading "trop."). The difference between the longitudes in the sidereal and tropical zodiacs can be determined from the next entry; VP = vernal point.

Alongside VP is listed the location of the *synetic vernal point,* i.e. the location of the vernal point in the sidereal zodiac as defined in the *American Sidereal Ephemeris* (compiled by Neil Michelsen, Astro Computing Services, San Diego, 1981). The difference between the tropical and sidereal longitudes is the difference between the VP's longitude and zero degrees Aries in the sidereal zodiac.

Planetary entries: For each of the planets both the sidereal and tropical longitudes – both geocentric and heliocentric – are listed under the appropriate headings, and in each case the planet's (geocentric/heliocentric) latitude is also listed.

```
Addey, John
Birth of  John Addey
at Barnsley
on Tuesday,  15 June  1920 A.D. - Gregorian
Comments: Stated birth time corrected by applying the hermetic rule.
Became partially paralysed at 23 years 6 months.
Source: ASTROLOGICAL JOURNAL 1982 p135
Reference/Group: Ch.6, Chart 16
      GEOCENTRIC              HELIOCENTRIC
      Sid.   Trop.   Lat.        Sid.   Trop.  Lat.              Sid.        Trop.
SU  0GE15  23GE52          *  TE   0SG15 23SG52         *   Time 08.31
MO 12TA21   5GE59   1S53   *                            *   ZT  , DST 1
ME 21GE 0  14CN38   1N58   *  ME   1VI49 25VI27   5N31  *   ST  0.58
VE 25TA10  18GE47   0S 6   *  VE  17TA59 11GE37   0S15  *   LO  1W29
MA 28VI55  22LI33   0S37   *  MA   4SC39 28SC17   0S18  *   LA 53N34
JU 21CN29  15LE 7   0N49   *  JU  29CN59 23LE37   0N54  *   AS 14CN51    8LE29
SA 12LE29   6VI 7   1N50   *  SA  18LE26 12VI 4   1N53  *   MC 22PI10   15AR47
UR 12AQ 1   5PI38   0S46   *  UR   9AQ17  2PI55   0S46  *   MN 19LI57   13SC34
NE 15CN58   9LE36   0N 0   *  NE  17CN21 10LE59   0N 0  *   MP  2GE59   26GE36
PL 13GE17   6CN55   3S36   *  PL  13GE35  7CN13   3S40  *   VP  6PI22

Addey, John
Conception of  John Addey
at Barnsley
on Friday,  17 October  1919 A.D. - Gregorian
Comments: Reincarnation of Michael Maestlin.
Born one month premature.
Source: See Chapter 6.
Reference/Group: Ch.6, Chart 15.
      GEOCENTRIC              HELIOCENTRIC
      Sid.   Trop.   Lat.        Sid.   Trop.  Lat.              Sid.        Trop.
SU 29VI24  23LI 1          *  TE  29PI24 23AR 1          *  Time 10.51
MO 14CN58   8LE35   5S 0   *                             *  ZT  , DST
ME 12LI50   6SC27   0S46   *  ME  12SC43  6SG20   2S17   *  ST 12.25
VE 20LE33  14VI11   3S 8   *  VE  20AR25 14TA 2   1S48   *  LO  1W29
MA 10LE48   4VI25   1N24   *  MA  13CN49  7LE26   1N49   *  LA 53N34
JU 20CN54  14LE31   0N31   *  JU  10CN48  4LE25   0N33   *  AS 12SC28    6SG 6
SA 14LE19   7VI56   1N31   *  SA   9LE56  3VI34   1N37   *  MC 13VI 5    6LI42
UR  4AQ20  27AQ57   0S46   *  UR   6AQ42  0PI19   0S45   *  MN  2SC46   26SC23
NE 17CN42  11LE19   0S 3   *  NE  15CN54  9LE31   0S 3   *  MP  6TA 3   29TA40
PL 14GE 7   7CN44   3S55   *  PL  12GE51  6CN28   3S54   *  VP  6PI23
```

Appendix II: Computations 405

```
Addey, John
Death of  John Addey
at London
on Saturday,  27 March  1982 A.D. - Gregorian
Comments: Astrologer/philosopher. Pioneered new astrological ideas.
Wrote HARMONICS IN ASTROLOGY.
Source: ASTROLOGICAL JOURNAL 1982 p135
Reference/Group: Ch.6, Chart 17.
     GEOCENTRIC              HELIOCENTRIC
       Sid.    Trop.   Lat.       Sid.    Trop.    Lat.         Sid.      Trop.
SU  12PI14   6AR43           TE  12VI14   6LI43          *   Time 17.17
MO  12AR27   6TA56  4S46  *                              *   ZT , DST
ME  28AQ 0  22PI29  2S14  *  ME  21CP26  15AQ56  6S59    *   ST  5.36
VE  25CP54  20AQ23  1N54  *  VE  22LI11  16SC41  1N41    *   LO  0W05
MA  17VI17  11LI47   3N 5 *  MA  14VI12   8LI42  1N12    *   LA 51N32
JU  14LI19   8SC48  1N26  *  JU   8LI43   3SC13  1N12    *   AS   1VI16  25VI45
SA  25VI23  19LI53  2N45  *  SA  24VI 2  18LI32  2N29    *   MC  29TA59  24GE28
UR  10SC 3   4SG33  0N10  *  UR   7SC27   1SG56  0N10    *   MN  24GE 9  18CN39
NE   2SG34  27SG 3  1N17  *  NE   0SG42  25SG11  1N17    *   MP  25TA59  20GE29
PL   1LI31  26LI 1 17N22  *  PL   0LI52  25LI21  16N50   *   VP   5PI31
```

```
Addey, Paralysis of John
Embryonic correspondence of  Paralysis of John Addey
at Barnsley
on Saturday,  17 January  1920 A.D. - Gregorian
Comments: Planetary configuration at moment in embryonic period
corresponding to paralysis at 23 years 6 months. Moon = 24 SCOR.
Source: See Chapter 6.
Reference/Group: Ch.6, Chart 18.
     GEOCENTRIC              HELIOCENTRIC
       Sid.    Trop.   Lat.       Sid.    Trop.    Lat.         Sid.      Trop.
SU   2CP44  26CP21           TE   2CN44  26CN21          *   Time 18
MO  24SC12  17SG49  2N 7  *                              *   ZT , DST
ME  20SG43  14CP20  1S13  *  ME  24SC37  18SG14  3S36    *   ST  1.38
VE  22SC15  15SG52  2N 0  *  VE  19VI45  13LI23   3N 1   *   LO  1W29
MA   0LI39  24LI16  2N 4  *  MA  24LE21  17VI58  1N37    *   LA 53N34
JU  21CN37  15LE15  0N51  *  JU  18CN11  11LE48  0N42    *   AS  21CN36  15LE13
SA  17LE29  11VI 6  1N52  *  SA  13LE12   6VI49  1N44    *   MC   2AR40  26AR17
UR   6AQ 6  29AQ44  0S44  *  UR   7AQ41   1PI18  0S45    *   MN  27LI52  21SC30
NE  16CN55  10LE32  0S 2  *  NE  16CN27  10LE 5  0S 2    *   MP  16TA19   9GE57
PL  12GE41   6CN19  3S54  *  PL  13GE 8   6CN45  3S49    *   VP   6PI23
```

```
Demotic horoscope 3
Birth of  (Unknown person) Demotic horoscope 3
at Medinet Habu
on Friday,  25 February  18 A.D. - Julian
Comments: 3rd. demotic horoscope. Birth at "4 o'clock in the evening"
equates with 4 hours after sunset, i.e. about 8.45 p.m.
Source: O.Neugebauer,DEMOTIC HOROSCOPE
Reference/Group: Ch.7, Figure 17.
     GEOCENTRIC              HELIOCENTRIC
       Sid.    Trop.   Lat.       Sid.    Trop.    Lat.         Sid.      Trop.
SU   7PI51   5PI 8            TE   7VI51   5VI 8         *   Time 20.45
MO   0SG14  27SC31  4S30  *                              *   Local Time
ME  20PI30  17PI47  0N15  *  ME   5TA33   2TA51  0N58    *   ST  6.58
VE  18PI33  15PI50  1S14  *  VE   3AR25   0AR42  2S52    *   LO 29E55
MA  25TA 5  22TA22  1N37  *  MA   1CN32  28GE49  1N31    *   LA 31N13
JU  12PI44  10PI 1  1S10  *  JU  13PI43  11PI 0  1S24    *   AS  15LI 8  12LI25
SA  14CP20  11CP37  0S 2  *  SA   9CP42   6CP59  0S 2    *   MC  15CN57  13CN14
UR  10GE26   7GE43  0N 5  *  UR  13GE28  10GE45  0N 5    *   MN  29CP32  26CP49
NE  29SG53  27SG10  0N48  *  NE  28SG 7  25SG24  0N49    *   MP  21GE55  19GE12
PL  13SC45  11SC 2  12N15 *  PL  11SC59   9SC16  12N 5   *   VP   2AR43
```

John of the Cross

Birth of St. John of the Cross
at Fontiveros
on Saturday, 24 June 1542 A.D. - Julian
Comments: Poet and Christian mystic of sixteenth century Spain.
Helped Teresa of Avila found the Carmelite Reform.
Source: L.Christiani,JOHN OF THE CROSS
Reference/Group: Ch.2, Chart 5.

```
     GEOCENTRIC              HELIOCENTRIC
     Sid.   Trop.  Lat.        Sid.   Trop.   Lat.           Sid.      Trop.
SU  23GE11 11CN33          TE 23SG11 11CP33             Time 12
MO  17SC36  5SG57  5S 6                                 Local Time
ME  15GE25  3CN46  0N41    ME 18TA47  7GE 9   2N53      ST 6.47
VE  14TA 0  2GE21  4S20    VE 16CP 1  4AQ23   2S40      LO 4W58
MA  17LI14  5SC35  1S48    MA 26SC24 14SG46   0S53      LA 40N55
JU   5VI20 23VI41  1N17    JU 15VI33  3LI55   1N20      AS 20VI57    9LI19
SA  13LI50  2SC12  2N29    SA 19LI22  7SC44   2N23      MC 22GE27   10CN49
UR   4LE34 22LE55  0N43    UR  6LE40 25LE 2   0N44      MN 15AQ 9    3PI31
NE   2AR10 20AR32  1S43    NE  0AR15 18AR36   1S43      MP 19VI35    7LI57
PL  28CP 8 16AQ29  9S20    PL 27CP15 15AQ37   9S 8      VP 11PI38
```

John of the Cross

Death of St. John of the Cross
at Ubeda
on Saturday, 14 December 1591 A.D. - Gregorian
Comments: Died at midnight. Reincarnated at midnight 254 years later in nineteenth century Germany as King Ludwig II of Bavaria.
Source: Gerald Brenan, LIFE p.81.
Reference/Group: Ch.2, Chart 6.

```
     GEOCENTRIC              HELIOCENTRIC
     Sid.   Trop.  Lat.        Sid.   Trop.   Lat.           Sid.      Trop.
SU   2SG33 21SG35           TE  2GE33 21GE35             Time 00.00
MO  10SC50 29SC53  3N 9                                  Local Time
ME  14SC16  3SG19  1N 7     ME 26VI54 15LI56   3N15      ST 5.28
VE  11SG43  0CP46  0N49     VE 29TA 8 18GE11   0N18      LO 3W22
MA  16AQ11  5PI14  0S58     MA 27PI45 16AR48   0S55      LA 38N01
JU  14SC43  3SG46  0N40     JU 11SC29  0SG32   0N47      AS  4VI29   23VI32
SA  21GE46 10CN49  0S33     SA 19GE43  8CN46   0S30      MC  3GE40   22GE43
UR   6PI 4 25PI 7  0S45     UR  8PI51 27PI54   0S44      MN 18GE 8    7CN11
NE  21CN 1 10LE 4  0N 3     NE 19CN36  8LE39   0N 3      MP 20AR50    9TA53
PL  24PI18 13AR21 17S 2     PL 25PI26 14AR29  16S55      VP 10PI57
```

Kepler, Johannes

Birth of Johannes Kepler
at Weil der Stadt
on Thursday, 27 December 1571 A.D. - Julian
Comments: German mathematician and astronomer who discovered the laws of planetary motion through analysis of Tycho Brahe's observations.
Source: A.Koestler SLEEPWALKERS p.227.
Reference/Group: Ch.8, Chart 22.

```
     GEOCENTRIC              HELIOCENTRIC
     Sid.   Trop.  Lat.        Sid.   Trop.   Lat.           Sid.      Trop.
SU  26SG42 15CP28           TE 26GE42 15CN28             Time 14.30
MO  15TA15  4GE 1  4S28                                  Local Time
ME  16SG49  5CP35  1S12     ME 25SC33 14SG20   3S37      ST 21.31
VE  29SG50 18CP36  0S56     VE  4CP 4 22CP50   2S11      LO 8E53
MA  19VI30  8LI17  2N25     MA 13LE37  2VI23   1N47      LA 48N45
JU  29AQ54 18PI40  1S14     JU 10PI 6 28PI52   1S19      AS  3GE55   22GE42
SA  25LI 1 13SC47  2N16     SA 20LI 1  8SC47   2N22      MC  1AQ27   20AQ14
UR  19SG5B  8CP44  0S20     UR 19SG36  8CP22   0S21      MN 14CN 0    2LE46
NE   5GE 4 23GE50  1S16     NE  5GE46 24GE32   1S13      MP 19CP55    8AQ41
PL   3PI16 22PI 3 15S43     PL  4PI28 23PI14  15S51      VP 11PI14
```

Appendix II: Computations   407

Louis the Pious
Death of Emperor Louis the Pious
at Ingelheim
on Sunday, 20 June 840 A.D. - Julian
Comments: Louis the Pious was the third son of Charlemagne and succeeded
him as Holy Roman Emperor. Reincarnated as Wallenstein.
Source: A. Cabaniss LIFE.
Reference/Group: Ch.8, Chart 20.

```
    GEOCENTRIC              HELIOCENTRIC
     Sid.    Trop.  Lat.      Sid.    Trop.  Lat.           Sid.       Trop.
SU 23GE53   2CN30          *  TE 23SG53   2CP30       *  Time 10
MO 10CP55  19CP32  4N18    *                          *  Local Time
ME 13CN 4  21CN41  1N41    *  ME 10VI28  19VI 5  4N59 *  ST   4.11
VE 28CN44   7LE22  0S52    *  VE  5SG42  14SG19  0S28 *  LO   8E04
MA  8LE30  17LE 7  1N10    *  MA  4VI14  12VI51  1N34 *  LA  49N58
JU 11CN47  20CN24  0N29    *  JU 15CN10  23CN47  0N35 *  AS   1VI55   10VI32
SA 11SG52  20SG29  1N 3    *  SA 13SG 4  21SG41  0N57 *  MC  26TA12    4GE49
UR  1AR 4   9AR41  0S40    *  UR 28PI10   6AR47  0S41 *  MN  12SC58   21SC35
NE 25SG35   4CP12  0N49    *  NE 25SG32   4CP 9  0N48 *  MP  23TA18    1GE55
PL 17PI57  26PI34 16S46    *  PL 16PI39  25PI16 16S43 *  VP  21PI23
```

Ludwig II of Bavaria
Birth of King Ludwig II of Bavaria
at Nymphenburg
on Monday, 25 August 1845 A.D. - Gregorian
Comments: Known as the "fairy-tale king". Died mysteriously at age 40.
Reincarnation of St. John of the Cross.
Source: D.Chapman-Huston, LIFE.
Reference/Group: Ch.2, Chart 7.

```
    GEOCENTRIC              HELIOCENTRIC
     Sid.    Trop.  Lat.      Sid.    Trop.  Lat.           Sid.       Trop.
SU  9LE 1   1VI36          *  TE  9AQ 1   1PI36       *  Time 00.30
MO 11TA28   4GE 3  1S16    *                          *  Local Time
ME  4VI 0  26VI35  3S27    *  ME 22SG 5  14CP40  5S57 *  ST  22.42
VE  6VI 4  28VI39  1N 1    *  VE 15LI33   8SC 8  2N 3 *  LO  11E30
MA  1AQ14  23AQ49  6S40    *  MA  6AQ55  29AQ30  1S49 *  LA  48N08
JU 18AR14  10TA49  1S21    *  JU  7AR16  29AR51  1S14 *  AS  15GE50    8CN25
SA 21CP47  14AQ22  1S 7    *  SA 23CP31  16AQ 6  1S 0 *  MC  16AQ25    9PI 0
UR 17PI 2   9AR37  0S44    *  UR 15PI15   7AR50  0S42 *  MN  27LI49   20SC24
NE  1AQ45  24AQ20  0S28    *  NE  1AQ59  24AQ34  0S27 *  MP  20SG12   12CP47
PL  2AR12  24AR47 17S 2    *  PL  1AR12  23AR47 16S50 *  VP   7PI25
```

Ludwig II of Bavaria, R. Wagner
First meeting of R. Wagner and Ludwig II of Bavaria
at Munich
on Wednesday, 4 May 1864 A.D. - Gregorian
Comments: This chart is the planetary configuration at the first meeting
between Richard Wagner and Ludwig II of Bavaria.
Source: Martin Gregor-Dellin, LIFE.
Reference/Group: Ch.3.

```
    GEOCENTRIC              HELIOCENTRIC
     Sid.    Trop.  Lat.      Sid.    Trop.  Lat.           Sid.       Trop.
SU 21AR27  14TA17          *. TE 21LI27  14SC17       *  Time 14.00
MO  2AR42  25AR33  2N 5    *                          *  Local Time
ME 11TA28   4GE19  2N31    *  ME 10VI 4   2LI55  4N51 *  ST   4.51
VE  1AR21  24AR12  1S32    *  VE  2PI49  25PI40  3S20 *  LO  11E30
MA 19AQ47  12PI38  1S36    *  MA 10CP20   3AQ10  1S47 *  LA  48N09
JU  0SC59  23SC49  1N11    *  JU 29LI12  22SC 3  0N58 *  AS  24LE27   17VI17
SA 19VI44  12LI34  2N43    *  SA 22VI53  15LI44  2N29 *  MC  21TA11   14GE 2
UR  0GE 0  22GE50  0N 9    *  UR  1GE51  24GE42  0N 9 *  MN  26LI 0   18SC51
NE 14PI21   7AR12  1S26    *  NE 13PI12   6AR 3  1S28 *  MP   0AQ34   23AQ24
PL 19AR 0  11TA51 15S20    *  PL 18AR57  11TA48 15S38 *  VP   7PI 9
```

Ludwig II, R. Wagner
First meeting of R. Wagner and Ludwig II
at Leipzig
on Tuesday, 2 March 1813 A.D. - Gregorian
Comments: This chart is the embryonic correspondence (in Wagners embryonic period) of his first meeting with Ludwig II of Bavaria.
Source: Moon's longitude = 16 AQUARIUS
Reference/Group: Ch.3, Chart 9.

```
     GEOCENTRIC              HELIOCENTRIC
     Sid.    Trop.   Lat.         Sid.    Trop.   Lat.            Sid.       Trop.
SU  19AQ35  11PI43            TE  19LE35  11VI43             Time 15.13
MO  15AQ59   8PI 7   1S43                                    ZT , DST
ME  15AQ 4   7PI12   1S59     ME   3AQ38  25AQ45  6S53       ST  2.40
VE  28CP 9  20AQ17   0S55     VE  28SG16  20CP24  1S58       LO 12E20
MA  29SC18  21SG26   0N12     MA  20LI30  12SC38  0N11       LA 51N15
JU   7CN44  29CN52   0N44     JU  14CN54   7LE 2  0N38       AS  2LE37   24LE45
SA  24SG42  16CP49   0N24     SA  20SG 5  12CP12  0N26       MC 20AR15   12TA23
UR   5SC47  27SC55   0N15     UR   2SC54  25SC 2  0N14       MN 26CN29   18LE37
NE  23SC22  15SG30   1N29     NE  21SC30  13SG37  1N29       MP 19AR 2   11TA 9
PL  26AQ40  18PI48  14S39     PL  26AQ50  18PI58  14S58      VP  7PI52
```

Maestlin, Michael
Birth of Michael Maestlin
at Goeppingen
on Tuesday, 30 September 1550 A.D. - Julian
Comments: Professor of mathematics at Tubingen University. Believed in the validity of the Copernican system. Taught Kepler astronomy.
Source: DSB
Reference/Group: Ch.6, Chart 13.

```
     GEOCENTRIC              HELIOCENTRIC
     Sid.    Trop.   Lat.         Sid.    Trop.   Lat.            Sid.       Trop.
SU  28VI 1  16LI30            TE  28PI 1  16AR30             Time 12
MO  19TA49   8GE17   5S 2                                    Local Time
ME   0LI51  19LI20   0N38     ME   7LI23  25LI52  2N 4       ST 13.14
VE  20LE54   9VI23   1N 1     VE  24GE 5  12CN34  1N42       LO  9E38
MA  20GE23   8CN52   0N34     MA   9TA35  28TA 3  0N23       LA 48N43
JU  12GE11   0CN39   0S24     JU   1GE24  19GE52  0S22       AS  1SG40   20SG 9
SA  14CP59   3AQ28   0S51     SA  20CP29   8AQ58  0S50       MC  1LI27   19LI55
UR  16VI 8   4LI36   0N41     UR  15VI28   3LI56  0N43       MN  5VI 7   23VI35
NE  19AR18   7TA47   1S52     NE  18AR37   7TA 5  1S49       MP 25LE55   14VI23
PL   7AQ36  26AQ 5  11S59     PL   8AQ43  27AQ11  11S48      VP 11PI32
```

Maestlin, Michael
Death of Michael Maestlin
at Tubingen
on Thursday, 30 October 1631 A.D. - Gregorian
Comments: Pioneering astronomer; amongst the first to proclaim the Copernican heliocentric system. Reincarnated as John Addey.
Source: DSB
Reference/Group: Ch.6, Chart 13.

```
     GEOCENTRIC              HELIOCENTRIC
     Sid.    Trop.   Lat.         Sid.    Trop.   Lat.            Sid.       Trop.
SU  17LI13   6SC49            TE  17AR13   6TA49             Time 12
MO  29SG22  18CP58   4S43                                    Local Time
ME   3SC 3  22SC39   2S14     ME  11PI37   1AR13   4S45      ST 14.34
VE  27SC50  17SG27   4S57     VE  24PI49  14AR25   2S54      LO  9E04
MA  20CN44  10LE20   1N36     MA  12GE15   1CN51   1N19      LA 48N32
JU  22PI13  11AR49   1S36     JU  27PI 4  16AR40   1S18      AS 19SG 5    8CP41
SA  28LI43  18SC19   2N 0     SA  29LI51  19SC28   2N11      MC 21LI18   10SC54
UR   3VI41  23VI17   0N44     UR   1VI36  21VI12   0N46      MN 26AR16   15TA53
NE  15LI56   5SC32   1N45     NE  15LI53   5SC29   1N48      MP 22LI57   12SC33
PL   3TA32  23TA 8  13S54     PL   3TA12  22TA48  13S39      VP 10PI24
```

Nero

Birth of Emperor Nero
at Anzio
on Sunday, 15 December 37 A.D. - Julian
Comments: 5th. Roman emperor. Involved in numerous scandals. Fire of Rome.
Murdered his mother. Persecuted Christians. Committed suicide.
Source: B.W.Henderson NERO p.19.
Reference/Group: Ch.8, Chart 23.

```
     GEOCENTRIC             HELIOCENTRIC
     Sid.   Trop.   Lat.        Sid.   Trop.   Lat.              Sid.      Trop.
SU 24SG42  22SG16           * TE 24GE42 22GE16          *    Time 07.28
MO 13LE28  11LE 1   3S14    *                           *    Local Time
ME  2SG55   0SG29   2N49    * ME 21LE56 19LE30   6N20   *    ST 12.55
VE 25CP25  22CP58   1N13    * VE 11GE 7  8GE40   0N33   *    LO 12E38
MA 28SG13  25SG46   0S53    * MA  0CP41 28SG14   1S30   *    LA 41N27
JU 16SC54  14SC27   0N51    * JU 10SC25  7SC58   0N58   *    AS 24SG29   22SG 2
SA 28VI54  26VI28   2N27    * SA 23VI 8 20VI41   2N28   *    MC 17LI30   15LI 4
UR 17VI44  15VI18   0N46    * UR 14VI46 12VI20   0N46   *    MN  6CP15    3CP49
NE  9AQ58   7AQ32   0S36    * NE 11AQ19  8AQ52   0S37   *    MP 17VI27   15VI 0
PL 24SG31  22SG 4   0N30    * PL 24SG31 22SG 4   0N31   *    VP  2AR27
```

Nietzsche, Friedrich

Birth of Friedrich Nietzsche
at Rocken
on Tuesday, 15 October 1844 A.D. - Gregorian
Comments: One of the great German philosophers of the nineteenth century.
Reincarnation of St. Peter of Alcantara.
Source: E. Forster-Nietzsche
Reference/Group: Ch.1, Chart 2

```
     GEOCENTRIC             HELIOCENTRIC
     Sid.   Trop.   Lat.        Sid.   Trop.   Lat.              Sid.      Trop.
SU 29VI33  22LI 8           * TE 29PI33 22AR 8           *    Time 10.00
MO 16SC29   9SG 3   0N17    *                            *    Local Time
ME 11VI35   4LI10   1N52    * ME 22GE37 15CN12   5N59    *    ST 11.36
VE 13LE48   6VI22   0S 3    * VE 21TA38 14GE13   0S 4    *    LO 12E09
MA  5VI22  27VI56   1N 6    * MA 21LE 8 13VI43   1N40    *    LA 51N15
JU  3PI29  26PI 3   1S36    * JU  8PI33  1AR 7   1S18    *    AS  6SC40   29SC14
SA  8CP 9   0AQ43   0S37    * SA 13CP50  6AQ24   0S36    *    MC  0VI53   23VI28
UR 10PI59   3AR34   0S45    * UR 11PI52  4AR27   0S43    *    MN 14SC26    7SG 0
NE 28CP27  21AQ 1   0S24    * NE  0AQ 6 22AQ40   0S23    *    MP 15SC17    7SG51
PL  0AR23  22AR57  17S12    * PL  0AR22 22AR56  16S51    *    VP  7PI26
```

Steiner, Rudolf

Birth of Rudolf Steiner
at Kraljavec
on Monday, 25 February 1861 A.D. - Gregorian
Comments: Spiritual teacher active 1900-1925. Developed spiritual science.
Founded the Anthroposophical Society. Taught reincarnation.
Source: See HERMETIC ASTROLOGY I Ch.10
Reference/Group: See Ch.4 for chart.

```
     GEOCENTRIC             HELIOCENTRIC
     Sid.   Trop.   Lat.        Sid.   Trop.   Lat.              Sid.      Trop.
SU 14AQ33   7PI21           * TE 14LE33  7VI21           *    Time 23.26
MO 24LE51  17VI39   4S16    *                            *    Local Time
ME  2PI28  25PI16   1N 9    * ME 25TA25 18GE13   3N40    *    ST 9.49
VE 25CP34  18AQ22   0S56    * VE 29SG17  22CP 5   2S 2   *    LO 16E00
MA 12AR48   5TA36   0N33    * MA 16TA20   9GE 8   0N39   *    LA 46N22
JU 27CN16  20LE 4   1N 7    * JU  0LE25 23LE13   0N55    *    AS 19LI50   12SC38
SA 13LE14   6VI 2   1N56    * SA 13LE22   6VI10   1N43   *    MC  2LE10   24LE58
UR 15TA16   8GE 4   0S 2    * UR 18TA11 10GE59   0S 2    *    MN 27SG40   20CP28
NE  5PI27  28PI15   1S18    * NE  6PI 9 28PI57   1S20    *    MP 20VI58   13LI47
PL 14AR56   7TA44  15S47    * PL 15AR59  8TA47  15S56    *    VP  7PI12
```

Stroke patient
Birth of Stroke patient
at Stuttgart
on Thursday, 10 September 1936 A.D. - Gregorian
Comments: After a normal life occurred a sudden stroke at age 46 years &
5 months. This led to a paralysis of the right side of the body.
Source: Patient's sister
Reference/Group: Ch.6, Chart 10.

```
     GEOCENTRIC              HELIOCENTRIC
     Sid.  Trop.   Lat.          Sid.  Trop.   Lat.              Sid.     Trop.
SU 23LE13 17VI 5         *   TE 23AQ13 17PI 5          *    Time 00.30
MO 16GE14 10CN 6  0S51   *                              *   ZT  -1, DST
ME 19VI30 13LI21  3S 8   *   ME 23SG55 17CP47  6S 4    *    ST 23.20
VE 13VI 1  6LI52  1N 1   *   VE 11LI10  5SC 1   2N14   *    LO  9E15
MA 25CN42 19LE33  1N11   *   MA  9CN12  3LE 4   1N47   *    LA 48N45
JU 22SC 1 15SG52  0N18   *   JU  3SG 2 26SG53   0N18   *    AS 22GE51   16CN42
SA 25AQ25 19PI16  2S18   *   SA 25AQ11 19PI 2   2S 4   *    MC 25AQ21   19PI12
UR 15AR28  9TA19  0S29   *   UR 13AR 8  7TA 0   0S28   *    MN  5SG40   29SG31
NE 22LE41 16VI32  1N 0   *   NE 22LE39 16VI30   1N 2   *    MP  3AR27   27AR18
PL  4CN22 28CN13  2N19   *   PL  3CN16 27CN 7   2N22   *    VP  6PI 9
```

Stroke patient
Conception of Stroke patient
at Stuttgart
on Thursday, 12 December 1935 A.D. - Gregorian
Comments: Normal length embryonic period. Applying the hermetic rule, the
Moon at conception was at the place of the Ascendant at birth.
Source: See Chapter 6.
Reference/Group: Ch.6, Chart 11.

```
     GEOCENTRIC              HELIOCENTRIC
     Sid.  Trop.   Lat.          Sid.  Trop.   Lat.              Sid.     Trop.
SU 25SC33 19SG24         *   TE 25TA33 19GE24          *    Time 08.44
MO 23GE 7 16CN58  0S23   *                              *   ZT  , DST
ME 26SC42 20SG33  1S18   *   ME 29SC 8 22SG59   4S 4   *    ST 14.39
VE 10LI22  4SC13  2N29   *   VE 23CN38 17LE28   2N59  *    LO  9E15
MA 10CP11  4AQ 1  1S18   *   MA 10AQ14  4PI 4   1S47   *    LA 48N45
JU 13SC32  7SG23  0N38   *   JU 11SC20  5SG11   0N45   *    AS 16SG 5    9CP56
SA 10AQ41  4PI31  1S47   *   SA 16AQ18 10PI 9   1S49   *    MC 18LI28   12SC19
UR  8AR 4  1TA55  0S31   *   UR 10AR 9  3TA59   0S30   *    MN 20SG 7   13CP58
NE 22LE54 16VI45  0N59   *   NE 21LE 2 14VI53   0N59   *    MP  3PI 6   26PI56
PL  3CN 9 26CN59  2N 6   *   PL  2CN17 26CN 8   2N 4   *    VP  6PI 9
```

Stroke patient, Stroke of
Embryonic correspondence of Stroke of Stroke patient
at Stuttgart
on Thursday, 11 June 1936 A.D. - Gregorian
Comments: Configuration at moment in embryonic period corresponding to the
occurrence of stroke at age 46 years 5 months. Moon = 10 AQUA.
Source: See Chapter 6.
Reference/Group: Ch.6, Chart 12.

```
     GEOCENTRIC              HELIOCENTRIC
     Sid.  Trop.   Lat.          Sid.  Trop.   Lat.              Sid.     Trop.
SU 26TA17 20GE 8         *   TE 26SC17 20SG 8          *    Time 06.30
MO 10AQ12  4PI 3  4N35   *                              *   ZT  , DST
ME 11TA43  5GE34  4S 9   *   ME 15SG54  9CP45   5S32  *    ST  0.23
VE 21TA20 15GE11  0S12   *   VE 14TA20  8GE11   0S28   *    LO  9E15
MA 26TA13 20GE 4  0N34   *   MA 26TA11 20GE 2   0N57   *    LA 48N45
JU 25SC36 19SG27  0N34   *   JU 25SC44 19SG35   0N27   *    AS  4CN50   28CN41
SA 28AQ15 22PI 6  2S 0   *   SA 22AQ13 16PI 4   1S59   *    MC 12PI19    6AR10
UR 14AR 8  7TA59  0S27   *   UR 12AR 9  6TA 0   0S28   *    MN 10SG28    4CP20
NE 20LE12 14VI 4  1N 1   *   NE 22LE 7 15VI58   1N 1   *    MP 23PI21   17AR12
PL  2CN 5 25CN56  2N13   *   PL  2CN56 26CN47   2N16   *    VP  6PI 9
```

Appendix II: Computations 411

Swedenborg, Emmanuel
Birth of Emmanuel Swedenborg
at Uppsala
on Sunday, 29 January 1688 A.D. - Julian
Comments: Swedish scientist, theologian and mystic. Experienced a divine
revelation at age 57. Wrote voluminously on spiritual mysteries.
Source: CBC (with place correction)
Reference/Group: Ch.8, Chart 21.

```
     GEOCENTRIC              HELIOCENTRIC
     Sid.    Trop.   Lat.       Sid.    Trop.   Lat.              Sid.      Trop.
SU 29CP 3  19AQ26          * TE 29CN 3  19LE26          *  Time 05.15
MO 24AR 6  14TA29  0N39    *                            *  Local Time
ME 10CP 9   0AQ32  1S23    * ME 26SC44  17SG 7  3S46    *  ST 14.28
VE 12SG29   2CP52  3N 0    * VE 17VI33   7LI56  3N 6    *  LO 17E35
MA  7AR47  28AR10  0N34    * MA 14TA57   5GE20  0N35    *  LA 59N52
JU 24SG55  15CP18  0S 2    * JU 18SG48   9CP11  0S 3    *  AS 29SC59   20SG22
SA  4LI38  25LI 2  2N37    * SA 29VI19  19LI42  2N30    *  MC 18LI55    9SC18
UR 24AR27  14TA51  0S19    * UR 27AR20  17TA43  0S19    *  MN 17AR 2    7TA25
NE 17AQ17   7PI40  0S52    * NE 17AQ52   8PI15  0S54    *  MP  2PI 5   22PI28
PL  1CN44  22CN 7  2N 6    * PL  2CN23  22CN46  2N 3    *  VP  9PI37
```

Teresa of Avila
Birth of St. Teresa of Avila
at Avila
on Wednesday, 28 March 1515 A.D. - Julian
Comments: One of the great Christian mystics of 16th. century Spain.
Founder of the Carmelite Reform with St. John of the Cross.
Source: M. Auclair, TERESA OF AVILA
Reference/Group: Ch.1, Chart 3.

```
     GEOCENTRIC              HELIOCENTRIC
     Sid.    Trop.   Lat.       Sid.    Trop.   Lat.              Sid.      Trop.
SU 28PI14  16AR13          * TE 28VI14  16LI13          *  Time 05.30
MO  5VI 1  22VI59  2N40    *                            *  Local Time
ME 26PI30  14AR29  0S58    * ME 21PI20   9AR19  3S51    *  ST 18.27
VE 11PI 8  29PI 7  6N 8    * VE  5LI16  23LI15  2N34    *  LO 4W42
MA 20TA48   8GE47  1N11    * MA 20GE28   8CN27  1N28    *  LA 40N39
JU 24TA21  12GE20  0S17    * JU  3GE42  21GE41  0S19    *  AS 23PI48   11AR47
SA 18SC44   6SG42  1N58    * SA 14SC19   2SG18  1N50    *  MC 18SG16    6CP15
UR  7AR28  25AR27  0S32    * UR  7AR56  25AR55  0S33    *  MN  2LE26   20LE25
NE  1AQ43  19AQ42  0S22    * NE  0AQ 7  18AQ 6  0S22    *  MP 21LE27    9VI25
PL 11SG57  29SG56  4N47    * PL 10SG13  28SG12  4N44    *  VP 12PI 1
```

Teresa of Avila
Death of St. Teresa of Avila
at Alba de Tormes
on Thursday, 4 October 1582 A.D. - Julian
Comments: Died around sunrise. Reincarnated at sunrise 231 years later
in nineteenth century Germany as the composer Richard Wagner.
Source: M. Auclair, TERESA OF AVILA
Reference/Group: Ch.1, Chart 4.

```
     GEOCENTRIC              HELIOCENTRIC
     Sid.    Trop.   Lat.       Sid.    Trop.   Lat.              Sid.      Trop.
SU  1LI36  20LI31          * TE  1AR36  20AR31          *  Time 06.15
MO  5TA42  24TA37  3N13    *                            *  Local Time
ME 25VI18  14LI13  1N26    * ME  9VI11  28VI 6  4N59    *  ST 7.44
VE 27LE20  16VI16  1N17    * VE  6CN 2  24CN57  2N16    *  LO 5W30
MA 26GE58  15CN54  0N51    * MA 16TA28   5GE24  0N36    *  LA 40N50
JU 23CP25  12AQ21  1S 4    * JU  4AQ 2  22AQ58  0S58    *  AS  1LI44   20LI39
SA 15AQ43   4PI38  2S 2    * SA 19AQ57   8PI53  1S53    *  MC  5CN18   24CN13
UR  0AQ28  19AQ23  0S45    * UR  2AQ56  21AQ51  0S43    *  MN 15SG32    4CP27
NE  1CN25  20CN20  0S35    * NE 29GE31  18CN26  0S35    *  MP  8AR 0   26AR55
PL 15PI44   4AR39  17S 2   * PL 16PI 5   5AR 0  16S42   *  VP 11PI 5
```

Wagner, Richard

Birth of Richard Wagner
at Leipzig
on Saturday, 22 May 1813 A.D. - Gregorian
Comments: Given birth time of 4.00 a.m. corrected to 3.58 a.m.
Reincarnation of St. Teresa of Avila. Earlier Merlin.
Source: A. Leo NATIVITIES
Reference/Group: Ch.1, Chart 1

```
     GEOCENTRIC              HELIOCENTRIC
     Sid.   Trop.  Lat.          Sid.   Trop.  Lat.              Sid.     Trop.
SU   8TA28  0GE36          *  TE  8SC28  0SG36          *  Time 03.58
MO  23CP58 16AQ 6  0S14    *                            *  Local Time
ME  13AR27  5TA35  3S19    *  ME  7CP30 29CP38  6S42    *  ST  19.55
VE   7TA34 29TA42  0S24    *  VE  6TA20 28TA28  0S58    *  LO  12E20
MA  11CP45  3AQ53  2S23    *  MA  3SG22 25SG30  1S 7    *  LA  51N20
JU  11CN33  3LE41  0N42    *  JU 21CN19 13LE27  0N45    *  AS   5TA31   27TA39
SA  26SG48 18CP56  0N21    *  SA 22SG30 14CP38  0N19    *  MC   4CP41   26CP49
UR   3SC34 25SC42  0N14    *  UR  3SC53 26SC 1  0N14    *  MN  22CN13   14LE21
NE  22SC26 14SG34  1N31    *  NE 21SC58 14SG 6  1N29    *  MP  27AR59   20TA 7
PL  28AQ23 20PI31 14S54    *  PL 27AQ 5 19PI13 15S 0    *  VP   7PI52
```

Wagner, Richard

Conception of Richard Wagner
at Leipzig
on Saturday, 15 August 1812 A.D. - Gregorian
Comments: Conception date and time computed according to the hermetic
rule. Confirmed by way of astrological reincarnation comparison.
Source: See Chapter 3.
Reference/Group: Ch.3, Chart 8.

```
     GEOCENTRIC              HELIOCENTRIC
     Sid.   Trop.  Lat.          Sid.   Trop.  Lat.              Sid.     Trop.
SU   0LE33 22LE41          *  TE  0AQ33 22AQ41          *  Time 19.02
MO   5SC33 27SC41  5N17    *                            *  Local Time
ME  27LE50 19VI58  1S40    *  ME 22SC38 14SG45  3S22    *  ST  16.38
VE  10CN19  2LE26  7S36    *  VE  9AQ 8  1PI15  3S18    *  LO  12E20
MA  24CN18 16LE25  1N 9    *  MA 20CN28 12LE35  1N51    *  LA  51N20
JU   3CN47 25CN55  0N14    *  JU 28GE47 20CN55  0N17    *  AS  23CP48   15AQ55
SA   9SG38  1CP45  0N44    *  SA 14SG 6  6CP13  0N41    *  MC  18SC57   11SG 4
UR  27LI20 19SC28  0N16    *  UR  0SC29 22SC36  0N16    *  MN   7LE 1   29LE 9
NE  18SC30 10SG38  1N31    *  NE 20SC19 12SG27  1N30    *  MP  26PI53   19AR 0
PL  26AQ48 18PI55 15S11    *  PL 26AQ12 18PI19 14S53    *  VP   7PI53
```

Wallenstein, Albrecht von

Birth of Duke Albrecht von Wallenstein
at Hermanitz (nr. Prague)
on Saturday, 24 September 1583 A.D. - Gregorian
Comments: Reincarnation of Emperor Louis the Pious. Pluto's sidereal
longitude is the same as at the death of Louis the Pious.
Source: Kepler OPERA VIII p.350.
Reference/Group: Ch.8, Chart 19.

```
     GEOCENTRIC              HELIOCENTRIC
     Sid.   Trop.  Lat.          Sid.   Trop.  Lat.              Sid.     Trop.
SU  11VI56  0LI52          *  TE 11PI56  0AR52          *  Time 16.36
MO  18SG 8  7CP 4  1N50    *                            *  Local Time
ME   4VI 5 23VI 1  1N48    *  ME 11LE24  0VI20  6N41    *  ST  16.47
VE  27LI54 16SC50  2S32    *  VE 19CP29  8AQ25  2S48    *  LO  14E24
MA   9LI 4 28LI 0  0N 1    *  MA 26LI17 15SC13  0N 2    *  LA  50N40
JU   3PI39 22PI35  1S37    *  JU  5PI19 24PI15  1S18    *  AS   1AQ59   20AQ55
SA   0PI 3 18PI59  2S25    *  SA  1PI17 20PI13  2S10    *  MC  24SC17   13SG13
UR   4AQ58 23AQ54  0S46    *  UR  6AQ40 25AQ36  0S44    *  MN  27SC14   16SG10
NE   3CN23 22CN18  0S31    *  NE  1CN36 20CN32  0S31    *  MP  16TA28    5GE24
PL  17PI11  6AR 7 17S 5    *  PL 17PI 4  6AR 0 16S44    *  VP  11PI 4
```

Appendix III

The Jewish Calendar

The central theme of this work on astrological biography is that the human being's life on Earth unfolds through definite stages related to the Sun, Moon and planets. The historical tradition concerning this is outlined in Appendix I, which includes Shakespeare's poetic rendition of the *seven ages of man*, starting with the words: "All the world's a stage". Just as the Earth is the "stage" for the human being's earthly life, so the cosmic world is the realm in which the human being exists between incarnations upon the Earth. Here the Sun – as the central cosmic body – is the human being's primary abode in the world of spirit. The Sun realm is the central sphere for the life as a spiritual being; similarly, the Earth is the domain where human life unfolds on the physical plane of existence. In between, just as the Moon mediates between the Sun and the Earth, the human being's soul life is placed between that of the spirit (Sun level) and that which belongs solely to existence on the physical level (Earth).

The lunar calendar, based on the Moon's phases, evolved in antiquity in response to the attunement of the human soul to the Moon as a mediator between the cosmic world and the Earth. As referred to in Chapter 10 ("The hermetic calendar"), both the Babylonians and the people of Israel developed a lunar calendar; and the hermetic calendar – as a modern lunar calendar – represents a synthesis of these two ancient lunar calendars. The hermetic calendar is thus a kind of modern-day "calendar of the soul", and as described in Chapter 10 it is intended to help enable the soul to attune to one of the fundamental rhythms of the cosmic world coming to expression on the Earth in the cycle of nature during the course of the year.

It will be recalled that the starting point taken for the definition of the hermetic calendar in Chapter 10 is related to that defining the Jewish calendar. The hermetic calendar and the Jewish calendar thus have a similar foundation, without being identical. In actual fact, as we shall see, there are historical reasons for considering the Jewish calendar as a valid calendar of the soul. Moreover, the Jewish lunar calendar is still in use to the present day. As any Jewish diary, usually available in August or September each year (for the coming year), lists the day of the Jewish month alongside the calendar date, it is quite straightforward to follow. All that it is necessary to know is the correspondence between the lunar months of the Jewish calendar and the signs of the zodiac.

	Jewish month	zodiacal sign
1.	Nisan	Aries
2.	Iyyar	Taurus
3.	Sivan	Gemini
4.	Tammuz	Cancer
5.	Ab	Leo
6.	Elul	Virgo
7.	Tishri	Libra
8.	Heshvan	Scorpio
9.	Kislev	Sagittarius
10.	Tebeth	Capricorn
11.	Shebat	Aquarius
12.	Adar	Pisces

For example, referring to a Jewish diary for the year 1987, the first day of the month Nisan (Nisan 1) is listed as coinciding with the calendar date March 31. As the day in the lunar calendar begins at sunset – or rather dusk – this means that Nisan 1 started at dusk on March 30 and extended to dusk on March 31. (The day in the Jewish calendar always commences at dusk on the evening prior to the corresponding calendar date.) Taking the Jewish calendar, therefore, in 1987 the first day of the lunar month of Aries (Nisan 1) coincided with March 30/31, the second day of the lunar month of Aries (Nisan 2) equated with March 31/April 1, etc. In this way the lunar calendar (as based on the Jewish calendar) can be followed through the course of the year, with the help of a Jewish diary for the relevant year. (Standard reference work: Arthur Spier, *The Comprehensive Hebrew Calendar*, Feldheim Inc., Jerusalem, 1981.)

But what are the historical reasons for considering the Jewish calendar as a valid calendar of the soul?

The answer to this question is to be found through a study of the historical foundations of Christianity. Jesus Christ was born in Palestine and he lived within the framework of the Jewish culture, where the Jewish calendar was in use. He came as the "Sun of righteousness", but his mission was fulfilled in Israel, among whose people there prevailed a calendar based on the phases of the Moon. The date of his death – through the Crucifixion on Golgotha – is communicated in the *Gospel of St. John* as the day of preparation for the feast of the Passover, which equates with the fourteenth day of the month of Nisan in the Jewish calendar. Thus the end of Christ's earthly life was on the afternoon of Nisan 14, around the middle of the first month of the Jewish lunar year, i.e. close to the Full Moon in the month of Nisan. This was the original Good Friday, which was followed two days later by the Resurrection on Easter Sunday (Nisan 16).

Appendix III: The Jewish Calendar

This fact is utilized in Christianity by specifying Easter Sunday as the first Sunday after the Full Moon after the vernal equinox, which – generally speaking – is the first Sunday after Nisan 14 in the Jewish calendar. On the whole it is true to say, therefore, that the Jewish calendar implicitly underlies the Easter festival. Whenever Easter falls in the month of Nisan (as it usually does), it follows that Ascension (forty days after Easter Sunday) and Whitsun (ten days later) are also implicitly related to the Jewish calendar, with Whitsun falling in the third month (Sivan). Historically these dates were as follows:

event	Jewish calendar date
Crucifixion	Nisan 14
Resurrection	Nisan 16
Ascension	Iyyar 25
Witsun (Pentecost)	Sivan 6

The above Jewish calendar dates relate to events following on from the death of Jesus Christ. By means of research – the results of which are presented by the author in *Christian Hermetic Astrology: The Star of the Magi and the Life of Christ* and also in the companion volume *Chronicle of the Life of Christ* – it has been possible to determine with a high degree of exactness the Jewish calendar dates of major events in the life of Jesus Christ. Including the above four dates, these may be summarized as follows, where it needs to be borne in mind that the Jewish day (starting at dusk) has the pattern evening, night, morning, afternoon.

The Jewish calendar – with its festivals – is of historical significance to the Jewish people. For, in terms of this calendar the great events in the history of Israel, such as the revelation to Moses on Mt. Sinai (commemorated on Sivan 6/7), are celebrated. Over and above this, for those seeking to attune to the life of Christ, the above list of historical dates of major events in his life – in terms of the Jewish calendar – offers the possibility of enabling these events to be commemorated by following the Jewish calendar each year. Just as the Crucifixion and Resurrection are commemorated each year at Easter (Nisan) and Pentecost is celebrated each year at Whitsun (Sivan), so do the major events in the life of the Messiah deserve to be commemorated yearly. It is this historical aspect which serves to qualify the Jewish lunar calendar as a valid "calendar of the soul". In terms of this calendar the deeds of Christ, which are of inestimable significance to the life of the soul, may be commemorated each year. And in the age of the second coming the Jewish calendar is again of significance to Christians – as a framework for the renewed activity of the Risen One – just as it was the framework for the life of Jesus Christ at his first coming two thousands years ago.

event	time of day	calendar date
Feeding of the 4000 (Mk. 8:1–9)	afternoon	Nisan 2
Founding of the Church (Mt. 16:13–20)	dawn	Nisan 6
Crucifixion	3 p.m.	Nisan 14
Resurrection	dawn	Nisan 16
Transfiguration (Mt. 17:1–8)	midnight	Nisan 22
Ascension	noon	Iyyar 25
Witsun (Pentecost)	dawn	Sivan 6
Raising of Lazarus (Jn. 11:1–44)	morning	Tammuz 28
Healing of the nobleman's son (Jn. 4:43–54)	1 p.m.	Ab 15
Baptism in the Jordan	morning	Elul 26
Start of the 40 days in the wilderness	dusk	Tishri 26
Raising of the youth of Nain (Lk. 7:11–17)	morning	Heshvan 28
End of the 40 days in the wilderness	sunset	Kislev 6
Birth of Jesus	night	Kislev 12
Raising of Jairus' daughter (Mk. 5:35–43)	evening	Kislev 17
Wedding at Cana (Jn. 2:1–12)	morning	Tebeth 4
Beheading of John the Baptist	evening	Tebeth 20
Healing of the paralysed man (Jn. 5:1–14)	evening	Shebat 7
Feeding of the 5000 (Jn. 6:1–15)	afternoon	Shebat 16
Walking on the water (Jn. 6:16–21)	night	Shebat 17
Triumphant entry into Jerusalem (Mt. 21:1–11)	morning	Adar 28

Apart from the new spiritual significance of the Jewish calendar in the twentieth century on account of the second coming, there is a practical aspect to it. For, as it is made available each year in diary form, it is convenient to utilize and is directly applicable in place of the hermetic calendar in Chapter 10. For example, if instead of the hermetic calendar the Jewish calendar is taken as the basis for the meditations – *sanctification of the New Moon* and *sanctification of the Full Moon* – discussed in Chapter 10, then the following considerations apply. In the lunar months of the Jewish calendar the astronomical New Moon occurs at the end of the month, usually on day 29 or day 30, and the Full Moon occurs in the middle of the month, generally on day 14 or day 15. Hence the day-by-day meditative preparation for the sanctification of the New Moon can be started on day 16 and continued through to the end of the month (day 16 to day 29/30), and similarly the daily meditative preparation for the sanctification of the Full Moon can be commenced on day 1 and continued through to day 15 (inclusive). This means that the sanctification of the New Moon builds up towards the end of the month, culminating on the last day of the month (day 29 or day 30), whilst the climax of the sanctification of the Full Moon is attained on day 15, in the middle of the Jewish lunar month.

Afterword

In these two volumes on hermetic astrology some guidelines have been given concerning the basis of an astrology leading to a new wisdom of the stars (astrosophy). The line of development involved here can be stated quite simply as: astronomy → astrology → astrosophy. Astronomy, astrology and astrosophy comprise the "body", "soul" and "spirit" of star wisdom, viewed as a whole. And, considered from a general point of view, the trilogy of hermetic-astrological works – *Astrology and Reincarnation, Astrological Biography, The Star of the Magi and the Life of Christ* – relate, respectively, to the body, soul and spirit of a new star wisdom.

What are the main features of the astronomy ("body") of a new star wisdom as presented in Volume I: *Astrology and Reincarnation?* These may be stated concisely as follows:

(1) the authentic astronomical-astrological zodiac is the sidereal zodiac of the Babylonians, Egyptians and ancient Greeks;
(2) in addition to the geocentric planetary positions, the heliocentric positions of the planets in the sidereal zodiac, as these come to expression in Tycho Brahe's astronomical system, are astrologically significant.

These two findings, discovered by way of the astrological reincarnation research presented in Volume I, form the astronomical pillars upon which hermetic astrology is based, and the latter, in turn, provides a foundation for a new wisdom of the stars. At this stage, therefore, it is helpful once again to briefly consider these two astronomical pillars supporting the new star wisdom outlined in this trilogy of hermetic-astrological works.

Concerning the zodiac, the initiates of antiquity spiritually beheld the signs of the zodiac embedded in the stellar constellations: the Ram, the Bull, the Twins, etc. With clairvoyant vision they perceived that the twelve visible stellar configurations of the zodiac are the outer manifestation ("body") of twelve highly evolved spiritual beings known as the *holy living creatures*. In the Apocalypse of St. John four of these twelve holy living creatures are referred to, one on each side of the throne of God:

And round the throne, on each side of the throne, are four living creatures, full of eyes in front and behind: the first living creature like a lion, the second living creature like an ox, the third living creature with the face of a man, and the fourth living creature like a flying eagle. And the four living creatures, each of them with six wings, are full of eyes all round and within, and day and night they never cease to sing: "Holy, holy, holy, is the Lord God Almighty, who was, and is, and is to come! (Revelation iv, 6–8)

Here St. John depicts his clairvoyant vision of the holy living creatures whose "bodies" are visible externally in the zodiacal constellations of the Lion, the Bull (Ox), the Waterman (Man), and the Scorpion (Eagle). (For a discussion as to why the Eagle came to be seen as the Scorpion, see *Christian Hermetic Astrology: The Star of the Magi and the Life of Christ.)* St. John refers to only four of the holy living creatures – those manifesting through the four fixed zodiacal signs – but each of these four is flanked on either side by two holy living creatures, so that the full circle of holy living creatures surrounding the throne of God comprises twelve.

In contemplating the inner reality of the sidereal zodiac, we draw near to the throne of God. The inner side of that which is presented to us externally as the twelve sidereal signs (zodiacal constellations) is revealed to clairvoyant vision as the twelve holy living creatures who assisted in the divine creation, and who continue to assist in the guidance of the evolution of the world and in the shaping of the destiny of mankind. In trying to delineate the spheres of influence of the twelve holy living creatures, as hermetic astrology – both ancient and modern – sets out to do, an attempt is made to take account of the spiritual influence of these divine beings upon the Earth and humanity. In this respect hermetic astrology aspires to the same sphere of divine reality as that of the age-old star wisdom of antiquity, cultivated by Zarathustra in ancient Persia, Hermes in ancient Egypt, Zoroaster (Zaratas) in Babylon, and which radiates through the revelations of the prophet Ezekiel of Israel and the Christian initiate John the Evangelist.

It was the deed of Zoroaster, who lived in Babylon in the sixth century B.C. and was known to the priests there as Zaratas, to first arrive at a scientific understanding of the spheres of influence of the twelve holy living creatures comprising the being of the zodiac. On the basis of Zoroaster's indications the Babylonians defined the twelve sidereal signs, each 30 degrees long, such that the star Aldebaran (the Bull's eye) is located at 15° Taurus and the star Antares (the heart of the Scorpion) is placed at 15° Scorpio. It is this zodiac, defined on the basis of the revelation of the great initiate Zoroaster, which is the original astronomical- astrological zodiac of the spiritual tradition to which hermetic astrology belongs. Now known as the sidereal zodiac, this zodiac of the ancient mystery wisdom tradition became reintroduced into western astrology in the middle of the twentieth century by Cyril Fagan with the publication of his book *Zodiacs Old and New* (Anscombe: London, 1951), and received a formal astronomical definition in the work by Robert Powell and Peter Treadgold *The Sidereal Zodiac* (American Federation of Astrologers: Tempe, 1985). This is the first of the two astronomical pillars upon which hermetic astrology rests.

Often the idea is put forward that the sidereal zodiac may well have been valid in antiquity, but that since the Mystery of Golgotha it is the tropical zodiac – defined by Greek astronomers and now used by the majority of western astrologers – that is the true astrological zodiac. Here it is only necessary to point out that St. John's vision of the holy living creatures from the post-Christian era is more or less in agreement with that of Ezekiel from the Old Testament. The continuity in visionary experience of these two initiates – one from the pre-Christian and one from the post-Christian era – indicates that the twelve holy living creatures did not depart from the zodiacal constellations at the time of the Mystery of Golgotha to take up their abode elsewhere.

Moreover, the twentieth-century Christian initiate Rudolf Steiner – in agreement with the initiates of antiquity such as Hermes and Zoroaster – also described clairvoyantly the passage of the Sun through the constellations of the sidereal zodiac and not through the signs of the tropical zodiac. To emphasize that it is the passage of the Sun through the zodiacal constellations which is spiritually significant, Rudolf Steiner published the *Kalender 1912/1913* describing this phenomenon, and wrote in the preface:

Just as we can describe the simple experience of "I feel the nocturnal darkness giving way to the light" with the words, "the Sun is rising", so the more complicated soul experiences such as "I feel how in springtime the Earth prepares itself for new growth and for taking in the power of Sun" may find itself expressed in the words, "the rising Sun is perceived in the constellation of Pisces."*

Here the word "perceived" does not refer to physical perception, as the Sun cannot be observed physically against the background of the stars (except at the moment of a total solar eclipse). Rather, Rudolf Steiner is referring here to *clairvoyant perception* of the Sun in the constellation of Pisces.

The second astronomical pillar underlying the foundation of hermetic astrology is the astronomical system of Tycho Brahe, which, as described in Volume I, represents a modern scientific definition of the hermetic world system of the ancient Egyptians. While not denying the validity of the Ptolemaic system as the basis for classical geocentric astrology, astrological reincarnation research not only demonstrates that the sidereal zodiac is the authentic astrological zodiac but also shows that the heliocentric movements of the planets through the signs of the sidereal zodiac are definitely an astrological reality. (See, for example, the second "law" of reincarnation described in Appendix IV of Volume I.) Moreover, although the Copernican heliocentric system is applicable with regard to physical phenomena (planetary motion, orbits of comets, etc.), it is the Tychonic helio-geocentric system that applies to the soul-spiritual side of existence which is the domain of astrology. For, whereas returning comets (such as Halley's) orbit around the Sun as their focal point, human beings reincar-

---

* quoted from Powell-Treadgold, *The Sidereal Zodiac* (AFA: Tempe, 1985), p. 24

nate upon the Earth, and therefore the Earth is central from an astrological point of view.

As described in *Christian Hermetic Astrology: The Star of the Magi and the Life of Christ*, whereas the Copernican heliocentric system applies well on the physical plane of existence, on the astral (soul) plane it is Ptolemy's geocentric system which holds good, and on the devachanic (spiritual) plane the Tychonic system comes into its own. Each plane of existence – physical, astral, devachanic – has its own laws and requires a corresponding astronomical system. From the physical point of view the Tychonic system may seem "stupid", but from the devachanic plane of existence it has a definite validity. That there is a deeper significance to Tycho Brahe's astronomical system is hinted at in the following words of Rudolf Steiner:

The world really knows nothing about Tycho Brahe except that he was "stupid" enough to devise a plan of the cosmos in which the Earth stands still and the Sun together with the planets revolve around it. That is what the world in general knows today. The fact that we have to do here with a significant personality of the sixteenth century, with one who accomplished an infinite amount that even today is still useful to astronomy, that untold depths of wisdom are contained in what he gave – none of this is usually recorded, for the simple reason that in presenting the system in detail, out of his own deep knowledge, Tycho Brahe saw difficulties which Copernicus did not see. If such a thing dare be said – for it does indeed seem paradoxical – even with the Copernican cosmic system the last word has not been uttered. And the conflict between the two systems will still occupy the minds of a later humanity.*

As outlined here, there need not to be a conflict between the Copernican and Tychonic systems if it is recognized that they apply to different levels of existence. Similarly, the replacement of the Ptolemaic geocentric system by the heliocentric system of Copernicus meant that by the sixteenth century A.D., when Copernicus published his system, the transition by human consciousness – effected over centuries – from the astral plane to the physical plane was at its final stage of completion. The Ptolemaic system in its turn had replaced the still earlier hermetic world system of the ancient Egyptians, signifying the transition made in antiquity by human consciousness (again over a long period of time) from the devachanic plane to the astral plane. By continuing to adhere to the Ptolemaic system right down to the present time, traditional geocentric astrology shows that it is a science applied to the astral plane and not to the physical plane. And by re-introducing the hermetic (Egyptian-Tychonic) system in the twentieth century, modern hermetic astrology is simply taking account of the fact

---

*Rudolf Steiner, *Occult History* (Rudolf Steiner Press: London, 1983), p. 79.

that man's deeper spiritual nature — rooted in the devachanic plane — can only be explored by means of an astronomical system appropriate to that plane. This deeper spiritual nature comes to expression in the seven lotus flowers (chakras) of the human being; and by way of the correspondences between the seven lotus flowers of the microcosm and the seven planets of the macrocosm it is possible to arrive at insight into the human being's deeper spiritual talents and faculties. This is achieved by casting a horoscope, within the framework of the Tychonic system, for the moment of birth of the human being, the resulting horoscope being called the *hermetic chart*. The hermetic chart, relating more to man's spiritual nature (belonging essentially to the devachanic plane), complements and supplements the traditional geocentric chart, cast within the framework of the Ptolemaic system, which offers a picture more of the human being's soul nature (belonging essentially to the astral plane).

Having briefly reviewed some essential points concerning these two astronomical pillars — the sidereal zodiac and the Tychonic system (see Volume I) — let us turn to the main astrological pillar upon which hermetic astrology rests. Here we shall make the transition from the "body" (astronomical level) to the "soul" (astrological level) of a new wisdom of the stars, and correspondingly redirect our attention from the content of Volume I to that of Volume II of *Hermetic Astrology*. Fundamentally, the central astrological pillar underlying the science of astrological biography outlined in *Hermetic Astrology* II can be summarized as follows:

> The human being's destiny is mapped out in the cosmic world during the embryonic period between conception and birth and unfolds in seven-year periods between birth and death according to the correspondence between each seven-year period of earthly life and each lunar orbit of the sidereal zodiac during the embryonic period.

This key correspondence between the embryonic period and the course of life was discovered by Willi Sucher during the 1930's. Intrinsic to any practical application of this correspondence underlying astrological biography is the use of the hermetic rule (rule of Hermes), which has been handed down from the days when hermetic astrology flourished in Hellenistic Egypt during the first and second centuries B.C. (see Appendix I of Volume I for a description of the hermetic rule in a historical context). The hermetic rule, therefore, is an astrological rule essentially belonging to the central pillar underlying the foundation of hermetic astrology.

Although there is some evidence from the corpus of astrological manuscripts surviving from antiquity that a few astrologers were interested in delving into the cosmic mysteries belonging to the embryonic period, there is no explicit mention of the key correspondence discovered (or rediscovered) by Willi Sucher in the 1930's. There were certainly astrologers in antiquity who utilized the hermetic rule for determining the moment of conception, but even if they had known of the above-mentioned key correspondence, the sheer complexity of following the planetary movements throughout the embryonic period would surely have been a sufficiently daunting reason for them not to have undertaken this. But now, given modern ephemerides and computing facilities, the mapping out of an individual's astrological biography – by following the planetary movements during the embryonic period and applying the key correspondence in order to transpose to the course of life – has become quite feasible. Willi Sucher, without ever making use of a computer, was adept at applying the hermetic rule and mapping out the astrological biography of a person. He even developed a graphical method for plotting the geocentric and heliocentric movements of the planets throughout the entire embryonic period, a feat which no astrologer in antiquity could ever have attempted without an enormous expenditure of time and energy. From his graphs of planetary movements during the embryonic period, he could see at a glance the destiny images, prefigured in the formation of the web of destiny during the embryonic period, relating to events taking place in the course of the individual's life. Willi Sucher was therefore not only the pioneer of astrological biography, he was also an exceptionally accomplished practitioner of this arcane discipline.

In this respect, just as Zoroaster and Tycho Brahe are the names associated with the two astronomical pillars underlying a new star wisdom, so the names of Hermes and Willi Sucher will always be remembered in connection with the central astrological pillar – Hermes having inspired the hermetic rule for the computation of the moment of conception retrogressively from the moment of birth, and Willi Sucher having pioneered the science of astrological biography for exploring the unfolding of destiny in relation to the planetary movements between conception and birth. Just as Volume I of *Hermetic Astrology* is intended as a source work concerning the two astronomical pillars underlying a new star wisdom, so Volume II can be thought of as a practical handbook outlining the central astrological pillar and its application.

In turning to a brief consideration of the next step: astrology → astrosophy, our attention is directed to the third volume in this trilogy of hermetic-astrological works: *Christian Hermetic Astrology: The Star of the Magi and the Life of Christ*. Here the explicitly Christian nature of a new star wisdom becomes apparent, for the entire work is devoted to the stars at the time of Christ, starting with the Star of the Magi. For some readers of this trilogy, in which in the first two volumes the Christian aspect has also been emphasized throughout, the question has surely arisen: Are not Christianity and astrology essentially incompatible, since any Christian who believes in divine providence is bound to reject the idea that man's life is linked to the movements of the planets against the background of the stars? Yet the very fact that the Magi were led to the birth of the Messiah by way of a revelation connected with a specific planetary-stellar configuration, as discussed in *Christian Hermetic Astrology,* shows that Christianity from its very inception had a relationship with the star wisdom of the ancients, of whom the Magi were perhaps the last true representatives. The whole of *Christian Hermetic Astrology* is written in the same spirit as that which prevailed when the Magi learnt from the world of stars concerning the birth of the Messiah. In the same way which the Star of the Magi – connected with the divine birth – is discussed, so the planetary configurations at the most significant events in the life of Christ are looked at in the same spirit. But, as many readers will undoubtedly ask, to what purpose? Can this help our understanding of the human being's relationship to the world of the stars?

Here it should be pointed out that Willi Sucher also placed great importance upon contemplating the geocentric and heliocentric movements of the planets against the background of the stars at the time of Christ. For him this was the heart of astrosophy, through which an immeasurable deepening of the human being's relationship to the star world can take place. How is this to be understood?

Just as the twelve zodiacal constellations, considered in their outer aspect, comprise the "body" of the twelve holy living creatures surrounding the throne of God, so the planets – or rather the spheres traced out by the planets on their orbits – are the abodes of spiritual beings in the service of God the Father. The movements of the planets against the background of the zodiacal constellations, taken in their totality, represent the bringing to realisation of the will of the Father through manifold spiritual beings. In this respect the cosmos as a whole can be considered as an expression of the Father. But since the Mystery of Golgotha the words of Christ apply: "No one comes to the Father, but by me" (*John* xiv, 6). This means to say, no mortal can find a true relationship with the cosmic world without the mediation of Christ. The step from astrology to astrosophy – astrosophy being concerned with the spiritual side, the spiritual beings of the cosmos – can be undertaken by way of Christ, who acts as the Great Guardian to the Threshold of the cosmic world.

In view of the central importance of the Being of Christ for a new wisdom of the stars, already in Volume I, especially in Appendix II ("The second coming"), an attempt was made to indicate a path towards a new understanding of Christ in the twentieth century. It was precisely this, however, which gave rise to misunderstanding and even outright criticism of *Hermetic Astrology* I, although on the whole the purely astronomical and astrological content has been well-received.

The criticism directed against the content of Appendix II of *Hermetic*

Astrology I generally overlooked the central idea – or rather ideal – of this appendix, an ideal towards the realisation of which the Russian philosopher Vladimir Soloviev (1853–1900) devoted much of his life. The significance of this ideal for a new understanding of Christ in our time should be evident from the following train of thought: there is only one Christ Being, and all true Christians are united in this Being, therefore on a higher level there exists only one Christianity. UNITY IN CHRIST was the ideal which inspired Soloviev, and it is this ideal which inspired the writing of Appendix II, which is nothing other than a modern-day exposition of Soloviev's line of thought, taking account of certain developments in mankind's spiritual life since Soloviev's death.

The main difference between Soloviev's time and our own can be summarized with the words: the second coming. When Soloviev was alive, there existed only traditional Christianity. As he described in poetic form in his work *A Short Narrative about Antichrist* (written towards the end of his life), traditional Christianity comprises three streams: Roman Catholic, Eastern Orthodox, and Protestant. These in turn, using an analogy with the human being, correspond to the will, feeling and thinking aspects of Christianity, which may be represented in the form of a triangle.

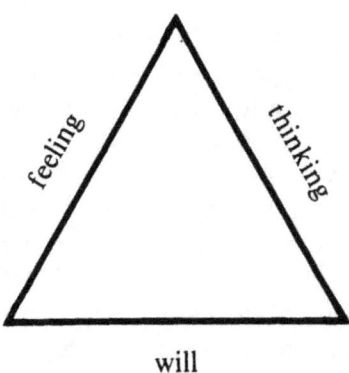

As described in Appendix II, continuing further the analogy with the development of the human being, Rudolf Steiner (1861–1925) came as a messenger of the Self of Christianity, as opposed to the will, feeling and thinking aspects represented by the three main Christian confessions. The message of Rudolf Steiner – Anthroposophy ("spiritual science") – signified the beginning of the instreaming of the Being of Christ taking place through the second coming, the onset of which commenced in the twentieth century. The second coming of Christ signifies the coming to birth of the Self of Christianity, which can be represented in the above diagram by placing a point in the middle of the triangle.

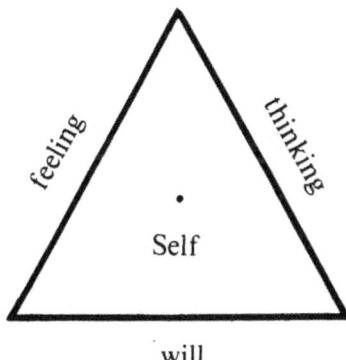

In this analogy with the human being, what is new since the time of Soloviev is the advent or birth of the unifying principle, the self, which alone can truly unite thinking, feeling and the will. Applying this analogy to Christianity as a whole, there still remains the question as to how the unifying principle (the Self of Christianity, the Being of Christ) can accomplish the task of unification, and in Appendix II of Volume I, although it was possible to give only the briefest of indications there, mention was made as to how the spiritual teachers of mankind (known in the East as Bodhisattvas) assist Christ in this work. Here in Chapter 9 of Volume II, concerning the descent of Christ from cosmic realms, this has been expanded upon further. However, just as Soloviev met with incomprehension and antagonism when he espoused the ideal of UNITY IN CHRIST, so this immeasurably powerful and inspiring ideal, which is capable in our time of leading to an inner nearness to the Being of Christ, may well again evoke misunderstanding and even outright criticism.

Part of the criticism directed against Appendix II, where certain time indications are given relating to the second coming, concerns the application of the correspondence: one year of human life corresponds to one century in the history of Christianity. After the publication of Appendix II in Volume I of *Hermetic Astrology*, I came across a reference by Rudolf Steiner (lecture of January 10, 1915) to a similar correspondence: one year of human life corresponds to one century in the history of the Sophia Being. (Sophia is the inspiring Being of philosophy and astrosophy, and is described in the vision of St. John as "a woman clothed with the Sun, with the Moon under her feet, and on her head a crown of twelve stars" – *Revelation* xii, 1.) Rudolf Steiner traced the history of the Sophia Being in the history of philosophy, looking at 700-year periods corresponding to 7-year periods in the development of the human being. If this correspondence holds for the Sophia Being, whom Rudolf Steiner described as Jesus' "Sister Being", it is not unreasonable to look at 700-year periods of development in the history of Christianity as undertaken in Appendix II of Volume I.

Rudolf Steiner also emphasized the necessity for the permeation of astrology with the Christ Impulse:

It became clearer and clearer to me – as the outcome of many years of research – that in our epoch there is really something like a resurrection of the astrology of the third epoch (that of the Egyptian and Babylonian civilizations), but permeated with the Christ Impulse. Today we must search again among the stars in a way different from the old ways, but the stellar script must once again become something that speaks to us.*

These words of Rudolf Steiner summarize the essence of hermetic astrology as represented in this trilogy of works. The original hermetic astrology, which was cultivated in and around Alexandria during the first two or three centuries B.C. and A.D., was a continuation of the star wisdom of ancient Egypt stemming from the great initiate Hermes Trismegistus. Modern hermetic astrology is a resurrection of this ancient star wisdom, arising in our time as a result of the permeation of the ancient astrology with the Christ Impulse.

However, it is not only the inclusion of an explicitly Christian orientation which distinguishes modern hermetic astrology from its predecessor in antiquity, it is also the inclusion of reincarnation. As presented in Volumes I and II, reincarnation research opens up altogether new dimensions for the science of the stars, but this has only become possible, as Rudolf Steiner pointed out, since the Age of Michael (1879–2233) began in 1879.

We see here how great the difficulties are when one wishes to approach the wisdom of the stars rightly and righteously. Indeed the true approach to the wisdom of the stars, which we need to penetrate the facts of karma, is only possible in the light of a true insight into Michael's domain. It is only possible at Michael's side. I have shown you a single example today... It will show you once more, how through the whole reality of modern life there has come forth a certain stream of spiritual life which makes it very difficult to approach with an open mind the science of the stars, and the science, too, of karma. But difficult as it is, it can be done. Despite the attacks that are possible from those quarters which I have described today, we can nevertheless go forward with assurance, and approach the wisdom of the stars and the real shaping of karma.**

---

*Rudolf Steiner, *Christ and the Spiritual World. The Search for the Holy Grail* (trsl. C. Davy and D.S. Osmond, Rudolf Steiner Press, London, 1963), p. 106.

** Rudolf Steiner, *Karmic Relationships* vi (trsl. G. Adams, Anthroposophical Publishing Company: London, 1957), p. 111.

Afterword

The call issued by Rudolf Steiner (in the above words, from 1924) for a new science of the stars as a science of karma provided the central motivation for the writing down and publication of Volumes I and II of *Hermetic Astrology*, which I began writing at Easter 1983. *Hermetic Astrology* thus arose in response to Rudolf Steiner's call issued fifty-nine years previously. And just as Rudolf Steiner's reincarnation research provided the initial material forming the foundation for modern hermetic astrology – indeed, it would not have been possible without it – so Willi Sucher's example in pioneering a new star wisdom inspired *Hermetic Astrology* to come into being.

Between Rudolf Steiner (1861–1925) and Willi Sucher (1902–1985), it is important to mention Elisabeth Vreede (1879–1943), who not only was a co-worker of Rudolf Steiner but also was Willi Sucher's mentor. In the introduction to her book concerning the foundations of a modern star wisdom, she wrote: "Knowledge of the universe ascends in three stages: from astronomy to astrology, to astrosophy."* Elisabeth Vreede actively encouraged Willi Sucher in the development of a new and Christian wisdom of the stars, and it was she who pointed out to him the importance of the hermetic rule for determining the moment of conception, given the moment of birth. In this way she contributed at an early stage to the resurrection of hermetic astrology in the twentieth century.

In making the transition from astronomy to astrology, in passing from Volume I to Volume II, we move from study of the "body" to consideration of the "soul" of star wisdom. Whereas Volume I is essentially concerned with the right astronomical frame of reference for casting horoscopes (the sidereal zodiac, the Tychonic system, the hermetic chart, etc.), Volume II is devoted primarily to biography, through which the "soul" of star wisdom is revealed in the unfolding of human destiny, as indicated by Rudolf Steiner.

*If we make the attempt with the kind of knowledge I have described, we begin to gaze upon the destiny of a single human being with holy awe. For what is it that works in the destiny of each human being? In very truth it is star wisdom – all-embracing star wisdom!***

A sacrifice has to be made, in making the transition from the body to the soul of star wisdom, in that the more technical astronomical aspects have to be left aside in order to "gaze upon the destiny of a single human being with holy awe", as attempted here in Volume II with respect to the destiny of Richard Wagner. As long as one is concerned primarily with casting

---

*Elisabeth Vreede, *Astronomie und Anthroposophie* (Philosophisch-Anthroposophischer Verlag: Dornach, 1980), p. 11.

**Rudolf Steiner, *Karmic Relationships* iv (Rudolf Steiner Press: London, 1971), p. 119.

horoscopes, it is difficult to devote oneself in the right way to the more subtle task of contemplating the unfolding of destiny through human biography. Yet it must be remembered that the horoscope and all computations resulting therefrom provide only the "bare bones", and it is by way of contemplating the biography that "life and soul" are allowed to enter in. The deep and intensive study of biography – the more biographies of historical personalities that are studied the better – is indispensible for a new and "all-embracing star wisdom."

A further sacrifice is called for in order to make the transition from astrology to astrosophy. Whereas reincarnation research plays an important role in hermetic astrology, this activity presents something of a hindrance to contemplation of the cosmic mysteries in the domain of astrosophy, e.g. those connected with the life of Christ, as described in *Christian Hermetic Astrology: The Star of the Magi and the Life of Christ*. For example, the knowledge that Richard Wagner was the reincarnation of a nun who was one of the greatest mystics in the history of Christianity, although it helps to illumine Wagner's biography, may divert our attention from the cosmic mystery surrounding Richard Wagner's life work, which was bound up with the Grail mystery. Here this Grail mystery can only be hinted at. (For a deeper study see my article "The Grail in Relation to the Stars" in *Shoreline* vol. I, 1988.) Briefly, Wagner's life work culminated with *Parsifal*, in which "the urge to give a musical expression of the Christ Impulse existed. It was anticipated in Richard Wagner and was ultimately responsible for the creation of *Parsifal*."*

What was this Christ Impulse to which Wagner sought to give musical expression in *Parsifal*? It had little to do with traditional Christianity, with which Wagner had hardly any relationship. No, it was the beginning of a radiating in of the Christ Impulse in connection with the descent of Christ from cosmic realms through the ranks of the hierarchies, as described in Appendix II ("The second coming") of Volume I (see p. 325). Exactly at the time that Wagner was composing *Parsifal* (1877–1879), the Russo-Turkish war was taking place, which mirrored on Earth the resistance encountered by Christ on his passage – within the sphere of the Sun – through the ranks of the spiritual beings known as *Dynamis*. The Russo-Turkish war signified a negative reflection of the descent of Christ through the realm of the Dynamis, whereas the composition of *Parsifal* was a positive reflection of this event. Such knowledge, concerning the spiritual dimensions of cosmic events, belongs to the domain of astrosophy. We are led into this domain through contemplation of the Christ Mystery. This Mystery oc-

---

*Rudolf Steiner, *True and False Paths in Spiritual Investigation* (Rudolf Steiner Press: London, 1969), p. 219.

cupies the central position in astrosophy, and *Christian Hermetic Astrology: The Star of the Magi and the Life of Christ* is intended as a contribution towards this highest level of a new wisdom of the stars.

There is still a further reason for making this point here. The reader may have gained the impression in Volumes I and II of *Hermetic Astrology* that reincarnation research can be undertaken without too much difficulty. Nothing could be further from the truth. According to Rudolf Steiner, true reincarnation research can be undertaken only through a special spiritual calling. As he indicated in 1924, it is a matter of destiny – a preparation in the previous incarnation – if one is able to carry out reincarnation research in the present incarnation. In the intervening time since Rudolf Steiner spoke of this in 1924, the possibility of reincarnation research has become opened up on a wider scale – through the grace of Christ, through the onset of His second coming in 1933. Nevertheless, an intensive preparation is required in order not to fall into error when engaged in reincarnation research. Guidelines concerning an appropriate preparation for reincarnation research are outlined in Volume I, Chapter 7.

It cannot be emphasized strongly enough that without appropriate preparation it is better to leave reincarnation research alone. This preparation helps to minimize the possibility of making a mistake. Otherwise, the risk of arriving at false conclusions concerning previous incarnations is very great. This is one of the most formidable temptations facing mankind in the twentieth century and on into the future. Already in esoteric circles in the twentieth century serious mistakes have been made in the domain of reincarnation research, mistakes which have wreaked havoc in the lives of numerous people.

One example suffices to illustrate how damaging false reincarnation statements may be: the example of the Indian boy Alcyone (Krishnamurti), who was put forward in the Theosophical Society by Annie Besant and C.W. Leadbeater as the reincarnated Jesus or Jeshu, the new World Teacher. Thousands of people were taken in by this, and it was only through Krishnamurti's honesty that the spiritual movement surrounding him became disbanded, in that he publicly disavowed himself from the false reincarnation statement attached to him. Since most people are not in a position to prove or disprove the authenticity of a reincarnation statement, if a reincarnation statement is attached to a spiritual teacher, either his followers have to believe it, or else they will question it or reject it. In the case of Krishnamurti, the false reincarnation statement propagated by C.W. Leadbeater and Annie Besant had a hypnotizing effect on large numbers of people who accepted it unquestioningly, and at the same time it created an aura of mystery and spiritual authority surrounding the young Indian. His words, because they were believed to be those of the new World Teacher, acquired formidable power and authority. In a mood approaching fanatical devotion, thousands of people accepted uncritically everything he said. Fortunately, Krishnamurti was honest enough not to perpetuate the illusion built up around him. Indeed, he shattered this illusion when he proclaimed publicly that he was not the One whom his followers believed him to be.

The lesson that may be learnt from this example is clear. There is a deep-seated tendency to look to spiritual authority, and this may be misused – as it was by C.W. Leadbeater and Annie Besant. The ultimate spiritual authority, however, is to be found within, and may be approached through moral deepening. It is here, within the inner light of conscience, aided by reasoning and common sense, that discrimination has to be learnt as an essential step on the spiritual path. Whosoever learns to discriminate is offered a high measure of protection from falling prey to the subtle temptations presented in the domain of the esoteric life.

Discrimination involves weighing up, subjecting to scrutiny, but without making an over-hasty judgement. Both openmindedness (tendency to believe) and scepticism (tendency to disbelieve) are called for, and these two attitudes should balance each other out in a healthy and harmonious way. It is precisely a combination of these two attitudes which is alluded to in the Introduction as being appropriate with regard to the results of reincarnation research presented in this volume of *Hermetic Astrology*.

www.ingramcontent.com/pod-product-compliance
Lightning Source LLC
Chambersburg PA
CBHW060228240426
43671CB00016B/2887